Colonial Justice in
Western Massachusetts
(1639–1702)

THE PYNCHON COURT RECORD

LEGAL STUDIES OF THE WILLIAM NELSON CROMWELL FOUNDATION

WILLIAM PYNCHON, 1590–1662

Colonial Justice in Western Massachusetts

(1639–1702)

THE PYNCHON COURT RECORD

*An Original Judges' Diary of the Administration
of Justice in the Springfield Courts in the
Massachusetts Bay Colony*

EDITED WITH A
LEGAL AND HISTORICAL INTRODUCTION
BY Joseph H. Smith
OF THE NEW YORK BAR

Massachusetts (Colony) Courts (Hampshire Co.)

(1)

PUBLISHED UNDER THE AUSPICES OF
The William Nelson Cromwell Foundation
BY Harvard University Press
Cambridge, Massachusetts
1961

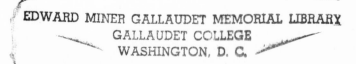

Distributed in Great Britain by Oxford University Press, London

Library of Congress Catalog Card Number 61-7394

Printed in the United States of America

TRUSTEES
OF
THE
WILLIAM NELSON CROMWELL
FOUNDATION

Foreword

In generously establishing the Foundation which bears his name, Mr. William Nelson Cromwell charged the Trustees thereof to use his gift for a variety of purposes related to the law. The recital of these in the Purposes clause of the Trust Indenture points up the universality of his interest in legal matters.

First in the long list of projects to which the Trustees are directed to devote his funds and their energies is that of "Research of the laws, judicial systems, legal procedure and legal history of the Colonial period of the United States of America."

By a fortuitous circumstance, the Trustees ascertained that the Law School of Harvard University is the owner of a unique Diary kept in large part by William Pynchon and John Pynchon, from 1639 to 1702, covering their judicial acts and judgments as magistrates or commissioners in Springfield, in the Massachusetts Bay Colony.

An examination of the document, which is in longhand, but well preserved, and largely legible, disclosed that it is a most interesting record, from the legal, the historical, and the human viewpoint.

Therefore, the Trustees offered to publish the same. Harvard University accepted the offer, and, by direction of Mr. William Dean Embree, the Chairman of the Board of Trustees, the undersigned was assigned the interesting task of supervising the publication.

The work required the preparation of the text, carrying with it the deciphering and modernizing of the seventeenth-century script in which it is written, and researches in many places for the purpose of tracing down the ultimate determination of those cases which were appealed or transferred to a higher tribunal.

Upon Mr. Joseph H. Smith, of the New York bar, has fallen the major portion of the work. His most able treatment of the Massachusetts Bay judicial system and the jurisdictions and procedures of the Springfield courts adds immeasurably to our understanding and appreciation of the Diary, and speaks volumes for his erudition and for the thoroughness of his work. To these, he has added most interesting biographies of the compilers of the Diary. His articles present clearly the legal aspects of the Diary and the light it sheds upon some of the legal practices and procedures of our colonial ancestors.

But the Diary is also a colorful record of the mores of that colonial community. Witchcraft, juvenile delinquency, bootlegging— they are all there. There, also, are the determinations of the guardianships of children, the just distributions of estates of decedents, the protection of widows and orphans, and the resolution of the financial disputes of the community.

Follies and foibles; prejudices and petty quarrels; crimes and misdemeanors; jealousies, hopes, and fears—the Diary runs the gamut of human frailties and human passions. It is enlivened every so often by pungent pronouncements, such as the following:

The answer of the man accused of card playing, who pleaded to the Court: "I did not so well know the Law against it and I was willing to have recreation for my wife to drive away melancholy," adding, when pressed by the Court, that he was willing to do any thing when his wife was ill to make her merry.

The case of the "Goodwife," who, found guilty of the "continuall Trade upon every occasion to be exorbitant with her Toung," was dealt with as follows: "I sentence her to be Gagged or else set in a ducking stoole and dipped in water as Law provides: Shee to choose which of them shee pleases within this halfe howre: or else I to determine and order either as I see cause. She not choosing either: I ordered her to be Gagged and so to stand halfe an hour in the open streete which was done accordingly."

This gem of Pynchon wisdom, tempered by mercy: "Though at first he was alitle saucy yet afterward Confessing all and being admonished and told of the evill, he seemed very Penitent and promised to be more watch full against such like disorder: I therefore dealt more gently with him by a small fine bearing Testymony against such disorders."

Compiled on the spot and by the judges themselves, it is, indeed, a fascinating legal and human document.

Acknowledgments, in addition to the one to Mr. Joseph H. Smith, heretofore noted, are made to:

Professor Mark DeWolfe Howe, of the Law School of Harvard University, who, despite his many duties, made himself available at all times for consultation, and gave most helpful advice;

Mr. Charles McClumpha, formerly of the New York bar, now of Northampton, Massachusetts, who ably carried on the preliminary stages of the investigation until forced by illness to relinquish, reluctantly, the task;

Miss Juliette Tomlinson, Director of the Connecticut Valley Historical Museum, in Springfield, Massachusetts, for most helpful cooperation in modernizing the text of the Diary, in making available manuscript material relating to the Pynchons, and in connection with the biographical portion of the Introduction;

The respective staffs of the New York Public Library, the Massachusetts Department of Archives, the Massachusetts Historical Society, the Connecticut State Library, the Connecticut Historical Society, the Registry of Probate, Northampton, Mass., the Office of the Clerk, Superior Court, Northampton, Mass., the Office of the Clerk, Superior Court, Springfield, Mass., the Office of the Clerk, Superior Court, East Cambridge, Mass., the Columbia Law School Library, the Boston Public Library, the American Antiquarian Society and the Library of Congress for cooperation in making available manuscripts or printed material in their custody;

Miss Ruth A. McIntyre, who has transcribed a portion of the Pynchon Account Books, for expert guidance concerning biographical details relating to John Pynchon;

Miss Madeleine Conners, formerly of Harvard University, who originally transcribed the Diary;

Mrs. Margaret M. Emmison, M.A., for research on William Pynchon in the Essex Record Office in Chelmsford, England;

Mrs. Joseph H. Smith for editorial assistance in connection with the Introduction and the supplemental court records interspersed with the text of the Diary; and

My fellow Trustees, for their tolerant understanding as the work progressed slowly toward its goal.

In thus rescuing from the secluded files of a law school and giving to the profession and the public this Diary, the Trustees are certain that they are carrying out Mr. Cromwell's wishes, and are hopeful that the publication thereof may reveal the existence of like records in other sections of our land, so that one day a series of books similar to this one may adorn the shelf holding the publications of The William Nelson Cromwell Foundation, a result which we are certain would meet with the unqualified approval of Mr. William Nelson Cromwell.

JOHN F. BROSNAN

New York, N.Y.
May 15, 1960

CONTENTS

ILLUSTRATIONS

frontispiece:
William Pynchon at the age of 67, painted by an unknown artist in 1657. (Reproduced through the courtesy of the Essex Institute, Salem, Massachusetts.)

facing page 203:
Page 2 of the Pynchon Diary, showing the entry of February 14, 1638/9 appointing William Pynchon magistrate for Agawam. (Reproduced through the courtesy of the Law School of Harvard University.)

LEGAL AND HISTORICAL INTRODUCTION

TO

THE PYNCHON COURT RECORD

BY

JOSEPH H. SMITH
OF THE NEW YORK BAR

I. The Pynchon Manuscript

AMONG the material preserved in the Treasure Room of the Law School of Harvard University is a small manuscript volume known as the *Pynchon Diary* or the *Pynchon Magistrate's Book*. Neither designation is quite accurate and for the purpose of this publication the volume is called *The Pynchon Court Record,* or for brevity, the *Record*. The bulk of this manuscript consists of a record kept by William Pynchon, the founder of Springfield, Massachusetts, by his son-in-law, Elizur Holyoke, and by his son, John Pynchon, of matters coming before various courts on the lower jurisdictional levels (below the county level) held for Springfield and the vicinity during the period from February 14, 1638/9 to January 9, 1701/2.[1] The present publication makes available the complete text of the manuscript with the exception of a few pages not deemed of sufficient interest to warrant publication.

The manuscript was acquired by Harvard in May 1927 from Goodspeed's Book Shop in Boston. From 1899 until then the *Record* had been owned by a Boston collector, Sumner Hollingsworth, who had obtained it from another Boston bookseller. It appears probable that it was in the possession of historian Judge Henry Morris of Springfield in the latter part of the nineteenth century.[2]

In appearance the manuscript consists of approximately 360 pages measuring $7\frac{1}{2}$ by $5\frac{1}{2}$ inches. A few pages are torn and fragmentary; a few have been removed or mutilated by cutting; some have been left blank. The present binding dates from the latter half of the eighteenth century, but most likely the volume was originally bound

[1] The word "courts" is used in the broad sense of a person or persons exercising judicial powers, although the laws of Massachusetts, during the seventeenth century, did not normally comprehend within the term "court" the jurisdiction exercised by a magistrate, by commissioners for ending small causes or by a justice of the peace.

[2] See C. D. Wright, *Report on the Custody and Condition of the Public Records of Parishes, Towns and Counties* (1889) 345. An 1826 address to members of the bar of western Massachusetts indicates access to the *Record,* but not ownership. See George Bliss, *An Address to the Members of the Bar of the Counties of Hampshire, Franklin and Hampden at Their Annual Meeting at Northampton, September 1826* (1827).

in vellum. The entries on the first forty-nine pages (1638/9–1650) are in the handwriting of William Pynchon, with the exception of a few entries inserted at later dates by John Pynchon or Elizur Holyoke. Following six pages of entries by John Pynchon, pages 61 through 90 (1653/4–1660) are in Holyoke's hand. The remaining pages are in the hand of John Pynchon, with the exception of pages 102–105 written by Elizur Holyoke, one page by John Holyoke, a copy of a General Court order in William Pynchon's hand, and a page in an unidentified hand (perhaps John Pynchon, Jr.'s) listing persons joined in marriage during the period 1711/2 to 1716/7. Many of the later entries of John Pynchon are extremely difficult to read being closely written with numerous abbreviations and interlineations.

For use in this publication the text of the *Record* was modernized in accordance generally with the Rules for Style adopted for use in the American Legal Records Series by the Committee on Legal History of the American Historical Association. The same rules have been adopted in the interspersing of extracts from the *Hampshire County Probate Court Records*, the *Records of the Acts of the County Courts Holden in the County of Hampshire*, and the *Hampshire Book of Records for the Court of Pleas begun March 7th, 1692/3*, all manuscript sources which supplement material in the *Record*, and, as an appendix, a return made to the County Court at Cambridge by John Pynchon and Elizur Holyoke in a criminal matter.[3] Any material from other contemporary sources quoted in this Introduction has been modernized in accordance with the same rules.

That portion of the *Record* not included in the present publication consists of eleven pages listing persons joined in marriage by John Pynchon as magistrate or justice of the peace, commencing April 1665, as well as the later list of persons joined in marriage and

[3] The three manuscript volumes referred to in the text appear to be engrossed minutes or records; the first is in the Registry of Probate Office, Northampton, Mass.; the second, in the Office of the Clerk, Superior Court, Northampton, Mass.; the third, in the Office of the Clerk, Superior Court, Springfield, Mass. The *Pynchon Waste Book for Hampshire*, a manuscript in possession of the Connecticut Valley Historical Museum, Springfield, Mass., contains rough minutes of the County Court for Hampshire for the period from April 1663 to January 1676/7. The American Antiquarian Society in Worcester, Mass., has two more manuscript volumes of rough minutes. One covers sessions, mostly at Springfield, of the County Court for Hampshire and the later Court of General Sessions of the Peace and Inferior Court of Common Pleas for the period March 1677 to June 1694. The other volume covers sessions, held almost entirely at Northampton, of the same courts for the period March 1677 to June 1696, plus the incomplete record of a court of oyer and terminer held at Northampton in October 1696. There are also some entries of the County Court for Hampshire for the period covering September 1690 to April 1692 in *Volume A, Registry of Deeds, Springfield, Hampden County, 1690–1692*. This abundance of judicial records for the County of Hampshire derives from the practice of keeping records at both Springfield and Northampton.

the copy of the General Court order. Included are seventeen pages of entries, found toward the end of the *Record,* of meetings of the freemen of Springfield for the period 1660/1 to 1696—material closely connected with the public career of John Pynchon.

While the manuscript volume was maintained as a judicial record for approximately sixty-three years, it is obvious that entry was not made therein of all judicial acts of the various courts held at Springfield on the lower jurisdictional levels during the period. There are several substantial periods of time for which no entries of a judicial nature are found. Internal evidence and the records of the County Court for Hampshire confirm that, in the case of offenders let off with a warning or bound over to the County Court, no entry might be made in the *Record.* For the years 1660–62 some entries (which have been included) were made in the *Hampshire County Probate Court Records* rather than in the *Record.* However, apart from these entries and one enigmatic reference in the manuscript, there is no evidence that either Pynchon or Elizur Holyoke maintained any other records of a judicial nature on the jurisdictional levels covered by the *Record.*[4] Apparently none of the file papers kept by the Pynchons or Holyoke has survived.

Legal historians of colonial Massachusetts have tended to concentrate upon the courts of higher jurisdiction of the Bay. This book is the first to print *in extenso* any colonial court records for western Massachusetts or, with one exception, records of any court below the county level for that portion of the Massachusetts Bay colony now included within the Commonwealth of Massachusetts.[5] The *Record,* supplemented by records of the County Court and successor courts for Hampshire, affords a representative and vivid portrayal of the administration of justice on the lower jurisdictional levels—the "grassroots" level—in western Massachusetts during the seventeenth century.

[4] *Rec.* 134.
[5] See *Early New England Court Records, A Bibliography of Published Materials,* prepared by W. Jeffrey, Jr.; published for The Ames Foundation, Harvard Law School (n.d.); also contained in *The Boston Public Library Quarterly,* July 1954.

I I. William Pynchon

WILLIAM PYNCHON who was primarily responsible for the establishment of the first court in western Massachusetts and for the administration of justice in that region until 1651 was born in England on or about December 26, 1590. His birthplace was the village of Springfield, some thirty miles northeast of London, near Chelmsford, the shire town of Essex.[1] His name, spelled in various ways, appears to have been Norman in origin. His ancestry can be traced to William Pynchon, a yeoman of Writtle (the ancestral village of the Pynchons, also near Chelmsford), who died in 1552 possessed of substantial holdings. His eldest son, John Pynchon, grandfather of the founder of Springfield, seemingly established the family properties and prestige on a sounder basis by marriage to a daughter of Sir Richard Empson. John, the second son of this marriage, inherited the family properties at Springfield upon his father's death in 1573 and received a bachelor's degree at New College (Oxford) in 1581.[2]

When John Pynchon, described as "gent." in his will, died in 1610, he provided that William, his elder son, should receive during the life of decedent's wife, a portion of the rents and profits of certain lands and tenements in the parish of Writtle, and, after her death, in fee, all the houses, lands, and tenements of decedent in Springfield. Some biographers of William Pynchon have stated that he was educated at Oxford, matriculating at Hart Hall (afterward Hartford College) in 1596; however, since he was born in 1590, this

[1] The date of birth is based upon the statement in *Chancery Inquisitions post Mortem C.* 142, 321/130, taken October 7, 1611, that, at the time of his father's death on September 4, 1610, William Pynchon was aged 19-1/2 years and 10 weeks. See 87 *N. Eng. Hist. and Gen. Reg.* 224. Since the age is expressed in years and weeks, there may have been some rounding. This dating is consistent with the inscription appearing on the well-known portrait of Pynchon at the Essex Institute, Salem, Mass., reading in part, *Delin. Anno. Dom. 1657 Aetat 67.*

[2] For the Pynchon genealogy see 2 Waters, *Genealogical Gleanings in England* (1901) 854–857, 859, 863–867, and the more recent article by S. E. Morison, "William Pynchon, The Founder of Springfield," 64 *Mass. Hist. Soc. Proc.* (1931) 67–107.

appears highly unlikely.[3] Where he acquired his education, which, judging by his published works, included extensive knowledge of Latin, Greek, and Hebrew writers and of theological doctrines remains unexplained, but biographers have unanimously regarded him as a "gentleman of learning." He married Anna Andrew (or Andrews), daughter of William Andrew of Twiwell, Northamptonshire, and member of an old Warwickshire family, and had one son and three daughters when he embarked for New England.[4]

Presentments found in the Essex Quarter Sessions Rolls reveal that Pynchon was a churchwarden of Christ Church in Springfield in January 1619/20 and in December 1624.[5] However, the assertion that Pynchon served as justice of the peace in Essex is not supported by an examination of the Essex commissions of the peace for the period. Similarly no evidence appears that Pynchon was a "lord of the manor." The Manor of Springfield with Dukes was held by the Tyrells; the manor court records show that William Pynchon, "gent.," did fealty to the lord for certain lands inherited from his father.[6] His social status is brought into sharper focus by noting that the Pynchon family was included in the Heralds' Visitations of Essex in 1612 and 1634, although not in the earlier visitation of 1558, and that the widow of the earlier John Pynchon married Sir Thomas Wilson, Secretary of State under Elizabeth. A cousin of William Pynchon married Richard Weston, later first Earl of Portland and Chancellor of the Exchequer.[7] Thus, while not a lord of the manor, William Pyn-

[3] Morison, *William Pynchon* 69; 2 Waters, *Genealogical Gleanings* 854–855, 866. Andrews states, without citation of authority, that Pynchon owned many houses and lands in the parishes of Writtle and Widford. 2 *Col. Period Amer. Hist.* (1936) 126.

[4] 2 Waters, *Genealogical Gleanings* 866–867; Morison, *William Pynchon* 69.

[5] Q/SR 227/13 (Epiphany Session, 1619/20) and Q/SR 247/48A (Epiphany Session, 1624/5) in Essex Record Office, Chelmsford, England. For this and other material from the Essex Record Office we are indebted to Mrs. Margaret M. Emmison, M.A. of Chelmsford, one-time acting Archivist, Essex Record Office. Several biographers have referred to the tablet in the Springfield parish church showing Pynchon as churchwarden in 1624.

[6] The statements are based upon research conducted by Mrs. Emmison at the Essex Record Office. An October 1622 entry in the *Ms. Court Rolls for the Manor*

of Springfield with Dukes shows William Pynchon doing fealty to the lord in court for a parcel of lands called Varneswell Fields and Varneswell Moores, conveyed to his father in February 1596/7. An October 1631 entry reveals that the lands were later sold to a William Bentall. There is no reference to William Pynchon in the Manor Court Rolls of Writtle. The Manor of Writtle, one of the largest in Essex, was held by the Petres. By a May 1, 1612 document Sir Edward Pynchon released to his cousin William Pynchon all rights in some farms and other lands in the parishes of Writtle, Broomfield, and Chignall St. James. Sir Edward Pynchon was lord of the Manor of Roman's Fee (probably identical with the Manor of Turges), one of the nine sub-manors of Writtle.

[7] *The Visitations of Essex*, 13 Harleian Soc. Pub. 266, 319, 470; Morison, *William Pynchon* 68. Earlier, John Pynchon of Writtle had been overseer of the will of Richard Weston, Justice of Common Pleas,

chon was on the fringe of the social class which usually held manors
and served as justices of the peace.

The available facts do not indicate how or when Pynchon became interested in the Massachusetts Bay Company project. His extensive and successful business activities in the colony suggest that
his motivation was in part economic. His profoundly religious nature
and his proximity to Chelmsford, the center of a strong Puritan
group, suggest a less worldly motive. Passages in his later writings
indicate that political considerations may have played a part. Evidence is lacking that personal friendship influenced his decision.[8]

William Pynchon was one of twenty-six patentees and one of
eighteen assistants named in the charter to the Governor and Company of Massachusetts Bay in New England which passed the seals
March 4, 1628/9. Confirmed and taking his oath as assistant on May
13, 1629, he was a regular attendant at the meetings of the General
Court and of the Court of Assistants held in England and also a sig-
natory of the well-known Cambridge Agreement of August 26, 1629.[9]
His subscription to the joint stock in the amount of £25 was recorded
August 29, and he disposed of some of his Springfield holdings prepar-
atory to leaving England.[10] He was on the committee appointed by

former solicitor-general who acquired the
Manor of Skreens in Roxwell, Essex; the
will was proved July 29, 1572. 74 *N. Eng.
Hist. and Gen. Reg.* 69; *The Visitations of
Essex* 319. The lengthy DNB article on
Richard Weston, first Earl of Portland,
shows that his wife was buried on Febru-
ary 10, 1602/3, before he was knighted.
His father, Sir Jerome Weston, had been
high sheriff of Essex in 1599.

[8] Thomas Hooker was an Essex neighbor for many years but nothing indicates
that Pynchon was among the many whom
he induced to emigrate to New England.
The supposition that the Reverend John
White of Dorset influenced Pynchon to
join the Massachusetts Bay Company rests
largely upon inference. Morison, *William
Pynchon* 70–71. Rose-Troup in *John
White, the Patriarch of Dorchester (Dorset) and the Founder of Massachusetts,
1575–1648* (1930) refers only to the fact
that White authorized Pynchon to demand, receive and, if necessary, sue for
certain debts owing from New England
inhabitants (pp. 463–466). See also 2 *Winthrop Papers* (1931) 268; 47 *Mass. Hist.
Soc. Proc.* 346–347 and the supposition in
Wright, *The Genesis of Springfield* (1936)
6–7. In the same vein, the later business

relations between Pynchon and the Win-
throps lend support to the inference that
Pynchon was acquainted with John Win-
throp and the Downings prior to 1629.
See 1 Winthrop, *Hist. New England* 449;
2 *Winthrop Papers* 306; 3 *ibid.* 116; 6
Mass. Hist. Soc. Coll. (4th ser.) 40. Andrews makes the sweeping statement that
Saltonstall, Downing, Dudley, Johnson,
Ward, Ludlow, Bradstreet, Bellingham,
Eaton, Endecott, Nowell, and Pynchon
"were all non-conformists, forming a close
corporation of friends and relatives." 1
Col. Period Amer. Hist. (1934) 370. The
same inference is possible in the case of
Richard Andrews, one of the Plymouth adventurers, and a so-called London partner.
5 *Winthrop Papers* (1947) 2–4.

[9] 1 *Rec. Mass. Bay* 6, 10–11; Young,
*Chronicles of the First Planters of the Col-
ony of Massachusetts Bay* (1846) 281–282.

[10] 8 Mass. Hist. Soc. Coll. (2nd ser.)
228; 2 Waters, *Genealogical Gleanings*
863; *supra*, note 6. The subscription is reproduced in J. T. Adams, *The Founding
of New England* (1921), opposite p. 128.
Compare the recital of John Pynchon in a
1659 petition to the General Court that
his father had laid out £50 in furtherance
of planting the colony, in consideration of

the General Court on October 15 to draw up articles of agreement between the adventurers remaining in England and those intending to remove and again elected an assistant on October 29, 1629, when it had been decided to transfer the government to New England. By December 1629 he was engaged in assembling the ordnance for the Winthrop fleet.[11]

Pynchon left England on March 29, 1630 with John Winthrop's fleet, accompanied by his wife and three daughters and perhaps some servants. His son John apparently came over on a later ship.[12] Upon arrival in New England Pynchon first settled at Dorchester, but within a short time removed to Roxbury, an adjoining settlement nearer to Boston. He is said by Thomas Prince, the annalist, to have been the "principal Founder" of Roxbury and by John Eliot to have been "one of the first foundation of the church" in that town. Shortly after her arrival in the plantation his wife succumbed to the widespread sickness and Pynchon then married Frances Sanford, characterized by Eliot as the "grave matron of the church at Dorcester." Her son by her first marriage, Henry Smith, a "Godly, wise young man," later married Anne Pynchon and figured prominently in the settlement of the plantation of Agawam on the banks of the Connecticut River.[13]

---

which he had been promised land. 45 *Mass. Archives* 82.

[11] 1 *Rec. Mass. Bay* 40, 47, 49, 50–51, 54–56, 58–60; 6 Mass. Hist. Soc. Coll. (4th ser.) 30. When John and Samuel Browne, lawyer and merchant respectively, arrived in England in September 1629, having been sent back from the plantation by Captain Endecott as "men factious and evil conditioned," the General Court authorized a committee of ten to determine the differences. Pynchon was one of four chosen by the Brownes. As to whether this selection by the Brownes, patentees and men of substance, was based on friendship (they came from Roxwell where Sir Edward Pynchon had lived) or on their conception of Pynchon's religious views, the record is silent. The dispute had its origin in charges by the Brownes that the ministry in the plantation were Separatists, departing from the orders of the Church of England. Young, *Chronicles* 88–91; 1 *Rec. Mass. Bay* 51–53; Salisbury, *Memorial of Gov. John Endecott*, Antiquarian Papers (1879) 21–26; 3 *Archaeologia Americana*, Trans. and Coll. Amer. Antiq. Soc. (1850) lxxiv.

[12] Morison, *William Pynchon* 72. A 1659 petition of John Pynchon to the General Court for a grant of land recited that his father had brought over several servants promising them 50 acres of land apiece, which the Company had agreed should be allowed each person, and that some of these servants were still importuning petitioner for their land. 45 *Mass. Archives* 82. Banks (*The Winthrop Fleet of 1630* (1930), 53–54) refers to a contemporary news report found in the Public Record Office in London that "Mr. Pinchin and his wife and 3 daughters" had recently sailed to New England. Lockwood refers to a document in the Massachusetts Archives as showing that John remained behind and came over in a later ship. 1 *Hist. Western Mass.* 88.

[13] Morison, *William Pynchon* 72; Drake, *The Town of Roxbury; Its Memorable Persons and Places* (1878) 12; Prince, *Annals of New-England*, 7 Mass. Hist. Soc. Coll. (2nd ser.) 14; *A Report of the Record Commissioners Containing The Roxbury Land and Church Records* (2nd ed., 1884) 74.

Pynchon, after his arrival in the colony, was chosen assistant and magistrate annually until the May 1637 session of the General Court. He also served as treasurer of the plantation from August 1632 until May 1634.[14] He may have served in a military capacity at Roxbury; he was one of the eleven members of the commission for military affairs established by the General Court in March 1634/5.[15]

During his tenure as assistant, the Court of Assistants was the principal judicial body in the plantation. Whatever Pynchon's previous lack of judicial experience or training, his extensive participation in hearing and determining causes, both civil and criminal, coming before the Court of Assistants must have given him considerable experience with the judicial process as it operated in Massachusetts Bay. However, the fact that in 1630 Pynchon was not one of the assistants granted the powers of a justice of the peace for the reformation of abuses and the punishing of offenders and that prior to 1637 he was named by the Court of Assistants in only one commission and one reference indicates that he was not regarded as a judicial stalwart.[16]

While virtually all the records of his business activities have been lost, William Pynchon is regarded as one of the most important fur traders in Massachusetts Bay prior to 1650. An entry in Winthrop's *Journal* for October 30, 1631 concerning the wreck of "Mr. Pynchon's boat, coming from Sagadahock" indicates that he had brought over some capital and was engaged in trade with the port established on the Sagadahoc River by inhabitants of New Plymouth.[17] A year later he agreed to give twenty-five pounds for his beaver trade for the year in return for remission of the twelve pence per pound imposed by the plantation in June 1632 on all beaver skins received in trade with the Indians. However, this agreement was made "in regard of a benefit by an order of Court . . . that there should be but one in a town to trade in beaver," and, since the order was not observed and Pynchon's trade was less, he only made allowance at the twelve pence per pound rate. However, Pynchon's recomputed allowance of twenty pounds for his trade made up a substantial portion of the monies he accounted for, in his capacity of treasurer, as

14 1 *Rec. Mass. Bay* 99, 128, 136, 148; 8 Mass. Hist. Soc. Coll. (2nd ser.) 228–235. Perhaps because of his experience as Treasurer, Pynchon in September 1634, was charged by the General Court with the receipt and distribution of some military supplies furnished by Dr. Edmund Wilson for use of the plantation. A fine of a noble (6s., 8d.) for nonattendance on September 7, 1630 may have helped make Pynchon a regular attendant at meetings of the Court of Assistants. 1 *Rec. Mass. Bay* 75.

15 1 Wright, *Story Western Mass.* 119; 1 *Rec. Mass. Bay* 138; 1 Winthrop, *Hist. New England* 186–187. See also Brennan, "The Massachusetts Council of the Magistrates," 4 *N. Eng. Quart.* 54, 58–59.

16 1 *Rec. Mass. Bay* 74, 96, 144.

17 1 Winthrop, *Hist. New England* 76.

received from the beaver trade.[18] In addition to his fur trading, it seems likely that he engaged in farming at Roxbury.[19]

It has been assumed that William Pynchon removed from Roxbury to the banks of the Connecticut River to obtain a more advantageous location for his beaver trade but supporting evidence is scant.[20] Massachusetts Bay had lagged behind the Dutch and New Plymouth in settling the Connecticut Valley and it was not until May 1635 that the inhabitants of Roxbury were granted liberty to remove to another location, provided they continued under the Bay government. In the last half of 1635 settlers arriving in substantial numbers from the Bay made an effective beginning of the settlements along the Connecticut at Hartford, Windsor, and Wethersfield.[21]

[18] 1 *Rec. Mass. Bay* 96, 100; 8 Mass. Hist. Soc. Coll. (2nd ser.) 231–232. The justice of Pynchon's account was recognized by the General Court in March 1634/5 when it remitted five pounds due under its agreement with Pynchon at the time it repealed the June 1632 order. 1 *Rec. Mass. Bay* 140–141. See also the imposition by the General Court in May 1634 of a five-pound fine upon Thomas Mayhew and Pynchon for violation of an order against employing Indians to use firearms and of five pounds upon the Court of Assistants which authorized such conduct, the fines being remitted. 1 *Rec. Mass. Bay* 118. Wright states that Pynchon had asked to have the Indians armed because beaver could not be obtained otherwise. 1 *Story Western Mass.* 120. The same court imposed a five-pound fine, also remitted, upon Pynchon for refusal to pay his part of the last rate for Roxbury without distraint, on the ground that Roxbury was not equally rated with other towns. 1 *ibid.* 136. See also Winthrop's account in 1 Winthrop, *Hist. New England* 186. Wright states that the basis of Pynchon's objection was that the Roxbury lands were not the same fertile meadows as in other towns. 1 *Story Western Mass.* 119.

[19] See the description of the town in Wood's *New England's Prospect*, the earliest topographical account of Massachusetts (1634), reprinted in 1 *Memorial History of Boston* (ed. J. Winsor, 1880) 403.

[20] Moloney, *The Fur Trade in New England, 1620–1676* (1931) 49–50. One publication attributes Pynchon's motivation to his "instinct for adventure."

Springfield 1636–1936, p. 4, published by the 300th Anniversary Committee, May 1936. A recent writer states that Pynchon was not in sympathy with the rigid Calvinism of the church at Roxbury. J. L. Cox, "Governor William Pynchon," 3 *Hist. Pub. Soc. Col. Wars in Commonwealth Pa.,* No. 3 (1950) p. 5. No evidence found supports the statement (see 1 Lockwood, *Hist. Western Mass.* 1) that Pynchon was much interested in accounts furnished Governor Winthrop in 1631 by the Indian sachem Wahginnicut of fertile regions in the west. John Winthrop gave as reasons for the migration to the Connecticut Valley: the lack of accommodation for cattle in the Bay; the fruitfulness and commodiousness of Connecticut; and the "strong bent of their spirit to remove thither." Byington, *The Puritan in England and New England* (1896) 189. It has been stated that the Dutch in 1633–34 attempted to secure exclusive trading rights from the Indians in the vicinity of what was later to be Springfield and that Pynchon was aware of such attempt. 1 Wright, *Story Western Mass.* 123; 1 Lockwood, *Hist. Western Mass.* 90–91. The basis for the statement as to the Dutch is Bradford. *Of Plymouth Plantation, 1620–47* (ed. S. E. Morison, 1953) 270.

[21] 1 *Rec. Mass. Bay* 146; 2 Andrews, *Col. Period Amer. Hist.* 73; Andrews, *The Beginnings of Connecticut, 1632–1662* (Pub. Ter. Comm. State Conn., 1934) 3; Bradford, *Of Plymouth Plantation* 281; 1 Stiles, *The History and Genealogies of Ancient Windsor, Connecticut* (1891) 28–30.

When Pynchon made his first trip to the Connecticut River and how extensive his explorations were before he settled upon a site at Agawam, on the west bank of the Great River where it is joined by the Agawam or Westfield River, are subjects of speculation. An accepted view is that Pynchon with a few followers, coming in a shallop from Boston, visited the site of the proposed settlement in September 1635, entered into an oral agreement with the Indians to purchase the requisite lands, and erected a house on the west bank of the Connecticut.[22] The first permanent settlement was made in April or May of 1636 on the east bank of the River (Agawam being too encumbered with Indians) ; most of the settlers came overland. On May 14 Pynchon and seven others entered into "articles and orders to be observed and kept" by the signatories. These articles, largely concerned with the division of the plantation lands, expressed the intent to procure "some Godly and faithfull minister" and contemplated a settlement not exceeding fifty families.[23]

Pynchon's role in establishing the plantation is indicated by a recital in the articles that "Mr. William Pynchon, Jehu Burr and Henry Smith have constantly continued to prosecute this plantation when others fell off for feare of the difficultys, and continued to prosecute the same at greate charges and at great personall adventures." The minister procured was George Moxon, a Cambridge graduate ordained in 1626 and a former chaplain to Sir Edward Brereton; he had been censured several times by the Bishop of Chester for ignoring the ceremonies of the Church while serving in a Lancastershire parish.[24] He makes several appearances in the *Record*.

An agreement whereby title to the lands was obtained from the Indians was entered into on July 15, 1636; it reserved certain hunting and fishing privileges to the Indians.[25] It is probable that by this

22 1 Lockwood, *Hist. Western Mass.* 92; 1 Wright, *Story Western Mass.* 124–128. *Cf.* 1 Burt, *Hist. Springfield* 156 that the trip was overland. The references in the Dutch records to the establishment in 1635 of a trading post above Fort Hope on the Connecticut by a "Pinsen" or "Prinsen" apparently confuse Pynchon with Captain Holmes. See 1 *Doc. Rel. Col. Hist. N.Y.* 543, 565; 2 *ibid.* 134. Oliver B. Morris in his *Bi-Centennial Address at First Church in Springfield, May 25, 1836* (reprinted in 1 *Papers and Proc. Conn. Valley Hist. Soc.* 298, 305–306) stated that: "From a somewhat minute examination of our ancient records, and manuscripts, I am induced to believe that Mr. Pynchon with his son-in-law Henry Smith, and Jehu Burr, and per-

haps others of Roxbury, visited this river in 1634, explored the valley, and selected a place for their future settlement."

23 1 Wright, *Story Western Mass.* 130–131, 144–145; 48 *Mass. Hist. Soc. Proc.* 29; 1 Burt, *Hist. Springfield* 156–158. On March 17, 1635/6 Pynchon sold approximately £200 of goods at Roxbury, largely cloth, to John Winthrop, Jr. 3 *Winthrop Papers* 238, 255, 314.

24 1 Burt, *Hist. Springfield* 157; 1 Wright *Story of Western Mass.* 183–184; DNB article on George Moxon. The statement that Moxon moved to Agawam to be near his "old friend and neighbor," William Pynchon, is without support.

25 *Indian Deeds of Hampden County* (ed. H. A. Wright, 1905) 11–12. The con-

time Pynchon had commenced his trading operations. A warehouse constructed later on the lower end of Enfield Falls, the head of navigation for seagoing vessels, at what is still called Warehouse Point, played a large part in the success of these operations.[26] This site afforded easy access to the upper reaches of the Connecticut, to the Bay via overland paths, and to the Mohawk country via the Westfield River.

At the time of the Agawam settlement the General Court had already taken steps to govern those inhabitants who had settled or intended settlement along the Connecticut River by granting a commission on March 3, 1635/6, limited to a one-year period, to Roger Ludlow, William Pynchon, John Steele, William Swaine, Henry Smith, William Phelpes, William Westwood, and Andrew Ward, or the greater part of them, with full authority to hear and determine all differences which might arise between party and party, as well as misdemeanors, to inflict capital punishment or imprisonment, and to impose fines. Also granted was the power to make such orders for the peaceable and quiet ordering the affairs of the plantation as best conduced to the public good. The powers granted were to be exercised as a court to which the inhabitants of the River towns were to be convented, although the power to inflict corporal punishment might be exercised by two commissioners, if the occasion warranted.[27]

Under this commission a number of meetings were held in the River towns of Hartford, Windsor, and Wethersfield, although Pynchon attended only one. After the expiration of the commission by its terms in March 1636/7 the inhabitants of the River towns in effect set up an independent government by electing magistrates, including Pynchon and Henry Smith, and sending "committees" of deputies from each town to join with magistrates in a Connecticut "General Court." [28] From the start the relation between Pynchon and this *de facto* government was marked by friction. Having declared war against the Pequots at a meeting at which he was not present, the government, cautioning Pynchon to avoid betrayal by friendship with the Indians, not only failed to afford any protection

sideration, £30 of wampum, blanket-coats, hatchets, hoes, and knives, was advanced by Pynchon who was not reimbursed until 1647. 1 Lockwood, *Hist. Western Mass.* 98–99.

26 See the June 2, 1636 letter to John Winthrop, Jr., in charge of the Saybrook plantation at "the Rivers Mouth," acknowledging receipt of some wampum. 48 *Mass. Hist. Soc. Proc.* 38–39. An October 5, 1684 reference in the Enfield com-

mittee book refers to the former warehouse at Warehouse Point built fortyeight years earlier by William Pynchon. 1 Allen, *The History of Enfield, Connecticut* (1900) 92–93. Wright also refers to a Pynchon warehouse at Saybrook under the charge of Stephen Winthrop. 1 *Story Western Mass.* 152.

27 1 *Rec. Mass. Bay* 170–171.
28 1 *Pub. Rec. Col. Conn.* 1–3, 5–7.

to outlying Agawam, but even pressed into service one of Pynchon's boats. Later, when a tax to defray the costs of the war was levied upon Agawam, Pynchon protested a prior understanding "that if we would look to ourselves you would expect no more at our handes," that the defensive measures employed at Agawam "have not been chargeable to any of you" and that, in any event, he had been rated for the war in the Bay for his whole estate.[29]

Another source of annoyance was the adoption of a system, similar to that formerly in effect in the Bay, of granting rights in the beaver trade to one or two persons in each town in return for a payment of one shilling per skin. Pynchon, granted the monopoly at Agawam, may have doubted the enforceability of the exclusive features of such grants. Or, he may have been concerned that he was being taxed for a monopoly he in fact already enjoyed when he complained that, "I cannot see how it can well stand with the public good and the liberty of free men to make a monopole of trade." [30]

The most serious controversy developed over a shortage of corn, with its threat of ensuing famine, which developed in the River towns as a result of the poor crop harvested in 1637, the year of the Pequot hostilities. To alleviate the shortage, the General Court of the towns in March 1637/8 instructed Pynchon to purchase corn from the Indians at about five shillings per bushel. Others were forbidden to trade for corn with the Indians, except in case of necessity. When Pynchon attempted to carry out his mandate, he found the Indians at Agawam unwilling to sell at the stipulated price and so informed the Hartford authorities. The General Court promptly sent Captain John Mason, conqueror of the Pequots, up the river to obtain the necessary supply. Mason obtained little or no corn at the prices he offered and returned to Hartford convinced that Pynchon was attempting to profit by the shortage.[31]

Shortly after Mason's return the General Court summoned Pynchon before it on charges of "unfaithful dealing in the trade of corne" and breach of his oath as a magistrate, alleging that Pynchon had obstructed Mason in the performance of his mission by forbidding the Indians to trade with the Captain and by refusing to procure a canoe needed for their transportation to Woronoco. Pynchon replied that he had sought to have the Indians do business with Mason and that, even when his own family and neighbors were in want of corn, he had refused to exceed the maximum price fixed by his

29 8 Mass. Hist. Soc. Coll. (2nd ser.) 235–237; 58 Mass. Hist. Soc. Proc. 387–388; 64 ibid. 83. Bliss found no indication that Agawam contributed either money or troops to the Pequot war. An Address, De-livered at the Opening of the Town-Hall in Springfield, March 24, 1828 (1828).
30 58 Mass. Hist. Soc. Proc. 388.
31 1 Pub. Rec. Col. Conn. 11, 13, 16; 48 Mass. Hist. Soc. Proc. 40–48.

instructions in order to induce the Indians to sell. The use of the canoe had been refused by its owner who needed it during the planting season.[32]

The General Court, in the course of its hearings, sent for the Reverend Thomas Hooker, then pastor of the Hartford Church, and Samuel Stone, teacher, for an opinion on the questions involved. Hooker accused Pynchon of holding off buying in order to obtain a monopoly and delivered his judgment that Pynchon had broken his oath. Following Hooker's opinion, the Court fined Pynchon forty bushels of corn as "he was not soe carefull to promote the publicque good in the trade of corne as hee was bounde to doe." Pynchon's justification came within a few months when Mason, with a show of arms and threats of force, still was compelled to pay twelve shillings a bushel in order to obtain any corn from the Indians.[33]

Pynchon did not submit tamely to the General Court's judgment. A statement of his, probably presented to the General Court, shows reliance upon principles of English law, buttressed with a reference to "Sir John Fortescue in his treatise of Rights."[34] The charges against Pynchon in connection with the corn purchases were also taken up to the elders of the church at Windsor but, after several years delay, were apparently referred to the church at Roxbury which eventually, it has been assumed, cleared Pynchon of any fault in the matter.[35]

Despite the judgment passed upon Pynchon by the Connecticut General Court, Roger Ludlow on May 29, 1638, in behalf of that body, commissioned John Haynes, William Pynchon, and John Steele to treat with the Massachusetts authorities as to some "rules, articles and agreements" for the purpose of combining and uniting the Connecticut plantations with Massachusetts Bay, in accordance with some preliminary discussions held in Boston the previous summer. While the records of the meeting have not survived, it appears that in June at a meeting in Cambridge of the Massachusetts General Court, Pynchon, to the consternation of his fellow commissioners, expressed a desire to remain under the Massachusetts Bay government.[36] Some

[32] 48 ibid. 40–51.

[33] 48 ibid. 43–48; 1 Pub. Rec. Col. Conn. 19. See also Perry Miller, "Thomas Hooker and the Democracy of Early Connecticut," 4 N. Eng. Quart. (1931) 663, 710–711, and the same author's more recent account in Errand into the Wilderness (1956) 45–46.

[34] 48 Mass. Hist. Soc. Proc. 47–48.

[35] 48 ibid. 48–50; Morison, William Pynchon 87; Cox, Governor William Pynchon 8.

[36] Morison, William Pynchon 87; Cox, Governor William Pynchon, 8. Baldwin, "The Secession of Springfield from Connecticut," 12 Pub. Col. Soc. Mass. 68–69. See also Ludlow's communication to the Bay authorities on the mission of the Connecticut commissioners. 4 Winthrop Papers, 36–37. At a July 23, 1649 meeting of the Commissioners for the United Colonies the Connecticut commissioners stated that Pynchon's "apprehension that Springfield

light is cast upon this meeting by a passage from Winthrop's *Journal* written at a later date:

> The differences between us and those of Connecticut were divers; but the ground of all was their shyness of coming under our government, which, though we never intended to make them subordinate to us, yet they were very jealous.[37]

The attitude of the River towns toward Pynchon's desertion is most vividly expressed in a famous letter from Thomas Hooker to John Winthrop, written in December 1638, concerning the "business of Agaam." As might be expected, the characterization of Pynchon's conduct is harsh.[38]

Hooker, in emphasizing the inconvenience and charges of Agawam settlers seeking justice in small causes in courts located in the Bay, failed to appreciate that, following the example of the River towns, the Agawam inhabitants might also establish their own court. Such establishment in fact took place on February 14, 1638/9 and constitutes the first entry in the *Record*.

However, it was not until June 2, 1641 that Agawam, by then called Springfield after the birthplace of its founder, was integrated into the Massachusetts Bay frame of government. On this date, the General Court made answer to a petition of William Pynchon and others of Springfield that some of their neighbors upon the Connecticut had taken offense at petitioners for adhering to Massachusetts Bay and withdrawing from the General Court on the River, on the supposition that petitioners had been dismissed from the Massachusetts jurisdiction and that the General Court of the Bay had bound itself by its own act from claiming any jurisdiction or interest in Agawam, now Springfield.[39]

To this petition the General Court replied that support for the supposition rested upon misrecital of passages from the March 3, 1635/6 commission for government of those settling upon the Connecticut; that such commission was not granted with the intent either to dismiss persons from the Bay government or to determine any jurisdictional limits; and that the limitation of the commission to

would fall within the Massachusetts line" had not been declared prior to June 1638 and arose "from a present pang of discontent upon a sensure hee then lay under by the Government of Conectacutt." Baldwin, *Secession* 70.

[37] 1 *Winthrop's Journal, "History of New England," 1630–1649* (ed. J. K. Hosmer, 1908) 287.

[38] 1 *Conn. Hist. Soc. Coll.* 12 ff. For Winthrop's letter of August 28, 1638, see *Winthrop's Journal* 290; 4 *Winthrop Pa-*

pers 53–54. On Hooker's letter, see also Miller, *Thomas Hooker* 700–701, and *Errand Into the Wilderness* 39–40. In April, 1640 the Reverend Moxon anxiously sought advice from Winthrop as to the status of Springfield. 4 *Winthrop Papers* 254.

[39] 1 *Rec. Mass. Bay* 320–321. As to derivation of the town name see Hubbard, *History of New England*, 6 Mass. Hist. Soc. Coll. (2nd ser.) 308.

one year showed an intent by the grantor to reserve an interest upon the River and by the grantees to stand to the condition of the license of departure given most of them, that they remain part of the body of the commonwealth. The General Court thereupon granted William Pynchon authority to govern the inhabitants of Springfield and to exercise certain judicial powers.[40]

Relatively little is known concerning William Pynchon's activities once Agawam returned to the Massachusetts Bay fold. As the settlement grew slowly in size, its founder continued to engage extensively in the fur trade, although most statements as to the volume of this trade are based upon the later trade of his son John.[41] In 1640 Timothy Cooper was sent to Woronoco to tap the flow of furs from the Mohawks. When Connecticut sought to grant trading rights at this location to Governor Edward Hopkins and William Whitney, Pynchon complained to the Bay authorities who successfully asserted the jurisdiction of Massachusetts before the Commissioners for the United Colonies in 1644.[42] Pynchon may have had some interest in the Winthrop graphite workings at Tantiusque for he endeavored to keep the surrounding Indians friendly and interested in searching for further deposits, as well as supplying provisions.[43]

There is some indication that during the late 1640's the Connecticut Valley beaver trade began to decline. In 1650 the Dutch from New Amsterdam complained to the Commissioners for the United Colonies that Pynchon had ruined the beaver trade by paying too high prices for skins. Johnson, in his *Wonder-working Providence of Sion's Savior in New England,* published in London in 1654, de-

[40] 1 *Rec. Mass. Bay* 321. See also the four heads of a reply to George Fenwick which Governor Dudley was directed to make by the General Court on June 2, 1641. 87 *Mass. Archives* 251; reprinted in Jones, *The Life and Work of Thomas Dudley* (1899) 283, note.

[41] At the September 1642 General Court Pynchon was appointed to pay according to the order for the beaver trade. A year later he was ordered to pay for his beaver trade from the time of the running of the line. 2 *Rec. Mass. Bay* 31, 44. The only surviving account book of William Pynchon, kept by his son, contains entries of what amounted to a "country store" supplying the Springfield inhabitants with a variety of manufactured goods, largely in exchange for produce and services. See volume catalogued as *William Pynchon record of accounts with early settlers and Indians carried forward from previous book around September, 1645 and to a new book*

around March, 1650 at the Forbes Library in Northampton, Mass. For the allocation of lands in Springfield c. 1645, see map opposite p. 84 of Wright, *Early Springfield and Longmeadow, Massachusetts, with Special Reference to Benjamin Cooley, Pioneer,* constituting C. IV of *The Cooley Genealogy* (1941). See also Bailyn, *The New England Merchants in the Seventeenth Century* (1955) 53–54.

[42] Moloney, *Fur Trade in New England* 52–53; 9 *Rec. Col. New Plymouth* 21; 1 Lockwood, *Hist. Western Mass.* 16; Bagg, "Ruling Spirit and Good Genius of First Settlers of Western Massachusetts—William Pynchon," 20 *Americana* 220–221. See 2 *Rec. Mass. Bay* 44 for reference to the Warwick patentees' claim to Woronoco.

[43] 4 *Winthrop Papers* 495–496. See also Haynes, "'The Tale of the Tantiusque', An Early Mining Venture in Massachusetts," 14 *Amer. Antiq. Soc. Proc.* (ns) 471–497.

scribed Springfield as "fitly seated for a Bever trade with the Indians, till the Merchants encreased so many, that it became little worth, by reason of their outbuying one another, which hath caused them to live upon husbandry." [44] Closely related to Pynchon's trading activities was his opposition before the Commissioners for the United Colonies to the imposts which Connecticut sought to impose upon the corn and beaver skins of Springfield inhabitants, shipped to sea via the Connecticut River, in order to defray the expense of maintaining a fort at Saybrook. Although Pynchon's view was rejected by the Commissioners, fear of retaliation by Massachusetts Bay ultimately brought the Connecticut authorities to heel.[45]

By virtue of geography and economics Pynchon was in close contact with Indian matters. In April 1636, even before the Agawam settlement, Pynchon cautioned John Winthrop, Jr., that he take careful information on the killing of two English by the Indians so "that a course of justice may be taken so as may be cleere to all that the course is just." [46] In August 1637 Ludlow, Pynchon, and others brought to Boston the scalps of Sassacus and other Pequot sachems whom the Mohawks had slain when the Pequots, fleeing from the English, had sought refuge with them.[47]

In July 1648 Pynchon may have averted a dangerous Indian war by refusing a request of several of the magistrates, spurred on by John Eliot, to assist some Indians of Quabaug in apprehending some murderers at Naucotok (Northampton) on the basis that the murdered Indians were subjects and the offenders within the colony jurisdiction. While self-interest may have dictated the answer, Pynchon, refusing the request, stressed the danger of a war and resorted to legal principles in stating that the culprits were not subjects within the Bay jurisdiction. Governor Dudley apparently accepted the views of Pynchon who proposed a safer, if less efficacious, method of bringing the offenders to justice. This stand has caused Pynchon to be hailed as a champion of Indian rights; however, complaints about his punishment of an Indian at Agawam had earlier led the Connecticut General Court to adopt an order regulating the punishment of Indians.[48]

[44] 9 *Rec. Col. New Plymouth* 172, 178; Johnson's *Wonder-Working Providence, 1628–1651* (ed. J. F. Jameson, 1910) 237.

[45] 9 *Rec. Col. New Plymouth* 80, 89–93, 128–136, 151–158; 5 *Winthrop Papers* 89–92, 134–137, 142–143, 271. See also 2 *Rec. Mass. Bay* 182, 268–270; 1 *Pub. Rec. Col. Conn.* 119–120.

[46] 3 *Winthrop Papers* 254–255.

[47] 1 Winthrop, *Hist. New England* 281. For Pynchon letters to John Winthrop on Indian matters, see 4 *Winthrop Papers* 443–444; 5 *ibid.* 5, 114–115.

[48] 2 Winthrop, *Hist. New England* 397, 467–471; H. Morris, *Early History of Springfield* (1876) 68–71; 1 *Pub. Rec. Col. Conn.* 13–14.

At a December 10, 1641 General Court Pynchon and several others were mentioned to be proposed to the towns as new magistrates. Accordingly, when the General Court met in May 1642 William Pynchon again took an oath as assistant. He continued to be chosen an assistant each year until 1651 by which time he had become embroiled with the General Court on a charge of heretical writings.[49] In his capacity as assistant he not only attended the General Court but also sat on the Court of Assistants; in both capacities he exercised a judicial function.

Only a few documents have survived to indicate Pynchon's attitudes on the many political events of the 1640's in both Massachusetts and England.[50] Of particular interest is his attitude toward the criticism of the administration of justice in Massachusetts Bay which welled up in 1646, principally in connection with the "Remonstrance and humble Petition" presented to the General Court by Robert Child and six others in May of that year. This document, political in nature, was severely critical of existing conditions and advocated drastic reforms unacceptable to the authorities.[51] Probably Pynchon's best known letter was written March 9, 1646/7 to John Winthrop in connection with the documents seized when Child was about to embark for England. This letter reads, in part:

But how soever their endevors cannot but have an ill construction; yet I thinke the Courte both of magistrates and deputies, should not turne of[f] all the particulars wherin they desyre a Reformation, without making a right use of so much of their petition as doth justly calle for reformation: for as we had the happinesse to be bredd and borne under such lawes for civill goverment as I conceive no nation hath better, so it should be our care, in thankefulnesse both to God and that state to preserve and adhere to what ever lawes or customes they have except those that be contrary to God, and therin we must obey God and not man, and yet we have liberty from that pattent to make what soever by lawes may tend to the good of this place; and I cannot but apprehend that your spirit lies this way for I remember at our first comminge, as soone as ever

[49] 1 *Rec. Mass. Bay* 345; 2 *ibid*, 2; 3 *N. Eng. Hist. and Gen. Reg.* 189.

[50] See 4 *Winthrop Papers* 443–444; 5 *ibid.* 90–92, 271.

[51] For the remonstrance, see Hutchinson, *Collection of Original Papers relative to the History of the Colony of Massachusetts Bay* (1769) 188 ff. The most detailed accounts of the episode are found in G. L. Kittredge, "Dr. Robert Child the Remonstrant," 21 *Pub. Col. Soc. Mass.* 146; W. T. R. Marvin in his introduction to a reprint of Major John Child's *New-England's Jonas Cast Up at London* (1647; reprinted 1869) ; 2 Palfrey, *History of New England* (1892) 165–179; Hubbard, *General History of New England* (1815) 499–519; Oliver, *The Puritan Commonwealth* (1856) 420–430; 1 Hutchinson, *Hist. Col. and Prov. Mass. Bay* (ed. L. S. Mayo, 1936) 124–127; 1 Osgood, *The American Colonies in the Seventeenth Century*, 257–264; 3 *ibid.* 111–112; Smith, *Appeals to the Privy Council from the American Plantations* (1950) 45–47.

the people were divided into severall plantations, you did presently nominate a conestable for each plantation as the most common officers of the Kings peace, and gave them their oath in true substance as the conestables take it in England: likewise all controversies about meum and tuum were tryed by Juries after the manner of England, and after a while grand Juries were appointed for further inquiry into such matters as might tend to the Kings peace; and still thes courses I thinke are continued and thes courses are the best courses that this commonwealth can take if they have free liberty to alter: as Fortescue in commendation of the lawes of England [to] my satisfaction doth shew he gives good Reasons for the necessary use of Juries for all tryalls shewing that it is consonant to the word of God and preferrs it far above the course of Justice in France which is also of high respect.

But that wherin I feare the Generall Court is most faulty is, in that they doe not issue out all warrants in the name of the Kinge: I know no hurt in it: for what though the Kinge be never so corrupt in Religion and manners yet if his subjectes will be faithfull to the lawes of England he cannot hurt his subjectes, for when warrantes are issued out in the name of the Kinge, they are not issued out in the name of his personall prerogatives, but in the name of his power which is his lawes and therefore if his subjectes will sticke to his lawes (as the Parliament do at this day) the King cannot wrong them. Thes things you know much better than my selfe.

Again by the lawes of England if any of our people will stand uppon the priviledge of an English subject: they may I conceive lawfull disobey warrants of processe or Attachments and the like In case the warrants be not made in dew fourme accordinge to the lawes of England: as for example if they be not dated or if they be dated in any place out of the Jurisdiction or if they be not subscribed by such as are in authority. Thes and many such like circumstances may mak warrantes illegall and so a nullity as Dalton in his Country Justice sheweth at large and to my greefe I have seene many warrantes failing in thes circumstances But above all if warrants be not sent out in the name of the King they are not legall: we are not a Free state neather do I apprehend that magistrates Elders or deputies doe think we are a Free state, neather do I think it our wisdome to be a Free state though we had our liberty we cannot as yet subsist without England.[52]

William Pynchon has been closely linked by historians with two of the earliest witchcraft proceedings in Massachusetts Bay—those against Mary and Hugh Parsons of Springfield. Their first connection with witchcraft appears in the *Record* when Pynchon, on May 30, 1649, in a case of criminal defamation sentenced Mary Parsons to

52 5 *Winthrop Papers* 134–137; 6 Mass. Hist. Soc. Coll. (4th ser.) 381; reprinted in part in 1 *Records of the Court of Assistants of the Colony of the Massachusetts Bay, 1630–1692* (1901) ix.

twenty lashes or payment of three pounds to the widow Marshfield for spreading reports that the widow was suspected of being a witch.[53]

This sentence seems to have had little effect upon Mary Parsons who had married Hugh Parsons, her second husband, in 1645. Obviously a mental case, she now concentrated upon spreading reports that her husband was a witch. However, it is not until a year and a half later that there was further mention of the Parsons in connection with witchcraft. At the New York Public Library is a record, largely in William Pynchon's hand, of examinations in Springfield of Hugh Parsons who had been "attached upon Suspition of Witchcraft." [54] The manuscript refers to two examinations, one on March 1, 1650/1 and one later, perhaps on March 18. However, the manuscript contains statements made under oath before Pynchon on thirteen different days, starting as early as February 25, 1650/1 and extending to April 7. It indicates that Mary Parsons was also examined by Pynchon on the same suspicion but no record of her examination appears to have survived. Whether complaint was made against either of the Parsons or whether William Pynchon acted upon his own view of the case is not discernible. In its broader aspects the Parsons incident may be related to the first witchcraft cases in the Bay and in Connecticut and the stern repression of witchcraft in England by Matthew Hopkins a few years earlier.

Apart from the Parsons, thirty-five persons testified under oath or volunteered information; few prominent Springfield names were absent. The case against Hugh rested in large part on the testimony of his wife, his "biggest Accuser," that he was a witch. Others testified as to the unpleasant things that happened to people or their possessions when Hugh threatened "to get even" with them, to the presence of Hugh when events took place without natural explanation, to his unnatural lack of grief when his child died, and to his frequent appearance in the hallucinations of those subject to fits. Several witnesses testified that when Hugh, in paying the widow Marshfield for his wife's defamation, was refused an abatement, he threatened that the corn would avail her little.

Mary appears to have been taken into custody at some point during Hugh's examination and was probably transported to the Bay to stand trial late in March or early April 1651. Hugh was in chains in custody of the constable on March 2; when he was transported to the

[53] *Rec.* 32–33. For Pynchon's earlier (1645) problems with Mary Parsons, then Mary Lewis, see 5 *Winthrop Papers* 45, 50.
[54] The manuscript has been printed in Drake, *Annals of Witchcraft in New England, and Elsewhere in The United States from Their First Settlement* (1869) 219–258.

Bay does not appear. Despite some contentions to the contrary, neither Mary nor Hugh was "tried" at Springfield; the offenses charged were beyond Pynchon's jurisdiction to hear and determine. There is nothing in the *Record* regarding the examination of either Mary or Hugh.

On May 8, 1651 the General Court "understanding that Mary Parsons, now in prison accused for a witch, is likely, through weaknes, to dye before triall if it be deferred," ordered that she be brought before it and tried the next morning at 8 o'clock, "the rather that Mr. Pinchon maybe present to give his testimony in the case." However, it was not until May 13 that Mary, "being committed to prison for suspition of witchcraft, as also for murdering hir oune child" was called forth and indicted for witchcraft. Mary pleaded not guilty to the indictment, and after the evidences against her were heard and examined, the Court found that they "were not sufficcient to proove hir a witch"; therefore she was cleared in that respect.[55]

Mary Parsons, then indicted for the murder of her child, acknowledged herself guilty of this charge. The Court, finding her guilty of murder by her own confession, sentenced her to death by hanging. However, a marginal notation in the General Court records states that Mary was reprieved until May 29. No official record has been found of her execution; most writers accept the view that she died in prison shortly after sentencing.[56]

What happened to Hugh Parsons between his apprehension in March 1651 and his trial in May 1652 is far from clear. On May 20, 1651, Henry Smith, who by this time had been granted judicial au-

[55] 4 *Rec. Mass. Bay* (*Part I*) 47–48; 3 *ibid*. 229. There is no indication that Pynchon gave testimony against the accused.

[56] 4 *ibid* (*Part I*) 48. William F. Poole in "Witchcraft in Boston" (chapter IV of 2 *Memorial History Boston*, pp. 137–138), in concluding that Mary Parsons was executed, relied largely on a London newspaper, *Mercurius Publicus*, of September 25, 1651, in which a letter "from Natick, in New England, July 4, 1651," attributed to John Eliot, the Indian apostle, stated with respect to witchcraft that: "Four in Springfield were detected, whereof one was executed for murder of her own child, and was doubtless a witch; another is condemned, a third under trial, a fourth under suspicion." Poole also construes a passage in Cotton Mather's *Wonders of the Invisible World* as a reference to Mary Parsons. Hutchinson, finding no record or contemporary account of the execution of Mary Parsons (mistakenly called Mary Oliver) concluded that, "I do not find that she was executed." 2 *Hist. Col. and Prov. Mass. Bay* 12. Johnson in his *Wonder-working Providence of Sion's Savior in New England*, which carries the history of New England to 1651, only states of Springfield that: "There hath of late been more than one in this Towne greatly suspected of witchcraft, yet have they used much diligence, both for the finding them out and for the Lord's assisting them against their witchery, yet have they, as is supposed, bewitched not a few Persons, among whom two of the reverend Elder's children." Hale's *Modest Inquiry Concerning Witchcraft* (p. 19) mentions "two or three of Springfield" being executed but has one whose circumstances are reminiscent of Mary Parsons.

thority in Springfield, took further testimony in Boston.[57] Seemingly Parsons was in prison in October 1651, for we find an order by the General Court on October 24 that a Court of Assistants be held in January to try those in prison accused of witchcraft. The most material witnesses in Springfield were to be summoned to the Court of Assistants to give in their evidence against the prisoners. There is no explanation of the plurality of prisoners, but Mary Parsons in her examination may have implicated others.[58]

On May 12, 1652, a grand jury at the Court of Assistants indicted Hugh Parsons for witchcraft. The trial jury found him guilty. The assistants not consenting to the verdict of the jury, the cause came before the General Court. This body, on May 31, 1652, calling the prisoner to the bar and considering the evidences brought in against him, judged that he was not legally guilty of witchcraft. Acquitted, Parsons never returned to Springfield.[59]

Much of the tarnish upon William Pynchon's reputation stems from the treatment accorded the Mary and Hugh Parsons cases by historian Samuel G. Drake in his *Annals of Witchcraft,* a treatment that contains glaring errors, important omissions, and no understanding of the legal procedure of the period. Distorting a contemporary reference, Drake asserts that "Witches were disturbing the Peace of the People of Springfield ten Years" before William Pynchon "felt compelled to set up his Inquisition," and insinuates that, since the offenders "were at first among a Class of Denizens of too high social Standing to admit an Interference," Pynchon waited until suspicion fell upon Hugh Parsons, an "honest, sensible laboring Man, a Sawyer by Occupation." [60]

There are no facts to support such insinuations. If Hugh Parsons had anybody to blame for his plight, it was his wife and himself for

[57] Smith took the evidence of Symon Beamon, a Pynchon servant, on May 20. This testimony and related testimony of Jonathan Taylor, originally given before Pynchon on March 21, 1650/51, are followed in the manuscript examination of Hugh by a notation "Deposed before the court 17.4 mo: 1651," signed by Edward Rawson, Secretary of the General Court. This deposition was probably not made before the General Court; it may have been made before the Court of Assistants. Three other depositions were taken during the period May 20–26th. See 35 *N. Eng. Hist. and Gen. Reg.* 152–153.

[58] 3 *Rec. Mass. Bay* 273. The testimony as to Mary Parsons' conversation with Thomas Cooper, who was appointed to watch her in March, certainly implicated Goodwife Merrick and Besse Sewell. Drake, *Annals of Witchcraft* 244–245.

[59] 4 *Rec. Mass. Bay (Part I)* 96; Drake, *Annals of Witchcraft* 68–70. It would appear that Jonathan Taylor, George Colton, Hannah Langton and Samuel Marshfield were the witnesses summoned from Springfield who appeared at Hugh Parsons' trial on May 13th.

[60] Drake, *Annals of Witchcraft* 65–66. The contemporary reference was to the passage from Johnson's *Wonder-working Providence of Sion's Saviour in New England* set forth in note 56. Drake's views were given further currency in Burt, *Cornet Joseph Parsons* (1898) 8,

his foolhardy habit of threatening to "get even" with those who crossed him. His inept answers at his examination must have confirmed any doubts as to his guilt, being characterized by evasions, equivocation, falsehoods, refuge in rules of evidence (one witness not sufficient), and pregnant silences. The contention that "there was Something like Conspiracy against Parsons," seems to be based upon the fact that, prior to his examination, Parsons was not informed of the identity of his accusers; yet he must have known his wife would be the principal accuser. Once the examination started it appears that most, if not all, the accusing witnesses testified in his presence, and he was given frequent opportunity to answer the charges. Most laudable in Parsons' conduct was his steadfast refusal to allow Pynchon to "saddle the right horse" by casting suspicion on others.

Drake comments that "the Testimonies amount to Nothing, being a collection of as childish Nonsense as ever was got together." [61] By present-day standards this condemnation is just. However, the evidence was typical of that received in seventeenth-century witchcraft trials in Massachusetts Bay and elsewhere, and Pynchon had no alternative but to receive it. What is harder to justify is that the examinations reveal that William Pynchon, enlightened as he may have been in some respects, clearly accepted the existence of witchcraft as a supernatural phenomenon. [62]

It should also be remembered that Pynchon, in conducting the examinations of the Parsons, was not entirely a neophyte. In June 1648, he had sat on the General Court at which Margaret Jones of Charlestown was indicted, found guilty of witchcraft, and hanged— the first case of capital punishment for witchcraft in the colony. [63]

[61] Drake, *Annals of Witchcraft*, 70–71.

[62] Drake, *Annals of Witchcraft* 233, 253. Two depositions, those of William Branch and Thomas Stebbins, taken in Parsons v. Bridgman, a slander action tried in the County Court of Middlesex County at Cambridge on October 7, 1656, reveal William Pynchon admitting inability to explain supernatural events connected with another Mary Parsons, the wife of Joseph Parsons of Northampton, formerly of Long Meadow, and no relation to the wife of Hugh Parsons. (The identity of names and the fact that the Mary Parsons of Northampton was involved in both a civil action for defamation and a criminal proceeding for witchcraft has confused historians over the years.) Most of the depositions in this case are in the Office of the Clerk, Superior Court, Middlesex County, Mass. (East Cambridge) in Folder 16 (1656) of file papers. Photostatic copies are in the Harvard Law School Library in two volumes entitled *Papers in Cases Before The County Court of Middlesex County, 1649–63*, running from about item 646 to item 674. The depositions have been summarized in 1 Trumbull, *Hist. Northampton* 43–50. For the judgment for plaintiff in the manuscript court records, see 1 *Middlesex County Court Records, 1649–62*, 110. An account in Burt, *Cornet Joseph Parsons* 45–46 is inaccurate and unreliable.

[63] For a treatment of this case, see Poole, *Witchcraft in Boston* in 2 *Memorial History Boston* 133–137.

This Court had resorted to a forced search of the prisoner's person to determine if she had "the Devil's mark" in some secret place and to the same course adopted in England of watching for her familiar or imp.[64]

In the absence of the record of the examination of Mary Parsons one cannot tell whether Pynchon ordered the accused searched for "the Devil's mark"; however, there is nothing in the examination of Hugh to suggest that either was exposed to such indignity. Such examination does show that several persons were appointed by Pynchon to "watch" Mary. What form the watching took and what results were obtained is not clear. Nothing indicates that watchers were appointed for Hugh.[65] On the whole, the conduct of Pynchon appears much less vigorous than that of the General Court in the case of Margaret Jones. And, if, as certain contemporary accounts indicate, Springfield in 1650–51 was threatened with a rash of witchcraft cases, his skillful handling of the situation kept Springfield from being linked with Salem in the annals of witchcraft.

While William Pynchon was sitting in the examinations of the Parsons he himself was under a cloud as the result of the publication in London in June 1650 of a book entitled *The Meritorious Price of Our Redemption, Justification, etc. Cleering it from some common Errors . . .* by "William Pinchin, Gentleman, in New England." In the form of a discourse between "a Trades-man and A Divine" the book was designed to prove that "Christ did not suffer for us those un-utterable Torments of Gods Wrath, which commonly are called Hell-Torments, to redeem our Souls from them" and that "Christ did not bear our Sins by Gods Imputation, and therefore he did not bear the Curse of the Law for them." The reader was notified that the argument set forth was "framed by M. Henry Smith a godly Preacher, neer thirty years since, in my presence." [66]

[64] Poole, *Witchcraft in Boston* 135, refers to Gaule, *Select Cases of Conscience touching Witches and Witchcraft* (1646) who describes the mode of "watching a witch" in England.

[65] Mary Parsons testified in the course of the examination of her husband that she had made an inconclusive search of Hugh's body while he slept, while Hugh testified that his wife had denied him the same privilege. Drake, *Annals of Witchcraft* 240–241, 244, 248.

[66] In 16 *Bibliotheca Americana* (1886) 153 Sabin places publication on or about June 2, 1650. The fact that the title page states that the volume was "Printed by J. M. for George Whittington, and James Moxon" has led to the assumption that a relative of the Reverend Moxon was connected with the publication. James and Joseph Moxon were printers in London in 1650; the latter became famous as the first practical English writer on the mechanics of typography. See Reed, *A History of the Old English Letter Founders* (Rev. ed., 1952) 168 ff. The DNB accounts of George Moxon and Joseph Moxon show both were born in or near Wakefield in Yorkshire. Once thought exceedingly rare, at least eight copies have been located; they are in the British Museum, New York Public Library, Connecticut Valley Historical Museum, Congregational Library in Boston, Bodleian, Balliol College (Oxford), Hunt-

Henry M. Burt, Springfield historian, has this to say of the book:

This work was a protest against the Calvinistic theology as preached by the clergy of that day, and proves Mr. Pynchon to have been a profound scholar, a logical writer, and an independent thinker. He read his Bible in the original tongues, and while a sincere believer in the literal truth of the Scriptures and in the exact fulfillment of prophecy, he was his own interpreter and he would not accept as a part of his faith the system which Calvin had framed in all its terrible details. In his book he condemned specially the doctrine that Christ suffered the wrath of God and the torments of hell to pay man's debt to his Creator. His theory of the atonement was that, inasmuch as sin came into the world through Adam's disobedience, so Christ by his perfect obedience, paid the full price of our redemption. The killing of Jesus was not the display of God's wrath, but was the work of the devil through his instruments, the Jews and the Roman soldiers. The theory that the guilt of the world was laid upon or imputed to Christ he denounced unsparingly.[67]

What motivated William Pynchon to put into print the product of thirty years intellectual gestation is one of the darker corners of his career. He must have known it would arouse wrath and indignation in Boston. The first copies of the book apparently arrived in Boston in the second week of October 1650. The General Court, then in session, after a quick examination of the volume, on October 15, 1650, ordered: first, that a protest be drawn to notify all men that the Court, far from approving the volume, did "utterly dislike it and detest it as erronious and daingerous"; secondly, that the book be answered by one of the elders; thirdly, that the author be summoned to appear before the next General Court to answer for his publication; and, fourthly, that the book be burnt by the executioner, or such other person as the magistrates should appoint, in the market in Boston the next day after the lecture. A "Declaration and Protesta-

ington Library, and The Free Library of Philadelphia. There may be others still in private hands, such as the Hollingsworth copy referred to in 1 Wright, *Story Western Mass.* 200–201. No support has been found for the statement that the edition was "quite large and quickly exhausted." See 1 Lockwood, *Hist. Western Mass.* 101. Several standard reference works state that Pynchon published the book "during a visit to England in 1650." This could not have been so since the *Record* shows Pynchon was in Springfield on June 10th (*Rec.* 39). The *Record* refers to several

indentures between Pynchon and servants in Barnett, England, entered into on April 22 and 29, 1650 but these must have been entered into by an agent since it further appears from the *Record* that Pynchon was in Springfield on May 7. See *Rec.* 38, 42–43, 45.

[67] 1 Burt, *Hist. Springfield* 80. See also F. H. Foster, *A Genetic History of the New England Theology* (1907) 16–19 and Byington, "William Pynchon, the Founder of Springfield," 2 *Papers and Proc. Conn. Valley Hist. Soc.* 32.

tion" was drawn up to be signed by the Secretary and sent to England to be printed.[68]

The General Court also ordered that the Reverend John Norton of Ipswich be entreated to answer Pynchon's work and that the latter be summoned to appear before the next General Court to answer for it. On May 7, 1651 William Pynchon appeared before the General Court and owned the book to be his. The Court, out of its "tender respect" to the author, then offered him liberty to confer with the reverend elders present. Pynchon, taking this offer under consideration, returned "his mind" in a writing, dated May 9, 1651, in which he stated that he had "conferred with the Reverend Mr. Cotton, Mr. Norrice, and Mr. Norton, about some points of the greatest consequence in my booke, and I hope I have so explained my meaning to them, as to take of the worst construction," and admitted "that I have not spoken in my booke so fully of the prize and merit of Christs sufferings as I should have done." [69]

The Court on May 13, finding by Pynchon's writing that he was "in a hopefull way to give good sattisfaction," granted him liberty to return home. He was to have Mr. Norton's answer with him to consider so that at the October session of the Court he might appear and give "all due sattisfaction as is hoped for and desired." On October 24, 1651 the Court judged it meet that patience be exercised toward Pynchon that, if possible, he might be reduced into the way of truth and renounce the errors and heresies published in his book. To that end the Court gave him time to the next General Court, in May, more thoroughly to consider of such errors and heresies and to weigh Norton's answer, so that he might give full satisfaction for his offense. In case he did not give satisfaction, the Court ordered that judgment be suspended till the Court in May next, and that Pynchon be enjoined, under the penalty of one hundred pounds, to make his personal appearance to give a full answer to the Court's satisfaction or otherwise to stand to its judgment and censure. It was also ordered by the Court that Norton's answer to Pynchon's book be sent to England to be printed. This volume, not published in England until 1653, bore the short title of *A Discussion of that Great Point in Divinity, the Sufferings of Christ* and was dedicated to the General Court.[70]

[68] 4 *Rec. Mass. Bay (Part I)* 29; 3 *ibid.* 215. A letter written at a later date by certain "considerable" elders throws further light on the vigorous action of the General Court. This letter is an appendix to Norton, *A Discussion of that Great Point in Divinity, the Sufferings of Christ* (1653).

[69] 4 *Rec. Mass. Bay (Part I)* 48–49. For

the only contemporary reference to the incident found, apart from official records and Norton's reply, see 6 Mass. Hist. Soc. Coll. (4th ser.) 285.

[70] 4 *Rec. Mass. Bay (Part I)* 72; 3 *ibid.* 248. Foster, *Genetic History* 19, commenting on Norton's reply states that: "The reply was keen and able, but it was sim-

During this period it seems likely that Pynchon turned to England for support. This support apparently took the form of letters to several influential elders in the colony who were requested to intercede with the magistrates to deal favorably with Pynchon "as a Gentleman pious and well deserving." This intercession proved unsuccessful.[71]

When the May 1652 session of the General Court arrived, it seems likely that William Pynchon had returned to England beyond the reach of the General Court. The date of departure is not known; the fact that the General Court records for May 1652 contain no reference to proceedings against Pynchon indicates he was no longer in the jurisdiction.[72] The fact that he published a second book in London in 1652, a short work with the title of *The Jewes Synagogue: or, A Treatise Concerning the ancient Orders and manner of Worship used by the Jewes in their Synagogue-Assemblies,* is somewhat equivocal evidence as to his whereabouts, since the author is carried on the title page as "William Pinchin of Springfield in N. England." [73] However, there is in existence at least one copy of *The Meritorious Price of Our Redemption* composed of previously unbound sheets used in the 1650 edition, with a cancel title page bearing a 1652 date.[74] This 1652 issue, if authorized, must have been published after Pynchon arrived in England. The fact that the author was still described as "of New England" may have been deliberate goading of the Massachusetts authorities. Support for the view that Pynchon arrived in England prior to April 15, 1652 and intended to return to the colony is derived from a well-known letter of that date, written from England to the Massachusetts authorities on his behalf by his friend Sir Henry Vane the Younger, a former governor of the colony.[75]

---

ply a defense of the old theology according to the command of the General Court, and added nothing to the common understanding of the theme." Byington characterizes Norton's reply as a "very able and learned work, thoroughly scientific in its methods." *William Pynchon, The Founder of Springfield* 34. See also 1 Mather, *Magnalia Christi Americana: or, The Ecclesiastical History of New England* (1853 ed.) 291–292.

71 See the letter referred to in note 68.

72 Reasons of appeal in Pynchon v. Collicott indicate that William Pynchon returned to England from Boston but not the date of his departure. 1 *Records of the Suffolk County Court, 1671–1680,* 29 Pub. Col. Soc. Mass. 320. No support appears

for the statement (1 Lockwood, *Hist. Western Mass.* 109) that £100 forfeited for nonappearance was "honorably paid."

73 McCutcheon, "Americana in English Newspapers, 1648–1660," 20 *Pub. Col. Soc. Mass.* 88.

74 The copy is owned by The John Carter Brown Library; the conclusion was reached by Lawrence C. Wroth, now Librarian Emeritus, in 1938 as the result of correspondence with H. A. Wright. See 1 Wright, *Story Western Mass.* 200–201. The title page includes the following: "London,/Printed for William Ley at Paul's Chain neer Doctors Commons. 1652."

75 *Hutchinson Papers,* 1 Mass. Hist. Soc. Coll. (3rd. ser.) 35–37. Lockwood makes the statement that Pynchon passed

Pynchon on his return to England was accompanied only by his wife. Henry Smith, his son-in-law, seemingly returned in October 1652: his daughter Anne, late in 1654. The Reverend Moxon and his family probably left in the autumn of 1652 but had no further association with Pynchon after arriving in England. John was left to carry on the various Pynchon enterprises at Springfield. Also remaining in New England were John's other sisters, Margaret (who had married William Davis, a wealthy and enterprising Boston apothecary, later chosen deputy from Springfield several times) and Mary (who had married Elizur Holyoke).[76] Pynchon first lived at Hackney, a suburb of London. Later the Pynchons and the Smiths settled down at Wraysbury, Buckinghamshire, twenty miles from London on the Thames opposite Runnymede.[77]

through Hartford with Moxon on his way to England in July 1652. 1 *Hist. Western Mass.* 108. Wright takes the view that Pynchon went to England for business reasons and that Moxon went to England later than Pynchon, remarking that on September 22, 1652 Moxon conveyed all his real property to the town. 1 *Story Western Mass.* 193, 199. The fact that Pynchon conveyed to his son John certain lands and buildings on April 17, and September 24, 1651, indicates that a decision to leave for England at an early date had been arrived at. 1 Lockwood, *Hist. Western Mass.* 107; 1 Wright, *Story Western Mass.* 200. Andrews (2 *Col. Period Amer. Hist.* 98) states that Pynchon returned to England because of his difficulties with the authorities and, in part, because of the necessity of looking after extensive properties there.

[76] Bagg in his article on William Pynchon (20 *Americana* 210) prints in facsimile a deed by Anne Smith to John Pynchon of August 18, 1654 which refers to a power of attorney from her husband of October 17, 1652 at the time he "went into England." The return of Moxon and his family has been ascribed to the Parsons witchcraft episode. Morris, "Bi-Centennial Address," 1 *Papers and Proc. Conn. Valley Hist. Soc.* 311–312. A deposition by Symon Beamon, quondam Pynchon servant, made September 19, 1656 in Parsons v. Bridgman, relates that "about the time that witches were apprehended to be sent to Boston Mr. Moxon's children were taken ill with their fits (which we took to be bewitched)." The deposition

is in the Treasure Room, Widener Library, Harvard University. A statement by George Bliss, one of the earliest writers on the subject, that the Moxons left with William Pynchon, but that Henry Smith left a year later, cannot be reconciled with known dates. *An Address, Delivered at the Opening of the Town-Hall in Springfield March 24, 1828* (1828) 14. For Davis, see "Note on William Davis the Loyalist," 6 *Pub. Col. Soc. Mass.* 124.

[77] The deed to the lands at Wraysbury, dated December 5, 1653, is in possession of the Connecticut Valley Historical Museum. Photostatic copies are in the Library of Congress (Genealogical Division) in a collection entitled: *Facsimiles of some English deeds, leases and other documents, about 1525 to 1686 relating to William Pynchon and his son John who settled Springfield, Massachusetts in 1636.* Mary, a sister-in-law of John Pynchon of Writtle (grandfather of William) and also a daughter of Sir Richard Empson, married for her second husband Edward Bulstrode of Bulstrode Park, Buckinghamshire, not far from Windsor and in the immediate neighborhood of Horton and Wraysbury. See Crawford, *Maternal Ancestry of Charles Whiting MacNair* (1912) 57; *The Visitation of the County of Buckinghamshire,* 58 Harleian Soc. Pub. 12–13. For purchase of lands in Wraysbury from Edward Bulstrode by John Pynchon in 1662, see documents in the above Library of Congress item and Gyll, *History of the Parish of Wraysbury, Anderwycke and Magna Charta Island* (1862) 21. This work also makes reference to later land

From this rural retreat Pynchon continued at a safe distance his doctrinal struggle with the Massachusetts Bay authorities. Following publication in 1654 of *The Time when the First Sabbath was Ordained,* he returned to his controversy in the next year with *A Further Discussion of That Great Point in Divinity the Sufferings of Christ . . . Being a Vindication of a Dialogue, Intitled [The Meritorious Price of our Redemption, Justification, etc.] from the exceptions of Mr. Norton and others.*[78]

No support has been found for the statement that Pynchon was one of the Puritans returning to England who rose to a position of prominence during the Commonwealth and Protectorate.[79] Some controversy was, however, aroused in England by his writings.[80] No further volume came forth from Pynchon's pen until 1662 when his last work, *The Covenant of Nature made with Adam Described, and Cleared from sundry great mistakes,* saw publication. This book was an enlargement of the author's earlier reply to Norton.

William Pynchon died on October 29, 1662 and was buried in the churchyard at Wraysbury; presumably he had returned to the Church of England. He outlived both his second wife and his daughter Mary, who had died within a few days of each other in October 1657.[81]

Posterity paid little attention to Pynchon's theological writings and he exerted no positive influence upon the development of theo-

transactions of John Pynchon and litigation over titles involving Henry Smith. *Ibid.* 21, 46. In a November 20, 1672 letter to his son Joseph in England, John Pynchon gave him, among other things, "all my land and housing bought of Mr. Bulstrode." Mass. Hist. Soc. Photostat. Some writers have the Moxons living with William Pynchon at Wraysbury but the DNB account of George Moxon does not support such statements.

78 Some copies were issued with the title *The Meritorious Price of Mans Redemption, or Christ's Satisfaction Discussed and Explained* and have been mistaken for a second edition of Pynchon's first work. The New York Public Library copy with this title has corrections and additions in the author's hand.

79 1 Andrews, *Col. Period Amer. Hist.* 497. No support appears for the statement that Pynchon had a part in writing Sir Henry Vane the Younger's book, *A Healing Question, Propounded and Resolved,*

published in 1656. *Cf.* 1 Wright, *Story Western Mass.* 227.

80 In 1656 Nicholas Chewney, "MA and Minister of Gods word," published a refutation entitled *Anti-Socinianism; or . . . the confutation of certain gross errours . . . in a dialogue . . . called, The Meritorious Price of our Redemption.* The postscript to Pynchon's last work (*infra*) notes that the author, when his book was mostly in print, received "a copy of Anthony Burges, The True Doctrine of Justification, the second part wherein I found he hath opposed some things in my Book."

81 A letter of William Pynchon is quoted in 1 Lockwood, *Hist. Western Mass.* 110, that, "I am the more solitary, as son Smith is of a reserved melancholy and my daughter (Anne) is crazy." William's will left certain bequests to John and Anne and to his grandchildren, his surviving sisters and other members of the Pynchon family. John, named as executor, was the residuary legatee. 2 Waters, *Genealogical Gleanings* 859.

logical doctrines in New England or in the land of his birth. One writer has evaluated his contributions in the following words:

Thus Pynchon's work was one-sided, incomplete, and immature. It was essentially a protest, not in any way a constructive effort. It had no immediate effect in producing modification of theory in New England, for most of the following writers pass over all he said as if they had never heard of him, or at least never read him; and doubtless few had. No trace of positive influence exerted upon the later New England writers has yet been discovered. The book seems to have exhaled its life in the flames in which it was burned upon Boston market place.[82]

William Pynchon was obviously a man of many attributes and accomplishments. Enjoying substantial means and social status in Essex, by his able, shrewd, and energetic conduct he became one of the foremost fur traders of Massachusetts. Despite his preoccupation with trade and husbandry, he was a man of learning and intellectual accomplishments. He was intensely religious, although his writings in the field of theology, while stamping him as a man of independent thought, failed to attract a following. While his accomplishments as a public servant were not on the level of those of John Winthrop, Endecott, or Dudley, it was through his efforts that the upper portion of the Connecticut Valley became part of the Massachusetts Bay colony. His counsel in Indian matters was characterized by wisdom and insight.

While Pynchon was familiar with Fortescue and Dalton, his treatment of legal matters lacks a professional touch. It is doubtful that he brought to the administration of justice the same interest or capacity which he did to fur trading or theology. That his interest in the law may have been largely philosophical appears in the dedication of his last publication to Oliver St. John, Lord Chief Justice of the Common Pleas, which gives considerable insight into his views of the relation between the common law of England and scripture law. However, the part played by William Pynchon in the early administration of justice in western Massachusetts may be discovered through a reading of the *Record*.

---

[82] Foster, *Genetic History* 19–20. Pynchon's principal work has been characterized by Morison as "devoid of literary merit." *The Intellectual Life of New England* (1956) 170. His other published writings fall into the same category.

III. John Pynchon

JOHN PYNCHON'S date and place of birth are uncertain, but it seems probable that he was born at Springfield in Essex in 1626.[1] It is doubtful that he arrived in New England with the remainder of the Pynchon family. The records do not reveal the nature or extent of John's education, which may have been under the tutelage of John Eliot at Roxbury and of the Reverend Moxon at Springfield.[2] In October 1645 he married Amy Wyllys of Hartford, daughter of the late Governor George Wyllys of the Connecticut colony. He became a freeman of the Bay colony on April 13, 1648.[3] Upon attaining maturity, he presumably participated in the fur trading and other pursuits of his father.

However, few facts are known as to John until November 1650 when he first held public office, being elected a selectman and also town treasurer of Springfield. He was chosen selectman again in 1651 and 1652, but was discharged from this office on November 27, 1652, when he, Samuel Chapin, and Elizur Holyoke, by order of the General Court, took their oaths before the selectmen as commissioners for the town of Springfield. In the same month Pynchon was also

---

1 Some biographical details on John Pynchon are found in *Record of the Pynchon Family in England and America*, originally compiled by J. C. Pynchon (1885), revised by W. F. Adams (1898) 5–7; A. P. Clarke, *Clarke's Kindred Genealogies* (1896) 139–140. Wright (1 *Story Western Mass.* 300) refers to an entry in the "Springfield register" that "the Honourable Colonel John Pynchon, esquire, was sick and died in the seventy-seventh year of his age." The date of his death was January 17, 1702/3.

2 The earliest writings of John we have seen are some notes taken in a form of shorthand of some of Moxon's sermons in February and March 1639/40; these are at the Connecticut Valley Historical Museum. Cf. 1 Wright, *Story Western Mass.* 134–135, 189–190.

3 37 N. *Eng. Hist. and Gen. Reg.* 33; *Rec.* 24. A study by John Pynchon of the Indian names for various months of the year has survived (10 N. *Eng. Hist. and Gen. Reg.* 166; 1 Wright, *Story Western Mass.* 253), but it is doubtful that Pynchon attained fluency in any Indian tongue. A receipt, dated November 1, 1645, by John Pynchon for £150 received from Mrs. Mary Wyllys, the executrix of Governor Wyllys, as the first part of a legacy to his daughter is in 7 *Wyllys Mss.* (Connecticut Historical Society, Hartford, Conn.)

chosen recorder, to record lands, town orders, and "the publike occasions of the Towne." [4]

John Pynchon was named in each of the commissions issued by the General Court after November 1652 for the administration of justice in Springfield and its environs. Presumably by virtue of certain of these commissions he sat initially on the County Court for Hampshire which heard its first causes in March 1663. In May 1659 and again in May 1662 and the two succeeding years Pynchon was chosen deputy for Springfield.[5] On May 3, 1665 he was chosen an assistant—an office which he retained until May 1686.[6]

During these twenty-one years Pynchon held court at Springfield by virtue of his authority as magistrate; he sat on the County Court, with associates (and for part of the period, another assistant, Peter Tilton), by virtue of such position; and, of course, he sat on the Court of Assistants (although not too frequently), and participated in the judicial work of the General Court. As a member of the General Court Pynchon appears to have played a minor role. In his years as assistant he was named to only a few committees, apart from those relating to protection and settlement of the frontiers of the colony. In February 1659/60 he was again chosen town treasurer, serving for three successive terms, and clerk or recorder of Springfield. He was also elected selectman in which capacity he served the town for most of the next eleven years. Lastly, he was chosen moderator to preside at town meetings; with a few intervals he continued in this office until 1694.[7]

During the period between 1660 and 1685 scarcely a year passed that Pynchon was not appointed to some *ad hoc* town committee. These committees dealt with such matters as town rates, town boundaries, accounts of selectmen, settlement of the county government, county rates, laying out of highways, disposition of town lands, establishment of mills, lands at Woronoco, poor relief, Indian matters, a new meeting house, defense measures, lands at Freshwater Brook, and land grants to the minister.[8]

[4] 1 Burt, *Hist. Springfield* 217, 218–219, 223; *Rec.* 54.

[5] See *Pynchon Waste Book for Hampshire* 2; 1 *Hamp. Cty. Probate Ct. Rec.* 28; 4 *Rec. Mass. Bay (Part I)* 364; 4 *ibid (Part II)* 41, 117.

[6] See *Rec. Mass. Bay, passim,* for the composition of the General Court each year. Records of the choice of magistrates indicate Pynchon reached the peak of his popularity at about 1683–1685. 1 Mass. Hist. Soc. Coll. (6th ser.) 1–2; 5 *ibid.* 48, 77, 133, 137; 3 New Hampshire Hist. Soc.

Coll. 99–100; Hutchinson, *Collection Original Papers* 541, 543.

[7] 4 *Rec. Mass. Bay (Part II)* 476; 39 *Mass. Archives* 391. The town offices may be traced in Burt, *Hist. Springfield*, vols. I, II.

[8] 1 Burt, *Hist. Springfield* 282, 284–285, 289, 291, 297, 300, 307, 352–353; 2 *ibid.* 80, 81, 85–86, 105, 110, 114, 120, 129, 142–143, 149, 169, 186; 5 *Rec. Mass. Bay* 376. For material before the General Court on the Glover controversy, see 11 *Mass. Archives* 9–12, 20, 170, 178–182.

On the county level Pynchon headed the County Court for Hampshire. The records of this court, and those of the later Court of General Sessions of the Peace, in a number of instances show him charged with the duty of providing for or maintaining the house of correction at Springfield.[9]

The *Record*, commencing in March 1660/61, contains entries of annual meetings of the freemen of Springfield at which they chose deputies to the General Court and gave in their votes for nomination of assistants, and, after the establishment of a county, choice of associates on the County Court and of county treasurer. John Pynchon was the commissioner appointed to carry such votes sealed to the shire meeting for the first two meetings recorded. He was chosen and allowed County Treasurer at least twelve times between 1664 and 1679, and may have served consecutively during the entire period.[10]

John Pynchon was extremely active in connection with new plantations in the Connecticut Valley, an activity which had economic as well as political aspects. At the May 1653 General Court, upon the petition of Springfield inhabitants craving liberty to erect a new plantation at Nonotuck (Northampton), Pynchon, Holyoke, and Chapin were appointed a committee to divide the land petitioned for into two plantations, the petitioners to have liberty to settle on the one of their choice, under certain conditions.[11] In May 1659, settlement having commenced on the east side of the Connecticut, the General Court empowered a committee of five including Pynchon, Holyoke, and Chapin to lay out the bounds of the "town at Norwattocke" (Hadley) on either or both sides of the river, "so as shall be most suitable for the chohabitation and full supply of those people, that this wildernes may be populated and the maine ends of our coming into these parts may be promoted." [12]

In May 1667, upon petition of the inhabitants of Quabaug (later Brookfield), the General Court appointed Pynchon and four others with power to admit inhabitants, grant lands, and order all the pru-

---

[9] *Rec. Cty. Ct. Hamp.* 73, 129, 148–149; *Pynchon Waste Book for Hampshire* 52, 154; *Hamp. Rec. Ct. Pleas* 61. See also Morris, "The Old Main Street Jail and House of Correction," 1 *Papers and Proc. Conn. Valley Hist. Soc.* 29–30.

[10] *Rec.* 318–335. As to County Treasurer see the entries in *Pynchon Waste Book for Hampshire* and *Rec. Cty. Ct. Hamp.*

[11] 4 *Rec. Mass. Bay (Part I)* 136; cf. 3 *ibid.* 308. For the return of the committee see 4 *ibid.* 213; 3 *ibid.* 360. When a dis-

pute arose later as to the boundary between Northampton and Springfield, committees from both towns met on April 28, 1685 and reached agreement. The Springfield committee included Pynchon, who, as survivor of the original committee, explained the intent in settling the original boundary. 5 *ibid.* 480–481; 112 *Mass. Archives* 403, 407–408.

[12] 4 *Rec. Mass. Bay (Part I)* 368; 112 *Mass. Archives* 116.

dential affairs of the place until the Court judged it meet to grant the full liberty of a township. In November 1686, Pynchon and five others were appointed a committee for Quabaug to receive the claims of the old inhabitants, to grant lots to others, and to give the necessary orders for some orderly settlement of the town. In 1692 Pynchon was a member of a committee reestablished for Brookfield.[13]

In October 1670, upon petition of Springfield inhabitants, liberty was granted to erect a new plantation, later known as Suffield, on the west side of the Connecticut River. For the purposes of managing the affairs of the township, receiving inhabitants and granting land, and ordering all prudentials the Court appointed a committee of Pynchon, Holyoke, and four others. The committee delayed laying out the bounds of the plantation in hope of settlement of the boundary line between Massachusetts and Connecticut, but when the latter did not accept a Massachusetts concession, the committee proceeded and made its return, per Pynchon and Holyoke, to the General Court in June 1674.[14]

In May 1671 a petition, largely by Northampton inhabitants, sought liberty to settle at "Squawqueque and Wissquawqueque," both deserted by the Indians. A committee headed by Pynchon reported favorably on the petition but the magistrates did not approve the return. At the May 1672 Court, when the petition was renewed, the General Court offered to grant land at Squakeag for a village, provided qualified householders gave their engagement to settle twenty families within eighteen months. Such engagement was presented by Pynchon at the October Court and a grant was made for a new plantation; however, Pynchon was not named to the committee.[15] In May 1672 Hadley inhabitants were granted additional lands on the northern boundary, later called Swampfield (still later Sunderland); Pynchon and two others were named a committee to order prudential affairs and grant lots.[16] In May 1683 the General Court granted a new township at Freshwater Brook below Springfield, to

[13] 4 *Rec. Mass. Bay* (*Part II*) 342; 21 *Acts and Res. Prov. Mass. Bay* 667; *Quabaug, 1669–1910* (comp. and ed. C. J. Adams, 1915) 45; 2 *Ms. Mass. Council Rec.* 85; 112 *Mass. Archives* 426–427; 113 *ibid.* 294. For the early history of Quabaug, see 35 *N. Eng. Hist. and Gen. Reg.* 332.

[14] 4 *Rec. Mass. Bay* (*Part II*) 469; 5 *ibid.* 12–13; 112 *Mass. Archives* 208, 210, 235, 440–441. For an earlier petition to which the deputies did not consent, see Sheldon, *Documentary History of Suffield* (1879–88) 47–48. For the report of Pynchon and Holyoke see *ibid.* 49–50. For the

acts of the committee, largely concerned with land grants, covering the period January 12, 1670/1 to January 2, 1681/2 see *ibid.* 53–78.

[15] 4 *Rec. Mass. Bay* (*Part II*) 528–529, 542; Temple and Sheldon, *A History of the Town of Northfield, Massachusetts* (1875) 59–63; 1 *Hist. and Proc. Pocumtuck Valley Mem. Asso.* 116–117.

[16] 4 *Rec. Mass. Bay* (*Part II*) 557–558; 5 *ibid.* 9; 113 *Mass. Archives* 760; 1 *Hist. and Proc. Pocumtuck Valley Mem. Asso.* 174–175.

be called Enfield, and for the admittance of inhabitants, granting
allotments and ordering all the prudential affairs of the town, appointed Pynchon and four others to be a committee. An earlier appointment, in September 1679, of a committee to settle a town at
Freshwater had been made by the County Court with Pynchon one
of the members.[17]

In a number of cases Pynchon assisted settlement of new plantations on the Connecticut River on lands purchased from the Indians
by advancing the purchase price from his own funds, taking a conveyance of lands in trust, and obtaining reimbursement from the settlers at a later date. Such arrangements were made in connection
with Northampton, Hadley, Westfield, Pocumtuck (Deerfield), Enfield, and Suffield.[18]

Closely related to Pynchon's work in laying out new plantations
was his participation in determining the boundaries of the commonwealth. Since by marriage, geographic location, and military necessity Pynchon was closely tied to neighboring Connecticut, he was a
natural choice to represent Massachusetts in ascertaining the boundary line between the two colonies, made controversial by an error in
the Woodward-Saffery line. Therefore, on May 31, 1671 the General
Court authorized him to run the south line of the patent twenty
miles or more westward from the Connecticut River. This move was
prompted by a letter from the General Assembly of Connecticut expressing fear that a recent grant of lands toward Windsor by Massachusetts could prove prejudicial, if not ruinous, to the people of
Windsor.[19]

Pynchon, unaccompanied by any Connecticut representatives, although opportunity was afforded, carried out his mission between

[17] 5 *Rec. Mass. Bay* 410–411; 112 *Mass. Archives* 238, 339; *Rec. Cty. Ct. Hamp.* 32. For the committee book see 1 Allen, *The History of Enfield, Connecticut* 60–135.

[18] Wright, *Indian Deeds* 27–28, 33–35, 37–38, 51–53, 61–62, 65, 69–71, 84–85, 89–92, 94–96, 97–98, 99–100. See also 1 Wright, *Story Western Mass.* 254–258, 261. See 1 *Hist. and Proc. Pocumtuck Valley Mem. Asso.* 80, that four conveyances were made at Pocumtuck to Pynchon by the Indians on behalf of the Dedham proprietors, Pynchon advancing £40. For the manner in which Pynchon was reimbursed for his advances in connection with the Enfield plantation see 1 Allen, *The History of Enfield, Connecticut* 76. For Pynchon's reimbursement for £41/15 expended in connection with Stony Brook or Suffield see

Sheldon, *Documentary History of Suffield* 20, 21, 62–63. For references to Pynchon in the settlement of Pocumtuck see *Early Records of the Town of Dedham, Massachusetts (1659–1673)* 103, 117, 133–134, 136–138, 162, 173, 192–193, 219–220. It was not until 1674 that Pynchon was entirely repaid his advances. *Ibid. (1672–1706)* 17, 23.

[19] 4 *Rec. Mass. Bay (Part II)* 487, 502–503. On the boundary question see Bowen, *The Boundary Disputes of Connecticut* (1882) 53–55; Hooker, *Boundaries of Connecticut* (Pub. Ter. Comm. State Conn., 1933) 16–19. Many of Pynchon's dealings were with Lieutenant Colonel John Allyn, secretary of the Connecticut colony, who had married Henry Smith's eldest daughter, Anne.

October 31 and November 3, 1671 and made his return to the General Court in May 1672. The Court allowed and approved the return and ordered that Pynchon have its thanks for "his great paines Therein." The General Court, in order to accommodate the town of Windsor, offered to make some concession on its boundary and to have Pynchon, joined by Connecticut representatives, run the new line before winter. However, Connecticut never saw fit to accept this offer, and this failure to settle the boundary line gave rise to controversy for many years.[20]

In most New England histories John Pynchon makes but a fleeting appearance, usually as a military leader in King Philip's War and in later defensive actions against Indian and French marauders. Under the First Charter he was successively confirmed as lieutenant (1653), captain (1657), and sergeant major (1671) in the military establishment of western Massachusetts. However, prior to the outbreak of King Philip's War Pynchon was rarely called upon to act in a military capacity.[21] In August 1664 Captains Thomas Clarke and Pynchon were dispatched by the General Court to inform the English commissioners engaged "in reducing the Dutch at the Monhatoes into the obedience of his Majestie" of the military assistance to be furnished by the Bay colony. As deputies, both men were signatories to the articles of capitulation consented to later in the month at New Amsterdam.[22]

John Pynchon took no conspicuous part in King Philip's War as a field commander; his role was largely confined to pressing the Bay and the Connecticut authorities for succor and to coordinating the

[20] 4 Rec. Mass. Bay (Part II) 517–519, 529–530; 5 ibid. 12; 3 Mass. Archives 23a. For the correspondence exchanged between Pynchon and John Allyn in October 1671, see 2 Mass. Archives 188–190. For the map drawn by James Taylor, dated June 6, 1672, by order of the General Court of May 15, 1672, see 3 Conn. Archives, Colonial Boundaries 3–4. For an example of the controversy see the November 12, 1679 letter to Windsor from the committee for Suffield, of which Pynchon was a member. Wolcott Mss. (Conn. Hist. Soc.)

[21] 4 Rec. Mass. Bay (Part I) 135, 314; 4 ibid. (Part II) 82, 488. For Pynchon's role in various Indian matters, see 1 Sheldon, Hist. Deerfield 62–67; Sheldon, "The Pocumtuck Confederacy," 2 Papers and Proc. Conn. Valley Hist. Soc. 78–79; 1 Conn. Archives, Miscellaneous 88k–m; Thornton, "The Gilbert Family," 4 N. Eng. Hist. and

Gen. Reg. 232, 339; O'Callaghan, Calender of Historical Manuscripts in the Office of the Secretary of State, (Dutch Manuscripts, 1663–64) 304; 8 Mass. Hist. Soc. Coll. (5th ser.) 89.

[22] 4 Rec. Mass. Bay (Part II) 123–125; 2 Doc. Rel. Col. Hist. N.Y. 253; N.Y. Hist. Soc. Coll., 2 Pub. Fund Series (1869) 333–336; CSP, Col., 1661–68, #788 (p. 228), #794. See also 6 Mass. Hist. Soc. Coll. (4th ser.) 527–529; letter, dated Aug. 15, 1664, from John Pynchon to John Endecott, Boston Public Library, Rare Book Room, Ac. Ms. 586. For Pynchon's connection with Indian matters in 1665–66 see 6 Mass. Hist. Soc. Coll. (4th ser.) 531; CSP, Col., 1661-68, #1379; 67 Mass. Archives 170; 3 Doc. Rel. Col. Hist. N.Y. 146, 148. See also the references to Pynchon in letters of John Winthrop, Jr. to Colonel Nicholls. 8 Mass. Hist. Soc. Coll. (5th ser.) 105, 111.

activities of the local, the Bay, and the Connecticut forces. When, on August 4, 1675, he confirmed Indian intelligence of the attack on Brookfield by the Nipmucks, Pynchon immediately sent to Hartford for aid in securing Springfield, succoring Brookfield, and giving "present chase" to the Indians, stating:

> We are very raw and our People of this Towne extreamely scattered so that our owne Place needs all and how soone these Indians may be upon this Towne we know not.[23]

On the same date he informed John Winthrop, Jr. of the presence of Philip and a small band of followers at Ashquoash, no more than twenty-three miles from Springfield, having escaped from the Pocasset swamp on the night of July 29. He urged swift action to destroy Philip, but the Connecticut authorities were skeptical of the intelligence.[24]

On August 12 Pynchon, who was in command on the River, apparently feeling the weight of responsibility too great, sent a messenger to inform the Council at Hartford that he "is alone and wants advice what to doe in this Juncture." Major John Talcott with a small force of dragoons was sent to his assistance with a recommendation that an agent be sent to Albany to enlist the aid of the Mohawks, if the enemy should go in that direction. Governor Andros, being at Albany when Pynchon's messenger arrived, engaged the Mohawks not to join the war or entertain the hostile Indians.[25]

Headquarters was established at Hadley, but extensive scouting uncovered no hostile Indians. By August 22 Pynchon was engaged upon a task, often repeated in coming years, of persuading the Connecticut authorities to garrison remote locations such as Squakeag (Northfield) and Deerfield, since it was feared that the Indians would fall upon these areas. The first combat along the River took place when a party of English was ambushed on August 25 below Deerfield while pursuing some River Indians who formerly occupied a fort on the west bank of the River between Northampton and Hadley. Although disarmed by the committee of militia, these Indians, pretending great fidelity to the English and promising that they

---

[23] Mather, *The History of King Philip's War* (ed. S. G. Drake, 1862), appendix B, pp. 234–235; 1 *Conn. Archives, War Colonial* 162. For the attack on Brookfield see *Quabaug, 1669–1910*, 46 ff.

[24] 1 Sheldon, *Hist. Deerfield* 87; Mather, *Hist. King Philip's War*, appendix B, pp. 234–239; 1 *Conn. Archives, War Colonial* 11a, 11c, 11d, 163.

[25] Sheldon, *Hist. Deerfield* 87–88; 2 *Pub.*

Rec. Col. Conn. 345–350; *Wyllys Papers,* 21 Conn. Hist. Soc. Coll., 221; 1 *Conn. Archives, War Colonial* 164. For a letter, dated August 28, 1675, from the Massachusetts Council entreating Connecticut's assistance see 2 *Pub. Rec. Col. Conn.* 362. For a September 8, 1675 letter from Pynchon to the Albany authorities see 67 *Mass. Archives* 250.

would fight against Philip, had been rearmed in the hope they might do the same service as the Mohegans and Naticks. When it became plain that they were not trustworthy, the council at Hadley demanded their arms on August 24 but met a show of defiance which culminated in their quitting their fort. Advice to Pynchon from the Connecticut Council to forbear from forcibly disarming the Indians, "least it might prove to be provoakeing or discourageing to our Indian Neighboures," arrived too late. Pynchon, who was "of a differing mind" from those favoring disarming, thus offending some, wrote that "when I Recollect things: I cant but conclude that this was a Contrived busyness of the Indians." [26]

All the marching and countermarching provided no effective answer to Indian tactics which included an attack upon Deerfield and the ambushing of forces marching to the relief of Northfield, for, as Pynchon despondently noted, "when we go out after the Indians they doe so sculk in swamps we cannot find them and yet do waylay our people to there destruction." Perhaps influenced by Pynchon's pessimistic attitude in matters military, a council of war on September 8 decided to give up operations in the field and only garrison the towns. This view proved unacceptable to Connecticut which urged a more aggressive campaign. However, a few days after the initial decision bolder counsels had prevailed at Hadley and, a vigorous campaign having been agreed upon, Major Treat was sent up the River with a large force of Connecticut troops. [27]

The concentration of large bodies of troops in the Valley made it necessary to lay in an adequate store of provisions. At this time Major Pynchon and others had a large quantity of unthreshed wheat at Deerfield which had been spared by the Indians in expectation that it would soon be theirs. About September 15 Pynchon sent orders to have some of this wheat threshed and to impress teams and drivers for its transportation. Captain Thomas Lathrop was sent up with his company from Hadley to convoy the supply train to headquarters. On September 18 Lathrop with a train of carts laden with wheat commenced his return march from Deerfield, taking no precautions against hostile activity. In a swampy area on the narrow Pocumtuck Path, later known as Bloody Brook, Lathrop's force was ambushed by a superior force of Indians and virtually annihilated. Pynchon, realizing the difficulty of holding Deerfield, sent to Hartford for advice which led to the abandonment of the town and of an expedition

[26] 1 Sheldon, *Hist. Deerfield* 88–93; 2 *Pub. Rec. Col. Conn.* 352–354; *Wyllys Papers* 222–223; Mather, *Hist. King Philip's War* 71, 73–76; 1 *Conn. Archives, War Colonial* 14, 17, 166–167.

[27] 1 Sheldon, *Hist. Deerfield* 95–100; 2 *Pub. Rec. Col. Conn.* 365, 367–368; Mather, *Hist. King Philip's War*, appendix B, 241–243.

planned to regain Northfield as a center for offensive operations by Connecticut troops.[28]

On September 21 the council of war at Hatfield was notified by the Commissioners for the United Colonies at Boston that they had decided to raise a thousand men. Pynchon was appointed commander-in-chief; the council chose Major Treat as second in command. The letter from Thomas Danforth stated that, "considering the great trust and dependance that is upon Major Pinchon, for the constant management of the publicke affaires in those parts we do not expect that he should be personally present in every expedition against the enemy, further then himselfe, and his Councill of officers shall See a necessity off." With Pynchon's commission, received on September 22, came instructions, drawn up before Bloody Brook, to employ all forces in field operations and not in garrisoning towns. Though against his judgment, Pynchon set in motion plans to assemble at Hadley a force large enough to sweep the valley clear of hostile Indians, but also persevered in attempts to resign his command.[29]

In the meantime the Indians were continuing their hit-and-run tactics. On September 26 Pynchon's farmhouse, barns, and crops on the west side of the River were burned. A few days later Pynchon sent in his resignation as Commander-in-Chief, stating that "my sad state of affairs will necessitate your discharging me, and truly I am as full of troble and overwhelmed with it that I cannot act." [30]

Although Pynchon had tendered his resignation, he remained in command of the Valley forces and on October 4 led all the troops from Springfield to Hadley where a force had been assembled to move out in a large-scale operation to clear the Valley. However, these plans were upset when an Indian informant on the evening of October 4 revealed at Windsor plans of the "friendly" Indians at Long Hill to join with hostile Indians in an attack on Springfield the next morning. Messengers were dispatched in haste to Major Treat at Westfield and to warn Springfield. The Springfield inhabitants, who had received the firmest assurances and pledges of friendship and faithfulness from the Long Hill Indians both by covenant and hostages given as security (but cunningly enticed away from Hartford), took to the shelter of their palisaded houses and sent a messenger to Pynchon at Hadley. The next morning, believing the report to be false, two defenders started to ride out to the Indian fort

28 1 Sheldon, *Hist. Deerfield*, 100–103, 110–112.

29 *Ibid.* 112; 67 *Mass. Archives* 263–264, 270; 1 *Conn. Archives, War Colonial* 19a.

30 1 Sheldon, *Hist. Deerfield* 113–114. Contemporary accounts estimated Pynchon's loss at Suffield at £1100–1200. 1 Wright, *Story Western Mass.* 268.

to ascertain the facts. A short distance from the town they were fired upon; one was killed and the other mortally wounded. The town was then attacked. Although the defense was successful, most of the town was put to the torch. Late in the morning Treat reached the west bank of the River but could not cross in the face of the enemy. Finally, a few hours later a force of almost two hundred men led by Major Pynchon and Captains Appleton and Sill approached from Hadley and the Indians abandoned the attack.[31]

In a letter to Governor Leverett, dated October 8, Pynchon related the disaster, stating that he had "Called off all the Soldiers that were in Springfield leaving none to secure the Town the Commissioners order was so strict." Scouts had been unable to locate the enemy and Pynchon could not take the field with the troops since his presence was necessary at Springfield, the inhabitants being discouraged and threatening to leave. To desert Springfield would encourage the "Insolent Enemy" and lead to abandonment of the towns above. However, to hold Springfield required many soldiers while lack of a mill made provisioning of a garrison difficult.[32]

As to himself, Pynchon declared:

Sir I am not capable of holding any Command being more and more unfit and almost confounded in my understanding, the Lord direct your Pitch on a meeter person then ever I was: According to Liberty from the Councill I shall devolve all upon Captain Appleton unless Major Treat return againe.

In closing, Pynchon reiterated that, "All these Towns ought to be Garrisoned," and reminded the Governor that he had advised this earlier and, had he been allowed to follow this course, the disaster might have been averted.

Governor Leverett wrote a letter of consolation to Pynchon, but indicated that, in some quarters at least, the plight of Springfield was laid at Pynchon's door, even though his suggestion for disarming the "friendly" Indians had been rejected by the Connecticut Council.[33]

Pynchon received the news that he had been relieved by Captain

[31] 1 Sheldon, *Hist. Deerfield* 113–115; *A Narrative of the Indian Wars in New England* (1803) 117–118; 1 Wright, *Story Western Mass.* 268–269.

[32] 1 Sheldon, *Hist. Deerfield* 117. For the effect of the attack in Connecticut see 2 *Pub. Rec. Col. Conn.* 372–373; *Wyllys Papers,* 226–228.

[33] 1 Sheldon, *Hist. Deerfield* 116; 1 Wright, *Story Western Mass.* 274. On the attitude of Connecticut toward disarming

the Indians at Springfield see 2 *Pub. Rec. Col. Conn.* 353–354, 356; Bodge, *Soldiers in King Philip's War* (1891) 97; 1 *Conn. Archives, War Colonial* 167. Captain Mosely had written Leverett on the day of the attack that the Springfield Indians were thought "to be ready att any times when the enemy comes to oppose the towne to fall upon the English along with the enemy." Bodge, *Soldiers* 26.

Samuel Appleton on October 12, "the Councill having seriously considered the earnest desires of Major Pincheon and the great affliction upon him and his family." Pynchon thanked Leverett for discharging him from a trust which he had "noe ability to manage," and pledged that he would "cast in his mite and help Appleton and the cause and interest of God and the people." He hoped that the orders for the Captain would be less "strict," reminding the Governor that "Springfield was destroyed for this reason." Although urged to attend the General Court ("it may be of great use to the publique and not disservice to yourselfe"), Pynchon decided to stay "to encourage the Pople" for if he should go to Boston "all would fall here." [34] It seems doubtful that Pynchon played any significant advisory role in the later fighting in the Valley; his activity appears to have been limited to commanding the garrison at Springfield.

Under Appleton, who lacked tact and personal ties, the reluctance of Connecticut to have its troops remain in garrison in Massachusetts towns, intensified by fear that Hartford and Wethersfield would become the scene of hostilities, constituted a serious operational handicap. An October 18 attack upon Hatfield was followed by harassing activities at Westfield, where the Springfield inhabitants had to grind their grain, and Northampton. On October 27, Pynchon and other Springfield inhabitants were ambushed returning from a search for ore at Westfield. However, after early November there were no significant operations in the Valley, although a few Indians lurking in the swamps did some small mischief upon the outer dwellings at Springfield until the middle of next March when an attack upon Northampton was repulsed. Then on March 26 an attack was made upon a group of Longmeadow settlers going to meeting at Springfield by a small band of "known" Indians. Only one of four captives survived when a party sent out by Pynchon overtook the fleeing Indians. In late April an Indian raiding party was surprised near Springfield and three warriors slain. In the massacre at the Indian camp at Turners Falls on May 19 and the disastrous retreat, many Springfield inhabitants served in the forces of Captains William Turner and Samuel Holyoke. A June 12 assault upon Hadley was the last offensive action by the Indians in the Valley; during July

34 67 Mass. Archives 246; 1 Sheldon, Hist. Deerfield 113, 116–118; 1 Wright, Story Western Mass. 270; Record of the Pynchon Family 21. There were some ties between Pynchon and Leverett in that John Pynchon, Jr. had married Margaret, the daughter of William Hubbard, the Ipswich historian, while her brother, John, had married Ann, the daughter of Governor Leverett. 1 Hubbard, A Narrative of the Troubles with the Indians in New England (ed. S. G. Drake, 1865) xxxii. The John Pynchon listed in Leverett's funeral cortege on March 25, 1679 was probably John Pynchon, Jr. A Memoir, Biographical and Genealogical of Sir John Leverett, Knt., Governor of Massachusetts, 1673–9 (1856) 86.

and August numerous Indians traveling westward were seen in the vicinity of Westfield, some of whom were successfully attacked by forces from Connecticut.[35]

The Indians who fled to the west were secured by Governor Andros by putting them under the watch of the Five Nations. Pynchon wrote Leverett on August 15, 1676 that "surely it is the worst of Indians that are gone thither, our Indians who most Treacherously ruined this Town and some of them that we know murdered our people without any provocation" and that Andros should be requested to deliver up the murderers. Andros never surrendered any fugitives to the Massachusetts authorities but with the death of Philip on August 12 and the refusal of the New York governor to allow an expedition against fugitives collecting on the Hudson, the war ground to an end and the soldiers under arms were discharged.[36]

Pynchon's military duties did not end with King Philip's War. In April 1677 Pynchon and James Richards of Hartford made a "long, troublesome and hazardous" journey to Albany on behalf of Connecticut and Massachusetts to renew ancient friendships with the Mohawks and to settle and conclude a "league of Freindship and amity between the English of New England" and the Mohawks, looking to protection for the "friendly Indians" and destruction of "enemy" Indians allied with the French. The Mohawks made a great show of friendship for the English and bitter enmity toward the Eastern Indians, promising to pursue their quarrel against them to the utmost of their power. However, as was expected, distance of place and difficulty of journey prevented any great effect. In September 1677 when a group of Indians from Canada under Ashpelon carried off captives from Hatfield and Deerfield, Pynchon sought, without success, to have the authorities at Albany incite the Mohawks to pursue the retreating war party.[37]

---

[35] 1 Sheldon, *Hist. Deerfield* 116, 124–125, 128, 132, 135–136, 149, 154, 169–170, 173–175; *A Narrative of the Indian Wars in New England* 123, 127; 1 Mass. Hist. Soc. Coll. (3rd ser.) 68–70. For the predicament of Appleton, see his correspondence in *Memorial of Samuel Appleton of Ipswich, Massachusetts* (comp. I. A. Appleton, 1850) 96–148. See also Bodge, *Soldiers* 101–104 and the most recent account in Leach, *Flintlock and Tomahawk: New England in King Philip's War* (1958) 97–100. For opposition to an order to abandon Westfield see *The Westfield Jubilee* (1870) 124–127; Greenough, "Historical Relations of Springfield and Westfield," 2 *Papers and Proc. Conn. Valley Hist. Soc.* 252–263.

[36] 1 Sheldon, *Hist. Deerfield* 175–177. Andros, protesting charges by the Bay that Philip received gunpowder from Albany, received support from Edward Randolph. Hutchinson, *Collection Original Papers* 477, 490. In May 1677 the Connecticut authorities were still writing Andros that certain Indians on the Hudson should be delivered to justice. 1 *Conn. Archives, War Colonial* 120d.

[37] 5 *Rec. Mass. Bay* 138, 165–168; 1 *Conn. Archives, War Colonial* 117a, 119, 120, 123, 224–225; 2 *Pub. Rec. Col. Conn.* 492–494, 496–497, 506–507; 1 Sheldon, *Hist.*

In October 1677 the towns in Hampshire "being in more hazard of the incursions of the heathen ennemy than some others," the General Court ordered that a committee of John Pynchon and five others contrive that each town endeavor "the new moddelling the scittuation of their houses, so as to be more compact and live neerer together, for theire better deffence against the Indians." At the same time the Major was to treat with Connecticut to join in keeping a garrison at Deerfield. In June 1680 the County Court of Hampshire, which Pynchon headed, was empowered, as far as concerned that county, to receive any Indian peace offers and to conclude such terms as were judged by them most conducive to the safety of the English inhabitants.[38]

In October 1680 Pynchon was commissioned by the General Court to repair to Fort Albany where, with the advice and consent of Sir Edmund Andros, he was to endeavor a treaty with the Mohawks "in order to the stopping of any invassions, depredation, and insolencys towards our neighbors, Indians and freinds, that live within this jurisdiction." His instructions make it clear that the April 1677 agreement had been disregarded. At a meeting on November 9 Pynchon, with some inner qualms, presented a bold front in accusing the Mohawks of breaching the earlier agreement. However, the next day he presented them with gifts "which they said sweetened the hard speech as they termed it." The answer received from the Mohawks, termed a "finall conclusion of peace," was returned to the General Court on May 27, 1681.[39]

In addition to holding many offices and engaging in numerous activities on the public behalf, John Pynchon was the foremost trader, merchant, and landowner of western Massachusetts. While the fur trade in the Connecticut Valley declined in importance after 1652, it still remained an important source of income for John Pynchon until a few years before King Philip's War.[40] Most of his fur trading

Deerfield 183–184; Hubbard, *General History of New England* (1815) 629–630; 8 Mass. Hist. Soc. Coll. (4th ser.) 81; 2 *Hist. and Proc. Pocumtuck Valley Mem. Asso.* 497–498; D. W. Wells and R. F. Wells, *A History of Hatfield, Massachusetts* (1910) 467–470; *Papers Concerning the Attack on Hatfield and Deerfield by A Party of Indians from Canada, September Nineteenth, 1677* (ed. F. B. Hough, 1859) 51, 54–61. For the effect of news of the attacks when communicated to the Connecticut Council by Pynchon, see 1 *Conn. Archives, War Colonial* 228.

[38] 5 *Rec. Mass. Bay* 170–171, 238–239, 277.

[39] 5 *Rec. Mass. Bay* 299–300, 319–321; 30 *Mass. Archives* 252–255, 277. At an August 1682 Albany meeting the Mohawks stated: "The Ax which Major Pinchon (for New England) and wee have been buryed in the ground in this house, remaines so (and we do not look out anymore) that way to go a fighting." 3 *Doc. Rel. Col. Hist. N.Y.* 328.

[40] Data compiled by Sylvester Judd, Hadley historian, from the *Pynchon Account Books*, now in the possession of the Connecticut Valley Historical Museum, show that during the period 1652–1657 Pynchon shipped to England almost 9,000 beaver skins valued at £13, 139. During

JOHN PYNCHON

activities were carried on through agents at such locations as Westfield, Northampton, Hadley, and Albany.[41]

In 1659 Pynchon joined a number of influential merchants of Salem and Boston to form a company having as its objective a share in the western fur trade and an end to the Dutch monopoly. The objective of the company was concealed under a grant by the General Court of a plantation ten miles square about two-thirds of the way from Springfield to Fort Orange. William Hathorne, the most active of the promoters, and Pynchon traveled to Fort Orange in August 1659, announced their intention of making a settlement east of the Hudson, provided the proposed site did not lie within Dutch jurisdiction, and expressed a desire to supply the fort with cattle. The matter being referred to New Amsterdam, Director-General Stuyvesant expressed fear that this was another attempt by the New Englanders "to get into our beaver-trade with their wampum and divert the trade"; he was instructed by the West India Company to prevent the English settlement by all means.[42]

Persuasion having failed, the company sought to apply pressure through the United Commissioners and the General Court, the latter writing Stuyvesant for free passage up the Hudson for agents of the company. At the same time the objective of the company was revealed by a grant to the company of a monopoly of trade within fifteen miles of the Hudson for twelve years and liberty to trade in commodities such as the Dutch usually sold. Stuyvesant, under pressure from the Dutch traders, flatly refused the request for free passage, and with the Restoration Massachusetts was in no position to press the matter. Although supplemental grants were obtained from the General Court and boundaries run, the company, after 1662,

the period 1658–1674 he shipped over 6,000 beaver skins and a substantial number of muskrat, moose, otter, fox, raccoon, fisher, and other miscellaneous skins. He also had substantial losses to the Dutch. "The Fur Trade on Connecticut River in the Seventeenth Century," 11 *N. Eng. Hist. and Gen. Reg.* 217–219. See also the agreement in October, 1658 by which Pynchon for £20 secured the trading rights for one year at Springfield and Northampton. 4 *Rec. Mass. Bay (Part I)* 354.

41 Burt, *Cornet Joseph Parsons* 16–17; 1 Wright, *Story Western Mass.* 41; Leder and Carosso, "Robert Livingston (1654–1728): Businessman of Colonial New York," 30 *Business History Review* 18. See also Elizur Holyoke, Jr.'s letters of October 3, 1678 and May 8, 1679 and Timothy Cooper's of October 2, 1678 to Robert

Livingston in *Livingston Mss.*, Redmond Library, Hyde Park, New York. A frank comment on the treatment by the Albany authorities of New Englanders attempting to reach Canada to ransom Indian captives, when intercepted, ended the Albany venture. See the March 18, 1677/8 letter from Cooper to Pynchon. 2 *Hist. and Proc. Pocumtuck Valley Mem. Asso.* 500–501. For the October 23, 1678 New York Council minutes as to Cooper's unsatisfactory explanation of his letter to Pynchon and ordering him to remove from Albany in the spring see O'Callaghan, *Calendar of Historical Manuscripts in the Office of the Secretary of State (English Mss., Part I, 1664–1776)* 75.

42 Buffington, "New England and the Western Fur Trade, 1629–1675," 18 *Pub. Col. Soc. Mass.* 176–178.

disappeared from view for ten years. The project was renewed in 1672, the settlement being urged as valuable in keeping the New England Indians loyal and in winning over the Mohawks. The General Court in 1673 granted Governor Leverett and John Pynchon powers to regulate the affairs of the projected plantation, but nothing came of the grant, probably due to the Dutch occupation of New York in 1673–74 as well as the outbreak of King Philip's War.[43]

Pynchon, through his "country-store" activities, was the principal supplier of manufactured goods to Springfield and the upper towns. By sale or barter he obtained quantities of products such as corn, wheat and other grains, peas, flax, hay, beef, pork, tar, and timber. These products plus those from his own extensive lands were shipped from Warehouse Point to Boston and other New England ports, to New York, and even to the West Indies. Cattle might be driven overland to points such as New London and even Boston. John Pynchon, Jr. was a merchant in Boston for a number of years but the integration of the commercial enterprises of father and son has not been studied. John Pynchon was also a partner in land speculation with James Rogers, the foremost New London merchant of the sixties and seventies, and it seems likely they were engaged in joint mercantile enterprises.[44] At various times Pynchon owned and operated grist-mills, corn-mills, and sawmills.[45]

John Pynchon's far-flung ventures included an interest with Samuel Wyllys and Richard Lord of Connecticut (c. 1682–87) in a sugar plantation called Cabbage Tree in Antigua in the Leeward Islands.[46] During the period between 1652 and 1689 he owned or had interests in at least five vessels, apparently engaged largely in the coastal trade. In 1692 he had an interest in a plant for the distillation of turpentine and the production of rosin. In 1696/7 the town of Springfield granted Pynchon and Joseph Parsons the right to operate an ironworks within the town bounds but there is no evidence that the project bore fruit. At a November 1700 Suffield town meet-

[43] *Ibid.* 178–181, 183–187. Pynchon's expenditures in connection with this venture are to be found in the *Pynchon Account Books* which are in the possession of the Connecticut Valley Historical Museum.

[44] 1 Wright, *Story Western Mass.* 309; Caulkins, *History of New London, Connecticut* (1852) 96, 133–134, 201–202. In a November 20, 1672 letter to his son Joseph in England Pynchon stated he was giving him 1000 acres of land at New London. Mass. Hist. Soc. Photostat. The Connecticut authorities in 1679 sought to acquire from Pynchon lands on which to settle some Pequots and Niantics. 3 *Pub. Rec. Col. Conn.* 42, 54, 117, 125.

[45] For Springfield see 1 Burt, *Hist. Springfield* 72, 247, 352, 354; 2 *ibid.* 84, 221; 1 Wright, *Story Western Mass.* 288. For Enfield see 1 Allen, *History of Enfield, Connecticut* 117; 3 *ibid.* 1919–1920. For Suffield see Sheldon, *Doc. Hist. Suffield* 21, 23–24, 62, 303.

[46] For litigation concerning this plantation see *Wyllys Papers* 281, 282–287, 295–296, 313–316, 383–385.

ing the undertaking of Pynchon and John Eliot of Windsor to set up an ironworks was approved. Pynchon might also finance local artisans, such as blacksmiths, who could furnish goods useful in the Indian trade.[47]

Pynchon was also interested in several mining ventures. In the period 1657–59 he apparently had some interest in the "black lead" or graphite workings at Sturbridge. At the June 1685 General Court, upon petition of Pynchon and two others, a grant was made of 1000 acres above Deerfield, provided it was improved by settlement within twelve years. Petitioners alleged that they had been at much pains and costs in searching for metals. Trumbull indicates that Pynchon had an interest in a mining venture near Northampton and also one in Connecticut.[48] Richard Wharton, writing from London in March 1687/8 concerning his attempts to secure a patent for all the mines in New England, stated that £13,000 had already been subscribed and that "without order" he had subscribed for Pynchon and a number of others prominent in business in the Bay. However, this patent never issued.[49]

As already indicated, Pynchon was a large landowner. Some of these lands he inherited from his father; some he was granted by the General Court; some were purchased or obtained by exchange; some were taken in payment of debts; some were obtained as an allotment to a town proprietor; some were obtained by town grants in connection with the erection of sawmills, corn-mills, grist-mills, or ironworks. While Pynchon devoted much time and energy to service of the commonwealth, such services were rewarded in some instances by the General Court by grants of land.[50]

Although Pynchon has been accused in effect of immoral, if not illegal, conduct in using his "monopolistic" position to accumulate extensive land holdings, no evidence has been found supporting such accusations. An examination of his holdings at Deerfield, for instance, indicates that he made a bona fide attempt to improve his lands by use of long-term leases to tenant farmers who in return for low rents were obligated to build dwellings and barns. However, the statement has been made that Pynchon and James Rogers of

[47] 1 Wright, *Story Western Mass.* 41, 290; 2 Burt, *Hist. Springfield* 346–347; Sheldon, *Doc. Hist. Suffield* 137, 151–152; Banks, "Scotch Prisoners Deported to New England by Cromwell, 1651–52," 61 *Mass. Hist. Soc. Proc.* 13–14.

[48] 10 *N. Eng. Hist. and Gen. Reg.* 160; 5 *Rec. Mass. Bay* 482; Jones, "An Early Silver Mining Venture in Massachusetts Bay," 62 *Mass. Hist. Soc. Proc.* 374–375; 1

Trumbull, *Hist. Northampton* 262–263. See also the reference to iron ore on land sold by Pynchon. 1 Lockwood, *Westfield and Its Historic Influences* (1922) 218.

[49] 5 Mass. Hist. Soc. Coll. (6th ser.) 11–14.

[50] 4 *Rec. Mass. Bay* (Part I) 402; 5 *ibid.* 329–330, 410, 486; 2 *Mass. Archives* 206; 3 *ibid.* 37a; 45 *ibid.* 82; 112 *ibid.* 414, 414a; 243 *ibid.* 4.

New London, as partners in land speculation, "engrossed" over 2000 acres in Groton from small holders.[51]

Local historians have tended to overlook the impact upon John Pynchon's fortunes of the decline of the fur trade in the Connecticut Valley and the damage wrought by the Indians upon the buildings, crops, and goods of Pynchon and of those inhabitants indebted to him. Between 1671 and 1675 several letters to his son Joseph, a Harvard graduate (1664) then intending to practice medicine in England, reflect these straitened circumstances.[52] However, such pessimism may have been designed to prevent further drains on the parental purse.[53]

Although John Pynchon had ties of family, trade, and property with England and made occasional trips to the mother country, it is hard to detect his attitude in the political struggle between the Crown and the commonwealth which culminated in the scire facias proceeding against the First Charter.[54] An intriguing question is whether Pynchon, the chief law enforcement officer of western Massachusetts, was ever aware of the presence in Hadley of the regicides William Goffe and Edward Whalley for a number of years after their arrival in October 1664. Seemingly, the principal protectors of these fugitives were the Reverend John Russell and Peter Tilton, both of whom were closely associated with Pynchon on various occasions. Some mystery surrounds the part played by Pynchon in the Crown's attempts to take the regicides. An August 20, 1661 letter from Colonel Thomas Temple to Secretary Morrice in England states that the writer had joined in a secret design with "one Pinchin, and Captain Lord" (assumed to be John Pynchon and Captain Richard Lord, an eminent merchant of Hartford), two of the most considerable persons in the southern parts of the country,

51 Burt, *Cornet Joseph Parsons* 66, 72–73; 1 Sheldon, *Hist. Deerfield* 180; Caulkins, *Hist. New London* 96.

52 *Record of the Pynchon Family* 21 ff.; photostatic copy of November 20, 1672 letter in Mass. Hist. Soc.; November 14, 1671 fragmentary letter in Connecticut Valley Historical Museum. In the same tenor is a February 1, 1672/3 letter in the Yale University Library.

53 Between 1669 and 1674 Pynchon acquired lands in Boston from Edward Rawson, Secretary of the General Court. In 1680 £475 of the funds of the New England Company were placed with Pynchon. 1 Mass. Hist. Soc. Proc. (2nd ser.) 319; Winship, "Samuel Sewall and the New England Company," 67 *Mass. Hist. Soc.*

Proc. 58–59. Pynchon retained his Wraysbury holdings until July 1686. The July 6, 1686 indenture of release, signed by John Pynchon and his wife and John Pynchon, Jr. and his wife, is at the Connecticut Valley Historical Museum. A photostatic copy is in the Library of Congress (Genealogy Division) in *Facsimiles of some English deeds, leases, and other documents . . . relating to William Pynchon and his son John.* For a May 30, 1688 letter of Samuel Sewall regarding failure to pay off some mortgages see 1 Mass. Hist. Soc. Coll. (6th ser.) 82–83.

54 See, however, *Clarendon Papers*, N.Y. Hist. Soc. Coll., Fund Pub. Series (1869) 127–128, 132–134 and 5 *Rec. Mass. Bay* 185.

to use their utmost endeavors to apprehend the fugitives. Whether this was a bona fide design, whether Temple was placating his superiors, or whether he was duped cannot be determined at this date.[55]

Edward Randolph, New England's "evil genius," adverted to Goffe and Whalley on several occasions in his reports, but usually credited Daniel Gookin with harboring and protecting them. However, one report to Secretary Coventry in June 1676 mentions that Goffe, "still in this Country, narrowly escaped the Major in the Southern parts, where he and others are harboured by Their Antimonarchicall Proselites." Whether or not "the Major" referred to was Pynchon is not known; the date of the report is about the time that Goffe is believed to have quit Hadley for Hartford. If Pynchon was playing a double role, he completely deceived Randolph, who in September 1685 named the Major to the Committee for Trade and Foreign Plantations as a person well disposed and fit to be concerned in the temporary government.[56]

Whatever his inner convictions, John Pynchon encountered little difficulty in adjusting to the loss of the First Charter. When Joseph Dudley arrived in May 1686 Pynchon was one of those named councilors. Samuel Sewall noted in his *Diary* that, on May 14, "Major Pynchon and Mr. Stoughton are sent to the Magistrates to acquaint them with the King's Commands being come." At Dudley's meeting with the "Old Government" on May 17 the diarist indicates that Pynchon filed in next to the President. Pynchon was one of the Council nominated a committee to take the accounts of Nowell, the late Treasurer, as well as to make recommendations as to collection of duties on imported wines and liquors. In June Pynchon and two others were charged with examining and reporting on the acts of the proprietors of the "Narragansett Country." [57]

[55] Judd, *Hist. Hadley* 214 ff.; Dexter, "Memoranda Respecting Edward Whalley and William Goffe" in *A Selection from the Miscellaneous Historical Papers of Fifty Years* (1918) 24–29; CSP, Col., *1661–68*, #160. For biographical details on Lord, see 1 Trumbull, *The Memorial History of Hartford County, Connecticut, 1638–1884* (1886) 249. Lord's son Richard married Mary Smith, John Pynchon's niece, on April 15, 1665, was one of the wealthiest merchants of his time, and engaged in at least one venture with John Pynchon. Among the *Mather Papers* is a copy of a March 26, 1662 letter coded by Goffe as "from Mr. Pinchon to Mr. Daven-

port" (presumably John Davenport). 8 Mass. Hist. Soc. Coll. (4th ser.) 170–171. Perhaps Davenport, active in harboring the fugitives in the early days of their flight, had turned Pynchon's letter over to Goffe.

[56] 1 *Edward Randolph* 59, 100, 173, 196; 2 *ibid.* 207, 314; 3 *ibid.* 43–45. It is extremely doubtful whether Gookin maintained any relationship with Goffe and Whalley. See Gookin, *Daniel Gookin, 1612–1687* (1912) 106–110; Hutchinson, *Collection Original Papers* 419–420.

[57] 2 *Ms. Mass. Council Rec.* 15, 56, 77, 79, 80, 94; 5 Mass. Hist. Soc. Coll. (1st ser.) 246; 6 *ibid.* (6th ser.) 475–476; 5

In July Pynchon and Wait Winthrop were "persuaded" to undertake a visit to the Connecticut authorities at Hartford to encourage alliance with Massachusetts; they were received with respect if not interest. In the same month Edward Randolph visited Pynchon at Springfield in a swing around New England, perhaps in connection with the Connecticut mission. The *Record* also reveals that during July and August Pynchon delivered commissions to the various military officers in western Massachusetts, administering the oath of allegiance.[58]

When Governor Andros arrived in Boston in December 1686, Pynchon was again nominated a councilor, a post which he retained under the second commission to Andros. Apparently he was named a justice in the commission of the peace for Hampshire and sat on the quarterly Court of Sessions and, by virtue of a commission as judge, headed the Inferior Court of Common Pleas for that county. By June 1687 he was serving in the capacity of judge of the Prerogative Court of Hampshire.[59]

There is reason to believe that Pynchon became too identified with Andros for his own good. The two were not strangers when they met in Boston; earlier Pynchon had dealt with Andros as Governor of New York in Indian matters and probably in connection with Pynchon's trading venture at Albany with Robert Livingston. A December 28, 1686 letter from Edward Randolph to Pynchon concerning the opposition of Connecticut to becoming part of the Dominion is extremely revealing as to the latter's relations with the Crown representative. Almost a year later, when Connecticut was made part of the Dominion of New England, Pynchon was one of the cavalcade accompanying Andros from Boston to attend the Council meeting held in Hartford on November 1st. Apparently Pynchon also played a part in explaining or gaining acceptance by Connecticut of Dominion legislation.[60]

Springfield's exposed position also made it mandatory that Pynchon, made Lieutenant Colonel and then Colonel, maintain close relations with the Dominion executive. On July 27, 1688 a

ibid. (5th ser.) 137–138; *Dudley Papers,* 13 Mass. Hist. Soc. Proc. (2nd ser.) 251, 254, 272–273; *CSP, Col., 1685–88,* #702.
[58] 13 Mass. Hist. Soc. Proc. (2nd ser.) 282, 284; *CSP, Col., 1685–88,* #2140, 2144; *Rec.* 198. For the visit to Hartford see 3 *Pub. Rec. Col. Conn.* 358–359, 363–365; 1 *Conn. Archives, Miscellaneous* 5a, 7a–b, 8; 1 *Edward Randolph* 299. For Randolph's visit see 6 *ibid.* 191.
[59] 1 *Laws N.H.* 143, 235; 2 *Edward Randolph* 19; 2 *Hamp. Cty. Probate Ct. Rec.*

141–145. For the form of a commission for a judge of the Superior Court of Common Pleas and of a fragmentary commission of the peace see 40 *Mass. Archives* 243–244.
[60] 4 *Edward Randolph* 139–140 (*cf.* the variant version in 2 *ibid.* 11); Bates, "Expedition of Sir Edmund Andros to Connecticut in 1687," 48 *Amer. Antiq. Soc. Proc.* (ns) 276–299; 3 Coll. Conn. Hist. Soc. 139; Barnes, *The Dominion of New England* (1923) 94.

small party of Indians from Canada penetrated to the vicinity of Springfield and killed five friendly Indians at Spectacle Pond. A "diary" account reveals a picture of Pynchon springing into action upon receipt of the news, sending out scouts and a burial party, dispatching messengers to the nearest towns, and putting Springfield in a posture of defense. A few days later he was off to New London to await orders from the Governor; on August 3 he was back in Springfield. On August 6, upon intelligence of strange Indians in the vicinity, he moved up to Northfield with a few followers, picking up additional soldiers in the upper towns, and assisted in putting that town in a state of defense. Matters appearing quiet at Northfield, Pynchon ordered some Connecticut Indians assembled at Springfield sent home and returned to Springfield on August 11, where, with misplaced optimism, he discharged all the soldiers assembled for the trip. However, on August 16 the same war party killed six settlers at Northfield. Pynchon immediately sent a party of soldiers from Springfield in a vain attempt to take the murderers. On August 19 a small force was sent to Quabaug, "the people then being about to remove: ordering and urging their continuance"; it was, however, to fetch off such women as desired to come away. Despite some attempts to safeguard Northfield in August, a more permanent garrison was not established until Captain Jonathan Ball with some fifty men left Hartford November 9 and remained at Northfield until the overthrow of Andros.[61]

Governor Andros at New York expressed great concern at the "mischief and the actors escaped." Later he sent a strong representation to De Nonville, Governor of Canada, demanding that the murderers be sent to him forthwith, without success. In October Andros spent a short time at Hartford with John Allyn and other "principal officers and magistrates" of Connecticut, held a consultation with Pynchon at Springfield, and reached Hadley on October 14 or 15. From Hadley, Andros and his group went to Brookfield and then to Worcester and Marlborough. The inquiries made in this eyre were scarcely calculated to endear Andros or his adherents to the Valley inhabitants. This was strongly reflected in a letter written by Pynchon in early November when a report of enemy demonstrations at Northfield caused him to dispatch some men from Springfield, who readily attended, and to give orders to the defiant upper towns, who would not "give 3 skips of a louse" for Pynchon's authority, to supply additional men.[62]

Pynchon does not appear to have held strong views on the subject

---

61 Temple and Sheldon, *Hist. Northfield* 113–117, 215; *CSP, Col. 1685–88,* #1877, I, II, III.

62 Temple and Sheldon, *Hist. Northfield* 117–120.

of the Revolution of 1688. He took no part in the overthrow of the Andros regime in April 1689.[63] One historian has sought to explain Pynchon's role in the Andros government by stating that "although utterly opposed to the arbitrary measures of that day . . . he deemed it his duty to hold the office [on the Council], that he might be the better enabled to subserve the interests of the people." [64] However, this explanation apparently did not enjoy contemporary currency.

Pynchon was not on the Council for the Safety of the People and Conservation of the Peace, formed on April 20, 1689, ostensibly because he had never taken the oath as assistant, although chosen to serve in May 1686, prior to Dudley's arrival. He was not chosen an assistant during the interim prior to the granting of the Second Charter.[65] However, in September 1689, in June 1690 and in May 1691, Pynchon was allowed and confirmed as associate for the County Court of Hampshire and invested with magistratical power. In March 1692 he was again chosen an associate. Pynchon was not named a member of the Council in the 1691 Charter, but no disappointment is evident in his comments on those appointed. The *Record* shows that at a meeting of the freemen of Springfield in May 1693 John Pynchon was chosen representative to the General Assembly but "being taken to the Council The Freeholders made a choise of Captain Benjamin Davis for their Representative." Pynchon continued a member of the Council until his death.[66]

Pynchon was commissioned a justice of the peace in 1692 and headed both the Court of Inferior Pleas and the Court of General Sessions of the Peace of Hampshire established under the Second Charter. He was appointed Judge of Probate for Hampshire in June 1692 and continued in this office until his death.[67] There are

[63] See letter, dated January 16, 1688/9, to Robert Livingston in *Livingston Mss.*, Redmond Library. For an appeal by Lieutenant Governor Nicholson to Pynchon, see *Documents Relating to the Administration of Jacob Leisler*, N.Y. Hist. Soc. Coll., Pub. Fund Series (1868) 248–249; 2 *Conn. Archives, War Colonial* 4. Washburn, quoting from an unidentified document, states that Pynchon, among others, was empowered by Andros "to bind over all persons *suspected* of riots, outrages, or abusive, reflecting words and speeches against the government." *Sketches of the Judicial History of Massachusetts* (1840) 102. However, Pynchon is not mentioned in the pamphlets justifying the overthrow. See *Andros Tracts, passim.*

[64] Oliver B. Morris, "Bi-Centennial Address at First Church in Springfield, May

25, 1836," 1 *Papers and Proc. Conn. Valley Hist. Soc.* 323–324.

[65] For the 1690 and 1691 choices of assistants, see *CSP, Col., 1689–92*, #904–905, 1399.

[66] 1 *Laws N.H.* 327, 406; *Rec. Cty. Ct. Hamp.* 143, 151; *Vol. A, Registry of Deeds, Springfield, Hampden County, 1690–92*, 301, 313; 14 *Mass. Hist. Soc. Proc.* (2nd ser.) 215–217; *Rec.* 335.

[67] Whitmore, *The Massachusetts Civil List* (1870) 46–47, 91, 94, 139. The results of the 1696 and 1697 choice of councilors indicate that Pynchon's popularity and influence had waned. 5 *Mass. Hist. Soc. Coll.* (5th ser.) 426, 454. Pynchon's tenure as Judge of Probate is confirmed by the *Hampshire County Probate Court Records.*

also references to Pynchon as County Treasurer in 1690 and again in 1693.[68]

For several years after the overthrow of Andros there is no record of Pynchon's appointment to *ad hoc* town committees. Then, in August 1691, and again in the next year, Pynchon was appointed a commissioner to join with the selectmen in taking a list of the town's estate for presentation at a shire meeting. In 1692–93 Pynchon was active in several church matters and on a committee to settle boundaries with representatives of Northampton. In 1694 and in 1696, Pynchon and two others were named assessors for the public tax. With one other he was delegated the duty of examining the constable's accounts. In the closing years of his life Pynchon, still at work as a public servant, was authorized with one other, in 1698, to present certain circumstances on the local church establishment to the General Court, and again with one other, in March 1699/1700, to make inquiry as to the payment of rates to constables in Andros' time and report to the General Court. His last appointment came in November 1701 when he was named to a committee dealing with the perennial problem of the settlement of a ministry in the town.[69]

Between May 1693 and June 1694 Pynchon was active in seeking action by the Massachusetts Council on complaints by Suffield and Enfield that Windsor inhabitants were forcibly entering on their lands and carrying away their hay, timber, and so on. In October 1694 he was on a committee to perambulate the Massachusetts-Connecticut boundary line and to examine what had been done formerly in order that the line might be settled. In June 1700 Pynchon and three other councilors were constituted a committee to join with a committee of the House of Representatives to treat with Connecticut commissioners concerning the boundary line.[70]

Under the Second Charter Pynchon played little part in the settlement of new plantations. However, in February 1700/1, when some inhabitants of Springfield petitioned for a tract of land to the east

68 *Rec. Cty. Ct. Hamp.* 118; *Hamp. Rec. Ct. Pleas*, volume reversed. As a public servant Pynchon was handicapped by "many losses and charges" and advancing years. 3 *Mass. Archives* 51; 2 *Conn. Archives, War Colonial* 99a–c, 103; 4 *ibid., Private Controversies* 163.

69 2 Burt, *Hist. Springfield* 202, 204–205, 207–208, 212–213, 330, 332–335, 343, 345, 347, 350, 356, 358. See also 7 *Acts and Res. Prov. Mass. Bay* 38; 113 *Mass. Archives* 102.

70 2 *Mass. Archives* 214–218a, 258a; 112 *ibid.* 438–439, 444, 447, 449; 3 *ibid.* 54.

CSP, Col., 1700, #545. For the June 13, 1700 proposal of the Massachusetts commissioners, see 21 *Acts and Res. Prov. Mass. Bay* 695–696. For an enigmatic secret letter from Pynchon to Governor Treat see *Conn. Archives, Colonial Boundaries* 10a. See also 4 *Pub. Rec. Col. Conn.* 161 and the May 5, 1696 letter from John Allyn to Pynchon re quieting some Enfield inhabitants who threatened to take tar away from Windsor people burning candlewood on lands claimed by Enfield. *Wolcott Mss.* (Conn. Hist. Soc.)

INTRODUCTION

of the town and reference was made to a committee to admit inhabitants, grant allotments of land, and order all the prudential affairs, the petitioners were "bold to suggest to your Consideration that the Honourable Colonel John Pynchon be one of the committee having been Improved in Continuing and Settling new Places." The committee appointed consisted of Pynchon and five others.[71]

Even if Pynchon was out of favor after April 1689, and may have reverted to the rank of major, he still was continued in his military duties. In July 1689 he was active in garrisoning Northfield. In September he was again prevailed upon to travel to Albany, this time accompanied by Major Savage, Captain Belcher, and representatives of other New England governments, for a meeting with the Five Nations. However, the New Englanders "mist their chiefe expectations," when the Five Nations refused to make war on the Eastern Indians until they found whether the latter sided with the French against them.[72]

In February 1689/90 Pynchon wrote to the Connecticut authorities in connection with garrisons at Northfield and Springfield that:

Stephen Lee reported here that the French and Indians had a special aime to this Towne and a particular designe against me and that he was afraid this place might be laid in ashes before he returned to Boston, which is a greate discouragement to many of our people . . .

We are extreame naked and open and cant agree upon fortification some being for one way and some another . . .[73]

In March 1690, following news of the attack upon Schenectady by the French and Indians, Pynchon approved a weekly scout for discovery of the enemy, which was accordingly ordered by the County Court. He was also empowered by the General Court to dispose the Hampshire Indians to such place or places as might prevent exposure to danger and with such limitations as might least disquiet the Indians. In May 1690 Pynchon was consulted on raising troops from Hampshire for an expedition against the enemy and directed to consult with the Connecticut authorities whether a combined Hamp-

[71] 113 *Mass. Archives* 256, 258; 21 *Acts and Res. Prov. Mass. Bay* 712–713.
[72] Temple and Sheldon, *Hist. Northfield* 117, 121–123; 35 *Mass. Archives* 18–19, 21, 32–33, 274; 107 *ibid.* 253, 258; 4 *Pub. Rec. Col. Conn.* 2; 3 *Doc. Rel. Col. Hist. N.Y.* 621; 2 *Conn. Archives, War Colonial* 6, 12, 15. The account in Colden, *The History of the Five Nations of Canada* (1747 ed.) 100–105 states that, while proclaiming publicly that they could not declare war on the Eastern Indians, representatives of the Five Nations "with some

Art" said in private they would war against them. See also Buffington, "The Isolationist Policy of Colonial Massachusetts," 1 *N. Eng. Quart.* 175–176. For an informative Pynchon letter to Governor Bradstreet on frontier problems, see 35 *Mass. Archives* 102–103 (letter dated December 5, 1689).
[73] Letter, dated February 24, 1689/90, from Pynchon to Samuel Wyllys and Colonel John Allyn at Hartford. Mass. Hist. Soc. Mss.

shire-Bay force should advance to Albany or be deployed in defense of the Hampshire frontier. To a proposed levy of sixty soldiers from Hampshire, Pynchon objected that the towns were "weake scattered and next to the enymy." Finally, not "desyring in the least to withdraw from the Publike service, or to be wanting thereunto," Pynchon left the determination of the Hampshire quota to the Governor and Council, requesting only leave to designate the commissioned officers.[74]

During the summer of 1690 Pynchon was in an unenviable position. From the Bay he was under pressure to have Connecticut supply troops for the proposed land expedition against Canada, despite the friction between Jacob Leisler and Major Fitz-John Winthrop and the unwillingness of the Connecticut contingent to serve under Jacob Milborne. From Hartford he was under pressure to hasten the preparations of the Massachusetts authorities for the coordinated assault by water against Canada. At the same time, signs of hostile Indians near Deerfield and Swampfield and complaints from the Mohawks against the detention of two alleged Albany Indians (suspected of participating in the attacks in the Eastern parts) made it necessary to seek the retention of Connecticut troops in the Valley. In December 1690, the Connecticut Council was again asked by Massachusetts to provide garrisons for the upper towns, to be disposed of as Pynchon and the Council best advised.[75]

In November 1691 a group of about 150 Indians from Albany, many former enemies, settled near Deerfield. Pynchon, fearing that these Indians might prove to be false and betray the towns, suggested that a company be raised in the upper towns to march to Deerfield once or twice during the winter to let the unwelcome intruders know that the settlers were in a "warlike Posture." The Council accordingly directed Pynchon in January 1691/2 to keep a sharp lookout, to organize the company as suggested, to continue the weekly scout, to send a message of inquiry to Albany, and, if necessary, to maintain a garrison of Connecticut men at Deerfield. These directions were complied with, Pynchon sending Samuel Partrigg with a form of proclamation to parley with the Indians. However, the winter passed without incident and in May the inhabitants were relieved when the Indians returned home.[76]

[74] *Rec. Cty. Ct. Hamp.* 121; 1 Sheldon, *Hist. Deerfield* 221–226; 1 *Laws N.H.* 373; 36 *Mass Archives* 56–57; 8 Mass. Hist. Soc. Coll. (2nd ser.) 238; 5 *ibid.* (5th ser.) 320–321; 5 *ibid.* (4th ser.) 253, 258.

[75] 2 *Conn. Archives, War Colonial* 84, 86, 91–92, 98–99, 103, 113, 120, 127; 36 *Mass. Archives* 439. For a typical letter to Pynchon on frontier conditions see June 2, 1690 letter from Thomas Wells of Deerfield. 8 Mass. Hist. Soc. Coll. (2nd ser.) 239.

[76] 1 Sheldon, *Hist. Deerfield* 222–223; 37 *Mass. Archives* 214–215, 223–224, 246, 306a; 2 *Conn. Archives, War Colonial* 156a. See also letter, dated January 18, 1691/2, from Pynchon to William Stoughton and Samuel Sewall regarding frontier

In February and March of 1692/3 Pynchon was again active in transmitting intelligence to the Bay and in securing a Connecticut garrison for Deerfield upon news of assaults upon the Mohawks by French and Indians from Canada. Since the garrison would have to be provisioned by the country, Pynchon sought directions from Governor Phips as to hastening the garrisoning, "for I am in Paine least my good husbandry in delaying them (to ease the Country's charge) should prove of any dangerous consequence." In June 1693 several Deerfield inhabitants were murdered by Indians. Based upon identifications in dying declarations, a Mohawk and an "Albanian" Indian, hunting in the vicinity of Deerfield, were accused of the crime and imprisoned at Springfield. The Mohawks immediately brought pressure to bear upon Governor Fletcher to secure the release of the prisoners, asserting that weapons left at the scene of the crime bore the marks of Canadian Indians. Fletcher in turn brought pressure upon Pynchon and the Massachusetts authorities for release of the prisoners, sending Major Wissells, "a greate man with the Indians," and a group of Mohawks to investigate the matter. Pynchon, who "verily supposed" the Indians guilty of the murder, first requested that a suitable time and commission be appointed for the trial, but soon weakened in his resolution.[77]

On July 4 Phips wrote to Fletcher, commenting on certain evidence supplied by the latter that Canadian Indians were guilty of the crimes, that the accusation and evidences were direct and positive against the prisoners, but that he proposed "to defer a present Tryal if Probably Providence may make a fuller and more clear discovery of the matter." [78]

On July 28 Phips, writing Pynchon that his letters and same material supplied by Governor Fletcher and others in New York had been laid before the Council, said:

The Council have likewise procured the Examinations and Evidences taken from the wounded people being chiefly what others report to have heard them say, and not directly from themselves, besides that it's much doubted whether they were of sound mind, and upon consideration of the whole, are of opinion, the Indians cannot be convicted by those Evidences, advising that they be dismissed if no further material evidence

defense matters in *Misc. Mss. IV. 1683–93* (Mass. Hist. Soc.) and 4 *Pub. Rec. Col. Conn.* 14.

[77] 1 Sheldon, *Hist. Deerfield* 229–235, 241; 7 *Acts and Res. Prov. Mass. Bay* 378 ff., 390; 2 *Pub. Rec. Col. Conn.* 89; letter of Governor Phips to Governor and Council of Connecticut, dated February 24, 1692/3, 2 *Mass. Archives* 212; 2 *Conn. Archives, War Colonial* 167a.

[78] 1 Sheldon, *Hist. Deerfield* 236. See also the July 12 letter from Pynchon to Phips concerning a meeting with Lieutenant John Schuyler and some Mohawks at Springfield. 2 *Davis Papers, 1681–1747* (Mass. Hist. Soc.)

appear against them, which I accordingly order, and that care be taken that they may pass homeward without any violence being offered them . . .

In conclusion Phips stated that:

It is of great concernment to the whole of there Majesties Interest in these Teritories that the English be in good termes with the Maquas etc at this Critical hour when they are so much Solicited to go over to the side of the Enemy and that no just provocations be given them for a Rupture. As all caution ought to be used that no muther escape Justice, so it being plainly evident beforehand that these Indians cannot by this evidence be found guilty upon Tryal, its thought more advisable to dismiss them without and to avoid the inconvenience that may ensue there being longer detained which the Indians (not understanding the formalities of Law) may improve to disaffect them to the English Interest.[79]

However, Phips's letter crossed one from Pynchon, dated July 29, relating that, two days earlier, the Indians had escaped from prison, supposedly having been secretly provided with files by other Indians.[80]

In July, after an attack on Brookfield, a party from Springfield pursued the invaders northward and rescued several captives. Pynchon, requesting instructions, advised a small garrison for the town. Discovery of traces of hostile Indians near Deerfield led to proposals for a constant scout and an allowance for the fortification of the town.[81] In August 1694 Pynchon and two other commissioners of Massachusetts were present in Albany when Governor Fletcher entered into a treaty with the Five Nations, Pynchon noting that this was "a very hard service in my age." On the same trip he was consulted by the New York Governor and Council regarding defense measures.[82]

In December 1694, Pynchon wrote Secretary Addington requesting advice concerning the continuance of garrisons at Deerfield and Brookfield, being "loath upon my owne head to discharge them, least If any thing fel out not wel, I should deservedly be Blamed." In March 1694/5 a garrison of Connecticut men was withdrawn from

---

[79] 1 Sheldon, *Hist. Deerfield* 238; 7 *Acts and Res. Prov. Mass. Bay* 382. See 30 *Mass. Archives* 335a for a July 26, 1693 letter from Governor Phips to Governor Fletcher.

[80] 1 Sheldon, *Hist. Deerfield* 240, 243–244, 246–247; 7 *Acts and Res. Prov. Mass. Bay* 382.

[81] 7 *ibid.* 389–390. For a detailed account by Pynchon of the pursuit see *ibid.*

395–398. See also *Quabaug, 1669–1910* 52–54.

[82] 7 *Acts and Res. Prov. Mass. Bay* 440–441, 444–445; 2 *Conn. Archives, War Colonial* 236a; Wraxall, *An Abridgment of The Indian Affairs* (ed. C. H. McIlwain, 1915) 25–27. See also the Reverend Benjamin Wadworth's *Journal* in *Mass. Hist. Soc. Coll.* (4th ser.) 102–110.

Deerfield after ten weeks and Pynchon was compelled to furnish a garrison; the withdrawal led to an acrimonious exchange of letters between Lieutenant Governor Stoughton of Massachusetts and John Allyn, Secretary of the Connecticut Council.[83]

On December 12, 1695, having been called out of bed by news of a war party near Northfield, Pynchon quickly had Captain Colton and twenty-four troopers moving up the east bank of the Connecticut. On August 21 some Deerfield inhabitants, who in the words of Pynchon were "in a sense in the enemy's Mouth almost, and are often and so continually pecked at," were ambushed with one fatality. Vigorous pursuit proved futile, but, upon Pynchon's application, a garrison force was again supplied by Connecticut. In September Pynchon sent further reinforcements to Deerfield when an Indian attack threatened.[84]

Pynchon's labors in defense of the western frontier had virtually ended by the autumn of 1695. In November 1696 he petitioned the Governor and the General Court for "a meete Compensation for his Past and already chearful service hithertoe in this time of War," setting forth his services at length. Almost a year later he was allowed ten pounds for his "extraordinary service and expenses with the regiment under his command, lying frontier to the enemy." [85]

When, in July 1698, two settlers were killed by Indians at Hatfield and two others taken captive, Pynchon in a blistering letter to Governor Bellomont of New York laid the blame on their "counterfeit friends," the Scagadacooks, accusing them of having a hand in all the Indian outrages in the Valley since 1688. But Bellomont took no effective action to curb these Indians.[86]

Pynchon played little part in Queen Anne's War. However, in June 1702 upon a report by Pynchon and Samuel Partrigg that some French were ranging the Hampshire woods and hunting with the Indians, the Council ordered that all civil and military make strict search and cause the strangers to be apprehended and sent down to Boston to give an account of themselves to the governor. In July the Council advised that the Governor write Pynchon to send his Lieutenant Colonel to Deerfield to view and have repaired the fortifications, covering the work with a scout out of other towns, and to per-

[83] 43 Mass. Hist. Soc. Proc. 505–506; 7 Acts and Res. Prov. Mass. Bay 460–464; 2 Mass. Archives 227a, 230, 232–233, 234a; 3 Conn. Archives, War Colonial 1a, 2a, 3a–b, 4a, 5, 7a.

[84] 1 Sheldon, Hist. Deerfield 247–253, 259; 7 Acts and Res. Prov. Mass. Bay 486; 4 Pub. Rec. Col. Conn. 149; 5 Mass. Hist. Soc. Coll. (5th ser.) 430.

[85] 7 Acts and Res. Prov. Mass. Bay 165, 570–571. A good example of Pynchon's interest in the election of militia officers is a December 5, 1690 letter to Joseph Hawley in 36 Mass. Archives 242.

[86] CSP, Col., 1697/8, #822, IV. See also ibid. pp. 431–432, 439–440; 7 Acts and Res. Prov. Mass. Bay 605–606; 4 Doc. Rel. Col. Hist. N.Y. 364–367.

form the same task at Brookfield. A list of the militia and civil officers of the province, compiled in December 1702, shows Pynchon as colonel of the Hampshire regiment, mustering over 800 soldiers.[87]

When John Pynchon died "about sun-rise" on January 17, 1702/3, probably at the age of seventy-seven, he had outlived most of his contemporaries, being characterized by one diarist as "an old man and full of days." His wife had died a few years earlier; his second son, Joseph, a physician in Boston, had died unmarried in 1682; his daughter Mary, married to Josiah Whiting, also predeceased him; two children had died in infancy. His only surviving child was John, Jr., who had become a merchant in Boston and later removed to Springfield. Final settlement of Pynchon's estate was not made until 1737 when it was valued at £8,446/16/6 of which only £165/18/2 consisted of personalty.[88]

While the funeral sermon delivered by Solomon Stoddard, a well-known Northampton minister, is largely couched in generalities studded with classical allusions, the following passages constitute a fitting eulogy:

Observe, That God has removed one that has been along while Serviceable. That has been improved about Publick Service for above Fifty Years: he has been Serviceable unto the Country in General, and in special among our selves. He hath had the principal management of our Military Affairs, and our Civil Affairs; and laboured much in the setling of most of our Plantations, has managed things with Industry, Providence and Moderation. He has been careful in time of War and as there has been occasion, has been a Peace Maker among us, and helpfull in composing differences: he has discountenanced Rude and Vicious Persons, bearing his Testimony against Them.

It is to be feared that we shall feel the sorrowful effects of his removal a long while . . . He was honourable and had great influence upon men in Authority abroad, and upon the People at home, and had more experience by far, than any other among us.[89]

[87] CSP, Col. 1702, #607, 696; ibid, 1702–03, #30, V; 1 Sheldon, Hist. Deerfield 284.

[88] Record of the Pynchon Family 6–7; 6 Mass. Hist. Soc. Coll. (5th ser.) 73; "Diary of John Marshall of Braintree," 14 Mass. Hist. Soc. Proc. (2nd ser.) 22; photostatic copies of Hampshire County Probate Court Records at Connecticut Valley Historical Museum.

[89] Stoddard, Gods Frown in the Death of Usefull Men. Shewed in a Sermon Preached at the Funeral of the Honourable Colonel John Pynchon Esq. Who deceased January the 17th, 1702/3. (1703).

I V. Elizur Holyoke and Samuel Chapin

A S already noted, a portion of the *Record* was kept in the hand of Elizur Holyoke. Born in Tamworth, Warwickshire, about fifteen miles northeast of Birmingham, and educated in England, in 1637 or 1638, when about twenty years old, Holyoke accompanied his father, Edward Holyoke, to New England and settled on a farm at Rumney Marsh, near Chelsea. Termed by Eliot "Mr. Pynchon's ancient friend," the older Holyoke was apparently a farmer of good estate who served as deputy for several terms during the 1640's, and in May 1650 was chosen deputy for Springfield.[1]

The first mention of Elizur Holyoke is his marriage to William Pynchon's daughter Mary on November 20, 1640, at which time he was granted lands at Springfield. His first appearance in the *Record* is as a juror in January 1641/2.[2] In January 1642/3 and in May 1645 he was on town committees to view and to allot lands; in September 1646 he was chosen a selectman for the ensuing year and in May 1651, constable. He was sworn a freeman April 13, 1648.[3]

Holyoke first assumed judicial duties in October 1652 when, as noted, the General Court empowered Pynchon, Holyoke, and Chapin as commissioners for the government of the inhabitants of Springfield and then continued to act under successive commissions until May 1665. After this date Holyoke, until his death on February 5, 1675/6, sat as an associate on the County Court for Hampshire.[4] He was chosen recorder for the commissioners in March 1660, and an entry in the Registry of Probate supplemental material notes

[1] 1 Burt, *Hist. Springfield* 590; Morris, "Elizur Holyoke," 1 *Papers and Proc. Conn. Valley Hist. Soc.* 62; *Rep. Rec. Comm. Roxbury Land and Church Rec.* (2nd ed., 1884) 74; 2 *Rec. Mass. Bay* 1, 22, 33, 186, 238; 4 *ibid.* (Part I) 2. Edward Holyoke and other patentees of lands on the Piscataqua put themselves under the jurisdiction of the Massachusetts colony in June, 1641. 1 *Doc. and Rec. Prov. N.H.* 155–157. He was appointed to assist in holding courts at Salem in May 1643. 2

Rec. Mass. Bay 35. A scholar and writer in the field of religious doctrines, he published in London in 1658 a substantial work entitled *The Doctrine of Life, or of Mans Redemption*.

[2] 1 Burt, *Hist. Springfield* 590; *Rec.* 17.

[3] 1 Burt, *Hist. Springfield* 170, 179–180, 185, 218; *Rec.* 24.

[4] 4 *Rec. Mass. Bay* (Part II) 148; *Pynchon Waste Book for Hampshire* 25, 30, 36, 37, 46, 54, 65, 70, 83, 94, 106, 112.

that on September 25, 1660 he was "chosen and appointed Recorder for this Court and County." Apparently he was recorder for the County Court until his death. In 1665/66, he became clerk of the writs for Springfield when Chapin declined the office.[5]

During his period of judicial tenure Holyoke also held legislative office, being chosen deputy for Springfield eleven times between 1656 and 1675 (in some cases for only one session). He was elected selectman for Springfield nine times between February 1660/1 and February 1673/4.[6] In November 1656 he was chosen recorder or clerk of the town in John Pynchon's absence, in which capacity he served during the period 1661–76. Between 1663 and 1673 Holyoke was frequently chosen to carry up to shire meetings the sealed votes of the freemen of Springfield for nomination of assistants and choice of county treasurer and associates on the County Court. Once he was chosen moderator of a town meeting.[7]

In a number of instances Holyoke was commissioned by the General Court to act with others in matters relating to the settlement and pacification of the western frontier of the colony. Several on which he served with John Pynchon have been noted. In October 1663 Holyoke and David Wilton were authorized to lay out the bounds of a grant of lands to Major General Dennison near Northampton and Hadley. In May 1664 he and two others were designated to settle a grant of lands to Indians near Quabaug. In October 1669 he was one of seven empowered to determine what lands at Hadley belonged to the several ministers, and four years later one of three directed to report on a petition of the inhabitants of Swampfield.[8]

Holyoke, like John Pynchon, was on a number of *ad hoc* committees concerned with various Springfield town matters. He served on several committees concerned with the settlement of Woronoco, and on one charged with laying out lands granted Westfield by the General Court. In February 1661/2 Holyoke, Pynchon, and Timothy Cooper constituted a committee to consider settling the towns of western Massachusetts into a county. He was also on committees to dispose of town lands, to examine the accounts of the selectmen, to make rates, and to obtain a minister for the town. During 1656–57 he sometimes filled in for the minister on the Sabbath.[9] Other scattered committees on which Holyoke served dealt with such matters

5 *Rec.* 86; 1 *Hamp. Cty. Probate Ct. Rec.* 3.

6 4 *Rec. Mass. Bay (Part I)* 255, 416; 4 *ibid.* (*Part II*) 2, 331, 448, 551; 5 *ibid.* 2, 42; 1 Burt, *Hist. Springfield* 26–28.

7 1 *ibid.* 46–47, 251; *Rec.* 321 ff.; 2 Burt, *Hist. Springfield* 119.

8 4 *Rec. Mass. Bay (Part II)* 96–97, 109, 322, 446–447, 459; 5 *ibid.* 22; 2 Burt, *Hist. Springfield* 107.

9 1 Burt, *Hist. Springfield* 218, 247, 250, 256, 261–262, 278, 281–282, 297–298, 307, 309; 2 *ibid.* 83.

as a new meeting house, a claim against the town, poor relief, the location and maintenance of highways, and treating with the Indians. As town recorder he might be charged with drafting petitions to the General Court on matters such as inequitable county rates and imposts.[10]

Although Holyoke was commissioned an ensign in 1653, a lieutenant in 1657, and later appears as captain in the records, he played no important role in King Philip's War or in earlier defensive measures.[11]

Holyoke's income was derived largely from farming his substantial land holdings in and around Springfield, but he also owned lands near Lynn and Reading received from his father. Through his wife he had an interest in a sawmill which in March 1663/4 was conveyed to John Pynchon in settlement of a debt. Judging from the fact that he was chosen recorder for several bodies and from the manner in which the duties of such offices were performed, he must have been a person of some education and intellectual accomplishments. His father, in leaving all his books and manuscripts to Elizur, significantly noted that "he onely cann make use of them." [12]

The last of the four persons prominent in the early administration of justice at Springfield is Samuel Chapin, better known to posterity as Deacon Chapin. Baptized in October 1598 in the parish church of Poignton, Devonshire, he married in February 1623/4 and probably came to New England in 1635 with his father and family. At Roxbury, where he settled and engaged in agricultural pursuits, he was a member of the church and became a freeman on June 2, 1641.[13]

Chapin first appears in the Springfield records in January 1642/3 when he, with Holyoke, Henry Smith, and three others, was authorized to lay out lands on the west side of the River. He may have been elected a Deacon soon after his arrival but is not designated as such in the town records until 1649/50. In May 1645 he and Holyoke were on a committee to apportion planting grounds to each home lot and on another to make allotments of lands. He was one of the first se-

[10] 1 ibid. 144, 282, 302; 2 ibid. 85–86, 110, 114. For a committee settlement of the claims of certain Indians to lands east of the river see Wright, Indian Deeds 89–91. For the petition to the General Court from the inhabitants of Springfield, February 2, 1668/9, protesting the requirement of payment of imposts in specie see 9 N. Eng. Hist. and Gen. Reg. 86–87.

[11] 4 Rec. Mass. Bay (Part I) 135, 314.

[12] For an abstract of Edward Holyoke's will, dated December 25, 1658, see 9 N. Eng. Hist. and Gen. Reg. 345–346. Mary Pynchon Holyoke died October 26, 1657. For the sawmill see Morris, Elizur Holyoke 65; 1 Burt, Hist. Springfield 322; 2 ibid. 22.

[13] 1 Chapin Book of Genealogical Data (comp. G. W. Chapin, 1924) 1; H. M. Chapin, Life of Deacon Samuel Chapin of Springfield (1908) 12–14.

lectmen chosen in 1644 and continued in that capacity until October 1652, when he resigned to become a commissioner. In 1661 and in 1664 he was again chosen a selectman. Chapin, along with John Pynchon and Holyoke, continued to act as a commissioner under successive commissions until May 1665. While Chapin attended the first few sessions of the County Court for Hampshire, he was never elected an associate.[14]

The first reference to Chapin found in the *Record* is on December 21, 1643, as a juror in *Merick* v. *Ashley*. On February 13, 1643/4 he was sworn constable in the place of John Leonard who was removed for swearing to a lie in the evidence he gave on review of the above action. He apparently continued in the office until March 12, 1645/6 when James Bridgeman was sworn constable. In 1648 and 1649 Henry Smith and Chapin were chosen to seal up the votes of the freemen for magistrates and to send them to the deputy from Roxbury representing Springfield at the General Court.[15] As already noted he was on committees appointed by the General Court in connection with the settlement of Northampton and Hadley. In the Springfield hierarchy around 1650 Chapin probably ranked next after William Pynchon, Henry Smith, and Elizur Holyoke.

Deacon Chapin served on many *ad hoc* committees. In September 1652 he was on the committee which treated with the Reverend Moxon for the purchase of his house and lands; twice he was on committees concerned with securing a minister for the town; and in 1656–57 was one of several charged with administering to the spiritual needs of the town in the absence of a minister. In the period 1665–67 he was on several committees charged with poor relief. In 1659 and 1662/3 the seating arrangement in the meeting house was ordered by Chapin and the selectmen.[16] In 1661/2 he was on a committee with two others for altering certain lots; later he was on a committee charged with the distribution of town lands and a committee on highways. In August 1665 he was a commissioner for the town to join with the selectmen in making the county rate. In 1669/70 and upon two subsequent occasions Chapin and one other were charged with examining the selectmen's accounts. These were the last appointments for the Deacon who died on November 11, 1675.[17]

At Springfield, Chapin, like Holyoke, was principally engaged in farming. Nothing is known of his education or of his activities in England, but on the basis of his "educated hand" and his phraseol-

[14] Chapin, *Life* 17; 1 Burt, *Hist. Springfield* 26–27, 144, 179–180.
[15] *Rec.* 22–24; 1 Burt, *Hist. Springfield* 178.
[16] 1 *ibid.* 125–127, 146–147, 222, 247, 250, 254, 256, 261–262, 359; 2 *ibid.* 85–86.
[17] 1 *ibid.* 292, 310, 315, 323–324; 2 *ibid.* 68, 104, 111, 119; Chapin, *Life* 37; 38 *N. Eng. Hist. and Gen. Reg.* 121.

ogy in drafting legal documents such as deeds, he may have had some legal training.[18]

Holyoke and Chapin, although less enterprising and aggressive than John Pynchon, were able public servants. The *Record* indicates this competence extended to the exercise of judicial functions.

[18] 2 Burt. *Hist. Springfield* 22–24. See also Chapin, *Life* 48–49.

V. The Massachusetts Bay Judicial System

I N general, descriptions of the judicial system of seventeenth-century Massachusetts Bay display a marked disregard for its jurisdictional complexity and *ad hoc* qualities. While the General Court, the Court of Assistants, and the County Courts have received treatment by commentators, little attention has been paid to the jurisdiction, under the First Charter, of a single magistrate, two magistrates, or persons vested with magistratical powers, of the commissioners for ending small causes, of the special commissions for western Massachusetts and the eastern regions, of the Associate Courts and Commissioner Courts, of the selectmen of the towns, and of various miscellaneous courts. Similarly, little interest has been shown in the lower jurisdictional levels of the judicial establishment under the Second Charter. In addition, the changes wrought by Dudley and Andros are far from clear in their application to the lower levels.

This discussion of the Massachusetts judicial system provides the background necessary to a proper understanding of the relation of the courts held at Springfield, as reflected in the *Record,* to the Massachusetts Bay judicial establishment. It also serves to indicate the statutory jurisdiction conferred upon such courts from time to time. The treatment is divided into three periods: the period of the First Charter (1639–1686) ; the intercharter period (1686–1692) ; and the period of the Second Charter (1692–1702) .

1639–1686. THE FIRST CHARTER

At the time of the first entry in the *Record,* in February 1638/9, the Massachusetts Bay judicial system had attained, in the main, the form which was continued until superseded in June 1686 by the courts set up by the President and Council for New England. At the apex of the judicial hierarchy was the General Court, consisting of the governor, deputy governor, assistants, and deputies. Below the General Court was the Court of Assistants which consisted of the governor, deputy governor, and the assistants. Below this court were the several Inferior Quarter Courts, which later evolved into the County Courts. Below the Inferior Quarter Courts were the magistrates (assistants) who exercised limited jurisdiction in the town in which they resided and the commissioners for ending small causes in certain towns in which no magistrate resided. In addition, the selectmen of the several towns were given judicial and quasi-judicial powers in certain narrow areas.

General Court

The General Court, the only body specifically granted judicial powers in the charter, exercised original jurisdiction, both civil and criminal, and also review jurisdiction over the acts of the Court of Assistants and, to a lesser extent, of the County Courts and other inferior tribunals.[1] Its original jurisdiction was rarely set forth in the laws. Similarly, its amorphous jurisdiction upon petition or review was seldom specifically defined by order or law.[2]

Several self-imposed jurisdictional limitations were not strictly adhered to so that the General Court continued to exercise original jurisdiction in civil causes from time to time.[3] However, in numerous cases petitioners were directed to pursue their remedies at law or to apply to an inferior court for relief or the matter was referred to an inferior court to hear and determine. In others, petitions were referred to County Courts to hear and report back to the General Court or to the Court of Assistants.[4] The General Court also heard cases, largely civil, transferred from the Court of Assistants in which the magistrates had refused to accept a jury verdict,[5] and even cases of disagreement between bench and jury in the County Courts and other inferior courts.[6] While normally appellate recourse from the inferior courts was to the Court of Assistants, in a few cases the General Court reviewed directly judgments of the inferior courts.[7]

[1] 1 *Rec. Mass. Bay* 17.
[2] Cf. *Col. Laws Mass., 1660* 122 and Liberty No. 36, *ibid.* 41. On the controversy concerning the right of appeal to the King in Council, see J. H. Smith, *Appeals to the Privy Council from the American Plantations* (1950) 45–51, 54–58, 60–62. For the relative judicial roles of the magistrates and the deputies, see Howe and Eaton, "The Supreme Judicial Power in the Colony of Massachusetts Bay," 20 *N. Eng. Quart.* 291.
[3] 2 *Rec. Mass. Bay* 16; 4 *ibid.* (Part I) 184; *Laws and Liberties Mass.* 51. See also the committee appointed in May, 1653 to attempt to restrict the General Court's

jurisdiction in small matters. 4 *Rec. Mass. Bay* (Part I) 134.
[4] 3 *ibid.* 400; 4 *ibid.* (Part I) 262, 282, 285, 412–414; 5 *ibid.* 39.
[5] 3 *ibid.* 197, 329, 400–401, 405–406, 413; 4 *ibid.* (Part I) 73, 145, 193, 212, 269; 4 *ibid.* (Part II) 47, 89, 93, 293, 308–309, 340–341.
[6] 4 *ibid.* (Part I) 14, 132, 174, 295, 318, 331, 394; 4 *ibid.* (Part II) 539.
[7] 4 *ibid.* (Part I) 97, 111, 174, 217–220, 247; 4 *ibid.* (Part II) 17, 26, 80, 85, 453–454; 5 *ibid.* 252. Cf. 4 *ibid.* (Part I) 189 where the General Court would not assume jurisdiction in a case on appeal to the Court of Assistants and *ibid.* 194 where

The General Court might also grant an appeal from a County Court to the Court of Assistants,[8] grant a bill of review or new hearing below,[9] allow a suit or review *in forma pauperis* in an inferior court,[10] remit or abate fines, or direct inferior courts therein, or otherwise mitigate punishment and issue pardons.[11] A recalcitrant in the lower courts might be ordered to appear before the General Court.[12]

The General Court, in its judicial capacity, played relatively little part in the administration of justice in western Massachusetts. Mention has already been made of its role in the censure of William Pynchon and in the witchcraft cases of Mary and Hugh Parsons. Its connection with another serious offense reported to have been committed at Northampton appears in a May 22, 1656 entry to the following effect:

Whereas the Court hath bin informed that Robert Bartlett, of Northwottuck, alias Northampton, hath committed a great misdemeanor, in attempting to force the wife of one Smyth of the same towne, and some report that he did force the said Smyths wife, this Court doth therfore order Mr. John Pynchon, and Mr. Elitzur Hollioke to heare the case, and examine the wittnesses, and if they judg the case capitall, then to cause the offendor to be forthwith sent to the prison at Boston, to answer the same at the next Court of Assistants, whither all the testemonyes and examinations are to be sent, and the wittnesses required to appeare at the said Court; but if it be only found by them a misdemeanor, in that case they shall bind over the said Bartlett to the County Court at Cambridge, in October next, with suffycient securitie, to answer for his offence, and cause all the testemonyes and examinations in the case to be sent to the clarke of the said Court, sealed up, and the Court doth hereby give full powre to the said commissioners, by warrent, to send for partyes, and make full process in the case for the fulfilling of this order.[13]

The original return made by Pynchon and Holyoke to the County Court at Cambridge denying the existence of a capital case is in the possession of the Connecticut Valley Historical Museum. (It is printed as an Appendix to illustrate the judicial integration of the frontier and the Bay.) Apparently the County Court took no action upon the return.

---

it refused to take a case referred by a County Court.

[8] 2 *ibid.* 198; 4 *ibid.* (*Part II*) 500.

[9] 2 *ibid.* 207; 4 *ibid.* (*Part I*) 420; 4 *ibid.* (*Part II*) 45, 79, 541.

[10] 4 *ibid.* (*Part II*) 351, 406, 501, 540 (review), 555; 5 *ibid.* 397, 427.

[11] 4 *ibid.* (*Part I*) 191, 227–228, 297, 396–397, 398; 4 *ibid.* (*Part II*) 91, 327, 353, 427; 5 *ibid.* 7, 69, 117, 147, 173, 264.

[12] 4 *ibid.* (*Part II*) 290, 316, 373–375 (Anabaptists); 5 *ibid.* 272, 330.

[13] 3 *ibid.* 414.

Court of Assistants

The Court of Assistants, also known as the Great Quarter Court, was held quarterly at Boston until 1649 when its sittings were reduced to twice a year. This judicial body at first exercised broad original jurisdiction, both civil and criminal, including exclusive jurisdiction in capital and criminal causes extending to life, member, or banishment and, later, in divorce cases.[14] It also exercised appellate jurisdiction over the Inferior Quarter Courts, which later developed into the County Courts; over Associate Courts until 1670; and over single magistrates and commissioners for ending small causes until at least 1648, and perhaps later.[15] Several General Court orders limited the original jurisdiction of the Court of Assistants. By an order of September 6, 1638 a plaintiff in such court bringing a civil action under twenty shillings, cognizable by a single magistrate or by commissioners to end small causes, was to lose his action and pay defendant costs. A May 1649 order provided that the Court of Assistants was not to take cognizance of any case or action triable in any County Court or of any debt or action cognizable by any one magistrate or any three commissioners for trial of causes under forty shillings, except by way of appeal. Under the laws of 1660 the Court of Assistants was to hear and determine all and only actions of appeal from inferior courts, plus cases of disagreement between bench and jury in such courts.[16] However, original jurisdiction was retained over serious offenses and divorce causes.

In some instances the laws of the colony specifically provided for concurrent jurisdiction by the Court of Assistants and the County Courts.[17] In a few cases the General Court and the Court of Assistants were given concurrent jurisdiction; in others, the General Court, the Court of Assistants and either two magistrates or the County Courts.[18] In several laws provision was made for binding over of offenders or recalcitrants to the Court of Assistants by magistrates, commissioners, or a County Court.[19]

The part played by the Court of Assistants in the administration

14 2 ibid. 285. 1 Col. Laws Mass., 1672 36.

15 4 Rec. Mass. Bay (Part II) 452; Laws and Liberties Mass. 2. Cf. note 16 below.

16 1 Rec. Mass. Bay 239; 2 ibid. 279; Col. Laws Mass., 1660 143, 167.

17 Laws and Liberties Mass. 17–18, 22, 25–26. Information or complaints of gates or rails erected on common highways might be made to the Court of Assistants, the County Courts or a single magistrate (ibid. 25).

18 Ibid. 28, 36–37, 45.

19 Grantors refusing to acknowledge a previous grant, in certain cases (ibid. 13); suspected Jesuits not cleared by "some of the Magistrates" (ibid. 26); traders refusing to account on oath to a magistrate as to furs traded (ibid. 26); and stranger Quakers apprehended (Col. Laws Mass., 1672 61–62). Persons refusing to take the oath of fidelity before a magistrate or County Court might be bound over to the Court of Assistants (Col. Laws Mass., 1660 183–184).

of justice in western Massachusetts was limited to handling a few cases involving witchcraft or unlawful trading with the Indians.[20]

County Courts

By 1639 Inferior Quarter Courts (sometimes called Particular Courts) were held each quarter at Ipswich, Salem, Newtown (Cambridge), and Boston by designated magistrates and associates. These courts exercised jurisdiction in all civil causes in which the debt or damage did not exceed ten pounds and all criminal causes not concerning life, member, or banishment. Any person aggrieved by any sentence might appeal to the Court of Assistants.[21]

In May 1642 four shires or counties were set up in the Massachusetts Bay colony—Suffolk, Middlesex, Essex, and Norfolk. By 1648 the use of the term "County Court" had been generally accepted, and the jurisdiction of such courts—all civil causes and criminal causes not extending to life, member, or banishment, subject to appeal to the Court of Assistants—corresponded to the territorial limits of the respective counties.[22] Later, County Courts were authorized for Piscataqua (Dover and Portsmouth), York, Hampshire, and Devonshire.[23]

In addition to such general civil and criminal jurisdiction the County Courts were given jurisdiction in specific judicial and administrative matters by various laws. Included were such matters as probate and administration, apportionment of charges for the repair of bridges, provision for the maintenance of the ministry, punishment of interference with church elections, punishment of heretics, ordering highways laid out, licensing of ordinaries, violation of town orders regulating wages, settlement of the poor, settlement of houses of correction, licensing of new meeting houses, and punishment of vendors charging excessive prices.[24]

The County Courts exercised concurrent jurisdiction in certain matters with the Court of Assistants or even with the General Court.

20 For the trial of Mary Parsons, wife of Joseph Parsons of Northampton, for witchcraft see 1 Rec. Ct. Assistants Mass. Bay 31, 33. For the trials of James Fuller of Springfield and of Mary Webster of Hadley on witchcraft charges see ibid. 228–230, 233. For further material on the charges against Mary Parsons at the County Court level see 1 Hamp. Cty. Probate Ct. Rec. 158–159; Pynchon Waste Book for Hampshire 120, 122–125. For further reference to Mary Webster see Rec. Cty. Ct. Hamp. 65; 2 Mather, Magnalia Christi Americana (1853 ed.) 454–456. The witchcraft charges against John Stebbins of Northampton in April 1679 were transferred by the County Court to the Court of Assistants. Rec. Cty. Ct. Hamp. 25, 27. For the cases of John Westcarr and Benjamin Waite, guilty of selling liquor to the Indians without license, see Section VII.

21 1 Rec. Mass. Bay 169, 175.

22 2 ibid. 38, 41, 227; Laws and Liberties Mass. 15–16.

23 3 Rec. Mass. Bay 308; 4 ibid. (Part I) 124, 127, 131–132; 4 ibid. (Part II) 82; 5 ibid. 16–17, 30.

24 Col. Laws Mass., 1672 12, 45–46, 59, 61, 64, 79, 84, 104–105, 118, 123, 127, 157–158, 236, 267.

In a large number of instances the County Courts exercised concurrent jurisdiction with a single magistrate,[25] or with two magistrates.[26] In a few cases they exercised concurrent jurisdiction with a single magistrate or with commissioners or a single commissioner.[27]

In some cases a single magistrate was given power to bind offenders over to the County Court. Commissioners for ending small causes, having no authority to commit to prison, might charge a constable with carrying a defendant before a magistrate or the County Court, if sitting, to be further proceeded with according to law in the event such defendant, having been sentenced, refused to give his bond for his appearance or satisfaction.[28] Under some laws the power of the County Courts might be limited to the punishment of habitual offenders.[29] By virtue of a few scattered laws jurisdiction was vested in "any court"; [30] such terminology was probably intended to give the County Courts jurisdiction.

25 Administering oaths to clerks of the markets (*Laws and Liberties Mass.* 3) ; appointing gaugers to view casks (*ibid.* 6) ; unauthorized taking and using of horses or draft animals (*ibid.* 7) ; making fires on commons or enclosed grounds (*ibid.* 22–23) ; appointing and swearing leather sealers and searchers and punishing violation of regulations concerning leather (*ibid.* 31) ; requiring the taking of the oath of fidelity (*Col. Laws. Mass., 1660* 183–184) . Also punishing the keeping of unlicensed ordinaries (*ibid.* 233) ; the performing of servile work on the Sabbath (*ibid.* 259) ; the taking of certain fish at unseasonable times (*Col. Laws Mass., 1672* 53), being a scold (*ibid.* 206) , misbehaving at meeting houses (*ibid.* 234) and failing to assist in apprehending suspected pirates (*ibid.* 315–317) .

26 Assisting selectmen to place unruly, neglected children (*Laws and Liberties Mass.* 11) ; determining differences concerning the settling and providing for poor persons (*ibid.* 44) ; punishing failure to pay fees for selling or bartering guns, lead or powder with Indians (*Col. Laws Mass., 1660* 240–241) ; failure to pay imposts on liquors (*ibid.* 241) ; assisting selectmen in putting orphans out to service (*ibid.* 260–261) ; punishing those leaving towns to avoid military service (*Col. Laws Mass., 1672* 248) .

27 Offenses by innkeepers (*Col. Laws Mass., 1660* 165) ; rude singing in houses of public entertainment (*ibid.* 228–229) ;

selling inferior beer (*Col. Laws Mass., 1672* 80) ; riotous and unsober conduct (*ibid.* 236–237) . A 1675 law gave jurisdiction in cases involving the wearing of unlawful apparel to the County Courts, a single magistrate and the Boston Commissioners Court (*ibid.* 233) . Prior to the enactment of this law the County Courts had sole jurisdiction in such cases. One 1668 law gave jurisdiction in assault and battery cases to the County Courts, a single magistrate, a commissioner or an associate (*Col. Laws Mass., 1660* 261) .

28 Under a 1661 law a magistrate might inflict corporal punishment on youthful offenders or bind them over to the County Court (*ibid.* 136) . See also *Laws and Liberties Mass.* 37, sub "Marriage," third offense. For commissioners see *ibid.* 8–9.

29 Drawing away the affections of any maid under pretence of marriage without consent of the parents, third offense (*ibid.* 37) ; Sabbath violations, after third offense (*Col. Laws Mass., 1660* 189–190) ; vagabond Quakers, after third conviction (*ibid.* 219) .

30 A 1674 act authorized "any Court or Magistrate" to punish single women, or married women whose husbands were absent, who took in male lodgers despite the disapprobation of selectmen, magistrate, or commissioners (*Col. Laws Mass., 1672* 216) . Laborers receiving excessive wages and sellers charging excessive prices might be fined by the "Court to which is presented" (*Laws and Liberties Mass.* 43) .

Under the laws of 1648 the County Courts were to hear appeals from the sentences of one magistrate and of commissioners for ending small causes. In May 1649 the County Courts were deprived of original jurisdiction in civil actions properly cognizable by a single magistrate or by commissioners to end small causes.[31] A few laws supplemented the above general appellate provision as to specific offenses or matters.[32]

Associate Courts and Commissioners Courts

Commencing in 1642 the General Court at various times authorized associates and/or commissioners, without a magistrate being joined with them, to exercise a limited jurisdiction in civil and criminal matters.[33] These courts, made up of associates chosen or commissioners appointed to hold County Courts, were, however, confined to the eastern portions of the colony. The Commissioners Court at Boston and its predecessor, the Boston "Smal Cort," exercised limited criminal jurisdiction as well as civil.[34]

Two Magistrates

Two magistrates exercised concurrent jurisdiction with the Court of Assistants and with the County Courts in certain matters. They also were given sole authority in a few administrative areas.[35] In view of the difficulty of assembling two in some localities, a 1673 law provided that, in counties where only one magistrate resided, action taken by such magistrate, joined with an associate of the County Court, was as valid as if done by two magistrates. In counties having no magistrate, any person with magistratical powers, joined with two associates of the County Court, likewise had the power of two magistrates.[36] An examination of practice manuals shows that in England the jurisdiction of two justices of the peace was much more extensive than that of two magistrates in Massachusetts Bay.

[31] *Ibid.* 2; 2 *Rec. Mass. Bay* 279.

[32] Appeal provided from sentence of single magistrate for offense of lying (*Laws and Liberties Mass.* 35) ; complaint against order of magistrates or Boston Commissioners Court compelling idle to work at suitable employment (*Col. Laws Mass., 1672* 294).

[33] See 2 *Rec. Mass. Bay* 31, 37, 120, 153; 4 *ibid.* (*Part I*) 127–128, 131–132, 135–136, 361; 4 *ibid.* (*Part II*) 424, 451, 520; 5 *ibid.* 5, 17, 23, 30.

[34] 1 *Rec. Mass. Bay* 276; 2 *ibid.* 28; 3 *ibid.* 244–245.

[35] Authority to grant exemption from military duty (*Laws and Liberties Mass.* 40–41) ; power to require strangers brought in by masters of ships to give an account of themselves (*Col. Laws Mass., 1660* 193) ; disposition of orphans without their consent (*Laws and Liberties Mass.* 12).

[36] *Col. Laws Mass., 1672* 208.

Special Commissions

At various times the General Court granted commissions to one or more persons, in some cases magistrates or commissioners for ending small causes, conferring jurisdiction which in most cases was *sui generis* in terms of the established laws. Several such commissions granted for Springfield, Northampton, and Hadley are discussed in Section VI.[37] Others were granted for various localities on the eastern frontier.[38]

A Single Magistrate

In discussing the respective jurisdictions of the Court of Assistants and the County Courts it has been noted that, in certain cases, a magistrate exercised concurrent jurisdiction with these courts. The first general grant of civil jurisdiction to a magistrate appears in a September 6, 1638 order that any magistrate in the town in which he lived might hear and determine by his discretion, that is, without a jury, all causes wherein the debt, trespass, or damage did not exceed twenty shillings. Any party finding himself aggrieved by any sentence of any such magistrate might appeal to the Court of Assistants. Although the Court of Assistants was at the same time in effect deprived of jurisdiction in such causes, it appears that the Inferior Quarter Courts retained concurrent jurisdiction. In the laws of 1648 the jurisdictional limitation was changed to all causes arising in the county not exceeding forty shillings and the County Courts were designated as the proper appellate bodies.[39]

The laws of 1648 and those prior thereto, with one short-lived exception, made no provision for exercise of general criminal jurisdiction by a single magistrate. Instead, jurisdiction was granted over certain specified offenses. For instance, it was provided that upon complaint any magistrate might hear and determine certain cases of theft committed by settlers or Indians, provided the treble damages awarded or fine imposed did not exceed forty shillings or corporal punishment four stripes.[40] It was also provided that a magistrate have

[37] See also the authority of the governor in October 1660, in connection with a grant of lands to Major William Hathorne and others on the Hudson River near Fort Orange, to commission some meet person or persons to exercise in the plantation the authority of a magistrate or that of a County Court. 4 *Rec. Mass. Bay* (*Part I*) 438. No evidence appears that such a commission ever issued.

[38] 4 *ibid.* (*Part I*) 69–70, 109–110, 159, 162–163, 360; 5 *ibid.* 5, 17.

[39] 1 *ibid.* 239; *Laws and Liberties Mass.* 2, 8–9. See also the provision that unpaid ferrymen might complain to a magistrate and obtain satisfaction (*ibid.* 22).

[40] *Ibid.* 5. See also 2 *Rec. Mass. Bay* 193. A 1645 law, not incorporated in the *Laws and Liberties* of 1648, provided that a magistrate might hear and determine any offense against order and fine the offender. 2 *ibid.* 100.

jurisdiction over refusals to aid constables in the execution of their office, contempts toward ministers or their preachings, absences or withdrawals from church meetings, gaming offenses, failure to pay certain imposts at trading posts, violations of the law regulating inn-keepers and prohibiting tippling and drunkenness, willful making or publishing of lies, cattle rescues or pound breaches, profane swearing, and refusals to watch and ward. In only one law was an appeal specifically reserved (the making or publishing of lies), but the law regulating appeals appears to contemplate appeals in criminal matters from the jurisdiction of one magistrate to the County Courts.[41] In addition, magistrates were given the power to marry,[42] to perform various administrative functions,[43] and to assist in the apprehension of offenders or suspected offenders.[44]

In 1649 the Court of Assistants and the County Courts were forbidden to assume jurisdiction of any civil action properly cognizable by a single magistrate. Shortly thereafter it was further provided that in all trespass actions in which damages in excess of forty shillings were alleged, but upon hearing it appeared to the court that the damages were under this figure, plaintiff was to lose his action and pay defendant costs. In the 1660 laws the prohibition upon the original jurisdiction of the County Courts was relaxed in defamation and battery actions.[45]

Among the laws of 1660 were several authorizing a magistrate to declare forfeited defective casks, to punish gaming and dancing offenses, to seize the estate of persons transporting money out of the colony, to commit to prison idlers, runaways, common drunkards, pilferers, common nightwalkers and wanton persons, and to punish willful defacers of public records. In small theft cases, as well as in profane and wicked cursing offenses, jurisdiction was broadened to give courts (presumably the County Courts), as well as magistrates,

---

41 *Laws and Liberties Mass.* 2, 13, 19–20, 24, 30–31, 35, 44–45, 52.

42 *Ibid.* 37.

43 These included imprisonment of grantors refusing to acknowledge previous grants (*ibid.* 13); administering oaths to persons adjudging the value of hides ruined by poor workmanship (*ibid.* 29); permitting offers of marriage (*ibid.* 37); putting out to service persons unable through poverty to provide themselves with arms and ammunition (*ibid.* 41); appointing impartial persons to settle disputes concerning servants' wages paid in corn (*ibid.* 38); administering oaths to viewers of pipe staves (*ibid.* 44); adjudg-

ing the amount of charges to be paid to recover strays (*ibid.* 48); allowing entertainment of or sale of lands to strangers (*ibid.* 49); and certifying as to killing of wolves in connection with bounty payments (*ibid.* 49).

44 Persons indicted for capital crimes were to surrender to a magistrate (*ibid.* 29). The next magistrate or constable or two of the chief inhabitants had the power to impress men and boats to apprehend runaway servants and persons suspected of ill intentions going away secretly (*ibid.* 38).

45 2 *Rec. Mass. Bay* 279; *Col. Laws Mass., 1660* 121, 132.

cognizance.[46] In the case of offenses by innkeepers, jurisdiction was given to the County Courts and commissioners for ending small causes, as well as to magistrates. Both magistrates and such commissioners were given authority to punish youthful offenders by corporal punishment (or to bind over to the next County Court), to punish those unlawfully entertaining servants, students, children, and so on, and to levy penalties on those not recording births, deaths, and marriages with clerks of the courts within the time specified.[47] Nightwalkers apprehended by constables were to give satisfactory explanations before a magistrate or a commissioner. Those found drunk or abusing a constable were to be dealt with by a magistrate or if there were none, by a commissioner or one or more selectmen, who for this purpose were given the power of a magistrate. Certain Sabbath violations were to be dealt with by a magistrate, commissioner or selectman; other proscribed activities on Saturday or Sunday evenings were to be disposed of by a magistrate or commissioner.[48] During this period magistrates were also given additional administrative functions.[49]

Later acts empowered a magistrate to administer corporal punishment to vagabonds, to commit strange Quakers to prison without bail until the next Court of Assistants, to apprehend Quakers who returned to the colony, to administer the oath of allegiance, and to commit idlers to prison or to compel them to labor at suitable work.[50] A single magistrate or commissioner was authorized to whip vagabond Quakers through the town and to commit hardened offenders until the next Court of Assistants, to punish drunken Indians or those possessing liquor without authority, to punish persons taking away canoes, to commit to prison those attending Quaker meetings, and to

[46] Ibid. 124, 127, 153, 182, 187, 189, 194.

[47] Ibid. 136, 165, 188.

[48] Ibid. 164, 189–190, 198–199.

[49] These included the power to impress workmen to repair bridges (Col. Laws Mass., 1660 127); to administer oaths to gaugers or packers (ibid. 124); to impress laborers on public works and to establish their wage rates (ibid. 160); to allow liquor for medicinal purposes to Indians (concurrent with two commissioners) (ibid. 163); and to constitute the committee of militia in each town, along with the three chief military officers (ibid. 178). See also a May 1662 law that the plaintiff in a civil cause was to stand the charges of defendant's imprisonment if the latter deposed before a magistrate that he was not worth five pounds (ibid. 221).

[50] Col. Laws Mass., 1660 221; Col. Laws Mass., 1672 60–62, 236, 237, 262–263, 294. See also the requirements that all Quaker books and writings and certain other banned books be turned over to a magistrate (ibid. 60–61); that dice be turned over to a magistrate or a commissioner (ibid. 58); and that piratical practices be disclosed to a magistrate or some other person in authority (ibid. 211). A temporary law empowered any magistrate to commit, without bail or mainprise, certain Anabaptists not leaving the jurisdiction within a specified time until they gave sufficient security to depart (ibid. 246–247).

punish those failing to report profane oaths and curses. Authority was given to a single magistrate, a commissioner or selectmen to enforce the law against tippling and to return to the County Court all keepers of private unlicensed houses of entertainment.[51]

Persons Vested with Magistratical Powers

Since the number of magistrates was limited, the General Court found it advisable to vest certain persons from time to time with what it termed "magistratical powers." The first instance is found in May 1657 when certain persons were authorized by the General Court to act in criminal matters as one magistrate might act. Less wholesale appointments were made later for various parts of the colony, particularly the eastern portions, frequently at the request of a particular locality.[52] Such powers might also be granted for *ad hoc* purposes such as the examination of Quakers. In some cases the commissioners for ending small causes in a particular town might be vested with magistratical powers. In at least one instance the powers granted were limited to offenses not punishable by fines of more than ten shillings or corporal punishment exceeding ten stripes.[53]

On May 24, 1677 the status of persons vested with magistratical powers was formalized by the following order of the General Court:

Whereas, for the preservation of the peace, suppression of vice, and accommodation of justice in severall parts of this jurisdiction where no magistrate dwells, it hath binn customary for this Court to authorize meet persons of quallity and skill, and them to invest with magistraticall power, it is ordered by this Court, that henceforth all such persons so appointed and allowed shall have commission granted them accordingly from this Court and under the seale of this colony, according to the direction of the charter, wherein, shall be incerted the preservation of the peace, taking recognizances and binding over offendors to the County Court to which they belong, punishing all offences whose poenalty is stated by law under forty shillings, or corporall punishment not exceeding tenn stripes, in such cases as are by law refferred to the judgment of any one magistrate, taking depositions, joyning persons in marriage according to lawe, ending small causes and actions not exceeding forty shillings; and all this for the time being, and within the precincts of the toune where they dwell.[54]

[51] *Col. Laws Mass., 1660* 219, 222 (*quaere* if the later act required more than one commissioner), 236 (the selectmen or a majority thereof were also given the power to punish drunkenness in towns not having a magistrate or commissioner); *Col. Laws Mass., 1672* 212, 234, 235.

[52] 4 *Rec. Mass. Bay (Part I)* 288, 348, 375, 420; 4 *ibid. (Part II)* 335, 377, 406, 424, 425, 451–452, 467, 496, 516, 554; 5 *ibid.* 5, 88, 101, 145, 187 205, 226. *Cf.* 3 *ibid.* 423.

[53] 4 *ibid. (Part II)* 5, 21, 536; 5 *ibid.* 5, 30.

[54] 5 *ibid.* 139.

Commissioners for Ending Small Causes

The General Court in its order of September 6, 1638 conferring jurisdiction upon magistrates to hear small causes, also provided that, in any town in which no magistrate resided, it would from time to time nominate three men, two of whom were to constitute a quorum, with like power to hear and determine all causes wherein the debt, trespass, or damage did not exceed twenty shillings. Any party aggrieved by the sentence of such commissioners might appeal to the Court of Assistants. In June 1641 the General Court authorized the next magistrate to advise with any commissioners for hearing small causes who might desire assistance and to administer oaths to witnesses for better deciding causes according to justice.[55]

In 1647, when the jurisdictional limitation upon magistrates in civil causes was raised, it was also ordered that any three commissioners (of which two constituted a quorum) have like power to hear and determine by their discretion (without a jury) all causes arising within the county wherein the debt, trespass, or damage did not exceed forty shillings. It was further provided that the appointment of such commissioners, in towns in which no magistrate resided, should be made from time to time by the Court of Assistants or the several County Courts upon request of such towns signified under the hand of the constable. An oath was to be taken by the commissioners before the County Court or some magistrate in the county for faithful discharge of the trust and power committed to them. They were also to keep a true record of all causes which came before them for determination and to publish their times of meeting.[56] The *Laws and Liberties* of 1648 gave commissioners powers to send for parties and witnesses by summons or attachment directed to the constable, to administer oaths to witnesses, and to give defendants time to answer if they saw cause. It was also stated that commissioners had no power to commit to prison in any case. In the event the party sentenced refused to give bond for his appearance or satisfaction and had no goods in the town in which the plaintiff resided or the commissioners sat, the commissioners were authorized to direct the constable to carry such party before a magistrate or the County Court, if then sitting, to be further proceeded with according to law. From the sentences of the commissioners an appeal was to lie to the County Court. In the event the cause concerned one of the commissioners, then the selectmen of the town were authorized to hear and determine the cause and to grant execution.[57]

[55] 1 *Rec. Mass. Bay* 239, 327.

[56] 2 *ibid.* 188, 208; *Laws and Liberties Mass.* 8–9.

[57] *Ibid.* 2, 8–9. An October 1652 order of the General Court provided that any three commissioners to end small causes

Commissioners for ending small causes were rarely granted general jurisdiction in criminal matters comparable to that of a magistrate.[58] However, commissioners were in the case of certain offenses given concurrent jurisdiction with a single magistrate.[59] In still other instances a single commissioner might exercise jurisdiction concurrent with that of a single magistrate, or, more rarely, with a single magistrate or one or more selectmen.[60] In a few cases, concurrent jurisdiction was lodged in the County Courts, a magistrate, and a commissioner, and, in one case, an associate. In some instances, concurrent jurisdiction was granted to a single magistrate and to a "commissioner authorized by law in such cases" or some similar language.[61] The meaning of such clauses is obscure and jurisdiction in such cases may have been limited to commissioners specifically granted jurisdiction in criminal matters.

Selectmen of Towns

In March 1635/6 the General Court ordered that the freemen of each town have the power to make such orders as might concern the well-being of their towns, as also to lay mulcts and penalties for the breach of such orders and to levy and distrain the same to an amount not exceeding twenty shillings. At later dates the General Court granted the freemen or selectmen specific authority in such matters as the fixing of commodity prices and wage rates, the disposition of single persons, and the making of orders with respect to ringing of swine, the maintenance of fences, and the maintenance of watches.[62] No. 66 of the Liberties of 1641 provided that the freemen of every township should have power to make such laws and constitutions as might concern the welfare of their towns, provided they were not of a criminal but only of a "prudentiall nature," that the penalties did not exceed twenty shillings for one offense, and that they were not repugnant to the public laws and orders of the colony. If any inhabitant neglected or refused to observe such laws, the freemen were to have power to levy the appointed penalties by distress.[63]

While these various grants clearly contemplated the exercise of

---

should have the same power to give oaths to witnesses in any civil case as a magistrate. 4 *Rec. Mass. Bay (Part I)* 103. It is doubtful that this order added to the powers already granted under the 1648 laws.

[58] See, however, the criminal jurisdiction granted to the commissioners of Souther Town in October 1658. 4 *ibid. (Part I)* 353.

[59] *Col. Laws Mass., 1660* 136, 165, 188, 198–199; *Col. Laws Mass., 1672* 80.

[60] *Col. Laws Mass., 1660* 164, 189–190, 198–199, 219 (*cf.* p. 222), 228–229, 236; *Col. Laws Mass., 1672* 58, 234, 235.

[61] *Col. Laws Mass., 1660* 236, 261; *Col. Laws Mass., 1672* 212, 236–237.

[62] 1 *Rec. Mass. Bay* 172, 183, 186, 215; 2 *ibid.* 220–221; 4 *ibid. (Part I)* 153, 293.

[63] *Col. Laws Mass., 1660* 47.

judicial or quasi-judicial powers by the freemen or selectmen, the
laws contained virtually nothing as to process or procedure in connection with such exercise. For the most part, no provision was made
for judicial review of the enforcement of town orders by the freemen
or selectmen.[64] The town records examined usually merely record
the imposition of a fine or penalty and afford no insight into the procedure employed. In certain cases the selectmen of Springfield, empowered, as in most towns, to order the "prudential affairs" of the
town, held hearings on violations of town orders which appear judicial in nature.[65] In other cases, they sought to recover penalties for
such violations in the courts held at Springfield, rather than imposing
and levying their own penalties.

It has already been pointed out that selectmen were given power
to hear and determine civil causes in those cases in which the magistrate residing in a town or one of the commissioners was a party and
that selectmen, or even a single selectman, might exercise concurrent
jurisdiction with a magistrate or commissioners for ending small
causes or a single commissioner, in cases of certain offenses against
the laws of the colony. A colony law also authorized selectmen to issue warrants to levy upon the estates of delinquent land owners or
tenants the double recompense to which fence viewers were entitled
for repairing certain defective fences. A 1647 law made nonfreemen
who were church members liable to serve as constables, jurors, selectmen, and surveyors of highways and, if they refused to serve, liable
to pay such fine as the town imposed, not exceeding twenty shillings.
Presumably these penalties could be imposed by the selectmen. This
would also appear to be the case under a law which permitted towns
to assess inhabitants for damage done to the corn fields of Indians for
which the town had made satisfaction.[66] A 1666 law granted selectmen, or the majority thereof, power to fine or whip Indians convicted of drunkenness in towns in which there was neither magistrate
nor commissioners. Another authorized selectmen to make orders for
increasing the production of saltpeter and to provide penalties up to
ten shillings for violation thereof. A 1668 act authorized selectmen to
impose penalties for letting stallions run loose, unless allowed by the
majority of the selectmen.[67]

[64] Violations of town orders fixing
prices or wage rates were apparently to
be punished at the discretion of the General Court, not by the freemen or selectmen. 1 Rec. Mass. Bay 183. Persons aggrieved by town orders disposing of single
persons were to have liberty to appeal to
the Governor and Council or to the General Court (ibid. 186).

[65] 1 Burt, Hist. Springfield 336–338, 376,
377, 381, 386, 405, 407–408, 419, 421, 431;
2 ibid. 197.

[66] Laws and Liberties Mass. 9, 23, 28.

[67] Col. Laws Mass., 1660 236–237, 243–
244.

Miscellaneous Courts

From time to time the General Court provided for the establishment of courts limited in jurisdiction to such matters as causes concerning strangers, matters arising among the Indians, causes relating to the rights of creditors or employees, cases arising under the Acts of Trade and Navigation, and certain land claims.[68] However, these establishments had no significance for western Massachusetts.

In June 1665 the royal commissioners (Carr, Cartwright, and Maverick) appointed a number of justices of the peace for the eastern parts of the colony. Three or more were to have jurisdiction to hear and determine all causes, both civil and criminal, "proceeding in all cases according to the lawes of England as neere as maybe." Except for these appointments for the eastern parts, no use was made of justices of the peace under the First Charter.[69]

1686–1692. THE INTERCHARTER PERIOD

The President and Council of the Territory and Dominion of New England, on June 10, 1686 published An Order for the Holding of Courts and execution of Justice which established a new judicial system for Massachusetts. At the apex was a Superior Court of Grand Assize and General-Gaol Delivery to be held three times a year at Boston by the President and Council. This body had jurisdiction of all cases of appeal, all capital cases and all such pleas of the crown and "other matters of greater Concernment as are above the Cognizance of Inferior Courts." [70]

The same order provided for the erection in each county or province of a County Court "to be held and kept as a Court of Pleas and of General Session of the Peace." The court in each county or province was to consist of the resident member or members of the Council together with such justices of the peace as were particularly commissioned thereunto. Jurisdiction extended to all civil causes and all criminal causes, excluding those concerning life or limb, with an appeal in all civil cases to the President and Council. The order further provided:

And for the more ready Dispatch of small Causes, where the Dammage besides Cost shall not exceed the Summe of Forty Shillings, It is Ordered

[68] 1 *Rec. Mass. Bay* 264; 2 *ibid.* 188; 4 *ibid.* (*Part I*) 155–156, 334; 4 *ibid.* (*Part II*) 15, 83–84; 5 *ibid.* 337–338, 398. *Cf.* 3 *ibid.* 322; 4 *ibid.* (*Part II*) 63; *Col. Laws Mass., 1672* 38, 207.

[69] 4 *Rec. Mass. Bay* (*Part II*) 250–251, 401–403. *Cf.* the references at 5 *ibid.* 193, 263, and the powers of justices of the peace conferred upon the governor and certain magistrates in August 1630. 1 *ibid.* 74.

[70] 1 *Laws N.H.* 104. Compare the judicial powers, granted in the commission, to the President or any seven of the Council. *Ibid.* 96.

and declared that the President and each Member of the Council hath Power to hold Plea of, and to give Judgment, and award execution in all such Causes, as heretofore hath been in use. The like Power have any two of the Justices joyning together. And from the Sentence and Judgment in these Cases to be given, there shall be an Appeal to the next Court of the County and no higher.[71]

The President and Council had in May appointed justices of the peace in order "that speedy and effectual Care be taken for the maintenance and preservation of the peace." [72] However, the order of June 10 made no reference to the jurisdiction of such justices of the peace in criminal matters, nor for that matter, of members of the Council. No copy of any commission of the peace for this period has been found but it seems unlikely that criminal jurisdiction was spelled out in detail in such commissions. Presumably the Council members exercised jurisdiction in criminal matters comparable to that of a justice of the peace, an assumption supported by the scant entries in the *Record,* but there is no specific authority for the exercise of such jurisdiction, and it is unlikely that, as at a later date, each councilor was made a justice of the peace.[73]

Following the arrival of Governor Andros in late December 1686, a new court system was erected by means of an Act for Establishing Courts of Judicature and Publick Justice, passed on March 3, 1686/7. The principal court, the Superior Court of Judicature, was:

Authorized and Impowred to have Cognizance of all pleas reall personall or mixt as well in all Pleas of the Crowne and in all matters relating to the Conservacion of the Peace and Punishment of Offenders as in Civill Causes or accions betweene party and party; and betweene his Majestie and any of his Subjects; Whether the same doe concerne the Reallity and Relate to any Right or Freehold and Inheritance Or whether the same doe Concerne the personallity and relate to matter of Debt Contract Damage or personall Injury And alsoe in all mixt accions; which may Concerne both realty and personalty.[74]

This court was not, however, to have any jurisdiction over any matter or cause of action not exceeding ten pounds, unless freehold was concerned. Appeal was to lie "in case of Errour" to the Governor or President and Council in all civil causes, provided the value ap-

[71] *Ibid.* 103–104.
[72] *Ibid.* 100.
[73] See the provision for a five-pound penalty for drawing drink without license upon conviction before any member of the Council or any two justices within the county (*ibid.* 106); the fine for selling liquor to any Indian or Negro without ex-press license from a member of the Council or two justices of the peace (*ibid.* 117); and the allowance of amounts to defray public charges of towns by two justices of the peace or a member of the Council (*ibid.* 115).
[74] *Ibid.* 192–193.

pealed for exceeded one hundred pounds sterling. The criminal jurisdiction of the Superior Court of Judicature might yield to a commission of oyer and terminer in the case of capital offenses.[75]

The act further provided that in each county a quarterly Court of Sessions be held by the justices of the peace to hear and determine all matters relating to the conservation of the peace and punishment of offenders and "whatsoever else is by them Cognizable, according to Law." An Inferior Court of Common Pleas was to be kept at the same time and place by a judge assisted by two or more justices of the peace. This court had jurisdiction over all causes wherein freehold was not concerned to the value of ten pounds with costs, except in any matter not exceeding the value of forty shillings. Appeals were to lie to the Superior Court of Judicature in cases of error. By a December 29, 1687 act these inferior courts were given "power and Jurisdiction in all Causes and Cases personall and mixt, Wherein Tittle of Land is not Concerned To any Summ or value whatsoever," with defendant having the right of removal to the Superior Court of Judicature by habeas corpus or certiorari.[76]

A further act of March 3, 1686/7 provided that "all manner of Debts Trespasses and other matters not Exceeding the value of Forty shillings (wherein the Title of Land is not Concerned)" should be heard and determined by any justice of the peace within his precinct. In criminal matters, jurisdiction presumably was spelled out, if at all, in the commissions of the peace, although a few acts specifically conferred jurisdiction in criminal and administrative matters. In a few instances, two justices, of whom one was of the quorum, were given jurisdiction.[77]

Statutes and records during the Andros regime leave obscure the jurisdiction of members of the Council in civil and criminal matters. Statutes which might be expected to treat justices of the peace and Council members on the basis of parity refer in only one case to the issue of a warrant by a Council member. The evidence as to inclusion of members of the Council in commissions of the peace is inconclusive.[78] A proclamation of the Governor and Council, issued March 8, 1687/8, ordered that:

. . . the severall Justices Town Officers and other persons concerned do proceed in their severall places and trusts according to former usage and

[75] *Ibid.* 193, 253. See also the commission to Andros, *ibid.* 149.

[76] *Ibid.* 190–191, 193, 213–214. For later statutory jurisdiction in administrative matters, see *ibid.* 198, 207, 209, 220–221.

[77] *Ibid.* 194–196, 198, 199, 201, 203, 215, 217, 219–220, 222.

[78] *Ibid.* 195–196. On February 15, 1686/7 upon reading in Council a commission of the peace for Rhode Island, "Upon the question whether the members of Councill ought to be Inserted in it, It was resolved in the Negative." *Andros Records*, 13 Amer. Antiq. Soc. Proc. (ns) 250–251.

directions given by the late President and Councill, and such other Locall Laws in the Severall parts of this Dominion, as are not repugnant to the Laws of England, his Majestie Commission for Government and Indulgience in matters of Religion, nor any Law or Order already made or passed by the Governour and Councill untill further Order.[79]

This proclamation may be construed as permitting Council members to exercise whatever judicial powers they had exercised during Dudley's period of office.

A provision in the royal instructions to Andros suggests the possibility that members of the Council might be regarded as the equivalent of the former magistrates and exercise the jurisdiction vested in magistrates under the First Charter.[80]

Within a few months after the overthrow of Andros, Massachusetts, in effect, returned to the form of government which had existed under the First Charter. On June 5, 1689 the Governor, Deputy Governor, and assistants declared their acceptance of the government of the colony according to the Charter rules by the name of Governor and Council of the Massachusetts Colony. On June 22nd the Governor and Council and representatives declared that all laws made by the Governor and Company in force on May 12, 1686, except any that might be repugnant to the laws of England, were the laws of the colony and were to continue in force until further settlement.[81] On July 3 it was declared that:

. . . all Courts of Judicature as formerly held within this Collony according to the Direction of the Law Title Courts, made by the Governor and Company; be holden at the stated times and places, as mentioned in said Law.[82]

This declaration in its reference to the "Law Title Courts" presumably intended the 1672 edition of the laws which, under such title, made no reference to the jurisdiction of magistrates, of persons vested with magistratical powers or of commissioners for ending small causes. However, the several appointments of commissioners for small causes and of persons vested with magistratical powers by the General Court clearly demonstrate an intention to restore the entire pre-Dudley judicial system.

1692–1702. THE SECOND CHARTER

Under the October 7, 1791 charter for the Province of Massachusetts Bay the Governor with the advice and consent of the Council was authorized to nominate and appoint judges, commissioners of

[79] 1 *Laws N.H.* 249.
[80] *Ibid.* 157.
[81] *Ibid.* 281, 294.
[82] *Ibid.* 303.

oyer and terminer, justices of the peace, and other officers of the judicial establishment. The General Assembly was given full power and authority to enact and constitute judicatories and courts of record and other courts to be held in the King's name.[83]

Governor Phips arrived in the province with the new charter on May 14, 1692. Whitmore in his *Civil List* indicates that various justices of the peace were commissioned shortly thereafter. While no commissions of the peace for Hampshire have been found, a May 30, 1692 commission for York County is virtually identical with the contemporary English form. A later York commission from Bellomont, dated July 26, 1699, was more suited to local conditions in that it omitted reference to certain specific offenses (such as forestalling, regrating, and engrossing) not important in colonial law enforcement. We assume that the forms of the Hampshire commissions of the peace were identical with those for York. We have seen no evidence that the jurisdiction actually exercised was enlarged by the reference to offenses not covered by the province laws.[84]

It appears likely that until late in November 1692 administration of justice in the province centered in the justices of the peace. By a June 15 act all local laws ordered and made by the late Governor and Company of Massachusetts Bay, not repugnant to the laws of England nor inconsistent with the present constitution and settlement by royal charter, were to continue in full force until November 10 next, except where otherwise provided. The "several justices" were empowered to the execution of such laws as the magistrates formerly enforced. A June 28 act provided for the holding in each county by justices of the peace of Courts of General Sessions of the Peace and of County Courts or Inferior Courts of Common Pleas.[85]

Within the next several months a number of acts were passed which gave jurisdiction to a single justice of the peace or to "any justice or justices" or to one or more justices of the peace in such matters as violations of the law regulating casks, cursing and swearing, drunkenness, theft (as long as the treble damages did not exceed forty shillings), lying, or libeling, violations of a law against unlicensed ordinaries and gaming in ordinaries, violation of the Lord's Day, slaughtering outside assigned slaughterhouses, cruelty to animals en route to market, pulling down marriage notices, neglect or refusal to maintain common boundaries, neglect of constables in having certain town officers take their oaths, breach of town orders

[83] 1 *Acts and Res. Prov. Mass. Bay* 10–12, 14–15, 19.
[84] Whitmore, *Mass. Civil List* 139; 4 *Prov. and Ct. Rec. Me.* 21–23, 245–246.
[85] 1 *Acts and Res. Prov. Mass. Bay* 27, 37.

and by-laws, neglect of constables to settle their accounts, idling, neglect of constables to call town meetings, failure to comply with the law regarding weights and measures, and improper curing of fish or use of nets in fishing.[86]

In addition, every justice of the peace in the county where the offense was committed had jurisdiction over all affrayers, rioters, disturbers or breakers of the peace, and such as rode or went armed offensively before any justice or other officer or minister or uttered menacing or threatening speeches; also in cases of breach of the peace and forcible entrys and detainers. He also was authorized to make out hues and crys after runaway servants, thieves, and other criminals. Some offenses were reserved for quarter sessions. Little use was made of the jurisdiction of two justices as such.[87]

It was not until November 25, 1692 that a comprehensive judicial system was established by An Act for the Establishing of Judicatories and Court of Justice within this Province. This act provided for a Superior Court of Judicature held by a chief justice and four justices with cognizance over all pleas, real, personal, and mixed, as well as all pleas of the crown, and all matters relating to the conservation of the peace and punishment of offenders. However, the court was to have no jurisdiction in actions under ten pounds unless an appeal of freehold was concerned. On the criminal side the justices constituted a Court of Assize and General Gaol Delivery for each county.[88]

The act also provided for Courts of Quarter Sessions of the Peace held by the justices of the peace in each county who were empowered to hear and determine all matters relating to conservation of the peace and punishment of offenders and whatsoever was cognizable by them by law. At the same times and places Inferior Courts of Common Pleas were to be held by four justices of the peace (three constituting a quorum) with power to hear and determine all civil actions arising in the county triable at common law of whatsoever nature, kind or quality, except those under forty shillings, with liberty of appeal to the next Superior Court of Judicature held in Boston or Charlestown. It was also provided that all manner of debts, trespasses, and other matters not exceeding the value of forty shillings (wherein the title of land was not concerned) should be heard, tried, adjudged, and determined by any justice of the peace within the county in which he resided. The party cast was to be free to appeal to the next Inferior Court of Common Pleas.[89]

---

[86] *Ibid.* 49–53, 56–57, 58–61, 64–66, 67–68, 69–70, 71.

[87] *Ibid.* 52–53. For those reserved for quarter sessions see *ibid.* 49, 52, 59, 62–63, 67, 69–70. For the jurisdiction of two justices see *ibid.* 67–68. See also *ibid.* 34.

[88] *Ibid.* 72–74.

[89] *Ibid.* 72–74.

This act of 1692 made no provision for review in criminal cases tried by justices of the peace or at quarter sessions. However, a June 1695 act remedied this omission by providing that any person sentenced for any criminal offense by one or more justices of the peace out of sessions might appeal to the next Court of General Sessions of the Peace held within the county. It was also provided that any person aggrieved by the sentence of justices of the Court of General Sessions of the Peace might appeal to the next Court of Assize and General Gaol Delivery held within the county, there to be finally issued. However, this act was disallowed by the King in Council in November 1698.[90]

When the act of 1692 was disallowed by the King in Council in August 1695, an act was passed in September 1696 which reëstablished the judicial system of 1692, except that the objectionable restriction of appeals to the King in Council to personal actions was omitted. However, this act suffered disallowance in November 1698, along with a June 1697 Act for Establishing of Courts which substantially reënacted the 1692 judicial system, with the exception of the civil jurisdiction of justices of the peace in matters not exceeding the value of forty shillings, which was covered by a separate act of the same session and escaped disallowance. Finally, in June 1699 three acts were passed which placed the judicial establishment on a permanent footing substantially in the manner provided in the earlier disallowed acts, with those modifications necessary to avoid further disallowance.[91]

The charter's authorization allowing the Governor to issue commissions of oyer and terminer was invoked on several occasions, one of which involved Hampshire. On October 5, 1696 Richard Church, a Hadley inhabitant, was killed while hunting by four Albany Indians encamped near Hatfield. The culprits were quickly apprehended and examined by several justices of the peace in the presence of the ministers of Northampton and Hatfield. On October 13 Governor Stoughton issued a commission of oyer and terminer to John Pynchon, Samuel Partrigg, Joseph Hawley, Aaron Cooke, and Joseph Parsons to try the offenders. On October 21 a Court of Oyer and Terminer was held at Northampton, John Pynchon, 3rd, acting as clerk and Ebenezer Pomery as King's attorney. The four Indians were indicted by a grand jury, two as principals and two as accessories. A petty jury found all four guilty and the principals, sentenced to be shot, were executed on October 23; the accessories were reprieved. The records show that the court scrupulously sought to give the accused fair trials. This attitude was wisely taken for some of

<hr/>

[90] *Ibid.* 217.   [91] *Ibid.* 248, 282–283, 367–372.

the Albany Indians immediately complained to Governor Fletcher of alleged lack of due process. Stoughton, to whom the complaints were relayed, defended the action taken, and in April 1697 sent the New York governor a narrative of the proceedings.[92]

In the decade following the establishment of the provincial judicial system various acts were passed giving jurisdiction to the Courts of General (or Quarter) Sessions of the Peace in various criminal, regulatory, and administrative matters.[93] Other acts supplemented or reiterated the powers of a justice of the peace in such matters as failure to register births or deaths with town clerks or to pay the registration fees, breach of the peace, profanation of the Sabbath, unlawful gaming, drunkenness (including Indian offenders), profane swearing and cursing, failure to work on the highways when called, allowing horses to graze on common lands, regulation of inns and tippling, forfeiture of cord wood not of the requisite size, false returns of ratable estates, regulation of the movement of certain Indians, delaying the post, violation of the assize regulating shingles, selling goods by measure not conforming to the established standards, refusal of grantors to acknowledge their deeds, inspection and suppression of disorders of licensed houses, failure to ward, apprehension of suspected Jesuits, selling wine and such without a license, returning inhabitants to their towns, and observation of the laws respecting schools and school masters.[94] Jurisdiction was given to one or more justices in offenses such as serving liquor to proscribed persons, disorderly firing of guns and forcible entry and detainer.[95]

In certain cases a person aggrieved by a statutory violation might recover damages not exceeding forty shillings before a justice of the peace and, if in excess of such amount, before an Inferior Court of Common Pleas. Such cases included action by fence viewers for repair of fences, failure of shipowners to pay tonnage imposts, suits by commissioners of the excise for duties, regulation of tanners, carriers, and cordwainers, replevin of cattle from pounds, cutting or carrying away wood from another's lands, and actions by finders of strays.[96] Cases involving unlawful cutting of hay, robbing gardens, breaking down fences, and damaging or taking away of trees might be tried in any court or by one justice. While not specifically stated,

92 Judd, *Hist. Hadley* 263–265; 7 *Acts and Res. Prov. Mass. Bay* 523–530. For various documents relating to this incident see 30 *Mass. Archives* 378–412.

93 1 *Acts and Res. Prov. Mass. Bay* 76–78, 93, 103, 127–128, 136–137, 141, 152, 183, 188, 191–192, 210, 218, 256, 312, 329–332, 435–436.

94 *Ibid.* 104, 122–123, 136, 138–139, 154, 157, 168, 175, 183, 212, 219, 298, 327–328, 382, 423–424, 434–435, 436–437, 453, 470.

95 *Ibid.* 192, 268, 397, 469.

96 *Ibid.* 138, 164–165, 208, 274, 312–314, 322, 324, 326–327, 393.

the jurisdiction of the one justice was presumably limited by the forty-shilling ceiling. Similarly, in the case of certain offenses, such as selling liquor to the Indians and cutting down or carrying off wood from another's land, a single justice had jurisdiction if the penalty did not exceed forty shillings; if in excess of such amount, then quarter sessions had jurisdiction.[97]

In connection with the military establishment, a justice of the peace was given jurisdiction to punish persons evading listing for military service and those neglecting military duty, to apprehend deserters and runaways, to return French prisoners to neighboring provinces, to imprison deserting seamen and to apprehend nonfreeholders deserting frontier towns or persons pressed into military service.[98]

A single justice had power to appoint shipwrights to survey the building of certain vessels (jurisdiction to fine for refusal to correct faults of workmanship uncovered by the survey was at first in one or more justices; later quarter sessions was given concurrent jurisdiction) ; to appoint commissions of two or more to view encumbrances on highways and cause their removal; to authorize by warrant and administer the oath to ship's carpenters for determining the tonnage of ships for impost purposes; to appoint shingle viewers; and to appoint persons to determine whether leather seized by searchers and sealers was defective.[99] A single justice was also to join with the selectmen in appointing suitable watches in towns. He also had power to swear in surveyors of the highways, fence viewers, assessors, town treasurers, and those freeholders authorized to set forth dowry.[100]

In certain cases a single justice had power to grant warrants to commissioners of the excise to search for liquors, and other things concealed to avoid payment of excise; for part of the period this power was lodged in two justices. A justice, the selectmen, or a majority thereof might issue warrants to fence viewers to impress workmen. Persons receiving licenses as innkeepers or retailers out of doors were to be bound in recognizance before one or more justices.[101]

Penalties for failure to attend ferries and to keep the boats in repair, for refusal to serve as tithingman, for violation of certain provisions regulating licensed houses, for refusing to accept or neglecting the office of surveyor of the highways might be imposed by a single justice of the peace or at quarter sessions.[102] A person refusing

[97] Ibid. 150–151, 156, 324.
[98] Ibid. 128, 133–135, 142–143, 295, 399, 400, 402–403.
[99] Ibid. 114, 137, 164–165, 212, 275, 312–313, 352.
[100] Ibid. 136, 138, 361, 381–382, 384, 451.
[101] Ibid. 119, 154, 271, 306–307, 328, 334, 345.
[102] Ibid. 137–138, 183, 190–191, 224, 328–329.

to accept the office of assessor might be fined by a single justice or the Inferior Court of Common Pleas. Masters failing to give in a list of passengers to the receivers of imposts might be bound over to quarter sessions by a single justice. A justice of the peace might order whipped persons convicted of adultery or incest who did not wear their letter A or I as sentenced.[103]

Some jurisdiction was granted to two justices; in some cases one was to be of the quorum. Two justices were given power to commit to prison French subjects living in seaport or frontier towns without gubernatorial permission or keeping shop or practicing a trade in any town without consent of the selectmen, to put indigent inhabitants out to service to enable them to equip themselves with arms, to punish selectmen who failed to make rates to buy arms, ammunition, and so forth, and to commit certain persons to the workhouse.[104] In case of neglect by a town two justices might appoint three or more assessors; they were also authorized to investigate cases in which banns were forbidden, to license ships visited with sickness to enter port, to allow Indians to bind themselves out, to make restitution in cases of forcible entry, to impress lodgings in sickness cases, and to issue warrants to levy rates for the support of the ministry.[105] Two justices or quarter sessions were vested with jurisdiction over forfeiture of excess liquors, persons absconding after enlisting, and the support of the ministry. Selectmen of a town, with two justices of the peace, had authority to assign places at which stills might be operated.[106]

While the judicial establishment under the Second Charter was clearly influenced by English standards, experience under the commonwealth was not ignored. The prototype of the Superior Court of Judicature was certainly the Court of Assistants. The Inferior Courts of Common Pleas and the Courts of General (or Quarter) Sessions of the Peace were comparable to the County Courts, and the justices of the peace, to the magistrates. The experience under the First Charter is particularly noticeable in the practice, under at least two governors, of commissioning all councilors as justices of the peace. Under the Second Charter the complexities of the lower jurisdictional levels were simplified; in part, at least, this was at the expense of the towns as judicial units.

---

[103] Ibid. 166, 209, 452.
[104] Ibid. 90, 130–131, 132, 380.

[105] Ibid. 166, 210, 377, 435–436, 442, 469, 505.
[106] Ibid. 224, 256, 499.

VI. The Jurisdictional Bases of the Springfield Courts

HE *Record* covers a period of over sixty years during which the jurisdiction exercised was far from constant. This section is concerned with the delineation of the authority by which the various courts whose acts are recorded in the *Record* were held from time to time and, to the extent not generically described in Section V, the jurisdiction of each such court.

THE AGAWAM APPOINTMENT

The first entry in the *Record,* under date of February 14, 1638/9, records the appointment of William Pynchon to execute the office of magistrate in the plantation of Agawam until further directions were received from the General Court. This appointment, made by the general vote and consent of the inhabitants, recognized the many inconveniences which might befall the inhabitants, now under the jurisdiction of Massachusetts Bay, for want of a fit magistracy and the impracticality of attendance at the constituted courts of the colony.[1]

The appointment authorized Pynchon to give oaths to constables or military officers, to direct warrants (including process, attachment, and execution), to take the depositions of witnesses, to inflict corporal punishment (such as whipping or putting in the stocks) upon proof of misdemeanor, to bind offenders to the peace or to good behavior, to require sureties in proper cases, and, if the offense required, to commit to prison. In default of a common prison, delinquents were to be committed to the charge of some fit person or persons until justice was satisfied. In the trial of actions for debt or trespass Pynchon was authorized to administer oaths, to take the depositions of witnesses, to direct juries, to take verdicts, and to keep a record of verdicts, judgments, and executions.

[1] *Rec.* 2.

In addition to the specific, Pynchon was granted generally power to do whatever else might tend to the King's peace, to the manifestation of the fidelity of the inhabitants to the Bay jurisdiction, to the restraining of any that should molest God's laws, and, lastly, to do whatsoever might fall within the power of an assistant in Massachusetts Bay.

It was also agreed that, since a jury of twelve fit persons could not be presently had, six persons should be a sufficient jury to try any action of debt or trespass under the sum of ten pounds. This provision was to continue until the inhabitants by common consent altered the number or until the General Court directed otherwise.

This assumption of power by the inhabitants of Agawam to establish a court with powers far exceeding those of any magistrate or commissioners to end small causes was ultra vires since under the Massachusetts charter the sole power to establish courts or to grant judicial powers resided in the General Court. However, regardless of any lack of authority under the charter, William Pynchon held courts for well over two years solely by virtue of the authority conferred upon him by the inhabitants of Agawam and the appointment was never disapproved by the General Court. It is hard to believe that Pynchon, presumably the draftsman, did not fully realize that his appointment had no de jure status. Yet, having put practical considerations ahead of legal, the frequent references to adherence to the jurisdiction of Massachusetts Bay were shrewdly calculated to appease the General Court if it should be resentful of the invasion of its prerogative.[2]

Several aspects of this appointment merit notice. In the first place, although civil jurisdiction was apparently limited to acts of debt or trespass, to be tried by jury, there was no limitation on the amount involved, unless the ten-pound reference is construed as a jurisdictional limitation similar to that of the Inferior Quarter Courts. It would appear that the reference to the powers of an assistant was designed to add to, and not to subtract from, the powers previously enumerated. However, it is doubtful that the reference was designed to give Pynchon power to hear and determine civil causes not exceeding twenty shillings "by his discretion," that is, without a jury, as in the case of a magistrate. Secondly, Pynchon was given broad criminal jurisdiction, although presumably causes concerning life, member, or banishment were not comprehended. While the power to impose fines was not specifically conferred, Pynchon in one case in early

[2] The fact that a copy of the appointment, in the hand of Henry Smith, is among the *Winthrop Papers* (vol. 4, p. 98) indicates that the Bay authorities had due notice of the appointment.

1641 did impose a small fine for swearing. On the other hand, magistrates exercised no general criminal jurisdiction until May 1645. Thirdly, there was no provision for an appeal to the Court of Assistants or to the General Court from any sentence or judgment of Pynchon. Fourthly, six instead of twelve jurors were to constitute a petty jury in causes under ten pounds. Fifthly, while Pynchon was authorized or required to keep records of verdicts, judgments, and executions, it was not until 1647 that magistrates and commissioners were required by order of the General Court to "keep a true record of all such causes as shall come before them to be determined." [3]

The clause "whatever else may tend to the Kings peace" is one not usually found in grants of judicial power in Massachusetts at this period when even process did not run in the King's name. The enlarging phrase, "the restraining of any that shall molest God's laws," may reflect a May 25, 1638 order of the General Court that until laws agreeable to the word of God were drawn up by a committee appointed for that purpose "the magistrates and their associates shall proceed in the courts to hear and determine all causes according to the lawes now established, and where there is no law, then as neere the lawe of God as they can." [4]

THE GENERAL COURT COMMISSION OF 1641

Pynchon's appointment as magistrate was to continue only until the General Court directed further. On June 2, 1641, the General Court declared that Springfield was and always had been within the Bay jurisdiction and ordered that Pynchon, not then an assistant, have full authority for the year to govern the inhabitants at Springfield and to hear and determine all causes and offenses, both civil and criminal, that did not reach to life, limb, or banishment, according to the laws established for the colony. In "matters of weight or difficulty" any party might appeal to the Court of Assistants at Boston, provided they prosecuted such appeal according to the order of the General Court. It was also provided that "these tryalls bee by the oathes of 6 men, until they shall have a greater number of inhabitants for that servise." [5]

This 1641 commission which did not specifically term Pynchon a "magistrate" or refer to magistratical powers placed the Pynchon-held court upon a de jure basis. It broadened the civil jurisdiction to all causes, still without limitation of amount, and in criminal causes made explicit the implied limitation in cases extending to life, limb,

[3] *Rec.* 14; 2 *Rec. Mass. Bay* 100, 208.   [5] 1 *ibid.* 321–322.
[4] 1 *ibid.* 174–175.

or banishment. In providing for appeals it integrated the Springfield court into the judicial system of the colony. It retained trial by jury in civil causes and was open to the construction that a petty jury was required in trial of criminal offenses. For a vague body of law it substituted the established laws of the colony. It omitted, however, any requirement that a record be kept of causes heard and determined.

THE GENERAL COURT COMMISSION OF 1643

The June 2, 1641 commission was limited by its terms to one year. However, it was not renewed by the General Court in June 1642. Perhaps this body felt that, since Pynchon was chosen an assistant on May 18, 1642, it was unnecessary to renew the earlier commission. However, after the lapse of a year (in which no entries appear in the *Record*), the General Court on June 22, 1643, granted a commission to Pynchon, for the year ensuing and until the court made further order, with full power to govern according to the 1641 order, reiterating the power to try causes by a jury of six if twelve could not be conveniently had.[6]

The duration of the 1643 commission depends upon the construction placed upon the clause "till the court make further order." On May 14, 1645 the General Court ordered that the Massachusetts Bay commissioners for the United Colonies for the year, together with Pynchon, have power to keep a court at Springfield and to hear and determine all causes, both civil or criminal, either by a jury of six freemen, or otherwise, according to law, and to give the oath of freedom to such as they found capable thereof.[7] Certainly this is a "further order" of the General Court and the 1643 commission must be regarded as at least suspended for a period of a year. However, there is no evidence that the three-man court thus authorized ever sat. (John Winthrop, Deputy Governor, and Herbert Pelham were the Massachusetts commissioners, with Captain Cooke and William Hathorne, deputies, as alternates.) The *Record* contains no entries for the period April 1645 to April 1648; the printed records of the Commissioners for the United Colonies afford no assistance. The Springfield town records for the period indicate that judicial authority was regarded as residing in a single magistrate.[8]

However, whether or not the court authorized on May 14, 1645 ever sat does not answer the question as to whether or not such order in effect terminated the June 23, 1643 commission to Pynchon. If the latter commission was terminated by the May 14, 1645 order, then

---

[6] 2 *ibid.* 41.

[7] 2 *ibid.* 109.

[8] 1 Burt, *Hist. Springfield* 181–185.

the entries from 1648 to 1650 were made in Pynchon's capacity as magistrate rather than under the broader authority of the 1643 commission. It seems more likely that during this period Pynchon exercised judicial powers by virtue of the 1643 commission.

THE HENRY SMITH COMMISSION

Out of favor for his published religious views, William Pynchon was not chosen an assistant at the May 1651 session of the General Court. Therefore, the court on May 22 issued a commission, until further order, to Henry Smith, Pynchon's son-in-law and a deputy, in substantially the same terms as the 1641 commission to William Pynchon, with the addition that Smith was authorized to give oaths to constables legally chosen and to examine witnesses under suitable oath.[9] This reiteration of the 1641 commission provisions indicates that the General Court, or perhaps the Springfield inhabitants, entertained the view that Pynchon had been acting under the 1643 commission. If Pynchon had only the power of a magistrate, there was no apparent justification for granting Smith any greater powers. However, the order recited that the inhabitants of Springfield were at present destitute of any magistrate or others to put issue to such cases and differences as might arise amongst them. Since no "further order" had apparently issued terminating the 1643 commission, the fact that Pynchon had ceased to be a magistrate must have been regarded as putting an end to judicial authority at Springfield.

There is no trace of any courts held by Henry Smith under this commission in the *Record* nor has any reference to such a court been found. However, Henry Smith did not remain long in New England after his father-in-law's departure, and the General Court was again faced with the necessity of issuing a new commission.

APPOINTMENT OF THREE COMMISSIONERS

On October 26, 1652 the General Court granted to John Pynchon, Elizur Holyoke, and Samuel Chapin a commission, until further order, to govern the inhabitants of Springfield virtually identical in terms with the Smith commission. The court also provided for an oath which was taken before the selectmen of Springfield on November 12 when the commissioners commenced the exercise of their powers. In May 1653 Pynchon and Holyoke were also empowered by the General Court to administer the freeman's oath. On September

9 3 *Rec. Mass. Bay* 230; 4 *ibid.* (*Part I*) 49.

10, 1653 the General Court renewed this commission for one year more. On November 1, 1654, the 1653 commission having expired, the General Court empowered Pynchon, Holyoke, and Chapin as commissioners to act at Springfield according to the commission granted Henry Smith in May 1651 until the court took further order. They were to take the same oath as appointed in 1652 at some public meeting of at least ten Springfield inhabitants.[10] The oath was presumably taken, but it is not recorded in the *Record*. After April 1655 there are no entries in the *Record* until September 28, 1658.

The last date has significance. At first Springfield alone had a court on the western frontier of the colony. But on May 23, 1655, upon petition of the inhabitants of Nonotuck (Northampton), the General Court empowered three commissioners to end small causes in this town—William Holton, Thomas Bascom, and Edward Elmer. These commissioners and the constable were directed to repair to Springfield and have their oaths administered by the Springfield commissioners. A similar order was made on May 14, 1656.[11] No appointment of the General Court has been found for 1657, but on February 8, 1657/8 William Holton and Thomas Bascom were chosen commissioners for the year ensuing at a town meeting at Northampton.[12] Then in May 1658, a new court made its appearance in the Connecticut Valley.

On May 26, 1658 the General Court, during its pleasure, authorized the commissioners of Springfield and Northampton, jointly, or any four of them, to keep courts yearly in Springfield on the last Tuesday of March and in Northampton on the last Tuesday in September with jurisdiction to hear and determine, by jury or without (according to the liberty the law allowed in County Courts), all civil actions not exceeding twenty pounds damages and all criminal cases, not exceeding five pounds fine or ten stripes. Appeal was reserved to the County Court at Boston. This court was given power to grant licenses for the keeping of ordinaries or houses of common entertainment selling wine, cider, or strong liquors, to give the oath of freedom or fidelity to qualified persons, to bind to the peace or good behavior, and to commit to prison felons and malefactors, all

---

[10] 4 *ibid.* (*Part I*) 115, 135, 180, 213–214; *Rec.* 54.

[11] 4 *ibid.* (*Part I*) 227, 271. A petition to the General Court by several Northampton inhabitants, dated April 10, 1656, requested that Holton, Bascom, and Elmer be continued as commissioners; that they might appeal to the Court of Assistants in cases of capital crimes and causes of great discernment; that in other causes they might be tried by the three Springfield and the three Northampton commissioners, with jurors equally chosen from the two towns. 1 Trumbull, *Hist. Northampton* 32.

[12] 1 *Ms. Northampton Town Rec.* 9.

according to law.[13] In effect, the commissioners of the two towns were authorized to hold courts twice yearly comparable in jurisdiction to the County Courts in the more settled parts of the colony.

Presumably this commission in no way derogated from the authority previously exercised by the Springfield and the Northampton commissioners respectively. Yet such construction admits of some doubt in the case of the Springfield commissioners since the powers exercised in civil actions and criminal cases by such commissioners under their existing commission were in some respects greater than those to be exercised jointly with the Northampton commissioners under the May 26, 1658 commission. Further, under the former commission the appeal provided was to the Court of Assistants, under the latter, to the County Court at Boston, a court lower in the judicial hierarchy. An uncharitable explanation is that the General Court, in issuing the commission, erroneously assumed that the Springfield commissioners exercised only the usual powers of commissioners for ending small causes, as in the case of Northampton.

In any event, the first joint court authorized by the May 26, 1658 commission was held at Northampton on September 28, 1658. The *Record* does not disclose the commissioners present, with the exception of Pynchon and Holyoke, but it may be that several Northampton commissioners also attended.[14] One of the matters heard was a complaint of Elmer, apparently chosen the third commissioner at Northampton, against William Holton, one of the other commissioners, and Robert Bartlett, for defaming Elmer by saying that he had come to Springfield in a disorderly way to take his oath.[15]

The second and last meeting of this joint court took place at Springfield on March 29, 1659. At this court the three Northampton commissioners appeared and presented themselves by certificate under the hand of the constable of Northampton to be sworn. At this point some present from Northampton objected "against their three men as being not legally appoynted to the work they came for, in that they were not allowed by any superior Power as the Law provides; and in that they were nonfreemen as to this Commonwealth, and for other causes." The entry then states that "after the busyness was longe debated the result was that there could be noe Corte Legally kept here without further Order from superior Powers: and soe the Assembly brake up." No causes were heard except one in which the

---

[13] 4 *Rec. Mass. Bay (Part I)* 335. The General Court order was entered in the *Record* (p. 73).

[14] *Rec.* 73–76. See Wright, *Indian Deeds* 31–32.

[15] The Northampton town records actually do not show that Edward Elmer was chosen commissioner. 1 *Ms. Northampton Town Rec.* 9.

parties agreed that the Springfield commissioners should determine an action of debt.[16]

What was behind the objection made to the Northampton commissioners is not apparent, but it may have been another facet of the feud reflected in Edward Elmer's complaint. The Northampton town records reveal that on March 11, 1658/9 Holton, Williams, and Lyman were "chosen Commissioners for this Town for the year ensuing to end small causes." [17] The apparent basis of the objection was that the commissioners had not been allowed of by the General Court or a County Court and, secondly, that they were not freemen as required by law in the case of commissioners.

The inhabitants of Springfield quickly sought relief from the General Court which on May 28, 1659 ordered that Pynchon, Holyoke, and Chapin, for the year ensuing and until further order, have full power and authority to govern the inhabitants of Springfield in terms virtually identical with the 1651 commission to Henry Smith, except that there was no reference to the power to give oaths to constables and to examine witnesses under oath. The order also referred Northampton commissioners to Springfield, "in reference to County Courts," which courts were to be held at Springfield on the last Tuesday in March and on the last Tuesday in September, unless the commissioners saw just cause to hold one session at Northampton. These courts were to have in all respects "the power and priviledges of any County Courte" until the General Court saw cause to determine otherwise. However, only four jurors from Northampton were to be warned to Springfield and vice versa. All fines, as well as payments for entry of actions, were to go toward defraying the charges of these courts. The commission granted in 1658 respecting Northampton was repealed. Lastly, the order provided that, out of court, the commissioners, or any two of them, agreeing, might act in all respects as one magistrate might, either at Springfield or at Northampton.[18] The intent of this order is far from clear. In effect, three jurisdictional standards are referred to but the powers first granted seem inconsistent with either of the others.

On the same date John Pynchon took an oath before the General Court for the faithful discharge of the commission, was authorized to give an oath to the other two commissioners in the form appointed by the Court in October 1652, and was empowered to solemnize marriages. At the same time William Holton, Arthur Wil-

---

16 Rec. 77–79.
17 1 Ms. Northampton Town Rec. 43.

See also 1 Trumbull, Hist. Northampton 97.
18 4 Rec. Mass. Bay (Part I) 378–379.

liams, and Richard Lyman were allowed of by the General Court as commissioners to end small causes at Northampton.[19]

The *Record* contains only two meetings of the "County Court" established by the May 28, 1659 order; these were held at Springfield in September 1659 and March 1660.[20] However, a volume of records in the Registry of Probate at Northampton, Massachusetts, in which the records of the duly constituted County Court for Hampshire were later entered, reveals that the above "County Court" held sessions at Springfield or Northampton (and once at Hadley) in September 1660 and in March and September in 1661 and 1662. In order to show the development of this jurisdiction of the commissioners, those entries appearing in the Registry of Probate volume through the September 30, 1662 session are included along with the *Record*.

Prior to the formal establishment of a County Court for Hampshire several other orders of the General Court supplemented the powers or modified the structure of the Springfield court. On November 12, 1659, the General Court granted the commissioners of Springfield power to administer the freeman's oath to any capable by law of taking it in the plantations on the Connecticut River. In addition, the "new towne" upon the Connecticut, Hadley, was to be under the power of the Springfield commissioners in reference to County Courts until further order of the General Court. Later, on May 31, 1660, the General Court commissioned John Webster, Sr., of Hadley with magistratical powers for the ensuing year to act in all civil and criminal cases as one magistrate might do and ordered that he join with the commissioners "in keeping the Courts at Springfield," presumably the "County Courts." Webster, a former governor of Connecticut, sat with the Springfield commissioners in September 1660 and in March 1661. He died within a fortnight of the latter sitting.[21]

On October 16, 1660 the following entry appears in the records of the General Court:

It is ordered by this Court, that Springfeild County Court be and is heereby impowred to erect and improove a prison and house of correction, as other countys have, any deficiency for want of magistrates notwithstanding, and that the commissioners for that Court, or any two of

[19] 4 *ibid.* (*Part I*) 373, 379–380. The Northampton town records show no election of commissioners for ending small causes between March 10, 1658/9 and March 19, 1660/1 when William Clark, William Woodward, and Henry Cunliffe were chosen commissioners. 1 *Ms. Northampton Town Rec.* 15, 25.

[20] *Rec.* 82, 84.

[21] 4 *Rec. Mass. Bay* (*Part I*) 406, 420

them, be impowred to act in any case concerning the same, and for the committing of offendors thereto and releasing of them againe, as any one magistrate may doe.[22]

On May 22, 1661 the General Court, upon motion of the inhabitants, granted town status to Hadley and ordered that "for the better government of the people, and suppressing of sinns there" some meet persons, annually presented by the freemen, should be commissioned and empowered to hear and determine all civil actions, not exceeding five pounds, without a jury, to deal in all criminal cases according to law, where the penalty did not exceed ten stripes for one offense, and, together with the commissioners for Springfield and Northampton, or the greater part of them, to keep the courts appointed at Springfield and Northampton. Any person sentenced by the Hadley commissioners, either in civil or criminal cases, might appeal to the court at Springfield or Northampton. However, the Hadley commissioners did not sit as a "County Court" with the Springfield and Northampton commissioners until March 31, 1663. They did, however, appear before John Pynchon on July 12, 1661, as ordered by the General Court, and took their oaths for the faithful discharge of their duties.[23]

The same May 22 order, recognizing the lack of a grand jury system, also ordered that the jurymen freemen for trials at the Springfield and Northampton courts should take information and make presentments to the court of misdemeanors as grand jurors usually did or ought to do.[24] This order is probably the genesis of the practice which later obtained in the Hampshire County Court of having petty jurors double in brass as grand jurors.

Finally, on May 7, 1662, in order that public affairs might with more facility be transacted according to the established laws of the colony, the General Court ordered that the towns of Springfield, Northampton, and Hadley constitute a county called Hampshire and enjoy the liberties and privileges of any other county. Springfield was to be the shire town and the courts and shire meetings were to be held alternately at Springfield and Northampton.[25] Apparently the establishment of this new county was not regarded as ipso facto terminating the existing authority to hold "County Courts." The first shire organizational meeting was not held until April 2, 1663; the first County Court for Hampshire, described as such in the records,

[22] 4 *ibid.* (*Part I*) 434.
[23] 4 *ibid.* (*Part II*) 11–12; *Rec.* 94.
[24] The complaint of Thomas Stanley of Hadley against Robert Williams "by Thomas Coleman Juryman" for violently taking away cattle being driven to pound (1 *Hamp. Cty. Probate Ct. Rec.* 15) may have been pursuant to this power.
[25] 4 *Rec. Mass. Bay* (*Part II*) 52.

did not sit until March 31, 1663.[26] While the record is not explicit, the personnel of this and several succeeding courts probably was based upon the provisions of the above May 22, 1661 commission to the Hadley commissioners.

The extent of the powers exercised by the Springfield commissioners after May 7, 1662, or perhaps March 31, 1663, must have depended upon the terms of the 1659 commission, since there is no record of the town's having elected Pynchon, Holyoke, and Chapin as commissioners for ending small causes. This meant that these commissioners, or any two of them, had the powers of a single magistrate. This view is consistent with the entries in the *Record*, except that in one instance Pynchon, sitting alone, imposed fines for drunkenness upon two Indians.[27]

JOHN PYNCHON AS MAGISTRATE

Whatever powers the commissioners of Springfield retained after the events of 1662–63 were terminated on May 3, 1665 when John Pynchon was chosen assistant, an office to which he was reelected annually until 1686 when a new government was organized by Dudley. The entries in the *Record* from May 3, 1665 to May 25, 1686 (the date of the first meeting of the President and Council of New England), are thus of jurisdiction exercised by Pynchon as a magistrate. There are no entries for the period between May 1665 and September 1670 other than notations of the swearing of constables and the taking of the oath of a freeman or of the oath of fidelity. One enigmatic entry which follows several as to swearing constables—"Afterward: I entred them in my Law Booke"—indicates that Pynchon may have kept another book in which he entered cases heard in his capacity as magistrate.[28] However, no such volume has been found nor any further reference to one.

The election of John Pynchon also affected the composition of the County Court, for on May 3, 1665 the General Court ordered that the County Court for Hampshire should thenceforth be kept by John Pynchon, as magistrate, and by such associates elected as the law directed. It also ordered that the commissioners for small causes in Northampton and Hadley continue in their commissions in other respects as formerly. As to the Springfield commissioners, there had been a cessation of their commission by Pynchon's election as magistrate and the town's affairs now properly belonged to his care and oversight.[29]

---

[26] *Pynchon Waste Book for Hampshire* 1–2.

[27] *Rec.* 100.

[28] *Rec.* 134.

[29] 4 *Rec. Mass. Bay* (*Part II*) 148.

PYNCHON AS MEMBER OF THE DUDLEY AND ANDROS COUNCILS

The General Court records for May 12, 1686 show that Pynchon was again elected assistant but that he apparently did not take the oath of office. Technically, this may have terminated his power as magistrate but in any event the lapse was short-lived. On May 25 Joseph Dudley, at the first meeting of the President and Council in Boston read his October 8, 1685 commission as President of the Council for New England. This commission nominated and appointed seventeen councilors, including John Pynchon. On the same day the members of the Council were authorized to hear all causes under forty shillings.[30]

The first case heard by Pynchon as a member of the Council, on June 23, 1686, involved the misdemeanor of disturbing the peace and swearing, and resulted in a fine of five shillings for breaking the peace and three and six for swearing.[31] This case raises the question previously noted as to what jurisdiction members of the Council exercised in criminal offenses, and for that matter, what jurisdiction justices of the peace had in such matters. The records of the President and Council are silent; the commissions of the peace might afford at least a partial answer but none have been uncovered.[32] Thus Pynchon's jurisdiction in criminal matters during this period is not known. It may be that members of the Council assumed the same jurisdiction in criminal matters as magistrates under the First Charter.

On December 20, 1686 Sir Edmund Andros arrived in Boston. His June 1686 commission as governor of the Dominion of New England named John Pynchon as a member of the Council, as did the instructions accompanying his second commission of April 17, 1688.[33] However, no order has been found relating to the jurisdiction of councilors in civil matters comparable to the June 10 order under Dudley, nor any commission of the peace for Hampshire during the Andros regime, although undoubtedly Pynchon would have been included in such commission. The entries in the *Record* during such period (the last being in September 1688) relate to civil actions, with the exception of a presentment for failure to ward, but

---

[30] Matthews, *Notes on the Massachusetts Royal Commissions, 1681–1775* (1913) 5, 29–30; *Dudley Records* 229–231.

[31] *Rec.* 199.

[32] The records of the President and Council and entries in the *Record* indicate that during July–September 1686, Joseph Hawley, William Clark, John Hol-

yoke, Peter Tilton, Samuel Partrigg, and a "Mr. Haley" were commissioned justices of the peace. Pynchon, Tilton, and Clark were commissioned to hold the County Court for Hampshire. *Dudley Records* 258, 271; 2 *Ms. Mass. Council Rec.* 54, 77, 79; *Rec.* 198.

[33] 1 *Laws N.H.* 143, 235.

do not disclose the capacity in which Pynchon held court. It may be that the June 10, 1686 order referred to was continued in effect by the March 8, 1686/7 proclamation noted earlier.[34]

PYNCHON EXERCISING MAGISTRATICAL POWERS

Since Pynchon did not regain the status of assistant following the overthrow of Andros, Peter Tilton, as magistrate, became the top judicial figure in Hampshire. However, on September 8, 1689 the General Court ordered that Pynchon among others be allowed and confirmed an associate for the County Court of Hampshire and be invested with magistratical power until further settlement. There are no entries in the *Record* for the period covered by this appointment. On June 2, 1690 Pynchon was again confirmed and approved by the General Court as an associate of the County Court and invested wtih magistratical power.[35] An entry in the County Court records relates that on May 20, 1691 he was further invested with magistratical power by the General Court. A March 29, 1692 County Court entry notes that Pynchon and three others were chosen associates for the year ensuing, but no further investment of Pynchon with magistratical powers has been found.[36] However, the *Record* contains no entries between July 22, 1691 and September 12, 1692.

PYNCHON AS JUSTICE OF THE PEACE

No first-hand evidence appears as to the date when Pynchon became a justice of the peace under the Second Charter. Whitmore indicates that Pynchon and four others were commissioned justices of the peace and collectively the Court of General Sessions of the Peace for Hampshire on May 27, 1692 (Pynchon being of the quorum).[37] However, the Act for the Holding of Courts of Justice was not passed until June 28, 1692, and the first meeting of the Court of General Sessions of the Peace for Hampshire was not held until July 26, 1692.[38] A June 15, 1692 law, continuing in effect certain earlier laws, in providing that "the several justices are hereby impowered to the execution of said laws as the magistrates formerly were" indicates that justices of the peace may have been commissioned soon after the arrival of Governor Phips on May 14.[39]

---

[34] *Ibid.* 249. That some commissions of the peace issued see *Andros Records* 466–467, 473.

[35] 1 *Laws N.H.* 327, 406.

[36] *Rec. Cty. Ct. Hamp.* 143, 151; *Vol. A, Registry of Deeds, Springfield, Hampden County, 1690–92* 301, 313.

[37] *Mass. Civil List* 139.

[38] 1 *Acts and Res. Prov. Mass. Bay* 37; *Rec. Cty. Ct. Hamp.* 126.

[39] 1 *Acts and Res. Prov. Mass. Bay* 27; *Rec. Cty. Ct. Hamp.* 158.

In any event, Pynchon did not hear his first case until September 12, 1692; presumably he had been commissioned a justice of the peace by that date. As was the case for the earlier period, no commission of the peace has been found for Hampshire for 1692–1701. However, the form of the commission of the peace for York County and the statutory jurisdiction conferred upon justices of the peace under the Second Charter have been referred to. A few *Record* entries relate to the jurisdiction of two justices of the peace, also referred to.

Whitmore indicates that Pynchon continued as justice of the peace until omitted from the June 29, 1702 commission of the peace issued by Governor Dudley. However, the Council minutes for June 29th reveal that Dudley appointed all members of the Council to be justices of the peace in each county and that Pynchon was also named a judge of the Inferior Court of Common Pleas for Hampshire.[40] Further, the records of the Court of General Sessions of the Peace for Hampshire contain a July 21, 1702 entry of the reading of a commission empowering John Pynchon, among others, as a justice of the peace and of the justices being sworn according to law. Pynchon also sat at the September 1, 1702 Court of General Sessions of the Peace held at Springfield, but the last judicial entry in the *Record* was made January 9, 1701/2.[41]

40 *CSP, Col. 1702*, #679.   41 *Hamp. Rec. Ct. Pleas* 141, 147; *Rec.* 254.

V I I. Criminal Jurisdiction

MOST of the laws of the various American colonies are readily available in printed form; most of the court records are still in manuscript form and difficult of access. As a consequence, some historians of the colonial period have tended to describe law enforcement solely or largely on the basis of an examination of printed laws and legislative records. The results are at times misleading. In the two preceding sections the jurisdiction conferred by the printed laws upon the various courts at Springfield was set forth. In this section the *Record* is examined against such statutory background to determine, compare, and evaluate the jurisdiction actually exercised from time to time by the several courts at Springfield. This jurisdiction may be conveniently grouped into the following: sexual offenses, other moral offenses, offenses against the peace, offenses against property, contempts of authority, defamation, neglect of duties, offenses against licensing laws, offenses involving Indians, and violations of town orders. The latter were not in a strict sense criminal offenses, but are treated here for convenience of presentation.

SEXUAL OFFENSES

A 1642 law, embodied in the later printed laws, provided that if any man committed fornication with a single woman, they should be punished by enjoinment to marriage, fine, or corporal punishment or any or all of such punishments as the judges should appoint, most agreeable to the word of God. Under later commonwealth laws the measure of punishment was to be "as the Judges of the Court that hath Cognizance of the Cause shall appoint." [1] A 1649 law provided that no person should, directly or indirectly, draw away the affections of any maid under pretense of marriage before he had obtained permission from her parents or governors, or, in their absence, from the nearest magistrate, under penalty of forfeiting five pounds

---

[1] *Laws and Liberties Mass.* 23; *Col. Laws Mass., 1660* 153; *Col. Laws Mass., 1672* 54.

for the first offense, with more severe penalties for subsequent offenses. It was not until 1668 that the laws provided that a person found the father of a bastard should have the care and charge of maintaining such child.[2]

While the operation of these laws in a few instances may be observed in the *Record*, the first matter involving a sexual offense antedated the laws and was apparently decided by William Pynchon in his discretion, guided perhaps by the practice of the Court of Assistants. In one of the earliest cases in the *Record* Pynchon ordered that John Hobell be whipped by the constable for getting promises of marriage from Abigail Burt, despite her father's prohibition, and for offering and attempting fornication with her. Abigail was likewise ordered whipped.[3] What crime she was regarded as having committed is not clear, unless it was participation in unchaste or unclean behavior.

Only two other fornication cases appear in the *Record*. The March 1654/5 case involving Samuel Wright, Jr. is significant in that a jury of twelve was used to try a paternity charge, that Wright was ordered to make certain payments toward the maintenance of the child, and that Mary Burt, who made the charge, was ordered whipped twice—for fornication with Wright and with Joseph Bond.[4] In the February 1670/1 case, Richard Barnard was discharged from prison so he could marry Sarah Clark and then bound over to appear at the next County Court where the offenders were fined forty shillings apiece.[5] The supplemental material from the Registry of Probate records shows that the commissioners, in September 1661, concluded, from the date of birth of their child, that Samuel Terry and his wife "did abuse one another before marriage" and accepted a four-pound fine in lieu of punishment of ten lashes apiece.[6] This offense was frequently punished on the county level by the courts of the Bay.

While no entries appear in the *Record*, the records of the County Court for Hampshire show that John Pynchon, as magistrate, examined and bound over to the County Court a number of others charged with sexual offenses. In practice the severe punishments imposed placed fornication cases outside the ambit of a magistrate. At a September 26, 1671 County Court Joshua Barsham, lately of Hatfield,

[2] *Laws and Liberties Mass.* 37; *Col. Laws Mass., 1660* 172, 257; *Col. Laws Mass., 1672* 101.

[3] *Rec.* 12. Fornication was punished by the Court of Assistants as were filthy and unchaste behavior and tempting maids to uncleanliness. 2 *Rec. Ct. Assts. Mass. Bay* 30, 32, 48, 60, 64–65, 79, 81, 87, 90.

[4] *Rec.* 63–64.

[5] *Rec.* 137–138; 1 *Hamp. Cty. Probate Ct. Rec.* 126; *Pynchon Waste Book for Hampshire* 81.

[6] 1 *Hamp. Cty. Probate Ct. Rec.* 8.

having been sent down to Major Pynchon and bound over to answer Ruth Butler's accusation of forcing her, appeared but was allowed costs of court when no accuser appeared. A March 31, 1674 County Court entry reveals that in the previous July Pynchon had examined Hannah Merick who was suspected of being with child by fornication, and, when she confessed that she feared it was so and on oath accused Jonathan Morgan of having knowledge of her body, had bound both over to the September 1673 court at Springfield.[7]

A few years later William Brooke of Springfield was bound by Pynchon in the sum of twenty pounds that his daughter Patience, being with child out of wedlock, appear at the September 1680 County Court and answer "to her Crime and guilt of that vile sin of fornication." The court, being "desirous to shew their detestation of such forbidden and dangerous carnal Lusts and if possible to prevent such like God provoking wayes," adjudged the offender to be whipped with fifteen lashes or else to pay a fine of four pounds to the county treasurer. Thomas Taylor, with two sureties, also gave bond to Pynchon in the sum of twenty pounds to appear at the same court and answer what Patience Brooke had to lay to his charge, as well as for his good behavior in the meantime.[8]

John Riley of Springfield was also bound by Pynchon in the sum of twenty pounds for his daughter Margarite's appearance at the same court "to answer to her foul Crime of Fornication." The court, "being desirous to beare due Testimony against this Growing and provoking sin of whoredom and to restrain the like abhorend practices," ordered the offender forthwith whipped with fifteen lashes and to receive a further fifteen stripes when Pynchon saw cause to have them inflicted or to pay a fine of four pounds to the county. Roco, a Negro, being examined by Major Pynchon, acknowledged to him and later to the court "that he had (upon the said Riley's tempting him) the carnal knowledge of her body" and was sentenced to fifteen lashes or to pay a fine of three pounds.[9]

At its March 25, 1684 sitting the County Court noted that Thomas Granger and his wife, as well as Esther Spencer, all of Southfield, had been presented for fornication, but that the women were in no condition to be brought to court. It therefore ordered the clerk to draw up what the court had considered as to these offences and to send it to Major Pynchon, desiring him to send for the offenders, examine them and bind them over to the next court at Spring-

---

[7] *Pynchon Waste Book for Hampshire* 88, 117.

[8] *Rec. Cty. Ct. Hamp.* 43.

[9] *Ibid.* 43. This may have been the

Roco mentioned in a December 1, 1687 entry by John Pynchon in the *Record* (p. 313): "Roco and Sue my Negroes, Joined in Marriage."

field or otherwise. However, no entry of such examination appears in the *Record*. At the September 1685 court John Webb of Northampton, having been bound over by John Pynchon to answer "to his notorious Crime in abusing the little maide Mary Bennet in a Shameful uncleane way," appeared, was convicted and sentenced to twenty lashes, the court being desirous to bear "testimony against such abominable fruits and issues of corrupt nature, and to restraine al other Persons (God affording his restraining Grace) that such or such like woful effects of original Sin in al Persons may not be Committed amongst us to the defiling the Land." At the March 1686 County Court Joseph Ashly, being bound over by John Pynchon "for that he was accused for Commiting fornication by Deborah Miller and with her; which Said Joseph and Deborah upon Examination by the Worshipfull Major John Pynchon Esq. was found guilty of said Sin by their own acknowledgment," was adjudged to pay a fine of six pounds to the county and provide maintenance for the child according to law. Deborah Miller was adjudged to pay a fine of four pounds and clerk's fees.[10]

Only two fornication cases have been found after the period of the First Charter in which Pynchon bound over offenders. At the September 1686 County Court Richard Waite of Springfield, being bound over by Pynchon to answer for his offense of fornication with the widow Sarah Barnard, appeared with the widow whom he had married in the interim. The court, being "Sensible of the growth and increase of this abominable Sin, and desirous to use all wayes to curb (as God shall Assist) the further breakings out of such provoking Sins," adjudged the offenders to be well whipped or to pay a fine of five pounds. At the same court Gregory McGregory and Sarah Kent of Springfield, "being by their own confession upon their examination before the Worshipfull Major Pynchon Esq. (August 19th: 1686) found guilty of defileing one the other by the sin of fornication," appeared. McGregory was adjudged to be whipped with twenty lashes or to pay a three-pound fine, and to give security for the payment of forty pounds maintenance for the child to be born and for his good behavior or to be committed to prison. Sarah Kent was adjudged to be whipped with fifteen lashes or to pay a three-pound fine, but, being near her "time of travel" and this punishment dangerous of execution, a surety was allowed to stand bound for a period of six weeks to see the fine paid or to deliver her up.[11]

A few cases concerned what might be termed lewd or lascivious conduct. In July 1650 William Pynchon gave an offender private

[10] *Rec. Cty. Ct. Hamp.* 73, 100–101, 105.   [11] *Ibid.* 109–110, 111–112.

correction upon report by the watch of lascivious conduct on the Sabbath.[12] This is the only case in the *Record* in which correction was private. In September 1660, the commissioners, exercising the powers of a County Court, imposed a ten-pound fine for "gross Lascivious carriage and misdemeanor toward the wife of John Stebbins." [13] In February 1672/3, following examinations held on three separate days, several persons were fined in modest amounts by Pynchon for their "uncivill Immodest and beastly acting" in a play. In June 1678 a drunken soldier was fined thirty shillings for wicked, lascivious and unclean carriage toward Mary Crowfoot.[14] No laws have been found specifically dealing with offenses constituting lewd conduct; in most cases the entries do not spell out the details of the offense. Presumably the scope of the crime and the punishment to be imposed resided within the discretion of the court. From the early years of settlement the Court of Assistants had assumed wide jurisdiction over such offenses.

OTHER MORAL OFFENSES

A 1646 law provided for a forfeiture of ten shillings "if any person within this Jurisdiction shall swear rashly or vainly either by the holy Name of God, or any other oath." Later, profane and wicked cursing of any person or creature carried the same penalty.[15] However, even before 1646 the Court of Assistants had punished swearing and cursing. The offenses of profane swearing or cursing appear several times in the *Record*. In a February 1640/1 case William Pynchon obviously adopted the punishment provided by act of Parliament (21 Jac. 1, c. 20). In two cases in 1675–76 the offenders, accused of being in drink and swearing "by God," were fined the statutory ten shillings to the county.[16] In some instances swearing or cursing was merely one facet of conduct in breach of law and order.[17]

Under the First Charter willfully making or publishing any lie which was pernicious to the public weal, tended to the injury of any particular person, or was intended to deceive people with false news

[12] *Rec.* 41. Compare the 1675 charge against Robert Hinsdall in the County Court for Hampshire for "Wanton and Lascivious carriage" in which the testimonies were read to him in private, being "Loathsomely obsceene and exceeding Nocious to any honest heart to heare or Mention." 1 *Hamp. Cty. Probate Ct. Rec.* 161. See also the examination of witnesses in private by the County Court for Essex when Henry Phelps was bound to answer for keeping company with his brother's wife. 2 *Rec. and Files Quart. Cts. Essex Cty. Mass.* 261.

[13] 1 *Hamp. Cty. Probate Ct. Rec.* 3.

[14] *Rec.* 144, 166.

[15] *Laws and Liberties Mass.* 45; *Col. Laws Mass., 1660* 195; *Col. Laws Mass., 1672* 144–145.

[16] *Rec.* 14, 160, 162.

[17] *Rec.* 165, 177, 199, 209–210; 1 *Hamp. Cty. Probate Ct. Rec.* 23.

or reports was made punishable with a ten-shilling fine for the first offense.[18] In only two instances under the First Charter was a fine imposed *secundum legum*. Apparently no action was taken upon a 1685 complaint of Springfield tithingmen against Mary Towsley for "Notorius lying." [19] Under the Second Charter fines for lying were also imposed in only two instances. The last entry in the *Record*, the sentencing of a Negress to ten lashes, was based in part on the utterance of some lurid lies.[20]

In several cases not appearing in the *Record*, John Pynchon as magistrate bound over to the County Court persons accused of lying among other offenses. An entry at the March 29, 1670 court held at Northampton notes that Robert Williams of Hadley, a former servant, was bound over to the court by John Pynchon in ten-pounds bond and, for want of sureties for his appearance, committed to prison. The ground for this action was the offender's "notorious Lyinge," but he was also suspected of witchcraft. The evidence of witchcraft was not of sufficient force to keep Williams in prison or to warrant sending him to superior authority. However, for his lying, Williams was adjudged to pay a five-pound fine to the county, to be whipped with fifteen stripes, to pay all charges of his imprisonment, and to stand committed until the court's order was performed.[21] This punishment, harsher than that appointed by law, was undoubtedly influenced by the suspicion of witchcraft.

At the September 24, 1678 County Court, Jane Jackson, a Hadley servant, having been bound over the previous summer by John Pynchon to answer "as being guilty of most notorius evils," appeared and by the court's examination, and that of Pynchon, was found guilty of "wretched and vile Contradictions or Lyings" and "vilely guilty of filching or stealing" from her master. The court ordered that she be whipped with twenty lashes and serve her master an additional six months in recompense for his troubles and expenses about "his misdemeaning Servant." [22]

Under the First Charter the General Court in 1653 and 1658 made orders with respect to profaning the Sabbath.[23] Enforcement of these orders is reflected in the *Record* in cases during the period 1654–1685 which cover such diverse violations as not coming to ordinances, playing and sporting, laboring, engaging in an affray or disturbance, and driving cattle or a laden cart. In one case a charge of idleness against a servant was combined with charges of profaning the Sabbath. In most cases small fines were imposed or the offenders

---

18 *Laws and Liberties Mass.* 35; *Col. Laws Mass., 1660* 171; *Col. Laws Mass., 1672* 91.

19 *Rec.* 70, 97–98, 193.

20 *Rec.* 228, 251, 254.

21 *Pynchon Waste Book for Hampshire* 69; 1 *Hamp. Cty. Probate Ct. Rec.* 114.

22 *Rec. Cty. Ct. Hamp.* 17.

23 *Col. Laws Mass., 1660* 69; *Col. Laws Mass., 1672* 132.

admonished.[24] There is no case of a Sabbath violation in the *Record* after 1685. However, at the March 1691 sitting of the County Court the case of Isaac Morgan of Enfield, presented by the grand jury for unnecessary travel on the Sabbath, was referred to Pynchon to give sentence as the law directed.[25] There is no entry in the *Record* of such sentencing.

One aspect of profanation of the Sabbath consisted of misconduct during sermon time. At one of the earliest courts held by William Pynchon, John Woodcock, the plantation troublemaker, was warned to answer at the next court for his laughing during sermon time and also for his misdemeanor of idleness. However, there is no entry in the *Record* that he was ever tried for these offenses. In a June 1661 case a five-shilling fine for misbehavior during sermon time was imposed according to law, the offender having been earlier admonished for the same offense.[26] At a court held in March 1671/2 a Northampton inhabitant, summoned before John Pynchon by order of the County Court, was fined ten shillings to the county for his "unseemly and prophane carriage" on the Sabbath at the Northampton meeting house during the time of public ordinances.[27] Whether such fine was for a third offense, as provided by the law, does not appear.

A case might concern profanation of the Sabbath, among other offenses. This is true of the February 1670/1 fine imposed on Thomas Stebbing, Jr. for posting the publication of the intended marriage of Richard Barnard and Sarah Clark, referred to above, without consent or knowledge of the parties or parents, accompanied "with a foolish and reproachful Rime casting reproch upon the Towne and the Maides in Towne." [28] In view of the "shotgun" circumstances of the marriage Pynchon's finding the offense "very greate" appears unduly sensitive.

Several laws of the commonwealth imposed punishments for allowing games at a house of common entertainment or for playing at such games.[29] The *Record* shows fines of from five to twenty shillings being imposed in two instances in 1661–62 for playing cards or commonly suffering the unlawful game to be played in one's house. One offender acknowledging that card games took place at his house, said that he was willing to have recreation for his wife "to drive away melancholy," and would do anything when his wife was ill "to make her merry." However, his plea of recreational therapy was disregarded.[30]

Another instance of less innocent merriment is found in March

[24] *Rec.* 65, 91, 104, 151, 152, 194, 201. See also 1 *Hamp. Cty. Probate Ct. Rec.* 8.
[25] *Rec. Cty. Ct. Hamp.* 142.
[26] *Rec.* 5, 93.
[27] *Rec.* 142; *Pynchon Waste Book for*

Hampshire, 83, 88; 1 *Hamp. Cty. Probate Ct. Rec.* 127.
[28] *Rec.* 138.
[29] *Col. Laws Mass., 1660* 153.
[30] *Rec.* 97–98, 101.

1677/8 when some youths confessed to having played cards in the cellar of William King's house in Hatfield at an unseasonable time of night and to have defiled King's loom. One offender was fined for card playing, for being out playing at an unseasonable time of night, and "for being at so Nasty a busyness." He was also to answer for any damage to King's property. The evidence on file against the other offenders was transferred to the Northampton County Court where they were fined, whipped, and ordered to pay charges and to make good the damage suffered by King. One offender, in addition, received eighteen stripes for fornication.[31]

OFFENSES AGAINST THE PEACE

The most serious offenses against the peace involved riotous assemblies, although the commonwealth laws contained no specific provisions dealing with riots, routs, or unlawful assemblies. On February 16, 1675/6 John Pynchon, sitting at Hadley, imposed fines ranging from five to forty shillings on several persons who, the day previous, had participated in an unlawful and riotous assembly in an attempt to prevent the execution of a sentence upon a delinquent by order of the committee of the militia. Several participants in the riot, unnamed in the *Record,* were bound over to the County Court. An examination of the March 28, 1676 entries of the County Court reveals that of those persons bound over by Pynchon, most received five-pound fines.[32]

At the March 30, 1686 County Court Samuel Kent of Suffield, apparently bound over by John Pynchon, appeared to answer "for raising or abetting a Mutinous and Riotous Behaviour at Suffield, and himselfe very much active in such Carriages, besides Several unworthy Speeches, as in an high and violent manner, saying, that All Persons might vote at the Town Meeting, in Choice of Townsmen and Constables, etc. That the Lawes of this Government Some of them were not worth a Chip, and being present when there was a Tumult and disorder in the Town Meeting, abettinge said non voters and saying they might vote." These offenses the court found "high abusive Carriages, tending to breakeing of Order, and in reallity a breach of Law, and greivous violation of his Religious Tye which is upon him" and adjudged that Kent pay a fine of five pounds to the county and witness and other charges.[33]

At the same sitting Peter Rhoe, another disturber of the peace of

31 *Rec.* 165–166; *Rec. Cty. Ct. Hamp.* 8.
32 *Rec.* 161; 1 *Hamp. Cty. Probate Ct.*
Rec. 168–169; *Pynchon Waste Book for Hampshire* 134–136.
33 *Rec. Cty. Ct. Hamp.* 104.

Suffield, also bound over to the County Court by John Pynchon, was accused "of approbrious Speeches, and violent Carriages and voteing for Townsmen and Constables in a Publique Towne Meeting, when he hath no Liberty in Law so to doe, to the great disturbance of the Peace and Greife of the Moderator of said Meeting, in so much as he withdrew out of his Place, and said Rhoe was so bold as to Supply and Occupy in his Place, besides an Abettor of an evil Spirit against the Minister of the Place." The court, adjudging Rhoe's conduct "to be high handed Rebellion, and tending to confusion, and Every Evil thing," sentenced him to pay a fine of five pounds to the county and witness and other charges. David Winchel, bound over by Pynchon, was adjudged to pay a fine of four pounds and witness and other costs for scurrilous speeches reflecting upon the Suffield minister and for pressing at the town meeting for the choice of a constable contrary to the mind of the town. (Winchel figured in an earlier disorder at a Suffield town meeting which is referred to in a March 15, 1681/2 entry in the *Record*.) Edward Burlison, also bound over, was fined five pounds and court costs for his part in being a disturber and molestor of the peace at the Suffield town meeting.[34]

A later Suffield matter reflects the disturbed state of the western frontier. An entry at the March 14, 1693/4 sitting of the Court of General or Quarter Sessions of the Peace at Northampton reveals that during the previous winter the constable of Suffield had complained to John Pynchon, as justice of the peace, that several persons had "made an Alarum" in the town of Suffield to the great disturbance of the people. The constable by summons from Pynchon was authorized to bring these offenders before him or to take security in the amount of five pounds for the delinquents to appear before the next Court of General Sessions of the Peace at Northampton. Security was given and largely forfeited when the offenders failed to appear at the appointed court at which fines of twenty shillings apiece were imposed and, in addition, twenty-four shillings in charges.[35]

More numerous were breaches of the peace involving such aspects as assault and battery, drunkenness, use of abusive language, abusing the watch, and so on. These offenses tended to overlap and appear to have been segregated at times only for the purpose of building up the amount of the fine in aggravated cases. It is not until 1672, however, that the title "Breach of the Peace" is found in the laws. This title provided that any person beating, hurting, or striking any

---

[34] *Rec. Cty. Ct. Hamp.* 104–105; *Rec.* 181. Upon complaint of some of the principal inhabitants of Suffield, the court also declared the town meeting null and void and of no effect and directed a new meeting for the election of selectmen, constable, and other officers.

[35] *Rec. Cty. Ct. Hamp.* 161.

other person might be compelled to pay the party struck, as well as a fine to the county at the discretion of the court. Since the circumstances surrounding each breach of the peace might vary widely, it was left to the court to impose such penalties as in their discretion might seem just, equal, and proportionate to the merit of the offense.[36]

However, even prior to this law there was manifest in case of breaches of the peace a tendency to award compensatory damages to an injured party, as well as to impose fines of five or ten shillings.[37] In an aggravated case the offender might be bound over to the County Court. For example, at the March 1675 County Court James Brown, having been bound over by John Pynchon to answer the complaint of John Graves of Hatfield for breach of the peace in falling upon and beating complainant, was adjudged to be whipped with ten stripes, to pay a three-pound fine to the county and twenty shillings as damages to Graves.[38]

In other cases Pynchon might find the complaint a "squobling business," but nevertheless impose a five-shilling fine for breach of the peace. In a May 1697 entry the offender, having compounded the damages, was fined six shillings and court costs, Pynchon seeing no reason to bind him over to the Sessions, "he being Penitent and very Ingenious also Ingaging watchfulness and good cariage for future." [39]

In one case, in July 1679, in which John Pope complained of being abused and struck by Philip Matoone, he tendered an oath that he stood in fear of his life, and craved the peace of Matoone. Pynchon ordered Matoone bound in the sum of £10 for his appearance at the next County Court and in the meantime to keep the peace. At the September 1679 County Court Matoone, confessing his fault and promising to carry himself better in the future, was discharged of his bond.[40] In another case in 1681 a runaway Negro who stole a knife from Anthony Dorchester and then attempted to draw a cutlass on him was committed to prison to remain there until discharged by authority. The County Court records show his imprisonment but not his discharge. When John Stewart was accused of stabbing John Bliss and endangering his life, the offender was "quickly after the fact done committed to prison" by Pynchon and not bound over to the County Court until Bliss was out of danger.[41]

Closely akin are cases involving use of abusive language. Although this was not a specified offense under the commonwealth laws, it had

[36] *Col. Laws Mass., 1672* 11.
[37] *Rec.* 83, 89, 147, 172, 177, 199, 232.
[38] *Pynchon Waste Book for Hampshire* 126.
[39] *Rec.* 160, 208, 233.
[40] *Rec.* 170–171; *Rec. Cty. Ct. Hamp.* 30.
[41] *Rec.* 178–179; *Rec. Cty. Ct. Hamp.* 52, 132.

been punished by the Court of Assistants from the early years of settlement. In these cases covering the period from 1661 to 1678, punishment ranged from reproves to forty-shilling fines.[42]

A few cases involved abuse of the watch, another offense not specifically treated in the commonwealth laws, but which was punished by the Court of Assistants and at the county court level. In May 1674 a five-shilling fine for abusing the watch was imposed, although apparently Pynchon considered the conduct of the watch provocative. In August 1690 John Crowfoot and John Buck, participants in a drunken brawl described in considerable detail in the *Record,* were sentenced to be whipped for abuse of the watch, among other offenses.[43]

Fines in the amount of ten shillings for drunkenness, as provided in the commonwealth laws, are found scattered through the *Record.*[44] Except for the bibulous misadventures of Sam Owen in the widow Barnard's house, none of the entries has the colorful detail of the Crowfoot and Buck incident. In one case a fine of three shillings, four pence for being in drink, rather than drunk, was imposed.[45] The term "disguised with drink" found frequently in the records of the County Court for Essex, for one, is not used in the *Record.*

The institution of the pound with the inevitable pound breaches and rescue of cattle or swine going to pound would seem a likely source for breaches of the peace.[46] Although the offenses were specifically covered in the commonwealth laws, only two instances involving pound rescues are found in the *Record*—one in 1679, the other in 1687.[47] In several cases, after the period of the First Charter, group offenders engaging in foolish or high-spirited actions were let off with admonitions by John Pynchon.[48]

The task of preservation of the peace encompassed the ordering of family relations. In May 1655, John Stebbins, being bound in the amount of forty pounds to appear and answer the charge of misbehaving toward his aged father was discharged when "there was not found full proofe of such evill carriage." Under the colony laws a disobedient and disorderly child might be punished by whipping,

---

[42] 1 *Hamp. Cty. Probate Ct. Rec.* 8; *Rec.* 135, 162; *Rec. Cty. Ct. Hamp.* 5. Cf. *Rec.* 164.

[43] *Rec.* 153, 209–210. See also *Rec. Cty. Ct. Hamp.* 127 for the interrogation of Buck by the County Court leading to a confession that the liquor consumed was purchased from an unlicensed seller. For cases in the Court of Assistants see 2 *Rec. Ct. Assts. Mass. Bay* 133, 135.

[44] *Rec.* 91, 102, 163, 166, 167, 172, 194–

195. For the statutory provisions see *Col. Laws Mass., 1660* 163–164; *Col. Laws Mass., 1672* 80.

[45] *Rec.* 162.

[46] For the governing statutory provisions see *Laws and Liberties Mass.* 44–45; *Col. Laws Mass., 1660* 66; *Col. Laws Mass., 1672* 125.

[47] *Rec.* 169, 203. *Cf.* the civil action at *Rec.* 204.

[48] *Rec.* 200, 216–217, 225.

not exceeding ten stripes, or bound over to the County Court.[49] In March 1655/6 Joane Miller, upon complaint by her husband of very evil behavior toward him, was adjudged to receive as many stripes as the commissioners saw cause to inflict. However, because of her earnest protestations of better carriage, the punishment was remitted in favor of a sentence that for the least miscarriage to her husband in the future she was to receive a good whipping well laid on. Actually, there was no express penalty for the offense in the commonwealth laws. Some ten years later, in August 1665, Miller and his wife were bound over to the County Court by Pynchon, "haveing had Sad bickeringe and Strife between themselves." Upon their appearance they owned they had not carried it well with each other formerly but asserted that, since being bound for their appearance, they had lived in peace and quietness. After being admonished by the court they were released of their bond upon promises of better carriage.[50]

On March 25, 1684 the County Court noted that John Hodge of Suffield, presented at the last Springfield court for beating his wife and wasting his time and estate in drinking, had not appeared, although summoned. The clerk was accordingly ordered to inform John Pynchon in writing how the case stood and to desire him to send for the offender, examine him and bind him over to the next court at Springfield or otherwise.[51] The *Record,* however, contains no entry as to any such action by Pynchon. In October 1673 Goodwife Hunter, accused of railing and scolding, was sentenced to be gagged or to be set in a ducking stool and dipped in the water as the law provided—a 1672 enactment providing the first express punishment for scolds. When she failed to elect her punishment, Pynchon ordered her gagged and to stand in the open street for a half hour.[52]

OFFENSES AGAINST PROPERTY

The *Record* reflects the fact that, although burglary and the more serious cases of theft were handled on the County Court or General Sessions of the Peace level, petty pilfering was handled by the courts at Springfield.

At the March 1672 sitting of the County Court, Philip Barsham of Hatfield, having been sent down to John Pynchon upon a charge of theft and bound over, appeared and was fined forty shillings or to

49 *Rec.* 69; *Col. Laws Mass., 1672* 27.

50 *Rec.* 71; *Pynchon Waste Book for Hampshire* 31; 1 *Hamp. Cty. Probate Ct. Rec.* 66.

51 *Rec. Cty. Ct. Hamp.* 73. The laws provided that a man striking his wife, or

vice versa, might be fined not exceeding £10 or such corporal punishment as the County Court should determine. *Col. Laws Mass., 1672* 101.

52 *Rec.* 148. For the 1672 law see *Col. Laws Mass., 1672* 206.

be whipped with fifteen stripes. In addition, he was to pay Eleazir Frary three pounds and costs of court as treble damages for the wheat and flour stolen.[53] However, there is no entry with respect to this case in the *Record*. In July 1674 Benjamin Allyn of Hatfield and James Brown were brought before John Pynchon, examined concerning their breaking into a house at night and stealing a barrel of liquor, and bound over to the next County Court where they received stiff sentences.[54] In August 1686 Joseph Deane, brought before John Pynchon for stealing some clothes and money at Hadley, was ordered jailed unless he found two sureties in the sum of twenty pounds for his appearance at the next County Court.[55]

Among the chronic offenders found in the *Record* are Michael Towsley and his family. Several offenses by members of this family involving theft were handled by Pynchon but ultimately, in 1691, punishment was imposed on the County Court level.[56] A September 1694 incident involved a charge of theft arising out of property taken by way of distress by virtue of the accused's office of clerk of the band at Suffield for a fine taxed for defects in training.[57] This case illustrates the remedy available where extra-judicial distress was resorted to.

In April 1697 William Pierce of Suffield was brought before John Pynchon and John Holyoke, sitting as justices of the peace, and found guilty of entering a house and feloniously taking away certain goods. Since Pierce had confessed his crime and restored the goods and the owner had not prosecuted, he was let off with a light sentence. In August 1699, John Webb was fined ten shillings by Pynchon for theft of a gun, the owner being left to his remedy at law.[58]

In several cases involving property rights the circumstances were unusual. In November 1653 the commissioners ordered William Brookes "for defrauding sundry persons in withholding from them, and converting to his owne use the goods of severall persons" to make satisfaction in the sum of eighteen pounds, besides restoring the principal amounting to nine pounds. The entry is obscure but the order appears to rest upon the theory of an award of treble damages. In March 1686 a number of inhabitants of Windsor, Connecticut were brought before Pynchon for gathering candlewood within the town boundaries of Enfield and burning it into tar. After consulting with the committee for Enfield, Pynchon, "to Moderate the Busyness," de-

[53] *Pynchon Waste Book for Hampshire* 93; 1 *Hamp. Cty. Probate Ct. Rec.* 135.
[54] *Rec.* 155; 1 *Hamp. Cty. Probate Ct. Rec.* 158; *Pynchon Waste Book for Hampshire* 121.
[55] *Rec.* 200.
[56] *Rec.* 186–187, 192, 212; *Rec. Cty. Ct. Hamp.* 144.
[57] *Rec.* 222–223. For the authorizing act see 1 *Acts and Res. Prov. Mass. Bay* 129.
[58] *Rec.* 230–231, 242.

clared forfeit one-half the tar seized and returned the other half to
the intruders. In January 1700/01, when Josiah Marshfield complained that Luke Hitchcock and Joseph Williston had "in a clandestine way tooke a Deed of Sale of Land" by complainant to them
out of the hands of John Holyoke, Pynchon ordered the deed returned to Holyoke but not recorded until all parties were in agreement.[59]

Several cases involved the taking of or damage to animals. In one
1679 case Pynchon imposed the statutory ten-shilling penalty for taking another's horse without leave.[60] While not mentioned in the
Record, a County Court entry for March 28, 1665 shows that Walter
Lee was bound over by the Springfield commissioners on suspicion
of killing a steer of one Cornish at Woronoco. The court, judging
that the evidence was strong against him, ordered that he pay fifty
shillings for the steer, plus costs of court.[61] At the March 30, 1675 session of the County Court Joseph Selden was presented for cutting a
horse and for uttering a falsehood. Selden not appearing, John Pynchon was directed to send for the offender, examine him, and deal
with him accordingly. However, the Record contains no record of any
action by Pynchon in this matter. In March 1673/4 when a dog killed
a sheep, the owner agreed to hang his dog as required by law.[62]

Several miscellaneous cases involved injury or threat of injury to
property rights. A September 27, 1681 County Court entry reveals
that Peter Hendricks (Hennix) was bound over by John Pynchon in
a bond of thirty pounds to answer with respect to burning a house
in Northampton. Although Hendricks did not appear, the court discharged him of his bond, since he had been given some latitude as to
his appearance and nothing further was chargeable against him.[63]
Under the First Charter smoking outdoors was prohibited as a fire
hazard. In May 1649, following the reading of the printed Laws and
Liberties of 1648, several persons were fined ten shillings for taking
tobacco out of doors. In March 1652/3, two persons were presented
for the same offense.[64]

DEFAMATION

From the early years of the colony the Court of Assistants treated
defamation or slander as a criminal offense, although not prohibited
by any specific law or order. At least one Quarterly Court, that at Salem, followed suit. Perhaps the courts tacitly accepted the view of the

59 Rec. 59, 196–197, 251.
60 Rec. 171. For the law see Col. Laws Mass., 1672 19.
61 Pynchon Waste Book for Hampshire 20; 1 Hamp. Cty. Probate Ct. Rec. 48.
62 Pynchon Waste Book for Hampshire 130; 1 Hamp. Cty. Probate Ct. Rec. 163; Rec. 150.
63 Rec. Cty. Ct. Hamp. 50.
64 Rec. 31, 56. For the law see Laws and Liberties Mass. 50.

Star Chamber that such offences tended to breach of the peace (12 *Coke Rep.* 35). In 1641 the General Court ordered (the order appears as follows at the start of the 1672 laws) that "no mans person shall be arrested, restrained, banished, dismembered, nor any wayes punished; no man shall be deprived of his wife or children, no mans goods or estate shall be taken away from him, nor any wayes indamaged, under colour of Law, or countenance of Authority, unless it be by virtue or equity of some express Law of the Country warranting the same, established by a General Court, and sufficiently published; or in the case of the defect of a Law, in any particular case, by the word of God." On its face the 1641 order appears to exclude any implied reception in the colony of the laws of England establishing criminal offenses. However, after 1641, although no express law making defamation or slander a criminal offense is found, such conduct was still generally regarded as criminal (by the Court of Assistants and the County Courts of Hampshire, Suffolk, Essex, and Norfolk, among others) —whether regarded as such by reason of the word of God or of tendency to breach of the peace does not appear. (It is believed that slander offenses were not regarded as covered by the law against lying; the penalties imposed for slander are not consistent with those provided by law for lying.) As indicated above, this was not peculiar to the offense of defamation; it was also true of such offenses as lascivious conduct, abusive speeches, and certain contempts of authority.

How, as a practical matter, the inhabitants of western Massachusetts received notice of the specific laws and orders of the General Court, prior to receipt of a copy of the printed *Laws and Liberties* of 1648, is far from clear. There is no indication that any copy in manuscript form of the laws distributed earlier to some of the colony towns was made available to Springfield.

The first reference to defamation or slander as a crime in western Massachusetts, as previously noted, is found in a May 29–30, 1649 entry in the *Record* in which the widow Marshfield complained against Mary Parsons of Springfield for reporting her to be suspected for a witch. Pynchon found that the accused had defamed the good name of the widow Marshfield and sentenced her whipped with twenty lashes, unless she procured payment of three pounds to the widow toward the reparation of her good name. The *Record* does not show the payment of the money, but, at William Pynchon's later examination of Hugh Parsons on suspicion of witchcraft, payment is revealed in a statement by the widow Marshfield.[65] Since not an ex-

[65] *Rec.* 32–33; Drake, *Annals of Witchcraft in New England* 250–251. For early libel or slander cases before the Court of Assistants see 2 *Rec. Ct. Assts. Mass. Bay* 65, 72, 93.

press offense by law, the measure of punishment and the scope of the offense were matters of judicial discretion. Presumably the rationale for regarding defamatory statements as criminal offenses was that they tended to provoke breaches of the peace or perhaps that "Truth in Words, as well as in Actions is required of all men." [66]

In the next defamation case, in April 1655, John Stiles of Windsor complained against John Bennett for defaming his wife in saying she was a "light woman." When Bennett was unable to substantiate the accusation, it was ordered that he be whipped with eight lashes and pay a fine of forty shillings to the complainant. This is consistent with English practice, in criminal proceedings, which permitted a spoken, as opposed to a written, defamatory statement to be justified by proving that it was true. A September 1658 case in which John Elmer complained that Goodwife Hilton had accused him of theft was settled among the parties. [67]

The other defamation proceedings found in the *Record* are under the Second Charter. The March 1697/8 case involving Abraham Temple was transferred to the Court of General Sessions of the Peace. A week later, a ten-shilling fine was imposed for publishing a false report that Westwood Cooke had given false evidence under oath. An appeal taken to the next Court of General Sessions of the Peace was afterward withdrawn. In December 1698 an offender was discharged when he acknowledged his offense in imputing theft. In October 1701, an accused was convicted of spreading false reports tending to the defamation of particular persons and fined five shillings. The sentence of ten lashes for a Negress in January 1701/2 was based in large part upon defamatory statements about members of the Glover family. [68] Whether this jurisdiction was exercised under the law providing punishment for lying is not clear.

CONTEMPT OF AUTHORITY

Only one case in the *Record* involved contempt of the ministry. The punishment inflicted, a five-shilling fine, was far short of that provided in the laws for reviling the office or person of a minister. [69] An earlier case involving the same minister was handled at the County Court level. In March 1669 John Matthews of Springfield, having been bound over by John Pynchon to answer for his "exceedinge contemptuous behavior" toward the Reverend Pelatiah Glover, appeared at the County Court, and, the evidence being pro-

[66] See the preamble to the law entitled "Lying." *Col. Laws Mass., 1672* 91.
[67] *Rec.* 72, 75.

[68] *Rec.* 235–36A, 244, 253–254.
[69] *Rec.* 138. See *Col. Laws Mass., 1672* 61.

duced and read, it appeared that his carriage was "very odious and Shamefull" toward Glover "much after the custome of the Quakers." Accordingly, Matthews was sentenced to fifteen stripes and ordered bound in the sum of ten pounds for his good behavior till the September court and to pay costs of court.[70] While the commonwealth laws extensively regulated the activities of Quakers, this sect did not constitute a law enforcement problem in western Massachusetts.

A September 27, 1692 entry of the Court of General Sessions of the Peace relates that Edward Burlison of Suffield had previously been presented to John Pynchon by the grand juryman for that town for "Scurrilous vile Speeches" against the town's late minister. When Burlison, having been summoned, failed to appear in court, the witnesses were sworn and the clerk directed to issue out a special warrant to the Suffield constable to apprehend Burlison and bring him before Pynchon who was to proceed against him "according to Law for Contempt of Authority and for his Lying and Scandalous Speeches against said Mr. Philips," or to bind him over for his appearance at the next court.[71] However, no entry appears with respect to Burlison in the *Record*.

The punishment imposed upon John Crowfoot was for contempt of the constable among other things. Another offense of this nature is found in December 1670 when Joseph Leonard and Sam Fellows were brought before John Pynchon for their contemptuous behavior toward the constable of Hatfield. Bound over to the County Court, they were fined in substantial amounts for contempt of judicial authority, as well as of the constable, and for unlawful trading with the Indians.[72] In January 1677/8, James Carver of Hatfield, venting his rage upon the constable for interfering with his attempt to "mischief" John Downing, was sentenced to pay fairly substantial fines and charges. Earlier, in 1659, John Matthews, presented for refusal to obey a summons sent by authority and for his "contemptuous and high carriage" toward the process server, who may have been a deputy constable, was fined five shillings.[73] In two other cases small fines were imposed for contempt of the constable. One, in 1673, involved refusal to go post with a letter to Quabaug; the other, in February 1675/6, refusal to go scouting on horse.[74]

In a related type of case Stephen Lee was presented by a Westfield tithingman at the Court of General Sessions of the Peace of Septem-

[70] *Pynchon Waste Book for Hampshire* 63; 1 *Hamp. Cty. Probate Ct. Rec.* 101.
[71] *Rec. Cty. Ct. Hamp.* 159–160.
[72] *Rec.* 137; 1 *Hamp. Cty. Probate Ct. Rec.* 128; *Pynchon Waste Book for Hampshire* 84.

[73] *Rec.* 83, 164–165.
[74] *Rec.* 146, 160. See also the attitude of John Woodcock toward a warrant to the constable to distrain for damages. *Rec.* 6.

ber 27, 1692, for refusing to listen when reproved for entertaining young persons in his house "to sing and make a rout at unseasonable time of Night, viz. after midnight." The justices agreed that John Pynchon should send for Lee and deal with him according to the merits of the case, but no entry appears in the *Record* respecting this matter.[75]

An entry in the County Court records in March 1665 reveals an instance of punishment for contempt of the Springfield commissioners. Walter Lee, being presented for profaning the Sabbath at Woronoco by threshing corn, for calling Isaac Shelden "a member of old nick and a member of the Devill and for his contempt of the authority in Springfeild in Saying he thought he might as well beleeve his boy when he Said Springfeild Commissioners threatned him with the Stocks and promised him Some new clothes as the Said Commissioners in declaring what his boy Said against him," the court fined him twenty shillings to the county and four shillings, sixpence allowance to three witnesses. This was a mild sentence as the laws provided for punishment by "whipping, fine, imprisonment, disfranchisment or banishment, as the quality or measure of the offense shall deserve." The only case of contempt of court in the *Record* is found in December 1684 when Obadiah Abbee, strenuously arguing a point of law with John Pynchon, exceeded the proper bounds.[76]

NEGLECT OF DUTY

Several cases involved neglect of various duties imposed by law. In August 1698 two former constables of Springfield were found guilty of neglecting to collect the town rates committed to their care and fined forty shillings each as provided by law.[77] The laws under the First Charter imposed fines up to five shillings upon any person who upon lawful warning refused to watch or ward in person or by some other sufficient to the service. Two cases appearing in the *Record* involved this situation.[78]

When William Hunter harbored his daughter, who had unlawfully left service, instead of sending her back to her master, he was fined twenty shillings "due by Law to the Country" but sentence was

[75] *Rec. Cty. Ct. Hamp.* 160.

[76] *Pynchon Waste Book for Hampshire* 22; 1 *Hamp. Cty. Probate Ct. Rec.* 54; *Rec.* 191. For the applicable law see *Col. Laws Mass., 1672* 36. See also the admonition by the Reverend Moxon of Henry Gregory for criticizing a jury verdict (*Rec.* 8); the refusal of Francis Ball to pay some wampum to an Indian complainant as or-

dered by William Pynchon (*ibid.* 25); and the five-pound fine imposed on Joseph Fellows by the County Court for contempt of John Pynchon and the Hatfield constable (1 *Hamp. Cty. Probate Ct. Rec.* 128).

[77] *Rec.* 191, 237–239.

[78] *Rec.* 61, 207; *Col. Laws Mass., 1672* 154.

respited until another time.[79] However, it is not clear which law was intended by this reference. At the County Court of March 31, 1691, George Granger of Suffield, being presented for neglecting the public worship of God, pleaded his sickness, weakness, and want of clothes. The court ordered that Pynchon send for and admonish him, but no such action appears in the *Record*.[80]

VIOLATION OF REGULATORY LAWS

As already noted, the sale of liquors was subject to extensive regulation in Massachusetts Bay in the seventeenth century. A County Court entry of September 26, 1682 records that Thomas Day, being warned, had appeared earlier before Pynchon as magistrate to answer for his breach of the law in selling liquors in small quantities without a license. The evidence being read, the Major informed Day that there were three witnesses to his having rum in his house and offering it for sale and three witnesses who had bought rum from him and that his breaking of the law was proved by this testimony. Pynchon therefore advised Day, a tithingman, to pay five pounds to the county treasurer rather than have the matter brought out further. However, Day replied that he would appeal to the County Court and there be tried by a jury. Pynchon accordingly referred the whole case to the County Court where a jury found Day guilty "if Testimonys to the same thing though not the same time be valid and Sufficient in Law." The court, judging "Such Testimonys valid and Sufficient" and "this course of Lodging and retailing Liquors without License . . . so Contrary to Laws and the good Intent and End of the Law forbidding such practises," fined Day five pounds and charges.[81]

In January 1700/1 Josiah Marshfield came before Pynchon and informed against himself for selling strong liquor without a license. At the same time he informed against Joseph Williston and/or his wife for the same offense. The *Record* is damaged at this point so that the exact disposition of these cases cannot be determined. However, the records of the Court of General Sessions of the Peace indicate that both cases were transferred to that court which fined Williston and Marshfield four pounds apiece.[82] A December 3, 1700 entry in the same records reveals that Pynchon and John Holyoke, sitting as two justices of the peace, had fined Jonathan Pease of Enfield four pounds for selling strong drink without a license but this fine is not entered in the *Record*.[83]

[79] *Rec.* 141.
[80] *Rec. Cty. Ct. Hamp.* 138.
[81] *Ibid.* 59, 67.

[82] *Rec.* 248, 253; *Hamp. Rec. Ct. Pleas* 124–125.
[83] *Ibid.* 103.

Several cases involved unauthorized trading with or selling liquor to the Indians. The widow Horton's case in October 1640 involved the sale of her husband's gun to Indians.[84] In June 1655 Robert Munro was fined five pounds for selling liquor to the Indians without a license. In the same month the Springfield commissioners issued an "order of restraint" prohibiting Robert Ashley and his wife (who apparently kept the ordinary) from selling wine or strong waters to the Indians without a license. As far as the *Record* shows, this order was issued without the benefit of any trial or hearing. At the March 1662 sitting of the commissioners at Northampton, with the powers of a County Court, John Sackett was fined forty shillings for selling liquor to the Indians and one hundred pounds for violating the law against trading for furs with the Indians; however, the latter fine was remitted because of weakness of proof.[85]

While not referred to in the *Record,* entries in the County Court records for September 1670 show that John Pynchon, upon complaint of certain Indians, bound over to the County Court John Westcarr of Hadley and Benjamin Waite of Hatfield for selling liquor to the Indians without a license. Both were found guilty of selling large quantities of liquor to the Indians, Westcarr being fined forty pounds and Waite forty-four, and both appealed to the Court of Assistants. At the appellate level the magistrates and jury disagreed; ultimately the fines were remitted in part.[86] At the September 1671 County Court Samuel Greene, Joseph Butler, and Samuel Martin were fined for trading prohibited goods with the Indians at Pochasick, selling liquors, powder, shot, and lead and buying beaver skins. The entry notes that Butler and Martin had been bound over to the County Court by Major Pynchon in the previous May; however, no entry of such action appears in the *Record.*[87] The unlawful trading activities of Joseph Leonard and Sam Fellows of Hatfield have already been noted.

A September 1681 County Court entry reveals that, complaint having been made to Pynchon that Samuel Ely of Springfield had sold forbidden drink to the Indians, Ely was examined and confessed that he had let the Indians have some cider. The court, taking notice of his "Ingenuity" in confessing his offense and desiring to encourage others to such conduct, let Ely off with an admonishment and advised him "to beware of Such dangerous practices in time to

84 *Rec.* 12. *Cf.* the ten-pound fine imposed by the Court of Assistants in 1637 for lending a gun to an Indian for four days. 2 *Rec. Ct. Assts. Mass. Bay* 71.
85 *Rec.* 69–70; 1 *Hamp. Cty. Probate Ct. Rec.* 8, 11.

86 *Pynchon Waste Book for Hampshire* 73, 75, 91; 4 *Rec. Mass. Bay (Part II)* 375.
87 *Pynchon Waste Book for Hampshire* 91–92.

Come, that he do no more So offend, and become an occasion of bringing down Gods Judgmente upon the Land, as is most Certaine the Custome and trade of Selling Strong drinkes thus in this manner to them doth demerit, in as much, as such their Cravings of such drinkes are not to Satisfy needy Nature, but beastlike to fil a Sensual appetite." [88]

OFFENSES INVOLVING INDIANS

Considering the frontier position of Springfield, relatively few other cases involving Indians are found in the *Record*. The most serious offense occurred in May 1660 when Thomas Miller and his wife were beaten by some Indians from the Nipmuck country. An Indian who broke into Rowland Thomas' house in June 1650 and stole some goods was not brought to justice but a sachem at Woronoco finally gave some wampum to William Pynchon in satisfaction.[89] This incident reveals that in the case of Indian offenders justice might have to yield to expediency. In May 1671 an Indian was found guilty of breaking into Samuel Bliss's house on the Sabbath and stealing some wampum. Two months later two Indians were punished for stealing some wampum and other goods from Obadiah Cooley's house. In the last two cases corporal punishment was imposed.[90]

Two Indians, charged in December 1674 with stealing a trap eighteen months earlier, were discharged when other Indians engaged that the offenders would return the trap and pay some wampum toward the charges. A runaway Indian from New York was apprehended by hue and cry in November 1694 after stealing a horse and other goods. Following examination by John Pynchon, although none offered to prosecute, he was committed to prison by mittimus and later returned to his New York master—an example of informal extradition.[91] At a March 1664/5 sitting of the Springfield commissioners an Indian who owned to breaking the windows of Captain Pynchon's farm house some years ago and to other misdemeanors was ordered to pay treble damages.[92] Despite the legendary aboriginal thirst for strong waters, only two cases of Indian drunkenness are found in the *Record*, one in 1662 and one in 1674; in both cases ten-shilling fines were imposed.[93]

A few cases concerned damage to the person or property of Indians. In May 1648, for striking an Indian squaw, Francis Ball was

[88] *Rec. Cty. Ct. Hamp.* 51.
[89] *Rec.* 39–40, 87–88.
[90] *Rec.* 139–140, 141.
[91] *Rec.* 156, 224.
[92] *Rec.* 132. See also 1 *Hist. and Proc. Pocumtuck Valley Mem. Asso.* 173.

[93] *Rec.* 100, 156. An examination of the *Pynchon Account Books* would undoubtedly disclose other fines. See 1 *Hist. and Proc. Pocumtuck Valley Mem. Asso.* 79.

ordered by William Pynchon to pay the injured Indian two hands of wampum, but Ball refused to make payment. Two years later, William Pynchon, with the advice of the Reverend Moxon and others who were present, adjudged that Thomas Miller receive fifteen lashes for breach of the peace in striking an Indian with the butt end of his gun. However, Miller avoided the whipping by paying down four fathom of wampum.[94] In August 1659, when some Indians complained of damage done by cattle to their cornfields on the western side of the Connecticut River, the damage was viewed and judged at eight shillings. The Springfield commissioners accordingly ordered the constable to raise this amount from the inhabitants on the west side of the River. In June 1664 the commissioners, finding that some youths had damaged a canoe left by an Indian, ordered the constable to gather up for the Indian twopence apiece from each person implicated.[95] At the March 1665 County Court an Indian sought help in respect of a sentence of the Springfield commissioners taking two guns from him for Thomas Miller. The court ordered the commissioners to review the case, but no entry appears in the *Record*.[96]

VIOLATION OF TOWN ORDERS

In outlining the Massachusetts judicial system note was taken of the power of the town freemen or selectmen to make orders of a "prudential nature." Although Agawam had not been recognized as a town by the General Court, on February 14, 1638/9, the same day that they commissioned William Pynchon with judicial powers, the inhabitants issued the first of many "town" orders. One provided a five-shilling fine for anyone selling or transferring out of the plantation a canoe under five years old; the other provided for payment for damage done by cattle put over the River to graze in violation of a restrictive order.[97] In the next few years a number of town orders covered a wide variety of subjects such as attendance at training exercises, trading, selling or giving powder to Indians (a forty-shilling penalty), fixing laborers' wages, keeping highways clean and in repair, felling "canoe trees," failure to possess certain arms and ammunition, failure to possess ladders (as protection against fires on roofs), carrying fire in the open without covering, making and maintaining ditches, allowing strangers to live on one's land without the consent of the inhabitants, and fixing prices of sawed wood.[98]

---

94 *Rec.* 25, 39.
95 *Rec.* 82, 104–105.
96 *Pynchon Waste Book for Hampshire* 22; 1 *Hamp. Cty. Probate Ct. Rec.* 52.

97 1 Burt, *Hist. Springfield* 164.
98 *Ibid.* 165–171.

The first election of selectmen was held on September 26, 1644, when by general vote of the town it was agreed that Henry Smith, Thomas Cooper, Samuel Chapin, Richard Sikes, and Henry Burt:

. . . shall have power to order in all the prudential affaires of the Towne, to prevent anythinge they shall judge to be to the dammage of the Towne or to ordr any thing they shall judge to be for the good of the Towne: and in these affaires they shall have power for a yeere space and that they, 5, or any three of them shall also be given full power and virtue, alsoe to here complaints, to Arbitrate controversies, to lay out High ways, to make Bridges, to repayr High wais . . . to see to the Scouring of Ditches, and to the killing of wolves, and to training up of children in some good caling, or any other thing they shall judge to be to the profitt of the Towne.[99]

The September 1646 appointment of selectmen specifically authorized them to impose five-shilling fines upon those neglecting to keep their chimneys clean or carrying fire uncovered in the open. In the event of refusal to pay such fines the selectmen were "to complaine to the magistrate who will grant his warrant to distraine for the said fine." Their authority was also "to reach to reconsile disgrements and disputes between neighbor and neighbor."[100]

Later town orders, most of which were issued by 1653, covered such subjects as sweeping of chimneys, taking canoes without leave, absence from town meetings, restrictions on grazing of cattle, work on highways, removal of wood and timber, attendance at town meetings, the burning of tar, the keeping of swine, clearing of highways, transporting building lumber outside the town limits, watering hemp or flax in streams near habitations, gathering of hops, recording of land grants, maintenance of fences, the location of houses, entertaining and selling lands to strangers, regulation of wages, refusal to accept town offices, leaving gates open, laying out land boundaries, children playing near the meetinghouse, riding of horses in town, regulation of seating in the meetinghouse, misbehavior of children in the meetinghouse, misbehavior at town meetings, and the gathering of turpentine.[101]

Considering the wide range of subject matters covered by town orders, there are relatively few instances of violations of town orders to be found in the *Record*. On November 17, 1648 John Clark was presented by Griffith Jones, presumably one of the recently elected "presenters" for the town, for leaving an offensive carrion by the

[99] *Ibid.* 175–176.
[100] *Ibid.* 185.
[101] *Ibid.* 177–178, 180–181, 183–184, 186–189, 191–194, 200–217, 229, 252–255, 256– 257, 259, 269–270, 273–276, 280, 307, 314, 317, 334–335, 359, 371–373, 379, 385–386, 405–406, 418–419, 423–424, 428–430; 2 *ibid.* 54–71, 123–124, 145, 154–155.

brookside. Whether this was regarded as a violation of a town order or came within the category of "any other misdemeanor" which the presenter had authority to present is not clear. The next May a number of inhabitants were presented for leaving their oxen over the Connecticut River in violation of a town order. In March 1652/3 the wife of Griffith Jones was presented for carrying uncovered fire in the open and fined five shillings. During the following November seven persons were presented for unspecified breaches of town orders and ordered to pay sums ranging from sixpence to ten shillings.[102] At the March 27, 1660 court three selectmen of Springfield presented a complaint against John Wood for staying in the town contrary to a legal warning to depart. (Wood in May 1659 had been fined forty shillings for taking up residence in the town without consent of the inhabitants, contrary to town order.)[103] In July 1685 several inhabitants complained against the appointed fence viewers for neglect of their duties in violation of the colony laws and of a town order. In February 1687/8 suit was brought for penalties for taking some swine out of pound in violation of both a town order and a "Publike act of the Council."[104]

THE ROLE OF THE CHURCH

The role of the church in the administration of justice in western Massachusetts in the seventeenth century is difficult to assess since the only church records remaining for the period are those for Northampton and Westfield. A recent study based largely upon unpublished manuscript records makes reference to only four instances of church intervention in western Massachusetts during the seventeenth century. In 1682 John Maundesly, charged by the church at Westfield with violation of the Eighth, Ninth, and Tenth Commandments in presenting a petition to the General Court, confessed his errors, and was restored. In 1685 Joseph Pomeroy, constable at Westfield, publicly confessed in church his embezzlement of county funds. In 1697 Abigail Bush, apparently suspended, was restored with an admonition to be "very tender of Parentall honour." In 1698 the church at Northampton excommunicated John Taylor who, upon release from the Springfield jail to attend church, profaned the Sabbath by absenting himself from public worship to elude authority.[105]

102 *Rec.* 28, 33–34, 56.
103 *Rec.* 85; 1 Burt, *Hist. Springfield* 264, 276.
104 *Rec.* 193, 204.
105 See Oberholzer, *Delinquent Saints* (1956) 59, 124, 190–191, 206–208. For the manuscript sources see 1 *The Publick Records of the Church, 1679–1836* 125–129, at the Westfield Athenaeum, Westfield, Mass., and 1 *Northampton First Congregational Church Minutes, 1661–1833* 25, in the possession of said church.

The *Record* itself shows the Reverend Moxon present on several occasions in a role other than litigant but there is no indication of any close relation between church and commonwealth in the administration of justice on the local level.

Certain generalizations can be made concerning the criminal jurisdiction appearing in the *Record*. The various jurisdictions exercised ranged widely in taking cognizance of different offenses, but there was at no time any substantial volume of any one class of offenses. While jurisdiction was exercised in various capacities, there was no great contrast in the nature of the offenses handled from time to time, except perhaps for the earliest years and the years under the Second Charter. In terms of volume and variety, the period during which John Pynchon acted as magistrate is foremost. Another outstanding feature is the flexibility of administration, both in taking jurisdiction without seeking support in the letter of the laws and in awarding punishment. Lastly, the significance of the magistrate or justice of the peace in examining and binding over offenders to courts on the county level and in dealing with cases referred back from such level can be seen. From the first volume of County Court records for Hampshire it appears that Pynchon was responsible for almost one-half of the offenders bound over to that court; most of the remainder were bound over by the commissioners for Northampton, Hadley, and Hatfield.

In evaluating the jurisdiction exercised in the *Record* from a statistical standpoint it must be kept in mind that the County Court of Hampshire exercised concurrent jurisdiction in minor offenses for about twenty-three years. Of the almost two hundred offenses handled in the first volume of the County Court records (to 1675), many were minor offenses such as breach of the peace, drunkenness, swearing, lying, abusive speeches, neglect of duty, theft, lascivious carriage, profanation of the Sabbath, and offenses by Indians. The use by the County Court of grand jury presentments served to account for a substantial volume of the jurisdiction exercised.

A comparison of the jurisdiction in criminal matters appearing in the *Record* with that exercised on comparable judicial levels in the Bay during the period of the First Charter (county court level until 1665, magistrate or commissioners level from 1665 to 1686) shows a much greater volume of cases handled in the Bay, covering, particularly on the county level, a wider variety of offenses in a more settled, but less homogeneous, society, with a better defined and, to some extent, hardened criminal class. However, it is obvious that in both areas law enforcement was primarily based upon the laws and orders of the General Court. As to offenses not specifically covered by such laws and orders, there was no cleavage in treatment between the two geographic areas. It seems likely that both found guidance in this respect in the activities of the Court of Assistants, or perhaps in the word of God. If there was any significant reliance upon substantive laws supposedly received from England, it is not patent in the *Record* or in any of the printed and manuscript material examined for comparative purposes. This conclusion is not intended to derogate in any way from the importance of the laws of England as precedents or models in founding the laws and orders of the General Court and in furnishing standards in procedural matters not covered by colony laws and orders.

V I I I. Criminal Procedure

THE Massachusetts laws of the seventeenth century devoted much space to the enumeration and description of criminal offenses and to granting jurisdiction to various courts over such offenses. However, little space was devoted to the procedures to be employed in the exercise of the jurisdiction thus conferred. Perhaps such neglect was beneficial in that it permitted each court to shape its procedure, to some degree, in accordance with its own circumstances.

ACCUSATORY DEVICES

The cases appearing in the *Record* and related County Court records reveal that flexibility was the principal characteristic of the initial step in setting in motion the judicial process in criminal matters. Thus, such step might be found to take any one of the following forms:

(a) Complaint or presentment by a private person;
(b) Complaint or presentment by a constable or the watch, including those cases in which an offender was taken without warrant by the constable or watch and brought before the court for examination;
(c) Complaint or presentment by the selectmen of Springfield or another town;
(d) Presentment by the elected town presenters of Springfield;
(e) Presentment by tithingmen;
(f) Presentment by a grand juror;
(g) *Qui tam* action by an informer;
(h) Reference from the County Court or the Court of General Sessions of the Peace;
(i) The court's own view of the offense.
(It should not be assumed that all these devices were in use for the entire period.)

Conspicuously absent from this list is presentment or indictment by a grand jury. No use was made of the grand jury by any of the courts whose acts are recorded in the *Record;* the evidence in the supplemental Registry of Probate material is equivocal. Largely because of the sparse population, the grand jury did not thrive as an institution in western Massachusetts. Although it was employed by the County Court, petty jurors were compelled to double as grand jurors. Formal informations were not used as there were no commonwealth or Crown attorneys or clerks of the peace. A few instances appear in the *Record* and the supplemental Registry of Probate material of the use of a jury of inquest in case of "any suddain, untimely or unnatural death."[1]

While it received little recognition in the laws, the most widely used device for initiating judicial action in criminal offenses during the period covered was the complaint made to the court by a private person. This was in effect what Lambard stated was most aptly termed a "suit of the party"—whether in the form of a bill, plaint, complaint, or information.[2] Normally the complainant was the person injured or aggrieved, as in the case of offenses such as assault and battery, defamation, and theft.[3] In a few cases the complaint might stem from the relation of master and servant, husband and wife, or parent and child. A 1668 law provided that any person, whether or not twenty-one years of age, might "inform and present any misdemeanor to any magistrate, Grand-juryman or court." However, little use of "presentments" by private persons appears in the records examined, with the exception, perhaps, of those made to grand jurymen on the county level. No requirement appears that such complaints be made in writing or in any particular form and most complaints probably were made orally. However, a notation of August 1681 shows Jonathan Winchel "Presenting his suspition" of Robert Old taking away a bushel of complainant's wheat meal from Westfield. Old being sent for, what Winchel had presented in writing was read to him. No requirement that complaints or presentments be made under oath was found, nor any evidence that complainants were bound or summoned to prosecute, the practice in some instances by the county courts.[4]

[1] For the inquest juries see *Rec.* 87, 158; 1 *Hamp. Cty. Probate Ct. Rec.* 3. For the law see *Col. Laws Mass., 1672* 39. Perhaps several presentments made at the September 1661 court held by the commissioners were made by petty jurors acting as a grand jury. 1 *Hamp. Cty. Probate Ct. Rec.* 8.

[2] For some acts referring to complaints under the Second Charter see 1 *Acts and Res. Prov. Mass. Bay* 136, 138, 219, 256. See Lambard, *Eirenarcha* (1607) 502.

[3] See also the appointment by the commissioners in March 1661, when the widow Bliss complained of the annoyance from Elizur Holyoke's mill. 1 *Hamp. Cty. Probate Ct. Rec.* 5.

[4] For the Winchel "presentment" see *Rec.* 180. For the 1668 law see *Col. Laws Mass., 1672* 2. The 1652 law entitled "Inditements" appears to contemplate that a written complaint, presentment or information be "made and exhibited" but most of the complaints in the *Record* would be

Next in importance to complaint by a private person was the complaint or presentment by a town constable. While the role of the constable in criminal law enforcement was of greater importance prior to 1692, the *Record* does not reflect its decline as sharply as does a reading of the laws passed under the Second Charter with their emphasis, derived from English practice, upon the role of the sheriff. By laws under the First Charter every constable was given full power where no magistrate was near, to make, sign, and put forth pursuits or hues and cries after murderers, manslayers, peace-breakers, thieves, robbers, burglars, and other capital offenders. He also had power to apprehend without warrant such as were overtaken with drink, those swearing, Sabbath-breaking, or lying, vagrant persons, and night-walkers. The constable was to act upon his own view of the offenses or upon present information from others. He was directed to make search for all such persons, either on the Sabbath or any other day when there was occasion, in all houses licensed to sell beer or wine, or in any other suspected or disorderly places, and to apprehend offenders and keep them in custody until they could be brought before a magistrate for further examination.[5]

Under the law regulating inns the constable was given power, in the case of persons found drunk or in their drunkenness abusing the constable or others, to commit such persons to safekeeping or imprisonment or to take bond for their appearance, as he saw cause, and to inform the next magistrate thereof. If there was no magistrate in town, he was to convent such person before one or more commissioners for ending small causes. Several acts gave constables power to apprehend without warrant persons found at Quaker meetings. A 1662 act provided that constables might apprehend vagabonds, with or without further warrant, and bring them before the next magistrate for examination. The law regulating Indians provided that any person finding any Indian with strong liquors, obtained without authority, was empowered to seize such liquors and deliver them to the constable of the town where the Indians were found, together with the persons of the Indians, to be conveyed before a magistrate or commissioner with power to deal with such cases.[6]

Various laws regarding the watch gave power to the constable or

excepted from the operation of this law. *Ibid.* 79. No fine distinction is drawn between complaints and presentments in the County Court records. Some offenders are "presented and complained of"; a complaint might be presented; a complaint at one session might be designated a presentment at another. For complainants bound

or summoned to prosecute see 1 *Hamp. Cty. Probate Ct. Rec.* 41, 89, 132; 2 *Rec. and Files Quart. Cts. Essex Cty. Mass.* 70. For what amounted to a complaint under oath see 2 *ibid.* 152.

[5] *Col. Laws Mass., 1672* 31.
[6] *Ibid.* 77, 153, 234, 250.

the watch to apprehend certain offenders without warrant. The laws of 1672, for instance, provided that:

And the Constables in every Town from time to time, are hereby enjoyned to give in their charge to Watch-men, that they duely examine all Night-Walkers after ten of the clock at night (unless they be known peaceable Inhabitants) to inquire whether they are going, and what there business is; and in case they give not reasonable satisfaction to the Watch-men or Constable, then the Constable shall forthwith secure them till the morning, and shall carry such person or persons before the next Magistrate or Commissioner, to give satisfaction for their being abroad at that time of night. And if the Watch-men shall finde any Inhabitant or Stranger, after ten of the clock at night, behaving themselves any wayes debauchedly, or shall be in drink, the Constable shall secure them, by commitment or otherwise, till the Law be satisfied.[7]

In those cases in which the constable, or perhaps the watch, apprehended offenders without warrant the initial step appearing in the *Record* was the examination of the offender by the court. Presumably this examination would be preceded by the constable's explanation of the circumstances of the apprehension, which in effect served as a complaint or presentment. However, the number of cases found in the *Record* in which constables apprehended offenders without warrant are relatively few, but certain brief entries merely recording imposition of fines may also be cases of apprehension without a warrant. By law a constable was required to carry a five-foot black staff tipped with brass when executing his office (later modified where the constable was acting under warrant from authority).[8] Such badge of office seems somewhat incongruous for western Massachusetts but cases in the Essex County Court records show that importance attached to the requirement.

In addition to those cases in which constables were authorized to arrest without warrant, several acts under the First Charter especially enjoined them to search out all offenses against such laws, presumably with a view to presenting the offenders. Such acts included that regulating inns and an act prohibiting the entertainment of young people in ordinaries. A 1677 act provided that constables were to present to the magistrate the names of all persons transgressing a law prohibiting horse racing for money. Under the law regulating "Idle Persons" constables were to use special care to take notice of persons spending their time idly or unprofitably, especially of "common Coasters, unprofitable Fowlers, and Tobacco takers" and present them to the next magistrate.[9]

[7] *Ibid.* 154.
[8] *Ibid.* 31, 221.

[9] *Ibid.* 27, 66, 83, 347.

Presumably a more general duty to present offenders against the laws of the commonwealth was comprehended within the constable's oath of office which, in the laws of 1672, read as follows:

Whereas you [E.G.] are chosen Constable within the Town of [C.] for one year now following, and until other be sworn in the place: You do here Swear by the Name of Almighty God, that you will carefully intend the preservation of the Peace, the discovery and preventing all attempts against the same: You shall duely execute all Warrants which shall be sent unto you from lawful Authority here Established, and shall faithfully execute all such Orders of Court as are committed to your care: And in all these things you shall deal seriously and faithfully while you shall be in Office, without any sinistre respects of favour or displeasure: So help you God, etc.[10]

Substantially the same language was retained and supplemented in the constable's oath provided under the Second Charter.[11] However, the laws enacted between 1692 and 1702 appear to contemplate that the principal duties of constables would be in enforcing observance of the Sabbath, assisting officers of the excise or impost in searches, and informing of breaches of the licensing laws. A 1701 act authorized presentment of violations of a licensing law by grand jurors, sheriffs, undersheriffs, constables, tithingmen, and such other persons as should be appointed by the respective Courts of General Sessions of the Peace for that service.[12]

Several complaints or presentments by the selectmen of Springfield and one by the selectmen of Hatfield are contained in the *Record*. The subject matter of these complaints covered a stranger remaining in Springfield contrary to town order, unseasonable playing at cards and other misdemeanors, and neglect by constables to collect town rates committed to them.[13] No authority has been found in the laws for this type of proceeding but it may be an extension of the device of complaints or presentments by private persons.

Grand juries probably were not employed in western Massachusetts until the establishment of the County Court for Hampshire. With an awareness of this deficiency the town of Springfield, commencing with the year 1648, provided for the election of "presenters." The town order of November 6, 1648 establishing this office, which appears to have been *sui generis,* reads as follows:

It is alsoe ordered that on the first Tuesday of Novembre there shall be yearly chosen by the Inhabitants two men in their stead of Grand Jury men who shall by virtue of an oath imposed upon them by the magistrate

---

[10] *Ibid.* 168.
[11] 1 *Acts and Res. Prov. Mass. Bay* 79.

[12] *Ibid.* 32, 59, 119, 271, 273, 393, 477.
[13] *Rec.* 85, 165–166, 237.

for that purpose, faithfully Present on such Court days [those established by an order of the same date] all such breaches of Towne orders or Court orders, or any other misdemeaners as shal come to theyr knowledge either by theyr owne observation or by credible information of others, and shall take out process for the appearance of such as are delinquents, or witnesses to appeare the said day, when all such Presentments by the said partys shall be Judicially heard and examined by the magistrate and warrants for distresses granted for the Levying of such fines or penaltys as are anexed to the orders violated, or which shall seeme meete or reasonable to the magistrate to impose or inflict accordinge to the nature of the offence. These two men to stand in the office for a yeare or till others be chosen in theyr roome.[14]

How long the office of presenter was continued by virtue of this town order we do not know. Presumably the need disappeared in large part with the establishment of the County Court and a system of grand jurors. The town records show one or two presenters chosen in 1651, 1654, 1655, 1656, and 1657.[15] The only presentments in the *Record* which are definitely attributable to the town presenters are found at four sittings from November 1648 to November 1653 and cover about a dozen violations.[16] An entry for November 30, 1659 shows "John Matthews beinge presented for refusinge to obey a summons sent from Authority," but there is no indication as to the identity of the presenter.[17] There is some evidence in the *Record* that an informal system of presenters existed as early as 1640 when Goody Gregory was "accused by oath of John Woodcoke and Richard Williams" of swearing.[18]

By a May 1677 law the selectmen of each town were ordered to see to it that tithingmen were appointed in their towns, each to inspect the families of ten neighbors with power, in the absence of the constable, to apprehend all Sabbath-breakers, disorderly tipplers, or such as kept licensed houses (later extended to public licensed houses as well as private and unlicensed houses of entertainment), or others that suffered any disorder in their houses on the Sabbath day or evening after, or at any other time, and to carry them before a magistrate or other authority, or commit to prison, as any constable might do, to be proceeded with according to law.[19] An October 1679 law provided that the selectmen should take care that tithingmen be annually chosen from the most prudent and discreet inhabitants and granted them powers of inspection of licensed and unlicensed houses

---

[14] 1 Burt, *Hist. Springfield* 195–196. As set forth in the town orders made and confirmed on February 5, 1649/50, "Two wise discreete men" were to be chosen. *Ibid.* 210.

[15] *Ibid.* 219, 235, 243, 251, 255.
[16] *Rec.* 28, 33, 56.
[17] *Rec.* 83.
[18] *Rec.* 14.
[19] *Col. Laws Mass., 1672* 250–251, 259.

and of seizure of strong liquors on such premises, an account of which seizure was to be made to the next magistrate or commissioner vested with magistratical powers to be proceeded against according to law.[20] The same law also provided that:

Also the Tything-men are required diligently to inspect the manner of all disorderly persons, and where by more private admonitions they will not be reclaimed, they are from time to time to present their names to the next Magistrate, or Commissioner invested with Magistratical power, who shall proceed against them as the Law direct, as also they are in like manner to present the names of all single persons that live from under Family Government, stubborn and disorderly Children and Servants, night-walkers, Typlers, Sabbath breakers, by night or by day, and such as absent themselves from the publick Worship of God on the Lords dayes, or whatever else course or practice of any person or persons whatsoever tending to debauchery, Irreligion, prophaness, and Atheism amongst us, whether by omission of Family Government, nurture, and religious dutyes, and instruction of Children or Servants, or idle, profligate, uncivil or rude practices of any sort, the names of all which persons with the fact whereof they are accused, and witness thereof, they shall present to the next Magistrate, or Commissioner, where any are in the said Town invested with Magistratical power who shall proceed against and punish all such misdemeanours by Fine, Imprisonment, or binding over to the County Court as the Law directs.

An oath provided read as follows:

Whereas you A. B. are chosen a Tything-man within the Town of D. for one year, until others be chosen and sworn in your room and stead, you do here swear by the living God that you will diligently endeavour, and to the utmost of your Ability perform and intend the duty of your place according to the particulars specified in the Laws peculiar to your Office, So help you God.[21]

Some evidence of the effect given to the earlier laws is found in the County Court records. At the March 26, 1678 County Court for Hampshire, at which six tithingmen for Springfield, six for Northampton, and four for Hadley were presented by the respective selectmen and approved by the court, the following entry appears in the records:

Al which persons abovenamed being authorized the titheing men for the Several Towns as aforesaid, are hereby required faithfully to act in their Inspecting of their Neighbors, so as that Sin and Disorder may be prevented and Suppressed in their Several precincts, and as occasion may be to Assist one the others, and act in one and others precincts, discharg-

20 *Ibid.* 270.   21 *Ibid.* 271.

ing the office of titheing men, according to the Laws made November 1675, May, 1677, and October 1677, they having reference thereunto.

And further this Court doth now commend to these titheing men, and require them diligently to take care that the Sabbath be not profaned by youth or Elder persons sitting or standing abroad out of their meeting houses in the time of Gods publique worship whereby they are exposed to many temptations and Diversions. And that they doe Check al such persons, and so Deal with them as thereby to enforce them to go in within their meeting houses, where they may attend better, and be in sight, or otherwise to present their Names in Case Such do not reforme, to the magistrates Comissioners or other Authoritie in the Several Townes to proceed against such as shal remayne refactory, according as they shal see Cause, as also to have a vigilant eye upon al persons that shal with out just and necessary Cause be unseasonably abroad in the Evenings from their parents or masters houses or familyes; Al persons being to repaire to their lodgings and homes by nine of the Clocke at night, or rather before; And what persons soever they find faultie herein, in being abroad unseasonably, or other waies faulty, they are to admonish and hasten to their own proper places of abode, whither they are to repaire when it draws toward nine of the Clocke at night, and in Case of their neglect hereof, or non attendance thereto, then to complain of Such to authoritie, that So they may be brought to better order, or proceeded against according to their demerit.[22]

With this elaborate background it is surprising that only two presentments by tithingmen are found in the *Record*. One, made in July 1685, was for "wicked and horrid desperate words of a Develish nature and Notorious lying"; the other, in September of the same year, for coming through the streets with a laden cart after sunset on a Saturday night.[23] No adequate explanation has been found for this paucity. It is doubtful that all the inhabitants of Springfield and neighboring towns were paragons of virtue. Nor is it probable that entries of presentments by tithingmen were omitted from the *Record* on a wholesale scale. The sentiments of the County Court expressed in cases involving sexual offenses at that time certainly indicate sympathy on the part of Pynchon with the legislative objectives. One can only surmise that the tithingmen adopted a live-and-let-live attitude to the neglect of their sworn duties, or perhaps, concentrated their presentments on the County Court level.

The office of tithingman apparently lingered on, surviving the loss of the Charter. In March 1693/4 it was rejuvenated by an act which provided that tithingmen be chosen annually in each town and that they have the power and duty to inspect all licensed houses and those selling at retail without license and to inform of all disorders

22 *Rec. Cty. Ct. Hamp.* 9.   23 *Rec.* 193–194.

and misdemeanors committed in such houses to a justice of the peace or to quarter sessions. They were also to present or inform of all idle and disorderly persons, profane cursers and swearers, Sabbath-breakers, and the like offenders. Where they informed, they were to have the informer's share.[24] There is, however, no entry in the *Record* of any presentment or informing by a tithingman pursuant to this act.

Under the First Charter a few laws, as a means of stimulating enforcement, included provisions that a portion of the penalty should go to the informer—in effect *qui tam* actions. Those laws designed primarily for informing at the magistrate's level included such matters as sale of defective casks, unlawful entertainment of young people, gaming for money, sale of adulterated beer, failure of a taverner or vintner to report purchases of wine, sale by a maltster of unclean malt, and unlawful taking of tobacco.[25]

An examination of the *Record* leads to the conclusion that use of *qui tam* actions by informers was not an important means of initiating prosecution in western Massachusetts under the First Charter. Only two cases, presentments in 1652/3 by the town presenter for unlawful taking of tobacco, refer to an informer; in both cases the presenter released his share of the fines imposed.[26] The *Record* does not disclose the accusatory process in several card-playing cases in 1661–62; the offenders may have been informed against.[27] The word "informing" had no precise procedural meaning in the laws; one law concerning the offense of lying, which made no provision for an informer's share in the penalty imposed, spoke of the "party complaining or informing." [28] It has already been pointed out that "presenting" was regarded as synonymous with "informing" in the 1668 law and in the case of the town presenter. Probably for procedural purposes there was little distinction made between a complaint, a presentment, and informing.

Under the Second Charter, while *qui tam* actions or suits by informers were provided for in many of the laws, in most cases they were required to be brought in a court of record. Apparently, a justice of the peace was not regarded as a court of record, contrary to the practice in England.[29] However, in January 1700/1 Josiah Marshfield informed against himself for selling strong liquors with-

---

[24] 1 *Acts and Res. Prov. Mass. Bay* 155. For the annual choice of tithingmen in Springfield commencing in March 1692/3, see 2 Burt, *Hist. Springfield* 211, 332, 342, 346, 349, 352, 353, 356, 359.

[25] *Col. Laws Mass., 1672* 16, 27, 57, 80, 82, 106.

[26] *Rec.* 56.

[27] *Rec.* 97–99.

[28] *Col. Laws Mass., 1672* 92.

[29] See 1 *Acts and Res. Prov. Mass. Bay* 138, that fence viewers might recover penalties for insufficient fences by "action, plaint or information" before a justice of the peace. That justices of the peace were judges of record in England, see Lambard, *Eirenarcha* (1607) 62–66; Dalton, *The Country Justice* (1635) 7–8.

out license and against Joseph Williston for the same offense. Both
matters were transferred by Pynchon to the Court of General Sessions of the Peace.[30]

  While grand juries were not utilized by any of the lower level
Springfield courts, mention has been made of one instance in which
a Suffield grand juryman presented to Pynchon an inhabitant of that
town for scurrilous speeches against the late minister. Pynchon took
no action on the presentment but brought it to the attention of the
Court of General Sessions of the Peace. However, when the offender
failed to appear, the matter was referred back to Pynchon to proceed
thereon.[31] Such a presentment made to Pynchon seems irregular in
that the oath of a grand juryman appeared to contemplate presentment to the Court of General Sessions of the Peace. In any event,
this device does not appear to have been widely employed, being expressly authorized only in connection with breaches of the licensing
laws.[32]

    In several cases the accusatory process operated on the County
Court level and, after coming to the notice of the County Court,
examination into the offense or sentencing was referred to John Pynchon as magistrate.[33] In the case of several persons presented for fornication the County Court ordered that Pynchon send for and examine them and bind them over to the next court or otherwise. Similar
action was taken in the case of a Suffield inhabitant presented for
beating his wife and wasting his estate in drink. Two cases of the
same type are found in September 1692 when the Court of General
Sessions of the Peace ordered Pynchon, as justice of the peace, to deal
with a Westfield offender who entertained youths in a riotous manner after midnight and with a Suffield offender for lying and scandalous speeches against the late minister.[34] In each of these cases it appears that the offender was not before the higher court and the
reference was apparently designed to accelerate law enforcement. Of
course, if the offender, having been summoned, failed to appear before the higher court, Pynchon might be ordered to proceed against
the offender for contempt of authority. The reference might order
Pynchon to send for the offender or a special warrant might issue
from the higher court to a constable to bring the offender before
Pynchon. An examination of the Essex County Court records reveals
that this court from time to time delegated to a magistrate (William

---

[30] *Rec.* 248.

[31] *Rec. Cty. Ct. Hamp.* 159–160. See also
the complaint made via a juryman to the
commissioners in September 1662, of cattle
being violently taken away en route to the
pound. 1 *Hamp. Cty. Probate Ct. Rec.* 15.

[32] 1 *Acts and Res. Prov. Mass. Bay* 191,
477.

[33] *Rec. Cty. Ct. Hamp.* 142; 1 *Hamp.
Cty. Probate Ct. Rec.* 127, 131, 163; *Pynchon Waste Book for Hampshire* 83, 88, 130.

[34] *Rec. Cty. Ct. Hamp.* 73, 159–160.

Hathorne) power to hear and determine all presentments undisposed of at the end of a session.[35] No such delegation has been found in the case of John Pynchon. However, the practice in other counties of referring certain cases to a magistrate to handle appears consistent with that of Hampshire.

The entries do not always reveal the accusatory device used; in some cases, only the examination and sentence is referred to and, in a few, only the sentence. In some cases at least, it seems likely that the court acted upon its own view or common knowledge of the offense. Certainly pregnancy attendant upon fornication in time must have become common knowledge. In several cases in 1655 the entries refer to offenses "being taken notice of" by the commissioners.[36] It may be that such entry denotes action upon the basis of common knowledge or report.

Apart from the several accusatory devices, merely coming into court might entail dangers for an offender. An Indian coming before the commissioners to acknowledge a debt confessed his misdemeanor several years earlier in breaking some windows of John Pynchon's farmhouse "and other miscariage" and was ordered to pay treble damages.[37] In several instances after a complainant's witnesses were heard, he himself ended up with a fine.[38] A person accused of one offense might be punished for another uncovered in the course of the hearing.[39]

INITIAL PROCESS

Once a complaint or presentment had been made to the court, process issued by the court to the constable to bring the alleged offender before it. (This would not be true, of course, if the offender had already been brought before the court without issuance of process, a possibility adverted to above.) Process might consist of either a warrant or a summons. In general, a warrant would require the constable to arrest the body of the person named in the writ and

[35] 2 Rec. and Files Quart. Cts. Essex Cty. Mass. 167, 311, 314, 338, 344; 3 ibid. 18; 4 ibid. 42, 273-275.
[36] Rec. 69-70.
[37] Rec. 106.
[38] Rec. 83, 102.
[39] See the additional penalty imposed upon William Armes for fornication (Rec. 165-166; Rec. Cty. Ct. Hamp. 8) and on Mary Burt for committing wickedness with Joseph Bond (Rec. 63-64). See also the 1698 act which provided that, if in

pleading any action of trespass, there be disclosed and proved any breach of the peace, the party guilty thereof should be fined or otherwise punished as the law provided. 1 Acts and Res. Prov. Mass. Bay 325. In 1669 the County Court for Hampshire fined the defendant, in a civil action for "abusing" the plaintiff, forty shillings for breach of the peace, as well as receiving a jury verdict for ten pounds damages. 1 Hamp. Cty. Probate Ct. Rec. 109.

bring him before the issuing authority to answer or be examined touching the offense charged; a summons would merely require such officer to notify the person named in the writ of the charge and require his appearance before the issuing authority on a day named to answer thereto.

In the period of the First Charter several laws contemplated the use generally of a warrant, without further specificity, as initial process in criminal matters.[40] Other laws dealing with specific offenses conferred upon the court the power to send for offenders or call them before it by warrant.[41] However, there are several laws which indicate that, in some criminal cases at least, it was contemplated that a summons would be used as initial process. The laws dealing with a few offenses provided that offenders were to be "summoned" by the courts having jurisdiction.[42] Several laws refer to offenders being "convented" before authority; there is some indication that consistent with statements in Dalton and Lambard, a warrant was used in cases in which offenders were "convented." In one case against a third offender, process provided was in the nature of a mittimus.[43]

The "Presidents and Formes" in the several volumes of printed laws of the commonwealth contain no form of "warrant." The form of summons provided for civil causes, while addressed to the defendant directly and not to the constable or any other officer, could by reason of the inclusive scope of its language be readily adapted to certain criminal offenses such as slander or assault and battery. Despite the form of the summons provided in the laws, it was customary under the commonwealth to have the summons in civil cases addressed to and served by a constable or his deputy. In only a few cases is there evidence that service was made by a party.

Since apparently no file papers have survived, process has to be reconstructed from the entries in the *Record*. With one exception, there is no reference to initial process in criminal causes until after 1660. In this case a warrant issued by William Pynchon to the constable of Springfield in July 1650 to take the body of an Indian who had broken into a house or the stolen goods, if the Indian should escape.[44] In the earlier years covered by the *Record* the term "warrant" was generally applied to initial process in civil causes. When the same term was used in connection with criminal causes it is not clear whether the instrument called for the constable to arrest or attach the body of the accused. Hugh Parsons was "attached" upon suspicion of witchcraft and presumably the same process was used

40 *Col. Laws Mass., 1672* 22, 31, 61, 153, 221, 324.

41 *Ibid.* 27, 52, 83, 145.

42 *Ibid.* 39, 88, 101, 233, 237.

43 *Ibid.* 22, 101.

44 *Rec.* 39.

in the case of Mary Parsons. An examination of the period from 1660 to 1692 indicates that in most cases, in which the method of initial process is determinable, a summons was used.[45] However, some caution must be used in this semantic inquiry for an entry that an alleged offender was "summoned" may mean "summoned by warrant," as in one 1679 entry.[46] Those cases in which the entry notes that the accused "appeared" were probably cases in which a summons was used.[47] A few entries record that the alleged offender "was sent for."[48] Only one reference *in haec verba* to such process appears in the laws which leads one to suspect that an inept draftsman intended the use of a summons. In one case several persons were "convented" before the commissioners.[49] In only two other cases in the *Record* does it appear that a warrant of arrest may have been used as initial process. One involved theft by an Indian, the other a riotous assembly at Hadley.[50]

The practice revealed by the *Record* is consistent with that in the Bay where the printed records of courts on the county level indicate that a summons (or a warrant to cause to appear) was used for minor offenses and a warrant of arrest or attachment (sometimes referred to as a "special warrant"), for more serious crimes. The records of the County Court for Hampshire show that a summons was normally used as initial process; if the summoned offender failed to appear, he might be fined for contempt of authority or ordered to be warned a second time or referred to a lower judicial level to be proceeded against for contempt, if he had "legall warning." Of course, on the county level many of the serious offenders had been bound over by a magistrate or commissioners for their appearance so that choice of initial process offered no problem.

To some extent the use of warrants by magistrates in criminal causes may have been a reflection of English practice by justices of the peace. This practice made a distinction between process and warrant or precept. The term process was limited to the use of venire facias and further process *ad respondendum* to bring in an offender at quarter sessions or the assizes after indictment found or other conviction. The warrant or precept of a justice of the peace was used only to attach and convent the accused before any indictment or conviction. During the seventeenth century the jurisdiction of a justice of the peace to hear and determine offenses was limited, and text writers such as Lambard, Dalton, and Keble questioned whether process in the sense used above could in any event issue by a single justice

45 *Rec.* 142, 186, 208, 209.
46 *Rec.* 171.
47 *Rec.* 135, 146, 150, 152, 177, 194, 200.
48 *Rec.* 165–166, 170, 172, 178, 180.
49 *Rec.* 101.
50 *Rec.* 141, 161.

without a prior indictment, except where the power of process upon information proceeded from a special statute. In such cases perhaps either a warrant or process could be granted.

When in Massachusetts Bay judicial powers were conferred by the General Court upon a single magistrate the analogy to a justice of the peace must have been obvious. Reliance upon the use of warrants in exercising these powers was perhaps natural. The fact that the jurisdiction of a single magistrate to hear and determine extended to a wide variety of offenses, in contrast to the limited jurisdiction of a single justice of the peace in England, may have been obscured. Perhaps the choice was deliberate in order to achieve greater flexibility in process and yet to retain apparent consistency with English practice in this one particular. In any event the availability to magistrates of a warrant of arrest made for more efficient administration of justice on the lower jurisdictional levels.

The law entitled "Burglary and Theft" (1652) provided that when any goods were stolen the constable "by warrant from Authority" was to search any suspected places or houses and if he found the goods or any part thereof or had any ground of suspicion, he was to bring the delinquent or the suspected party to a magistrate to be proceeded against according to law. Several entries in 1691 disclose the use of search warrants.[51]

By implication from the law entitled "Constables" a magistrate had the authority to put forth hues and cries against certain capital offenders. Perhaps magistrates were regarded as having the power of a justice of the peace in this respect. In May 1660 some Indians who had beaten Thomas Miller and his wife were pursued by hue and cry and three Indians who were taken were brought before the commissioners.[52] Since there was no magistrate at Springfield at that time, the hue and cry may have been put forth by the constable.

An obvious weakness in the use of a summons was that the summoned offender might not appear at the appointed court, as in the case of Samuel Harmon, complained of for misbehavior on the Sabbath in June 1661.[53] However, this was corrected by a 1672 law which provided that if any person presented by a grand jury for any offense, or summoned by a magistrate to answer any crime, did not upon summons appear at the time appointed, after having been three times called in the court by name, after the first forenoon of the court, such person was to be proceeded against by contempt, unless restrained or prevented from appearing by the hand of God.[54] Even

51 *Col. Laws Mass., 1672* 13–14; *Rec.* 212.
52 *Col. Laws Mass., 1672* 31; *Rec.* 87–88.
53 *Rec.* 93.

54 *Col. Laws Mass., 1672* 87–88. Compare the June 1672 case in which the County Court of Hampshire ordered a Quabaug

without this law it would appear that attachment of property might be resorted to in order to secure appearance in criminal cases. It was used at times by the County Court for Essex.[55] In one case in July 1690 in which the offender, being summoned, had withdrawn himself, John Pynchon issued a "special warrant" to the constable to apprehend the offender and bring him before the Court.[56] The *Record* affords no information as to the form of return used by the constable in connection with a summons, attachment, or warrant in criminal cases.

Under the Second Charter no specific provision was made for the form of initial process by justices of the peace in criminal matters. A table of justice's fees appears to contemplate the use of warrants in criminal matters.[57] However, in most cases appearing in the *Record* initial process seemingly consisted of a summons, although again procedural terminology tended to be loose.[58] However, warrants were used in a few cases involving disorderly conduct by youths, theft by an Indian, lying and cursing, and defamation.[59] In one case a constable of Springfield was "convented" upon presentment for failure to collect town rates; the term was apparently used as synonymous with "summoned." [60] Several laws referred to offenders being "convented" before a justice of the peace, but it is not clear whether a warrant or summons was intended.[61] In several theft cases search warrants issued. The constable remained the principal arm of the justice of the peace, but in one case a search warrant was addressed to "the Marshal and Sherifs Deputy." [62]

The *Record* affords no clue as to the form of summons or warrant used in criminal causes after 1692 or as to the form of return employed by constables in connection with such process. No instance of attachment in a criminal case is found for this period. The alteration in the statutory form of summons in civil actions obviously made more difficult adaptation for use in criminal causes.

HEARING OR EXAMINATION

Most of the laws or orders which gave jurisdiction in criminal matters to magistrates, commissioners, or justices of the peace in no

inhabitant who failed to appear to answer for his "evill demeanure" toward the minister to make public acknowledgment of his offense or appear at the next court to answer therefor. 1 *Hamp. Cty. Probate Ct. Rec.* 138.
55 2 *Rec. and Files Quart. Cts. Essex Cty. Mass.* 151; 4 *ibid.* 245.
56 *Rec.* 209.

57 1 *Acts and Res. Prov. Mass. Bay* 84–85.
58 See *Rec.* 225, 232–233, 235B, 237, 244, 251.
59 *Rec.* 216, 224, 228, 253.
60 *Rec.* 237.
61 1 *Acts and Res. Prov. Mass. Bay* 58, 64, 66–67.
62 *Rec.* 222, 242.

way specified the manner in which the jurisdiction conferred was to be exercised. A few laws under the First Charter provided that a magistrate "hear and determine" certain offenses. Under a 1662 law magistrates were to examine and proceed against vagabonds.[63] Probably the most articulate provision was in the laws of 1672, entitled "Inkeepers, Ordinaries, Tipling, Drunkenness," which ordered:

That al offences against this Law, may be heard and determined by any one Magistrate, who shall hereby have power by warrant to send for, and examine parties and witnesses concerning any of these offences: and upon due conviction either by view of the said Magistrate, or Affirmation of the Constable, and one sufficient witness with circumstances concurring, or two witnesses, or confession of the party; to leavy the said several fines, by warrant to the Constable to that end.[64]

No greater explicitness is found under the Second Charter, the term "hear and determine" being most commonly used. The commissions of the peace under the Second Charter also employed the "hear and determine" language, consistent with English usage.

An early law (1641) provided that in all "Actions of Law" the plaintiff and defendant were to be at liberty by mutual consent to determine whether they would be tried by the bench, or by the bench and jury, unless otherwise provided by law, and that "the like liberty shall be granted to all persons in any Criminal case." It was also provided that both plaintiff and defendant in actions of law, and likewise "every Delinquent to be judged by a Jury," were to be at liberty to challenge any of the jurors, and if the challenge was found just and reasonable by the bench or the rest of the jury, as the challenger should choose, and allowed, *tales de circumstantibus*, that is, other persons present in court, were to be impaneled in room of those challenged.[65]

However, only one jury trial of a criminal matter appears in the *Record* and in the supplemental material from the Registry of Probate records. In March 1654/5 Samuel Wright, Jr., charged with fathering an illegitimate child, desired to be tried by a jury of twelve and "tryall was made accordingly." [66] The bare entry affords no insight into how the jury was summoned or how the trial was conducted. This practice is consistent with that of the County Court for Hampshire where relatively few criminal cases were tried by juries. The same is true for those records of the County Courts of Suffolk, Middlesex, Essex, Norfolk, and York which have been examined and for some fragmentary records of courts on the lower jurisdictional levels in Essex, Norfolk, and York.

63 *Col. Laws Mass., 1672* 13, 66, 80, 153.
64 *Ibid.* 83.
65 *Ibid.* 152.
66 *Rec.* 63.

Under the Second Charter, despite some sweeping statutory statements concerning the right to jury trial, there is no indication that this right was regarded as extending to criminal matters within the jurisdiction of a justice of the peace.[67] The *Record* shows no offender seeking jury trial.

In the *Record* the procedural step following the appearance of the accused before the court was usually referred to as an "examination." This examination appears to have been judicial, rather than inquisitorial in nature; it would appear that witnesses, for example, were examined in the presence of the accused. In principle, English justice of the peace practice was followed in that before conviction it was necessary, as allowed by God's law, to give the accused an opportunity to make a sufficient defense or excuse against the charge. Although not specifically required by any law or order, the examination probably commenced with an informal arraignment by means of which the accused was informed of the offense with which he was charged. If complaint was made in writing, it was presumably read to the accused; an oral complaint or presentment was probably summarized. In one case the "arraignment" took the form of the constable "making his declaration" against the offenders.[68] In a late defamation case the offender was required to answer to the evidence which was read to him. This was basically the procedure followed in the attachment of Hugh Parsons for witchcraft.[69] In the event an offender had been taken without warrant or had been summoned, such an "arraignment" may have served only to determine whether the accused would own or acknowledge the offense or whether, guilt being denied, the court would have to proceed to an examination of the offender and of witnesses. (No traverse of a presentment appears.) In a substantial number of cases the accused owned or acknowledged the offense charged, but sometimes this confession only followed an examination of the accused or of witnesses or both. In a few cases the acknowledgment was made in writing, presumably subscribed, and filed by the court. (Whether made under oath as found occasionally in other courts is not clear.) There is no evidence of a plea, answer or defense made in writing or of any reply by a complainant. In only one case did an accused stand mute.[70]

[67] *Col. Laws Mass., 1672* 40, 286.

[68] *Rec.* 137. For English practice see Dalton, *The Country Justice* (1635) 22, 26.

[69] *Rec.* 235B. In the case of the 1675 witchcraft charges against Mary Parsons of Northampton various "diverse testimonyes on oath," exhibited to the County Court, were read before her when she voluntarily appeared in court. 1 *Hamp. Cty. Probate Ct. Rec.* 161.

[70] *Rec.* 138, 144, 225. Compare the entry in 1 *Hamp. Cty. Probate Ct. Rec.* 138 (March 1675) that "Westcarr put in his defense in writing and John Smith putt in a Reply thereto." In a 1675 case in the County Court for Hampshire in which the accused in an assault case, upon examina-

Apparently the accused was not examined under oath. Whether this was due to acceptance of the common law maxim given currency by Dalton, *Nullus tenetur seipsum prodere,* is not clear. There is some suspicion that John Pynchon and other magistrates upon occasion engaged in judicial browbeating of alleged offenders. Whether defendants were ever required to purge themselves on oath does not appear. (Such procedure was given statutory form in several acts prohibiting selling strong drink to Indians.) In no case did the accused claim privilege against self-incrimination. Some witnesses, consistent with English practice, testified under oath; others apparently did not; in most cases it is not clear from the entries whether or not testimony was given under oath. In the face of testimony under oath, the denials of the accused were probably accorded little weight. In seventeenth-century English practice, witnesses for the accused were not sworn on the theory that it was improper to have witnesses against the King. No specific law with respect to administration of oaths to witnesses in criminal causes has been found, but in other parts of the colony cases appear in which witnesses for the accused were sworn.[71] The form of oath to be taken by a witness, presumably in both criminal and civil causes, appears in the laws of 1672 as follows:

> You swear by the Living God, that the Evidence you shall give to this Court concerning the Cause now in question, shall be the Truth, the whole Truth, and nothing but the Truth: So help you God, etc.[72]

The measure of proof required for conviction of various offenses was usually expressed in the laws of the period, if at all, in general terms. Under the First Charter, for instance, the laws referred to such standards as "due proof," "good testimony," "due conviction by

---

tion saw "noe Reason to answer such Questions," the court proceeded to sentence upon circumstantial evidence. *Ibid.* 161. See also 5 *Rec. Mass. Bay* 323 where the General Court gave no answer to the question whether a court should proceed if a person complained of or indicted refused to put himself on trial.

71 For the acts permitting purgation see *Col. Laws Mass., 1672* 78; 1 *Acts and Res. Prov. Mass. Bay* 150–151. For cases under the earlier law at the County Court see the refusal of Nathaniel Ely to purge himself (1 *Hamp. Cty. Probate Ct. Rec.* 91) and the refusal of the court to allow Benjamin Waite and John Westcarr to purge themselves. *Ibid.* 119, 121. As to self-incrimination it was provided by law that "no man

shall be forced by Torture to confess any Crime against himself or any other." *Col. Laws Mass., 1672* 129. At a September 1671 sitting of the County Court for Hampshire John Stewart, accused of stabbing John Bliss, upon examination "refused to confess against himself though also he denyeth not the fact." The court limited itself to a "serious admonition" since Stewart had suffered commitment and the charge "was not legally proved against him." In addition, Stewart had apparently effected a settlement with Bliss. 1 *Hamp. Cty. Probate Ct. Rec.* 152. For an instance in which witnesses for the accused were sworn by the County Court for Essex see 2 *Rec. and Files Quart. Cts. Essex Cty. Mass.* 41.

72 *Col. Laws Mass., 1672* 167.

testimony or confession," "confession or other manifest proof," "sufficient testimony" brought against the delinquent, proof by oath of a public officer or "other sufficient witness," and "upon sufficient proof." [73] The law regulating ordinaries provided for conviction of offenders by view of the magistrate, or affirmation of the constable and one sufficient witness with circumstances concurring, or two witnesses, or confession of the party. The last standards probably stemmed from acts of Parliament regulating ordinaries in England or practice manuals commenting thereon.[74] However, in general, it should be noted that a May 1657 law stated in civil cases it behooved both court and jury "to see that the affirmation be prooved by sufficijent evidence, els the case must be found for the defendant and so it is also in a criminall case for in the eye of the lawe, every man is honest and innocent, unless it be proved legally to the contrary." [75]

Under the Second Charter most of the acts conferring jurisdiction upon justices of the peace made no reference to standards of proof. A few specified the view of a justice of the peace, confession of the party, or the oaths of two witnesses; confession or sufficient witness; the justice's own view, confession, or other legal conviction; due proof; the justice's own view or other legal conviction. An act relating to breaches of excise regulations permitted two witnesses to testify to different violations, if committed within a month.[76]

An examination of the *Record* indicates as implicit requirement that conviction, in the absence of confession or the court's own view of the offense, rest on the testimony of at least two "sufficient" witnesses to the same unlawful act or acts, unless otherwise specifically provided. No statutory basis for the requirement has been found, although commentators such as Dalton lend support to the rule in summary proceedings as in accordance with God's word.[77] File papers

[73] *Col. Laws Mass., 1672* 13, 16, 31, 52, 55, 59, 83, 131, 145; 4 *Rec. Mass. Bay (Part I)* 290–291.

[74] *Col. Laws Mass., 1672* 83. For the English statutes see 1 Jac. 1, c. 9, 21 Jac. 1, c. 7, 1 Car. 1, c. 4, 3 Car. 1, c. 3.

[75] 4 *Rec. Mass. Bay (Part I)* 290.

[76] 1 *Acts and Res. Prov. Mass. Bay* 51–53, 58, 60, 155–156.

[77] See Dalton, *The Country Justice* (1635) 156, 297. For a vague answer by the General Court to objections of the Crown law officers that the commonwealth laws did not absolutely bind to two or three witnesses. 5 *Rec. Mass. Bay* 199. For statutory implication of the need for two sufficient witnesses in unlawful gaming cases see *Col. Laws Mass., 1672* 58. For the question before the County Court for Hampshire see 1 *Hamp. Cty. Probate Ct. Rec.* 161; *Rec. Cty. Ct. Hamp.* 59, 67. For the Essex County Court see 3 *Rec. and Files Quart. Cts. Essex Cty. Mass.* 213 (civil); 5 *ibid.* 144. For Suffolk see 1 *Rec. Suffolk Cty. Ct.* 311; 2 *ibid.* 892–893. See also Howe, *Readings in American Legal History* (1949) 142, 184; Fortescue, *De Laudibus Legum Angliae* in 1 *Works* (ed. T. Fortescue, 1869) c. xxxii ("But the meaning of the law is this: that a less number than two witnesses shall not be admitted as sufficient to decide the truth in doubtful cases."); McBratney, "The One Witness Rule in Massachusetts," 2 *Amer. Jour. Legal Hist.* 155.

found in Essex and Suffolk make occasional reference to the prevailing judicial view of the inadequacy of one witness.

Although the large number of witnesses examined in connection with the Hugh Parsons witchcraft accusation has been noted, the *Record* fails to disclose any explicit evidentiary standards employed in cases in which offenders were examined and then bound over or committed to await trial in a higher court. In several cases the evidence in part was documentary in nature. In a battery complaint the commissioners took notice of the fact complainant's nose "was much bruised and bloody." [78] In relatively few cases was the evidence found insufficient to support the complaint or presentment, sufficiency being tested by such vague standards as "any proofe of Justice" and "full proofe." When some young people at Westfield, complained against for breaking down fences, "put al upon profe" and "desyred to know their accusers and se the Proofe," Pynchon, although suspicious of their guilt, dismissed them with admonitions. This is consistent with cases in the County Courts of Essex and Suffolk of admonishing the accused where there was a failure of proof.[79]

In a number of instances appearing in the *Record* witnesses appeared before the court and gave evidence and, in some cases, were examined viva voce. In other cases it appears likely that testimony had been taken down in writing earlier and sworn to before a magistrate or commissioner authorized thereunto and then read at the examination or hearing. Such procedure was authorized under the First Charter "in any Case, Civill or Criminal," provided that, in the case of a witness who lived within ten miles of the court and was not disabled by sickness or other infirmity, such testimony taken out of court was not to be received or made use of unless the witness was present to be further examined about it. A 1650 law which in effect required all testimony to be in writing (experience having shown the inconvenience of taking oral testimony in court), may not have been applicable to criminal proceedings but, undoubtedly, testimony taken down in writing by a complainant or presenter out of court could be sworn to in court.[80]

Under the Second Charter it appears by implication in a 1695 act that in both civil and criminal causes a witness was required to testify in person unless bound for sea before the time of trial. If so bound, the justice was authorized to take his deposition, the adverse

78 *Rec.* 89, 138, 235B.
79 *Rec.* 12, 69, 101, 102, 216, 225. For the Essex County Court see 2 *Rec. and Files Quart. Cts. Essex Cty.* 219; 3 *ibid.* 60. For Suffolk see 1 *Rec. Suffolk Cty. Ct.* 116, 307.
80 *Col. Laws Mass., 1672* 158–159; 4

Rec. Mass. Bay (Part I) 27. The requirement that all evidence be in writing resulted in so many badly written, illegible, and soiled evidences that every court, magistrate, or commissioner was empowered to order and regulate them. 4 *ibid.* (Part I) 85.

party being present or having received notification of the taking. In some cases *Record* entries refer to "testymonys" of witnesses being on file. It seems probable that such a notation usually indicated that the testimony was taken down out of court and read at the trial. However, in the Hugh Parsons case and various cases transferred to the County Court examinations were taken down in writing and sworn to in court; therefore a reference to "testymonys on file" may not always mean that testimony was taken out of court. A 1652 act, which required the keeping of "all the Evidences (which are to be given in, in writing, in fair and large papers)," was on its face limited to civil actions.[81]

A magistrate or commissioner taking the testimony of a witness out of court would seem to be performing a merely ministerial act. However, in one case in December 1684 "testimonys" were brought to John Pynchon who was desired to swear the witnesses thereto, prior to the making of a complaint. Pynchon, perusing the papers proffered, declared that he "did not find them to reach to a ly in the sence or words of the Law." The violent reaction this declaration evoked resulted in the would-be complainant being committed for contempt.[82] The importance of such a "screening" process in the administration of justice is not evident from the *Record*.

Little appears in the *Record* concerning the mechanics of securing the appearance of witnesses. The laws of 1672 designated the use of a warrant by a magistrate to send for witnesses in case of infractions of the law regulating innkeepers and ordinaries. A June 1690 entry in connection with a complaint refers to witnesses being summoned.[83] Although no general provision regarding process in the case of witnesses in criminal causes can be found, from the practice in the courts of the Bay it appears that a summons was normally used to secure the appearance of witnesses in criminal causes. Perhaps, in some cases, a summons or warrant to summon, addressed to the constable, might require the appearance of witnesses as well as of defendant.

In some cases the accused, instead of denying or owning the offense, interposed an affirmative defense or excuse. The reception accorded bona fide defenses or excuses attests to the pragmatic approach employed in the law enforcement appearing in the *Record*.[84]

SENTENCE

Following the examination and, in some cases, a more extended hearing, the court in most cases adjudged the offender guilty of one

---

[81] 1 *Acts and Res. Prov. Mass. Bay* 226; *Col. Laws Mass., 1672* 129.
[82] *Rec.* 191.
[83] *Col. Laws Mass., 1672* 83; *Rec.* 208.
[84] *Rec.* 12, 28, 31, 56, 61, 72, 97, 151, 207, 222.

or more offenses and usually sentenced him to pay a fine or to be whipped a specified number of stripes. In some cases, as already indicated, the offender was given the alternative of paying a fine (damages to the person injured in one case) or of receiving a whipping. In view of the small amounts of most fines imposed it was not the practice to demand sureties or to order the prisoner to stand committed until the sentence was performed. As debits in his account books show, Pynchon in his capacity of moneylender sometimes paid to the county the fines he imposed in a judicial capacity. Imprisonment was rarely resorted to, nor was the practice of some of the county courts followed of having the offender stand in a public place wearing a placard setting forth his offense in capital letters. The laws passed after 1692 show a preference for setting in the cage or stocks, rather than whipping in case of corporal punishment, with greater resort to imprisonment for more serious offenses. Some provided that an habitual offender might be bound with sureties for his good behavior. A thief, unable to make restitution or pay threefold damages, might be disposed of in service. In a scattering of cases only an admonition was restorted to. In the case of violations of town orders, not true criminal offenses, only fines were imposed. This pattern of punishment in general reflects the methods of punishment adopted by the colony or province laws.

In only a few cases were other punishments imposed. A person adjudged father of a bastard was ordered to make payments toward maintenance of the child. An offender who confessed to swearing was to pay a fine of twelve pence to the poor or sit in the stocks three hours. Some persons "in drink" at an unseasonable hour were to pay a fine of five shillings or sit in the stocks one hour.[85] Goods stolen were ordered returned to their owners; in one case an Indian offender posted security for such return. The fruits of trespass upon town lands were ordered forfeited in part. A scold was sentenced to be gagged or to be set in a ducking stool and dipped in the water.[86] In one defamation case, quasi-criminal in nature, the offender was ordered to make open and public acknowledgment of his faults.[87] The owner of a sheep-killing dog had to hang the animal. An "order of restraint" prohibited selling wine or strong waters to Indians without a license. A runaway servant was ordered returned to his master.[88] Treble damages were adjudged in cases of theft.[89] In a few cases fines which had been imposed were abated or abatement, being sought,

85 *Rec.* 14, 63, 210.
86 *Rec.* 141, 148, 156, 186–187, 192, 196–197.
87 *Rec.* 78. *Cf.* the use of public acknowledgment as an alternative to pay-

ment of damages in a civil action. *Ibid.* 196.
88 *Rec.* 70, 150, 179.
89 *Rec.* 212.

was referred to the County Court.[90] In one instance sentence was in effect suspended. In a few cases offenders were discharged or dismissed by the court. However, no use was made of discharge by proclamation, although recognized by order of the General Court and used in other courts of the colony.[91]

An October 1668 law provided that warrants for execution in both civil and criminal causes were to be signed by the clerk of the court. This was one of several enactments which somewhat vaguely assumed the existence of a clerk of the court in the case of a magistrate. Perhaps the clerk of the writs of the magistrate's town could be regarded as a clerk of his court but the *Record* is unrevealing. An October 1678 law indicates that the clerk of the writs signed warrants in the form of "AB, per curia, for the towne of C." This practice is confirmed by the calendared file papers of the County Court for Essex.[92]

Little use of recognizances appears in the *Record* except in those cases in which offenders were bound over to appear at the County Court or the Court of General Sessions of the Peace. However, such an offender would also, presumably, be required to give bond, with two sureties perhaps, for his good behavior in the meantime.[93] Such bonds might specify good behavior toward particular persons, such as the complainant, and perhaps, as found in some cases in Essex County involving sexual offenses, enjoin frequenting the company of a co-offender. Binding to good behavior, which imposed stricter limitations upon an offender or suspected offender than binding to the peace, was not usually granted by a single justice of the peace in England.

The justices' manuals in England devoted much space to binding offenders to the peace. Little use is found of this device in Hampshire or elsewhere in Massachusetts Bay. However, the *Record* shows that one culprit in 1686 chose to pay a five-shilling fine for breaking the peace rather than be bound to the peace.[94] At the 1658 examination of Thomas Miller and John Henryson the commissioners noted that both deserved to be bound to the peace, but bond was not required since the quarrel was not recent and the participants had become reconciled.[95] In only one instance, in 1679, did a complainant "swear the peace" against an offender; Pynchon ordered the offender bound in the sum of ten pounds for his appearance at the County Court

---

[90] *Rec.* 141, 162, 169, 251.
[91] *Rec.* 71, 216, 225, 239, 244. For the General Court order see 1 *Rec. Mass. Bay* 12.

[92] 4 *Rec. Mass. Bay* (*Part II*) 394; 5 *ibid.* 194.
[93] See, however, *Rec.* 192.
[94] *Rec.* 199. See also *Rec.* 2.
[95] *Rec.* 83.

and in the meantime to keep the peace.[96] This action was apparently based upon English practice as it was not specifically provided for in the commonwealth laws. The form of bond employed is not known but it may have been adapted from the statutory form in civil cases.

While most of the entries in criminal causes appearing in the *Record* make no mention of any imposition of costs of court or charges upon the offender, there are scattered cases in which such imposition appears. Several offenders were ordered to pay witnesses either one or two shillings apiece; in a case in which witnesses assisted the constable in the detention of a prisoner they were allowed five shillings each in charges. Presumably this was pursuant to a provision in the laws that in all criminal cases charges of witnesses were to be borne by the delinquent party.[97] In others, offenders were ordered to pay the constable's charges or "the charge of their apprehending." [98] In a 1690 entry a fine of five shillings was to include costs of court, that is, twelve pence to the constable. In 1697 one offender had to pay all charges occasioned by his crime; another was to pay "the charges summons serving it and attendance al being about .4s." [99] In two later cases defendants were ordered to pay all charges of prosecution. In a 1701/2 defamation case, where defendant was convicted, "though somewhat Barely," complainant and defendant were ordered "each to beare their owne Charges in the Case." [100] In the case of an unjust complaint the person complained of probably would be allowed costs. In those instances in which criminal and civil matters were intermingled costs of court were usually awarded in connection with the civil action.[101]

In most cases in which a complaint combined civil and criminal aspects the judgment in the civil cause was segregated from the criminal sentence. In other cases criminal sentences specifically left complainants to their remedies at law for damages suffered as a result of the offender's misconduct. However, in one case in which the offender was sentenced to answer for whatever damage was done to complainant's property, it is uncertain whether this policy of segregation was maintained.[102]

In two instances the court sought assistance in sentencing. In a 1650 case William Pynchon noted that the Reverend Moxon and four others were present at his hearing of a case between Thomas Miller and an Indian and "with their advise" he sentenced Miller to

---

96 *Rec.* 170–171.

97 *Rec.* 135, 165, 172, 192. For the law see *Col. Laws Mass., 1672* 159.

98 *Rec.* 152, 165, 210.

99 *Rec.* 208, 230–231, 233.

100 *Rec.* 236B, 242, 253.

101 *Rec.* 169, 232. No evidence appears

that the statutory fee for entry of an action was part of costs of court in a criminal cause but see such imposition in March 1671 by the County Court. 1 *Hamp. Cty. Probate Ct. Rec.* 128.

102 *Rec.* 151, 166, 242.

fifteen lashes. In 1686 when some Windsor inhabitants were brought in for gathering candlewood within the bounds of Enfield, John Pynchon advised with the committee for Enfield before sentence.[103]

BINDING OVER

A 1641 order of the General Court provided that "no Mans Person shall be Restrained or Imprisoned by any Authority whatsoever, before the Law hath Sentenced him thereto, if he can put in sufficient Security, Baile or Mainprize, for his appearance and good Behaviour in the mean time." [104] It was presumably pursuant to this law that, in a number of cases involving more serious crimes, the accused, following examination, was bound over for his appearance at the County Court. Included in this category were cases involving fornication and other sexual offenses, "notorious" lying, theft, burglary, breach of the peace, contempt of authority, illegal trading with the Indians, strained marital relations, riotous behavior, causing a disturbance at a town meeting, killing another's steer, and arson. The amount of the recognizance or surety demanded varied; bonds in the amount of ten or twenty pounds were commonly used. In one case involving a charge of arson the amount was thirty pounds. Failure to provide bond in the requisite amount would probably result in commitment of the accused. Under the Second Charter there were only three cases in which offenders were bound over to the Court of General Sessions of the Peace. One involved defamatory statements; the others, sale of strong liquor without a license.

In cases where the accused was examined and then bound over to appear and answer at the County Court or quarter sessions, the examination was usually taken down in writing, and, probably along with depositions under oath of complainant and other witnesses, laid before such court. Such procedure, in some cases at least, left little scope for trial at the higher level—particularly if the examination included a confession by the accused. Some flexibility in binding over is indicated in a 1697 case in which Pynchon saw no need to bind the offender over to the quarter sessions since he had compounded with the injured party and engaged good carriage for the future.[105] Similarly, in the case of an offender presented at the County Court, where trial was referred to Pynchon, the witnesses might give their testimony under oath at such court to be transmitted to Pynchon.

In several instances in which offenders were bound over to the

[103] Rec. 39, 197.
[104] Col. Laws Mass., 1672 74.
[105] Rec. 233. In the 1671 case of Zebadiah Williams three witnesses at the

County Court took their oath "as touching what they observed of his ill demeanour." 1 Hamp. Cty. Probate Ct. Rec. 127.

County Court or to the Court of General Sessions of the Peace, the complainant was required to give bond to prosecute at the next such court. Whether it was the practice to bind witnesses, other than the complainant, to appear at the County Court or quarter sessions to give evidence against the offender is not clear. Evidence of such practice has been found in Essex County. In general the practice followed that of an English justice of the peace in certifying examinations, informations, recognizances, and bailment to quarter sessions or the next general gaol delivery. However, as distinguished from English practice, the material certified was not used to secure a presentment by the grand jury. The court, in most cases, arrived at sentence without a grand or petty jury.[106]

Dalton stated that it seemed "just and right" that a justice of the peace upon examination should take and certify such information, proof, and evidence as went to acquitting or clearing the prisoner, as well as such as was against the prisoner. However, he doubted whether such proof against the King should be taken on oath. What practice generally prevailed in this respect in Hampshire and in Massachusetts Bay is not clear.

APPEAL

The 1641 commission to William Pynchon and several succeeding commissions made provision for appeals to the Court of Assistants. The May 1658 commission for Springfield and Northampton provided for an appeal to the County Court at Boston. After the establishment of a County Court for Hampshire, presumably this court constituted the appellate body for the commissioners for Springfield. From the court established in May 1659 with the powers of a "County Court," appeal was presumably to the Court of Assistants, as provided in the law entitled "Appeal" in the 1648 and 1660 printed laws.

The *Laws and Liberties* of 1648 and subsequent commonwealth laws provided for an appeal from the sentence of one magistrate or "other persons deputed to hear and determine small causes" to the County Court of the jurisdiction in which the cause was determined.[107] Appellant was required to tender his appeal and to put in security to prosecute it to effect, to satisfy all damages and for his good behavior and appearance at the County Court. The provision

---

[106] *Rec.* 155, 200, 212, 236A. For examples of the material certified to the County Court of Essex by an examining magistrate see 2 *Rec. and Files Quart.* *Cts. Essex Cty. Mass.* 155, 235–236; 5 *ibid.* 400–404, 411–413.

[107] *Laws and Liberties Mass.* 2.

that execution should not be granted until twelve hours after judgment, unless by special order of the court, presumably was concerned with civil causes. Undoubtedly execution of sentence in criminal causes was respited pending the outcome of the appeal, although not specifically provided by law.

Such laws also provided that all appeals with the security as aforesaid were to be recorded at the charge of the party appealing and certified to the court to which made. The further provision, added in 1651, and later modified, that the party appealing should briefly in writing "without reflecting on Court or Parties, by provoking Language" give in to the clerk of the court from which he appealed the grounds and reasons of appeal six days before the beginning of the court to which the appeal was made, was seemingly designed for civil causes, since defendant, if desired, was to be allowed a copy of the grounds and reasons filed. The right of the court to impose charges and fines upon appellant contained in the laws of 1648, apparently intended for civil causes, was omitted in later laws.[108] The 1651 provision that whoever should appeal from the sentence of any court and not prosecute the same to effect, according to law, should, besides his bond to the party, forfeit forty shillings to the county may also have been designed primarily for civil causes.[109]

An early law which gave magistrates jurisdiction over small thefts and other offenses of a criminal nature where the damage or fine did not exceed forty shillings specifically provided that it might be lawful for either party to appeal to the next court held in the jurisdiction, giving sufficient caution to prosecute the same to effect at such court.[110] Whether this provision was designed to carve an exception from the above general, more stringent, procedural requirements is not clear.

Under the Second Charter a June 1696 act made it lawful for any person sentenced for any criminal offense by one or more justices of the peace out of sessions to appeal from such sentence to the next Court of General Sessions of the Peace held in the county. Appellant was required to enter into a recognizance, not exceeding five pounds, with two sufficient sureties for his appearance at the appellate court, for his prosecution with effect of his appeal, and to abide the sentence of the court appealed to, which was to be final, and in the meantime to be of good behavior. No appeal was to be granted unless claimed at the time of the declaring of sentence and security given as directed within the space of two hours thereafter, the appel-

[108] *Col. Laws Mass., 1660* 122; *Col. Laws Mass., 1672* 4; *Laws and Liberties Mass.* 2.

[109] *Col. Laws Mass., 1660* 122.
[110] *Col. Laws Mass., 1672* 13.

lant remaining in the custody of an officer until such security was entered. Every such appellant was to file reasons of appeal in the clerk's office of the court appealed to seven days before the court sat and, at his own cost, to take out and present to the court an attested copy of the sentence and copies of all evidences upon which it was grounded. The fee for entering the appeal was the same as for entry of an action in civil causes, ten shillings. Although this act was disallowed by the King in Council on November 24, 1698, no law was passed in place of the disallowed act during the period covered by the *Record*.[111]

An examination of the *Record* discloses that the only appeals in criminal causes during the period were taken in 1698 to the Court of General Sessions of the Peace. However, in each case the appeal was later withdrawn and not prosecuted. One appeal was taken from a fine of ten shillings, plus fourteen shillings costs of prosecution, in a defamation case. In the other cases, former constables of Springfield appealed from forfeitures of forty shillings apiece for neglect to collect certain town rates.[112]

FINAL PROCEEDINGS

The laws under the First Charter provided that every offender fined for breach of any penal law was to pay his fine or penalty forthwith, or give security speedily to do it, or be imprisoned or kept to work until it be paid—unless the court or judge imposing the fine saw cause to respite the same. It was also provided that, when any magistrate or commissioner assessed a fine, he was to send a transcript or note of the fine within fourteen days to the treasurer of the colony or the county to whom it belonged who was forthwith to give warrant to the marshal to collect and levy the same. If no goods could be found to satisfy the fine, the marshal was to attach the body of such person and imprison him until satisfaction was made, provided that the Court of Assistants or any County Court might discharge from imprisonment any such person who was unable to make satisfaction.[113]

Under the Second Charter some laws specifically empowered a justice to retain or commit an offender until the fine imposed was satisfied (and perhaps sureties for good behavior found) or to cause the fine to be levied by distress and sale of the offender's goods by warrant directed to the constable. In other cases, only warrant by distress on the delinquent's goods was authorized. An offender un-

111 1 *Acts and Res. Prov. Mass. Bay* 217.   113 *Col. Laws Mass., 1672* 51.
112 *Rec.* 236B–240.

able to make restitution or pay threefold damages in theft cases might be disposed in service.[114]

To the question as to whether or not procedure in criminal causes, as revealed in the *Record,* differed substantially from procedure in such causes in the more settled portions of Massachusetts Bay, the answer, based on the available evidence, is that it did not. This conclusion has been arrived at with an awareness that no file papers for the courts covered by the *Record* have survived (excluding the proceedings in the Hugh Parsons witchcraft case), that only fragmentary records of comparable courts on the lower jurisdictional levels in the Bay have been found, and that, in part, this conclusion rests upon indirect evidence from the records of county courts for Hampshire, Suffolk, Essex, Norfolk, Middlesex, and York. In large part the procedure clearly stemmed from the laws of the commonwealth. While no models of statutory draftsmanship, these laws provided a frame of reference that was not substantially warped by either the stresses of a "frontier" society or the vagaries of judicial personnel.

There is no reflection in the *Record* of the "individualistic and democratic tendencies" or the "innovating" tendency noted by Turner in his well-known essay on the Massachusetts Bay frontier in the late seventeenth century.[115] It is very doubtful that a curbing of such tendencies in the field of law enforcement could be ascribed solely to the dominant position in the judicial establishment of a conservative, wealthy trader and landowner such as John Pynchon with his many political, cultural, and economic ties with the Bay, with neighboring colonies, and with England. The conditions which shaped and influenced law enforcement were not sufficiently different in western Massachusetts during the seventeenth century to vary in a substantial manner the development of criminal procedure on the lower jurisdictional levels or, for that matter, on the county level.

What does the *Record* disclose of the influence of the laws of England on law enforcement in western Massachusetts? William Pynchon had some familiarity with Fortescue's work, *On the Laws of England,* and Dalton's *The Country Justice.* There is some ground for belief that John Pynchon also had available some English law books. In the inventory of John Pynchon, Jr.'s estate, taken in May 1721,[116] the following works are listed:

---

[114] 1 *Acts and Res. Prov. Mass. Bay* 51–53, 57–58, 65–66, 70, 136, 154.

[115] F. J. Turner, *The Frontier in American History* (1920) 65.

[116] The inventory is found in the *Hampshire County Probate Court Records.*

Fortaques on the Laws   Finches laws
law Dictionary   Magna Charta
A New England Law Book   Daltons Statutes
Cook upon Littleton   Dalton on the Laws of England

Some of these books probably belonged originally to John Pynchon or even to William Pynchon—the presence of Fortescue is convincing evidence. However, there is no reference to any of these volumes in the *Record* or, for that matter, to any English authority, either text or case, to any Biblical authority, or to any case decided by the General Court, the Court of Assistants, or any other court of Massachusetts Bay. Howevei, in view of the general paucity of citation of authority in seventeenth-century Massachusetts judicial records, the state of the *Record* comes as no surprise.[117] File papers, if preserved, would probably havc shown, as in other parts of the colony, greater recourse to Biblical authority by offenders and litigants. If any of the above books belonged to John Pynchon, they were owned in the capacity of judge, legislator, administrator, soldier, and merchant, not that of a bibliophile. Unfortunately, the uses to which they were put and the degree of influence exerted upon the administration of justice in western Massachusetts is beyond present reconstruction. In conclusion, in those areas not specifically covered by the laws of the colony, the procedure found in the *Record* was probably as consistent with the laws of England as that found in the more settled parts of the colony.

[117] The records of the County Court for Hampshire differ little from the *Record*. One case made reference to Biblical authorities. 1 *Hamp. Cty. Probate Ct.* *Rec.* 161. Another contained the statement that "the complaint falls of its own accord: for *Ubi lex nullus etc.*" *Ibid.* 153.

I X. Civil Jurisdiction

IVIL jurisdiction in Massachusetts, in contrast to criminal jurisdiction, was usually conferred in general terms. William Pynchon's first appointment as magistrate by the inhabitants of Agawam in February 1638/9 conferred jurisdiction over actions for debt or trespass, apparently without any limitation in amount. However, the fact that use of a jury of six persons was limited to such actions under the sum of ten pounds imposed a practical limitation—at least in cases tried by a jury. In the 1641 General Court commission to William Pynchon jurisdiction was broadened to all civil causes without any limitation of amount; this same jurisdiction obtained in the subsequent commissions until May 1658 when jurisdiction may have been limited to civil actions not exceeding twenty-pound damages. In any event, the May 1659 commission again granted jurisdiction to the Springfield commissioners in all civil causes without limitation of amount although the relation of this grant to the powers of a "County Court" and to the jurisdiction to be exercised out of court is far from clear.

From May 1665 to May 1686 John Pynchon, as magistrate, exercised jurisdiction over all causes arising in the county not exceeding forty shillings. During Dudley's period of office, Pynchon, as a member of the council, had jurisdiction of small causes where the damage besides costs did not exceed forty shillings. During the Andros regime Pynchon, presumably as justice of the peace, had jurisdiction over all manner of debts, trespasses, and other matters not exceeding the value of forty shillings wherein the title to land was not concerned. For the period during which Pynchon exercised magistratical powers (1689–92) he again exercised jurisdiction over all causes arising in the county not exceeding forty shillings. As justice of the peace under the Second Charter Pynchon had, in general, the same jurisdiction as that exercised under Governor Andros.

Most significant is that for most of the period until May 1665 the several courts held at Springfield possessed unlimited jurisdiction in civil matters. After that date, John Pynchon's jurisdiction in various

...

capacities at Springfield was limited to causes not exceeding forty shillings, but two years earlier the establishment of the County Court for Hampshire had served to divert from the Springfield commissioners jurisdiction in the more important causes.

Prior to May 1686 there was no specific limitation of jurisdiction to actions wherein title to land was not concerned. However, except for a few causes jurisdiction as evidenced by the *Record* was confined to personal actions, both *ex contractu* and *ex delicto,* with the latter category predominating. After May 1686 jurisdiction was limited, with the exception of the years 1689–1692, to actions wherein title to land was not concerned. However, statutory provision was made in 1698 for transfer to the Inferior Court of Common Pleas of trespass actions in which title to land was pleaded.

The two forms of action specifically mentioned for jurisdictional purposes were trespass and debt. Presumably the term "trespass" comprehended "trespass on the case," commonly referred to in the *Record,* and in other Massachusetts court records of the seventeenth century, as "action of the case." The commonwealth laws entitled "Actions" referred to "Actions of the Case Concerning Debts and Accounts." [1] Most of the causes in the *Record* characterized as to form of action are actions of debt or actions on the case. More sparing use was made of actions of trespass, detinue, and slander or defamation. Only a few entries make reference to covenant or replevin. There are no references in the *Record* to general or special assumpsit, trover, ejectment, or action of account. An examination of the records for other jurisdictions indicates that such absence was not peculiar to Hampshire. One entry refers to an "action of theft," one to an "action of battery." [2] The action of unjust molestation, found in several jurisdictions, does not appear in the *Record.*

Many entries are not characterized in form-of-action terms. Perhaps this reflects the predilections of the person making the entry. It seems more likely that, for the period of the First Charter at least, it indicates adoption by litigants of the form of summons provided in the printed laws of the commonwealth. This "president" or "forme," which made only functional reference to any form of action, read as follows in the *Laws and Liberties* of 1648:

To (IB) Carpenter, of (D). You are required to appear at the next Court, holden at (B) on the ―――― day of the ―――― month next ensuing; to answer the complaint of (N C) for with-holding a debt of ――――

---

[1] *Col. Laws Mass., 1672* 2.
[2] *Rec.* 78, 199. For recognition of account and actions on the case upon account as forms of actions see 2 *Rec. Mass.*

Bay 16. In the Suffolk County Court records (c. 1671–1680) actions of the case upon account were frequently used.

due upon a *Bond* or *Bill;* or for two heifers etc: sold you by him, or for work, or for a trespasse done him in his corn or hay, by your cattle, or for a slaunder you have done him in his name, or for striking him, or the like, and heerof you are not to fail at your peril. Dated the ——— day of the ——— month 1641.[3]

The only significant change in this form under the First Charter was the insertion in the 1672 laws of the words "in His Majesties Name" after the word "required."[4] The form of attachment provided contemplated the same description of the complaint as in the form of summons.

However, despite this statutory form there may have been some judicial expectancy of use of forms of action since the entry in a 1659 action noted "noe case specifyed in the summons."[5] In any event, in seventeenth-century Massachusetts Bay failure to characterize as to form of action was not peculiar to the courts of western Massachusetts.

In the form of summons prescribed in 1692 for use in actions before justices of the peace defendant was required to answer plaintiff in a "plea of _____," later changed to an "action or plea of _____." Substantially the same language was employed in the form of attachment to be used by justices of the peace.[6] However, this statutory prescription apparently did not serve in every case to evoke characterization by form of action.

DEBT

No great use was made of the action of debt under the First Charter, about a dozen such actions appearing in the *Record.*[7] By comparison much greater use was made of this form of action in such jurisdictions as Essex, Suffolk, and Norfolk—at least on the county level. However, during this period the *Record* lists such actions as for "failinge in the payment of a debt" or "for not paying a debt" which, although not so designated, were in effect actions of debt or perhaps, as found in the Suffolk County Court records, actions of the case concerning debt.[8] In a number of cases the circumstances of the debt do not appear. However, actions arose out of such matters as the sale of land, goods sold and delivered, a bill obligatory held by plaintiff, the balance due on an account stated, a payment ordered by the commit-

---

[3] *Laws and Liberties Mass.* 55.
[4] *Col. Laws Mass., 1672* 162.
[5] *Rec.* 77.

[6] 1 *Acts and Res. Prov. Mass., Bay* 81, 462.
[7] *Rec.* 6, 66, 77, 96, 167–168.
[8] *Rec.* 35, 38, 99, 171, 173–174, 180.

tee for the meeting house at Springfield, work performed, and a debt due a decedent's estate.[9] Debts were frequently payable in commodities such as corn or wheat, and, in one case, although tender of the debt was made in Indian corn and rye, plaintiff unsuccessfully contended that the debt should have been paid in wheat.[10]

After 1686 greater use was made of the action of debt. Many of these actions were so-called "debts due by booke" in which plaintiff, frequently a merchant or artisan, sought to recover for goods sold and delivered or for work performed on the basis of entries in books of account.[11] A number of such actions were brought by James Moore in 1687–88 for debts due the estate of Patrick Cunningham, the merchant competitor of John Pynchon. (In allowing these debts to be collected Pynchon disregarded a 1684 holding by the Court of Assistants that the account books of a deceased creditor were not admissible as evidence of debts due decedent.)[12] As in the earlier period, not all such actions were specifically labeled actions of debt. Other actions of debt were brought for monies due under an agreement for keeping a field, under some assignments of debts, for drinks provided, on the balance of an account stated, and for work performed.[13]

There is only one reference to an "action of Debt due by Bil," presumably upon a bill obligatory—a promissory note under seal.[14] However, in several other instances suit was brought for debts due by bill without reference to any specific form of action.[15] These probably should be regarded as actions of debt, yet it should be noted that on June 30, 1685 an action on the case was brought for "neglecting or delaying to pay Money according to Bill." As noted, there was some recognition in the laws of "actions of the case concerning debts and accounts."[16]

Under English practice an action of debt would lie only for a liquidated or certain sum of money due plaintiff; damages awarded for the detention of the debt would be merely nominal. In general, these standards were adhered to in the cases appearing in the *Record*, although allegations as to the amount of the debt sued for were somewhat elastic in a few cases.[17] An obvious deviation from English practice appears in a "Plea for a debt of .15s" entered in 1693. In this

9 *Rec.* 35, 38, 77, 79, 99, 167, 171, 173, 180.

10 *Rec.* 173.

11 *Rec.* 201, 204, 206, 216, 217, 221, 227, 229, 233, 252–253.

12 *Rec.* 203–204, 206. See 2 *Rec. Ct. Assts. Mass. Bay* 269.

13 *Rec.* 220–222, 241–242.

14 *Rec.* 241.

15 *Rec.* 157, 211, 214, 227, 240–241.

16 *Rec.* 192; 2 *Rec. Mass. Bay* 16; *Col. Laws Mass., 1672* 2.

17 *Rec.* 77, 220.

case, defendant having owned receipt of fifteen shillings to stub plaintiff's field, Pynchon found for the plaintiff "a quarter of an acre of Land wel stubbed forthwith fit for Plowing," or fifteen shillings and costs of court.[18]

In contrast with the sparse use of the action of debt evidenced in the *Record* itself for the period of the First Charter, the supplemental material from the Registry of Probate records shows that about a dozen such actions were brought before the commissioners sitting with County Court powers between 1660 and 1662. Several of these actions involved debts due by bill or on accounts between the parties. In most of these cases the entries refer to "an action of debt and damage to the value of _____ pounds" or "an action of debt with damage to the value of _____ pounds." [19] Thus, from the entries at least, it does not appear that the amount of the debt and the amount of damages were pleaded separately, a significant deviation from English practice. Secondly, it appears that in a few cases, again contrary to English practice, plaintiff was allowed to prove a debt less than the amount alleged and recover judgment thereon.[20]

In the Suffolk County Court (c. 1671–1680) it was the practice to plead the amount of the debt and damages separately but judgments were frequently given for less than the amount of the debt pleaded. In some cases penal bonds were chancered by the Suffolk County Court, but no instance of chancering appears in the *Record*, probably because of the limited jurisdiction exercised. Whether, in any event, Pynchon or the commissioners had the power to chancer a penal bond is moot.

ACTIONS ON THE CASE

In the first years of the court held at Springfield most of the causes entered in the *Record* were termed "actions of the case." These covered a wide range of subject matters such as wages due for work on a house; the taking away or failure to return boards or planks (the subject matter of several actions, including two by William Pynchon) ; failure to perform sufficient work for a day's wages; felling some trees on plaintiff's lot; for some corn delivered into defendant's possession; failure to divide properly the recompense for driving home certain stray sows and taking more pigs with his sows than defendant was entitled to; laying "false imputations of money

[18] *Rec.* 219.
[19] 1 *Hamp. Cty. Probate Ct. Rec.* 4, 7, 10, 14. *Cf.* Potter v. Osborne, *ibid.* 14,

where the amount of damages was apparently not specified.
[20] *Ibid.* 4, 7. See also to the same effect *Rec.* 66, 96.

dealinge"; failure to deliver a gun according to bargain; failure to break up certain ground according to bargain; the detention of a rug; the use of some tools and the charges of two journeys to recover such goods; detention of a pig; stating that plaintiff "said he was sorry that he did not make an end of his Cow"; abusing plaintiff's child; failure to return monies paid toward building plaintiff's chimneys, which defendant had neglected to do; "unjust possessing" of plaintiff's land; and damage done by swine to plaintiff's corn.[21] In a 1641 case John Burt complained against Judith Gregory "in an action of the case for breach of Covenant" for molesting plaintiff's daughter Sarah.[22]

Some of the above causes should have been labeled actions of trespass. Others in English practice probably would have been termed assumpsit (which had evolved from case) or debt. It is possible that this widespread use of "action of the case" reflects William Pynchon's unprofessional attempts to have procedure in the Springfield courts conform to English standards. After the departure of the founder for England, there is a decided decline in the volume of such cases found in the *Record*. However, an examination of other court records for the commonwealth period shows that extensive and somewhat indiscriminate use was made of action on the case in some jurisdictions, such as the Suffolk County Court. (In Essex County Court, if the calendaring in the printed records can be trusted, few actions on the case are found.) Later actions of the case were brought for failure to perform an arbitration award; for striking plaintiff's wife "with a long stick to her great prejudice"; for "unjustly stealinge away the affections" of plaintiff's "Espoused wife"; for the forfeiture of a bond; for breach of an agreement; for taking away timber; and for "neglecting or delaying to pay Money according to Bill."[23] A 1659 action by four plaintiffs against the town of Northampton concerned the town's turning out of the office of selectmen some inhabitants so chosen.[24] A 1693 "plea of Trespass upon the case" alleged the wrongful taking of a swine from plaintiff's possession under color of a writ of replevin irregularly executed.[25]

For the period in which the commissioners exercised the powers of a County Court (1660–1662) the entries in the Registry of Probate records reveal actions on the case covering such diverse matters as refusing to deliver a steer according to bargain, wrongfully impounding swine, taking a mare without leave, refusing to deliver a bull, wounding a horse, taking away bricks, "fraudulent dealinge"

[21] *Rec.* 3–4, 6–8, 13, 17, 22–23, 25, 37, 61.
[22] *Rec.* 17.
[23] *Rec.* 61, 74, 82, 84, 192.
[24] *Rec.* 77.
[25] *Rec.* 219.

about a meadow, failure to make distribution to a legatee, and with-holding a debt due by book account.[26]

To some extent the decline in the use of action on the case is accounted for by an increase in actions of trespass and of detinue. In addition, causes, which earlier presumably would have been denoted as actions on the case, are entered without reference to any form of action. A number of such cases concerned failure to perform a bargain, such as "non-performance of a bargayne of fetchinge . . . some fencinge stuffe"; "for not deliveringe a Cow and calfe accordinge to bargayne"; for John Sackett's "not performing his bargayne in thatching the Town barne" (an action by the selectmen of Springfield) ; "for non performance of a bargayne of ploughing"; for with-holding monies which defendant had engaged to pay for "victualls" supplied defendant's servant; "for not weaving linnen yarne into cloth according to agreement"; refusal to make satisfaction promised when taking plaintiff "off from a peice of Joinery worke"; for taking away the best or English hay cut on certain fields without dividing it, "Contrary to agreement"; and for neglecting to perform an engagement to cut and deliver three loads of wood.[27] Again in English practice these probably would have been brought in assumpsit. However, lack of characterization as to form of action was not limited to "frontier" courts. Many examples can be found in the records of the Suffolk and Essex County Courts, among others.

Other entries involved recovery of personalty and/or damages for wrongful detention. The chattels so detained included a sword, a plane which plaintiff "had formerly agreed for," a "Sandy Swine," an iron spade (detained over twelve months) , and a canoe detained nearly a month.[28] A 1664 action for wrongfully impounding a horse was probably in the nature of an action on the case. A 1694 entry concerned a "Plea for unjust taking away Boards" from the sawmill at Enfield.[29] However, an earlier entry, in 1659, refers to an "action of Theft" for stealing an ax at the lead mines; a second action entered at the same time is described only as "for stealinge about 10 pounds of lead." [30] No recognition has been found of such a form of action in the commonwealth laws or any use of it by other courts. A 1679 action for hindering plaintiff "in the Improvement of Land" at West-field, in which suit was let fall, probably should be regarded as in the nature of an action on the case, judged by the standards disclosed by the *Record*.[31] Several actions before the commissioners in September

---

26 1 *Hamp. Cty. Probate Ct. Rec.* 3, 7, 10, 14.

27 *Rec.* 72, 74, 78, 90, 95, 151, 173, 223, 235A.

28 *Rec.* 82, 174, 182, 207, 218.

29 *Rec.* 103, 222.

30 *Rec.* 78.

31 *Rec.* 168.

1661, undesignated as to form of action, probably come within the scope of action on the case—actions for wrongfully attaching a brick kiln, for wrongfully attaching a bull, and for taking a cow "in a dishonest way." [32]

TRESPASS

Presumably the term "trespass" in the first jurisdictional grant at Springfield was designed to include trespass *quare clausum fregit* and trespass *de bonis asportatis,* as well as trespass on the case, but not until 1649 was an action of trespass entered in the *Record,* other than actions on the case. In this instance Joseph Parsons complained against Reice Bedortha "in an action of Trespasse for pulling downe his fence against his hay Rick in the long meddow." [33] Bedortha countered with an action on the case against Parsons for "unjust possessing of his land in the long medow." The jury found for Parsons in both actions but whether it determined the title to the land or only the possessory right is not certain from the brief entries. In comparison with this picture the records of certain county courts, such as those for Essex, Norfolk, and York, reveal extensive use of trespass, due in large part to jurisdiction over actions involving real property.

The next action of trespass was not entered until September 1693 when Robert Pease of Enfield in a "Plea of Trespase" alleged that Samuel Terry and John Mighil had unjustly taken from him two loads of hay cut and standing in his fields. The pleas and evidences being read, John Pynchon found for the plaintiff two loads of hay or fourteen shillings and costs of court, if the land was his on which the hay was made, and for defendants, costs of court, in case the land on which the hay was made was theirs. [34] While not indicated in the entry, presumably defendants justified and demurred upon plea of title and would be expected to pursue their plea and bring forward a suit for trial of their title at the next Inferior Court of Common Pleas held in the county. However, such procedure was not given statutory form until passage in June 1698 of An Act for Preventing of Trespasses. [35] In any event, there is no indication that defendants tried their title in the Inferior Court of Common Pleas. The *Pease* action, in its facts and the procedure followed, was very similar to two earlier wrongful hay-taking cases brought in 1684 in which the form of action was not specified. [36] However, no law under the First Charter contemplated transfer of trial of title to the County Courts.

In *Gun* v. *Noble* in February 1695/6 defendant was summoned in a plea of trespass for felling and taking away pine trees on ground granted plaintiff by the town of Westfield for turpentine, but the action was not prosecuted. In *Cooley* v. *Kibbee,* a plea of trespass for cutting grass on plaintiff's meadow at Fresh Water Brook, defendant refused to become bound to prosecute title at the Inferior Court of Common Pleas, as provided by the above act, and Pynchon accordingly found for plaintiff two shillings and costs of court. In both *Cooley* v. *Hale* and *Keepe* v. *Kibbee,* two similar actions of trespass heard in the next month, defendants justified and demurred upon plea of title and the statutory procedure was pursued.[37]

Only one action of trespass appears in the *Record* which was in effect trespass *de bonis asportatis*. This was *Bissell* v. *Miller* (1700), an "action or Plea of Trespase for unlawfully or unjustly taking away and withholding" plaintiff's "Plow Irons." An action a few years earlier for "disorderly and violently" taking some bags left in plaintiff's custody was not characterized as to form of action.[38]

BATTERY

In December 1695, in *Granger* v. *King*, there was "a Plea of Trespass and Battery for abusing" plaintiff "by Striking and wounding him." [39] This is the only use made of this particular form of action in the *Record*. The close relation between civil and criminal jurisdiction in assault and battery cases has already been noted; however, in only one instance was there any reference to a form of action. In June 1686 complaint was made against John Norton by Samuel Ely "in an action of Battery etc" for that Norton "strake abused and drew Blood" from plaintiff.[40] That "battery" was regarded as a separate form of action under the commonwealth laws appears in the forty-shilling restriction upon the original jurisdiction of the County Court "except in cases of Defamation and Battery." [41] In English practice battery would have been termed "trespass *vi et armis*" and not regarded as a separate form of action. Records for other parts of the colony are consistent with the *Record* in showing relatively little use made of battery as a form of action.

DETINUE

Only five actions of detinue appear in the *Record,* all during the period from 1692 to 1695. In the first case Richard Waite, the prison

37 *Rec.* 228, 245–246.
38 *Rec.* 232, 246.
39 *Rec.* 226.
40 *Rec.* 199.
41 *Col. Laws Mass., 1672* 21.

keeper, in a "Plea of detinue" sued Thomas Lamb for five shillings in fees due for defendant's commitment. In *Parsons* v. *Mills,* a month later, an action of detinue was brought for not returning or rendering a true account of some cloth. In *Philips* v. *Adams,* an action of detinue was brought for "neglecting the payment of 27s. or thereabouts." In English practice, of course, detinue could be brought for recovery of a specific chattel only and not for a sum of money; except that if the chattel could not be returned, plaintiff could recover its value. In December 1695 a plea of detinue was brought in *Petty* v. *Kibbee,* for withholding from plaintiff a steer and in *King* v. *Smith* for taking away or detaining some cloth.[42] Nothing in the statutes passed under the Second Charter suggests why the action of detinue, used chiefly in the field of bailment in England, was not used earlier. An examination of other court records of Massachusetts Bay for the commonwealth period reveals a practice, consistent with the entries in the *Record,* of using action on the case for recovery of chattels where, in English practice, detinue would have been employed.

COVENANT

One action of covenant, or what appears to be such an action, appears in the *Record,* when in June 1660 Hugh Dudley complained against Thomas Mirick "for not performinge Covenante in plowinge up" a half acre of ground in the previous month at plaintiff's demand "as by the Covenante, presented appeares." Plaintiff pleading great damages and that he still expected the plowing to be done, the commissioners adjudged that defendant pay ten shillings in damages and also plow up the half-acre by the next May—an obvious departure from English practice.[43] It does not appear from the entry whether or not the covenant produced was under seal. The "action of the case for breach of Covenant" in *Burt* v. *Gregory* has already been noted. Examination of other court records indicates that little use was made of covenant as a form of action in seventeenth-century Massachusetts Bay.

REPLEVIN

Only a few scattered cases of replevin appear in the *Record.* However, the laws of the commonwealth clearly contemplated the use of

[42] *Rec.* 215, 216, 220, 226.
[43] *Rec.* 88. Perhaps this should be regarded as special assumpsit. Compare the 1648 case in the Essex County Court (*Archer* v. *Fullar*) calendared as: "Defendant to set up the fence within one month according to the covenant, the stuff being brought to the place." 1 *Rec. and Files Quart. Cts. Essex Cty. Mass.* 147.

this form of action since the Presidents and Formes in the several volumes of printed laws set forth the form of a writ of replevin.[44] The records of other courts indicate greater resort to this writ. The first action of this nature was brought in June 1675 by John Aires against two selectmen of Brookfield, for unlawful distraint of some pewter dishes by the constable at their order.[45] This case indicates one method, at least, of judicial review of warrants of distress issued by selectmen in enforcement of town orders. The fact that this is the sole case of this nature in the *Record* indicates that fines leveled by selectmen were usually paid or distress acquiesced in.

Several acts passed under the First Charter make reference to the use of an action of replevin by the owners of impounded horses or cattle to secure their return.[46] In *Miller* v. *Day*, in August 1685, plaintiff replevied a mare impounded by defendant and demanded ten shillings in damages for defendant's refusal to return the animal when offered poundage. Defendant had demanded five shillings from plaintiff "not so much for damage" as that the mare, being unruly and found unfettered in defendant's oats, defendant was entitled to five shillings under an amendatory law of 1673. A reading of this act reveals provision for a five-shilling fine to the town, as well as for damages accruing as a result of the offense, but does not indicate that the injured party was entitled to the fine. Apparently John Pynchon made the same reading of this law for he found for defendant only three shillings and sixpence, presumably for damage accruing from the offense.[47]

One of the early acts passed under the Second Charter provided for forms of writs for use by justices of the peace. However, this list did not include a writ of replevin, and it was not until 1698 that, following the form of writ of replevin provided for use in the Inferior Courts of Common Pleas, the statement appears: "The like form of replevin to be observed for matters cognizable before a justice of peace, *mutatis mutandis.*" [48] In the September 1693 "plea of Trespass upon the case" in *Goulding* v. *Selden,* defendant was alleged to have taken out of plaintiff's custody a swine "under colour of Law and Countenance of Authority by vertue of a writ shewed and caled a Replevin . . . not regularly executing any writ and regardless of the Comands and direction of the Law." This case, in which Pynchon found for the plaintiff, may reflect doubts as to the status of replevin in view of the statutory omission. However, next year in

---

44 *Laws and Liberties Mass.* 56; *Col. Laws Mass., 1660* 203–204; *Col. Laws Mass., 1672* 162–163.

45 *Rec.* 159.

46 *Col. Laws Mass., 1672* 18, 125.

47 *Rec.* 193; *Col. Laws Mass., 1672* 209, amending *ibid.* 18.

48 1 *Acts and Res. Prov. Mass. Bay* 81, 320.

Booth v. *Hayward,* is found a "Plea of unjust Impounding" by defendant of a mare and two colts which had been replevied by plaintiff. In this case the parties "agreed al past matters" and plaintiff's bond was delivered up.[49]

ACTION OF SLANDER OR DEFAMATION

The laws of the commonwealth recognized the action of slander, sometimes referred to as defamation, as a separate form of action.[50] In English practice slander would fall under trespass on the case. As has been noted, slander or defamation was a criminal offense which might, however, result in an award of damages to the injured party—as in the widow Marshfield's case. The records of other courts in the colony reflect a substantial volume of actions of slander or defamation; the number of such actions appearing in the *Record* is comparatively modest.

In one of the earliest entries in the *Record* the Reverend Moxon brought an action of slander against John Woodcock for reporting that plaintiff had taken a false oath against him at Hartford. In the next year collateral reference is found to recovery by Henry Gregory of twenty shillings for three slanders, but the nature of the slander does not appear. John Woodcock also sought, apparently without success, a warrant to warn Henry Gregory to answer him in two actions of slander.[51]

In September 1658 Edward Elmer brought an action of defamation against William Holton and Robert Bartlett for affirming that plaintiff, in going from Northampton to Springfield to take his oath as commissioner for ending small causes, "went down in a disorderly way" and for charging that plaintiff had "made a breach or rent in the Town [Northampton] concerninge the Lords dayes meetings." The commissioners, while they could not wholly free plaintiff from blame on the first count, found no defamation—"the speaking of a mans faylings and infirmityes may be disorderly and yet not a defamation." On the second count, the commissioners found the charge to some degree defamatory but, in regard of "some blame worthy carriage" on plaintiff's part, awarded no damages. The related complaint of Edward Elmer's son against Goodwife Holton has already been noted.[52] Edward Elmer reappears in two actions of slander at the March 27, 1659/60 court. In a review of an action of slander, previously tried at Northampton, in which Elmer was charged with slandering William Clark in saying that he was "noe better than a

---

[49] *Rec.* 219, 224.
[50] *Col. Laws Mass., 1672* 2, 21, 92.
[51] *Rec.* 4–5, 9, 10.
[52] *Rec.* 74–75.

theefe," Elmer withdrew his action. In an action by Nathaniel Clark, son of William Clark, against Elmer for calling plaintiff a thief, the jury found for plaintiff. It seems probable that these actions of slander were related to an action on the case, tried at the same court, by Elmer against William Clark for "takeing away of tymber" in which the commissioners found for defendant.[53]

One of the three actions by William Deynes against John Bagg, in March 1659, for affirming that plaintiff "did convert a greate deal of lead from the right owner" was presumably an action of slander. These matters issued by arbitration, Bagg making public acknowledgment of his offenses and receiving an admonition. Another action of slander against John Bagg, for reporting that Joseph Crowfoot had stolen while he tended the mill at Windsor, was entered at the same sitting; a later entry indicates that Bagg was cast in the amount of six shillings.[54] In the next year Francis Hacklinton brought an action of slander against Mary Ely for saying that plaintiff was seen at an unseasonable time of night with Hester Bliss and that there were "unseemly passages between them," but the commissioners, finding the testimony of little weight, adjudged it no slander.[55]

Several actions of defamation were brought before the commissioners exercising County Court powers (1660–62). Two actions by Francis Hacklinton, one against Alexander Edwards "in Saying that he runne away with his mare," and the other against Henry Cunliffe "in Sayinge he is a man of noe good report" were withdrawn. In an action of defamation by Richard Fellowes against Judith Varlette, alleging two hundred pounds damages from her statement that he had played or would have played the rogue, the jury found damages of ten shillings, plus thirteen shillings, sixpence costs of court. William Pixley was awarded ten pounds by a jury in an action against Joseph Roote for "Saying that he had gott Sarah Lynsley with child." [56]

The complaint entered in March 1676/7 by Joseph Browne against Lidia Morgan "for her abusive cariage and Language towards him using reprochfull and Scandalous speeches to him and of him" appears to have been a civil action, but it was not characterized as to form of action. In December 1694 Isack Meacham recovered ten shillings damages in an action against Obadiah Abbee for defamation in saying plaintiff was a cheater and had cheated him and that plaintiff (who seemingly had by committee order laid out a highway) had "altered the Highway and made the East Lots fall back to bring

53 Rec. 84–85.
54 Rec. 78, 83.
55 Rec. 89.

56 1 Hamp. Cty. Probate Ct. Rec. 7, 10, 14.

the Pease out of the dirt." [57] In February 1685/6 Benjamin Knowlton brought an action against Charles Ferry for defaming plaintiff's wife by false reports and "aspersing her as being the Raiser of scandalous reports on Miriam Mirick deceased," in which public acknowledgment of defendant's fault was ordered. In the same year Deacon Jonathan Burt brought an action against Thomas Mirick, Senior for defaming plaintiff by saying "he lyed basely and was a Lying man," but forgave defendant upon "his owning his disorder and Ill speakings." [58]

The first action of this nature under the Second Charter is found in March 1697/8 when Hezakiah Dickenson brought a "Plea of Defamation" against Abraham Temple for "Saying writing or in a Libellous manner declaring or Publishing" that plaintiff was "a Theife a lyar and whore Master." Defendant denied the charge, but Pynchon found "to much Idle base and reprochful writing, speeches and carriage" by defendant "in Publishing or spreading that which Tends to the defamation" of plaintiff. However, the damage to plaintiff not being demonstrated and "supposing none believe any of the reports Concerning him," Pynchon left the matter for the present and plaintiff to further process as he saw cause.[59] The criminal aspects of Temple's conduct have already been noted. In September 1700 in *King* v. *Sexton* plaintiff recovered ten shillings and costs of court in an action of defamation in that defendant had called plaintiff a thief.[60]

PROBATE AND ADMINISTRATION

Matters of probate and administration were not normally comprehended within general grants of civil jurisdiction in seventeenth-century Massachusetts. None of the commissions discussed above made specific reference to jurisdiction in such matters and only a few entries relating to testamentary matters appear in the *Record*. The last will and testament of John Searles was recorded on April 20, 1642, probably in connection with the antenuptial agreement between the widow Searles and Alexander Edwards, recorded on the same date.[61] On March 5, 1654/5 the commissioners made an order relating to the estate of Nathaniel Bliss, who died intestate, but again this was in connection with an antenuptial agreement between the widow and Thomas Gilbert. On July 14, 1659 the commissioners en-

---

[57] *Rec.* 164, 188–191.
[58] *Rec.* 196, 202.
[59] *Rec.* 235B.
[60] *Rec.* 247.
[61] *Rec.* 18–21. See also the antenuptial agreements entered into by widows intending to remarry and approved by William Pynchon on August 7, 1641 (*ibid.* 15) and April 12, 1649 (*ibid.* 29).

tered an order of administration upon the estate of Symon Sackett. In a few cases orders were made as to guardianships.[62] A number of orders in matters of probate and administration appear in the supplemental Registry of Probate material for 1660–62 when the commissioners were exercising the powers of a County Court, since normally such matters were handled on the County Court level.

A review of the civil jurisdiction exercised by the several courts at Springfield and the vicinity indicates that some attention was paid from time to time to forms of action. However, in no case does it appear that, as in English practice, functional significance attached to the use of a particular form of action. With litigants acting as their own attorneys and with little or no professional guidance from judge, clerk, or recorder, it would be unrealistic to expect close adherence to the standards of Westminster Hall. This is especially true when it is considered that the colony laws for much of the period made only limited attempts to comply with such standards and the general Puritan attitude was one of reformation of, rather than strict adherence to, existing English practice and procedure. The laws of the General Court made accurate characterization as to form of action neither a virtue nor a necessity for the litigant. The Court of Assistants, as far as appears, imposed no more stringent requirements in its judicial rule-making.

[62] *Rec.* 67–68, 80, 178, 181.

X. Procedure in Civil Actions

THE entries appearing in the *Record* for civil actions during the First Charter reveal slight concern for recordation of procedural details. The original grant of authority to William Pynchon authorized him "to direct warrantes, both processe executions and attachmentes." The subsequent commissions of the General Court made no reference to power to issue process. However, such power was probably implied, as in the early laws conferring civil jurisdiction upon magistrates and commissioners for ending small causes.[1] The earliest cases indicate that in most instances an action was commenced by service upon defendant by the constable of a "warrant" warning defendant to answer plaintiff's complaint, this "warrant" being granted by Pynchon. It seems likely that the form of such "warrant" was in the nature of a "summons." [2] The entries for the later commonwealth period indicate use of a summons as the procedural norm.

Under a 1641 law each town was authorized to establish the office of clerk of the writs. This officer was authorized to grant summonses and attachments in all civil actions, replevins, and summonses for witnesses.[3] The first reference in the *Record* to a clerk of the writs is on May 29, 1649 when an entry indicates that Henry

---

[1] *Rec.* 2. Later laws assumed magistrates had power to issue "Warrants, Summons and Attachments" (*Col. Laws Mass., 1672* 28), but the December 10, 1641 order of the General Court establishing the office of clerk of the writs specifically authorized magistrates to issue "warrants for summons" in the interim. 1 *Rec. Mass. Bay* 344–345.

[2] *Rec.* 10. See the reference to defendant in Moxon v. Woodcock being "summond by warrant" (*Rec.* 4) and the

interchangeable use of "warrant" and "summons" in the colony laws. *Laws and Liberties Mass.* 12; *Col. Laws Mass., 1672* 7.

[3] *Laws and Liberties Mass.* 12. Cf. the first appointments by the General Court which did not include Springfield (1 *Rec. Mass. Bay* 344–345) and the 1640 appointment by the General Court of certain persons in various towns (not including Springfield) "to take caption or cognizance, and to make replevies." *Ibid.* 307.

Burt was chosen clerk of the writs for Springfield; on the same day William Pynchon noted that "all the printed laws" (the *Laws and Liberties* of 1648) were read, the whole town being present.[4] Whether after this date all initial process issued by the clerk of the writs is not disclosed by the *Record*. A magistrate resident in Springfield had specific authority under the 1648 laws to issue warrants, summonses, and attachments.[5] Presumably the various commissioners for Springfield had authority to issue process by virtue of the same law which conferred such authority upon commissioners to end small causes in the various towns lacking magistrates. While evidence is lacking, it is likely that after May 1649 the form of summons set forth under Presidents and Formes in the printed laws, probably directed to the constable, was used; perhaps process issued in the King's name prior to the date (1662) when required by order of the General Court. By virtue of a 1647 law a defendant was at liberty whether or not to appear if the first summons was not served six days before the court at which it was returnable and "the Case briefly specified in the Warrant." The same period prevailed in the case of attachments until 1685 when it was changed to fourteen days.[6]

The original authorization of William Pynchon, as well as the law establishing the office of clerk of the writs, made reference to the use of attachments. An early law (1641) provided that the clerk of the writs grant attachment only where defendant was a stranger, or going out of the jurisdiction, or about to make away with his estate to defraud creditors, or doubtful in his estate. It was later provided that such status be signified to the clerk in writing by two honest persons dwelling near defendant. In case of courts suddenly called on extraordinary occasions attachment might be employed and the six-day service requirement dispensed with.[7] In 1650 the law was liberalized so that every plaintiff should be at liberty to take out either a summons or an attachment against any defendant, except that no attachment was to be granted any foreigner in an action against a settled inhabitant unless sufficient security was given to prosecute the action and answer for such costs as should be awarded defendant. Under a 1644 law, in all attachments of goods and chattels, or of lands and hereditaments, legal notice had to be given to the party or left in writing at his house or place of

4 *Rec.* 31.
5 *Laws and Liberties Mass.* 8. On the power to issue replevins see 1 *Rec. Mass. Bay* 307.
6 *Laws and Liberties Mass.* 49 (for an instance where failure to comply with this law was raised, see *Rec.* 84) ; 5 *Rec. Mass. Bay* 503.
7 *Laws and Liberties Mass.* 12, 49; 1 *Rec. Mass. Bay* 344–345; 2 *ibid.* 163, 194.

legal abode; otherwise the suit was not to proceed to trial, except in the case where a defendant was out of the jurisdiction.[8]

With the exception of the years between 1678 and 1681, the *Record,* during the period of the First Charter, makes little reference to use of attachments. However, this should not be taken to mean that in every case in which the *Record* is silent as to process, a summons, rather than attachment, was utilized. The form of attachment employed is not set forth in the *Record;* however, an attachment issued by Henry Burt, as clerk of the writs, in *Parsons* v. *Bridgman* has survived,[9] reading as follows:

To the Constable of Northampton

By virtue hereof you are required to attach the body of Sarah Bridgman wife of James Bridgman of Northampton and to take bond of her to the value of an 100£ with suficient surty or suerties for her personall appearance at the next Countey Court held at Cambridg on the 7th of October next ensuing the date hereof   Then and there to answer at the Complaint of Joseph Parsons for Slandering of the [*illegible*] Parsons and to make a true returne thereof under your hand hereof fayle you not.

<table>
<tr><td>Springfield this
8 of September 1656</td><td>By the Court
HENRY BURT</td></tr>
</table>

This warrant was returned to the County Court at Cambridge by Alexander Edwards, constable, that he had taken the body of Sarah Bridgman "and for want of Suirtie hav commited her to Safe custody in North Hamton [Northampton] shee being weeke and with childe is not able to appear at this court without hassard to her life." The form of this attachment follows in substance that provided in the Presidents and Formes with some variations in wording.

The practice with respect to attachment found in the *Record* varies from that in Suffolk, Essex, and Norfolk where, on the county level at least, attachment was the usual method of commencing an action. The writ was usually served by the marshal in such counties; from the *Record* it is not clear by whom attachments were served. In most cases they probably were served by the constable, a practice in accordance with the laws of the commonwealth. The form of attachment used in the other counties followed in substance the form provided by the laws of the colony.

A 1641 law provided that every person should have liberty to replevy chattels or goods impounded, distrained, or seized, unless

---

[8] *Laws and Liberties Mass.* 3; 4 *Rec. Mass. Bay (Part I)* 5–6; 2 *ibid.* 80. For the form of summons for appearance on attachment see 5 *ibid.* 489–490.

[9] File Papers in Parsons v. Bridgman, Folder 16 (1656), Office of Clerk, Superior Court, Middlesex County, Mass. (East Cambridge).

upon execution after judgment or in payment of fines, provided he put in good security to prosecute the replevin and to satisfy such demand as his adversary should recover against him in law. Included among the Presidents and Formes provided by the laws was a writ of replevin which embodied the statutory requirement of security.[10] However, the only replevin action entered in the *Record* under the First Charter yields no information as to the procedure followed.[11]

While the *Record* is silent on the point, plaintiff presumably entered his action with the court at the opening of the sitting at which the cause was to be heard—at least a 1652 law provided that, in order to defray charges, every person impleading another in an action for less than forty shillings, triable before a magistrate or commissioners for ending small causes, should pay ten groats (three shillings, fourpence) before his case be entered.[12] What was entailed in "entering an action" does not appear from a reading of the *Record* or an examination of the colony laws. Perhaps the practice of the County Courts or Courts Baron in England was followed in this particular.

The colony laws made no provision for regular sittings by magistrates or commissioners for small causes, which must have posed a practical problem for the clerk of the writs. However, an order at a Springfield general town meeting on November 6, 1648 provided that there should be henceforth four courts kept yearly on the first Tuesdays of November, February, May, and September, except for special occasions when reasonable notice was to be given.[13] The *Record* indicates no adherence to this order; William Pynchon may have felt that the town had no authority to regulate the time of his sittings. The only other regulation of court days, except for the "County Courts" held at Springfield and Northampton, is found in the appointment by Pynchon, Holyoke, and Chapin, as commissioners, of the first Thursday in March and in September for the hearing and determining of differences or offenses that might arise in the township.[14] The *Record* does not indicate where the earlier Springfield sittings were held; after 1665 it seems likely that they were held at John Pynchon's house. At Northampton, as entries in the *Pynchon Account Books* show, the commissioners held court at the ordinary.

After an action had been entered plaintiff was supposed to make his appearance and prosecute when the cause was reached for trial. Due to failure of plaintiffs to attend the courts ready to enter an ap-

[10] *Col. Laws Mass., 1672* 132, 162–163.
[11] *Rec.* 159.
[12] *Col. Laws Mass., 1672* 2. See also the 1/6 fee mentioned in 2 *Rec. Mass. Bay* 208. The fee for entry of the action was waived in one instance when the parties, unprepared for trial, agreed to let the matter rest. *Rec.* 103.
[13] 1 Burt, *Hist. Springfield* 195.
[14] *Rec.* 55.

pearance and prosecute, which had been connived at by the courts, the 1672 laws provided that, if a plaintiff did not appear and prosecute after being three times called in court by name, he was to be non-suited and costs awarded defendant.[15] This sanction was not invoked in any entry appearing in the *Record*. Even in the absence of the reformatory law, as a March 1661 entry in the supplemental Registry of Probate material shows, a defendant might be awarded costs if plaintiff failed to appear to prosecute.[16]

After the plaintiff had been called to appear to prosecute, the defendant was called three times in court by the constable to appear to answer. This practice is found in an early entry in the *Record;* the 1672 law, which was also applicable to appearances by defendants, provided for an award of costs to the plaintiff if the defendant failed to appear when thus called. However, the supplemental Registry of Probate material shows such costs were awarded even prior to the enactment of this law.[17] Prior to any award of costs to plaintiff the constable or perhaps the marshal must have made return of service of the summons. (There is no indication in the *Record* of service of a summons by a plaintiff or his agent.) Nothing appears as to the form of return used. A 1679 case indicates that plaintiff was responsible for seeing that the constable made return of the summons and might be required to pay defendant's charges in case of failure to procure return of service of the summons. A constable failing to make return of a summons might be fined.[18]

In those cases in which attachment was used the court might proceed to an ex parte determination if defendant failed to appear. Late in the period the General Court provided a form of bond which plaintiff was required to give to prosecute the attachment to effect when such process issued.[19] Again a return of service would have to be made, either by the constable or marshal, before the court would proceed to an ex parte determination. (Under a 1675 law the constable or marshal might make his return on the back side of the attachment and deliver it to the plaintiff.) With the exception of a few cases where chattels were attached, it does not appear from the *Record* whether personalty or real property was attached or whether sufficient surety was given for appearance.[20] A form of "Bond for Ap-

15 *Col. Laws Mass., 1672* 87.

16 1 *Hamp. Cty. Probate Ct. Rec.* 4. At the same court a plaintiff was non-suited for failure to give defendant legal warning to appear and ordered to pay 10 shillings for entry of his action.

17 *Rec.* 17, 168; 1 *Hamp. Cty. Probate Ct. Rec.* 8.

18 *Rec.* 17, 168.

19 *Rec.* 170; 1 *Hamp. Cty. Probate Ct. Rec.* 8 (presumably attachment had been used in Kinge v. Elmer) ; 4 *Rec. Mass. Bay (Part II)* 509; 5 *ibid.* 489-490.

20 *Rec.* 38, 180; *Col. Laws Mass., 1672* 220.

pearance" in attachment cases was provided in the Presidents and Formes.

At common law in England attachment was used only to compel the appearance of the defendant; when he entered an appearance, the attachment was dissolved. In the commonwealth, after some inconvenience arising from the common-law rule, it was provided by law that the attachment should not be released by appearance and that the property attached or bond given by sureties was to respond to the judgment.[21]

With one exception nothing in the *Record* indicates that, when the action had been entered and both parties had appeared, written pleadings were used.[22] (A 1647 law requiring plaintiffs to deliver a written declaration in a fair and legible hand to the clerk of the court at least three days before the court so that defendant might answer and summon witnesses was short-lived.) Two cases indicate that the summons might serve the purpose of a declaration or complaint. In a March 1660 action of the case for breach of an agreement defendant pleaded that the case was laid down in such general terms in the summons that he knew not what agreement was intended and therefore was not prepared to answer. The commissioners judged the plea reasonable. In a December 1684 case a summons was held to have fully complied with the law in setting forth the defamation of plaintiff's name in several ways.[23] The term "answer" was used loosely to characterize defendant's plea. There are no references to any demurrers, dilatory pleas or pleas in bar, including pleas of the general issue such as *non est factum, nil debet,* not guilty, or *non cepit,* nor do the entries reflect the formalized language associated with recognized pleas in English practice. No mention is made of imparlances, replications, rejoinders, surrejoinders, rebutters, or surrebutters. The issue was apparently arrived at on the basis of pleadings *ad exitum* consisting of a declaration or complaint and answer. Apparently in most cases the issue was one of fact not of law.

In connection with use of written pleadings it should be noted that in Essex County, for instance, the records on appeal from judgments of magistrates to the County Court do not contain written declarations or complaints and answers. In cases in which the County Court for Essex exercised original jurisdiction any written pleadings were basically factual recitals, not couched in legal language, and with little attention paid to the essential allegations required by the

---

21 4 *Rec. Mass. Bay (Part I)* 26–27, 365; *Col. Laws Mass., 1672* 144. See also 2 *Rec. Mass. Bay* 187.

22 In Knowlton v. Ferry there is a reference to "all Pleas and Evedence in the case which are on file being heard, read and Considered." *Rec.* 196.

23 *Rec.* 84, 188. For the law see 2 *Rec. Mass. Bay* 208.

various forms of actions at common law. If written pleadings were used at any time in the courts of lower jurisdiction of Hampshire, they probably did not differ substantially from those used in Essex County.

In the causes heard by the commissioners as a "County Court" a substantial number of actions which had been entered were withdrawn before trial; in some a notation was made that the parties had agreed between themselves. No such wholesale withdrawals appear as to courts held in other capacities.[24]

As to the trial, with one or two exceptions, all civil actions were tried by jury until March 1654/5—six jurors constituting the jury. The wording of the various authorizations and commissions leaves some question as to whether or not jury trial could have been dispensed with without the consent of the parties. In the causes tried in 1659–1662 by the commissioners exercising the power of a County Court a jury of twelve was used. Apart from these sittings, no use of juries in civil cases appears in the *Record* after March 1654/5, with one exception in 1688.[25] John Pynchon, as magistrate, was, of course, authorized to hear and determine causes without a jury. In a few instances causes were referred to arbitrators rather than tried by a jury or the court, although it might still be necessary to bring an action to enforce the award of the arbitrators.[26] However, in a December 1639 action for slander plaintiff put it to the inhabitants present whether "it were fitter to be heard by a private refference below in the River, or tryed here publikly by a Jury." The general vote of the plantation was that, seeing the matter was public, it should be publicly heard and tried at Agawam by a jury.[27]

While the manner of summoning jurors does not appear from the *Record,* it seems probable that the statutory norm was followed —at least after the establishment of the office of clerk of the writs. This norm contemplated that the clerk of the writs, in convenient time before the sitting of the court, send a warrant to the constable of Springfield to give timely notice to the freemen of the town to choose as many able and discreet men as the warrant required for jury duty. Those so chosen were warned by the constable to attend the court and return of process was then made by the constable to the clerk of the writs.[28] Prior to the establishment of the office of clerk

[24] 1 *Hamp. Cty. Probate Ct. Rec.* 3, 7, 8, 11, 14; *Rec.* 85. *Cf. Rec.* 164.

[25] Bancroft v. Moore, action of review in May 1688. *Rec.* 207. The entries contain no reference to a jury foreman, although foremen were used in the Salem courts, for one, as early as 1636.

[26] *Rec.* 8, 61, 78. See also the reference of Thomas Burnam's case and Cooley v. Webb. *Ibid.* 77, 79.

[27] *Rec.* 4, 5.

[28] See title "Juries, Jurors" in the various printed laws.

of the writs it seems likely that the constable was directed by warrants from William Pynchon to warn jurors to appear. In the earliest period, since courts and town meetings appear to have coalesced, jurors may even have been chosen from those present at such gatherings without the necessity of a warrant. For the period when the commissioners for Springfield and Northampton sat jointly such warrant may have issued by the recorder of the "county," since jurors were drawn from several towns and the recorder was in effect the clerk of the court. At a court held at Northampton in March 1662, the constable of Hadley was fined twenty shillings for not returning the warrant for summoning jurymen (presumably to the recorder), but the fine was rebated.[29]

The jurors appearing in court were impaneled and sworn truly to try between party and party. The County Court records indicate that a juror warned to attend who failed to appear without justifiable cause would be fined. The following form of oath for petty jurors appears in the laws and was probably used—at least after the printed laws were available:

You Swear by the Living God, that in the Cause or Causes now legally to be committed to you by this Court; You will true Tryal make, and just Verdict give therein, according to the Evidence given you, and the Laws of this Jurisdiction: So help you God, etc.[30]

By virtue of an early law of the colony either plaintiff or defendant might challenge any juror. If the challenge was found just or reasonable by the bench or the rest of the jury, as the challenger might choose, it was to be allowed and *tales de circumstantibus* impaneled in room of those so challenged. In one 1649/50 case four jurors were thus challenged.[31] Until May 1647 it was not lawful to choose nonfreemen as jurors, but by force of circumstances this law was not strictly regarded at Springfield. In fact it was not until the law was changed to permit nonfreemen who had taken the oath of fidelity to be jurors that William Pynchon was authorized to make freemen in Springfield "of those that are in covenant and live according to their profession."[32]

The colony laws specifically defined the function of the jury to "finde the matter of fact with the damages and costs," according to

<hr />

[29] 1 *Hamp. Cty. Probate Ct. Rec.* 10. For later fines by the County Court see *ibid.* 78, 134, 140.

[30] See the "Petty-Juries Oath" in the Presidents and Formes in the several volumes of printed laws. For the fines see

1 *Hamp. Cty. Probate Ct. Rec.* 58, 125, 156.

[31] *Rec.* 37. *Cf.* the offer of liberty to except. *Rec.* 10. See title "Tryals" in the printed laws.

[32] 2 *Rec. Mass. Bay* 197, 224.

the evidence of the parties. The judge was to declare the sentence
or to direct the jury to find according to law. If there were matters of
apparent equity, as the forfeiture of an obligation, breach of covenant without damage, or the like, the bench was to determine such
matters of equity. The jurors, in all cases where the law was obscure
so that they could not be satisfied therein, had liberty to present a
special verdict, but no such verdict appears in the *Record*.[33]

Little appears in the *Record* as to the details of trial procedure.
Presumably plaintiff presented his case first. Such presentation might
entail a statement of the plaintiff's case to the court or jury, followed
by the production in court of witnesses, the production of depositions of witnesses not present in court, and the production of documentary evidence such as agreements, bonds, notes, and account
books. (No instance of profert and oyer of documents appears in the
Record nor in the other court records examined.) It is doubtful
whether plaintiff was allowed to testify in his own behalf. The requirement of two witnesses, mentioned in connection with criminal
procedure, is also referred to in civil cases. Witnesses were probably
summoned by the constable (or perhaps the marshal); the summons
(or attachment) was at first issued by William Pynchon and later by
the clerk of the writs or John Pynchon, as magistrate. No form of
such summons was contained in the Presidents and Formes until
1685. A witness was not required to appear unless paid his travel expenses by the party calling him; a witness, so paid, who did not appear was liable to pay the damages of the parties.[34]

By law any magistrate or commissioner so authorized by the General Court might take out of court the testimony of any person of
fourteen years of age or over, of sound understanding and reputation, in any civil action. (The magistrate or commissioner retained
the deposition until the court met or turned it over to the clerk of
the writs to be recorded so that it might not be altered.) However,
if a witness lived within ten miles of the court and was not disabled
by sickness or other infirmity, his testimony so taken could not be
received or made use of unless the witness was present to be further
examined about it.[35] This proviso indicates that witnesses were subject to cross-examination. (How such cross-examination could be
preserved for appeal purposes is not apparent.) The 1650 and 1652
laws requiring evidence in writing in civil causes have already been
noted. After the plaintiff had presented his case, the defendant was
presumably given an opportunity to present his witnesses or other

---

[33] See title "Juries, Jurors" in the printed laws.
[34] *Col. Laws Mass., 1672* 159.
[35] See title "Witnesses" in the printed laws and 5 *Rec. Mass. Bay* 489–490.

proof; a defendant, to a limited extent, might be allowed to testify in his own behalf. Trial might even be adjourned to permit a party to obtain and offer further evidence.[36]

While apparently no depositions used in any case entered in the *Record* have survived, an indication of the format used about 1656 may be obtained from the depositions in *Parsons* v. *Bridgman,* taken before John Pynchon, Elizur Holyoke, or some of the Northampton commissioners. The form is substantially that used in the courts of the Bay.[37]

Presumably witnesses gave testimony under oath. The form found in the printed laws, referred to in connection with criminal procedure, was probably used.[38] While perjury was punishable under the colony laws only in capital cases, in 1643 John Leonard was removed as constable "as a mark of disfavor for swearinge to a lie" in testimony given in a civil action.[39]

There is no indication that any party appeared by counsel. In one case a Boston plaintiff appeared by an "Atturney"—a use of an attorney in fact sanctioned by the commonwealth laws and found in many cases on the county court level in Suffolk, Essex, and Norfolk. The parties themselves must have introduced and offered evidence, questioned witnesses, argued points of law, and possibly made summations. Under these circumstances it is remarkable that more litigants, unlearned in the law but convinced of the justice of their cause, did not end up by being committed for contempt.[40] Presumably, as noted earlier, plaintiff was required to satisfy the burden of proof by "sufficient" evidence.

The *Record* fails to indicate the extent to which the court instructed juries as to the applicable law. Any jury or jurors, not clear in their judgments or conscience, had liberty under the colony laws to advise in open court with any person they thought fit to resolve or direct them, but the *Record* reveals no instance in which such advice was sought. In no case is a directed verdict found. Nor is there found any case, while the commissioners exercised the powers of a County Court, in which court and jury differed as to their verdict so that neither could proceed with peace of conscience, requiring determination at a higher level of the judicial hierarchy. In no case, apparently, jurors had difficulty in reaching a unanimous verdict.[41]

---

[36] *Rec.* 8–9, 23, 72. *Cf.* the 1665 law which would require all pleas to be made and all evidence presented to the jury without any delays. 4 *Rec. Mass. Bay (Part II)* 280.

[37] See note 9 above.

[38] See "Witnesses Oath" under Presidents and Formes in the printed laws.

[39] *Rec.* 23.

[40] 1 *Hamp. Cty. Probate Ct. Rec.* 4; *Rec.* 191.

[41] See title "Juries, Jurors" in the printed laws.

While the colony laws contemplated declaration of the sentence by the court following a jury verdict, the *Record* contains only the jury verdicts without any notation of declaration of sentence or entry of judgment upon the verdict. This was not peculiar to western Massachusetts. Lechford, in his comments on judicial procedure in the Bay, noted that the verdict taken and entered was "also called the judgment." Most of the verdicts or judgments were, in effect, that plaintiff recover a debt or chattels or receive damages. A few contemplated what amounted to specific performance. In slander cases an acknowledgment by defendant of the tort might constitute part of the judgment. In an early case the jury deferred its verdict until impartial men viewed some work and determined whether it was done according to bargain. A jury sitting until near midnight was granted leave to bring in its verdict by the next evening. The 1648 *Laws and Liberties* provided that every judgment in any court be recorded "with all substantial reasons," but the *Record* rarely indicates the grounds of the judgment.[42]

While the various commissions made no reference to awards of costs of court and the laws provided no comprehensive schedule of such costs, costs of court as well as charges were awarded in a substantial number of cases. In view of the small amount involved in most actions appearing in the *Record* an award of costs might constitute a relatively significant item. For instance, in one 1679 case plaintiff was given judgment for thirteen shillings, sixpence plus thirteen shillings costs. In a number of cases costs were awarded in a lump sum. However, some of the individual items of costs and charges found in the *Record* are as follows: entry of action, three shillings, fourpence, and later, three shillings, sixpence; summons and service thereof, one shilling, twopence; attachment and service thereof, one shilling, sixpence; attendance of plaintiff or defendant, two shillings per diem (usually increased if the party was required to travel any distance); witness fee, one shilling per diem (the colony laws provided for a fee of two shillings per diem unless the witness lived within three miles, in which case the fee was one shilling, sixpence); and summons for witness, threepence. In one case plaintiff was admitted to try his case *in forma pauperis,* although not provided by the laws at the time.[43]

Most of the verdicts or judgments were expressed in terms of specie. However, after 1660 the *Record* contains a scattering of cases in which the judgment was expressly made payable in Indian corn,

42 *Plaine dealing: or, News from New England* (ed. J. H. Trumbull, 1867) 67; *Laws and Liberties Mass.* 46; *Rec.* 4, 22.

43 *Rec.* 37, 170.

wheat, tar or pork; in most cases it appears that the debt sued for had
been incurred in forms of such commodities. This probably reflects
a 1654 law that "all Contracts and Engagements for Money, Corn,
Chattel [cattle] or Fish, shall be satisfied in kinde according to Covenant . . . and in no case shall any Creditor be forced to take any
other Commodities for satisfaction of his debt." [44]

Few cases make reference to the grant of execution upon a judgment. The form of one such warrant subscribed by William Pynchon in 1640 and directed to the constable is set forth in the *Record*.[45] Later laws provided that the warrant be signed by the clerk
of the writs, that it be directed to the marshal, who was to make return within five months, that it take a prescribed form, and that it
not issue until twelve hours after judgment entered, except by special order of the court. While the early writ referred to directed the
constable to attach the body of defendant, later practice apparently
permitted body attachment only if the judgment could not be satisfied from the defendant's goods or lands. Exempt from execution
were such necessary items as bedding, apparel, tools, arms, and house-
hold implements. By law a judgment debtor without property was
not to be kept in prison but at the requirement of the creditor
might be sold into service to satisfy the debt.[46] In the case of an attachment of goods or lands of a defendant out of the jurisdiction,
judgment was not entered until the next court, if defendant did not
then appear. Execution was not granted thereon before plaintiff had
given security to be responsible to defendant if he reversed the
judgment within one year or such further time as the court should
limit.[47] In cases where attachment was resorted to, execution had to
be taken out within a month after judgment or the attachment was
void, unless the court saw cause to grant respite of execution.
Whether execution had to issue within a year and a day after judgment entered does not appear; the laws made no provision for revival
by writ of scire facias.

Provision was made in the various commissions and in the laws
generally for appeals to a higher court from the court at Springfield.
However, it was not until the end of 1684 that an appeal is found
entered—to the County Court at Northampton. In this case appel-

44 *Rec.* 99, 167, 174, 192, 204, 211, 215, 220–221, 226, 229. For the law, see *Col. Laws Mass., 1672* 120–121.

45 *Rec.* 11.

46 *Col. Laws Mass., 1672* 3, 6, 30, 102, 104, 313, 320. *Cf.* the execution, dated Springfield, September 26, 1678, signed by John Holyoke, recorder of the County Court for Hampshire, in Partrigg v.

White and the October 12, 1678 return of the constable of Hatfield. Bliss, *An Address to the Members of the Bar of the Counties of Hampshire, Franklin and Hampden at Their Annual Meeting at Northampton, September 1826* (1827) 78.

47 *Col. Laws Mass., 1672* 7, 144; 4 *Rec. Mass. Bay (Part I)* 365; *Rec.* 174.

lant Obadiah Abbee and his brother, according to law, bound themselves in the sum of five pounds each to the County Treasurer for
Hampshire and to appellee to prosecute the appeal to effect at the
next County Court at Northampton and to satisfy all damages in not
having execution issue according to the judgment. Failure to prosecute to effect also entailed a forfeiture of forty shillings to the
county. This appears in the only other appeal taken prior to the
Second Charter, a County Court entry of April 23, 1690 noting that
appellant forfeited his bond of three pounds to defendant and forty
shillings to the county.[48] Appellant was also required to give in to
the clerk of the writs six days (changed to fourteen days in 1685) before the County Court sat the grounds and reasons of his appeal
briefly in his or his attorney's hand, without reflecting on the court
or parties by provoking language. The clerk was obliged to transmit
these reasons to the court to which the appeal was taken and to give
a copy to appellee, if desired. Appellee might file an answer to the
reasons of appeal.[49] Some copies of such reasons of appeal and answers thereto are to be found in the files of the County Court of Essex. An examination of these files shows much greater resort to appellate review of the judgments of magistrates than in Hampshire.

While at one time the General Court declared that appeals were
to be accounted in the nature of a writ of error, the record on appeal
bore no relation to the formalized common-law record found in English practice and a bill of exceptions was not used. The records on
appeal from the judgments of a magistrate or commissioners to the
County Court for Essex indicate that at this level the record consisted of an attested copy of the judgment, verdict, or proceedings
below, attested copies of the depositions taken by the parties and
documentary material received in evidence (such as copies of agreements or town orders), copies of the process, and copies of the bills
of costs. A certificate by the magistrate explaining or justifying action claimed to constitute error might accompany the record.[50]

An early law provided that, in civil actions, if the party against
whom judgment was given should have any new evidence or other
new matter to plead, he might have a new trial in the same court
upon a bill of review. Several such cases appear in the *Record* entitled actions of review, two involving actions heard in the first instance at Northampton. Another is found in the supplemental Reg-

48 *Rec.* 190–191; *Rec. Cty. Ct. Hamp.*
126 (The case, James Blinn (?) v. Samuel Lamb, does not appear in the *Record.*) For the law see *Col. Laws Mass.,*
1672 3–4.
49 *Col. Laws Mass., 1672* 3.

50 2 *Rec. Mass. Bay* 279; 2 *Rec. and
Files Quart. Cts. Essex Cty. Mass.* 21–22,
138–140, 298–299, 436–437; 3 *ibid.* 126–
130, 404, 444–445; 4 *ibid.* 6–7, 52–53, 54–
55, 216–217, 335–337; 5 *ibid.* 13–14, 19, 49–
51, 179–181.

istry of Probate material reviewing and sustaining an ex parte verdict.[51]

In the early years at Agawam the parties in one case agreed to a new trial by the same jury. In another William Pynchon offered to undertake to have plaintiff Moxon, who had judgment against John Woodcock, refer the matter to arbitration by "indifferent men" anywhere in the River, if Woodcock would put up security to answer such damages as should be awarded; in the alternative, Pynchon offered a writ of error to have the matter tried again by a new jury. Pynchon also offered a new trial by writ of error to Woodcock in an action in which a jury had found against him.[52]

The slight use made of appeals and reviews indicates that neither was regarded as a significant procedural device in the courts on the lower jurisdictional levels in western Massachusetts during the First Charter. In this connection it should be noted that the laws provided in a statute of jeofailes provision that "no Summons, Pleading, Judgement, or any kinde of proceeding in Courts or course of justice, shall be abated, arrested or reversed upon any kinde of circumstantial errours or mistakes; if the person and cause be rightly understood and intended by the Court." [53] Such a provision could serve as a damper upon appeals and reviews.

1686–1692. THE INTERCHARTER PERIOD

During the period between the First and Second Charters the *Record* reflects no sharp cleavage with the past from the standpoint of procedure in civil causes despite the passage of several laws affecting such procedure. However, it should be noted that, after the overthrow of Andros, the Governor and Council in June 1689 declared that all laws in force in the colony on May 12, 1686, except those repugnant to the laws of England, were again the laws of the colony.[54]

Both summons and attachments continued to be used for the commencement of actions, although greater use was made of the latter process. Since no new forms were provided by law, it seems likely that the forms in use were continued. Apparently the office of clerk of the writs was discontinued under Dudley for a law provided that original writs in small actions were to issue under the hands and seal of such as were to try them.[55]

Process in most cases continued to be served by the constable,

---

[51] *Col. Laws Mass., 1672* 152; *Rec.* 22, 77, 84; 1 *Hamp. Cty. Probate Ct. Rec.* 14.
[52] *Rec.* 8, 10, 13.
[53] *Col. Laws Mass., 1672* 7.
[54] 1 *Laws N.H.* 294.
[55] *Ibid.* 104.

although the marshal might serve attachments and writs of execution.[56] References in schedules of fees established by the laws and in bills of costs indicate that plaintiffs were still required to enter their actions with the court.[57] A defendant who failed to appear was still called three times by the constable. In the case of an attachment the court might proceed to an ex parte hearing and judgment if defendant, having been warned by a writing left at his usual place of abode, failed to appear, but execution might be delayed if defendant was out of the jurisdiction. In one 1691 case, no return of the attachment was made but defendant appeared and produced an acknowledgment under the constable's hand of receipt from defendant of the sum demanded.[58]

A March 3, 1686/7 act (An Act Impowering Justices of the Peace to Decide Differences not exceeding forty shillings), in the case of nonappearance of a defendant, summoned upon complaint made to a justice, authorized the issuance of a warrant of contempt directed to the constable.[59] While this act is the prototype of a law passed under the Second Charter, no use of a warrant of contempt is found during the intercharter period.

During this period no civil cases coming before John Pynchon were tried by a jury, although the March 1686/7 act allowed a jury if in matter of fact either party demanded it, at the cost and charge of the party so desiring. In one action of review, in May 1688, a jury of twelve was summoned and returned by the constable but the parties, reaching a settlement, did not proceed to trial.[60] How the jurors were chosen does not appear in the *Record;* the aforesaid act authorized a justice to "Summons a jury." The *Record* reveals no resort to arbitration during the years in question.

As in the earlier period, the *Record* contains scant detail as to trial procedure although there is a tendency to describe the evidence in cases involving "debt by book." For part of the period the taking of testimony was governed by a May 1686 law that no affidavit or testimony in any civil case was to be taken out of the court where the trial was held—except where the witness was a great distance from court, incapable of attending, or bound to sea before the trial—and then it was to be taken before a member of the Council and, if possible, in the presence of the opposite party upon reasonable notice.[61] While one plaintiff appeared by an attorney in fact, no

56 For service of attachments by the marshal see *Rec.* 201, 205. By law a constable might serve original writs and writs of execution in small causes. 1 *Laws N.H.* 104, 137.

57 *Ibid.* 107.
58 *Rec.* 199, 201, 205, 213, 215.
59 1 *Laws N.H.* 194–195.
60 *Rec.* 207.
61 1 *Laws N.H.* 105.

parties were represented by counsel. There is no indication that written pleadings were in use. In one case judgment was given for plaintiff unless defendant could prove certain facts. In another, execution was respited to give defendant an opportunity to satisfy the judgment. Presumably the form of a writ of execution followed that current under the First Charter.[62]

A 1686 law which provided for costs in the trial of small causes included the following: for attachment or summons, one shilling; subpoena to summon witness, threepence; entry of action, three shillings, fourpence; judgment, sixpence; execution, two shillings; an affidavit out of court, two shillings.[63] Entries of costs in the *Record* are consistent with this scale for the most part, although other items of costs appear which were not covered by the statutory schedule such as constable's fees, witness fees and charges to the parties.

While the laws provided for an appeal to the County Courts from the judgments of John Pynchon as councilor, none was taken.

1692–1702. THE SECOND CHARTER

One of the first acts passed under the Second Charter established the civil jurisdiction of justices of the peace in causes not exceeding forty shillings and defined the procedure to be employed in such causes. Each justice of the peace was empowered to grant a warrant or summons against a party complained of seven days before the day of trial or hearing, requiring defendant to appear and answer the complaint. If defendant failed to appear, the justice was to sue out a warrant of contempt directed to the constable or other officer to bring the contemner before the justice, as well to answer the contempt as the plaintiff's action. If he saw cause, the justice might also fine the contemner, provided the fine did not exceed twenty shillings.[64]

In either case, after judgment was given, the justice might grant warrants of distress directed to the constable or other officer to levy the fine, debt, or damage with charges upon defendant's goods and chattels, returning to him the surplus, if any, after sale. For want of such distress the constable or other officer was to take the body of defendant into custody and convey him to the common jail of the county or precinct, there to remain until he had satisfied the fine, debt or damage with charges. In case complainant or plaintiff was non-suited or judgment given against him, the justice was empowered to assess reasonable costs.

[62] *Rec.* 201, 206, 211.
[63] 1 *Laws N.H.* 107.
[64] 1 *Acts and Res. Prov. Mass. Bay* 72.

It was also provided by law that replevins, summonses, and attachments for any matter or cause triable before one justice of the peace and summonses for witnesses in civil causes generally might be granted by the town clerk and directed to the constable or to the party to be summoned as a witness. Another section of the laws provided that every justice of the peace might grant summons, capias, or attachment in all civil actions triable by him. The form of summons, warrant for contempt, attachment, and execution were all set forth in the laws; the form for a writ of replevin was not contained in the laws until 1698. Provision was also made that, if a summons was served and affidavit thereof made and defendant did not appear, judgment by default might be taken against him.[65]

A statutory schedule of fees for justices of the peace included such items as: attachment and summons, sixpence; subpoena for witness, twopence; entry of action, three shillings; and execution, two shillings. The constable's fees included: service of summons for trial, one shilling; service of capias or attachment, two shillings; if service required a journey of over a mile, threepence per mile.[66] Witnesses were entitled to a per diem allowance of two shillings for travel and expenses if they resided within three miles of a court and, when not required to cross any ferry, the allowance was one shilling, sixpence. A later law provided that the fee for a writ in any case before a justice of the peace should not exceed one shilling and the fee for service thereof, one shilling, any law, usage, or custom to the contrary. A plaintiff who was not a freeholder or settled inhabitant was required to put up security in double the amount sued for to cover costs before process was granted.[67]

The oath of a justice of the peace set forth in An Act for the Establishing of Forms of Oaths, published December 9, 1692, which drew heavily upon the English form, read as follows:

You, A B, [do] swear, that as justice of the peace in the county of S, according to the commission given you, you shall dispense justice equally and impartially in all cases, and do equal right to the poor and to the rich after your cunning, wit and power, and according to law; and you shall not be of council in any quarrel that shall come before you. You shall not let for gift or other cause, but well and truly you shall do your office of justice of the peace in that behalf, taking only appointed fees; and you shall not direct or cause to be directed any warrant (by you to be made) to the parties, but you shall direct your warrant to the sheriff, his undersheriff or deputy [constables] tythingmen, or other officers proper for the execution of the same in the county. And this you shall do without favor or respect of persons. So help you God.[68]

65 *Ibid.* 76, 78, 81, 316–317, 319–320.   67 *Ibid.* 76, 185, 222–223.
66 *Ibid.* 84–85, 87.   68 *Ibid.* 78.

Each justice of the peace was required to keep a record of all proceedings. The party cast was at liberty to appeal to the next Inferior Court of Common Pleas of the county upon entering into a recognizance with one sufficient surety in double the value of the debt or damage sued for and sufficient to answer all costs, to prosecute the appeal with effect, and to abide the order of the court to which the appeal was taken. Appellant was to bring copies of the whole case to the Inferior Court of Common Pleas and each party was to be allowed the benefit of any further plea or evidence. If upon any such new plea or evidence, judgment was reversed, appellant was to have no costs granted for the first trial. Probably appellant was also required to give to the justice a declaration setting forth briefly the reasons for his appeal fourteen days before the sitting of the Inferior Court appealed to.[69]

A June 1697 law, entitled An Act Impowring Justices of the Peace to Decide Differences Not Exceeding Forty Shillings, recapitulated the procedure in civil cases before a justice of the peace, making a few changes from the earlier laws. Process was to be directed to the sheriff or marshal of the county or to the deputy of either or to the constable of the town where the parties lived. The limit on fines for contempt of a summons duly served was reduced to ten shillings. The time within which an appellant was required to give in the reasons for his appeal was reduced to seven days before the sitting of the Inferior Court. A March 1700/1 act tightened up procedure in cases where an appellant neglected to prosecute his appeal.[70]

The June 1698 Act for Preventing of Trespasses provided that when, in an action of trespass brought before a justice of the peace, the defendant should justify and demur upon plea of title, a record should be made thereof and the matter of fact be taken *pro confesso*. The party making such plea should become bound with one or more sureties by way of recognizance unto the adverse party in a reasonable sum not exceeding twenty pounds, conditioned upon pursuing the plea and bringing forward a suit for trial of title at the next Inferior Court of Common Pleas held for the county in which the trespass was allegedly committed and upon paying and satisfying all such damages and costs as should be awarded. The justice was to certify the process and record of such plea together with the recognizance to the Inferior Court.[71]

If the recognizor neglected to bring forward the suit at the Inferior Court according to the tenor of the recognizance, the default was to be recorded and a writ of scire facias to issue from the clerk's of-

69 *Ibid.* 72–73.
70 *Ibid.* 282–283, 446.
71 *Ibid.* 324–325.

fice. If, upon trial at the Inferior Court, the recognizor did not make out title to the land or tenement paramount to the possession or other title of the adverse party, judgment was to be rendered for the party trespassed upon with treble damages and costs of suit. However, if a defendant, justifying on plea of title, refused or neglected to become bound, his plea was to abate, the justice was to proceed to try the cause, and, upon due proof of the trespass, award damages and cost of suit.

The entries in the *Record* during the Second Charter, although reflecting the various new enactments governing the jurisdiction of justices of the peace, also evidence continuity with the past in the administration of justice. In most cases the action was still commenced by the service of a summons by the constable, although in an increasing number of cases attachment was resorted to. No evidence appears of the use of a "warrant" or of capias as initial process. In a few instances process was served by the marshal or the sheriff's deputy rather than by the constable. The *Record* does not indicate whether process was issued by Pynchon or by the town clerk; recently published court records for York County indicate that at this time most process was drawn up by the justices or members of their families serving as clerks.[72]

The only form of return of a summons found in the *Record* appears at a March 1, 1693/4 hearing at which the constable made his return of service as follows:

This summons was served on Zachariah Booth and he warned to attend the same this 22th of February, 1693/94.[73]

In the case of attachments the return continued to note that defendant had notice of the attachment by a writing left at his place of usual abode.[74] Several entries state that this notice was given "according to law"; however, such a requirement was first contained in a law passed in March 1700/1. In most cases personalty was attached; in a few cases, real property.[75]

Judging from the schedule of fees of a justice of the peace, a plaintiff was still required to enter his action. (There was no provision in the laws for regular sittings by a single justice of the peace.) On the return date the summons or the attachment and the return thereof was read. If both parties were present, the justice proceeded

---

72 *Rec.* 221, 241, 243; 4 *Prov. and Ct. Rec. Me.* xix.

- 73 *Rec.* 220. See also the reference to the return in Philips v. Adams. *Ibid.*

74 *Rec.* 215, 221, 229.

75 See *Rec.* 233, 236, 252 for instances of attachment of lands. For the act, which does not specifically refer to justices of the peace, see 1 *Acts and Res. Prov. Mass. Bay* 448. For the form of summons to be used in case of attachment by a justice of the peace, see *ibid.* 463.

to consider the pleas and evidence. If defendant did not appear, he was then called three times by the constable, as was the earlier practice. The same procedure might be followed if plaintiff failed to appear. In one rather puzzling entry plaintiff did not appear, "not being summoned," and no proceeding was had. In a case in which neither party appeared on the return of the attachment, Pynchon entered "so it drops and wholy Fals." [76]

If a return was made by the constable or other officer that defendant had been summoned and defendant failed to appear, Pynchon might, as authorized by the laws, issue a warrant of contempt to the constable to take defendant's body and have him before the court on a date specified, as well to answer the action as for his contempt. The contempt might "issue" if defendant showed good reason for his failure to appear. If plaintiff were willing, the proceeding might be adjourned to a later date on the supposition that defendant, having notice, would agree and issue with plaintiff at that time. Or Pynchon might defer the issuance of a warrant of contempt until another time.[77] In a 1699 action of debt when defendant failed to appear and proof of service was made, Pynchon entered the default and upon plaintiff producing his evidence proceeded to judgment. However, Pynchon presently made the judgment "void and nul" because by law a writ of contempt should have gone out.[78] However, in the case of attachments where defendant failed to appear, Pynchon, consistent with earlier practice, usually proceeded to judgment upon presentation of plaintiff's evidence. In one case a warrant of contempt issued. A 1701 law specifically provided that if a defendant in any suit was duly served with a capias or attachment and did not appear on the return thereof, judgment was to be entered up against him by default.[79] However, in general, Pynchon exhibited considerable patience in waiting beyond the appointed time for parties to appear.

While no written pleadings are set forth verbatim in the *Record*, notation that pleas were "read" indicates that written pleadings were used in some cases. In others, where Pynchon noted that pleas were "heard," it seems likely that the pleadings were oral. The schedule of fees of a justice of the peace did not contemplate a written declaration.[80] As in the earlier period, there was no reference to recognized forms of pleadings or use of the formalized entries associated with such pleadings. All the actions entered in the *Record* under the Second Charter were heard by Pynchon without a jury. While

[76] *Rec.* 217, 224, 225, 246.
[77] *Rec.* 220, 231, 234, 252.
[78] *Rec.* 170–171, 243.

[79] *Rec.* 234. See 1 *Acts and Res. Prov. Mass. Bay* 464.
[80] *Ibid.* 86.

the laws provided that all matters and issues in fact arising or happening within the province were to be tried by twelve good and lawful men of the neighborhood, this provision apparently was not considered as extending to trials before a justice of the peace.[81]

Little appears of trial procedure in the *Record* but no marked deviation from the commonwealth period is evident. In some cases it is clear that witnesses appeared in person before Pynchon and gave testimony under oath. In other cases, where reference is made to "testimoneys" being read or "evidences" being on file, it may be that testimony of witnesses was taken down in writing out of court, although not specifically authorized by statute. None of these file papers has survived. Whether the disputed requirement of two witnesses carried over beyond 1692 is thus difficult of ascertainment. In a number of cases the evidence consisted largely of entries in books of account to which plaintiff or defendant, as the case might be, made oath. Strangely, the several acts of this period establishing forms of oaths made no provision for an oath for witnesses, nor was there any form of summons or subpoena provided for a witness in civil actions triable by a justice of the peace. Further the forty-shilling fine for witnesses failing to appear according to the tenor of process served upon them, without reasonable excuse, was limited to courts of record.[82]

In several instances plaintiff's case sounding in debt rested upon a bill under defendant's hand. In one case the hearing was adjourned for several days to give both parties an opportunity to present further evidence. In a dispute over the division of some hay Pynchon appointed two persons to view and judge who brought in their determination in writing.[83] In a few cases defendants confessed judgment so presentation of evidence was unnecessary.[84] A substantial number of cases were settled by the parties before or during trial.[85]

Under the laws each party had the liberty of pleading and defending his own cause in person or with the assistance of such other person as he should procure, such other person not being scandalous or otherwise offensive to the court. While some attempt was made to discourage use of attorneys in actions heard by justices of the peace by providing that there should be no allowance for fees for attorneys in such cases, scattered use of attorneys—presumably attorneys in fact rather than counsel—is found in the *Record*.[86]

For the most part no reference is made to the issuance of execu-

81 *Ibid.* 74, 286.

82 *Ibid.* 76, 78–79, 287, 374, 465.

83 *Rec.* 223, 227, 240–241. See also the adjournment when plaintiff's witnesses failed to appear. *Rec.* 221.

84 *Rec.* 227, 230, 233.

85 *Rec.* 224–227, 231–232, 235A, 236–237, 243.

86 1 *Acts and Res. Prov. Mass. Bay* 75, 287; *Rec.* 217, 220, 232, 240–241, 246, 253.

tion. However, in a few cases marginal notations appear that execution issued the same day as judgment was rendered or that it would issue if defendant did not satisfy the judgment in money or in kind. A December 1696 entry contains the only reference to a return by the constable of a writ of execution. Whether the writ was in the form provided by law does not appear.[87]

Many of the entries refer to "costs of Court as per bil allowed"; in some cases costs were substantial considering the amount involved. For the most part the individual items of costs are not listed but, to the extent they are set forth, they are consistent with the statutory schedule. Costs in some cases included an allowance to plaintiff for his attendance (usually two shillings per day) or for "coming for a summons." [88]

No reviews are found in the *Record* for the period of the Second Charter, not being provided for in the laws. In several trespass actions in which defendant pleaded title, the case was transferred to the Inferior Court of Common Pleas in accordance with the law referred to above upon defendant's posting the requisite security. In one case of this nature in which defendant refused to become bound, Pynchon proceeded to give judgment for plaintiff.[89] In a case of this nature which arose in 1693, prior to the passage of the above act, Pynchon rendered judgment conditioned upon decision as to title to the land.[90] Presumably such title would have to be determined by the Inferior Court of Common Pleas.

Appeals were taken to the Inferior Court of Common Pleas for Hampshire from seven judgments rendered by Pynchon, one being later withdrawn. The bonds given were in the amount of either four pounds or forty shillings; in most cases there were two sureties.[91] These probably did not differ substantially from those used in the commonwealth period on appeals to the county courts. The number of appeals taken in a relatively short period indicates that appellate review played a greater role on the lower jurisdictional levels under the Second Charter.

As to whether the procedure found in the *Record* under the Second Charter differed greatly from that employed by justices of the peace in other parts of the province is difficult to determine due to the lack of records for comparison. A justice of the peace, unnurtured in procedure as a magistrate under the commonwealth, might adhere more closely to or construe differently the province laws than

[87] *Rec.* 229. See 1 *Acts and Res. Prov. Mass. Bay* 81, 317, 463.
[88] *Rec.* 16–219, 226.
[89] *Rec.* 245–246.
[90] *Rec.* 219.
[91] *Rec.* 219, 222, 225, 235A, 245, 247, 252.

John Pynchon. Perhaps for such a justice resort to contemporary English texts and manuals as an aid in administering the laws would be more natural. It is difficult to believe that Pynchon, in his declining years and with forty years of judicial experience behind him, made any greater adjustment to the new laws than was necessary. The *Record* appears to confirm this belief.

X I. Conclusion

IN the Epistle to the *Laws and Liberties* of 1648 reference is made to an "old and true proverb" that "the execution of the law is the life of the law." In the pages of the *Record* the "life of the law" in western Massachusetts Bay may be studied at close range for much of the seventeenth century. Many of the people prominent in the early days of Springfield appear in the capacity of judges, law enforcement agents, criminal offenders, litigants, or witnesses. A wide variety of offenses and of civil actions are handled by a succession of courts on the lower jurisdictional levels.

The *Record* abundantly reveals the significant roles played by William Pynchon and John Pynchon and, to a lesser extent, Elizur Holyoke and Samuel Chapin, in the administration of justice in early western Massachusetts. Most court records are impersonal; the *Record* is unique in its reflection of the personal element in judicial administration, particularly as regards continuity, and, of the integration of such administration, through the court personnel, into the broader frame of local government in the Connecticut Valley. Through supplemental biographical data on the Pynchons, Holyoke, and Chapin a more rounded portrait of the judicial personnel has been obtained, as well as the economic, social, and political background necessary to full comprehension and evaluation of the entries in the *Record*.

While none of the four magistrates or commissioners was a trained lawyer, it is believed that the standards of judicial administration displayed in the *Record* compare favorably with that found in courts on the lower jurisdictional levels of the Bay. The few appeals taken and contempts of court recorded indicate that these standards were generally acceptable to offenders and litigants coming before the successive courts. John Pynchon with his diverse activities may have found it difficult to steer an impartial course at all times, but his detractors have limited their strictures to his conduct on the County Court. Certainly Pynchon did not fit into any of the categories of justices of the peace condemned by the Webbs—the Trading Justice, the Sycophant Justice, or the Rural Tyrant. His selection as head of a court of oyer and terminer in 1696 to try some New York Indians charged with murder indicates confidence in his judicial abilities on the part of the Bay authorities.

The *Record* affords substantial evidence that the administration of justice in western Massachusetts was based in great part on the laws and orders of the General Court. Any direct influence of Biblical laws, ecclesiastical laws, or the substantive laws of England is difficult to detect. Most of the offenses punished were violations of laws of the General Court. In the case of other offenses, seemingly not covered by express prohibitions, the precedents of the Court of Assistants appear to have been followed.

The *Record* shows no significant mutations or deviations, substantively or procedurally, attributable to so-called "frontier" influences. Ironically, the institutions of the petty jury and the grand jury did not flourish in a society which has been traditionally regarded as a forcing ground for democratic concepts. While the loss of records makes for uncertainty, perhaps the lack of widespread church discipline supplementing the sanctions imposed by the secular courts may be attributed to the weakness of the ministry on the frontier.

In those areas not specifically covered by the laws of the General Court, largely matters of procedure, the *Record* does not differ substantially from what appears in the records of the courts in the more settled portions of the colony and was probably as consistent with the laws of England.

In characterizing the jurisdiction exercised by the various courts at Springfield facile English analogies are of scant help. Leet jurisdiction in England in the seventeenth century differed greatly in its main outlines from the criminal jurisdiction and procedures found in the *Record*. The jurisdiction of a single justice of the peace in England likewise differed substantially, but from the standpoint of procedure, particularly in binding over offenders, the New England borrowing is apparent. The true answer is that in shaping the jurisdiction of the lower levels of the judicial hierarchy the General Court followed an eclectic policy grounded on expediency and pragmatism.

In the field of law enforcement the *Record* is not of great value from a statistical standpoint since not all offenses of which cognizance was taken were entered therein and, secondly, no substantial volume of any one class of offense appears. However, it is believed that the *Record* does afford a representative cross section of law enforcement on the western frontier of the Bay Colony for over sixty years—including the problem of the Indian offender. Such cross section of jurisdiction actually exercised must be read against that conferred by law which, particularly, under the Second Charter, clearly contemplated more extensive powers.

The *Record* itself does not accurately reflect the frequent binding over of serious offenders to the courts on the county level but this defect has been remedied by use of supplemental material from the records of the County Court and, later, the Court of General Sessions of the Peace. In the case of offenders referred back to the Springfield courts the absence of *Record* entries leaves uncertainty as to the efficacy of this method of reference. The *Record* is of great value in permitting evaluation of the various agencies of law enforcement such as the constable, the sheriff, the watch, tithingmen, town presenters, and individual complainants.

The *Record* can hardly be said to show that the inhabitants of Springfield were at all times afforded easy access to a court and prompt and inexpensive justice. John Pynchon, for instance, had many demands on his time and was frequently away from Springfield for considerable periods. To state, as some writers have, that procedure on the lower jurisdictional levels was informal is misleading. Certainly it was informal by the standards of Westminster Hall, but the procedural norms found in the *Record* and provided by law were not substantially more informal than those of the County Court for Hampshire and perhaps for other counties.

The *Record* cannot be approached as one would approach the lengthy annotations in fine print of a modern Civil Practice Act. The entries and the jurisdictional bases for most of the period have to be viewed against a statutory background consisting of the laws and orders of the General Court. Such background was the product of legislators disinterested in the technical details and niceties of statutory draftsmanship. This attitude of necessity also manifested itself in the administration of justice in the commonwealth. After all, such administration centered in and was dominated by the magistrates. The *Record* further indicates that such basic attitude was not extirpated solely by the passage of laws under the Second Charter establishing more rigid criteria of judicial administration.

Puritan pride of intellect in seventeenth-century Massachusetts Bay did not extend to mastery of mundane laws, whether substantive or procedural. Many would agree with Cotton's characterization of lawyers as unconscionable advocates who "bolster out a bad case by quirks of wit, and tricks and quillets of law." [1] Accordingly, the

---

[1] See Lechford, *Plaine dealing: or, News from New England* (ed. J. H. Trumbull, 1867) 68 note.

standards of judicial administration revealed in the *Record* must be viewed against the attitude revealed strikingly in the following extract from the Epistle to the 1662 laws of the commonwealth:

If any shall complain of incongruous expressions or obscurity in some passages, let them be sure it be so, before they affirm it; Considering the Supreme Court (which ought to be honoured) hath perused them, and hath judged meet to publish them as they stand: Neither would the time or their Honour permit them, as *Criticks,* to call every word to the Tryall before a Jury of Grammarians. Let it suffice that the meaning is intelligible, though the dress be not the most polished; nor is it necessary seeing *mens Legis est Lex.*

They, to whom these Laws are commended as Rules to which they ought to conform, may find better exercise for themselves by endeavoring to make them live by executing of them, which will add a greater lustre to them, then elegancy of expression: When Laws may be read in mens lives, they appear more beautiful than in the fairest Print, and promise a longer duration, than engraven in Marble. Weaker fences will secure against gentle Creatures, though walls of Brass be unsufficient against forcible Obtruders. If breach of order doth argue violence of men, more than weakness of the Law, it will be every mans prudence to defend the Authority of the Laws, to avoid the censure of Impetuous, and to cover rather than make gaps, whereat the most innocent may enter, and destroy that provision which was made for their preservation.

Some writers have been critical of the oligarchic tendencies inherent in the administration of justice under the First Charter which permitted the same person to sit at four levels of the judicial hierarchy—magistrate, County Court, Court of Assistants, and General Court. Such critics have failed to note the virtue of such a system in providing experienced personnel for the courts on the lower jurisdictional levels, in fostering uniformity of administration, and in discouraging judicial separatism. It is due in large part to such judicial hierarchy that many common attributes are found in the administration of justice in the purlieus of Boston, in the forests of York County, and on the banks of the Connecticut. Such achievement was of no small value to a colony frequently beset by perils both from within and from without.

The *Record* stands forth as a monument to the labors of William and John Pynchon in establishing and maintaining a judicial system in western Massachusetts in substantial conformity with that existing in the more settled portions of the Massachusetts Bay colony.

THE PYNCHON COURT RECORD

EDITED BY

JOSEPH H. SMITH

OF THE NEW YORK BAR

*The original manuscript of this Judges' Diary has been in
the Treasure Room of the Harvard Law School for the
past thirty-three years. For twenty-eight years prior
thereto, it was owned by Goodspeed's Book Shop, in Boston, and by Mr. Sumner Hollingsworth, of Boston. For
many years prior to 1899, it appears to have been in the
possession of Judge Henry Morris, an historian, of Springfield, Massachusetts.*

February the 14th 1638

We the Inhabitants of Agaam vppon Quinnetticot takinge into consideration the manifould inconveniences that may fall vppon vs for want of some fit magistracy amonge vs: Beinge now by gods providence fallen into the line of the Massachusets Jurisdiction: & it beinge farr of to repay or thither in suche cases of iustice as may often fall out amonge vs doe therfore thinke it meete by a generall consent & vote to ordaine (till we receive further direction from the generall court in the Massachuset Bay) mr William Pynchon to execute the office of a magistrate in this our plantation of Agaam viz

To give oathes to Constables or millitary officers to direct warrants, both processe executions & attachments, to heare & examine misdemenors to depose witnesses & vppon proofe of misdemenor to inflict corporall punishment, as whippinge stockinge byndinge to the peace, or good behaviour & in some cases to requiar sureties, & if the offence requier to comitt to prison, & in default of a comon prison to comitt the delinquents to the charge of some fit person or persons till iustice may be satisfied, Also in the tryall of actions for debt or trespasse, to give oathes, direct Juries depose witnesses take verdicts & keepe recorde of verdicts Judgments executions: & what ever else may tend to the kinge peace, & the manifestation of our fidelitie to the Bay Jurisdiction & the restraininge of any that shall violate gods laws: or lastly whatsoever else may fall within the power of an assistant in the Massachuset

It is also agreed vppon by a mutuall consent that in case any action of debt or trespasse be to be tryed: seinge a jury of 12 fit persons cannot be had at present among vs: That the partyes shall be agreed & chuse a sufficient Jury to try any action vnder the some of Ten pounde till we shall the raise to the contrary & by comon consent shall alter this number of Jurors or shall be otherwise directed from the generall Court in the Massachusetts

Jogn Cable is chosen & sworne to execute ye office of a Constable in this place for a yeare or till another shall be chosen in his roome. Maij 14 1636

The Pynchon Court Record

[*2] February the 14th 1638 [1639].

We the Inhabitantes of Agaam uppon Quinnettecot takinge into consideration the manifould inconveniences that may fale uppon us for want of some fit magistracy amonge us: Beinge now by Godes providence fallen into the line of the Massachusets Jurisdiction: and it beinge farr of to repayer thither in such cases of justice as may often fall out amonge us doe therefore thinke it meete by a generall consent and vote to ordaine (till we receive further directions from the generall court in the Massachuset Bay) Mr. William Pynchon to execute the office of a magistrate in this our plantation of Agaam viz

To give oathes to Conestables or military officers to direct warrantes, both processe executions and attachmentes, to here and examine misdemenors to depose witnesses and uppon profe of misdemenor to inflict corporall punishment, as whipping stockinge byndinge to the peace, or good behaviour, and in some cases to requier sureties, and if the offence requier to commit to prison and in default of a common prison to comit delinquentes to the charge of some fit person or persons till justice may be satisfied, Also in the Tryall of actions for debt or trespasse, to give oathes, direct juries depose witnesses, take verdictes and keepe Records of verdictes, Judgmentes executions: and what ever else may tend to the Kinges peace, and the manifestation of our fidellity to the Bay Jurisdiction and the restraininge of any that shall molest Godes lawes: or lastly whatsoever else may fall within the power of an assistant in the Massachuset.

It is also agreed uppon by a mutuall consent that in case any action of debt or trespasse be to be tryed: seinge a Jury of 12 fit persons cannot be had at present among us: That six persons shall be esteemed and held a sufficient Jury to try any action under the some of Ten pounds till we shall see cause to the Contrary and by common consent shall alter this number of Jurors or shall be otherwise directed from the Generall Court in the Massachusets.

John Cable is chosen and sworne to execute the office of a Constable in this place for a year or till another shall be chosen in his roome.

[*3] November 14. 1639.

A meetinge to order some Towne affaires and to try causes by Jury.

The Jury Henry Smyth, Jehew Burr, Henry Gregory, John Searl, Samuell Hubbard, Samuell Wright.

The Action.   John Woodcoke complaines against John Cable in an action of the case for wages due to him for certaine worke he did to a house that was built on Agawam side for the Plantation.

The verdict   The Jury findes for the defendant: But withall they find the promise that John Cable made to the plaintife to see him paid for his worke firme and good   But as for the 5 dayes in Comming up with John Cable we find them not due to be paid for he came not up purposely but in his Comminge he aimed at a lotte which end of his he did attain. Moreover we agree that John Cable is ingaged to the plaintife for worke don about the house: [*page torn*] we also Judge that John Woodcoke is fully satis[fied] in regard he hath had the use of the ould [*page torn*] ground and of the howse all that Sommer [so] far as John Cable had himselfe.

November 14. 1639.

William Pynchon complaineth against Thomas Merricke in an action of the Case for not delivering back the Boards he lent him.

The Jury Henry Smyth, Jehew Burr, Henry Gregory, John Searle, Samuell Hubbard, Samuell Wright.

The Jury find for the plaintife viz that the defendant is to make good 3 such like boards as we find not yet delivered with the rest.

[*4] December 12 1639.

William Pynchon complaineth against Thomas Horton in an action of the Case for taking away certaine plankes from the Maine Masse [?] at the mill and carieing them away to his house.

The Jury   Jehew Bur, Henry Smyth, Thomas Merick, Samuell Hubbard, John Searle, Samuell Wright.

The Jury returne this verdict That they cannot agree how to determine the Case as yet till the whole worke be finished and till it shall be vewed and judged by indifferent men whether it be don or no according to bargaine and therefore desyre that the matter in difference may be deferred till then and then we shall be the better able to determine the case.

Thomas Merick complains againste Thomas Horton in an action of the Case for 3 boards that the said Thomas Merick wantes, for he saith that Thomas Horton made use of some of the boards which he tooke without leave and knowes not of the redelivery.

The Jury find for the Plaintife that the defendant shall restore the said three boards or three shillings in mony.

John Woodcock beinge sommond by warrant to answer Mr. George Moxon in an action of slander for reporting that he tooke a false oath against him: The said John desyred that this difference might be tried by a private hearinge below in the River: Mr. Moxon referred himselfe to the Judgment of the plantation present [*5] present whether it were fitter to be heard by a private refference below in the River, or tryed here publikly by a Jury. The generall voa[t] of the plantation is that seeing the matter is publike it should be publikly herd and tryed her by a Jury: Liberty is granted to John Woodcoke to produce his witnesses against this day fortnight being the 26 of December. Also at the said tyme John Woodcoke is warned to answer for his laughinge in Sermon tyme: this day at the Lecture.

Also he is then to answer his misdemenor [of] idlenesse.

The meeting on the 26 of December is deferred till the 2d of January 1639 [1640].

1639 [1640] January 2d.

George Moxon complai[nes] against John Woodcoke in an action of slander that he saith that John Woodcoke doth report that he tooke a false oath against him at Hartford and he demandes of John Woodcoke for the said sland[er] 9£ 19s.

The Jury. Henry Smyth, Jehew Burr, Robert Ashly, Thomas Merik, John Searle, Samuell Hubbard.

Mr. Moxon produces thes witnesses Thomas Horton, John Cable, Robert Ashly, Henry Smyth, Samuell Hubbard.

The Jury find for the Plaintife damages 6£ 13s. [Page torn.]

When Mr. Moxon gave the Constable the warrant [*6] to distraine for the said damag the said John Woodcoke answered that he ought Mr. Moxon no mony nor none he would pay him.

Also John Woodcoke said that he had showed Mr. Moxon more respect and reverence than ever he would againe. Witnesse Henry Smyth, Samuell Hubbard and Thomas Horton

February 13 1639 [1640].

The Jury   Henry Smyth, Jehew Bur, Robert Ashly, John Leonard, Samuell Hubbard, Samuell Wright.

1   Thomas Horton complaines against Thomas Mericke in an action of the case for not doinge a sufficient dayes worke for the wages of a day.

2   the said Thomas Horton Complaines against Thomas Mericke in an action of the case for taking away certaine planks or boardes.

3 the said Thomas Horton complaines against Thomas Mericke in an action of the case for felling of two trees in the lot of Thomas Horton.

4 for changing of 4 bushells of corne after it was delivered.

1 Thomas Merick complaines against John Woodcoke in an action of debt of 2s 6d.

2 Also in another action of the Case for two bushells of corne that was delivered into his possession: and about two bushells more that he is to be accountable for.

[*7] June 19 1640.

1 John Leonard complaines in an action of the Case against Henry Gregory for taking more recompense for driving home of certaine stray sowes then his share comes to: and for taking of more pigges with his sows then his share comes to.

2 William Warrener complaines against Henry Gregory in an action of the case for layenge false imputations of money dealinge in taking of those pompions that Richard Everit gave to both of them which Henry Gregory affirmes to be contrary to the appointment of Richard Everit.

The Jury. Henry Smyth, Samuell Hubbard, Samuell Wright, Rowland Stebbing, John Dible, John Cable.

The .1. action the Jury find for the plaintife: viz the defendant is to make restitution the some of 8s to [be] paid to the plaintife to be devided amongst the rest that tooke like [paines] in bringing home of the said [sows] accordinge to [   ]nt between them:

[*The remainder of the page is damaged.*]

And for the dif[   ] the Divisions of the pigg[es] the Jury find [   ] life: for it was proved that the defend[   ] but 5 teates drawen and yet go to [   ] sixt pigg he [   ] manner: Th[   ] neighbors: and [   ] for the [   ] halfe to [   ] that had [   ] to be paid [   ] The 2d [   ] proved [   ] John Sear [   ]

[*8] The 10 day of September 1640.

Henry Gregory complaines against John Woodcoke in an action of the case for fower poundes fowerteene shillinges.

The Jury. Samuell Hubbard, Samuell Wright, Thomas Mericke, John Leonard, Robert Ashly, Rowland Stebbinge.

The Jury find due to the plainetife fower poundes seven shillinges three pence and for costes three shillinges.

The execution is respited because John Woodcoke pleades that there is an error in the Arbitration for part of that that mony that he was awarded by the Arbitrators to pay: and so by consent of both parties they referr themselves to a new tryall to the former Jury.

John Woodcoke complaines that there is an error in the former Arbitration and Henry Gregory is content to put it presently to a new tryall to the former Jury.

[*The remainder of the page is damaged.*]

1 The Jury [   ]endant in the matter [   ] in damages for his [   ] shillings and costes 3s [   ]rmer damages of ten [   ]he Arbitrators [   ] about the pigg [   ] of the hogges [   ]ber we want some [   ] saith he can produce [   ]en him to bring [*9] in what further proof he can on this day fortnight or else then the Jury is to give in their verdict and so it is agreed by mutuall consent of all parties to referr the conclusion till this day fortnight.

Sept. 24: 1640.

Accordinge to the former order by consent of the plaintife defendant and Jury this day they are all mett to determine the matter of Cheatinge: and Henry Gregory after 14 dayes to bring in what new evidence he can is present to certifie the Jury.

The Jury find for the plaintife about the pigg and gave to John Woodcoke in damages Twenty shillings and costes 4s.

For the last action about the double ingagment of the hogges we find for the plaintife in damages Two and Twenty shillings and in costs five shillinges.

Henry Gregory after the verdict was much moved and said: I marvill with what consi[deration] the Jury can give such damages: Seeinge in the case of John Searles I had of him but Twenty shillinges for three slanders: and he added: But such Juries: he was about to speake more But Mr. Moxon bid him take heed take heed, and so gave him a grave admonition: presently after the admonition Henry Gregory acknowledged his fault and earnestly craved pardon and promised more care and watchfulnesse for tyme to come: and so all the Jury acknowledged satisffaction in hope of reformation.

[*10] Sept. 28 1640.

John Woodcoke comminge to me for a warrant to warne Henry Gregory to answer him in 2 actions of slander: I then demanded of him why he did not satisfie Mr Moxon for the action of slander that he had recovered against him by way of action: he Answered that he purposed to have a new hearing of the matter: for he said that Mr. Moxons testimony to the Jury proved the things that he affirmed: Thereuppon I tould him that I would undertake that Mr. Moxon should put the matter to a refference of indifferent men any where in the River provided that he would put in security to answer such damages as should be laid uppon him if the Arbitrators saw cause: or else I put him to his choyse if he would he should have the matter tried againe by a new Jury here: and he should have a writ of error to try it againe: and also should have liberty to except against any of the jury if he could shew any reason for it: and I gave him tyme from this day till Thursday after to choose eather of thes courses or else if he refused to take any of thes courses Then I tould him if he did not presently pay Mr. Moxon the some of six poundes 13s and 4d according as the Jury did formerly damnifie him for the slander: Then I would delay no longer but I would deliver a warrant to the [*11] the Constable to attach his body or goods for the said debt.

October .1. 1640.

John Woodcoke not appearinge to give satisfaction to Mr. Moxon accordinge to the liberty tendered to him: Therefore I ordaine the execution as followeth.

To John Searles Constable of Springfeild   Thes are in his Majesties name to require you presently uppon the receite hereof That you attach the body of John Woodcoke uppon an execution granted to Mr. George Moxon by the Jury against the said John Woodcoke for an action of slander: and that you kepe his body in prison or irons untill he shall take some course to satisfie the said George Moxon: or else if he neclect or refuse to take a speedy course to satisfie the said execution of 6£ 13s 4d granted by the Jury January 2d 1639 [1640]. That then you use what meanes you can to put him out to service and labor till he make satisfaction to the said Mr. George Moxon for the said 6£ 13s 4d and also to satisfie yorselfe for such charges as you shall be at for the keeping of his person: And when Mr. Moxon and yourselfe are satisfied, Then you are to discharge his person out of prison: faile not at your perill.

Springfeild this 5 October 1640
Per WILLIAM PYNCHON

[*12] October 9. 1640.

The Examination of Widdow Horton about selling of her husbands peice to the Indians.

She saith that she hath not sould it but she confesseth that she lent it to an Indian for it lay spoilinge in her seller, but she saith that the Indian is suddenly to bring it againe and he hath lost about six fatham of wampam in pawne for it: and she saith that she knew of no order against it and doth promise to take it home againe: she cannot tell the Indians name but saith it is an Indian of Agaam.

I tould her if she would speedily get it home againe or else it would cost her dere for no commonwealth would allow of such a misdemenor.

January the 11 1640 [1641].

It is ordered that John Hobell shall be well whipt by the Constable for two misdemenors first for proceeding to get promises of Marriage from Abigall Burt, after that both he and she had been prohibbited by her Father severall tymes, and also for offeringe and attemptinge to doe the act of fornication with her as they both confesse though as far as we can discerne by any proofe of Justice the act was not don.

Also Abigall Burt is found guilty in both the said faultes and is also to be well whipt by the Constable for the said faultes:

[*13] February the 15. 1640 [1641].

Robert Ashly complaines against John Woodcooke in an action of the case for a gunn that he bought of him and paid him 22s 6d for it yet the said John Woodcoke did not deliver it to him accordinge to bargaine.

Also Robert Ashly complaines against John Woodcok in an action of the case for not breaking up of certain ground for planting according to bargaine.

The Jury Henry Smyth, Henry Burt, John Leonard, John Dible, Samuell Wright, Thomas Merick:

In the first action the Jury find for the plaintife 22s 6d and in costes 4s.

The 2d action John Woodcoke doth acknowledge it his dew to brake up the said ground and doth bynd over some of the Swine that he hath now in the hands of Thomas Mirick for the performance of the said ground in case it be not don before the first of Aprill, then he doth promise to allow for the damage out of the said swine as two indifferent neighbors shall prise the said swine and so to pay as much as the workmanship of the said ground shall be valued at.

After the Jury had given in their verdict John Woodcoke denied that Robert had paid for the said gunn notwithstanding the action was [illegible] before him and he never denied it: but I offered him a new tryall by a writ of error if he would present it.

Goody Gregory hearing him denie that he was paid testified uppon oath that she heard John Woodcock say [*14] that he did not owe above as 2s 6d in the plantation she said that she replied thus to John Woodcocke that she heard Robert say that John Woodcock ought him between 30 and 40s Then John Woodcok answered that Robert was a pratinge fellow for he had set of his gunn and now he did not owe him past 7 or 8s: Also Henry Gregory testified uppon oath that he heard him speak the same to his wife.

Goody Gregory being accused by oath of John Woodcoke and

Richard Williams for swearing before God I could break her head: she did acknowledge it was her great sin and fault and saith she hath bin much humbled for it:

She is fined 12d to the pore to be paid to Henry Smyth within a month: or if she doe not she is to sit 3 houers in the stocks.

[*15] August.7. 1641.

Know all men that whereas there is a mariage shortely intended betweene the widdow Horton and Robert Ashly both of Spring-feild: That the said widdow Horton in the presence of Robert Ashly doth assigne and set over her house and house lott conteininge about eleven akers and 4 akers of woodland afore the house Eastward all which is valued now at Twelfe pounds: and all her hogges litle and greate which are valued at eighteene pounds all together are valued at Thirty pounds into the hands of Robert Ashly for the use and be-hafe of her two sonns one sucking and the other about Three years ould caled Jermy to be paid to them that is to say to eather of them fifteene pounds apeice when they shall come to the age of Twenty and one yeares: and the said Robert is to have the use and profits of the said land and hogges for the educatinge of her said Two sonns: and when they shall come to the age of 13 or 14 yeares the said Rob-ert doth promise to put them out as apprentises to some usefull trade such as they shall like of: and if they cannot be put out with-out a portion of mony then so much is to be deducted out of their portion of 15£ apeace as shall be indifferently judged fitt for their bynding out: and for the rest of the said 15£ apeace the said Robert doth bynd himselfe his land goods and cattell to pay to them when they shall come to the age of .21 years: and in the meane tyme doth bynd himselfe to maintaine the present house and fencinge and if he shall leave it in better case than it is at present then he then shall injoy it shall pay such cost as shall be judged to make it better for his use by indifferent parties and if one of the two sonns of the widdow Horton shall die before the age of 21 yeares then the other shall have his portion also: And the widdow Horton being present before me at the wrighting hereof doth acknowledge that this is her will and meaninge and that she is fully consenting to what is above expressed and the said Robert Ashly being also present doth acknowledge that [*16] he is fully consentinge to all that is above expressed: and uppon this their mutuall Consent I have given them leave and liberty to proceed in marriage when they please: and the Inventory of her goods I have hereunto annexed as they were apprised under the hands of Samuell Wright and Samuell Hubbard.

WILLIAM PYNCHON

An Inventory of the Goods and Cattell of the widdow Horton of Springfeild this first July 1641 we whose names are underwritten do value things as followeth

Imprimis for all her linnen brasse pewter beddinge vessels and other implementes 17£ . 0 . 0

her hoggs litle and greate as they were rated by the appriser of the Towne Rate 18 . 0 . 0

her house and houselot 12 . 0 . 0

Samuell Wright
Samuell Hubbard

Robert Ashly was sworne Constable of Springfeild this 24 day of the 10 month 1641.

January the .5. January 1641 [1642].

Richard Hull of New Haven complaines against Thomas Merike in an action of the case for a Rugg which Thomas Merick had of his and for the use of certaine tooles which he kept a long tyme and for the charge of two journies which Richard Hull saith he made to Receive his goods.

[*17] The Jury: Henry Smith, Elizur Hollihoak, Henry Burt, Samuell Hubbard, John Leonard, Samuell Wright.

Robert Ashly beinge Constable came not in a due tyme to make retourne of his warrant and therefore it is thought meete to fine him in the some two shillinges six pence: it being now past ten of the clock neer eleven and he was ordered to appoint the meeting at nine aclock.

The Jury find for [five lines deleted] the plainetife Mr. Thomas Maik detained the Augur about 6 weeks after he sent downe the rest of the tooles for which we find him in damages 3 shillings.

2ly for the plainetifes last journey we find in damage eight shillings and costs three shillings but for the Rugg we cleer the defendant of that for wee do not find that he had any charge of that Rugg neather is it proved that he had any use of it after he was released from his masters service:

January the 13. 1641 [1642].

Accordinge to order given by warrant to the Constable: the Jury appointed are present to try the Action that Henry Burt hath laid against Judith Gregory viz

Henry Burt Complaines against Judith Gregory in an action of the Case for breach of Covenant in Molestinge him in his daughter Sara[h] Burt.

The Jury are Henry Smyth, Elizur Holioak, John Leonard, Samuell Hubbard, Samuell Wright, John Dible.

Judith Gregory was 3 tymes caled by the Constable to answer the action abovesaid and she appeared not.

[*18] A coppie of Record: of the last will and testament of John Searles of Springfeild dated the 21th day of the 10 month 1641 Recorded this 20 of the 2d month 1642.

I John Searles beinge very sicke in body doe make my last Will and Testament in manner and fourme followinge first I give to my brother in law William Warrener my best coate and my cullored hatt: and whereas in some reckonings betwixt him and me he owes me betwixt three and fower poundes: if he pay fortie shillinges thereof I am content that all the rest shall be remitted: The rest of my estate I devide betwixt my wife and my child equally: and doe appoint that my wife shall have for her use till my child come to the Age of 20 yeares that portion belonginge to my Sonn John Searles in consideration of his maintenance and education Provided that before she marry againe she shall give or in her behalfe cause to be given sufficient security for the payment of my childes portion which security shall be given to Mr. Moxon my brother Timothy Bawldwin and Samuell Wright whom I doe intrust to be overseers for the performance of this my last will:

witnesses hereof Henry Smyth, Elitzur Holioake

[*19] A Coppy of the Inventory of the Goods and Chattayles of the late deceased John Searle taken the 8 Feb: 1641 [1642].

Imprimis				
8 goates at 15s peace	6.	o.	o
6 boardes and rackes at 4s	o	4	o
9 hogges at	11.	o	o
3 small piggs at	o	4	6
a hogg lent William Warrener	2	11.	9
1 hogg in salt and 2 flitches of bacon	5.	o.	o
2 caske at 6s, tubb at 4s and other small things at 3s	o	13.	o
4 blankets a rugg a koverlit a bed and boulster of flaxes and bedsted	6.	o.	o
wearinge apparrell	3.	1.	o
20. yard dowlesse	1	10	o
linnin sheetes and shurtes etc.	4.	2.	6
a black hatt	o	2	o
pewter	1	.5.	3
a pair gloves and a brish	o	2	o
4 traies	o	4.	6

tooles and Iron things	3.	4.	0
iron potts and other things	1	1	4
3 chistes with bootes and shoes	2	3.	0
peeces powder and shott	3.	1.	0
brasse kettles and skilletes	[2]	17.	0
a wheelebarrow	0	5	0
a canoe lock and chaine	1	2	0
sackes pease and other things	1	15.	4
6 bushells of meale at 3s per bushell	0	18.	
2 tubbes and 2 skins	0	3.	0
28 bushells corne at 2s 4d per bushell	3.	5.	4
12 [illegible]	0	12	0
housing lotts fenceing [page torn] future dividends	35.	0	0
2 load of boltes	0	6	0
in debts that are owing from bretheren at Milford ——4£	97.	14	0

prisers Henry Smyth Richard Sykes.   Sume 101 14. 0
    R. S.

[*20] Aprill 20 1642.

Know all men that whereas there is a mariage shortly intended betweene the widdow Searles and Alexander Edwards both of Springfeild: That the said widdow Searles in the presence and with the full
consent of the said Alexander Edwards doth accordinge to the last
will and testament of John Searles deceased assigne and set over her
house and houselottes and all other dividentes of land with all other
moveables before mentioned in the Inventory or the value of them
to George Moxon Pastor of Springefeld Tymothy Baldwin of Milford and Samuell Wright of Springefeld for security of fifty pounds
to be paid to the sonne of John Searles caled John Searles at the age
of twenty yeares: viz. when the said child caled John Searles shall
come to the age of Twenty years as is expressed in the said last will
of his Father deceased: and in case the widdow named Sarre Searles
shall die before the said legacy be paid to the said child or the over-
seeres thereof above mentioned Then the said Alexander Edwards
doe bynd himself in the some of one hundred poundes to see the said
legacy performed to the said overseers above named: who have
power according to the last will to take care for securinge the said
legacy to the orphan and in case the said Alexander Edwards doe not
give sufficient security for the said legacy to the said overseers then
they shall have power to re-enter the said house and land or to distraine other goods of the said Alexander Edwards to the full value of

the legacy in the behalfe of the said orphant: And the said widdow Searles being [*21] present before me William Pynchon at the wrightinge hereof doth acknowledge that this which is expressed in wrightinge is according to her mind and meaninge and that she is fully consentinge to what is above expressed: And the said Alexander Edwards being also present doth acknowledge that he is also fully consenting to all that is above expressed: and George Moxon and Samuell Wright are also present and doe consent to accept of the said security and doe also testifie that Tymothy Bauldwine of Milford doth fully repose his trust in them so farr and doth fully consent to accept of the security they doe allow of for the security of the said legacy for the said orphant: and uppon this their mutuall consent I have given them leave and liberty to proceed in marriage when they please:

[*22] August 3. 1643.

John Leonard was sworne Constable of Springfeild for the yeare insuinge and till another be chosen in place.

December .21. 1643.

Thomas Merick complaines in an action of the case against Robert Ashley for kepinge a pig which Mr. Thomas Mericke saith is his.

The Jury   Elitzur Hollioak, John Dible, Allexander Edwardes, Henry Burt, Samuell Wright, Samuell Chapin.

The Jury find for the defendant: they find the pigg to be his and they give 7s Costes to the defendant and for the witnesses 5s.

Feb. 8 1643 [1644].

Thomas Mericke complaines against Robert Ashly in an action of Revew about a pigg.

The Jury   Thomas Cooper, John Dober, Benjamin Cooly, Richard Sykes, William Branch, John Gorman.

The Jury haveinge bin held most what in hering the plea and the proofes till nere midnight desyred liberty not to bring in this verdict till an houer before sunnsett which was granted.

[*23] February 9th 1643 [1644].

Both plaintife and defendant mett at the tyme appointed and the Jury: and the plaintife desyred a further hearing before the Jury brought in their verdict: which was granted provided he could produce any new profe or could nulifie any former allegation of the defendant.

And Goody Stebbing was herd what she could say uppon her oath:

The Jury returned this verdict: we find for the defendant The pigg to be his and we give him besides Ten shillings for costes and three shillings more for the Jury and Three shillings more for witnesses.

February 13. 1643 [1644].

Samuell Chapin was sworne Constable in the place of John Leonard who was put out of his place as a mark of disfavor for swearinge to a lie in the evidence he gave betweene Thomas Merik and Robert Ashly.

Aprill 10 1645:

John Dible complaines in an action of the Case against Morgan Johns for saying that John Dible said he was sorry that he did not make an end of his Cow.

The Jury are: Henry Smith, Thomas Cooper, Richard Sykes, Samuell Wright, Robert Ashly, and John Leonard.

The Jury find for the plaintife: and we give him in damages 15s Costes .6s.

[*24] the 12 day of the first month 1645 [1646].

James Bridgeman was Sworne Constable of Springfield according to the oath ordained by the Generall Court in the Bay.

This 2d of November 1647.

Thomas Stebinges was Sworne Constable according to the oath of the Generall Court: under Mr. Nowells hand.

Aprill 13. 1648.

These were sworne to be Freemen
John Pynchon, Elitzur Holioak, Henry Burt, Roger Pritchard, Samuell Wright, William Branch.

Aprill the 5 1649   These were sworne Freemen
Thomas Cooper, Griffin Jones, Daniel Chapen.

Aprill .24th 1654.

These persons were (before us John Pynchon and Elizur Holyoke) Sworne to be freemen of this Jurisdiction
Thomas Stebbins, John Lamb, Alexander Edwards.
Samuell Chapin, Richard Sykes made free in the Bay.

Aprill 25 1656: these were Sworne Freemen
John Stebbinge, Robert Ashly.

March 23d 1656 [1657] beinge a Trayning day these tooke the freemens oath: Benjamin Parsons, Thomas Gilbert.

[The freeman's oath, as contained in the printed Laws and Liberties *of 1648 (p.56), read as follows.]*

I (AB) being by God's providence an Inhabitant within the Jurisdiction of this Common-wealth, and now to be made free; do heer freely acknowledge my self to be subject to the Government thereof: and therefore do heer swear by the great and dreadfull Name of the Ever-living God, that I will be true and faithfull to the same, and will accordingly yeild assistance and support thereunto, and my person and estate, as in equitie I am bound, and will also truly indeavour to maintein and preserve all the Liberties and Priviledges thereof, submitting my self unto the wholsom Laws made and established by the same. And further that I will not plot or practice any evil against it, or consent to any that shall so doe, but will timely discover and reveal the same to lawfull authoritie now heer established, for the speedy prevention thereof.

Moreover, I do solemnly binde my self in the sight of God, that when I shall be called to give my voice touching any such matter of this State, wherein Free-men are to deal, I will give my vote and suffrage as I shall in mine own conscience judge best to conduce and tend to the publick weal of the Body, without respect of persons, or favour of any man. So help me God etc:

May .1. 1648.

These are chosen to seale up the votes of the Freemen to one of the deputies of Roxbury   Henry Smith and Samuell Chapen.

April 5 1649:

Henry Smith and Samuell Chapen now chosen to seale up our Freemens votes for magistrates and to send them seald up to John Johnson of Roxbury who is chosen for our deputy to the Generall Court.

[*25] Aprill 21. 1648.

Alexander Edwards complaines against Thomas Mericke in an action of the case for abusing his child named Samuell Edwards being about 5 or 6 years ould the 14 of Aprill last.

The Jury   Henry Smith, Thomas Cooper, Thomas Reeve, William Branch, Benjamin Cooly, Samuell Chapin.

The witnesses   John Mathews, Nathaniell Blisse.

They proved 3 batteries besides vilifieing words as hang him better kill him then he kill my child.

The Jury find for the plaintife damages 12s, costs 8s.

May 4 1648

Coe one of the Indians on the other sid did complaine against Francis Ball for striking of his wife two blowes with a stick. Francis Ball saith it was but two blowes with a litle shorte stick about two foote long and not so big as his litle finger and he strock her only on her beare skin coate.

I ordered him to pay her 2 hands of wampam but I also ordered that the boys that skared his cattell and hindered his cattell to pay 3 hands and when they paid the said 3 hands then Francis Ball should pay the two hands: he refused the said 2 hands and said he would give 2 blowes for it:

At the same tyme Coe desyred leave to plant corne in the Swamp over Agame River which was granted only for one yeare provided he would secure it against any cattell which he was entitled to doe or else if it were Spoiled he would aske nothing for it.

[*26] November .7th at a Court. 1648.

Thomas Mericke was Sworne Constable this present day [*The remainder of the page is blank.*]

[*27] At a Court this 6 February 1648 [1649].

Thes underwritten tooke the oath of Fidelity

Thomas Merick, Rowland Thomas, John Stebbinge, William Brookes, Nathaniell Browne, Thomas Cooper.

William Warrener, Robert Ashley, John Leonard, James Bridgeman, John Clark, Samuell Marshfield.

Rowland Stebbing, Jonathan Burt, John Herman, Nathaniell Blisse, George Langhton, John Mathewes, Thomas Sewell.

Richard Exile, Jonathan Taylor, Georg Coulten, Griffith Jones, Rice Bedorthe, Benjamin Cooly, Hugh Parsons, John Lumbard, Miles Morgan, Alexander Edwards.

March 23d 1655/56 being a Trayning day these underwritten took the oath of fidelity

Thomas Bancroft: John Stewart: James Warrener: Obadiah Miller: Symon Sackett: Nathaneel Burt: Hugh Dudley: Samuell Bliss: William Morgan: Lawrence Bliss: Jeremy Horton: James Taylor: Edward Foster: John Sackett: Josiah Chapin: Abell Wright: Richard Maund: John Riley: Anthony Dorchester: Francis Pepper: James Osborne: John Horton: John Earle:

And these underwritten did the same day before the Company affirme that they did on a Trayning day some yeeres past vizt. while Mr. William Pynchon was here in the Countrey, take this oath of fidelity, though their names be not on record: and therefore they were not willing to take the oath agayne: The persons were John Dumbleton, Nathaniel Pritchard, Symon Bemon: Thomas Miller.

[*The oath of fidelity, as contained in the printed* Laws and Liberties *of 1648 (p.56), read as follows.*]

I (AB) being by Gods provedence an Inhabitant within the Jurisdiction of this Common-wealth, doe freely and sincerely acknowledge my selfe to be subject to the Government thereof. And doe heer swear by the great and dreadfull Name of the Ever-living God, that I will be true and faithfull to the same, and will accordingly yield assistance thereunto, with my person and estate, as in equitie I am bound: and will also truly endeavour to maintain and preserve all the Liberties & Priviledges thereof, submitting myself unto the wholsome Laws made, and established by the same. And further, that I will not plot or practice any evil against it, or consent to any that shall so doe: but will timely discover and reveal the same to lawfull Authoritie now here established, for the speedy preventing thereof. So help me God in our Lord Jesus Christ.

[*28] Henry Burt was this day [*November 7, 1648*] sworne Clarke of the Band:

John Clarke is presented by Griffith Jones for leavinge A carrion by the brookside which was very offensive.

the 17. November 1648.

John Clark pleads that it was buried but uppon note of it he took it away for the swine had rooted it up: and by he pleads his case to remove it uppon the first notice I have passed it by: [*The remainder of the page is blank.*]

[*29] Aprill the 12th 1649.

Know all men that whereas there is a marriage intended to be this day sollemnised betweene the widdow Ball and Benjamin Mun of Hartford: That the said widdow Ball in the presence and with the consent of the said Benjamin doth condition to pay fourteene pounds in such pay as shall be estemed worth fourteene pounds to be paid to the two sonns of the said widdow that is to say eight pounds to Jonathan Ball now about 4. yere ould and six pounds to Samuell Ball now about the age of a yere to be paid to them when they shall accomplish the age of twenty yeres and in case either of them dye the other is to have all the said 14£: provided also that if the said Benjamin shall put out the said boyes to be apprentises to some trade then he shall lay out their said portions for their accommodation and so shall be freed of the said payment at 20 yeares of age and the said Benjamin doth acknowledge himself to stand bound in the some of 20£ for the

true performance of the said conditions: and uppon this their agreement I do give them leave to proceed in mariage:

The marke of Benjamin
Mun X in the presence
of me WILLIAM PYNCHON

[*Page 30 is blank.*]

[*31] Att a court this 29 of the 3d month 1649.

Henry Burt was chosen Clark of the writts for this Towne. This
day all the printed lawes were read: the whole Towne being present:

The perfectinge of the order about hogges and pigges is referred
to the select Townsemen and to set down the tyme when they shall
be yoaked and when they may go at liberty.

Hugh Parsons was complained on by the Constable for takinge
Tobacco in the open street and James Bridgeman did testifie the
same: he is therfore fined .10s and the Constable is to have the same.

Thomas Merick complaines against Richard Exile for taking to-
baco in the open streete this 30 day of May 1649 but the lawes were
published but yesterday and he not named to be present because he
takes himself to be no inhabitant therefore I thought it fitt to make
this a warning to him and others for after tyme except it appear that
he knew of the order before hand and then he is to pay it.

[*Four lines have been deleted.*]

James Bridgman was Complained of by Hugh Parsons for takinge
of Tobacco in his yeard without dores and is fined 10s therfore.

[*32] May 29 and 30 1649.

The widdow Marshfeild Complained against Mary the wife of
Hugh Parsons of Springefeild for reporting her to be suspected for a
witch and she produced John Mathewes and his wife for her witnesses: who were examined uppon oath.

John Mathewes said that Mary Parsons tould him how she was
taught to try a witch by a widdow woman that now lived in Springefeild and that she had lived in Windsor and that she had .3. children
and that one of them was married and at last she said it was the widdow Marshfeld.

The said John Mathewes answered her that he beleaved no such
thing of her: but thereuppon said he Mary Parsons replied you need
not Speak so much for Goody Marshfeild for I am sure (said she) she
hath envied every womans child in the end till her owne daughter
had a child and then said she their child died and their Cow died:
and I am persuaded said she they were bewitched: and she said moreover it was reported to her by one in Towne that she was suspected

to be a witch when she lived in Windsor and that it was publikely knowen that the divill followed her house in Windsor and for aught I know said she followes her here.

Goodwife Mathewes saith uppon oath that when Goody Parsons came to her house she said to her I wonder what is become of the half pound of woll. Goody Parsons said that she could not tell except the witch had witcht it away: I wonder said I that you talke so much of a witch doe you think there is any witch in Towne: then said shee, and she came into my house while the wooll was a cardinge: who is it said I: she said that An Stebbinge had tould her in Mr. Smiths Chamber that she was suspected to be a witch in Windsor and that there were divers stronge lightes seene of late in the meddow that were never seene before the widdow Marshfeild came to Towne and that she did grudge at other women that had Children because her daughter had none and about that tyme (namely of her grudging) [*33] the child died and the cow died.

Goody Parsons did stiffely denie the truth of their Testimonyes: but as the said witnesses had delivered their Testimony uppon oath and finding that she had defamed the good name of the widdow Marshfeild I sentenced her to be well whipped on the morrow after lecture with 20 lashes by the Constable unless she could procure the payment of 3£ to the widdow Marshfeild for and towards the reparation of her good name.

The Sworne Presenter of the breach of order did this 30 of May present Mr. Smith, Mr. Holioak, Mr. Moxon, Thomas Cooper, Samuell Chapen, William Warrener, Robert Ashly, Serjant Merick, James Bridgeman, Samuell Wright, John Herman, Benjamin Cooly and George Coulton for the breach of a Towne order in leaving their oxen over the great River since the first of May last without a keper.

The Towne order makes each Teame liable to a fine of 5s per teame if Any do kepe oxen over the River without a constant keeper after the first day of May.

Mr. Smith, Mr. Holioak and Serjant Merik had teames there of 4 oxen a peace Mr. Moxon and Thomas Cooper one: Samuell Chapen and William Warrener one, Robert Ashly and James Bridgeman one, Samuell Wright and John Herman one, Benjamin Cooly and George Coulton one: in all 8 teames.

A warrant to the Constable for the taking up these forfeites and to pay them presently to the Towne Treasurer Mr. John Pynchon.

These dues belonging to the Towne were all released by the Towne. [*Marginal notation.*]

These said Teames did also trespasse Henry Burt in his marshe wheate which was valued by Richard Sykes and [*34] George Lanckton to be to the value of 12 bushells in their best apprehensions: and they all were Content to refer themselves to my order for the severall proportions what every one is to pay.

I have considered of it and for want of proofe whose oxen did the damage in particular I have judged it most equall that all of said .8. Teames doe pay 1 bushell and halfe a peace the next winter by the first of December next. viz.

Henry Smith	1 bushell and half
Elitzur Holioak	1 bushell and half
Serjant Merik	1 bushell and half
Mr. Moxon and Thomas Cooper	1 Bushell and half
Samuell Chapen and William Warrener	1 bushell and half
Robert Ashly and James Bridgeman	one bushell and half
Samuell Wright and John Herman	one bushell and half
Benjamin Cooly and George Coulton	one bushell and half

[*35] December 2 1649.

Joseph Parsons Complaines against Thomas Sewell for failinge in the payment of a debt of 40s now 2 yeres: at first it was said Parsons for a bargaine of land that he had of me: but according to his desyer I released him of that bargaine but then by a new bargaine he was to pay uppon the Release of the former bargaine 40s.

Thomas Sewell saith that he was to pay him 40s uppon the Release of the said bargaine:

Joseph Parsons requiers damages for the forbearance and for Trouble of two witnesses viz Hugh Parsons and Serjant Merik for which I doe order the said Sewell to pay him 4s and the said Sewell doth promise to pay the said debt and damages being 44s by the latter end of February next: which Joseph Parsons is Consenting to:

[Page 36 is blank.]

[*37] At a Court this 5 February 1649 [1650].

John Mathewes Complaines against Hugh Parsons in an action of the Case for not restoring his mony which he hath paid towards the building of his Chimnies: which he hath neclected to doe. The bill of particulars of his debte is 1£ 14s 6d.

Joseph Parsons Complaines against Rice Bedornie in an action of Trespasse for pulling downe his fence against his hay Rick in the long meddow. [One line has been deleted.]

The Jury   Eliztur Holioak, Thomas Reeves, Leiftenant Henry Smith, Benjamin Cooly, Deacon Wright, Thomas Stebbinge, exceptions was made against Some and others were enterlined in there Rome.

[*The names of Miles Morgan, Deacon Chapin, Richard Sykes,
and Thomas Cooper are deleted.*]

Rice Bedornie complaines in an action of the case against Joseph
Parsons for unjust possessing of his land in the long meddow and was
admitted to try his case in forma pauperis.

The Jury find the first action for John Mathewes Plaintife

the debte	1	14	6
Charges	0	10	0
damages	0	1	0
	2	.5	.6

The Jury find the 2d action for Joseph Parsons plaintife

damages	0	.5	.0
Cost	0	.10	.0

The Jury find the 3d action for Joseph Parsons the defendant
damages 12d   Cost for witnesse 12d.

[*38] Serjant Merik Constable did by warrant atach certaine
goods of Nathaniell Brownes in the hands of Thomas Miller the next
day after the date of the warrant which was dated the 21 of the .1.
month 1649 [1650].

The goods he attached were   1 brasse bottell
1 iron pott
2 pewter platters
2 earthen dishes

Walter Fyler appeared this 7th of May 1650 to prove his Debt he
took his oath to his book of accountes that Nathaniell Browne of
Springfeld was indebted to him as followeth

whit starch	0	2.	8
2 pounds Reasens [*illegible*]	0	0	10
30 pounds Sugar at 16d per pound	2	0	0
vinegar 11 pintes this was feched by Miles Morgan for Nathaniell Browne as he testi-fied uppon oath.	0	3.	3
wine and cakes 6d another tyme caks 4d	0.	0	10
	2.	7.	7

To be paid in wheat the Spring following: and the said wares now
delivered nere .3. year since

he saith he Received of Goodman Watts	0	16.	0
so resteth due to Walter Fyler	1	11.	7

Also Anthony Dorcester testified this 7th May 1650 uppon oath
that he went with Walter Fyler to Nathaniell Brownes house a litle
before his going away: and that the said Nathaniell Browne did then
promise in his hering to bring downe corne for his debt to Goodman

Fyler which I apprehended was 10 bushells of wheat and deliver at Mr. Hills landing place in Windsor for Walter Fyler.

[*39] June 10. 1650.

Having herd the Case in difference between Thomas Miller and Nippinnsuite [?] Jones: Mr. Moxon beinge present Thomas Merick, George Coulton, Thomas Cooper and John Pynchon and with their advise I have judged Thomas Miller to receive 15 lashes for the breach of the pece in striking at the said Indian with the butt end of his gunn.

This whippinge was before the execution bought of by payinge downe 4 fathom wampam.

To Thomas Merick Constable of Springfeild
By virtue hereof you are to make inquiry amonge our Indians on the otherside what Indian hath broken open Rowlands house and taken away her best redd kersy petticote and some linin in a Baskett and you are to bringe the Indian before me or the goods if he make an escape that they may be delivered to the owner:
Springefeld this 20 July 1650

WILLIAM PYNCHON

If you find him at Woronoco you may persuade him to come and push him forward to make him come, but in case you cannot make him come by this meanes, then you shall not use violence but Rather leave him. Springefeld the day abovesaid.

WILLIAM PYNCHON

The Indians name is Munnuckquats of Hopauntaunck neer New Haven.

On the 23 of July 1650 Attumbesund of Woronoco and divers other Indians came to my house to excuse himself from blame in the said businesse: and that it was not he that did hinder the English from takinge away the prisoner but others of Ausatimik and other places that were many in opposinge and he durst not oppose them he found them and their prisoner: etc. I tould him that the English came to him as Friends and desyred him to let them have the prisoner, in a friendly way and because he being the Sachem [*40] did not only forbeare to speak but at last was Content that the prisoner should escape and in so doing he was to be accounted as one with the guilty person: he desyr he should live but desyred that his friends the English should be [illegible]: I tould him also that after the English had bound him with their cords (seeing others did hinder them from) they gave the end of their cords into his hands and praed him to kepe him till they went here and tould Mr. Pynchon and because he was content that other Indians should hinder the English: not [*illegible*] to them [*illegible*] and because he was content therfore should Proper Justice therefor I looked for satisffaction at his hands.

Thereuppon he praid me to Speak with him in private and tould me that he would put 3 fathom to the Corte: I tould him it was to litle but if he would put 5 fathome to the Corte I would take it and then all should live both Woronoco and the English: so after some pawse and conference together they gave me 5. fathome which I gave Rowland Thomas and his wifes Coate and willed him to pay out of it those that also paid him in this business:

I have put Goodman Coopers relation of their carriage of the Businesse among the last papers in this book.

[*This relation is not found in the* Record.]

[*41] July 28 1650.

Hugh Parsons and John Lombard testifi uppon oath that as they were warding the Sabbath day was Senight befor they saw Samuell Terry standing with his face to the meeting house wall nere the coner of the meeting house next the street chafing his yard to provoak lust, even in sermon tyme: and because they said they had kept it private I gave him private Correction with a rod on his bare back .6. lashes well set on.

[*The bottom half of the page is blank.*]

[*42] Whereas Hugh Dudly of Barnett did covenant promise and grant to and with William Pynchon of Springfeild in New England merchant his Executors and assignes from the day of the date herrof being the 29 April 1650 untill his first and next arivall at Boston in New England and after for and duringe the tearme of five yeares: The said William with the Consent of the said Hugh Dudly hath assigned and set him over to Mr. Henry Smith of Springfeild for the said tearme of .5. yeeres: and the said Mr. Henry Smith doth hereby promise to allow him three pounds and ten shillings per yeare to find him apparell: and to endevor at the end of his tyme to provide him a convenient allottment of land in witnesse whereof the parties above named have set to their hands this 9th day of September 1650. and his landinge at Boston was the 2d July 1650.

WILLIAM PYNCHON
the marke of
Hugh X Dudley
HENRY SMITH:

witnesse
ELITZUR HOLYOKE.
RICHARD MAUND

Memorandum that the said Indenture is delivered into the Hands of Mr. Henry Smith the day abovesaid,

[*43] Whereas James Wells of Barnet did covenant promise and grant to and with William Pynchon of Springfeild of New England merchant his executors and assignes from the day of the date hereof beinge the 22 day of Aprill 1650 untill his first and next arivall at Boston in New England and after for and during the tearme of nine yeares: The said William with the Consent of the said James Wells hath assigned and set him over to Mr. Henry Smith of Springfeild for the said tearme of nine yeeres and the said Mr. Henry Smith doth hereby promise to find the said James meate drink apparell and lodging with other necessaryes during the said tearme and at the end of the said tearme to pay unto him the sume of fifty shillings in mony or the true value thereof in such Comodities as the country doth afford as it is specified in his said indenture: In witnesse whereof the parties above named have sett to their hands this 9th day of September 1650. and his landinge at Boston was the 2d July 1650.

Witness   WILLIAM PYNCHON
ELITZUR HOLYOKE: the mark of
RICHARD MAUND   James X Wells
                   HENRY SMITH:

Memorandum that the said Indenture is delivered into the hands of Mr. Henry Smith the abovesaid day being the 9 September 1650.

[Page 44 is blank.]

[*45] Whereas Edmund Foster alias Edward Foster of Barnett did covenant promise and grant to and with William Pynchon of Springfeild in New England merchant his Executors and assignes from the day of the date hereof being the 22 of Aprill 1650 untill his first and next arivall at Boston in New England and after for and during the tearme of nine yeeres: the said William with the Consent of the said Edward alias Edmund Foster hath assigned him and set him over unto Mr. Elitzur Holioak of Springfeild in the Massachusett Colony and the said Elitzur Holioak doth hereby promise to find the said Edward Alias Edmund Foster meate drink apparell and lodging with the Necessaries during the said tearme and att the end of the said tearme to pay unto him fifty shillings in mony or the true value thereof in such comodities as the Country doth afford as it is specified in this said Indenture where he hath bound himself by the name of Edmund Foster. In witnesse whereof the parties above named have set to their hands this 9 September 1650: and his landing at Boston was the 2d July 1650.

Witness   WILLIAM PYNCHON
HENRY SMITH: EDWARD FOSTER
RICHARD MAUND   ELITZUR HOLYOKE

Memorandum that his Indenture is givenen into the hands of Mr. Elitzur Holioak this 9th September 1650.

[*Page 46 is blank.*]

[*47] October 15. 1650.

Know all men that I Samuell Terry with the consent of my present master William Pynchon of Springfeild gentleman have put my self an apprentense to Benjamin Cooly of Springfeild weaver his heires and assignes to serve him or them in any kind of Lawfull Imployment that the said Benjamin Cooly shall command me for and during the space of three yeeres 6 monthes and some odd dayes from the Tyme of the date hereof: In consideration whereof I the said Benjamin Cooly doe bynd myself my heires and executors to pay unto the said William his heirs or assignes the some of nine pounds viz fifty shillings at the 10 day of Aprill next 1651. and fifty shillings more at the 10 day of Aprill 1652 and fifty shillings more at the 10 day of Aprill 1653 and Thirty shillings the 10 of Aprill 1654 at the house of the said Mr. Pynchon in good and merchantable wheat at foure shillings per bushell or in sound merchantable pease at three shillings per bushell moreover I the said Benjamin Cooly doe bynd myselfe my heires and assignes to pay unto the said Samuell Terry now assigned and set over unto me as abovesaid, fifty shillings in merchantable wheat and pease at the prise abovesaid for his first yeeres service and fifty shillings for the 2d yeere and fifty shillings for the 3d yere and for the last halfe yeere and some odd days thirty and five shillings and also in the said space to find the said Samuell Terry meate drink and lodginge fitting as servants ought to have: and also I doe hereby bynd myselfe to instruct him and teach him the trade of linnin weaving accordinge to the use of it in this [*48] Towne of Springfeild provided he will be willinge and carefull to learne it:

This Nine Pounds due for Samuell Terrys tyme was sattisfied Mr. Pynchon according to ingagement: in specie: Per me JOHN PYNCHON [*Marginal notation.*]

And the said William Pynchon doth promise to the said Samuell Terry for his better incoragement to remitt his last yeeres service which he is bound by his Indenture made in England to serve him more than is expressed in this present agreement with Benjamin Cooly, and doth also freely give him all the apparell that he hath at present both wollen and linnin and doth also promise to give him Twenty shillings more in such necessaries for apparell as he shall call for in his first yeares service with Benjamin Cooly: and the said Samuell doth bynd himself to be dilligent in service to the said Benjamin and not doing him any damage accordinge to his Covenantes expressed in his Indenture to the said Mr. Pynchon which said Indenture the said Mr. Pynchon doth assigne set over and deliver into the hands of the said Benjamin Cooly for the use and behoof of himself or of any of the said persons mentioned in this Contract untill the said Samuell shall have performed the said service of 3. year 6 monthes and odd dayes from the date hereof: and for the sure Rattifienge of the said Agreement the said Mr. Pynchon hath Entered this agreement in his book of publik Records and also all the foresaid persons have hereunto set their hands this present 15 day of October 1650.

witnesse	SAMUELL TERRY
RICHARD MAUND	The Mark of
JOHN BENHAM	Benjamin ✕ Cooly
	WILLIAM PYNCHON

[*49] Memorandum that it is agreed by the parties expressed in the said Indenture that in case the said Samuell Terry dye in the tyme of his first yeeres service with the said Benjamin then the said Benjamin is to pay only 5£ to Mr. Pynchon at the yeares end: and that if he dye after the first yeere and before he hath served 3 yeeres then he is to pay half of that which remaines to Mr. Pynchon.

Also it is mutually agreed that whereas the said payments is expressed to be made in sound merchantable wheat or pease: yet if payment be made in any other thinge that the said Mr. Pynchon or Samuell Terry shall accept it shall be accounted a fulfillinge of their Covenant.

Memorandum that the 20s above promised to Samuell Terry is paid him this 25 October 1650   in a new hat and band   0 10 .0
in a moseskin   0. 10 .0

[Pages 50 to 53 are blank.]

[*54] A Coppy of our Comission:

For asmuch as there is a present necessity that some Care be taken respecting the Case of Springfeild they being destitute of any Magistrate: etc.

It is ordered by this Court and the authoritye thereoff, That John Pynchon, Elitzur Holyoke, and Samuell Chapin, of Springfeild aforesaid, for this yeare ensueing or till the Court shall take further Order, Shall hereby have full Power and Authority to Governe the Inhabitants of Springfeild and to heare and determine all Cases and offences both Civill and Criminall, that reach not to life, Limbs, or Banishment, according to the Laws here established, provided that in matters of weight or difficulty it shall be Lawfull for any party to appeale to the Court of Assistants at Boston, so as they prosecute the same according to the order of this Court provided also that theire tryalls be by the oaths of Sixe men If Twelve cannot be had for that service and the said John Pynchon, Elitzur Holyoke, and Samuell Chapin have Power to give Oaths to such Constable or Constables as shall be Legally Chosen, and to examine witnesses as any one Magistrate may doe:

By the Court etc:

The Oath:

Wee John Pynchon, Elitzur Holyoke, and Samuell Chapin Commissioners for the Towne of Springfeild By order of the Generall Court, Doe here sweare by the Living God that we will truly Indeavour to our best abilitys to demeane ourselves in our place according to the laws of God, and of this Jurisdiction and that we will dispence Justice on all occasions proper to our place and cognizance equally and Impartially during our aboade in this Jurisdiction, and continuing in Commission as aforesaid, so help us God in our Lord Jesus Christ: This oath is to be taken before the Select men of Springfeild, Before the Commission takes place: By the Court Edward Rawson: Secretary.

November 22th 1652.

John Pynchon, Elitzur Holyoke and Samuell Chapin Commissioners as abovesaid, tooke theire Oath before the Selectmen of Springfeild.

[*55] November 22th 1652.

John Stebbins was Chosen, and sworne to the office of a Constable in the Towne of Springfeild for the yeare ensueing, and till a new be chosen in his place:

Consideration being had, How necessary it is that some set time be appointed for the Hearing and determining of differences or offences that may arise in this Towneship:

Wee therefore appoint the first Thirsday in March, and also the first Thirsday in September for that worke, and shall attend them as Court days for that end and purpose:

[*56] March the .3d day, 1652/53.

Richard Sikes the sworne presenter for this Towne; doth present Reice Bedortha for Breach of an Order of General Court, namely, For Taking of Tobacco on his Hay Cock: Also Benjamin Mun, for the same offence:

We find them Gilty of the plaine breach of the law, which requires them to pay 10s a peice only Richard Sikes who Informed, being to Receive halfe the fine, he releases them of that So that we order each of them to pay .5s according as the Law requires: which is to be paid to the Deacon for the use of the poore.

Margarite the wife of Griffith Joanes being presented for breach of a Towne Order, in Carying fire we find not her excuse sufficient, and therefore adjudge her to pay .5s to the Towne Treasurer:

James Bridgeman was chosen and sworne to the office of a presenter in the Towne of Springfeild for the yeare ensueing: etc.

[*57] November .1st 1653.

William Warrinar was chosen and sworne to the office of a Constable in the Towne of Springfeild for the yeare ensueing and till another be chosen in his roome:

Jonathan Burt was only chosen for deputy in case of the constables absence.

Richard Sikes was Chosen and sworne to the office of a Sealer of weights and measures in the Towne of Springfeild.

November .1. 1653.

The persons underwritten being presented for breach of Towne orders are ordered to pay: as followeth

Hugh Dudly	o.	01s.	o
Thomas Merick	o.	10.	o
Samuell Wright	o	02.	o
Deacon Chapin	o	01.	o
Widdow Bliss	o	01.	o
James Bridgman	o.	00.	6
John Leanord	o	00.	6

[*Page 58 is blank.*]

[*59] November 26th. 1653.

William Brookes for defrauding sundry persons in withholding from them, and converting to his owne use the goods of severall persons was adjudged to make sattisfaction to the Sum of .18£ (besides the principall which (amounts to 9£ the which is restored) he being unable to pay the said sum of 18£ aforesaid was comitted to the custody of the Constable.

But this .1st day of December .1653. John Stebbins, Mistress Smith and Fraunes Pepper Ingages for him that he shall sattisfie the persons he hath wronged to the sum aforesaid by Michalstide next, whereuppon he is released from the Constables Custody only he is

not to depart out of the Towne till Michalstide that he have sattisfied the said sum:

[*Page 60 is blank and the next leaf has been cut out.*]

[*61] Att a Court holden for the tryall of Causes: March. 2d 1653
[1654].

Margarett Bliss Widdow complaynes against Thomas Mirack in
an action of the case for not performing the determination of certayne men chosen to Arbitrate a matter in difference betweene her
and him, concerning ditching and quick Setting a hedge in the Meddow of the said Margarett Bliss:

The Jury George Colton, Rowland Thomas, Miles Morgan,
Griffith Jones, Robert Ashley, and Anthony Dorchester.

The Jury returne this verdict: they fynd for the Plaintiffe vizt the
debt of 4£ 7. 6d to be due and 8s for forbearance withall that Thomas
Mirack pay the cost of the Court:

Jonathan Taylor and Anthony Dorchester beinge presented for
not wardinge on the Lecture day beinge February 9th 1653 [1654].
Jonathan Taylor pleadinge his inability of body at that tyme for the
service was freed: And Anthony Dorchester acknowledginge his offence and with all his plea beinge considered was judged to pay 2s
6d: which the Constable is to Levy for the use of the watch or ward:

Widdow Bliss complaynes against Anthony Dorchester in an ac-
tion of the case for damage done in her Indian corn by his swine:
The Jury Benjamin Cooley, Rowland Thomas, Robert Ashley,
Thomas Cooper, Miles Morgan, Griffith Jones.

The Jury fynd for the defendant that widdow Bliss shall pay the
charge of the Court:

[*Five lines on pages 61 and 62 are crossed out, possibly by a later
hand; the remainder of page 62 is blank.*]

[*63] At a Courte holden the 24th day of the first Month 1654
[1655].

This Court was holden for the tryall of Samuell Wright Junior
who is charged by Mary Burt to be the father of her illegitimate
child:

The said Samuel desired to be tryed by a Jury of 12 men: tryall
was made accordingly: The Jury were these Richard Sikes, John
Dumbleton, Benjamin Cooley, Alexander Edwards, George Colton,
William Branch, Miles Morgan, Anthony Dorchester, Griffith Jones,
James Bridgman, Joseph Parsons and David Chapin:

The verdict of the Jury: Wee fynd Samuell Wright Junior guilty
of committinge wickedness with Mary Burt in havinge the use of her

body 3 severall tymes, whereby wee fynd him to be the father of the said child:

Whereuppon the said Samuell Wright was ordered and adjudged to be the reputed father of the said child: And for his evill behaviour therein to be whipped with 12. stripes on the naked body well layd on: And to pay the charges of the Court, and towards the mayntenance of the said child to pay after the rate of One shillinge foure pence per week makeing payment every month, dureinge the tearme of Seaven yeares, and at the end of Seaven yeares to pay Forty shillings towards the putting of the child forth to be an apprentice and in the meane while to give good Security vizt a bond of 40£ with Sufficient Suretyes to perform this Order.

And Mary Burt for her great wickedness was ordered and adjudged to be whipped on the naked body with 12 lashes well laid on as also to keep her said child: And whereas shee hath been found guilty of Comitting wickedness with Joseph Bonde Shee was adjudged to be well whipped [*64] a Second tyme with 10 lashes about a month after the first whippinge, according as shee shal be called forth, except shee doe before pay into the Constable as a fyne to redeeme her Second whippinge the Sum of Thirty shillings.

Samuell Wright Junior was punished the 28th of May 1654 and Mary Burt by reason of inability to come forth and for other causes was protracted till   of May following at which tyme shee received her punishment and to redeeme the second whippinge shee paid the fyne of 30s above mentioned.

Likewise Samuell Wright Senior and Thomas Stebbins entred into a bond of 4£ for the performance of the Order above mentioned concerninge Samuell Wright Junior:

[*65] May 8th 1654.

Daniel a Scotchman Servant to Thomas Merick beinge found to prophane the Sabbath in idle walkinge about and not comeinge to the Ordinances of the Lord, yea though he had warninge to the contrary: and being also complayned off by his said Master for grievous idleness in neglecting his busyness for Severall dayes, yea Synce he was called before authority for the like misbehaviour formerly at which tyme he promised amendment; but grew worse and worse and therefore was adjudged to be whipped on the bare back with five lashes well laid on and Execution was done accordingly:

[*66] Att A Court holden the first of March 1654 [1655].

Thomas Mirick complaynes against Thomas Miller in an action of debt of Fourty shillings and 20s damage.

Thomas Mirack plantiffe against Hannah the wife of Richard

Exell defendant in an action of debt of 3£ 17s 9d due to the plantiffe on account from Thomas Reeves late husband to the defendant.

Thomas Miller plantiffe against Thomas Mirack defendant in an action of debt of One and Forty shillings.

Thomas Mirack plantiffe against Thomas Miller defendant in an action of debt of Fifteen shillings due from the defendant.

The Jury for the tryall of these causes were Thomas Cooper, George Colton, Benjamin Cooley, Benjamin Parsons, Robert Ashley, Anthony Dorchester.

The Jury fynd the first action for Thomas Mirack the Plantiffe the Debt 2£ os od costs 9s 4d.

The Jury fynd the 2d Action for Thomas Mirack plantiffe they fynd for the Plantiffe 1£ 17s 9d: 6s 8d damage and 9s 4d costs.

The Jury fynd the 3d action for Thomas Miller Plantiffe the debt 2£ 1s and costs 7s 4d:

For the 4th action the Partyes agreed between themselves in presence of the Corte:

[*67] An Inventory of the goods and Chattells of Nathaniell Bliss lately deceased: taken By Benjamin Cooley and Thomas Cooper Feb. 14th 1654 [1655].

	£	s.	d
Howsinge and Homelott—5 acres	06:	00:	00:
Wett Meddow before the house 3. acres	03:	00:	00:
woodlott—5 acres	01:	00:	00:
Over the great River 9 acres	04:	10:	00:
Att the Long Meddow 26 acres ¼	08:	10:	00:
Over Agaam River 5 acres	00:	05:	00:
Meddow on the Mill River 2. acres	00:	10:	00:
2 Cowes:—7£ 10s 3 swine .1£ 5s	08.	15.	00:
3 Kettles 1 skellet 1. pott	01.	13.	00:
7 peeces of Pewter 13s 7 peeces of Tin 4s	00:	17:	00:
a warming pan 5s a fryinge 2s	00:	07:	00:
Earthen ware 4s wooden ware 1£	01:	04:	00:
2 bedsteads—10s 2 chaires 3s 3. boxes a chest 7s 6d	01:	00:	06
Axes. Spades and how. 7s plough chayn and share 10s	00:	17.	00:
Certayn slayes 7s a cradle and a chest 5s	00:	12:	00:
a bedtike with flocks and feathers	00:	10:	00:
a Muskett Sword bandaliers	01.	02.	00:
1 hatt 5s 1 Jackett: 2 pair of breeches 18s	01.	03.	00:
1 pillow 3s bookes 10s a Spinning wheele 2s	00:	15.	00:
Debts	11.	13.	00:
total	54:	03.	06

Due from the deceased estate to others
   —02£ 06s 06:
The totall of the Estate debts being paid is   51: 17: 00:

[*68] Springfeild: March: 5th 1654/55.

Concerninge the disposinge of the estate of Katharine Bliss Widdow late wife of Nathaneel Bliss deceased who died intestate, It was Ordered that shee should enjoy all the Estate, left by her said Husband, and that shee may be carefull of the children which shee had by her said Husband which children are for present of very tender yeares: And it Is further Ordered that when her Eldest Son attaynes to the age of One and Twenty yeares shee shall pay unto him, the Summ of Eight pounds, and when the Two daughters attayn to the age of sixteen yeares shee shall pay to each of them the summ of Foure pounds: and Foure pounds to the youngest son at the age of One and Twenty yeares: And in case any of them dy under such ages aforesaid, the portion or portions of the deceased shalbe divided equally among the rest:

[*A marginal note is illegible.*]

Know all men by these presents that whereas there is a marriage intended to be solemnized between the above mentioned the Widdow Katherine Bliss of this Town, and Thomas Gilbert of Windsor. The said Thomas Gilbert doth for good causes and considerations him hereunto mooving covenante and promise, and hereby bynd himself his heires executors and administrators to pay or cause to be paid unto the children above mentioned of the said Widdow their Severall portions in the order above mentioned, and at the severall tymes of payment above mentioned: In witness whereof he hath hereunto sett his hand this 23d of May 1655.

X
The mark of
Thomas Gilbert

Signed before us ELIZUR HOLYOKE
            SAMUELL CHAPIN

[*The following September 26, 1665 order for settling the estate of Nathaniel Bliss appears in 1 Hamp. Cty. Probate Ct. Rec. 65–66. A variant form is found in Pynchon Waste Book for Hampshire 30–31.*]

The Corte at Northampton in March last past at the request of Widdow Margerett Bliss Guardian to her Granchild Samuell Bliss Son of Nathaneel Bliss late of Springfeild deceased haveing given their then apprehensions concerning the setling an estate on the children of the said Nathaneel Bliss, yet referring the full conclusion of the matter to this Corte, that for all persons concerned might have liberty to declare their exceptions, which this Corte now haveing heard doe see reason to revoke what they then declared touching the premises: And now after much tyme spent in hearing what is allegdged and pleaded, well weighing what was Ordered and determined by the Commissioners of Springfeild Anno 1654 for set-ling the estate of the said Nathaneel Bliss who died intestate; And al-though the want of an Inventory of the estate then proved doth some-what invalidate that determination, yet fynding it difficult now to gayne an Inventory of the estate and the friends concerned now refusing to take administration upon the estate and for the children: This Corte judgeth meet that the Summes formerly ordered to the children by the Commis-sioners of Springfeild shall Stand good, and is hereby determined to be their portions: vizt Eight pounds for the eldest Sonne Samuell Bliss and Foure pounds to Nathaneell Bliss the youngest Sonne and Foure pounds a peece to the Two daughters, Only in regard of Testimony now pre-sented to this Corte that the Said Nathaneell Bliss deceased did before his death declare that his son Samuell should have his lands after his de-cease, which till now or of late was not publikely known or manifested: This Corte doth therefore Order that the said Eldest Sonne Samuell shall have his Eight pounds and the youngest Son Nathaneell his Foure pounds in Land: which summes amounting to Twelve pounds shall be allowed and paid them out of the Land which was their fathers as the Land was then prized: And therefore now this Corte Ordereth that when they shall attayne the ages expressed in the Said Comissioners Order they shall have and enjoy the lott in the Long Meddow being Twenty Six acres and a quarter more or less then vallued at Eight pounds and ten shillings and Six acres of that Land in the neck at three pounds, and Two acres of Land vizt Meddow on the Mill River then vallued at Ten shil-lings: All being Twelve pounds as the Land was then vallued: And the Two Daughters shall have their foure pounds a peece paid to them in currant pay according as they shall attayne the ages determined in the said Comissioners Order.

[*69] May: the 2d 1655.

John Stebbins beinge taken notice for misbehavinge himself to-wards his aged Father calling him Old foole and uttering other un-seemly words towards him was the day abovesaid examined thereof: and the matter beinge not ripe for a fynall issue, the said John Steb-bin did before the Comissioners bynd himselfe in the summe of Forty pounds to appeare before Authority here established to make answer for the said misbehavinge himselfe to his Father when he shalbe thereunto required.

This matter beinge further considered there was not found full proofe of such evill carriage whereupon he was released and dis-charged of his bond above mentioned:

June 25t 1655:

Robert Monro a Scotchman being taken notice of to have brought diverse bottles of strong liquors to this Plantation which liquors he was suspected to have sold to the Indians: he being examined there uppon it was found and prooved that he had sold some of these liquors to the Indians: for which his offence against the law selling his liquors without a license and for a lye which he made to collour his offence affirminge that he brought up but three bottles when as it was proved that he brought up Foure bottles with a gourd shell besides with liquors   It was Ordered that he should pay 5£ 10s vizt 5£ for his unlawfull selling his liquors and 10s for his lye.

[*70] June 27 1655.

Symon Lobdell being taken notice of to come up with a Cannow with Cider and strong waters which he confessed he intended to have sold to the Indians: the strong waters beinge found hidden on shore were ceased on and Ordered to be kept in deposito: till the matter were further inquired into: uppon further consideration his strong waters were restored unto him:

The said Symon Lobdell beinge found in a lye was ordered to pay 10s Secundum legem:

The Coppy of an order of restraynt to Robert Ashley and his wife forbiddinge them to sell wine or strong waters to the Indians sent to them the 27 June 1655.

To Robert Ashley and his wife Keepers of the Ordinary in Springfeild.

Whereas it is famously known how the Indians abuse themselves by excessive drinking of strong liquors whereby God is greivously dishonoured, and the peace of this Plantation in great danger to be broken: And whereas you have noe lycence formally and according to Law to sell eyther wine or stronge waters to English or Indians: These are therefore to will and require you uppon your perill, that you henceforth forebear to sell eyther wine or strong waters to any Indians though for selling to the English wee would not restrayne you but doe allow thereof: Springfeild June 27 1655.

This was signed by the Comissioners of this towne.

[*71] March 13th 1655 [1656].

Obadiah Miller complaynes against Joane his wife for abusing him with reproachfull tearmes or names as calling him foole toad and vermine and threatninge him: as also for that yesterday shee fell uppon him indeavoringe to beat him at which tyme shee scratched his face and hands: The case being examined it was found that Joane the wife of Obadiah Miller was guilty of very evill behavior towards her said husband: it beinge prooved by the testimony of John Lamb and Thomas Miller:

John Lamb testifyed he heard her say shee would knock him on the head: and that shee did often call him foole and other reproachfull tearmes:

Thomas Miller testifyed that when his brother Obadiah and his wife lived with him, she did comonly call him foole and vermine: and he doth not remember he ever heard her call him husband: and that she said shee did not love him but hated him: yea shee here said shee did never love him and shee should never love him:

For which her vile misbehaviour towards her husband shee was adjudged to be taken forth to the whippinge post, there to receive Soe many stripes on the naked body as the Comissioners should see cause to inflict on her: whereuppon shee was brought forth; but by her humiliacon and earnest protestations for better carriage towards her said husband the punishment was remitted, and this Sentence passed, that for the least miscarriage to her husband after this tyme shee should be brought forth agayne to receive a good whipping on the naked body well laid on:

[*72] April 2d 1655.

Thomas Cooper complaynes against John Bliss for non-performance of a bargayne of fetchinge the said Thomas some fencinge stuffe.

John Bliss denyed the bargayne: but it was sufficiently prooved And therefore:

The result of the Comissioners was: that synce the bargayne is proved, the said John Bliss shall carry this fencinge stuffe soe soon as the way is fitt for cartinge and whereas the tyme is come that fences should be sett up; it was adjudged that John Bliss should be liable, to pay such damages as accrew for want of the fencing beinge done, because he neglected to cart the stuffe when there was convenient opportunity to cart it.

Aprill .9th 1655.

John Stiles of Windsor complaynes against John Bennet who at present resides in this Town for defaminge his wife, in saying shee was a light woman and that he could have a leape on her when he pleased:

This cause was upon the request of John Bennet deferred to the 18th of this instant that he might bring in what he had to prove his said accusation of the woman: John Clark beinge bound for his appearance.

Aprill .18th 1655.

The said John Bennet appearinge according to Order and not making any part of the slander to appeare against the woman: It was Ordered that John Bennet should be forthwith well whipped on the Naked body with 8 lashes and that he should pay unto the said John Stiles a fyne of Forty shillings:

[*73] At a Court holden at Northampton September 28 1658.

By order of the Generall Corte appoynting the Comissioners of Springfeild to joyne with the Comissioners of Northampton for the issuing of all Civill actions not exceedinge Twenty pounds etc. as in the said Comission hereunder written more at large appeareth uppon which day abovesaid Mr. John Pynchon and Elizur Holyoke of Springfeild attended for that service: According to the Comission following.

At a Generall Court held at Boston: May. 20. 1658.

In Answer to the Petition of Northhampton, It is Ordered that their Condition in relation to a Minister be forthwith commended to the Reverend Elders, and their help desired therein: Secondly, that there shalbe Two Courts kept yearely by the Comissioners of Springfeild and Northampton joyntly or by any foure of them, the one at Springfeild on the last Tuesday of the first Month and the other at Northampton on the last Tuesday in September, which Courts shall have power to heare and determine, by Jury or without according to the liberty the law allowes in County Cortes, all Civill actions not exceeding Twenty pounds damages, and all Criminall cases not exceeding five pounds fyne or corporall punishment not exceeding Ten Stripes, reserving appeales in all such cases to the County Court at Boston: and the said Court shall have power to grant licenses for the keeping of Ordinaryes or houses of comon entertainment, for Selling of wine cider or strong liquors, according to law and not otherwise, givinge the oath of freedome or fidelity to persons quallifyed according to law, to bynd to the peace or good behaviour to comitt to prison felons and malefactors as the law allowes, and this to bee during the Courts pleasure.

Per Edward Rawson Secretary

This is a true Coppy of the Courts Order which was sent up to Northampton:

As Attests ELIZUR HOLYOKE

[*74] Uppon which 28th Day of September

Thomas Roote complayned of Robert Bartlett in an action of the case for strikinge his the said Thomas his wife with a long stick to her great prejudice:

Robert Bartlett acknowledginge his offence in the Court: Both Plantiffe and Defendant agreed about the matter between themselves:

Joseph Parsons complaynes against John Webb for not deliveringe a Cow and calfe accordinge to bargayne, and thereupon Joseph demands 4£ of the said John which the said John owed him:

Upon hearinge of the busyness, Joseph Parsons was content to accept of the Cow though the Calf were lost, the said John allowinge the said Joseph 5s which he promised to allow and pay to the said Joseph.

Edward Elmer complaynes against William Holton and Robert Bartlett in an action of defamation in two perticulars: 1. for affirming that the said Edward Elmer went down in a disorderly way to take his oath, And 2ly: for charginge him the said Edward to be one that made a breach or rent in the Town concerninge the Lords dayes meetings.

To the first perticular in this action the Court did thus judge: Wee cannot wholly free Goodman Elmer from blame in the Transaction of the busyness in relation to the place [*75] that he was chosen to vizt a Comissioner for the Towne and Judge disorder in his proceedings, though in regard of the overhastyness of the Town in choosing another, which might be some occasion of his soe sudden goeinge down to Springfeild where he took his oath, we fynd not ground for William Holton and Robert Bartlett to charge him with disorderly taking his oath, seeing Edward Elmer did not seek for, or moove to have his oath given him till it was putt to him: yet we Judge it not a defamation: the speaking of a mans faylings and infirmityes may be disorderly and yet not a defamation:

For the 2d particular we see not ground for William Holton and Robert Bartlett to charge Edward Elmer for makinge a breach or rent in the Town: for it appeareth that the ill management of matters on both sides had been the occasion of the breaches in the Town But it doth not appeare that Edward Elmer was the cause of them, and therefore to charge him for makinge the breach, we fynd to be some degree of defaminge Him, though in regard of some blame worthy carriage found in Goodman Elmer about those matters we lay noe damage uppon the Defendants to pay to the plaintiffe:

John Elmer son of Edward Elmer complaynes against Goodwife Holton for charging him the said John to have stollen an axe: this action was taken up amongst them selves before any sentence passed uppon it:

[*76] Att the same Courte Joseph Parsons was chosen Clarke of the Band, and took his oath accordingly for the due execution of his office:

And the Town fyndinge a necessity for some one to keepe an Ordinary for entertayning strangers, they made choyce of John Webb for that service who had a license graunted him in that behalf, as also for the sellinge of wine Cider or stronge liquors: this license to continue for one yeare from this Courte: Provided the said John Webb doe not suffer any evil rule or disorder in his house dureinge the said tearme, and that he doe behave himselfe therein, in all things accordinge to the Lawes of this Jurisdiction of the Massachusetts:

[*77] Springfeild March 29th 1659.

Walter Lee of Northampton Plantiff against Edward Elmer of the same Town defendant, in an action of review of the case whereby the said Edward by Sute at Law in the Town of Northampton recovered of the said Walter, a hogg with damage to the vallue of Six pounds:

Edward Elmer, Samuell Wright, Senior, Alexander Edwards, and John Stebbin Plantiff against the Town of North-Hampton Defendant in an action of the case concerninge their turninge out some of the freemen from beinge select men to which office they were chosen.

Henry Burt Plantiff contra James Bridgman defendant in an action of Debt to the vallue of fifty five shillinges.

Thomas Cooper Plantiff contra John Lyman Defendant in an action of debt to the vallue of 27£ 19s 4d.

Thomas Burnam of Hartford Plantiff contra William Holton and Thomas Bascomb Defendant (noe case specifyed in the summons) Thomas Burnam and William Holton appeared but Thomas Bascomb appeared not The matter beinge referred to be issued by Mr Pynchon Elizur Holyoke and Ensign Cooper, the result was that William Holton could not justly deny the Plantiffe an Attachment when desired, and that the said William should pay the said Thomas for damages and charges the summe of ten shillinges.

Benjamin Cooley Plantiff contra John Webb of North-Hampton Defendant in an action of debt of 8£ and for damage 4£: issued, See forward:

Richard Fellowes Plantiff contra Edward Messenger of Windsor Defendant in an action of debt and damage to the vallue of about 20£ due to the said Richard by Bill assigned to him from Witt Hill of Hartford, of which there is already distreynd to the vallue of about 20s.

[*78] The selectmen of Springfeild complayne contra John Sackett of the same Town for not performing his bargayne in thatching the Town barne:

William Deynes Plantiff contra John Bagg Defendant in three severall actions: 1 for affirming that William Deynes did convert a great deale of lead from the right owner: 2ly in an action of Theft for stealinge an axe from the mines: 3. for stealinge about 10 pounds of lead which was found in John Baggs Custody: These matters between William Deynes and John Bag was issued by arbitration: vizt that John Bagg should make publike acknowledge of his offences etc which accordingly he did and was admonished for his miscarriages:

Joseph Crowfoot Plantiff contra John Bagg Defendant in action of slander in reporting him the said Joseph to have stollen while he dwelt at Robert Hawards at Windsor and tended the Mill there:

The 29 day of March 1659 above mentioned beinge appoynted by the Honored Generall Corte held at Boston, May 20th 1658 for the keepinge of a Corte at Springfeild, by the Commissioners of Springfeild and Northampton joyntly or any foure of them as in the Commission, (a Coppy whereof is before transcribed) more at large appeareth: The Three men chosen for Northampton Comissioners appeared here for the holdinge of the said appoynted and intended Corte which Three men were William Holton Arthur Williams and Richard Lyman, together with the Jury men [*79] that were chosen and warned to appeare at the Court for the tryall of causes vizt Thomas Cooper, George Colton, Rowland Thomas, Jonathan Burt, Thomas Mirack, Thomas Stebbin and Robert Ashley of Springfeild and Thomas Woodford, Robert Bartlett, Joseph Parsons and David Burt of Northamton. But the said William Holton, Arthur Williams and Richard Lyman not being under oath presented themselves by Certificate under the hand of the Constable of Northampton to be sworne. But then some of the said Town of Northampton objecting against their three men as being not legally appoynted to the work they came for, in that they were not allowed by any superior Power as the Law provides; and in that they were nonfreemen as to this Comonwealth, and for other causes, Therefore after the busyness was longe debated the result was that there could be noe Corte Legally kept here without further Order from superior Powers: and soe the Assembly brake up:

The diffrance above mentioned between Benjamin Cooley plantiff and John Webb defendant being by them referred to be ended by Springfeild Comissioners, it was by them concluded thus that beside the debt of 8£ due by bill to Benjamin Cooley, John Web should allow for forbearance of the debt to this tyme with some charges and damage accruinge the summe of Thirty shillings.

                    See the Record uppon the file:

[*80] An Order of Administration upon the Estate of Symon Sackett deceased who died the 9th day of July 1659: which Order was graunted by the Comissioners the 14th day of the Same Month.

Symon Sackett of Springfeild who deceased the Ninth of July 1659 dyinge intestate; and it beinge necessary that Administration be made upon the said Symons Estate; And William Blomefeild of Hartford appearinge to be assistant to his Daughter wife of the said deceased party to Administer to the aforesaid estate; therefore the said William Blomefeild is hereby allowed and appoynted to be Administrator and Sarah his Daughter wife of the said deceased party to be Administratrix to the Estate of the said Symon Sackett deceased:

An Inventory of the Estate of Symon Sackett deceased taken the 15th day of July 1659 by Richard Fellowes and Samuell Chapin:

Inprimis one barne	6. 00. 00
Item 3 piggs	1. 01. 00
Item one sow and a pigg	1. 00. 00
Item a chayne	0 08. 00
An axe 3s, a pott with the hookes. 6s 6d	0 09. 06
A parcell of brass with old Iron	0 02 00
See more the next page	9 00 06

[*81]

One chape for a cart	0. 02. 00.
a sickle 6d 2 fork tynes—2s	0 02. 06.
a bed tick with a pillow	0 06 06
a cellar .1£ 4 score rayles. 12s	1. 12. 00
1 tray, and a half bushell the ½ bushell John Dumbleton had	0 04. 00.
2 barrells	0 02. 00.
2 acre and neere a quarter of wheat at 38s per acre	4 05. 00.
7 bushel of wheat to be paid by William Brookes	1 04. 06.
4 bushel of wheat from Joseph Crowfoote	0 14. 00.
1 acre of pease	1 10. 00.
One parcell of Indian that Obadiah Miller bought	2. 00. 00
One parcell of Indian and the grass	1. 16. 00
A parcell of Oates with the Oates in the Orchard and water mill:	0 16. 00.
an acre of Oates	1 15. 00.

a plough share	0	12	00
a garden that Richard Fellowes bought	0	10	00
a cart with Irons to it	1	05	00
a spade 2s 3 pounds tallow 1s 6d	0	03	06
a steere	1	15	00
a yoke staple and ring	0	03	06
Item 8s due from Daniel Blomefeild	0.	08	00
An Oxe	6.	10	00
2 hoggs if found	2	00.	00
a Canow to Richard Fellowes	0.	08.	00.
	30.	04.	06.

All the Oates and pease and water-millions and the use
  of half the barn is for Richard Fellowes for to pay 3£

12: On the other side	09	00	06
	39	05	00

This is a true account as we judge witnes
both our hands: July.15. 1659
               Samuell Chapin, Richard Fellowes
theres due Goodwoman Sackitt from Goodman Bloom-
  feild 4s
Onely the heiffer and steere to Daniell for 3£ 17s that
  Simon oweth Daniell:
    1. Steere yeere and vantage 1£ 15s

[*82] Att a Corte holden at Springfeild Sept. 27 1659.

Benjamin Parsons complaynes against Joseph Crowfoote for with
holdinge Forty shillings and six pence due upon a bill.

Robert Ashley Plantiffe against Richard Fellowes Defendant for
detayninge a sword from him: the sword and damages he reckons at
40s. In this action the Plantiffe withdrew his action promisinge to
pay the cost of the Corte.

Samuell Allin of Northampton Plantiffe against John Bliss of the
Same Towne Defendant in an action of the case for unjustly stealinge away the affections of Hannah Woodford his Espoused wife,
damnifyinge the said Samuell to the vallue of Fifty pounds:

In this cause the Plantiffe withdrew his action before the case
was tryed, for that he found himselfe defective in his testimony:

Samuell Allyn agayne Plantiffe against Thomas Woodford of
Northampton defendant in an action of the case for the forefeitinge
of a bond, with damage to the vallue of Twelve pounds:

But upon Searchinge of the cause, the Plantiffe withdrew his action before the Jury tooke the matter to consider of: In both actions
Samuell Allyn is to pay 10s for entry of each action:

The Jury warned to attend this Corte were Thomas Cooper, Miles Morgan, William Warrener, Thomas Mirack, Thomas Stebbin, Benjamin Parsons, Benjamin Cooley, and George Colton of Springfeild: and of North-Hampton Joseph Fitch, Robert Bartlett, William Miller, and Alexander Edwards.

The Indians complayninge about the 10th of August of damage done in their Corne on the other side the great River; which damage was veiwed the next day by two men and judged at 8s which this Corte orders to be raysed on the Inhabitants on that side the River accordinge to the number of their cattell, And the Constable is to See it raysed and to gather it up:

[*83] November 30th 1659.

John Matthews beinge presented for refusinge to obey a summons sent from Authority and Served on him before witness by Francis Hacklington in August last and for his contemptuous and high carriage towards him that was sent with the Summons: comanding him off his ground and holding up his sickle at him and usinge other high words and unfitting carriage: and these things beinge made manifest he was fyned to the Countrey five shillings.

And John Henryson complayning against Thomas Miller for detayning a cart from him which he sayth he had right unto and for abusing him by striking him on the face making his mouth bleed and using reproachfull speeches callinge him Scottish dogg: the case beeinge examined, such strikinge and evill speeches were proved against Thomas Miller. And withal there was prooved against John Henryson that he threatned Thomas Miller in Saying that eyther he or Thomas Miller should dy before he should have the cart.

Thomas Miller and John Henryson for their making disturbance by their quarrelling together; contending in hot words and fur in breakinge the peace; one of them strikinge and the other threatninge Slaughter, are each of them fyned 10s apeece to the Countrey:

And Thomas Miller for abusinge John Henryson by reproachfull speaches and strikinge him whereby he drew blood is adjudged to pay John Henryson in way of satisfaction the summ of three shillings foure pence.

Wee find they deserved to be bound to the peace, but in regard these things were acted some tyme Synce, and the spirits now somewhat reconciled we doe not require that bond.

Jan: 13th 1659 [1660].

Joseph Crowfoote complaynes to the Comissioners of John Bagg in action of debt of 15s vizt. 6s which he was cast to pay him for a slander and 4s which the said Joseph sayeth he wrongfully took from him, and 5s on account for land, hired of Rowland Stebbin, and he says in 5s more for damage   John Bagg ownes the debt of 15s and is adjudged to pay the said Joseph 12d for damage and 3s 4d costs:

[*84] At a Corte held at Springfeild, March. 27th 1660.   Present Capt. John Pynchon, Mr. Samuell Chapin, Elitzur Holyoke Comissioners:

The Jury were Thomas Cooper, George Colton, Benjamin Cooley, Serjant Stebbins, Jonathan Burt, John Dumbleton, Thomas Gilbert, Benjamin Parsons, Samuell Marshfeild of Springfeild and Henry Cunliffe, Henry Woodward, Thomas Bascomb: of Northampton.

Edward Elmer of Northampton Plantiffe contra William Holton of the Same Town Defendant: in an action of the case for breach of an aggreement: The Defendant pleaded that the case was laid down in such generall tearmes in the summons that he knew not what aggreement was intended in the summons, and therefore could not be prepared to answer:

The Corte judged the Defendants plea reasonable and soe adjudged the Plantiffe to pay the Costs of the Corte vizt 10s for entry of his action, and 6s for his journey from Northampton.

Edward Elmer Plantiff contra William Clarke of Northampton Defendant in an action of the case for takeinge away of tymber to the damage of 39s.

Edward Elmer Plantiffe contra William Clark Defendant in an action of review of an action of slander formerly tryed at North-Hampton wherein Edward Elmer was charged to have Slandered the said William Clark in Sayinge that the Said William Clark was noe better than a theefe   And in this action the said Edward Elmer layes in damages the summe of 39s.

Nathaniell Clark son of William Clarke of North-hampton Plantiffe contra Edward Elmer defendant in an [*85] action of Slander in callinge the said Nathaniell theefe to the damage of Five pounds:

In which action the Jury fynd for the Plantiffe: vizt. that Edward Elmer should pay him the said Nathaneel the summe of Foure pounds besides the costs of the Corte vizt 10s for entry of his action and 12d for witnesses:

And in the action wherein Edward Elmer is plantiffe and William Clarke defendant about takeinge away tymber.

The Comissioners fynd for the defendant that is the tree cut or tymber in difference should belong to the defendant and that the

Plantiffe should pay 6 shillings for a witness comeinge downe from Northampton and 3s 4d for entry of his action.

And for the action of review between Edward Elmer Plantiffe and William Clark Defendant   The Plantiffe withdrew his action before any sentence passed uppon it: and soe was judged to pay 3s 4d for entry of his action, and 6s to William Clarke for his journey down to the Corte.

Miles Morgan Thomas Gilbert and Benjamin Parsons Selectmen of the Town of Springfeild presenting unto this Corte a Complaynt against John Wood for abidinge in this Township contrary to Order beinge legally warned to depart: And it appearing that the said Wood came from Richard Fellowes his farme at Chickuppe whereuppon the said Richard Fellowes did before the Corte enter into bond to cleare this Town of Springfeild of the said John Wood and his family within three weekes after Michalstide next which bond is hereafter specifyed:

[*86] The Freemen of Springfeild being assembled the —— of this Instant March for the Nomination of Magistrates choyce of County Treasurer etc the votes for the Treasurer being Sealed up were presented to this Corte where it appeared that Capt. John Pynchon was chosen to that Office.

Richard Fellowes his bond.

Richard Fellowes acknowledgeth himself bound to the County Treasurer in a bond of 40£ that he will cleare and discharge the Town of Springfeild of John Wood and his family within three weeks after Michalstide next.

Robert Ashley being chosen Sealer for weights, and measures for this Town of Springfeild for the yeere ensueing, was at this Corte sworne to the performance of his duty.

Samuell Marshfeild beinge presented to this Corte as chosen to keepe an Ordinary or house for Common Entertaynment in this Town of Springfeild, was by this Corte allowed for that worke.

Mr. Elizur Holyoke is chosen Recorder for the Court:

[*Substantially the same entries for March 27, 1660 appear in 1 Hamp. Cty. Probate Ct. Rec. 1–2, except that the actions by Edward Elmer against William Clark are omitted.*]

[*87] Aprill: 7th 1660.

This Day the youngest child of John Herman called Ebenezer was found dead in the brook in Nathaneell Pritchards yard: concerning whose death there was search and inquiry made by a Jury of 12 men of this Town of Springfeild how the said child came to its end: the Jurors were Thomas Cooper, William Branch, William Warrener, Thomas Stebbin, Thomas Noble, John Stewart, Samuell Marshfeild, Henry Burt, Benjamin Parsons, Abell Wright, Richard Sikes, John Clarke.

Whose returne upon oath before the Comissioners Elizur Holyoke and Mr. Samuell Chapin was that accordinge to their best light they could have in the case they judge the child to be drowned in the brought through its own weakness without the hand of any other person being any occasion or cause thereof.

[*Substantially the same entry regarding the death of John Herman (Harman) appears in 1* Hamp. Cty. Probate Ct. Rec. 2.]

May: 9th 1660.

Thomas Miller complayned against certayne Indians that came to his house: which as his wife Sayth Scarred his children by throwinge stickes at them: his wife comeing out of her house and callinge to her husband for help he was going into his house to fetch a Cudgell, and his wife followed him, and at the doore of his house one of the Indians stroke his wife on her head with his fist that shee fell down with the blow: and Thomas Miller turninge back layd hold on the Indian that struck his wife: then another of the Indians laid hold on Thomas Miller and rescued him that struck the woman: and the other Indians struck Thomas Miller diverse blowes while he and the Indian were scuffling: the Indians being pursued by diverse men and horses, three of them were taken, and brought before the three Commissioners two of which Indians were found guilty in the case, [*88] but the Indian that stroke the woman could not be taken: the Names of those that were taken and found guilty were Kollabauggamitt and Maullamaug who dwell in Nipmuch Countrey they were adjudged to pay for themselves and the rest that escaped, 14 fathom of wampam: the Indians payinge the wampam, 6 fathom was delivered to the Constable to defray the charges of 10 men and 5 horses that pursued them or that were required to waite on the service and 8 fathom was given to Thomas Miller in way of satisfaction for the injury done to him and his wife.

June 3d 1660.   Before Mr. John Pynchon and Mr. Samuell Chapin Commissioners.

Hugh Dudley complayninge against Thomas Mirack for not performinge Covenante in plowinge up $\frac{1}{2}$ an acre of new ground which should have been done in May last, at the said Hugh his demand as by the Covenante, presented appeares: the said Hugh pleadinge great damages and still expectinge the ploughinge of the ground: Thomas Mirack was adjudged to have damnified the said Hugh ten shillings which he is to pay him, and also to plow up the $\frac{1}{2}$ acre of ground by the first of May next.

[*89] July. 6. 1660.   Before Mr. John Pynchon, Mr. Samuell Chapin and Elizur Holyoke Commissioners:

William Morgan complaynes against John Earle for strikinge him the said William with a bowle uppon his face and nose:

It appearinge by the Testimonyes of John Stewart and Charles Ferry, that John Earle did strike the said William Morgan and broke his nose, which also was evident his nose beinge much bruised and bloody when he came before the Comissioners: John Earle was adjudged to allow the said William Morgan the sum of five shillings also five shillings to the County for breakinge the peace and Three shilling foure pence for entry of the Action:

July 13 1660.   By Capt. John Pynchon and Mr. Samuell Chapin

Francis Hacklinton complayning against Mary the wife of Samuell Ely in an action of Slander for sayinge that he was seen at an unseasonable tyme of the night with Hester Bliss and that there were unseemely passages between them: pleading 40s damadge. The testimonyes being found to be of little weight the two Comissioners adjudged it noe Slander:

[*90] Sept: 14th 1660.
Before the Three Commissioners for the Towne.

John Lamb complaynes against Thomas Mirack for non performance of a bargayne of ploughing for him the said John Lamb being bound thereto by Bill under penalty of 2s per day for every day the land should be unploughed after the tyme prefixt in the Bond: John Lamb pleaded for the forfeiture mentioned in the said Bill or bond for that the Land was not ploughed till 11 dayes after the tyme limitted in the Bill.

The case beinge considered The Commissioners apprehendinge the lateness in the yeere that the land was ploughed and that the penalty mentioned in the bond was not unreasonable they adjudged that Thomas Mirack should pay John Lamb 20s for damage and 3s 4d for the entry of the action:

[*The following entries for a court held by commissioners at Springfield on September 25, 1660, not contained in the* Record, *are found in 1* Hamp. Cty. Probate Ct. Rec. 3.]

At a Courte holden at Springfeild
September 25t 1660.

For holdinge this Corte there were present: Mr John Webster, Captain John Pynchon, Mr. Samuell Chapin And Elizur Holyoke Recorder.

The Jurors were Thomas Cooper, Henry Burt, Thomas Merick, William Warrener, William Branch, Mr. Jeanes, Mr. Williams, John Dumbleton, Robert Bartlet, Lawrence Bliss, Alexander Edwards And Benjamin Parsons.

John Scott Plantiffe contra Obadiah Miller defendant in action of the case for refusinge to deliver a steere accordinge to bargayne to the damage of 8£.

The Plantiffe withdrew his action before the cause was tryed and Soe was to pay the costs of the Corte vizt 10s. for entry of his action.

John Stebbins of Northampton beinge bound to prosecute Robert Lyman of the same Towne for misdeameaninge himselfe towards his the Said John Stebbins wife: he the said John Stebbins complaynes to this Corte for that the said Robert frequentinge the said Johns house did use very evill and miseemely behaviour towards his the said Johns wife inticeinge her severall tymes that he might ly with her, takeinge her in his armes and otherwise venting his unchast desires:

Robert Liman for his gross Lacivious carriage and misdemeanor towards the said John Stebbins wife, in assaulting with the tentacion severall tymes and profferinge to abuse her by lyinge with her and shewing much immodest behaviour towards her, is fyned to the County the summe of 10£. Also he is to pay For Deborah Bartletts cominge from Northampton as a witness .6s. But Robert Bartlett remitted that 6s.

Robert Lyman beinge bound under a 20£ bond for his appearing at this Corte and for his good abearinge, was discharged of his bond by this Corte.

Miles Morgan Plantiffe contra Robert Ashley defendant in an action of the case for wrongful impoundinge of his swine.

The Plantiffe withdrew his action, Hee and the defendant aggreeinge between themselves: And the Plantiffe is to pay 10s for entry of his action.

John Porter of Windsor Plantiffe contra James Osborne defendant in action of debt to the value of 4£ proved by Bill, the Plantiffe also pleading great damages by long forbearance of his money and making severall journyes to obtayne his due.

The Jury fynd for the Plantiffe vizt the debt of 4£ and damadge 1£ 15s and 10s for entry of his action.

Mr. William Jeanes of Northampton beinge chosen by that Towne for Clarke of the writts was by this Corte allowed of and appoynted to that Office.

Mr. Elizur Holyoke was at this Court chosen and appointed Recorder for this Court and County:

There was presented to this Corte from Northampton the verdict upon Oath of a Jury of 12 men who made Inquiry concerninge the death of David Burt of about 4 yeeres of age beinge the son of David Burt of that Town The childe beinge taken up allmost dead by the father neere his house: the Jury apprehendinge that the child being busy about the carte which carted his fathers corne he was trodden down by the carte or cattell noe person knowinge it: it beinge in the darke of the Eveninge. This sad accident fell out the 30th of 6th month 1660 the verdict of the Jury is one the file with the Recorder:

[*91] Jan. 22th 1660/61: By Mr. Holyoke, Mr. Chapin and John Pynchon.

John Mathews being found drunken and bereaved of his understanding which appeared both in his speech and behavior he was according to Law fined Ten shillings to the County:

This miscarriage of his was at Samuell Terrys wedding.

[*The following entries for courts held by commissioners at Northampton and Hadley on March 26, 1661, not contained in the* Record, *are found in 1* Hamp. Cty. Probate Ct. Rec. 4–6.]

[4] At a Corte held at Northampton March: 26th 1661.

For holding of this Corte were present Mr. John Webster, Captain John Pynchon, Mr. Samuell Chapin and Elizur Holyoke Recorder.

And for the Jury these David Wilton, William Clark, William Holton, Henry Woodward, John Lyman, John Stebbins, Andrew Warner, William Lewis, John White, Samuell Smith, Thomas Stebbins and Samuell Marshfield.

Thomas Cooper of Springfeild Attourney for Captain Thomas Savadge of Boston, complaynes against John Webb of Northampton in an action of debt and damage to the vallue of Threescore and Foure pounds: This 64£ is beside what the Plantiffe hath accepted of and received by a bill from Serjant William Clarke of Northampton to the vallue of Six pound thirteene Shillings: and by another Bill from Zachary Feild of Northampton to the vallue of Seaventeene pound ten shillings.

John Bliss of Northampton Plantiffe contra John Webb eiusdem Defendant for witholding a debt of Foure pounds:

In which Last Action John Bliss Plantiffe was non suted in that he gave not Legall warning to the defendant for his appearance at the Corte: And Soe is adjudged to pay 10s for the entry of his action.

And in the case depending betweene Thomas Cooper Atturney for Captain Thomas Savadge Plantiffe and John Webb defendant.

The Jury fynd for the Plantiffe vizt the Bills for Captain Savadge: which bills are 29£. 3s. 7d. of which there is owned to be received as above 24£ 3s. Soe there remaynes of the principall 5£. 0s. 7d. And in consideration of damage the Jury fynd to make the 5£. 0s. 7d. to be made 9£ to be paid according to the nature of the payment in the said bills:

But concerninge the account presented as out of Captain Savadge his booke, the Jury doe not fynd it prooved according to Law: Moreover the Jury fynd for the Plantiffe the Costs of the Corte:

Henry Cunleife makeing Complaint to this Corte that he beinge summoned to this Corte by Francis Hacklinton in an action of Slander done to the Said Francis in his Name, the said Francis not appearringe to prosecute his action, And the Said Henry pleading trouble and charge that he hath been at in attending on the Corte and for witnesses, the Corte adjudged that the said Francis shall pay unto the said Henry for his trouble in attendinge on the Corte two Shillings: and Eighteen pence a peece for five witnesses, and two pence for the summons:

Samuell Porter of the Newtowne [Hadley] haveinge assigned his right and interest in his Servant, Robert Williams to William Lewis of the said Newtowne with whom the Said Robert is to serve in husbandry for Five yeares from the 8th of May: 1660 as by his Indenture appeareth: the said Assignment was allowed of by this Corte:

Goodman Hannum of Northampton presentinge a petition to the Corte for freedome from trayninge watchinge and wardinge by reason of his age: and the weakness of his body:

The Corte consideringe his weakeness of body his age and meane estate have freed him from trayninge watchinge and wardinge.

Thomas Coleman of the New towne beinge presented to this Corte as chosen to the office of a Constable for the said NewTowne: In the presence of the Corte he tooke his oath for the execution of his office:

[5] Joseph Parsons licence to keep an Ordinary at Northampton.

Joseph Parsons of Northampton is by this Corte Lycensed to keepe an Ordinary or house of Common Entertaynment, in the Towne of Northampton for the yeare ensueinge. and he hath liberty graunted him to sell wines or strong Liquors as need shall require: Provided he keepe good rule and order in his house.

Samuell Marshfeilds licence renewed.

Samuell Marshfeild of Springfeild keeper of the Ordinary there, consideringe his yeere and lycence wilbe expired before he shall have opportunity at the next Corte to renew it, and therefore now desireing further liberty in that worke: this Corte doth renew his liberty and Lycence till the next County Corte.

Order for Widdow Bliss about the Mill at Springfeild.

Uppon complaynt made to this Corte by Widdow Margeret Bliss of Springfeild of that annoyance shee receives by the passage of the water to the Mill at Springfeild. This Corte ordered Leiutenant William Clark of Northampton and John White Senior of the New Towne should view and judge what they apprehend fitt to be done by Mr. Holyoke for her reliefe in that case:

Choyce of military officers for Northampton.

The Souldiery of Northampton presenting to this Corte the Names of certayne persons whom they had chosen for military Officers: vizt William Clarke for a Leiutenante: David Wilton for Ensigne bearer William Holton for a Serjant and John Hannum for a drummer the Company desireinge that the Corte would allow of them for those offices:

William Clark confirmed Leiutenante to Northampton.

The Corte declareth that they doe allow and approove of and confirme the said William Clarke to and in the place and office of Leiutenante to the Trayned band of Northampton: Also

David Wilton confirmed Ensigne Bearer to Northampton.

The Corte declareth that they doe allow and approove of and confirme the said David Wilton for and in the place of Ensigne Bearer to the trayned band of the Town of Northampton.

And William Holton not quallifyed according to Law for office, was by the Corte allowed and desired to doe the work of a Serjeant for the band at any tyme of military exercise till the next Generall Corte to whom they are to looke for his Confirmation in the Office.

It beinge presented to this Corte that this winter past John Holton killed a wolfe uppon the River betweene Northampton and New Towne the River beinge frozen: The Corte determined that the said Two Townes should pay 10s a peice to Goodman Holton for his son that killed the wolfe. This beinge in reference to different apprehensions between the Said Townes.

The Treasurers account and the Corts order upon it. Order for a house of correction at Springfeild.

Mr. Pynchon the County Treasurer presenting to the Corte his accounts of dues to, and disbursements for the County: his accounts were viewed and approved of by the Corte whereby it appeard that before this Corte there was due to the County 13£. 12s. which Said Summe this Corte determines shalbe allowed and improoved to the buildinge of a house of Correction in Springfeild, which buildinge the said Mr. Pynchon is appoynted to take care of, that it be carryed on to effect: The account abovesaid is on the file:

Persons that tooke the Oath of fidelity to the Common Wealth.

These 15 persons of the Town of Northampton whose names follow vizt Richard Fellowes, John Webb, Joshua Carter, Jonathan Hunte, James Wright; Zachary Feild: Thomas Copley: Joseph Barker, Thomas Hanchett, Ralphe Hutchison, Thomas Bascom, Samuell Bartlett, Nehemiah Allyn: Thomas Roote, and Judah Wright tooke the oath of fidellity to this ComonWealth in the presence of the Corte.

Order for Mr. Treat his 5£.

This Corte being informed of 5£ due to the Country by bill or bond made to William Holton and Richard Treat of Wetherfeild Junior which Bill is Said to be in the hands of John Barnard of [*page torn*] the Corte Ordered Captain John Pynchon to take up the Bill and to demand and recover the [*page torn*] to give an account thereof.

[6] The Votes of the Freemen of the Townes of Springfeild and Northampton for a County Treasurer for the yeere ensueinge were presented to this Corte which beinge opened and perused it appeared that Captain John Pynchon was chosen County Treasurer for this yeare.

There beinge presented to this Corte the great necessity that there is of makinge a bridge in the way to Springfeild on the East Side of the great River over that brook where there is an old cart bridge now out of repayre: The Corte impowred Joseph Parsons of Northampton and Goodman Dickenson Senior of the New Towne as a Comittee to make survey where they judge it most meet to make the bridge: who are also to take account of the charge of that bridge or of mendinge other passages that way, and to bring in the account to the next County Corte.

At the New Towne at Norwotuck [Hadley] March.26.1661.

These persons whose Names follow beinge Inhabitants of the said New Towne and quallifyed accordinge to Law to be made freemen of this CommonWealth tooke the freemans oath before Captain John Pynchon and Elizur Holyoke who are impowred by the Generall Corte to give the Said Oath accordinge to Law:

The Persons were these

Mr. John Webster, Mr. John Russell, Nathaneell Ward, William Markham, Thomas Dickenson, Andrew Bacon, Thomas Wells, John Hubard, Nathaneell Dickenson, Phillip Smith, Thomas Coleman, Robert Boltwood, Samuell Gardner, Peter Tilton.

[*The will and inventory of the estate of John Harman of Springfield who died March 7, 1660/61 are omitted.*]

Aprill. 17th 1661. By Mr. Holyoke, Mr. Chapin and John Pynchon.

Joseph Leanord being Complained of for Misbehaving himselfe on the Sabbath, Playing sporting and laughing etc.

Charls Ferry and John Stewart Testifie on oath that last Sabbath day: they saw Joseph Leanord sporting and laughing in Sermon tyme, and that he did often formerly misbehave himselfe also in the same way.

Symon Beamon also sweares that on Lords day was senight or Lords day was fortnight he saw Joseph Leanord come to Samuell Harmon at the metinghouse dore and beate of his hat and then ran away, and afterward came to him againe and offered to kick at him and run away and then Samuell Harmon ran after him.

Hannah Chapin Saith shee saw Joseph Leanord one Sabbath day and Samuell Harmon whip and whisk one another with a stick before the metinghouse in sermon tyme.

Joseph Leanord for his playing and sporting on the Sabbath as aforesaid, was fyned to the County five shillings being that he had formerly bin admonished for his misdemeanor on the Sabbath.

[*92] May 14th 1661. Before Leiutenant Holyoke and John Pynchon.

Henry Burt Complaines against John Henryson for not paying of Three bushells of wheate according to promise for spinning and knitting of Stockens.

To which John Henryson says that the debt which he owes Henry Burt is but 10s and this he ingaged .2. bushells of wheate towards it and noe more: and he hath paid Henry Burt in worke so that Henry Burt owes him 8s for worke: Henry Burt ownes his owing him 8s which says he John Henryson was to have a shurt cloth for and John owning it is adjudged to take the shurt cloth: and for the other 10s John Henryson is adjudged to pay Henry Burt Two bushells of wheate (7s) and Three shillings in a day and halfe worke:

May 31th 1661.

John King (of Northampton) was presented as chosen Constable And tooke his oath to execute the office of a Constable in Northampton.

[*93] June. 20th 1661. Before Samuell Chapin and John Pynchon.

Complaint being made against Samuell Harmon for misbehaving himself on the Sabbath.

Once formerly when he was sent for, but came not with Joseph Leanord and then testymony on oath came in against him as on the side over the leafe backward: Aprill 17. (1661).

And since, last Sabbath in sermon tyme Joseph Warrinar and Peter Swinck Testifie on oath that in the forenoone last Sabbath in sermon tyme they saw Samuell Harmon thrust and tickle Jonathan Morgan and Pluckt him of his seate .3. tymes and squeased him and made him cry.

William Morgan also testyfies the same For which Misdemeanors the said Samuell Harmon (being that he was formerly admonished) was adjudged to pay five shillings as a fine to the County:

[*94] July .12th 1661.

Mr. William Westwood, Mr. Samuell Smith, and Andrew Bacon, Comissioners for the Town of Hadley by order of the Generall Court; tooke their Oaths to dispence Justice there in Civill and Criminal Cases for the yeare ensueing, according to theire Comission: this 12th of July 1661.

Before me JOHN PYNCHON:

[*The following entries for a court held by commissioners at Springfield on September 24, 1661, not contained in the* Record, *are found in* 1 Hamp. Cty. Probate Ct. Rec. 7–9.]

[7] At a Corte held at Springfeild September 24th 1661.

For holdinge of this Corte were present Captain John Pynchon, Mr. Samuell Chapin and Elizur Holyoke Recorder.

The Jury men were Captain Cooke, Nathaneell Ely, Henry Burt,

George Colton, Thomas Gilbert, John Dumbleton, Robert Ashley, Jonathan Burt, William Holton. Henry Cunliffe, Peter Tilton, Phillip Smith.

Alexander Edwards of Northampton Plantiffe contra Francis Hacklinton defendant in an action of the case, for takinge away his Mare downe to Hartford downe to Hartford (sic) without his leave to the damage of 5£.

Francis Hacklington Plantiffe contra Alexander Edwards defendant for wrongfully attaching his Kilne of Brickes to 15£ damage.

Francis Hacklinton Plantiffe contra Alexander Edwards defendant in an action of defamation in Saying that he runne away with his mare.

Francis Hacklinton Plantiffe contra Henry Cunliffe of Northampton defendant in an action of defamation, in Sayinge he is a man of noe good report to the damage of 20£.

Mr. Caspar Varlete of Hartford Plantiffe contra Boltus Jacobus Lockermans a Dutch man residing in Springfeild defendant in an action of debt and damage to the vallue of 70£.

Garrett Dolley Plantiffe contra Richard Mountague defendant in an action of debt and damage to the vallue of ten pounds.

Richard Fellowes Plantiffe contra John Leonard defendant in an action of the case for refusing to deliver a bull which the Plantiffe challengeth for his.

John Leonard Plantiffe contra Richard Fellowes defendant in an action of wrong attachment of his bull.

John King of Northampton Plantiffe contra Edward Elmer defendant uppon Suspition that the said Edward tooke away the said Johns cow from Northampton in a dishonest way to the damage of 5£.

In the action depending between Alexander Edwards Plantiffe Francis Hacklinton defendant. The Jury fynd for the Plantiffe damage 3£ and the cost of the Corte vizt 10s for entry of his action.

As to the two actions wherein Francis Hacklington is Plantiffe contra Alexander Edwards defendant the Plantiffe withdrew both his actions without declaring and Soe was adjudged to pay 10s for entry of each action.

As to the action dependinge between Francis Hacklinton Plantiffe contra Henry Cunliffe defendant The Plantiffe withdrew his action, and Soe is to pay 10s for entry of his action.

As to the action dependinge between Mr. Caspar Varlete Plantiffe and Baltus Jacobus Lockermans defendant the Jury find for the Plantiffe debt and damage to the value of 43£. 15s. and the Cost of the Corte vizt 20s for entry of the action and 18d. for one witness: and for other charges appearinge about the case 1£. 10s. 2d: and the said Baltus was adjudged to pay for keeping his cow while shee was under attachment: and 3s for watchmen to keep him dureing the Corte 5s.

An Order about Baltus See forward:

[8] As to action dependinge betweene Garret Dolley Plantiffe and Richard Mountague defendant. The defendant not appearinge to make

answer the Plantiffe hath the costs of the Corte granted him: vizt 10s for entry of his action.

As to the two actions depending betweene Richard Fellowes and John Leonard, each Plantiffe withdrew his action and aggreed betweene them Selves: each Plantiffe beinge to pay 10s for entry of his action.

As to the action dependinge betweene John Kinge Plantiffe and Edward Elmer defendant the said Edward not appearinge the Jury fynd for the Plantiffe vizt. 2£. 2s. 6d damage and the costs of the Corte vizt 10s for entry of his action.

At this Corte Elizur Holyoke and John Lumbard tooke their oathes that they were present with John Harman of Springfeild a little before his death, at which tyme he made his last will and testament recorded on the leaf next before this.

Samuell Marshfeild of Springfeild upon his desires presented to this Corte hath his licence renewed for Keepinge an Ordinary and for sellinge wine and liquors. This licence to continue for one yeare next ensuinge provided he observe good Order and Keep good demeanor in his house:

Francis Hacklinton beinge presented for breach of the Sabbath in working by carrying of bricks at his Kilne at Northampton on the Sabbath day to the profaninge that holy tyme: The Corte judged him culpable: And it beinge his first offence of that Kind he was in the Corte admonished for his offence:

John Sackett beinge presented to this Corte uppon suspicion of Sellinge Strong Liquors to Indians: there appearinge some difficulty in it about the proofe of such offence, the matter was referred to the Corte at Northampton next March: And he was bound to this Corte in the summe of 10£ then and there to appeare to make further answer when he shalbe called: And his bond for appearance at this Corte is to be voyd:

Samuell Terry and his wife beinge presented for that they beinge married on the 3d of January last they had a Son born the 10th of the 5th month beinge about 12 weekes short of the ordinary tyme of womens goinge with child: This Corte concluded it manifest that they did abuse one another before marriage: and therefore did adjudge Samuell Terry for his offence and misdemeanor eyther to pay as a fyne to the County the summe of 4£ to be paid with 20 dayes or that he and his wife should be whipt on their naked bodyes with 10 Lashes appiece: Samuell Terry chusing the punishment by fyne: his choyce was accepted:

John King complayninge against Mr. Jacob Migate of Hartford for abusive speaches and chalenginge him to fight with him; he was by the Corte reprooved and checkt for his offence: And it beinge prooved that in the contest Mr. Mygate did sweare by this terme (Gods life) he was accordinge to the Law fyned 20s for his offence; for that he doubled the Said oath:

Richard Sikes presenting to the Corte his desires of freedome from Trayning by reason of his age and weakness; the Corte considering his case discharged him from beinge compelled to attend trayninge exercises.

[9] An Order Concludinge how Baltus Jacobus Lockermans a Dutchman resideing in Springfeild shall Satisfy Mr. Varlette of Hartford for his debt and damage above mentioned.

Mr. Caspar Varlete of Hartford complayninge against Baltus Jacobus Lockermans a Dutchman Liveinge at Springfeild in an action of Debt and damage to the vallue of Seaventy pounds: The Jury found for the Plantiffe: vizt that the said Baltus Jacobus Lockermans should pay unto the said Mr. Varlete for debt and damage to the vallue of Forty Three pounds Fifteen shillings together with and for the charges of the Corte and other charges and trouble about the said Baltus his person and his estate, Two pounds Nineteene shillings and Eight pence beinge in all 46£. 14s. 08d: For Satisfaction and full payment of which debt of 46£ 14s 08d to the Said Mr. Caspar Varlete: The comissioners for holdinge the said Corte adjudged and ordered, that what estate of the said Baltus is found beinge apprized according to Law, shalbe delivered to Mr. Varlete towards payment of the said debt of 46£: 14s: 08d: And for what falls short of full payment, the said Baltus Jacobus Lockermans and his wife beinge delivered to the said Mr. Varlete are to serve the said Mr. Varlete and his wife his heires and assignes after the rate of Eight pound per annum till the debt be fully Satisfyed, the said Mr. Varlete his heires or assignes providinge them and theires meat drink apparell and Lodginges Sutable for Servants: And it appearinge when the said Baltus his estate was examined, that his goods and wampum amounted to ten pounds Foureteen shillings and Seaven pence, the said Baltus remaynes 36£. 00s. .01d. in debt for which he and his wife are faithfully to Serve the said Mr. Varlete and his wife Their heires and assignes after the rate above mencioned, vizt Foure yeares and halfe.

[*95] December 2d 1661.   Before Leiutenant Holyoke and John Pynchon:

Richard Fellows Complaines against William Warrinar for withholding pay for his man Harmon Rowleys victualls at Chikkuppy as he passed to and from the Lead mines: to the vallue of which William Warrinar ingaged to pay for   Uppon the Testymonys of John Ginny and Garret Dolley which are on file it appeared that William Warriner had ingaged to pay Richard Fellows his just demand which being examened and rectified William Warriner is Adjudged to pay Richard Fellows the sum of eight and twenty shillings and sixpence.

[*96] Jan. 17th 1661 [1662].   Before Leiutenant Holyoke and John Pynchon.

John Scot complaints against Thomas Mirick in an action of debt, with Damadge, to the vallue of Thirty shillings:

Thomas Mirick excepting against one of the Rifles [?], which he says he had not ownes 10s 9d due to John Scot and John Scot not proving any more there is due to him for the forbearance of it .3.

yeares and about .10d or .12d damadge: in all 3s 6d which makes the whole .14s 3d whereuppon Thomas Mirick is adjudged to pay unto John Scot the aforesaid 14s 3d and 3s 4d cost for the entry of the action:

[*The following entries for February 26, 1661/2 and subsequent dates, not found in the* Record, *appear in 1* Hamp. Cty. Probate Ct. Rec. 9.]

Springfeild February: 26 1661 [1662].
                    Freemen of Springfeild
At a Publike meetinge these persons vizt Miles Morgan, Jonathan Burt, Anthony Dorchester, John Lumbard, and Lawrence Bliss being capable of beinge made Free of this Common Wealth, took the Freemans oath before Captain John Pynchon and Elizur Holyok who were appoynted to administer the Same by Order of the Generall Court: And May 8th 1663 Benjamin Mun and William Warrener were made free of this Comon Wealth.

At the Corte at Northampton Month 1st 31 1663 these persons were made free of this Comon Wealth: John Dickenson, William Patrick, John Marsh, Edward Church, Zachariah Field, Robert Bartlett, George Alexander, Isaak Sheldon, Joseph Leedes, Richard Weller [?], Nathaneel Phelpes and George Lancton. And on the 14th of 3rd month Richard Church and Aaron Cook Junior: more freeman See the Corte Record of Anni 1664 and September 1665. and January 17. 1665 [1666] and September 16.

[*97] March .20th 1661/62.   Before Leiutenant Holyoke: Samuell Chapin: John Pynchon:

Upon the examenation of Thomas Miller: John Scot: Edward Foster and John Bagg also John Henryson and his wife Concerning theire Playing at that unlawfull game of Cards.

William Brookes testifiing against them saith that one Night at John Henrysons house he saw Edward Foster: Thomas Miller: John Bag and John Scot all foure of them playing at Cards: and I staying in the house neere an houre they continued theire play at Cards all the while:

Edward Foster examend saith It is true I did then Play, but I am but a beginner to play at Cards and further saith, that those .3. before nominated viz John Scot: John Bag and Thomas Miller Played with him at John Henrysons howse that Night which William Brookes came thither:

John Bag: Thomas Miller and John Scot being asked they doe all acknowledge it that they did then Play at Cards at John Henrysons house.

John Henryson examened saith: it is true: they did Play at Cards at my howse but I did not so well know the Law against it and I was willing to have recreation for my wife to drive away melancholy.

And further he acknowledges Playing at Cards severall tymes at his howse (though he named not the persons) .3. or .4. severall tymes he owned, it maybe oftener: and said he was willing to any thing when his wife was Ill to make her merry:

Martha the wife of John Henryson being examened concerning her having of Cards being [*98] being they had said that they had the Cards of her: shee said shee had a Pack of Cards that shee brought up from Hartford with her and kept them by her and let them have those Cards her husband also owned that he had brought her up a Pack of Cards.

John Bag testifies against Martha the wife of John Henryson that he had seene her Play at Cards: which shee owned: Whereuppon John Lamb and his wife Joanna both of them gave in this Testymony upon oath That at a tyme (since they had herd these reports were about Towne) they asked Goodwife Henryson concerning her Playing at cards: and shee denyed it: and said moreover in theire hearing that shee never saw any Cards but once at a Pinnace and shee knew not what belonged to them and also shee said that shee brought up noe Cards to this Towne all which by her former confession and other profe appears to be a most gross ly: for it appeared That Card playing had been commonly used at John Henrysons house by his owne Confession.

From the Premises this Sentence: [*Marginal notation.*]

Thomas Miller: John Bag: John Scot: and Edward Foster are each of them adjudged to Pay five shillings according to Law for theire Playing at Cards:

Fines for Card Playing: [*Marginal notation.*]

Also John Henryson is adjudged to Pay Twenty shillings for that he hath Commonly suffered that unlawfull Game of Cards to be played in his howse: And Likewise Martha his wife is adjudged to Pay five shillings for her Playing at Cards And also Martha his wife is to pay Ten shillings for her ly:

[*The following entries for a court held by commissioners at Northampton on March 25, 1662, not contained in the* Record, *are found in 1* Hamp. Cty. Probate Ct. Rec. *10–13.*]

[10] At a Corte holden at Northampton March 25th 1662.

For holding this Corte were present Captain John Pynchon, Mr. Samuell Chapin, and Elizur Holyoke Recorder.

The Jurymen were Captain Aaron Cooke, Ensigne Cooper, Samuell Marshfeild, William Holton, William Woodworth, Richard Lyman, Thomas Bascomb, John Stebbin, Thomas Stanley, Mr. Russell Senior, Nathanell Dickenson, Senior, John Strong, Peter Tilton, Lieutenant Allys and John Hawkes.

William Lewis of Hadley Plantiffe Contra William Miller of Northampton Defendant in an action of the case for woundinge of a horse to the damage of Six pounds.

Richard Fellowes Plantiffe contra Alexander Edwards defendant in an action of the case for takeing away bricks which Richard Fellowes claimes for his to Six pounds damage:

Richard Fellowes Plantiffe contra Mistress Judith Varlette Defendant in an action of defamation for her saying that Richard Fellowes had played the Rogue or would have played the Rogue to the damage of Two hundred pounds.

Captain John Pynchon Plantiffe contra Boltus Jacobus Lockermans defendant in an action of debt with damage to the value of 3£. 10s.

Mrs. Judith Varlette Atturney to Mrs. Schreak of Hartford Plantiffe Contra John Webb defendant in an action of debt of 21£ due by Bill together with the damage thereof.

Mrs. Judith Varlette on the behalfe of her father Mr. Caspar Varlette of Hartford Plantiffe contra Richard Fellowes defendant in an action of debt to the value of 135£. oos. ood. due on account between them.

Bartholomew Barnard of Hartford Plantiffe contra William Holton of Northampton Defendant in an action of the case for Fraudulent dealinge in and about the meddow which was Edward Elmers late of Northampton to 40£ damage:

Samuell Marshfeild of Springfeild Plantiffe contra Francis Hacklinton defendant in an action of debt with damage to the vallue of 8£: Samuell Marshfeilds account in his book of Francis Hacklintons debt to which Samuell Marshfeild tooke his oath was 6£: 18s: o6d.

The Constable of Hadley for not returning the warrant for summoning of Jurymen was fyned 20s. The Constable afterwards appearing and acknowledging his error, with Some excuse was released of his fyne:

Northampton Comissioners.

Leiutenant William Clark Ensigne David Wilton and John Strong Senior of Northampton beinge presented as chosen for the three Comissioners for ending Small causes not exceeding 40s vallue; were allowed and well approved off by the Corte and Leiutenant Clark and John Strong took the oath for that Service: And Ensigne Wilton being out of town were impowred to give him his oath when he is returned.

Hadley Constable.

Mr. Steven Terry of Hadleigh being presented as chosen for Constable for that Town was approved of and tooke his oath accordingly:

Northampton Constable.

John Lyman of Northampton being presented as chosen Constable for that Town was allowed of and took his oath for the service.

William Holton Serjant for Northampton.

William Holton of Northampton being presented as chosen for a Serjant for the band and He being quallifyed accordinge to Law was approoved of by the Corte for that office and confirmed therein. At this Corte.

[11] Persons made free:

At this Corte William Holton, Mr. William Jeanes, Mr. Arthur Williams, Thomas Roote, Senior, Thomas Hanchett and Richard Lyman all of Northampton capable of being free of this Comon Wealth tooke the freemens oath accordingly: as likewise Samuell Marshfeild of Springfeild.

County Treasurer:

The Votes for County Treasurer beinge overlooked it appeared that Captain John Pynchon was chosen Treasurer for the County for the yeere ensueinge.

As to the action depending between William Lewis Plantiffe and William Miller Defendant they agreeing the Plantiffe withdrew his action paying 10s for entry thereof;

As to the action between Richard Fellowes and Alexander Edwards the partyes aggreeing the Plantiffe withdrew his action and payd entry of it.

As to the action dependinge betweene Richard Fellowes Plantiffe and Mrs. Judith Varlette Defendant the Jury fynd for the Plaintiffe 10s damage and the Costs of the Corte vizt 10s for entry of the action and 2s. for attending the Corte and for the attachment and serveinge it 1s. 6d.

As to the Action between Captain John Pynchon Plantiffe and Baltas Jacobus Lockermans Defendant the Jury fynd for the Plantiffe 3£. 8s. 4d. and the costs of the Corte vizt 10s. for entry of the action 6d. the Attachment 12d serving it and 2s. 6d other expences.

As to the action between Mrs. Judith Varlette for Mrs. Schreek Plantiffe John Webb defendant: The Partyes aggreeing the Plantiff withdrew her action: and paid entry thereof:

As to the action between Mrs. Judith Varlette for her father Mr. Caspar Varlette Plantiffe and Richard Fellowes Defendant: Shee withdrew her action paying 10s for entry thereof and 2s. for one witness and 2s for Richard Fellowes tyme and trouble.

As to the action between Bartholomew Barnard Plantiffe and William Holton defendant: the Partyes aggreed between themselves: and Soe the Plantiffe was to pay 10s for entry of his action.

As to the action between Samuell Marshfeild Plantiffe and Francis Hacklinton defendant.

John Sacketts fyne.

John Sackett beinge at the Corte at Springfeild September 24 1661 bound in a bond of 10£ to appeare at this Corte to answer to suspicions of his selling of liquors to Indians: He appearinge at this Corte and there beinge many grounds of suspicions that he had Sold much liquors to the Indians: and it beinge proved that he had Sold unto them 1 pinte he was fyned 40s to the County: And it beinge pleaded against him considering his estate how he could have soe much goods in his house of Indian trade as trayes kettles peltry of Beare and deere Skins he said he bought them of the Indians for wampam and corne. The Corte adjudged he had broken the law about trading peltry incurring the penalty of 100£ which the Corte adjudges him to pay to the County: only execution thereof shalbe respited till the first Sessions of the Generall Corte be ended.

John Sackett the next day pleadinge that these skins were traded above a yeere agoe and probability thereof appearinge: his 100£ fyne was remitted: Only he is to behave himselfe well in those respects for future. And if he be found suspicious in such matters hereafter: these things shall stand as witness against him which he consented to:

[12] At the said Corte James Bridgman beinge chosen Sealer for weights and measures for the Town of Northampton for the yeere ensueinge tooke his oath for the discharge of his office:

Ensigne Wilton of Northampton desiring liberty to sell strong liquors which for that though he still liquors yet by reason of the late law he may not sell in the Jurisdiction without lycence: And he haveing Some liquors by him: this Corte gives him Liberty to sell stronge liquors till the nexte County Corte: provided he sell not but to house Keepers of honest Conversation:

Cornelius Merry servant to John Lyman being by the Comissioners of Northampton fyned for severall misdemeanors in the summe of 30s: 10s whereof remaynes unpayd: his Master John Lyman engaging to pay the County Treasurer this 10s. for the use of the County (and 2s for an execution upon it:) The Corte Ordered that as soone as the said Cornelius his tyme is expired with his master he shall serve with his said master 12 dayes more for his satisffaction:

[*An inventory of the estate of Henry Curtis, late of Northampton, who died the last of November 1661, is omitted.*]

Elizabeth Curtis the wife of Henry Curtis late of Northampton decease (Dyinge intestate) desireing of this Corte liberty to administer to the estate of her said deceased husband: The Corte Ordered and graunted that shee should be Administratrix to the said estate: And concerninge the said estate the Corte further Ordered that the said Elizabeth haveing 2 Sons named Samuell Curtis and Nathaneell Curtis: the said Samuell her Eldest Son shall have out of the said estate the summe of Fifty pounds when he shall attayne the age of one and twenty yeares: And that her said son Nathaneel shall have the summe of Five and twenty pounds out of the said estate when he shall attayne the like age of one and twenty yeeres: [13] And that if eyther of the said Children shall dy before he shall attayne such age as aforesaid, then the other surviving shall enjoy his brothers porcion at such age as aforesaid: the rest of the estate is to pass unto the said Widdow Elizabeth Curtis:

[*An inventory of the estate of John Broughton, late of North-ampton, deceased, who died March 16, 1661/62, is omitted.*]

And concerninge the estate of the said John Broughton who died intestate Hannah his wife desireinge to administer to the Said estate: liberty therein was by the Corte graunted unto her: but because the estate is thought to be uncertayne: the Corte Ordered that Shee should have liberty till next Corte to improve the estate that shee may fynd out what debts are due to and from the estate: and in the meane tyme the land mentioned in the Inventory shall remayne as bound for security for the childrens portions be setled at the next Corte: And Thomas Bascum is desired to assist his Daughter with his councell and advice, which he promiseth to doe:

Joseph Parsons of Northampton uppon his desire hath liberty graunted him to continue in his work and employment of Keeping an Ordinary or house of Common Entertaynment in the Town of North-ampton for a yeare from this tyme: he hath also liberty graunted him to sell wines or strong liquors for the Same tyme: provided he Keepe good rule and order in his house:

[*99] June 20th 1662.   Before Capt. Pynchon, Mr. Holyoke:

Symon Lobdell Complaints against William Brookes for not paying a debt of Thirty nine shillings sixepence.

For profe: Symon produced an account made up dated the 19th of June 1659 written by Jonathan Burtt (wherein there was this written) Resting due to Symon Lobdell from William Brookes the Sum of one Pound seventeene shillings and all accounts cleared to be paid in wheate or Tar.

Symon Lobdell demands this debt being the Ballance of the account then made betwixt them.

Jonathan Burt also testifies upon Oath as followeth That the account was made up in my presence and that both Symon Lobdell and William Brooks did desire me to write it, and I writ nothing but what they both did order me, and to the best of my memory it was a chearfull account on both sides:

There is more to be added to this account (which William Brookes ownes) for bringing up .5. empty barells—8 or .06d the whole is Thirty nine shillings sixepence   The which William Brookes is adjudged to pay in wheate or Tar:

[*100] June: 1662:   .2. Indians fyned for Drunkeness.

Two Indians being brought before John Pynchon by the Constable of Springfeild for being drunk in the Night who were taken by the watch: They owned themselves drunk: and being demanded to pay theire fines of Ten shillings a peice: they ingaged to doe it and Left a gun with the County Treasurer till they make payment.

Theire Names were Pagamunt of Pacomtuck and Awasshaws:

[*101] September 22th 1662. Before Leiutenant Holyoke, Mr: Chapin and John Pynchon.

John Stewart fyned for Card playing.

Severall persons being Convented before us for playing at Cards, and suffering the said unlawfull Game in theire howses: There was only profe made against John Stewart: by John Bagg and Thomas Millers oath which is on file whereuppon the said John Stewart was adjudged to pay five shillings for his Playing at Cards, and Twenty shillings for that he Commonly suffered the said Game to be played at his house.

Nothing appearing against the other persons they were released only Henry and Japhet Chapin deferred till another tyme if we should se cause to call them forth againe.

[*The following entries for a court held by commissioners at Springfield on September 30, 1662, not contained in the* Record, *are found in 1* Hamp. Cty. Probate Ct. Rec. *14–17.*]

[14] At a Corte holden at Springfeild September 30th 1662.

For holdinge of this Corte there were present, Captain John Pynchon, Mr. Samuell Chapin And Elizur Holyoke, Recorder.

The Jury men were Nathaneel Ely, Thomas Coleman, Robert Bartlett, Joseph Parsons, Robert Ashley, Miles Morgan, Thomas Stebbins, Thomas Mirick, Lawrence Bliss, Thomas Bancroft, Richard Sikes, John Dumbleton.

Thomas Noble of Springfeild Plantiffe contra Widdow Sackett late of Springfeild defendant in an action of debt with damage to the vallue of 3£.

Captain Pynchon Plantiffe contra Widdow Sackett Administratrix above said, defendant and William Blomefeild administrator to the estate of Symon Sackett Late of Springfeild deceased defendants in an action of debt wtih damage to the vallue of 24£.

Susannah Cunliffe daughter of Henry Cunliffe of Northampton Plantiffe contra Medad Pomery Executor to the last will and testament of Eldad Pomery late of Northampton deceased defendant, in an action of the case concerninge a Legacy, vizt. for neglecting to make good what was bequeathed to her by the last will and testament of Eldad Pomery to the vallue of twenty pounds or thereabout.

This action was withdrawen by Plantiffe and defendant aggreeing to putt the matter to reference:

Mr. Caspar Varlette of Hartford Plantiffe contra Richard Fellowes of Hadleigh Defendant in an action of the case for witholding a debt of One Hundred thirty and five pounds due by booke accounts:

Thomas Stebbin Plantiffe contra Widow Sackett defendant in action of debt with damages to the vallue of Three pounds:

In this last action the Jury fynd for the Plantiffe vizt Thomas Stebbin the summe of forty shillings and the costs of the Corte vizt 10s for entry of the action:

Edward Elmer Plantiffe contra John King defendant in an action of reveiw respectinge an action commenced by the said John King Plantiffe and Edward Elmer defendant at the Corte in Springfeild September 24 1661. Wherein the Jury fynd for the Plantiffe costs of the Corte.

For prosecuting of this action Thomas Burnam of Hartford appeared as Atturney for Edward Elmer:

Mrs. Lord of Hartford Plantiffe contra Widdow Sackett late of Springfeild defendant in an action of debt to the value of 2£. 18s. 04d and 1£. 15s. od: damage:

William Pixley of Hadleigh Plantiffe contra Joseph Roote of Northampton defendant in an action of Slander to Forty pounds damage in Saying that he had gott Sarah Lynsley with child.

The Jury fynd for the Plantiffe the summe of ten pounds:

In the action depending betweene Thomas Noble and Widdow Sackett the Jury fynd for the Plantiffe the summe of three pounds:

In the action depending between Captain Pynchon Plantiffe and Widdow Sackett and William Blomefeild defendants the Jury fynd for the Plantiffe 20£. 15s. 08d. vizt 19£. 15s. 08d. and 20s for costs of the Corte:

[15] In the action dependinge between Mr. Caspar Varlette and Richard Fellowes: The Corte judged that Seeing Mr. Caspar Varlette is dead and none appearinge as declared heire executor or Administrator or assigne of the said Mr. Varlette etc: that therefore the case was not tryable at this Corte: And Richard Fellowes for prevention of future trouble did in the presence of the Corte acknowledge himselfe bound to any that are or shalbe found to bee eyther the heires executors or Administrators of the said Mr. Caspar Varlette in the summe of two hundred pounds Sterlinge: to appeare at any Corte at Hartford upon Six dayes warninge to answer the heires executors or Administrators of the said Mr. Caspar Varlette concerning any accounts of or debts due from the said Richard Fellowes to the said Mr. Varlette or to his estate:

In the action dependinge betweene Mrs. Lord and Widdow Sackett the Jury fynd the debt for the Plantiffe vizt 2£. 18s. 4d. and costs of the Corte:

Thomas Stanley of Hadleigh by Thomas Coleman Juryman complaynes against Robert Williams for violent taking away his cattell as they were driving to the pound:

Samuell Marshfeild of Springfeild being Plantiffe contra Francis Hacklinton at the Corte held at Northampton in March last in an action of debt with damage to the value of Eight pounds: the Jury then fynding for the Plantiffe the summe of 6£. 18s. o6d. and Costs of Corte: vizt 10s for entry for the entry of the action and 18d. for the attachment: and 4s. for the Plantiffe loss of tyme: This Corte approoves of the said Verdict, giveing liberty to the Plantiffe to take forth execution against Francis Hacklinton the Defendant: And the Said Samuell Marshfeild Plantiffe did in presence of the Corte acknowledge himself bound in a bond of 10£ to be responsible to the Plantiffe [sic] for what he shall take in execution of the Said Francis Hacklintons estate if he shall reverse the judgment within a yeare from this tyme:

There was taken in execution on the estate of Francis Hacklinton January 5 1662 [1663]: 3 ruggs at 4£. 10s. od: a cloake at 10s. and of James Osborne 14s. which he owed Francis Hacklinton:

In reference to Charges concerninge the house of Correction and other occurrences this Corte Ordered that there be a rate made and raysed uppon the County for defrayinge of the Same: which rate is to be Soe much as is a quarter part of the Single Countrey rate of these Three Townes this yeare, and is to be levyed upon the Inhabitants of the Same, to be paid unto the County Treasurer eyther before Winter or the next Springe.

In reference to the settlement of the estate of Richard Lyman, late of Northampton deceased, this Corte advised Some relations and freinds of the Deceased and the Widdow, to consider together how they would advise concerninge setling of the Said estate both in respect of the Widdow and also her children, (for that her husband dyed intestate): Whose advice the Corte approved of, and accordingly Ordered that the Eldest Son shall have out of the said estate the summe of Sixty pounds and the other Sons Forty, pounds each of them, and the Foure daughters thirty, pounds each of them: And that the Widdow their Mother should [16] have and enjoy all the rest of the estate as her own proper estate: And if any of the children shall dy before they come to such age as that their portions should be due unto them: that is to say, the Sons to the age of One and Twenty yeares and the daughters Eighteene yeares or Sooner in case they should come to a married estate; then such childs and childrens portions shall pass unto the rest of the children and shalbe proportioned among them as their mother shall judge of their deserts: And her husbands land shall remayn and stand as security for payinge the childrens portions:

[A copy of the inventory of the estate of Richard Lyman, late of Northampton, deceased, taken September 19, 1662, is omitted.]

To this Inventory the Widdow Lyman made oath before the Corte: And uppon the said Widdow Lymans desires the Corte graunted that shee should be administratrix to the estate of her deceased husband: and Also her father Thomas Fard of Windsor together with John Strong and Ensign Wilton of Northampton being desired by the said Widdow to be

Overseers of the said estate and assistinge to her and they consenting thereunto were well approved of by the Corte for such ends.

[17] Henry Burt of Springfeild who departed this life Aprill 30th. 1662. not leavinge any will under his owne hand for the disposing of his estate yet for that he did by words express his mind therein before Ensigne Thomas Cooper and Jonathan Burt who by a writing under their hands presented the Same unto this Corte: a coppy whereof hereafter followes, the Widdow Burt before the Corte consenting thereunto The Corte allowed the same to stand as the Last will and testament of the said Henry Burt.

We Thomas Cooper and Jonathan Burt doe testify, That after Henry Burt now deceased had disposed of part of his estate to his Son Nathaneell, the said Henry had Such expressions as these. vizt. that what estate he had then left should be at his wifes dispose as witness our hands This 29th of September 1662.

Thomas Cooper: Jonathan Burt

To the truth hereof as the mind of the said Henry Burt the said Ensigne Cooper and Jonathan Burt tooke their oath in the presence of the Corte:

[*Omitted are an inventory of the estate of Henry Burt of Springfield, deceased, taken September 11, 1662; a copy of the will of Eldad Pomry, late of Northampton, deceased, together with a copy of the inventory of his estate; a copy of the will and the inventory of the estate of Thomas Gilbert, late of Springfield, deceased; and a copy of the inventory of the estate of the Widow Gilbert, wife of the late Thomas Gilbert of Springfield.*]

[20] Their beinge presented into this Corte by Ensigne Cooper the Names of Severall persons who were by the trayned band of Springfeild chosen to severall places and Offices in the said Company, together with the desire of the said Company that this Corte would confirme the said Persons in such Places and offices to which they were chosen:

The Corte taking into consideration the desires of the Trayned Band of Springfeild thought fitt to confirm and ratify the choyce of the Souldery There: And therefore Doe accordingly declare That Samuell Marshfeild is and shalbe the Clark of the Trayned Band at Springfeild: And that Thomas Stebbins is and shalbe their Eldest Serjeant: And Miles Morgan their Second Serjeant: And that Jonathan Burt is and shalbe their first Corporall: Benjamin Parsons the Second Corporall: Rice Bedortha the third Corporall: And John Dumbleton the fourth Corporall:

John Nicholls a young man son of Goodman Nicholls of Hadleigh being upon the 27 of July 1662 drowned in the River at Hadleigh, and there being a Jury of twelve men of Hadleigh impannelled and sworn to make inquiry concerning the manner of his death: the verdict of the Jury remayning on the file was presented to this Corte: whereby it appeared they found his death casuall or accidentall not any way plotted by any person or persons:

In reference to highwayes and bridges between Springfeild and Hadleigh, this Corte Ordered that Ensign Cooper and Joseph Parsons and Nathaneel Dickison Senior be appoynted A comittee and impowred to consider of the bridge comonly called Batchelors bridge and other defective places in the said road whether they shalbe repayred by the County or by what particular place: and that being by them concluded: the said Joseph Parsons and Nathaneell Dickison are impowred to take effectuall courses for amendment of the Same: for which purpose they have power with any one of Hadleigh Comissioners to issue forth warrants to imprese men or carts out of eyther of those two Townes, as they shall judge needful for the work: Provided they Keepe not any Persons or Teames more than 3 dayes in a week to the work: And the work is to be done eyther before Winter or furthest by the tenth of Aprill next:

Samuell Marshfeild presenting his desires to this Corte for renewing of his Lycence to keep an Ordinary or house of Common Entertaynment and for Selling wine or liquors hath his licence renewed for one yeare next ensuing Provided he keep good Order in his house:

[*The will of John Webster, late of Hadley deceased, is omitted.*]

[*102] Feb. 2d 1662 [1663].

Joseph Crowfoote complayning against Thomas Thomson for abusing of him comeing lately from Windsor in that he tripped up his heeles and when he was down giveinge 3 thumps with his knee on his body: he not proovinge his charge before the Comissioners by the witness he produced:

The said Witnesses with others did testify that Joseph Crowfoote in their apprehensions was overcome with drink at that tyme whose testimonyes are on file:

Whereuppon the Comissioners adjudged the Testimoneyes of force against him prooving him to have abused himselfe with drinke and therefore fyned the said Joseph Crowfoote 10s to the County: And for that Thomas Thomson was prooved too active in that which concerned him not he was admonisht and reprooved therefore and Soe dismist.

[*103] March .17. 1662/63. Before the Comissioners Capt. Pynchon and Elizur Holyoke.

Serjant Stebbins of Springfeild Atturney for Mr Goodwin of Hadley complaynes against Widdow Sackett late of Springfeild Administratrix and William Blomfeild Administrator to the estate of Symon Sackett deceased in an action of debt due upon account together with damage to the vallue of Six and Thirty shillings.

The Plantiffe prooving the debt of 1£ o6s o1d the Comissioners adjudged the Defendant to pay the said Debt: and 6s 5d for costs and charges belonging to the said action: the debt was prooved as by account on the file:

June 22. 1664.   Before the Comissioners Samuell Chapin and Elizur Holyoke.

Nathaneell Ely complaynes against Joseph Leonard for wrongfully impounding his horse:

The Plantiffe and Defendant uppon debate of the case being found very insufficiently provided eyther to prosecute or to defend having noe testimonies at hand: The Comissioners propounded to them that if they would be content to lett the matter wholly rest and trouble each other noe further, this Entry of the sute should cost them nothing:

Whereupon both Plaintiffe and defendant were very willing and did yeeld and engage not to stir or trouble eyther the other about the busyness:

[*104] Ejusdem die.

Thomas Hobbe Constable presenting Thomas Thomson and John Horton for that last Sabbath was fortnight vizt June the .7. they made a fray in the street in the Evening and about $\frac{1}{2}$ an houre after sun sett: Samull and Elizur Holyoke being accessary in the said fray:

The Comissioners uppon examination of the case doe fynd that the said Foure persons did profane the Lords day: and therefore Doe determine that they all Shalbe admonished thereof and that Thomas Thomson John Horton and Samuell Holyoke shall pay a fyne of five shillings apeece to the County: or be whipped by the Constable on the naked body with 3 stripes apeece: whereupon they were all admonished and the 3 former desireing to pay the fynes than otherwise were Ordered to pay them to the County Treasurer:

Also an Indian called _____ haveing lately complayned to the Comissioners that haveing left a barken Cannow in Goodman Muns Garden it was taken forth and used and abused by diverse young persons at the brooke in the streete, whereby the Canow was made unserviceable:

The busyness being examined there were found fifteen young persons children and others that had a hand in playing with the Cannow: but who of them broke or splitt the Cannow it could not be [*105] certaynly determined: Whereuppon the Comissioners concluded that the said young persons should pay the said Indian 4d a peece and the Constable was ordered to gather up the money for the said Indian:

[*106] Springfeild March 4th 1664/65.   Before Mr. Holyoke and John Pynchon.

John Scott meeting with the Indian Watsaw Luncksin demanded of him a debt which he owned him and the Indian acknowledged before me John Pynchon and Mr Elizur Holyoke That he owed John Scot which he had taken up of him at severall tymes to the vallue of eight fadam of wampam.

Also he owned that for his misdemeanor some yeares agoe in breaking the glass windows of Capt. Pynchon farmehouse and other miscariage he was to pay .8. fadam of wampam: at treble is—24 fadam.

All which he did before us Ingage to take care for the Payment off when he could get any thing to doe it: and Ingaged his land above Hadly up to Mattampast for it which he made over for that end.

Aprill 24th 1668.
Richard Coy was sworne Constable of Quabaug.

[Pages 107–132 are blank.]

[*133] Dec. 22th 1669.
Thomas Gun of Westfeild Tooke the Oath of a Freeman: These Tooke the Oath of fidelity   Moses Cooke: George Sexton, Thomas Roote, Edward Neale, Jonathan Alvard, John Osborne, John Greete, George Fyler, Ambross Fowler, John Ponder and Jedediah Dewey.
[The lower half of the page is missing.]

[*134] Aug: 1669   Thomas Day was Sworne Constable of Spring-feild:

Aug: 28th 1670   James Warrinar was sworne Constable of Springfeild

Aug. 1671   Miles Morgan sworne Constable of Springfeild

Aug. 1672   John Hitchcock.

Aug. 1673   John Dorchester.

Aug. 19. 1674:   Samuell Bliss sworne Constable of Springfeild.

Afterward: I entred them in my Law Booke.
[The lower half of the page is missing.]

[*135] Sept. 16th 1670.

Reice Bedortha making Complaint against William Brookes and Mary his wife for theire abusing of his son Joseph Bedortha by Bad language flinging a stick at him and using Reproachfull words Threatning expreshons and Taunting speeches: William Brooke and Mary his wife appeared, and Although they partly deny what is charged upon them, yet I find them both gilty of a very great Misdemeanor Touching that busyness. And doe fine them as followeth

William Brooke, fyned 20s [*Marginal notation.*]

William Brookes for his Threatning High words, opprobrious speeches and villyfiing expresshons all which are evedenced by the Testymonys of John Scot, Isack Morgan and Thomas Lamb, which are on file and Reitterating the same: I sentence him, therefore To pay a fine of Twenty shillings to the County: and to pay 12d apeice to the witnesses:

Mary Brooke .10s. [*Marginal notation.*]

Also Mary his wife for her opprobrious and threatning speeches as by the Testymonys of John Bag, David Morgan, Edmund and Mary Pengilley [?] I fine her the Sum of Ten shillings to the County.

The Testymonys are on file.

Which fines of 20s and 10s William Brooke Ingaged to pay in to the County Treasurer within a very short tyme, as also to sattisfie and Pay the .7. witnesses .12d a peice.

[*Page 136 is blank.*]

[*137] December 26 1670.

Joseph Leanord and Samuell Fellows of Hatfeild being Brought before me for Contemptuous Behaviour towards Nathanell Dickenson the Constable of Hatfeild and finding they did contemptuously and in a most Boisterous manner affront the said Constable when he was in discharge of his office. I order the said Leanord and Fellows to be secured till the morning when the Jaylor is to bring them before me at 8 of the clock.

Dec: 27. (1670).

Joseph Leanord and Samuell Fellows appearing, and the Constable making his declaration against them: and presenting several Testymonys to prove theire cariage was very Contemptuous: I ordered them to become Bound to answer it and their Illegall Trading with Indians at Next County Court: And they accordingly became Bound in 20£ a piece with 2 suertys: and so I discharged them at present, refering the whole to next County Court at Northampton in March next.

[*The following March 28, 1671 entry regarding Fellows and Leon-*
ard appears in 1 Hamp. Cty. Probate Ct. Rec. *128. A variant entry is*
found in Pynchon Waste Book for Hampshire *84 where a marginal*
notation reads "were bound over to this Corte by Captain Pynchon
in December last."]

Samuell Fellowes and Joseph Leonard being accused for Selling of
Strong liquors to the Indians and for buying Beaver of the Indians without License for which they were both bound over to this Corte by the
Worshipfull Captain Pynchon in December last: they both appearing at
this Corte and their inditement read, they both desired to be tryed by
the Jury: And Soe both the cases being examined openly and committed
to the Jury and by them Searched into they brought in their verdicts,
That they fynd both the said Samuell Fellowes and Joseph Leonard
guilty of selling to the Indians Five pintes of Strong Liquors against the
Law page 41. Section 5. and therefore also fynd that they are to pay to
the County the summe of Ten pounds: the Jury also fynd the said Fellowes and Leonard guilty of buying of the Indians One Skin of Beaver
against that Law page 41. Section 4. they produceing noe Lycense soe to
doe, and according to that Law fynd them to pay to the County the
summe of One Hundred pounds:

These verdicts were received:

And the Corte Ordered the said Samuell Fellowes and Joseph Leonard
to pay forthwith to the County Treasurer for the use of the County the
tenne pounds for their soe selling of Liquors and they give security for
payment thereof:

And for the 100£ fine for their buying of beaver, they are to pay tenne
pounds thereof forthwith to the County Treasurer for the use of the
County and the rest of it to be at the pleasure of this or succeeding Cortes:

Also they are to pay Costs of Corte vizt for entry of the two actions or
cases 20s for the one actions and 15 shillings for the other and for other
charges as per bill 3£. 10s. ood. and the Recorders fees 5s.

And whereas the Said Samuell Fellowes absented himself before the
determination of the case and answered not when often called to answer
the case wherein Samuell Billing was bound for him in one bond and
Symon Lobdell and Samuell Bull in another bond, This Corte declareth
both Said bonds to be forfeited: yet that case of the forfeiture of those
bonds is referred to the Corte to be holden at Springfeild in September
next for further disquition:

Also Joseph Leonard for his contemptuous carriage particularly towards the Worshipfull Captain Pynchon as also towards Hatfeild Constable is fyned to the County in the summe of 5£ to be paid to the County
Treasurer for the use of the County:

And Samuell Fellowes for his contemptuous carriage in Corte and towards Hatfeild Constable is also fyned 5£ to the County to be paid to
the County Treasurer.

[*The following September 26, 1671 entries relating to Fellowes and Leonard appear in* 1 Hamp. Cty. Probate Ct. Rec. *129–30. A variant entry appears in* Pynchon Waste Book for Hampshire *85–86.*]

Samuell Billing of Hatfeild being bound in the summe of forty pounds for Samuell Fellowes his appearance at the last Corte at Northampton (to answer for his being suspected of Fellony) the said Billing petitioning this Corte for favour in the case for that his bond was by the Last Corte declared to be forfeited: this Corte to shew their readyness to hearken to the request of the poare doe abate Twenty pounds of the said forfeiture: And whereas the said Billings hath attached Four pounds of the estate of the said Fellowes it being delivered in to the County Treasurer is to be and is accounted as part of the pay of the other 20£ and the other 16£ remayning he is to pay to the County Treasurer for the use of the County with all convenient Speed:

Joseph Leonard petitioning for an abatement of his fyne wherein he and Samuell Fellowes were fyned Last Corte at Northampton for selling liquors to and buying bever of the Indians was abated 5£ provided he take a course Speedily to pay the rest of his dues to the County.

Feb. 2d 1670 [1671].

Richard Barnard examined concerning his getting Sarah Clarke (the daughter of John Clarke) with child acknowledged it and finding none that would become Bound for him was Comitted: till he should find suertys for his appearance at the County Cort to answer for his said fornication: And John Clarke Ingaged for his daughter Sarah to be then forthcoming: who by her owne Confeshion is above halfe gon with child: Richard Barnard having had carnall knowledge of her Body last English harvest at the very beginning of Reaping Ry: as she saith for which there fornication they are both to appeare at next Court in Northampton on the last Tuesday in March next, and so the whole case and examinations taken I Transmit thither.

Feb. 9 1670 [1671].

Richard Barnard who had also 2. or 3. times before signified his willingness to Marry Sarah Clark: came before me and manifested his desires to make ameans for his sin sofar as to take her in mariage: which I told him might be if her father consented to it shee being willing as was said: And In order to it John Clark Senior Ingaged with Richard Barnard in the sum of 10s to the County Treasurer that the said Richard should appeare at next County Court: and there answer for his fornication: and so I discharge him of the Prison: And [*138] And permit their Mariage together in meane tyme: which was accordingly sollemnized on the 13 of February and they declared Husband and wife:

[*The following March 28, 1671 entry regarding Richard Barnard appears in 1* Hamp. Cty. Probate Ct. Rec. *126. A variant entry is found in* Pynchon Waste Book for Hampshire *81.*]

Richard Barnard being bound over to this Corte to answer for his sin of fornication with Sarah Clark of Springfeild which he hath owned and confessed to the Worshipfull Captain Pynchon as also before this Corte, he also haveing marryed her, This Corte being sensible of disorders growing more and more upon us, and in Speciall of the gross miscarriages of the Said Richard and Sarah his now wife, doth Fyne them each in the summe of Forty shillings to be paid to the County Treasurer for the use of the County:

The said Richard Barnard is discharged of his bond for appearance at this Corte.

Feb. 6th 1670 [1671].   Thomas Stebbing Junior Fyned 20s.

Thomas Stebbing Junior being examined about Publishing a mariage intended betweene Richard Barnard and Sarah Clarke: which was set up on the Post in greate letters without order or knowledge of the partys or Parents: and was also underwrit in smaler Letters with a foolish and reprochful Rime casting reproch upon the Towne and the Maides in Towne: as by the Paper on file appeares: his offence being very greate besides the sin against God abusing the Parents, the Partys, profaning the Sabath, casting reproch on the Town and on the Maids together with other disorders, Though at first he was alitle saucy yet afterward Confessing all and being admonished and told of the evill: he seemed very Penitent and promised to be more watch full against such like disorder: I therefore dealt more gently with him by a small fine bearing Testymony against such disorders: and fine him 20s to the County which he Ingaged spedyly to pay in to the County Treasurer:

March 6th. 1670/71.   Nathanell Elys fine of 5s.

Nathanell Ely examened concerning his speaking Reprochfully of Mr. Glover the Reverend Teacher of the Church of Springfeild: By Symon Lobdells Testymony: and by the writing of Symon Lobdells and Mr. Glovers, of what he said before them which Nathanell Ely owned, and by Nathanell Elys owne acknowledgement all which are on file it appears That Nathanell Ely did most reprochfully villifie and revile Mr. Glover a faithfull minister of the Gospell, and Teacher of the Church of Springfeild, And declaring to him that he had broken the law which sentence such offence .5s. He the said Nathanell Ely said the law was good, and he would fall under it for he said he had broken it and he deserves worss: and Ingaged to pay the 5s accordingly in to the County Treasurer forthwith and upon this his Ingagement I discharged him.

[*139] Westfeild Constable

March 11th 1670/71 John Ingersoll was Sworne Constable of Westfeild:

Aprill. 28. 1671.

Praiseever Turnur, was Sworne Constable of North Hampton:

May. 1st 1671.   Indian whipped for stealling.

An Indian named Aquossowump alias Woquoheg being brought before me for stealing wampam out of Samuel Bliss his house yesterday being the Sabbath day: when the children were at hom who say it is this Indian, being he who kept there most of last weeke: and that he went to the chest and opened it against the childrens will who got on top of the chest to keepe it downe but the Indian being stronger then they: tooke out the wampam while Goodman Bliss and his wife was at meeting in the forenoone: Samuel Bliss his wife says that some of the wampam was her owne and in her owne Purse and other part of it was an Indian womans which shee left with them and was in the womans bagg: and they find all to be gon: The Indian examened ownes that he tooke away some wampam: and the wampam being found with him, he says that one parsell of it was Goodwife Bliss hers and that he tooke it out of her Purse and stript it loose of the strings for so it is found loose, whereas part of it Goodwife Bliss says was strung though Goodwife Bliss says this is much short of her due. And the Peice of Girdle he says himself: was of that which the Indian woman Left which he Challenges for his and says the woman that left it had it of him: But much of All is gon: His theft being evident and on the Sabbath also: and goeing into house stealing as is thought above 20 fadam of wampam I ordered him to pay his spare coate and the wampam found with him: (all which was delivered Samuel Bliss) and also sentenced to be well whipped with 20 lashes which was performed by the Constable.

[Page 140 is blank.]

[*141] July .27. 1671.

Obadiah Cooly makes complaint against 2 Indians for getting into his Howse and stealing from him wampam and some other small things: The Indians Missahump and Mahamatap: appeared (being brought by the Constable) who owne That last Satturday they went into Obadiah Coolys howse at the window noebody being at hom and tooke thence a knife: and a long Indian jewell: 7 hands of white wampam and 2 hands of black wampam and a fine workt Basket (though Obadia says there was about Ten fadam of the wampam; and the Basket he was offered .2. faddom of wampam for it: Missahump ownes that he was the chiefe actor and propounded it to the other Indian who Consented to watch: I ordered the Indians to be well whipped Missahump with 10 stripes and Mahamattap with 8 stripes well laid on the naked Body by the Constables and to restore the things they have taken away:

Which Punishment was accordingly inflicted. [*Marginal notation.*]

July 29th 1671. Katharin Hunter comitted to the House of Correction.

Katharin Huntur (of about 14 years old) servant to Robert Ashly Departing from her Masters service unlawfully: once last Tuesday and then Coming againe on Thursday and yet goeing away againe on Friday Morning to her fathers: and for noe Cause that shee can relate her selfe but only that her dame once only and that some time before gave her a blow or 2 with her hand: there being nothing to justifie her in her unlawfull departure I ordered her to the howse of correction there to abide till I discharged her:

And William Huntur her father for Harbouring his said daughter and not discharging her and sending her to her aforesaid Master (none Informing) I account 20s due by Law to the Country: But respited the sentence till some other tyme.

[*142] March 6th 1671/72: At Westfeild: Westfeild Constable.

Thomas Roote Sworne Constable of Westfeild.

March 8th. 1671/72. Zebediah Williams fyned 10s.

Zebadiah Williams of Northampton being Summoned before me (according to order of Last County Court) to answer for his not appearing at Said Court and also for prophaning the Sabbath: He appeared this day: And as to his not appearing at Last County Court he says he had noe warning and it not being proved that he had: that fell: But his profane cariage on the Sabbath was evident according to the Testymony on file.

Whence Zebadiah Williams for his unseemly and prophane cariage on a Sabbath in the meeting house at Northampton in the tyme of Publike ordinances. Laughing and Jutting others that sat by him to their disturbance thereby Rendring the ordinance unprofitable to himself and others. As a Testymony against such prophaness I fine him Ten Shillings to the County.

[*The following March 28, 1671 and September 26, 1671 entries regarding Williams are found in* 1 Hamp. Cty. Probate Ct. Rec. *127, 131. Variant entries are found in* Pynchon Waste Book for Hampshire *83, 88.*]

Zebadiah Williams being presented by the Jury for disorderly carriage on the Sabbath in the Meeting house in tyme of exercise of publike Ordinances this Winter (he being at present out of Towne) is to be warned to appeare at the Corte to be holden at Springfeild in September next: Samuell Davis Caleb Pomery and John Bridgman are testimonyes against him, who took their Oath at this Corte as touching what they observed of his ill demeanure:

[*September 26, 1671.*]

Zebadiah Williams being presented to the Last Corte at Northampton for profaning the Sabbath was to have been warned now to appear to answer it: but he not appearing this Corte Ordered that he be called before the Worshipfull Major Pynchon to be proceeded with for contempt if the Major fynd he had Legall warning now to appeare, if otherwise yet to answer for his said misdeameanor: Witnesses in the case are Samuell Davis, Joseph Edwards and Caleb Pomery:

[*Page 143 is blank.*]

[*144] Westfeild Comissioners

Capt. Aron Cooke, Mr. Joseph Whiting and George Phelps of Westfeild, allowed and appointed Comissioners for Westfeild at last County Court at Northampton: appeared this 27th July 1672. Before me: And tooke their respective oaths for ending small Causes according to Law.

Aug: 16. 1672.
John Hitchcock was Sworne Constable of Springfeild:

Aug. 18th 1673.
John Dorchester Sworne Constable of Springfeild.

Feb: 7th 13th and 18th 1672 [1673].
Severalls persons being examened concerning an uncivill play acted:
For theire uncivill Immodest and beastly acting (according to their examenations and acknowledgements on file) I fyned severall of them to the County as followeth

Samuel Terry: Timothy Cooper: John Holtum and Isack Morgan

13s 4d a peice

Samuel Taylor: Benjamin Leanord and Thomas
   Miller

5s a pece   04 . 08 . 04

And Benjamin Dunnidge 20s.

John Dumbleton Junior was only admonished:

[*145] March 5th 1672/73. David Ashley was sworne Constable of Westfeild.

October . 13. 1673: Westfeild Comissioners

This day Capt. Aron Cooke, Mr. Joseph Whiting and George Phelps Comissioners to end small causes at Westfeild for the yeare ensueing Tooke theire respective Oaths for the discharge of their Duty: Before me JOHN PYNCHON

Aprill. 10. 1675.

Capt. Aron Cooke and Mr. Joseph Whiting (being allowed commissioners for Westfeild at Last County Cort in Sept. 1674:) Tooke their Oaths, belonging theretoe this 10th of April 1675 from whence there yeare will begin.

And George Phelps tooke his oath to the said worke Aprill. 27th 1675.

[*146] Aug. 25th 1673. Isack Morgan: Fyned .10s.

The Constable William Warrinar Complaining against Isack Morgan for not attending him when he required him on Friday Night last to goe Post with a letter to Quabaug: The said Isack appearing and speaking for himselfe, yet it appeared That while the Constable went to fetch the letter to him, he slipt away and was not to be found, so that the Constable was forced to seeke another for which neglect of his the said Isack: I fine him Ten shillings to the County.

[*147] October 24th 1673.

William Huntur Complaines against John Petty for abusing him by striking him etc.: as also against James the son of John Petty for that the youth called him names and gave him bad and Ill Language.

That about the Boys language being denyed and not proved I only admonished him.

But as to John Petty striking Huntur besides the Testymony given in of Walter Holyday and his wife etc. John Petty owned the full and acknowledged that he being in a rage for Hunturs striking his Boy a Box under the Eare that he Run to him with a stick he tooke up and struck him a Blow which Blow having Lamed his arme at present and being scarse well now .2. or .3. days after: I doe order: John Petty to pay Ten shillings to said William Huntur in way of sattisfaction and five shillings as a fine to the County: which five shillings in regard of John Pettys acknowledgement of his fault and manifesting sorrow and Troble for it and upon his hearty acknowledgement of it I doe release and remit the fine and only order the 10s to be paid William Huntur.

John Petty complaines.

[*148] John Petty Complaines against Goodwife Huntur for offering to mischeife his wife and giving her Ill Language calling her as the Testymonys speake: Railing Scolding and other exorbitancys of the Toung appearing as by the Testymonys of Mary Brookes and Mercy Johns on file and Also the Neighbors declaring her continuall Trade upon every occasion to be exorbitant with her Toung as particularly Samuell Marshfeild and John Bagg so declared I sentence her to be Gagged or else set in a ducking stoole and dipped in water as Law provides: Shee to choose which of them shee pleases within this halfe howre: or else I to determine and order either as I see cause.

Shee not choosing either: I ordered her to be Gagged and so to stand halfe an hour in the open streete which was done accordingly: and for her reproching Goodwife Petty shee did openly cleare her of all shee spake against her and asked foregiveness which Goodwife Petty accepting off shee was released as to that.

[*149] December 18th 1673.

Thomas Parsons John Aires: Junior Also: Samuell Kent: of Brookefeild Tooke the oath of fidelity to this Government.

Jan. 28th 1673 [1674].

At Hadley These persons following tooke the oath of fidelity

Samuel Crow, John Ingram, Joseph Seldon, Isack Harrisson, Joseph Weld, James Bebee, John Loomis, William Gaylard, Thomas Hust, John Mountague, Charls Barnard, John Hubbard, Thomas Craft, Nathanell Crow, John Barnard, William Rooker: David Hoite.

Daniell Marsh, Joseph Grannis, Isack Warner, Samuel Boltwood, Edward Scott, Joseph Hovey, Nehemia Dickenson, Azaria Dickenson, James Leevens, Thomas Hovey, Peter Mountague, Joseph Kellogg, Junior, Samuel Gardner, Junior, John Gardner, Symon Beamon, Edward Grannis, John Taylor, John Dickenson, Junior, Timothy Nash, Thomas Wells.

[*150] March 9th 1673/74.

Nathanell Pritchard makeing Complaint against Obadiah Cooley for that the said Obadiah Cooleys Dogg with Goodman Dorchesters, had this last Night killed one of his sheepe: Goodman Dorchester having hanged his Dogg: Obadiah Cooly refused so to doe: The said Obadiah Cooley appearing, and it being proved to his face by the Testymony of Nathanell Pritchard and James Stevenson (which are on file) that his Dogg was there with Goodman Dorchesters in Wurrying and killing of the sheepe and eating up of part of it, being also gilty etc.

He resolved to Hang his dogg: and so Issued this matter:

Aprill .7th 1674.

Thomas Noble: being presented as chosen Constable of Westfeild; was sworne to discharge the said office in Westfeild.

Aprill: 12th 1676:

Jedediah Dewey being presented as Chosen Constable of Westfeild   Tooke his oath to discharge the said office in Westfeild for the yeare ensueing:

[*151] Aprill 27th 1674.

David Morgan Plantiffe against Charls Ferry for not weaving linnen yarne into cloth according to agreement: David affirming That Charls Ingaged to pay him for worke in building Charls a shop: Thirty shillings in weaving cloth which now Charls refuseth to doe: being to the Plantiffe damage 40s.

The Testymonys in the case produced being sworne and are on file I find for the Plantiffe That Charls Ferry make good the Thirty shillings in weaving or otherwise pay him Thirty shillings, in Current Pay: together with Costs of Court 3s 6d.

April 27 1674.   Samuell Allys fyned 5s.

Samuell Allys of Hatfeild being presented and Complained off for Throwing a Stone at James Browne at Hatfeild on the 12th of this Instant Aprill on the Sabbath Evening alitle after evening shut in Whereby James Browne was pritty much wounded on the eyebrows   James Browne giving in his Testymony that it was Samuell Allys: the said Samuell Allys also owning it only saying he did not intend to hurt him but only tossed it in waggery But hurt being done and it being on the Sabbath Night and he being out that Night (though he says it was as he was goeing up to the Barne to serve his Cattle) I order the said Samuell Allys to pay five shillings as a fine to the County and to defray the charge of John Colemans Coming downe with him to discharge all charges, and refer the sattisfaction to James Browne to his Complaint against him and as shall appeare so to be meete and Just.

[*152] April 30th 1674.   Butler and Omsted fyned 10s piece.

Daniell Butler and Samuell Olmsted being Complained off for prophaning the Sabbath in that they drove Cattle thorow the Towne on Sabbath day was Senight being the .19th. day of this Aprill: The said Butler and Omstead appeared who owne their lying at the Lower end of the Long meddow on Satturday Night and on the Lords day Morning they drove their Cattle from the Lower end of the meddow thorow the Towne and missing theire way almost to Sheepnuck and thence went on with their cattle so that they were at Quabaug on Munday Morning with their for Cattle by 10 of the clock.

For their so profaning the Sabbath I fine them 10s apiece to the County   That is to say Daniel Butler 10s and Samuel Omstead 10s and to pay the charge of their apprehending: and presently to pay the Monny or else to stand comitted.

[*153] May. 12. 1674:

Thomas Miller Junior being Complained off for abusing the watch last Thursday Night viz Thomas Lamb and John Lamb betweene .10. and .11. of clock at Night; as appeares by their Testymony which is on file: I Judge the said Thomas Miller (all Circumstances (the provocations) Considered) to Pay as a fine to The County five shillings.

[*The bottom half of the page is missing.*]

[*Page 154 is blank, with its bottom half missing.*]

[*155] July 17th 1674.

Benjamin Allyn of Hatfeild being brought before me for Breaking into Goodman Meakins his house last Lords day at night was Senight and stealing a Barrell of Liquors etc.

Being examined (as per his examination on file) he acknowledged it in part: As also that James Browne was with him and partner, he carrying away the Liquors into the woods, all which they did in the Dead of the Night about Midnight.

James Browne also appearing though denying the fact yet acknowledges he was with Benjamin Allyn that Lords day night in the evening: and they spake together: which tyme Benjamin Allyn says they concluded to doe the act that Night.

I required Both of them to become Bound in .20£ Bond a peice with .2. sufficient suertys for theire appeareance at Next County Court at Springfeild in September next as also for theire good Behaviour in the meane tyme. [Accordingly] Benjamen Allyn in Twenty Pounds and Israell Dewey as suerty in like sum of Twenty Pounds [*illegible*] to the Treasurer of Hampshire, Doe acknowledge themselves Bound: That Benjamin Allyn shall appeare at the Next County Court and abide the order of the Court answering to and concerning his felloni-ous taking Liquor and breaking open the Howse of Thomas Meakins Senior: as also that said Benjamin Allyn shallbe of Good Behaviour in the meane tyme and in case of default therein to forfeite the said sums:

This Done and acknowledged this .11. July 1674.

Before me: JOHN PYNCHON

James Browne finding noe Suertys was comitted and is to stand Comitted till the Cort or till he shall find suerty as aforesaid: Thomas Meakins Senior: Ingages in Ten Pound Bond to persecute Benjamin Allyn and James Brown at next County Court for their Breaking open his house and stealing Liquors as abovesaid.

Before me JOHN PYNCHON Asistant.

[*The following September 29, 1674 entry regarding Browne and Allyn is found in 1* Hamp. Cty. Probate Ct. Rec. *158. A variant entry is found in* Pynchon Waste Book for Hampshire *121.*]

James Browne and Benjamine Allin, both Late of Hattfeild being Bound over by the Worshipfull Major Pynchon to appeare at this Corte to answer for their gross miscarriages in Breakeing up the House and Sellar of Thomas Meakins Senior of Hatfeild and Stealeing of Strong Liquors and doeing other Damages etc. as in their examinationes and Confessions before the Worshipfull Major Pynchon Assistant appear-eth; They both made their appeerence at this Corte and their examina-tiones and Confessions (which are on File) being Reade to them they agayne acknowledged their wickedness, and they haveing Stolen nere nine gallones of Liquors, Besides what hath beene found and restored they are to pay treble according to Law viz twenty five gallons also they are adjudged to be Branded in their Forheades for their Burglary) with the letter B and to pay 3£ as a Fine to the County for Corte Charges, and Benjamin Allin is to pay 1£. 16s. ood for Charges in Persueing of him towards Albany etc as per Bill and Both of them are to pay 1£ 19s ood for Conveying them to Springfeild etc as per bill, and to Moses Croffts 10s. 06d. And to John Hawks 7s for Charges about them as per Bill: And for Breakeing Daniell Whites Windowes, to pay him 20s.

[*156] November .10th 1674.

Indian Wellawas being brought before me (by the Constable) for being Drunk it so appearing last Night that I comitted him till this Morning that he might be Sober: which he also Now ownes. I fyned him 10s, being a known Indian give him 8 days (at his desire) to pay it and if he pay not the Ten shillings in .8. days tyme to be appre-hended by the Constable and whipt with .10. stripes.

Dec: 22th 1674.

Indian Nowattassome and Wepuck, being apprehended for steal-ing a Trap of Timothy Coopers which had bin gon a yeare and halfe and Confessing they know where it is at Mohegan and owning also they saw it before it was caryed thither, other Circumstances plainly declaring them Tardy I ordered them to bring the Trap and 12 fadam toward the charges etc.: and Wequogan Cochapesnet and John Ingaged for theire bringing the Trap and paying 12 fadam and so the Indians are discharged.

[*157] Dec: 23: 1674:

Joseph Crowfoote Complaines against William Brookes for not paying him .34s due per Bill with due damages presenting the Bill (which hath bin due betweene .6. or .7. yeares:

Brookes affirmes the payment of it: and part of it appeares but other part being doubtfull and depending on acounts with Mr Gil-bert at Hartford I adjourne the busyness to this day a Month before Lecture:

Jan. 20 1674: [1675].

Both partys appearing: and a Testymony from Jonathan Gilbert being produced clearing that William Brooks Paid the old account about barels: it thence appeares that: William Brookes hath Paid to Crowfoote By a calfe from widdow Burt   14s 6d
more   03. o
and By Serjeant Stebbins   o6.
By Serjeant Morgan   o6
_____
1. 9. 6

So that there can be but 4s 6d due which I Judge William Brookes to pay: But inasmuch as William Brookes made a Journy to Hartford to cleare the busyness as above that is allowed and so the whole ac-counts between them Paid.

[*158] December 27th 1674.

The day being Sabbath day a child of betweene .3. or 4 year old of Abell Wrights: called Henry came to its end: and this 28th Dec: the Constable having Summoned a Jury to Inquire into the manner and Cause of its death: who were but .6. persons in regard of the remote-ness of the Place from the Towne over at Shepnuck and bad season and way: Theire Names follow viz   Rowland Thomas: Jeremy Horton, Thomas Stebbing: Thomas Mirick, John Clarke, Timothy Cooper, whose returne upon oath is That according to their best light evedence and Inquiry They find That the child went out to a sled without the dors and Indeavoring to get up upon the sled halfe Loaden with wood, a Log Rowled downe on the child and the Log falling on the childe which was a heavy log the child thereby came to its end:, the Log lying upon the child when it was found dead.

[*159] June .18th 1675:

John Aires, senior of Brookfeild Plantiff (according to Replevy) against William Pritchard and Samuell Kent selectmen of Brookfeild: for unlawfully distreining some Pewter dishes of his which the Constable did by occasion of their order:

William Pritchard and Samuell Kent appearing and putting it upon profes that they gave order for the distress, and plainly not owning it and John Aires not proving it: I allowed theire charges viz for .3. days each which is sixe shillings a peice in all .12s for John Aires to pay to William Pritchard and Samuell Kent and likewise Sixe shillings for Corporall Coys appearence as a witness by warrant:

[*160] December 11th 1675. Beardsly: fyned 10s.

Thomas Beardsly (a garrison Soldier) being accused for being in drink and swearing at least the swearing being evident that he swore By God owning it (the witnesses Benjamin Parsons and John Burnet were not sworne: I fyned the said Beardsly Ten shillings To the County and secured it out of his wages.

Dec. 24th 1675. John Bliss: fyned 5s.

Joseph Pike Complaines against John Bliss for that the said John Bliss did Beate him. It appearing by the Testymony of Jeremy Horton and John Burnet: as also that they were both disorderly in quarrelling and Contending I admonished them both for that: and fyned John Bliss .5s to the County for Breaking the Peace.

Feb. 8th 1675 [1676].

Thomas Day being complained off by the Constable for refusing to goe out Scout with his horse saying that If he must goe he would goe on foote and being sent for, and the Constable affirming it he not denying but owning it, and Justifiing himself in it saying he did enough to offer his person.

There being plaine Contempt and the Publike Service and safety neglected in such a perilous day as this is, I fine him .5s to be forthwith Paid to enable the carying on such service as this is and in case of Neglect the Constable to Levy it forthwith in Corne or mony or that which will be equivalent theretoe with all charges:

This .5s was Imployed accordingly. [*Marginal notation.*]

[*161] Hadley Feb. 16th 1675 [1675].

Severall persons of Hadley for their Riotous Assemblyng togithir yesterday in Hadly Disturbing the Peace, opposing Authority etc. some of them I Bound over to the County Court as by their Bonds. and Papers thither Transferred appeares and will be found in those Records: others I admonished: and some I fyned: as:

40s: [*Marginal notation.*]

Daniel Marsh: who being present at that unlawfull and Riotos Asembly yesterday with his Club or Stave and very active repairing to the Corporall who was to Execute a sentence on a delinquent by order from the Comittee of Militia: Indeavoring to rescue and deliver the delinquent, this owned by him, and he not declaring against but falling in and siding with that Mutinous Company manifesting much distemper in his Gestures, this attested by the Constable and Mr. Peter Tilton one of the Comittee of Militia: I fine him the said Daniel Marsh .40s to the County to be Paid in forthwith to the County Treasurer:

40s: [*Marginal notation.*]

John Dickenson Junior being present at that unlawfull and Riotous Assembly with his Club Siding with the Riotous Company and very active Indeavoring to Rescue the delinquent laying hold on the Corporall that should have executed the sentence, this being affirmed by many and he owning of it and John Prestons oath that he laid hold on the Corporall I fine him 40s to the County which he Ingaged to pay in to the Constable:

5s. [*Marginal notation.*]

Nathaniell Warner for refusing to asist the Corporall in Execution of a sentence against an offender, when required by the cheife Military officer, who was present saying to him (as he ownes) that he would not doe it: I fine him .5s. to the County.

5s. [*Marginal notation.*]

Samuell Marsh: when the Constable this morning required his Brother to goe along with him: saying, he would spend his Blood with such speed tending to disturbance and Plain spiting authority being also Justified by him I fine him .5s:

[*The following March 28, 1676 entries regarding the riotous assembly at Hadley are found in 1* Hamp. Cty. Probate Ct. Rec. *168–169. Variant entries appear in* Pynchon Waste Book for Hampshire *134–136, 140.*]

Edward Granis of Hadley being Bound over to the County Corte by the Worshipfull Major Pynchon for that he was Present at and Actor in an unlawfull and Rioteous Assembly att Hadley on the 15th February Last Past, Stirring up and anemateing Sedition, Breakeing the Peace, Contemning and affronteing Authority, being one amongst the Rest that did stopp and hinder the Execution of a Sentance which was Pronounced and ordered to be put into Execution by Authority) as likewise Saying it Should not bee, The Corte Considering the Heiniousness of his offence it being at such a time when many Soulders in the Town and soe an ill Example to others besides the evill Consequences that may fall out upon such beginnings and stirrings up of mutaney and sedition the Corte therefore have adjudged him to be well whipt on the naked Body with twelve Stripes well layd on which was accordingly Executed by the Constable.

Jonathan Gilburt being Bound over to the County Corte by the Worshipfull Major Pynchon for that he being one Yea a Cheife Actor in that Riotious Assembly at Hadley being then Present with them and haveing his Cudgell, Sideing with them in their Publique affronteing of Authority. This Corte yet Considering his humble Conffession and Acknowledgment, and manefestation of greate sence and Shame for his former actiones, Promiseing to Carry it Better for time to Come and Ernestly desireing that he may be put to the tryall upon that account, The Corte therefore doe ajudge him, to stand Bound in a Bond of ten Poundes (with two sufficient Suretyes in five Poundes appeice for his good Behaviour till this time twelve month—and then to appeare at the Corte at Northampton to be Discharged of the abovesayd Bond of Ten Poundes if he Carry it well or otherwise to Forfeite the Bond which is ten poundes.

His suretyes were Isacck Harrison and Luke Hitchcocke.

Thomas Dickenson being Bound over to this Corte by the Worshipfull Major Pynchon for that he being one of the Rioteous Assembly Yea a Leading man in itt, Highly afronteing authority that Considering his offence and for that it being an example of ill Consequence the Corte have therefore ajudged him to Pay a Fine of three Poundes to the County.

Nehemiah Dickenson, William Rooker, Thomas Crofft, Jonathan Marsh, being Bound over to this Corte by the Worshipfull Major Pynchon, for that they were Present at (with their Clubs) and Actors in that Rioteous Assembly at Hadly aforesayd Publiquely affronteing and resisting Authority, in the Stopping and hindering of the Execution of a Sentance Pronounct and ordered to be Executed. This Corte Considering the greatness of their offence and for that it is an ill Example and of ill Consequence such Stirings up of Sedition and mutuny This Corte have ajudged them to pay Five Poundes apeice as Fines to the County.

Joseph Selding being Bound over to this Court by the Worshipfull Major Pynchon on February 15th Last for that he was one of that Rioteous Assembly in Hadley being then Present where there was a Publique Affronteing of Authority in the Stopping and hindering of the Execution of a Sentance yet there appeareing some testemonyes that Seemed to take of blame from him Joseph Selding the Corte haveing Considered the Case with the Circumstances of it have ajudged him the sayd Selding to stand Bound in a Bond of ten Poundes with two sufficient suretyes in five Poundes apeice (acknowledgeing themselves Bound to the County Treasurer for Hampshire) for his good behaviour towards all men unto the next Corte of this County and then to appeare and in Case of Defualt to Forfeite the abovesayd Sum of ten Poundes.

Samuell Barnard on February Last being Bound over to this Corte at Northampton by the Worshipfull Major Pynchon, for that the sayd Samuell Barnard was one of that Rioteous Assembly in Hadley, being there present with his Clubb where authority was Publiquely Affronted, and that Notwithstanding his Fathers Comanding him not to be there and Likewise the Constable adviseing him to the Contrary And likewise for that he being before the Commissioners of Hadly Bound to his good behavior for that he with some of the Garrison Soldiers then in Hadly had been Privately Plotting and Contriveing a Disorderly designe off going to Narugansett. This Corte Considering the Heiniousness of his offences (it being not onely his Disobeydience to his Fathers Comand but high Contempt of authority as Likewise of ill Example and might be of ill Consequence if due testemoney be not Born against such Disorderly Carriages) have therefore ajudged him to be imeadiately well whipt on the naked Body with 12 Stripes, but by Reason the sayd Samuell Barnard gave in a humble acknowledgement to this Corte wherein he did Confess his greate Sin, Promiseing Reformation for time to Come, and likewise by the Mediation of his Father Francis Barnard Pleading his wives illness and Weakness of Body at that time as well the Loss of others of her Children not Long before which with this Afflection might be to hard for her The Corte therefore againe takeing the Case into Consideration did upon the aforesayd Reasons agree to alter the sayd Samuell Barnards Sentence Abateing one third Part of the Stripes he was to have, so that hee is to be whipt as afforesayd with Eight Stripes, or to pay a Fine to the County of five Poundes forthwith which Punishment by way of fine was accepted by the Delinquent his Father Francis Barnard Ingageing for the Payment of the Money to the County Treasurer or his Order.

[*162] Aprill. 12th. 1676.   40s.

John Williams of Westfeild being Complained off for affronting the Comissary John Roote using villifiing speeches to him and for striking Samuell Roote: which being owned by him, I fine him 40s to the County. But the said John Williams acknowledging his fault and Rashness noe way Justifiing himselfe but expresing great sorrow for it and promising to be more carefull for future I respit the payment of the fine till next County Court:

[The following March 26, 1678 entry regarding John Williams appears in Rec. Cty. Ct. Hamp. 5.]

John Williams his fine that was imposed upon Him for Resisting the Commissary of Westfeild was abated to twenty shillings, It being forty shillings at the first.

Aprill 13th 1676. John Cragg: 13s 4d.

John Cragg being accused for being Drunk at least in drink and for swearing by God: he owning his swearing: and Ensign Cooly and Isaack Cakebread affirming they toke him to be drunk: at least it is evident he was in drink and gave extream bad Language for which I fine him 3s 4d and .10s for his swearing: all is .13s 4d.

[*163] September 30th 1676.

Philip Butler brought before me for being drunk last Tuesday Night Samuell Terry and Isack Morgan doe both of them Testifie that being on the watch, that Night, about Midnight this Philip Butler came to them, and gave them Ill and high language: his Toung run excedingly and he spake we knew not what and coming in to the house would not goe out nor be ordered but said he had as much to doe there as wee though it were the house we were to watch in: we Judged him Drunk or at least well in drink.

Samuell Tery saith expressly that he was Drunk and Plainely Fudled which appeared to me by his words and cariage: his countenance and eyes also declaring it. heretoe he made oath.

Before me JOHN PYNCHON Asistant.

Isack Morgan says on oath that he was exceding much in drink: and I did Judge he was drunk.

Before me JOHN PYNCHON Asistant.

Hereuppon I adjudge the said Philip Butler to Pay for his drunkenness .10s to the County: and 12d a peice to the 2 witneses.

[*164] March 10th 1676/77.

Joseph Browne complaining against Lidia Morgan for her abusive cariage and Language towards him using reprochfull and Scandalous speeches to him and of him, as calling him base Baudy Rogue and saying of him he was so mad he was ready to gore out her Gutts etc.

Lidia Morgan appeared and putting all upon profe: severall Testymonys were taken which are on file: And at last said shee had not tyme to answer and desyred the Liberty of the Law, not having had that warning the Law allows: so the busyness was adjourned to next Friday at one of the clock: being 16th of this Instant March.

March 16: 1676 [1677].

Joseph Browne and Lidia Morgan appearing: They withdrew: etc:

Jan. 23. 1677 [1678]:

John Coale Constable of Hatfeild coming from Hatfeild with .3. or 4 men with him Complaines against James Carver of Hatfeild for that the said Carver abused him the Constable, both by Threatning words and abusive actions the Night before this: which was occasioned thus: The said Carver being in a rage against John Downing and saying he would Mischeife him etc. I Labouring to prevent him and bringing him from John Downings dore who had shut the Dore against him to my Howse whether we were forced to bring him, he fell into a rage against me calling me dog: Rouge etc and In his Rage and Pashon sounded away for which we tooke care of him and after he came to himself he raged also against me calling me foole Rogue etc: saying and offering to Beate out my Brains, etc. which I refer to the witnesses John Graves, John Courser, John Feild whose Testymonys are on file:

[*165] He the said James Carver also struck at me with his fist severall tymes, besides the Bad words, that he gave me so that I was forced to ty him fast and to have help to hold him and carry him in and keepe him he being in a Rage and resolving to kill damming: vowing and swearing he would be revenged of him, which made me also to set some to watch with him that Night: and for that he run out against me and said he would be Revenged of mee: and swearing by his soule he would kill me or beate out my Brains and Cursing: God damne him: etc: according to the Testymonys:

Jan. 24 1677 [1678].

I adjudge the said James Carver for his horible abusive Cariage to the Constable (Threatning him: villyfiing reproching him and heaping odious Termes on him: I say for his abusive words and also abusive actions striking him with his fist besides his saying he would kill him and beate out his Braines etc.) To pay as a fine to the County forty shillings and for his Swearing to Pay Ten shillings and Likewise Ten shillings for his Auging.

40s
10s
10s

3£ 00.00 [*Marginal notation.*]

And for the .3. witnesses their Journy from Hatfeild .2d a peice and charges at Springfeild .5s. a peice is togither for their watching with him and keeping him the Night before Fifteen shillings more: and Likewise to pay Ten shillings to the Constable for the abuse he hath offered him and Putting him to tend upon him etc:

March 20th 1677/78.   Philip Mattone

Having by letter from the Selectmen of Hatfeild, been Informed of severall persons unseasonably Playing at Cards in their Towne, and other Misdemeanors: one of whom they say Lived in this Towne viz: Philip Mattoone, I sent for him the said Philip Mattoone and ex- amening him, thereabouts: He very readyly and Ingeniously owned That Sometime in February last being at Hatfeild he did at an un- seasonable tyme of the Night at William Kings Cellar being there till about .10. or 11 of the clock at Night Play at Cards; with William Armes; Gershom Hawks and Steven Belding and was Consealing with William Arms and Steven Belding who layd their Tailes on Kings Beame and Loome etc: Having freely [*166] confessed his fault and given in his evedence against the other .3. which is on file and to be Transferred to Northampton Court where the other per- sons may be proceded against: I came to this Issue and sentence of Philip Mattone viz

That he Pay

for playing at Cards	5s	
for being out at that unlawfull Play etc. ⎫ at unseasonable tyme of the Night etc. ⎬	5.	15s fine to the County.
for being at so Nasty a busyness ⎫ as his Testymony speakes ⎭	5.	

and what damage is to William King he to answer besides: and so I discharged him at present:

[The following March 26, 1678 entry regarding Hawkes, Belding, and Armes appears in Rec. Cty. Ct. Hamp. 8.*]*

Gershom Hawkes, Stephen Belding, William Armes being bound over to this Corte for their being examined some of them at Hatfield, by the Selectmen there, and one of them by the Commissioners of Hadley, and found guilty of breaking into William King's Cellar of Hatfeild, and there being very vitious many wayes, viz: in playing at Cards and other foule and Shamful abuses of the Cellar and implements of the said Kings in the Cellar by their excrements in a shamful manner: and damnifying the said King otherways, This Corte have adjudged the said Gershom Hawkes, Stephen Belding, and William Armes to pay for their playing at Cards, and being out unseasonably and Disorderly (in King's Cellar) ten shillings apiece; and for their other offence, to be wel whipt with Seven lashes apiece on the naked body wel laid on; Thomas Armes his seven stripes to be added to the 18 stripes he is to receive for fornication. The abovesaid Persons are to discharge al charges that have been expended by Constables or otherwayes, as also to discharge what shalbe allowed to the said William King for the abuses he had, and wasting and spoiling his goods, to whom the Corte allowed forty shillings to be equally payd by the four persons in delinquencie, Philip Mattoon being one of them: the abovesaid punishments were executed on the said Armes, Gershom Hawkes, and Stephen Belding according to order and on Joanna Armes at Hatfeild.

June. 10. 1678: John Norton

John Norton (a Soldier) being Complained off by Mary Crowfoote and Hanah Morgan for offering abuse to them especially to Mary Crowfoote taking up her Coates and offering baseness to her etc. He being sent for appeared: and The Testomonys that are against him which are on file viz Nicholas Rust: Hanah Morgan and Mary Crowfootes Doe evedence his Lacivious and uncleane Cariage offering and attempting to be naught with Mary Crowfoote etc. as in the Testymonys for which I adjudge and order him: (he professing his not knowing what he did And it appearing by the Testymonys and otherwise that he was Drunk) to pay a fine of Thirty shillings for his wicked and Lacivious cariage and attempts and Ten shillings for his Drunkenness:

30s and 10s   all is 40s. [*Marginal notation.*]

[*167] June. 10th 1678.

Widdow Margarit Bliss plantiff against Florence Driskill defendant in an action of debt to the value of .35s shillings according to Atachment halfe in wheat and halfe Indian Corn: it being for Appls.

Florence Driskill ownes the Debt to be .35s remaining of a larger sum, since which he hath Paid Somthing which Widdow Bliss ownes to be only .1. bushel of Indian Corn: viz .2s 6d.

Which Taken out of the .35s the remaining due is 32s 6d. owned by said Driskill to be due to the said Widdow Bliss:

Whereupon I find for the plaintiff .32s 6d due 22s 6d of it in wheate and the rest in Indian Corn: with Costs of Court

3s   6d
1   6

Florence Driscoll plantiff against Isack Morgan in an action of Debt to the value of .35s according to Atachment. Isack Morgan appearing (after severall debates etc.) owned .31s 6d so I find for the Plantiff .31s 6d. (of which 11s 3d of it is to be Paid in wheate:) And Costs of Court viz. 6s 6d allowed as per Bill.

Samuell Moody of Hadley Being Drunk which he Confessed I fyned .10s to the County:

[*168] May. 6th 1679.

At a Court Called by Major Pynchon and held at Springfeild for Tryall of Small Causes: etc.

Leiutenant Walter Fyler Plantiff against Joseph Leanord in an action of Debt with damage to the value of forty shillings.

Leiutenant Fyler appearing to prosecute; and Joseph Leanord being .3. tymes called after the Marshalls return that he had warned him to appeare was read: and he not appearing The said Fyler requiring his Costs I granted him 3s 4d for entry of the action and foure shillings for this journy to be paid him by the said Leanord:

Also James Taylor the Marshal having warned him as per his return not appearing after the .3. times called the said Fyler requiring his Cost for his Journy .4s is allowed him.

Also Henry Rogers after .3. tymes called not appearing is cast to pay Leiutenant Fyler 4s.

Likewise Jonathan Taylor not appearing is to pay 4s to Leiutenant Fyler.

At a Court held July .2d. 1679.

John Hodge having Summoned Gabriell Cornish of Westfeild to appeare and answer for hindering him in the Improvement of Land there etc: John Hodge also appearing and Letting his sute fall: Gabriell Cornish and 2 witnesses appearing viz: Edward Adams and Noah Cooke and requiring their charge: I adjudge the said Hodge to pay them 2s apeice is sixe shilling and so discharge them at present.

Victory Sike plantiff against Thomas Taylor both appearing but the return of the sumons being wanted and the plaintiff not taking care to procure it the defendant Thomas Taylor requiring his charge I grant him .2s to be paid by Victory Sikes:

[*169] July 5th 1679. At A Court By Major Pynchon:

John Sackcut Plantiff against James Sexton for Beating and wounding his son William Sackcut: As also for Pound breach or rescuing of swine goeing to Pound.

John Sackcut appearing also his son William charges James Sexton with Beating him at the Pound dore when some of the hogs were in the Pound he gave him .3. blows with his fist and tooke him by the Throat and hindered the putting the rest of the hogs into the Pound.

It being not so cleare yet very suspicious by Samuell Loomis Oath I only Judge James Sexton to allow for the entry of action and sumons 3s 6d.

James Sexton fyned 20s I say: 20s. [*Marginal notation.*]

For the Rescuing of the swine It being evident by Testymony on file: I find for the plantiff himself and sons attendance   4s

.3. witness   6

Coming for Atachment 2s Atachment and for serving it   3.6   14.00

.2. sumons for witness   0.6

all is   17s. 6d

And likewise for Rescuing the swine I fine James Sexton to the County 40s which I afterward abated to 20s And so he is to pay to the County: I say 20s.

I gave 6 Months tyme for the payment and John Minor Ingaged with him and for the payment of [*illegible*] in 6 Months.

[*170] July 16th 1679.

Victory Sykes Plantiff against Thomas Taylor Defendant according to Atachment for withholding pay for a heifer he tooke up and kept to the Damadge of fifteene shillings.

The Plantiff appeared and the defendant being .3. tymes called and not appearing, after .2. or .3. houres waiting was againe Called by the Marshall at the Dore and not appearing: The Case Proceedede And it being evedenced by Testymonys on file that Victory Sike the Plantiff tooke up a heifer the .20th of December last and kept it neere .6. weekes which The Defendant challenged and had away I find for the Plantiff Thirteene shillings Sixpence and Costs of Court according to Bill on file viz 13s.

July 18th 1679.

John Pope complaining aginst Philip Matoone for abusing him by word, and striking him on the head yesterday etc. The said Philip Mattoone being sent for and appearing: denys all, but the said Pope affirming it and saying he goes in feare of life for that Philip formerly abused him .2. severall tymes and now came secretly behind him and strooke him on the head and Jawbone which seems to be dislocated: the said Pope also tendering oath: It was taken as followeth John Pope Demanding the Peace of Philip Mattone: Makes oath and Sweares by the Living God That he stands in feare of his life by Philip Mattoon who by abusive words and attempts to strike him seekes his Mischeife also striking him on the head or Jaw last Night to his great prejudice and displacing of his Jawbone disabling him from speech and this don secretly [*171] and privately coming behind him and unawars giving him a blow with his Fist and afterward profferring his Hatchet towards him: so that he is in very feare and therefore craves the Peace for the Needfull security of his Body To this John Pope made oath this 18th of July 1679.

Before me JOHN PYNCHON Asistant.

Hereuppon I ordered the said Philip Mattoone To find .2. sufficient suretys to become Bound in the Sum of Ten Pounds for his personal appearance at the next County Court then and there to answer the premises and in the meane tyme that he the said Philip Mattoone keepe the Peace Towards our Soveraigne Lord the King and all his Subjects and particularly towards John Pope.

Philip Mattoone as Principall: in the sum of Ten Pounds and John Stewart and Isack Gleson as Suertys in five Pounds a peice acknowledge themselves firmly Bound to the County Treasurer that Philip Mattoon keepe the Peace towards all men and appear at Next County Cort in September next.

July 18. 1679   Before JOHN PYNCHON Asistant.

[*The following September 30, 1679 entry regarding Philip Matoone appears in* Rec. Cty. Ct. Hamp. *30.*]

Philip Mattoon of Springfeild being bound over to this Corte for breach of the Kings peace, and confessing his fault, and promising to Carry himselfe better and more suitably in time to come, was discharged of his bond.

July 31 1679.

Joseph Ashly summoned by warrant to answer Isack Morgan for taking away his horse out of Pasture yesterday and Riding him to his great damadge and want of him for his owne use Joseph Ashly owneing it I ordered him to pay said Isack Morgan Ten shillings according to Law.

Sept. 24 1679.

John Pope Plantiff against James Warrinar for not Paying him as he says .7s ordered him by the Comittee for the Meeting house: There appearing some mistake in it as to the Sum James Warrinar being to be allowed for one Seate and so it should have bin for .3s down or beinge 3s 6d I find for the plantiff 3s 6d and Costs of Court 4 10d

This Atachment and serving it: 1 . 6⎫
      Entry of action   3 . 4⎬
               all is 8. 4d

[*172] Sept. 3d 1680.   Joseph Trumble 10s.

Joseph Trumble acknowledging his offence in being overtaken with Drink about .5. weekes since, and being very sorry and affected with it Confessing it himselfe and proffering to sattisfie the Law by paying Ten shillings for the same, I have accepted thereoff he paying it by the ordinary keeper Goodman Ely: and so discharge him.

Sept. 16. 1680.   John Pope 10s.

John Pope being Complained off for Drunkenness which evidently appeared by the Testymony of John Hitchcock and Thomas Stebbings which are on file   I fined him Ten shillings to the County according to Law and 12d a peice to the .2. witnesses:

Sept. 20th 1680.

Isack Gleson Complaining against Isack Morgan for that Isack Morgan Beate his servant Josias Miller at Chikuppy last Friday, and tooke away his Gun and knife.

Josias Miller says that Isack Morgan abused him by beating him and taking away his knife: the which also is testified by Samuell Chapin whose Testymony is on file: the Gun also and knife being evedent that it was taken from him and kept from him till I sent for him the said Isack Morgan who putts the beating of him on profe and saith that he tooke his gun and knife from him that he might doe him noe hurt he accounting him as a distracted fellow (whereas noe such thing appears)   But what he did was because Josias Miller tooke away and was eating his water Million. I adjudge the said Isack Morgan for taking a Gun: and beating him to pay but five shillings because of his taking his water Million to the said Josiah Miller and also a fine of five shillings to the County for quarrelling and disturbing of Peace:

[*173] Sept. 23th 1680.

John Pope plantiff against Thomas Stebbings Junior for non payment of Monys due to the sum of Ten shillings .6d with all due damages:

The Debt was owned to be Nine shillings .6d the which though John Pope demands it in wheate, yet Thomas Stebbins denying it to be such pay and noe profe being made by Pope that the Pay is to be wheate, but there being other evedences (as on file) to the Contrary: and profe being made by Thomas Stebbins producing Isack Gleson and Joseph Ely: whose Testymony are on file, that Thomas Stebbins caryed and tendered him .2. bushel of Indian Corn: and one bushel and $\frac{1}{2}$ of Ry which amounts to 9s 6d I Judge Pope should have taken said pay and is now to take up therewith, and pay Costs of Court Thomas Stebbing bearing his owne tyme:

Costs allowed is for .3. witnesses: .3s.

John Pope plantiff against Nicholas Rust for not paying five shillings etc: Pope declaring the debt to be for worke making tuggs etc. of cedar to serve instead of Cork for a net: which Popes Servant says he wrought halfe a day about it: besides his Master turning the wood etc: which Pope affirmes to be about .3. quarters of a day: I find for the Plantiff five shillings and Costs of Court only the small Bass fish which Pope had is to be acounted toward the five shillings.

John Pope plantiff against Leiutenant Thomas Stebbins for Taking him off from a peice of Joinery worke and promising him sattisfaction which he now refuses: to the Damadge of said Pope .39s.

Leiutenant Stebbins not owning it and noe profe being made either of Damage nor yet of any promise made by Leiutenant Stebbins to make him sattisfaction: I find for the defendant costs.

[*174] Nov. 26. 1680.

Isack Gleson plantiff against John Pope for detaining from him a plaine he Bargained for to the damadge of five shillings according to Atachment. John Pope Being Called .3. tymes and not appearing, the Atachment produced and read togither with the evedences in the case which are on file: I find for the Plantiff the Plaine sued for which he had formerly agreed for or in want thereoff Two shillings sixe pence and Cost of Court as per Bill allowed: .7s 4d.

Dec. 6. 1680.

Joseph Parsons plantiff against Nathanell Foote for non payment of a Debt of 19s 6d in wheate with due damadges according to Atachment. Nathanell Foote being .3. tymes called and not appearing the Atachment produced and read togither with the evedences in the Case which are on file it appeared that Nathanell Foote owes Joseph Parsons 19s 6d in wheate and 5s 6d damadge for forbearing is 25s the whole Costs of Court as per Bill allowed is 5s 10d.

I appoint a Court on Wednesday fortnight being the 22th of this Instant December: [*Marginal notation.*]

Dec. 22th 1680.

Joseph Parsons appearing at this Court and Craving Judgement and Grant of Execution against Nathanell Foote: (He being out of the Jurisdiction) Joseph Parsons acknowledges himselfe Bound to Nathanell Foote in the Sum of fifty shillings in Case the said Foote shall appeare in .12. Months to reverse the Judgement which hereby is Granted viz That I find for the Plantiff Joseph Parsons as at former Courte appeared 25s which Nathanell Foote is to pay him in wheate as also 5s 10d Costs of Corte and hereuppon I Grant execution to the said Parsons: for said Sum:

[*175] December. 24th. 1680.

Joseph Ashly and Thomas Hancock appearing Before me in refference to said Hancocks being under Atachments from said Ashly at Boston and thereby comitted to Prison there, and afterward the said Hancock Ingageing himselfe an apprentice to Joseph Ashly for one yeare he discharged him from Prison and tooke him up to Springfeild There being a condition only entred on one of the Indentures viz Hancocks: And Joseph Ashly before me owning the said writing to be the Condition of the Indenture And in order to fullfilling the same Thomas Hancock surrendring himselfe up to Authority:

Upon which finding that Thomas Hancock stood Comitted to Prison at Boston as by returne of the Atachment which Joseph Ashly produced appears for not finding Security to the Sum of five Pounds for his the said Hancocks apearing at the next County Cort at Northampton to answer the Complaint of Joseph Ashly as attourney to John Highlery according to said Atachment dated .13: Dec. 1680: I doe therefore in order to fullfilling the Condition of the Indenture order and Commit Thomas Hancock to Prison in Springfeild till he shall give Bond accordingly: And also .2. Cases being to be herd before myselfe on the .3d. of January next one of them to answer the Complaint of Joseph Ashly as assignee of Walter Fyler for a debt of 14s 1d and the other the Complaint of Samuell Ely for a debt of .18s 6d which Cases are mentioned in the Condition of the Indenture that they are to be herd before me   The Security required in the Atachments being the one 28s and the other 37s Joseph Parsons Junior apearing before me and Becoming Bound in the said Sums and doth hereby acknowledge himselfe Bound accordingly in the said Sums for Thomas Hancocks appearing before me on the 3d of January next and answering according to the Atachment.

I doe accept of the said Parsons Bond for Security: And so declare the Conditions of the Indenture and obligation of Thomas Hancock to Joseph Ashly to be fullfilled and thereupon order Joseph Ashly to deliver up to Thomas Hancock the Counterpart of the Indenture that is in his hand which I declare to be void and of none Efect Thomas Hancock having fullfilled the Condition thereoff.

Moreover: Joseph Ashly presenting a Bil of charges which he required of Hancock (being now released his service) for the expenses of his dyet and his Horse at Boston amounting to 10s I allowed the said Bill to be Paid by Hancock to Ashly .6s of it in Mony and 4s in other pay: upon which Joseph Ashly delivered up Hancock his Indenture: Thomas Hancock also presenting a Receite under Joseph Ashly hand that he had Received of him. .21s Mony I ordered Joseph Ashly to repay him said Mony part of which he said he Paid for Hancocks charge.

There was also a Bond of Hancocks to Joseph Ashly for .20s Mony on a Condition which Bond and Condition were distinctly and severally sealed I mentioned it to Joseph Ashly that it was not faire or honest to make [*176] make them seperable so as that the Bond which Posibly might prove nothing might be Cut of from the Condition of it: But having given this Caution I left this matter medling noe further with it because as I told Joseph Ashly he had Atached Hancock to answer it at next Court at Northampton, and had taken Bond of Hancock viz his owne Bond of 40s as the Constable Joseph

Bridgham of Boston had certified on the Backside of the Atachment that Joseph Ashly had accepted Thomas Hancocks owne Bond.

Dec. 28. 1680.

Thomas Hancock coming before me: and acknowledging a Judgment against himselfe for .14s 1d due to Leiutenant Walter Fyler: I accordingly enter the same: And this being one of the Cases to be herd before me on the .3d of January next Issues his attendance then: It being that Mony which Joseph Ashly says is assigned to him.

Samuell Ely: also told me that he and Thomas Hancock had Issued: Thomas Hancock having Paid his debt to him: and afterwards the said Ely appeared, and before Hancock declared the same that he was sattisfied the debt and so Thomas Hancock becomes discharged of attendance as well as of that debt to Samuell Ely.

[*The following March 29, 1681 entries relating to the controversy between Ashley and Hancock appear in* Rec. Cty. Ct. Hamp. *48.*]

Joseph Ashley Attourney to John Higley of Windsor Plaintiff per Contra Thomas Hancocke defendant, for not paying the Sum of two pounds Seventeene shilling ten pence money due as per booke shal appear with al due Damages and all according to attachment,

In the action wherein Joseph Ashley was attourney to John Higley of Windsor plaintiffe, and Thomas Hancocke defendant the attachment and Evidences in the Case being produced and read In Corte and transferred to the Jury they brougte In the verdict that they find for the Plaintiffe, two pounds Seventeen Shillings and ten pence and costs of Corte, by bill allowed of, two poundes fourteen shillings, six pence.

Joseph Ashley Attourney to John Higley Walter Filer Samuell Ely plaintiffe per Contra Thomas Hancocke Defendant in an action of Debt of Twenty pounds money due by bond under the hand and Seale of the said Hancocke as shal appeare with al due damages, and al acording to attachment.

In the Action depending in Corte between Joseph Ashley Attourney to John Higley Walter Fyler and Samuel Ely plaintiffe: and Thomas Hancocke defendant, the attachment and evidences in the Case being produced and read in Corte and transferred to the Jury, they brought In the verdict that they find for the Defendant Costs of Corte: one pound twelve shillings and Six pence.

Joseph Ashley of Springfeild acknowledged himselfe bound in the bond of ten pounds to Thomas Hancocke to Stand responsible out of his estate, to answer any further processe either by review or appeale or otherwise.

[*177] Springfeild   Jan. 25th 1680 [1681]:

James Barlow of Suffeild Complaines against Samuell Roe and Peter Roe of said Towne for striking him and abusing him the said

Barlow last Friday: Samuell Roe and Peter Roe appearing disowne much of James his accusation and refer to profe: Edward Burlison and John Taylor being present and by their Testymony which is on file it appears that there was quarrelling and that Samuell Roe struck James Barlow as well as Peter Roe and that Peter Roe Cursed.

Whereuppon I fine Peter Roe Ten shillings to the County: and Samuell Roe and Peter Roe each of them to pay 5s a peice to James Barlow and to Pay all charges in the Case viz for .2: witnesses 4s and .3s his attendance and former Journy with 1s 2d for Summons and serving it—all is 8. 2d.

[*178] April 15th 1681.   Widdow Margarite Bliss and Samuell Bliss Senior Guardians to Samuell Bliss.

Samuell Bliss the son of Laurence Bliss being brought before me by his father in Law John Norton for Disorderly goeing from him   It appearing that he was not Setled with him, and that at his Coming to him from Goodman Dorchester He was to be at liberty to goe away when it should be judged meete, and John Norton not Insisting upon his Continuance with him Longer: The lad is left to the Care and Disposure of his Guardians: and He being about 18 yeares of age: hath made choise off and doth here Publikely declare his choise of: his Grandmother Widdow Margarite Bliss and his uncle Samuell Bliss to be his Guardians who appearing also and accepting thereoff are accordingly allowed and Declared the Guardians of Samuell Bliss the Son of Laurence Bliss, who are to take care to dispose off and settle the Lad in some good honest service or trade:

Some debate being about new cloathes bought him by Goodman Norton   It is determined and agreed to that the lad shall have all his cloathes   Only that his Hat bought of Bracy Goodman Norton shall be Paid for and have 20s more allowed to him; out of that 40s which Goodman Norton is to allow him for the mare.

July .1. 1681.

A Negroe who says his Name is Jack, being sent for and examined saith That he came from Wethersfeild and is Run away from Mr. Samuell Wolcot because he always beates him sometimes with 100 blows so that he hath told his Master that he would sometime or other hang himselfe he says he ran away from him one weeke and halfe since:

He says he stole a Gun at the next Towne viz Southfeild and hath left it in the woods he laid it downe in a Path because it had noe flint in it:

Anthony Dorchester saith That to day about noone this Negroe came to his howse and after asking for a Pipe of Tobacco which I told him there was some on the Table he tooke my knife and Cut some and then put it in his Pocket, and after that tooke downe a Cutlass and offered to draw it but it Coming out stiff I closed in upon him and so [*179] Bound him with the help of my wife and daughter When he scrabling in his Pocket I suspected he might have a knife and searching found my knife naked in his Pocket which he would fain have got out but I prevented him and tooke it away:

I committed the said Negroe to Prison there to remaine and be safely secured till discharged by Authority.

[*The following September 27, 1681 entry concerning the negro Jack appears in* Rec. Cty. Ct. Hamp. *52*.]

Benjamin Knowlton, the Prison Keeper presenting his charges or an account of his charges about the Negro Jacke; viz: for two weeks diet, 5s and more 5s for two dayes and halfe time in looking after him, and five shillings more for Prison Keepers Fees, This Corte allows him his bil, viz: fifteen shillings.

Also the Corte allowes the Constables their bils respecting those that watched with the Negro Jacke, as that they have twelve [d.] per man per night.

July .8. 1681.

A young fellow of 18 or 19 yeares of age examened saith: My Name is George Fitting I came from Barbados above a quarter of a yeare since in one Mr. Brownes ship of 200 Tun and Landed me at Graves End about 3 months since from whence I went to Oister Bay and workt there 2 Months and thence went to NewHaven and so came to this Towne and went directly to Hadly with Symon Beamon where I have workt and with Samuell Boltwood for a Month, and came thence hither with Intent to goe to the Bay to Boston to my Father there but was afraid to goe alone.

My Master at Barbados was Mr. Felton Lived at Spikes whom I had Lived with 2 Years a quarter and was to have Lived with him a yeare and 3 quarters more But came away because I was badly used and had not victuals enough.

This man appeared afterward to be one of Collonell Morrice his Servants and that all above was a ly: his Name being James Cornwall as he owned upon an after taking and examenation and was delivered to Thomas Leechfeild by Collonel Morrices order according to Hud [*Page torn*].

[*180] Aug. 17th 1681.

David Morgan Plantiff against Nathanell Bissall as executor to the estate of Florence Driscoll and so is plantiff as referring to Florence Driscolls estate for Moneys due from said Florenc to David Morgan viz the sum of 27s. According to Atachment.

Nathanell Bissall Pleading what was Atached viz an iron Pot etc. was Inventored and producing the Inventory of it Though the debt appeares due to David Morgan could he find any other estate than what was Inventoryed yet In as much as this is of that estate I find for the Defendant Costs viz for his Journy up and attendance 4s. and being warned and attending before one Journy 4s.

Entry of the action: 3s 4d [*Marginal notation.*]

Nathanell Bissell plantiff against David Morgan for his the said David, not paying Monys due to the vallue of fifteene shillings in wheat according to Atachment.

Nathanell Bissell withdrew his action and so is to pay Costs [and .3s 4d entry]. [*Marginal notation.*]

Johnathan Winchel Presenting his suspition of Robert Old taking away a bushel of wheate meale, of his from Westfeild: I sent for said Old who appearing and what Jonathan Winchell presented in writing being read the said Robert Old denyed any knowledge of the Meale and said that Jonathan Winchell might put said Bag in Muddy Brook himselfe charged Winchell with being like to doe it and with slandering him and slandering better men than he calling him Theef and Saying it was Winchells Trade said he was well known in their Town what man he was and that he made it his Trade to abuse men.

[*181] March .15th 1681/82.

Leiutenant Anthony Austin Complaines against John Hodge, Jonathan Winchell and David Winchell for defaming him, and for other disorders as carying it disturbingly at a Towne Meeting on the .16th of December last etc.

By the Testimonys on file they apeare grosely faulty which also they acknowledged and fell under Ingaging also an open and Publike acknowledgement of it at Suffeild which I ordered them, and it was drawn up and accepted, and so Issued:

Aprill 30th 1683.

Nathanel Horton came before me presenting a Paper of his choise of Samuell Marshfeild and Charls Ferry for his Guardians and desyring my allowances and recording of the same which I accordingly doe.

JOHN PYNCHON, Asistant.

[*182] March 21 1683/84.

Michall Towsley against Hugh Roe for detaining a Sandy Swine etc. Each appearing and presenting their Evedences which are on file,

Duely weighing all both former and latter Evedencs I find the Swine for Michaell Towsley as also Costs of Court as per Bill—32s .6d allowed.

The Papers are Bundled up together where is the whole Case.
[*The remainder of the page is blank.*]

[*183] April. 9. 1684.

Thomas Dewey and Nathanell Bancroft Plantiff as per Atachment against James Sexton Defendant for that the said Sexton with Joseph his Brother, wrongfully tooke away from the said Thomas Dewey and Bancroft, a parsell of Hay which they had Laboured in and made sometime in August or September last to their great damadge as shall be made appeare:

The Plantiff James Sexton being .3. tymes Called and not appearing: The Atachment and evedences in the Case produced, and considered: I se cause to adjourne the Case to this day fortnight at 8 of the clock in the morning being 23th of this Instant Aprill.

April 23th 1684:

Thomas Dewey and Nathanell Bancroft appearing as Plantiff: James Sexton the defendant also appearing: after Pleas made and evedences in the Case being read (which are on file: I find for the Plantiffs In case the land on which the Hay was made be Nathanell Williams, and shall so appeare   Then Twenty shillings I find for the Plantiffs and Costs of Court: In case the Land be George Sextons and Ambrose Fowler, then I find for the Defendant, Costs of Court:

Thomas Dewey one of the defendants declared that he and James Sexton had agreed, which also the defendant James Sexton acknowledged: but that the agreement was only for his the said Deweys part in the Hay which was 10 Cocks: Moreover the said James Sexton declared he had but 22. Cocks and left .3. Cocks on the Place which he medled not with (as is owned) so that there is but .12 Cocks Of Nathanell Bancrofts to be under Consideration: and so I find for the said Bancroft Plantiff as aforesaid Eleven shillings in case the Land on which the Hay was made appears to be Nathanell Williams and Costs of Court viz 17s 9d as per Bill otherwise I find for the defendant, Costs.

[*184] Oct. .13. 1684:

Charls Ferry Plantiff against John Dorchester according to Summons for that said Dorchester tooke away a load of Charls Ferrys Hay, which is to his damadge as shall be made appeare.

Charls Ferry says he Mowed and Made the Hay: and Set it by Agawam River side, on his owne land as per the Testymonyes of John and Charls Ferry:

John Dorchester says I know noe Hay of Charls Ferrys that I fetched away: and can owne noe such thing   I carryed away Hay of my owne and none but what I tooke for my owne   I owne fetching Hay of my owne and none but what was my owne:

Charls Ferrys profe falling short I find for the Defendant Costs of Court viz   entry 8s.

sumons 3s:

John Dorchester after Charls was gon demanded .2s Costs.

October 20th 1684.

Charls Ferry Plantiff against John Dorchester Defendant on Reveiw of the Case about a load of Hay which John Dorchester tooke from Agawam River side in Septembr last which Charles Ferry Challenges and is to his said Ferrys damadge as he shall make appeare.

Charls Ferry says That the Hay was mine   I Mowed it and made it upon my owne Land as per the Testymonyes on file.

John Dorchester says That the Land was accepted Charls Ferrys as buying it of Widdow Harmon But Charls Ferry Sold it to my Father .16. yeares agoe and we have had it in Posession ever since without Molestation till now and therfore Land and Hay is mine: Putting it to Goodman Ferry why he Let them Injoy it [*185] it .16. yeares he the said Charls said He did not know who Improved the Land or who had it and produced a Deed that he Bought the Land of Widdow Harmon: To which John Dorchester replyed that that might wellbe and afterward he might sell it to his father, and did so: and hath owned it That he Let my father have it:

The Hay Goodman Ferrys .2. sons that made it say it was as they guessed a good Load and John says it was .24. Cocks John Dorchester ownes it to be about 14 or .15. Cocks and was Course Hay:

Upon the Pleas and evedences in the Case: I find for the Plantiff Charls Ferry In Case the Land be his on which the Hay was made and doe so appeare then I find for the plaintiff .15. Cocks of Hay or .15s and Costs of Court in Case the Land be John Dorchesters then I find for the Defendant Costs of Court.

3s 6d entry. [*Marginal notation.*]

After Judgment declared as above: each party agreed about the Title of the Land as follows: The Land being about an acre: Though John Dorchester says his father Bought it of Charls Ferry yet not producing any Deed and Charls Ferry saying he knows not that ever he sold it: John Dorchester relinquishes all his future right to the Land and allows Charls Ferry for Mowing and Making the Hay Ten shillings and Charls Ferry is to beare and allow all Costs of Court and to this agreement Each party are Consenting and desyred this Record to be made accordingly as a finall Issue of all matters Concerning the Hay and Land: and agreed it should so stand on Record under my hand:

JOHN PYNCHON Asistant.

[*186] Oct. 20: 1684.

Thomas Copley appearing and Complaining against Michall Towsley for stealing .2 barrow Pigs of about .2. Months old: and said Towsly appearing according to Summons.

Thomas Coply saith he sold 2 sow Piggs to Michall Towsly which he was to have at .6. weekes old when he came to Receive them I marked them with a halfpenny Cut in the off Eare, and he tooke them away with him afterward the Pigs came againe and Towsly came when I was not at home and carrys away other .2 Pigs I went and at his house found .2 of my Barrow Piggs which he had cut of both the eares of each Pig: which I challenged, and his wife owned they were not the Pigs he bought and yet he would marke them shee said.

Towsley examened saith That he did not know his owne Pigs and asked Goodman Coply children and they told me they were mine and I trusted to them   Why did you take away .2 that had Goodman Copleys mark and when you came hom cut of both their eares.

Answer: I was in hast and did not consider it:

The Constable says that when he went to Towsleys he told him he cut off both the eares to cut out Thomas Copleys marke his words were, that he cut them so because he would not keepe another mans marke on his Piggs.

Towsly ownes that he fetcht .2 Piggs and cut off the eares planning to Cut out the slit in the nere end and his wife fetched .2. Pigs when he was from hom because Goodman Copley had fetched away the Two I fetched last.

I sentence [*187] Michal Towsley for Taking .2. small Piggs from Goodman Copleys that were not his owne, and defacing Thomas Coplys marke upon them (notwithstanding his pretence that he tooke them for his owne wherein also he must needs be notoriously negligent If not wilfull in it) To pay to Thomas Copley (besides the Piggs againe) Sixteene shillings Thomas Copley defraying the charges which amount to .14s.

Nov. 4th 1684:

Thomas Vigors plantiff against Samuell Ely for wronging him in his accounts with him and advancing his debt when he reckned to a greater Sum then it was when he made a former account with him in his Booke to his the said Vigors damadge at least 40s.

Both partys appearing: Vigors says he owed Samuell Ely 37s in Monny which when he reckned he advanced to .2. 17s in Countrey pay: of which I Paid him .16s and then owed him 2£ 1s. But then coming to Reckne with him: he made this 2£ 1s 2£ 10s and so wrongs me 9s here, and in the first 2£ 17s above I account he wronged me .7s more then he ought to take allowance for not paying Monny: So that I am wronged 16s.

Samuell Ely says he hath not wronged him any thing at all that he knows of but made up a faire account with him as his Booke (which he produced) doth evedence: wherein Thomas Vigors is Debtor—   1.14.5 Mony (from May to July 1684)

which Vigor owns, and
there he is advanced
for not paying Mony   0.17.3.
                          _____
                           2.11.8

more in Page .82.
Vigor is Debtor   0. 3.0.
                          _____
                           2.14.8

And Vigors hath
credit 0.3.9.
            the rest is   2.11.0

But in Goodman Elys Booke, it is entered: That July 22 1684 They Reckned and Thomas Vigors owes by Joint Consent in Country pay 2. 10. 00 whereto his hand is subscribed.

Vigors ownes his hand But says he tooke it for 2£ 1s 00. [*Marginal notation.*]

To which Vigors says there is [*188] there is wrong to him, in not giving him credit for 16s of old, which it ought to be when as Samuell Elys account of credit is only 3s 9d.

Samuell Ely hereupon fetched and produced his old Booke where former accounts were Ballanced: April 2d and June .11. 1683. [which Thomas Vigors hand is too also and owned by him (*Marginal notation.*)] where and when the Ballance due to Thomas Vigors is 3s 9d which Goodman Ely hath given him Credit for as before so that there can be noe error I find for the defendant Costs of Court 18d his attendance and .3s 6d Vigors is to pay for entry and sum[mons.]

Dec: 9th 1684.

Isack Meachem Plaintiff according to Summons against Obadiah Abbee for his the said Abbees Defaming him the said Meachem several ways or by several Speeches to his Damage as he shal make appeare.

Meachem the Plaintiff appearing: The Defendant also Obadiah
Abbee who made exception against the Summons and Pleading to
Nonsuit because it did not express as he said what he was to answer
too   I told him it did express it in saying it was for defamation and
was according to the president for Summons which directs only to
mention for a slander or defamation in his Name, and this summons
was more full than the president because it mentions defaming
Meachems Name in severall things or speeches and answers fully to
the Law that says Only thus: the Case breifly specified, which is done
in this Summons mentioning a defamation of his Name several ways
or by several speeches to his damage, so that I se noe use for a Nonsuit nor is it to be Granted being the summons returned as served
that tyme enough to both partys being come and apearing. Although
the Constable Daniel Collins had said nothing about his serving it
which he being present did speake to, and said he served it the .3d. of
December: and so gave him full tyme and a day over according to
Law and moreover the Constable said that he told Obadia at serving
it, that Goodman Meachem Bid him tell Obadia: that severall
speeches he had used to defame him, but .2. of them particularly he
intended by the sumons should answer too 1st that he said Goodman
Meachem was a cheater and had cheated him and 2ly that he said
Goodman Meachem had altered the Highway and [*189] and made
the East Lots fall back to bring the Pease out of the dirt all which
said the Constable I told him Goodman Meacham did say and he
spake so to Obadia Abbee, at the tyme of summoning him which also
Obadiah owned, only said this was not expressed in the warrant or
Summons: Hereupon I replyd If the Constable had said nothing yet
I saw noe Legal exception against the termes of the warrant nor
Ground for any Nonsuit nor would I allow it now, or Countenance
such cavilling, seing he knew what he must answer to: and it being
breifely specified in the warrant and plainly that it was for speeches
to Goodman Meachams defamation   And also the Constable over
and above specially and particularly mentioning to him what the
speeches were   I therefore declared the case should proceed:

Whereuppon the Plaintiff made declaration That the defendant
had reproched and defamed him in saying he laid the Highway to
bring the Peases out of the dirt, and made the east lots fall back: and
was so earnest in contriving it, that he sweate and fomed with it:
which is much to my defamation, and a reprochfull speech: Being altogether false, nor did I ever so act or doe any thing in laying out
Lots or the Highway but by the express order of the comittee:

That Obadiah Abbee did so reprochfully and defamingly speake
as aforesaid I refer to the Testymony of John Pease Senior John Pease
Junior and Daniel Coolins which Testymonys are on file   The De-

fendant called to answer: refused to speake any thing saying he would not answer until he had another summons.

2ly: the Plantiff says, the defendant Obadiah Abbee charges me with cheating him of 4s 6d in Monny, and being a cheater: all which I Plainly and expresly deny nor had he any cause so to report   But that he did so report is proved by John Warner and Simon Booths Testymonys which are on file.

The defendant called said he would not speake to it and went away. Being again Called and desired to make his [*190] his answer and defence he refused, and said he had made a Nonsuit of it: I told him I never heard the defendant could make a Nonsuit at his pleasure: the Plantiff might nonsuit himself or withdrawe But if it came to Court seing he came upon summons the Court must Grant the Nonsuite and not the defendant at his will for then noe Case could proceed: and I had not allowed what he pleaded to be cause of Nonsuit, and therefor had herd the plantiff and would as readly hear him the defendant desiring him to speake what he could for himself But he still refused whereupon I said I could not refuse but must speak and find for one or other of them and I am sure clear Testymonys will carry it when nothing is said against them: and Therefore in the first particular referring to laying out the Highway and making the east lots fall back   It being proved by the Testymony of John Pease senior John Pease Junior and Daniel Collins that Obadiah the defendant so said in way of reproching Goodman Meacham which Goodman Meacham denying he did any such thing, I find for the Plantiff in this first particular 12d damage.

In the .2d. particular the Defendant charging Meachem to be a cheater and cheating him of 4s 6d in mony and his so charging being proved by the Testymonys of John Warner and Symon Booth I find for the plantiff .9. monny or as Money: The whole is 10s Monny which I find for the plantiff: and Costs of Court as per bill—eighteene shillings.

Judgment being entered for the Plantiff—   10s and
                                                   18s Costs
                                                   ―――――――――
                                                   1. 8. 00

And accordingly declared.

The Defendant Obadiah Abbee Appeales to the County Cort at North Hampton in March next. Obadiah Abbee appealing from this Judgment to the next County Court being told he must put in security (according to Law) to prosecute his appeale to effect and also to sattisfie all Damages to the present Plantiff Brought his Brother Thomas Abbee to be Bound with him accordingly.

As followeth: Obadiah [*191] Obadiah Abbee in the Sum of five

Pounds and Thomas Abbee his Brother in like Sum of five Pounds, doe Ingage and Bind themselves to the County Treasurer for Hampshire and to Isack Meachem of Enfeild: To prosecute this appeale at next County Court at North Hampton on the Last Tuesday of March next; To effect, And also to Sattisfie all Damages and Inconveniences in not having execution out according to Judgment Granted by Major Pynchon And in Case of any default in the premises, each of them to forfeite the aforesaid Sums.

This done and acknowledged by Thomas Abbee and Obadiah Abbee this .9th. of December 1684.

Before me
JOHN PYNCHON Asistant.

Obadiah Abbee Complaining against Goodman Booth which yet he said he did (not prosecute, but) only bring the Testymonys to me: and desyred me to sweare the men: which Obadiah did Improve to make Goodman Booth Culpable of a ly: In speeches Concerning a Training day: that he the said Booth should say he had gon to the Major about it and that by Goodman Pease his sending him: and yet said he had not gon in such a way.

I perusing the Testymonys (which are on file) and finding noe ly according to the Law but his owning of all, and explaining himselfe and his meaning: I declaring that I did not find them to reach to a ly in the sence or words of the Law. Obadiah Then affirmed with violente expressions: That Goodman Booth was lyable to the Law and was a ly and seing he would not take my sence or set downe by me I desyred him to take the chaire and be Judge, and when he was to be Judge I said I would Submit to his Judgment   But now it became him to rest in mine: but he would not have done and grew more violent in affirming it: and so feirce and Insolent exceeding all Bounds so that I was not able to quiet him till I writ his Mittimus and sent him to Jaile for his Contemptuous Insolent Cariage and Boisterous Speeches where he stood Comitted some houres .2. or .3. and on his Brothers motion was discharged [*illegible*].

Dec: 9. 1684.

[*The following March 31, 1685 entry relating to the appeal of Obadiah Abbey to the County Court appears in* Rec. Cty. Ct. Hamp. *89.*]

Obadiah Abbey Plaintiffe by way of Appeale from a Judgment past against said Abbey by the Worshipfull Major John Pynchon, in a case commenced against said Abbey by Isaac Meacham, which with Judgment being not Satisfyd, the defendant, viz. Abbey gave in Bond together with

Thomas Abbey as a Suretie to the Sum of five pounds to prosecute said appeale at this Corte.

In the Case depending in Corte, wherein Obadiah Abbey entred an Appeale from a judgment past by the Worshipfull Major John Pynchon, the Case and evidences being considered by this Corte, they Se no reason for an Appeale, and therefore have confirmed the Judgment past by the Worshipful Major Pynchon, viz. to pay to Isaac Meacham Ten Shillings in Money or as Money, and eighteen Shillings for charges, as alsoe Costs of Corte in this Action, viz. Ten Shillings entry money, and other charges as per bil allowed six Shillings.

[*192] June .30th 1685.

Samuell Osborne Plantiff against Isack Morgan Defendant in an action of the Case for neglecting or delaying to pay Money according to Bill:

The Bil presented and also owned by Isack Morgan I find for the Plantiff Samuell Osborne according to Bill .36s Due and to be Paid forthwith one .3d in wheat and the rest in Indian Corne according to Bill on file, as also Costs of Court,

Viz entry of the action—   .3s 6d ⎫
Atachment and serving   .1. 9 ⎬ o. 7s 3d
attendance   2. o ⎭
      1.16
and 0.07.3.
    2. 3.3.

July. 3d. 1685.

Joseph Segar Complaines against Michal Towsley and his wife for that his wife unlawfully tooke away out of His House a quart Pewter Pot, and violently caryed it away himself and his wife both seing her doe it and forbidding it   But shee said shee would have it and Caryed it away   And then he the said Segar following her to recover his owne Pot and demanding it of her shee denyed shee had it and Calling to her husband Michal Tousley He came and Both He and his wife struck the said Segar severall Blows He with His fist and shee with a stick:

He the said Michal Towsley Denys it altogether.

The former part of this charge appeares: By the Positive affirmation of Joseph Segar and his wife in Posession of their goods in theire House and Castle where their goods were taken from them and Goodwife Towsley owning she had the Pot.

The other part appeares partly by her owning that Segar followed her also Her Husband owning they were in Skuffle together: And Joseph Segar being in persuit of his stollen goods: And also Edward Burlisons Testymony which is on file.

Upon all, I sentence Goodwife Towsley for entring into Joseph Segars house, unlawfully taking of a Pewter quart pot of the said Segars, and violently carrying it away when he (and his wife) forbid her and afterward upon his the said Segars goeing after her to regain his Pot She denied she had it and struck the said Segar severall Blows calling him Rogue and other abusive carriage for all which, I order her to returne the Pot which cost .3s 6d mony in Boston and pay more either .9s in Monny or 10s in other pay and further stand Committed till shee give Bond with surtys to the vallue of .4£ for her good Behaviour and pay the witness Goodman Burlison 2s.

July 20 1685.
Michal Towsley became Bound in the sum of five pounds to the County Treasurer for his wifes good Behaviour and hertoe acknowledge.

Before me JOHN PYNCHON Asistant.
Til 29th September next [Marginal notation.]

[*193] July .3d 1685.
John Hanchet and James King Tithing men enter a Complaint against Mary the wife of Goodman Towsley for her wicked and horrid desperate words of a Develish nature and Notorious lying.
Refer to the Testymonys of John Scot: Thomas Hanchet and his wife: Thomas Taylor, David From and his wife about her lying.

July 22. 1685.
Thomas Miller, John Miller and Benjamin Leanord Complaine against Joseph Bodortha and Thomas Lamb for not doeing up fence in Chik Plaine or not taking care of fence there as fence veiwer to their the said Millers and Benjamin Leanords Damage which they sustaine thereby according as it shall appear:
They produce that the upper water worke was defective which appeares by the Testymonys of James Taylor and Henry Rogers on file it also appeares that the veiwers neither did the fence according to Countey Laws nor made the particular proprietors to doe it according to Towne order whereuppon I adjudge the veiwers according to Towne order to pay Ten shillings to be allowed and Paid to said Leanord and Millers because they sustained the damadge by veiwers neglect (and the Town prosecuts not).

Aug. 11. 1685.
John Miller Plaintiff (by way of Replevy of a Mare of his which Thomas Day had Impounded) against Thomas Day for said Day not delivering his Mare Impounded when he the said Miller tendered

pay unto said Day to his the said Millers damage .10s according to Bond and Summons.

Thomas Day says he demanded .5s of John Miller not so much for damage as for that his Mare being unruly was in the feild and according to Country Law it is due (the demand of 5s John Miller ownes) Thomas Day says the Mare was unfettered and as to Millers tendering him pay he knows not of any such thing   John Miller says his Mare was Hopled with a pair of with fetters and she might goe in when the gate was open however being so hopled and fetter not lyable to Country Law and I tenderd him for Poundage 2½ abushel of Indian Corn: good measure: Thomas Day says that he would have taken up with .5s according to Country Law though his damage was greater nere an acre of ots being spoild: and she was often in the feild, I find for the Defendant Thomas Day 3s 12d and it being by way of Replevy .5s for Miller to pay and also costs of Court .3s 6d and 12d for Thomas Days attendance.

[*194] Sept. 28 1685.

The Tithingman Samuell Bedortha presenting Benjamin Leanord for that Last Saturday Night he was out after Sunset and came thorow the streete with his Loaden Cart the said Benjamin Leanord appearing acknowledged it and said he was belated by the Gatherers of his Corne else had bene at hom before Sunset and is sorry for it acknowledging his disorder in it: I fine him only 5s to the County and so discharge him.

.5s certificate of it sent up. [*Marginal notation.*]

Jan. 21. 1685 [1686].

Widdow Sarah Barnard Informing that this day fortnight the .7th of this Instant January shee was much afrighted by a mans coming in to her House in the Night when she was in Bed and lying downe on her Bed wheruppon shee gat up and called when presently Thomas Lamb came in and speaking to him he gave noe answer to said Lamb till he Pulled him about to the fire and saw that it was Samuell Owen: the Bed lying close to the fireside he the said Owen lay upon it and would not speake.

So I the said Thomas Lamb run to David Morgan and called him and presently returned again: and Samuell Owen had not stirred to my apprehension and at first only opened his eyes and shut them again: I decerned that he had bene Drinking and smelled of it. When I came with David Morgan he lay across the Bed David Morgan also saith the same   Then Thomas Lamb Halling him on the floure: there he lay about a quarter of an Houre, and then Labord to

[*195] to get up though he staggered a pritty while before he could recover himself, but at last he stood up   I asked him Samuell what wil your wife say to this that you come to another womans Bed he made noe answer for some time, But at last askt after Josias Leanord and Jonathan Ball (asking him were they of your company, he made noe answer)   Samuell: said I Come goe hom, and leading him as far as my House He Inquird the way Hom I showed him and set him in it, and so parted (though as Goodman Foster told me he gat but to his House that Night, and that with some difficulty having fallen in the Snow as he saw next morning.

Goodwife Barnard says she Judged he was in drink because hee came in to the House in such a way and yet he never offered any abuse to her but that he lay on her bed and having formerly bene at her House shee never saw any uncivil carriage and doth now Freely forgive and Pass by this and must say and cleare him wholly further then that she Judged him in Drink and frighted her.

Samuell Owen saith He knows not how he got or went to her House not being sensible: nor where he left Josia Leanord having had drink at several Neighbors that Towne Meeting day had forget himselfe and where he was (as also Josia Leanord told David Morgan that Samuell Owen had bene where he had Drink and therfore was sorry he left him alone as he did   Uppon all I find and Judge that Samuell Owen was Drunk and not sensible whether he went or what he did   Wherfore (the woman Having forgiven him in rest save to his disorderly coming to her Huse)   I fine the said Owen for his Drunkkenness so to pay Ten shillings to the County Treasurer according to Law and so dismiss hime.

Certificate of it sent Mr. Tilton.

[*196] Feb. 25th 1685 [1686].

Benjamin Knowlton Plantiff against Charls Ferry defendant for his the said Ferrys defaming the wife of said Benjamin Knowlton By false reports and aspersing her as being the Raiser of scandalous reports on Miriam Mirick deceased to his the said Knowltons damage of forty shillings:

Both partys appearing: and all Pleas and Evedences in the Case which are on file being heard, read and Considered: I find for the Plantiff an acknowledgment from the Defendant and Costs of Court: The acknowledgment by Goodman Ferrey to be within .15. days at some Meeting where Goodman Knolton or his wife or Goodman Mirick are or may be present and .10. or more persons To the full effect of or in these words. I Did unadvisedly and sinfully say some words concerning Goodwife Knowlton as If shee had spoken re-

proachfully of Miriam Mirick deceased for which I am Sorry, and
that I have thereby unjustly aspersed Goodwife Knowlton this I now
acknowledge as to my owne shame so the vindication of her Name
and in Case of Defect herein by Refusall, or neglect Then the Defendant to pay therfor Twenty shillings and Costs of Court: Costs of
Court allowed as per Bill: is 11s 6d.

Goodman Ferrey made acknowledgement accordingly in the
words written: owning as abovesaid before the persons and above
.20. more present. [*Marginal notation.*]

March 27 1686.

The Constable of Enfeild Bringing before me some of Windsor
that had gathered Candlewood within the Bounds of Enfeild and
particularly Nathanell Watson and Nathanell Owen who (though
Enfeild men say it was within .4. or .5 Miles of their Towne Directly
East) yet owne it to be within .6. or .7. Miles of Enfeild and though
they say it is alitle to the Southward of the East yet it Plainly appeares
they owning it to be about .2. Miles Eastward of the great Meddow
[*197] over Scantuck that therfor It is considerably within Enfeild
Towns Bounds a Mile or Miles: wherefore it Plainly appeares (the
matter of fact being Evident) That said Nathanel Watson and Owen
are Intruders into the propriety of Enfeild and have unlawfully
taken Candlewood and Burned it into Tar to the Number of .18.
Barrels which they acknowledge: which Tar being Lawfully ceized
by the Constable of Enfeild and Brought into his Custody at Enfeild: The charges whereoff in prosecuting it were

.9 men on Thirsday Night and Friday is	
above a day	.1. 2. 6
.6 men on Satturday ½ the day	.0. 7. 0
.2. men this day attending part of the Night	0. 4. 0
.3. Teames to bring in the Tar	0.18. 0
	2.11. 06

the Cask .12. of them were Windsor mens and .6. bar-rells from Enfeild 18 .9. barrels of Tar at .13s. per barrell is 5£ 17s: 0.	The Candlewood being Enfeilds is accounted at 12 loads and so owned by them which at 12d per load is 48s after Treble damage	2. 02. 00 4. 13 06
	.6. of the Barrells Enfeilds are more to be allowed the Towne	1.01. 00 0.02. 06
		5 17. 00

which I give to the Examenance

Although the Tar is Justly forfeited The act being an unlawfully act yet to Moderate the Busyness, hoping it will be a warning to Windsor people (some whereoff have many tymes bene Tardy) It is adjudged to Let them have halfe their Tar: and so to take only .9. Barrells of Tar: which is by above 5. 17s. And so the Constable of Enfeild is ordered to take and keepe for the charges due as above only .9. barrells and deliver the rest to Windsor men who are discharged.

45s of the above Sum is the Townes that is belongs to Enfeild and must be Paid to them and the rest to particular persons.

John Pynchon advised with Samuell Marshfield and Decon Burt the Comittee for Enfeild. [*Marginal notation.*]

[*198] At Northampton July .5. 1686.

Mr. William Clarke: Sworn Justice of Peace as also tooke the oath of Allegeance.

July 12. 1686

Mr. Joseph Holyoke Sworne Justice of the Peace. Mr. Tilton and Mr. Partrig desyred alitle tyme to Consider and would attend it spedyly: who accordingly [Aug. 11th 1686] [*Marginal notation.*] Appeared viz Mr. Peter Tilton and Mr. Samuell Partrigg: and Tooke the oath of Allegeance and the oaths of Justice of Peace:

July .5. 1686.

I went up to Northampton Having appointed the Military Commission officers there to meete me: who accordingly attended: and Received their Commissions from my hands.

For North Hampton viz. Aron Cooke senior Captain, Joseph Hawley:—Leiutenant, Preserved Clap—Ensign.

Hadley: Captain Aron Cooke Junior, Leiutenant Joseph Kellogg, Ensign: Timothy Nash.

Hatfeild: Leiutenant John Allys, Ensign Daniel Warner.

Derefeild: Ensigne Thomas Wells.

Northfeild Ensign John Lyman.

Likewise goeing by Westfeild I there Delivered Comissions to Captain Joseph Maudsley, Leiutenant Samuell Lomes and Ensign Josiah Dewey.

I had before this delivered Springfeild Comissions viz to Captain Samuel Glover, Leiutenant Thomas Colton, Ensign Abel Wright.

All Sworne and Tooke the Oath of Alleageance.

Likewise to Leiutenant Anthony Austin, Ensign George Norton of Suffeild who swore August 11. 1686.

Enfeild: To Isack Meachem: Ensigne

The Troope also their Comissions I gave to them viz Leiutenant John Taylor, Cornet Thomas Dewey, Quartermaster Samuell Partrigg: swore Allegeance.

Clerks of the County Court Likewise Sworne viz Mr. John Holyoke and Mr. Samuell Partrigg.

[*The oath of allegiance, as printed in* Col. Laws Mass., 1672 *261–262, read as follows.*]

I (AB) doe truly and sincerely acknowledge, profess, testifie, and declare in my Conscience, before God and the world, that our Sovereign Lord King Charles is lawfull and rightfull King of the Realm of England, and of all other His Majestyes Dominions and Countryes; and that the Pope, neither of himself, nor by any Authority of the Church or See of Rome, or by any other means with any other hath any power or Authority to depose the King or to dispose any of his Majestyes Kingdomes or Dominions, or to authorize any foreign Prince to invade or annoy Him or His Countrey; or to discharge any of his Subjects of their Allegiance and Obedience to his Majesty; or to give licence or leave to any of them to bear Arms, raise Tumults, or offer any violence or hurt to his Majestyes Royal Person, State or Government, or to any of his Majestyes Subjects within his Majestyes Dominions.

Also I doe swear from my heart, that notwithstanding any Declaration, or Sentence of Excommunication or Deprivation made or granted or to be made or granted by the Pope or his Successors, or by any Authority derived, or pretended to be derived from him or his See against the said King, his Heirs, or Successors, or any absolution of the said Subjects from their Obedience, I will bear Faith, and true Allegiance to his Majesty, his Heirs and Successors, and him and them will defend to the uttermost of my power, against all Conspiracyes and attempts whatsoever, which shall be made against His or Their Persons, their Crown and Dignity by reason or colour of any such Sentence or Declaration, or otherwise: and will doe my best endeavour to disclose and make known unto his Majesty, his Heirs and Successors all Treasons, and traiterous Conspiracyes which I shall know or hear of to be against Him, or any of Them.

And I doe further swear, that I doe from my heart abhor, detest and abjure as impious and heretical, this damnable Doctrine and Position, that Princes which be excommunicated or deprived by the Pope, may be deposed or murdered by their Subjects, or any other whatsoever. And I doe believe, and in my Conscience am resolved, that neither the Pope, nor any Person whatsoever, hath power to absolve me of this Oath, or any part thereof; which I acknowledg by good and full Authority to be lawfully ministered unto me; and doe renounce all pardons and dispensations to the contrary. And all these things I doe plainly and sincerely acknowledge and swear according to these express words by me spoken, and according to the plain and common sense and understanding of the same words, without any Equivocation or mental Evasion, or secret Reservation whatsoever. And I doe make this Recognition and acknowledgment hearttily, willingly and truly upon the true Faith of a Christian: So help me God.

[*199] June. 23th 1686.

At a Court Per John Pynchon as a Member of his Majesties Council

Complaint was made against John Norton.

First for his Misdemeanor in disturbing the Peace of his Majesties Subjects and swearinge:

2ly By Samuell Ely in an action of Battery etc. For that on the 9th day of this Instant June He the said Norton strake abused and drew Blood from the said Ely, cutting a great Gash Just above his eye and sorely brusing his forehead: The occasion being: His denying him Cider when he told him he had had enough Then Norton rose up from the Tables end in his house and said By God I wil make you fetch me cider, and Coming to me struck me in the forehead with his hand or Fist with Somthing (I suppose a shilling which before I saw in his hand) which Cut a great Gash:

According to the Testymonys of Mary Ely: Daniel Beamon and Samuell Beamon which are on file I find the fact, and for damages by loss of tyme Smart or paine and Cure: I find for the Plantiff Twenty Shillings damage and Costs of Court as per Bill one Pounds .2s 9d.

Fine 8s 4d. [*Marginal notation.*]

For his Misdemeanor in Breaking the Peace (It being sometime since and over in his spt [?]) Instead of Binding him to the Peace he rather choosing a fine) I fine him 5s and 3s 4d for Swearing:

At Northampton July .6th 1686.

Samuell Porter Junior of Hadley Plantiff against John Steele of Hatfeild: The Constable of Hatfeild Returning the Atachment that he had Atached .45s of the Estate of said John Steele in the hands of William Armes and owned by said Armes.

The Defendant not appearing upon Call: The Plantiff Produced his Booke of accounts: John Steele being therein charged Debtor, where it is Manifest by the particulars of the Goods delivered in June and July 1685 that Steele the defendant is Debtor 1£ 5s 3d. To all which the Plantiff made oath: Whereuppon at request of the Plantiff I proceaded to Judgment, Finding for the Plaintiff
1. 5. 3
and costs of Court as per Bill allowed
0. 15. 2

2:00. 5

[*200] Aug. 23. 1686.

Thomas Lamb: John Lamb, and James Lewis appearing to answer for their disquieting The Towne by shooting of Guns Last Thirsday in the evening Just within Night.

They owning the thing and acknowledging their folly and being sorry for it and promising to be more carefull and for future to avoid all such foolery I Pass it by (except etc.) for the present.

Aug. 28. 1686.

Joseph Deane Brought before me for stealing several things from John Dickenson of Hadley which things he carryed away with him from Hadly as far as Sheepnuck where he was taken with the things he had stolen and taken out of John Dickensons chamber in which He lay at Francis Barnards House viz 1 white Hat a Serge wastcote .1. pair breechs all which he had on and ownes the taking them, also He is charged with Taking 12d of Money which John Dickenson says was in the Pocket: likewise a loafe of Bread.

But the monney the fellow denys.

He says he came from Bridgewater where he had lived .6. years and then went a whaling at Sandwich and since came to Hadley. [Marginal notation.]

He being evidently Gilty of Felony, I ordered him to Jayle unless he find .2. Surtys in the Sum of Twenty Pounds for his appearence at next County Court. I Ingaged John Dickenson to prosecute him at said Court.

Sept. 7. 1686.

John Dickenson coming to my house again I told him I Shold have Bound him to prosecute: and did now order him in the sum of .10s to prosecute Joseph Deane.

[*201] Springfeild: Sept. 20th 1686.

Luke Hitchcock as Attourney to Mr. William Gibbons of Hartford (whose Power of Attournyship clearly appeared to be so) Plantiff against Thomas Huntur Late of Springfeild, for a debt of .36s 9d due by Booke with due damages. The said Thomas Huntur .3. Times called appeared not. But the Atachment being produced which was served by the Marshall (according to his returne,) on a homlot lying on the west side of the River next above John Rileys etc. I Proceeded to examine the account presented out of Mr. William Gibbons Booke, the sum being .3. 5. 9d

whereis—credit 1. 9. 0
So the Ballance is 1. 16. 9

Which account produced is attested by Capt. Allyn of Hartford that it is a true Coppy out of Mr. Gibbons Booke to which he made oath Before said Capt. Allyn at Hartford.

And accordingly I find for the Plantiffs 1£ 16s 9d.

	Attachment .1s				
and Costs of Court	Entrance .3. 4d	5s 2d			
viz	Filing papers.o. 4	at 7s 9d pay	11. 6		
	Judgment .o. 6				
serving the Attachment		4. 6.			
the Time attendance of the Attorny		2. o.	2. 8. 3		

5s 2d if it to be money.

The Land I order to stand Responsible til execution, which I Respit (In regard of Hunturs absence) for .3. Months If Huntur shall appeare in said tyme to respond otherwise.

Execution Granted Feb. 5 1686/7. [*Marginal notation.*]

October 20. 1686.

James Cornish and Joseph Williston for their unseasonable walking and making Disturbance on the Sabbath day Night on or about the 19th of September 1686 it being in veiw and hearing of the Constable their Noise and walking in the streetes unseasonably for that day I admonished them and order them to pay the charges and so dismissed them only telling them especially Williston (who was most saucy) that If they did not reforme or were brought forth again this should be an evedence against him: and occasion more severity.

[*202] Oct. 20. 1686.

Deacon Jonathan Burt plaintiff against Thomas Mirick Senior for saying of Deacon Burt that he lyed basely and was a Lying man: to the damage of 40s in defaming his the said Burts name:

Thomas Mirick appearing said he was sorry for the words acknowledges they were grose Rash foolish and sinfull and desyred Deacon Burt to Pass them By who replyed he did not desire his Money But his owning his disorder and Ill speakings and now doeing it he did freely forgive him: He paying Costs viz 18d Mony and so Issued this matter.

Jan. 17. 1686 [1687].

The Complaint of Samuell Marshfeild: John Dumbleton, Benjamin Parsons and James Warrinar is, That in the yeare 1683/84. They then betrusted Thomas Mirick Senior Then Constable with the Collecting of a Towne Rate of .35£ or thereabouts, which was to be Paid out for Towne Disbursments of which they say there is yet behind and not come in or Paid in to their order the Sum of .2£ 9s

3d which they challenge and require of said Thomas Mirick: Thomas Mirick appearing Joines Issue with them that it come to a Judgment provided that what he makes appeare he hath Paid of this remaining Sum of .2£ 9s 3d towards Towne charges and disbursements be allowed off.

Upon hearing both partys I find 2£ 9s 3d due to the above persons Samuell Marshfeild, John Dumbleton, Benjamin Parsons and James Warriner for and towards the Townes disbursements from Thomas Mirick who had order to Receive it of particular persons with a greater sum The 2. 9s 3d being behind I adjudge Thomas Mirick who was betrusted with the collecting the sum or Rates then to Pay the sum behind viz 2£ 9. 3d which he must respond out of his owne estate unless he shal and doe make it appeare by this day senight that he hath Paid it or part of it towards the Towne disbursements not yet allowed him for what he doth make appeare that shalbe allowed of and He be discharged of: otherwise he the said Thomas Mirick is to respond for the whole 2£ 9. 3d or what of it shal not be allowed of by Samuell Marshfeild, John Dumbleton, Benjamin Parsons and James Warrinar as Paid toward Towne disbursements before this day senight: and the said Thomas Mirick shall require and collect it of the severall men behind.

[*203] October 5th 1687.

Fearenot King of Westfeild Plantiff against George Sexton Senior of Westfeild for that said Sexton refuses to give him the said King sattisfaction for taking away .8. Cattle from him which he was driving to pound about this time .12. month To his the said Kings Damage 40s or as shalbe made appeares and further for Threatning speeches towards said Kings person with due damages.

Upon hearing the Case: for as much as Fearenot King was Injustly disturbed and Interupted by George Sexton in driving the Cattle to the Pound wherby they were not Impounded as they ought to have beene: I find for the plantiff 5s and for the threatning him to knock him down therby stopping him when he was about a Lawfull designe I find for him .5s. In all Ten shillings and Costs of Court allowed .22s 2d whereof .9s 2d to myselfe.

Dec: 12. 1687.

James Moore Plantiff against Joseph Pomrey for not paying a debt of forty shillings due to Mr. Partrick Cunningham deceased.

The account which Mr. Moore shows in Mr. Cunninghams day Booke amounts to 4. 10. 7.½ of which Mr. Cunningham says Acounted and agreede

March 22. 8 ¾—that the rest is—   1.   6. 10½
and afterward March .16. 1684/85 for Gloves
    Stockens Cotten   14. 00
                                                       _____
                                All is 2. 00. 10½

Joseph Pomrey pleads payments which doe appeare to be allowed
or set of to the 22 of March 1683 [1684] to the sum of about .3£ 4. 0
and the remaine is above: And forasmuch as Joseph Pomrey produces several payments yet not exceding what Mr. Cunningham hath
allowed nor yet any payments since the date of the Reckning or setling of the acounts I therefore find for the Plantiff forty shillings and

Costs of Court viz ⎰ sumons   —0. 1.   0
                 ⎱ entry action   —0. 3.   4
                   Judgment   —0. 0   6
           Mr. Mors attendance   0. 2.   0
                                  _____
                                0. 6. 10
                   All is   2£ 6. 10d.

James Moore Plantiff against Walter Lee as above for about 40s
debt:
    The account produced is .2. 6. 8 whereof Lee disowns .1. yard
serge etc.   0. 9. 0
                        _____
              so 1.17 8 is the debt which Lee
                       produces payment of it and
                       more viz 2. 3. 6
So they withdrew and he must have his Costs If they doe not
agree.
    Mors Against Samuell Phelps for the debt   2. 14.   10d ⎱
                          Paid   1. 16 . 0 ⎰
                       rests   0. 18.   10
I find for the Plantiff .18s 10d and Costs to be Paid in Tar: as
Phelps owned.

    [*204] Dec. 12 [1687].
    Mr. James Moore Plantiff against Nathanell Bancroft for debt of
               Mr. Cunninghams of   1. 16. 6
               Wheroff Paid   1.   7. 5
                      Rest   .   9. 1
I find for the Plantiff .9s 1d and costs 6s 10d.
Moore Against Edward Neale for 14 bushels of Indian Corne.
    I find for the Plantiff .14. bushels of Indian Corne. He forgave
the costs:
    [Moore] Against William Randall for .1£ 13. 6 wherof Randal
Paid as he makes oath .4. bushels of Indian Corne: to Mr. Cunning-

ham himselfe at Sackcuts house which sets of .8s. I find for the plantiff
.25s 6d only If Randal prove .2 barrels of Tar Paid one at Windsor
per Thomas Nobl and .1. at Westfeild paid John Sackcut and to the
plantiff have bin paid since August 1685. or since the .16th of the
March Instant before: then I find but 3 and Costs of Court.

Westfeild Feb. 3d 1687 [1688].

Josiah Dewey Plantiff against Fearenot King in an action of Debt
of 8s 4d due to said Dewey from Fearnot King withal due damages
which shalbe made appeare:

The Plantiff and Defendant apearing and the Plantiff producing his account with evedences in the case also which are on file, the
defendant also not disowning the account yet saying that .2s 4d was
Paid him the debt since the summons which the Plantiff ownes: so
that the 6s remaining due to the Plantiff Josias Duee being a Just
debt for an Apple Tree that should have bene Paid in hay Last winter, but was denyed and refused to be delivered the Plantiff when he
came for it. Wherefore I find for the Plantiff .6s and for charge in
goeing for the Hay that Fearnot King would not let him goe away
with which appeares to be at least 2s 6d. In all eight shillings .6d. I
find for the Plantiff and costs of Court 16s 8d.

Fearenot King Plantiff against Capt. Joseph Maudsly, Ensign
Josia Dewey and Samuell Roote for taking out of Pound several
Swine viz .16. Impounded by said Fearnot King for which he demands .16s according to Towne order and 16s according to the Publike act of the Council and it being done without his allowance and
not giving him sattisfaction To his damage as he shal make appear:
Plantiff and defendants appearing:

The defendants say they tooke them not out of Pound without
leave, But by the Pound Keepers giving them the key and upon their
promising pay they had the Swine, and gave a note under their hand
accordingly which was produced and owned.

So that I doe not Find the defendants culpable as to disorderly
takeing the Swine out of Pound But It appearing the Swine were
Impounded and upon account of the Towne order of .12d per head
for being in the Feild I find for the Plantiff .16s, whereof .9s is owned
Received so that I find .7s to be paid him and costs of Court .19s 8d.

[*205] Feb. 8th 1687 [1688].

Benjamin Leanord appearing Before me and presenting the Case
of a Mare which he attached of Thomas Hunters for a Debt of Ten:
or .12s which the said Thomas Hunter owes him the said Benjamin
Leanord.

And the Case being thus that the Mare was formerly Benjamin Leanords and by him Sold to said Thomas Hunter, whereby it became his the said Hunters: only for that the said Huntur owes as aforesaid about .12s to Benjamin Leanord, Thereuppon he by the Marshal Atached the said Mare in another mans hands (viz James Foords who took her up in the woods) and Benjamin Leanord knowing the Mare to be that Bay Mare which he sold Thomas Huntur, which said Huntur oweing him as aforesaid about 12s He the said Leanord desyring some order from me concerning it and that he may have his 12s.

Considering what is presented and That Thomas Huntur is absent: I ordered Benjamin Leanord to keepe the Mare til Thomas Huntur may be sent to, or heard of and that he use al meanes to acquaint him with it, and in meane time to take Care for the wintering said Mare: and to Improve her for defraying the charges of Ataching and procuring her, that she may be preserved for Huntur in case he can be heard of within a .12. Month and so I wave the Issue of the case at present: ordering that he the said Leanord have the Mare forthcoming for Huntur in case he be heard of or otherwise as shalbe hereafter determined adviseing that the Mare be prized by Indifferent persons to know what she may differ from the price Benjamin Leanord at first sold her for (viz. 45s) to Thomas Huntur: and in order to what Further may be determined in case Huntur appear not by the time set That is to say a Twelve Month from this tyme for so long I order the Mare to be under Benjamin Leanords Custody and to be Responsible for the 10. or 12s abovesaid and for about 12s he owes to me John Pynchon (unless Huntur appear before) then to be determined that is this tyme 12 Month so long [?] the mare to be in the Custody of Law.

[*206] Feb. 18th 1687 [1688].

James Pettey Plantiff against Thomas Cooper defendant in action of Debt of one Pound 12s 2d due in Porke with al due damages.

The Plantiff producing his Booke To which he made oath wherein is charged 1£ 12s 2d and it appeares he Paid so much for the defendant to Mr. Gardner by Capt. Caleb Standlys attests from Mr. Gardners Booke which being presented I therefore find for the Plantiff 1£ 12s 2d and Costs of Court as per bil allowd 12s 8d.

May .4th 1688.

Mr. James Moore Plantiff against Walter Lee for not paying a debt as per Booke and due to Mr. Partrick Cunningham deceased.

Mr. Moore produces Mr. Cunninghams Booke where the Sum

due to Mr. Cunningham is 2£ 6s 8d most of which particulars the said Walter Lee ownes he had, only denys that Article of .1. yard of serge and Cotten riban .9s. The rest or other Articles he owne the having the goods only says he Paid for them and particularly 4s 6d for the salt, But produces noe evedence nor demonstration thereoff: yet Mr. Moore allows by a Paper he finds in Mr Cuninghams Booke of payment of .4. bushels of Indian Corne and 2 bushels of Winter wheat, which is the sum of   .15s 00

The first Article in the Booke being questioned by
Walter Lee, and disowned I therefore abate that   9. 00

which is	1. 4.	00
So remaines	1. 2.	08

I therefore find for the Plantiff one Pounds Two shillings eight pence, and Costs of Court viz summons —   0.   6d

serving it —	0.	6d
Coppy Judgment	0.	6.
Mr. Mors attendance	1.	6
	0 3.	0

Costs	3	
and	1. 2.	8
	1. 5.	8

Walter Lee promised to pay it by the .15th day of this May in Tar. and therfor execution is to be respited til after that day:

[*207] May 19th 1688.

Nathanel Bancroft. Plantiff against Mr. James Moore in an action of Review of a Judgment Granted Mr. Moore against said Bancroft on the 12th of December last where and when Judgment was Given for said More for 9s 1d besides Costs 6s 10d when as said Bancroft says the 9s. 1d. is Paid Moore and 2s 5d more is due to him wherefore he revews and sues for his due as aforesaid and for damages according as he shal make appeare: and said Bancroft desiring a Jury: accordingly a Jury was summoned and returned by the Constable, who are as followeth Jonathan Burt Senior, Benjamin Parsons, Samuell Bliss Senior, James Warrinar, John Hitchcock, Charls Ferry, Samuell Ball, Samuell Terrey, Johnathan Morgan, John Warner, James Dorchester, Luke Hitchcock.

The Jury Called: and Plantiff and Defendant appearing: and withdrew: so it falls.

They agreed only they desyre me to enter their Agreement which is That Nathanel Bancroft Ingages to pay to Mr. Moore 4 bushels ½ of Indian Corne and 2 Bushels of winter wheat to be Paid in next Munday at Joseph Sackcuts house.

May 31. 1688.

Widdow Mary Parsons Plantiff against Joseph Marks for detaining an Iron Spade above a 12 Month and Cost .8s in winter wheat I find for the Plaintiff the Spade to be delivered as good as it was forthwith or 8s in winter wheat and Costs 3s 6d.

Sept. 20. 1688.

The Constable of Enfeild Robert Pease Presents John Kibbee for refusing to watch last Sabbath day Night being warned per his order and saying it was not his turne wherby the Constable supplyed his Place: al attested to per the Constable: I sent Summons for him to answer it to Morrow at 8. of the Clock [Sept. 21.] Appearence being accordingly Elisha Kibbee saying his son was not wel: and it was out of his Turn and offering to watch for his son this Night and to allow the Constable .12d for his Paines and attendance so Issued this matter.

[*208] June. 4th. 1690.

Mr. Thomas Sweatman Complaining against Daniel Beamon, who being Summoned appeared accordingly to answer for his abusing said Sweatman yesterday by Reprochful words, calling him Rogue and Theife: Threatning his life; and by striking him, and breaking the Peace he affirming he gave him many Blows with his fist and kickt him when he was downe Tore the haire of his head and Tore his Jacket.

The witneses Summoned viz Obadia Cooly and Thomas Dyer not appearing I deferred the Case afterward they appeared.
[*Three lines are deleted.*]
Daniel Beamon ownes he said he was a Theife and said noe more and that was because he tooke a peice of eight from his Brother Josias: which Sweatman ownes but says his Brother Josias gave him it to Change because he Lent him 2s 6d.

I find it to be a squobling busyness between themselves only that Daniel Beamon is faulty in breaking the Peace as appears by Thomas Dyer and Sweatmans Testimony. So I fine Daniel Beamon five shillings to the County to be Paid in to the County Treasurer and Costs of Court as part of it viz .12d to the Constable: and 2 witness attendance which 12d being part of the .5s Tis .4s which I must certifie to the County Treasurer.

[*209] July 31th 1690.

John Crowfoote and John Buck being Complained of for being Drunk last Night and being abusive in their Carriage as also abusing the watch about or after Ten of the clock at Night: And appear-

ing according to Summons, that is to say John Crowfoote, Buck
having withdrawne himselfe: I gave out a special warrant to the Constable for apprehending said Buck and bringing him before me, and
deferred John Crowfoote til then, ordering him accordingly to appeare and answer for his disorders when Called:

　　Aug. 1st. 1690.
　　The Constable having apprehended and Brought John Buck:
went for John Crowfoote also whom he met with and required him
to Come along with him to my house forthwith, But said Crowfoot
Rid away and whipt his horse to make speed, and Riding by my
house in stead of Coming in went away which delayed proceeding til
late in the Evening when being light on I proceeded to examenation:
　　John Crowfoote: Examened saith: That the Drink we had was
mine, and I had a Bottle a quart of Rum which I caryed up to Capt.
Glovers new house: we had noe Company when I Carryed the Bottle
there, John Buck and I only was there; being asked where he had
the Drink he said I had it of Samuell Bliss in Towne, Old Samuell
Bliss that kept the ordinary: I had it of him last Wednesday and Paid
him for it before I had it: I Paid him in Corne, a bushel of Mislen
wheate and Ry he had of me for it, and at Night I and John Buck
drunk some of it, and Barrow Steele coming by I made Barrow Steele
and Thomas Rich: drink: Barrow Steele being by said I was goeing
by and seing them there I went towards them, and they gave me a
Dram Twas in the streete I was, But Thomas Rich was there before:
　　Asking Crowfoote why he abused the watch, He said that He
knows not that he medled with or abused the watch: and denys
much:
　　An evedence of his being in Drink. [*Marginal notation.*]
　　John Buck examened saith, I had noe drink at all only what
Crowfoote had in a Wooden Bottle, and I never saw it before it was
in Capt. Glovers house, and says he Remembers nothing [*210] nothing at al of drawing his knife or that he said anything to his Mistris
or saw her there which demonstrates also his being in Drink:
　　Testymony being ful and cleare concerning both of their Disorders, being at least in drink: and of their and each of their abusing
the watch, reviling them and others and roaring rudeness etc. which
evedences are on File: I accordingly proceeded to sentence them as
followeth:
　　John Crowfoote and John Buck for being last Wednesday Night
the .30th of July past In Drink, If not Drunk and that at a very unseasonable time being .10. a clock at Night If not past as the Testymonys speake: I Doe Sentence each of them forthwith to pay .5s a

peice according to Law or else by the Constable to be Set and stand in the Stocks to Morrow Morning one whole Houre: And for their and each of their Rude behaviour at that time of Night abuse of the watch, Offering at the watchman, and Daring him by words and actions, horribly reviling and reproching others also, John Buck grievosly swearing and prophaning the Name of God and Crowfoote shewing neglect and Contempt of the Constable now when called, though ordered to attend: Al being to the great dishonor of God, Scandal of Religion and of pernicious example If not borne witness against: I Doe therefore Sentence each of them for said various misdemeanors which are most evident by the Testymonys on File, To be wel Whipped by the Constable (or whom he shal procure) with Ten lashshes a peice well laid on upon the Naked Body to Morrow morning, and to stand Committed til the Sentence be performed, only Crowfoote in case of Paying downe a Fine of 40s to the County, to be discharged of this last Sentence of Whipping only: and is to pay al Charges to the Constable etc.

Each of them were accordingly Committed for this Night.

August .2d.

In the Morning: The Constable as he was ordered brought them forth to Receive their Punishment, which was duely Inflicted: John Buck being wel whipt, Crowfoote tendring the Fine, which Mr. Glover Ingaged payment of:

[*The following September 30, 1690 entry of the County Court relating to Crowfoot's offenses is found in* Rec. Cty. Ct. Hamp. *127. A variant entry appears in* Volume A, Registry of Deeds, Springfield, Hampden County, 1690–1692, *288.*]

John Crowfoot upon an Examination before the Worshipful John Pynchon Esq. where he had his drinke that he and others were abused with the summer foregoing this Corte, and also was amerced for by his Worshipful John Pynchon Esq. he the said Crowfoote did confesse that he had said Drinke of Samuell Bliss Senior and paid him for it, (which also he owned in open Corte) and in as much as said Bliss had no licence so to Sel, this Corte therefore doe order said Blisse to be brought into Examination and Tryall for it, either at the next Courte or before the Worshipfull John Pynchon Esq., if he Judge meet to do it.

[*211] Aug. 19. 1690: Samuell Lamb against Samuell Thomas.

Samuel Lamb Plantiff against Samuell Thomas, for that Samuell Thomas withholds from him a debt of .13s Ingaged to be Paid in a Barrel of Tar: with al due damages.

Samuell Thomas appearing ownes the debt that he owed him .13s But says he Paid it in a barrel of Tar To James Mun upon Samuell

Lambs Account: Samuell Lamb denys that Jams Mun owns the having of any barrel of Tar and will give him credit for none: So unless James Mun wil owne the Receiving or having the Barrel of Tar or that Samuell Thomas doe prove the delivering it to him: I find for the Plantiff Samuell Lamb: a barrel of Tar or .13s and Costs of Court viz.

Summons and Atachment	6d	
Entry of the action	3. 4d	
The Constables serving it	2. 6	o. 8s 6d
Samuell Lambs attendance the other day when Samuell Thomas appeared not and now	2. o	

Fearnot King Feb. 18. 1690:

Fearenot King and Thomas Mooreley Issued there busyness thus: that Thomas Moorely is to pay King .5s now in corne which he says is ready: and .4s in worke betweene this and Midsummer next: This was the ful Issue which I entred to prevent any after squoble betweene them.

April .6th 1691.

Widdow Benedicta Lawton administratix to John Lawton of Suffeild plantiff against Henry Rogers of Springfeild defendant for that said Henry Rogers neglects or delays to pay .1£ 3s 6d due by Bil which said Bil is presented in Court and owned by Henry Rogers and was payable the .15th of January last past: plantiff and defendant appearing and the debt not being Paid I find for the Plantiff said Bil of 1£ 3s 6d and Costs of Court .6s 1od.

[*212] April. 14. 1691.

James King of Suffeild Complaines against Michael Towsley of said Towne, for stealing certaine goods of his.

Michael Towsly appearing being Brought by the Constable who made search according to warrant sent him for that end; and returnes That he found some fine thrid and a Clout or child bed linnen in the house of said Towsly which James King challenged as his.

Further James King Complaines as per his Paper given in in writing of said Towsly and his wife Threatning them and offering Mischeife to their Cattle and threating to burne His house whereby he is in feare of Mischeife to him and his family said Kings wife also saying the same.

And that Towslys children were Theevish pilfering lying etc.

Burlisons axe which was in Towslys hands is lost said Burlyson not being here But the ax is found: and owned. [*Marginal notation.*]

James King demands of Towsly .21. knots of fine thrid which 20 of which knots are a Run: a Run at more than .4s Towsly ownes that is to say that they had 21 knots of Goodman Kings thrid.

The linnen and other things complained of and of his children not being made appear at present are deferred to another time.

But the thrid being evident that Towsly had it to the ful vallue of .4s I find Treble damages viz 12s for Michael Towsly to pay said King and al Costs and Charges both in the search and now at this time of appearence al amounting to .15s 6d.

```
[whereof    4s restored
 remains    8s
     and    15.6
           ────────
            .1.03.06.
```

May .23.1691.

Michael Towsley last week was complained off and now being again brought to me by the Constable some peices of linnen though worne much yet very evident of James Kings and .4. Trenchors of his being found in Towslys House also several Testymonys etc. about yarne he had was challenged by others besides vehement suspicions that he had killed and made use of others swine etc.

I required him to become Bound in .20£ Bond with .2. suretys for his (good behavior and) appearence at next County Court in Springfeild to answer for said Misdemeanor and Bound James King in like sum to prosecute against him at next County Court who acknowledged it before me and I accepted that and for Towsly he is to be under the Constable til Monday that he finds surtys or else be Comitted.

Munday May .25.1691.

Michael Towsly appearing several Testymonny etc. which are on file being produced, and Finding noe suretys for etc: I Sent him to Jaile til the Court or that he find suretys as aforesaid.

[*The following September 29, 1691 entry relating to Michael Towsley and his family is found in* Rec. Cty. Ct. Hamp. *144. A variant entry appears in* Volume A, Registry of Deeds, Springfield, Hampden County, 1690–1692, *303–304.*]

Michael Towsley and Mary his Wife and their daughter Mary, being al presented to this Court for divers misdemeanors and al appeareing, and each of them haveing been examined before the Worshipfull Collonel Pynchon, and divers Examinations and witnesses or testimonys being read in open Court, the Court do Judge them all to be guilty accordding to the respective testimonys of the crimes witnessed against them, viz. of lying of Stealing and of Killing Creatures, or some Creatures of some of their Neighbors, and of threatening some of their Neighbors, or expressing such things as that their Neighbors are affraid of greivous mischeifes to be done to them by the said presented partys. This Court therefore to beare due Witnesse against Such Sinfull and dangerous and to be abhorred practices doe adjudge as follows, first Since they find that the daughter Named Mary is guilty of lying, especially in that She charged her father before authority, as killing and Stealeing and teaching her to Steale, and again denying her Confession before this Court, the Corte doe adjudge her to be wel whipt on the naked body with eight Lashes and Ebenezer Parsons presenting himselfe in the Corte as willing to take said Mary as a Servant upon a months tryal, This Court do order that at the months end, if said Parsons desire it, that Indentures be drawn and confirmed, or otherwise the Corte do Order that the Select men of Suffeild do take effectual care to have said Mary put out to Some meet Person or Persons to Service with whom she may be wel educated, the child herself Saying, that she can do [no?] better or reforme whyle She continues with her Parents or father. And as to the woman the Wife of said Towsley, the Court do find her Guilty of desperate Speeches, and threatening Cursing to her Neighbors to the great disquieting of them and do adjudge her to be wel whipt on the naked body with ten Lashes: And to Michael Towsley, this Corte finde him Guilty of fellonious practices takeing away his Neighbors goods and in particalar Killing Some Swine or one Swine at Least, This Courte therefore do adjudge him to be well whipt on the naked body with fifteen Lashes, and that he pay al Charges respecting the prosecuting him for his hainous Crimes and particularly that he pay James King twenty shillings and Edward Burlison Ten Shillings And the Court do further adjudge the Said Michael Towsley and Mary his Wife to be bound in the Sum of Ten pounds apiece for their Good behaviour during the pleasure of the Corte.

[*213] June. 10. 1691.   Fearenot King against Thomas Mooreley.

Fearenot King and Thomas Moorly apearing noe Atachment being returned yet Thomas Morely produced under Constable John Guns hands, that said Thomas Morely had Paid in to the Constable what King demanded viz .2 bushels and $\frac{1}{2}$ of Indian Corne and .3s in other pay: for Kings charge so that the debt of .5s sued for being discharged I dismissed them that in the .2. bushels and .$\frac{1}{2}$. of Indian Corne and .3s in the Constables hands being Paid to King was to Issue the busyness (excepting that of the 4s) which I sent a note to the Constable Gun to deliver it to said King:

Se back one leafe: of their former agreement. [*Marginal notation.*]

July 22. 1691.   Victory Sikes against James King.

Victory Sikes Plantiff against James King for Taking Clapbords of his falaciously, though releasing them afterward yet not sattisfiing the said Sikes for his Troble and hindrance thereby to his damage 20s or as shal appeare.

Plantiff and Defendant appearing according to summons The Plantiff says he felled the Tree out of the Commons close and shaved the clapbords which King tooke away   King says he went for the clapbords because he tooke them to be on his Grounds and had measured it, but it seems mistooke and so released and left the Clapbords to Victory Sikes, and that the taking them was by a mistake and not falaciously; And an agreement also was made betwen Victory Sikes and him.

I find for the Plantiff the clapbords to be his: But noe Falacious taking them on Kings part. So that the plantiff having the clapbords which the defendant yeilded or left to hime I find for the defendant, and it being a case right meete for a Tryal: they having come to an agreement I order both of them to beare their owne charges: and so Issued it.

[*214] Sept. 12th 1692.

Thomas Day of Springfeild Plantiff against Richard Burk late of Springfeild Defendant according to Atachment for not paying a debt of about fifteene shillings due By Bil with al due damages.

Richard Burk being .3. times called and not appearing I proceeded according to Atachment, the Goods Atached being in the hands of Thomas Mirick Senior, Tilly Mirick and James Warrinar.

Thomas Day Bil from Buck produced, being at first 4£ .12s whereof is Indorsed on the Bil as I find: Paid   .3. 17. 6
so rests due—   .0 14. 6

I find for the plaintiff   14s 6d—14s 6d⎫   It is   1.3.10
and Costs of Court viz Constable   ⎬   and Execution   0.2. 0
                        twice   2s⎫   ⎪   is   1.5.10
attendance time etc.   ⎬ 4s⎫⎪
            of Days   2.⎭ ⎪⎪
                        ⎬ 9s 4d⎭ 1. 3. 10.
.2. Atachments is 1s ⎫
Entry of Action   .3s.4d⎬   5:4
and Fyling Paper   8d⎭

I deferred execution the defendant being absent for one weeke.

Sept. 12. 1692.

John Mirick Plantiff against Richard Burk according to Atachment etc. as above for not paying Ten shillings for Hay:

I find for that John Mirick declars .2. load of Hay he sold to Richard Burk at 10s per Load is 20s whereof he Received 10s remaines due 10s.

Ebenezer Graves and James Mirick Testify on oath that they carryed and delivered to Richard Burk .2. load of Hay into his Barne from John Mirick and John Mirick owning the Receit of 10s I find due 10s and Accordingly find for the Plaintiff .10s and Costs of Court

viz time	2s	
.2. witneses	.2.	8s 4d
Atachment and entry action	4.4	
Filing Papers	8d	

al is 17s 4d
with execution 2.0 } is .19. 4d

[*215] Jan. 17th 1692 [1693].

Richard Waite Prison Keeper Sueing for his Fees viz .5s which is due to him for Thomas Lambs Commitment, who refuses to pay his Fees which at first he had promised: Thomas Lamb being Summond as per return from the Constable and appearing: said Thomas Lamb: saying that he was wrongfully Imprisoned concerning which I Replyed that is not the worke now, But whether you wil pay the Prison keepers fees, which he not yeilding to: I Proceeded according to the writ returned:

Richard Waite being Plantiff in a Plea of detinue against Thomas Lamb for detaining .5s his fees: I find for the plaintiff .5s and Costs of Court viz

Withdrawne the persons agreeing: and so Issued the matter. [*Marginal notation.*]

Jan. 23. 1692 [1693].

Tilly Mirick Plantiff contra Samuell Davis defendant according to Atachment in an action of Debt of .40s due to said Tilly Mirick for a Saddle: Samuell Davis being Three times called the Atachment was read and returned being that it was served on a Crib of Corne in Samuell Lambs yard, Samuell Davis having notice of it, and warned also by writing left at his place of usual abode. I Proceeded upon Tilly Mirick presenting his Booke of accounts where in page 42. Samuell Davis is made Debtor To a Saddle .40s to be Paid in Corne, To which said Tilly Mirick made oath that it was accordingly a true and Just debt (ever since August last) for which he hath Received nothing: I find for the plaintiff .40s to be Paid accordingly that is in Corne and Costs of Court viz as per bil allowed .7s 2d.

[*216] Feb. 24. 1692/93.

Peter Mils Plantiff Contra Widdow Mary Parsons of Springfeild (according to Summons returned served) In an action of Debt to the value of Twenty five shillings Both partys appearing Peter Mils presented his Booke of accounts of several particulars of worke al which being cast up amounts to .25s. The particulars owned by the Defendant in everything: Only that the Widdow Parsons presents her Booke that 8s of it is Paid by her daughter Hesters worke with said Mils To which said widdow Parsons made oath to her Booke: which 8s abated from the debt I find for the Plantiff Seventeene shillings Costs of Court

entry etc.   .3s 8d $\Big\}$ 5s 8d
attendance 2.

    Eodem Die:

    Widdow Mary Parsons Plantiff (according to Atachment and Summons returned served) Contra Peter Mills defendant in action of Detinue for not returning or rendring a true account of .8. or .9. yards of linnen Cloth and some callico delivered him to the value of 33s with damages. The Plantiff presents her booke specifying 11 yards of Linnen Cloth delivered him whereof she had again only so much as was cut out for .3. stays To which she made Oath. So that it appeares there is about .7. or 8. yards stil in Mils his hands and the Callico Lining of a Manto a Patterne of the Cloth being presented and shown I find for the plantiff 6 yards $\frac{3}{4}$ of linnen Cloth that is sheere cloth at .3s. per yard is 01£ oos. ood and the calico not returned at 2s al is Twenty Two shillings And Costs of Court viz

an Attachment and Summons	1s		
entry of Action	3.0	4s 6d	6s 6d
Fyling Papers	.6d		
Attendance by an Attourney	2		

    They agreed after Judgment to Set both their actions according to their sums one against the other

Widdow Parsons sum with costs—1.8. 6d

      Mils his sum pays .1£.2s. 8d $\Big\}$ 1.8:6 which .5s 10d
          so rests   0. 5. 10

Peter Mils Ingaged to pay in to Mrs. Parsons in .3. or .4. days time: doeing which al Issues, both sides agreeing so that If Mils Faile in payment Execution may goe out for the .5s 10d.

    March. 9th 1692/3.

    Samuell Barnard (Prentice to Obadiah Miller) being Complained of and warrant sent for him to answer for his misdemeanor in throwing stones or sticks at Glass windows last Munday Night and appearing said he Threw none But these were in company Pelatiah, David and John Morgan as also Ebenezer Petty, William Scot and Thomas Stebbins, with himselfe: some said there must be noe throwing at Winddows, But Ebenezer Petty said he would throw and Did

Throw at Mr Holyokes window or to the house and it light on the
winddow: I ordered him said Samuell Barnard to appeare to Morrow in the evening about or before Sunset When I gave out warrant
for Ebenezer Petty (and others) appearing then:

March 10th 1692/93.

Ebenezer Petty: John and David Morgan and Thomas Stebbins
appeared: and al disowned the knowledge of Damadge to any window, and particularly Ebenezer Petty denying that he Throwd at the
window   Also Samuell Barnard further examined saying he thought
it only: I admonished the Lads and discharged them:

[*217] April .6th 1693.   Peter Mils against Banes.

Peter Mils Plantiff contra Benomi Banes defendant, in a Plea of
debt to the vallue of .1£ 19s 10d with damages: summons returned
and both partys appearing: Peter Mils produces his
Booke for several things to the sum of .2£ 19s od and allows for
Porke Received from Banes the sum of   o.   19.   9: which deducted
So the remaining debt due to Mills is   1.   19.   3
Banes produces payment By Silver 1s at   2s
                         By goeing to Hartford }   } o. 16.0
                           to take up a warrant } 4
                  By .2. yards ½ cotton cloth at 4s—   10
                  This appearing to be Paid viz——   16s and rests–
                                                          1.03.3d.
Each of them producing their Bookes [illegible] tendered to
make Oath to their several accounts as here Inserted, and made up:
and as they were goeing to Sweare, they agreed to accept and take
each others accounts without making oath.
    I find for the Plantiff——   01. 03. 03
       and Costs of Court:
    viz: summons   o.   6d }
          entry of the action   3:   } 3. 6d oo. 06. 06

          serving the summons—   1s. }
          .1. day attendance—   2   } 3. 0
Banes without execution Paid Mils by Charls Ferry .30s.

April .18. 1693.

Peter Mils Plantiff contra John Sackcut Junior of Westfeild in a
Plea of Debt according to summons to the vallue of .12. or 14s shillings with damages that shal appear:
    Summons returned and both partys appearing viz Peter Mils by
his servant and Attourney: said Attourny producing the account and

swearing thertoe for the sum of 11. I find for the Plantiff 11s and
Costs of Court .10s 4d viz sumons, entry action and

filing Paper	3.10
serving summons	2.
.2. day attendance	.4.

Peter Mils of Windsor Plantiff against Joseph Pomry of Westfeild
in a Plea of debt to 20s with damages: etc: summons returned and
both partys appearing: Joseph Pomry the Defendant Pleads that he
the Plantiff agred to take .11s owning the worke to be done I find
for the Plantiff .11s and Costs of Court.

viz summons entry of action and filing Papers—.3. 10d ⎫
   serving summons and travel .9. miles   3. 3 ⎬ —11s 1d.
   .2. day attendance   4. 0 ⎭
   .22s 1d. [*Marginal notation.*]

Peter Mils Plantiff against Samuel Ashley of Westfeild in a Plea
of debt to the value of Ten shillings with damages according to summons the plantiff not appearing and not being Summoned noe proceeding was:

[*218] May .23. 1693. Jacob Adams against George Granger.

Jacob Adams Plantiff against George Granger in a Plea concerning detaining his cannoe to .20s damage: Summons returned and
both partys appearing: The Plantiff affirming he detained his canno
nere a Month: The Defendant ownes that the streame and wind being to hard for him he could not bring the cannoe but left it at Hartford, and that it was .3. weeks and .3. days before she was returned:
The Plantiff Pleads the want of his canno to go to the Mil being as
his Horse and many ways a wrong to him: He was put to hire a Horse
to mil Twice. etc. I find for the plantiff .15s and Costs of Court

sumons	o	6d
entry	3	
filing paper	o.	4
serving summons	1.	o
Coming for summons:		
and attending twice	3.	6
	8.	4

     15.
      8. 6
  1. 3. 6 [*Marginal notation.*]

July 8th 1693.

There having beene some occasion of Discourse about Ebenezar
Scot his being at Liberty from his Father Terry: Disorderly goeing

off being noe ways allowable or Countenanced said Samuell Terry and his wife the lads Mother, as also his uncle Samuell Bliss being present: with the lad Ebenezer Scot: came to This Conclusion: That Ebenezer Scot shal be at liberty from his father in Law Samuell Terry at the end of October next Til when He the said Ebenezer Scot is to continue with Samuell Terry and under his Government, and to attend to doe him faithful Service: Samuell Terry Ingaging to Instruct him as he is Capable in the art of weaving and to Improve him for the most part as the season wil allow in that mistery or art that he may be as far as capable compleated in the art of weaving: When that is to say on the 30th day of October 1693 and after said Ebenezer Scot shal be at Liberty to Improve his time wholy for himself: and shal then be discharged from his fathers Service, his said father Samuell Terry Ingaging then to dismiss him with good and Sutable Cloathing in al respects as wel and better then he is now apparelled, that is to say with doble apparel in general and for most parts: To which agreement the Mother and uncle are consenting: as wel as father and son, who both doe hereunto Set their hands:

SAMUEL TERREY
EBENEZER SCOT
Before me JOHN PYNCHON

[*219] July .10th 1693.   William Randal against John Peirce.

William Randal plantiff against John Peirce of Enfeild in a Plea for a debt of .15s due for what he had to pay in Stubbing of Land in Randals Lot next to that Edmond Bemont stubbed for him to the vallue of 25s: Summons returned and both partys appearing: the evedences being on File that Peirce was to doe the stubbing sometime since; which also John Peirce ownes: I find for the Plantiff a quarter of an acre of Land wel stubbed forthwith fit for Plowing in that Lot of Randals where Edmond Beamont Stubbed and next to that Beamont Stubbed or for want thereof fifteene shillings and Costs of Court.

viz
- summons .6d filing Papers 6d
- entry of action 3s } 4s 00
- serving the summons   1. 08
- attendance .3 days or that
- part of .3. days   3. 00

Money   8. 08

Sept. 18. 1693.   Robert Pease against Samuell Terry and John Mighil.

Robert Pease Senior of Enfeild Plantiff against Samuell Terry and John Mighil both of Enfeild in a Plea of Trespase upon said

Pease according to Summons by unjustly taking from him, Hay about .2. load, made by him the said Pease and standing on a span or peice of Meddow of his in Enfeild at a place called Brooke Meddow, To his said Pease his dammage 40s as shal appeare:

Summons returned and both partys appearing The Pleas and Evedences in the case being read which are on File: I find for the Plantiff Robert Pease in case the Land be his on which the Hay was made and doe so appeare Then I find for the Plantiff .2. loads of Hay or 14s (that is to say .14s in Lew of the 2 loads of Hay in the woods at that Meddow) and Costs of Court: In Case the Land or Meddow on which Robert Pease made that Hay be Nathanel Horton by whose order the Hay was fetch away Then I find for the defendant Costs of Court

Summons	o 6d	⎫	
Filing Paprs	1 2	⎬ 4s 8d	
entry action	3	⎭	

Sept. 25. 1693.

Mr. Peter Goulding of Hadley Plantiff against Thomas Seldon of Hadley according to Atachment returned and read (and the returne upon it read The defendant Thomas Seldon being .3. times called appeared not, and time being out viz it being past .2. of the clock: The Plantiff proceeded: when also at entring into the case said Selden appeared) in a plea of Trespass upon the case for that said Seldon in September last year under Colour of Law and Countenance of Authority by vertue of a writ shewed and caled a Replevin Tooke out of said Peter Golding Custody a swine taken damage faisant not regularly executing any writ and regardless of the Comands and direction of the Law: whereby that is by irregular taking away said swine, and not acting according to Law the Plantiff said Golding is damnified 40s.

Atachment returned and both partys appearing The Pleas and evedences in the case being read which are on file: I find for the plantiff .12. bushel and halfe of good [*illegible*] merchantable Indian Corne in Hadly or Twenty five shillings in corne: and Costs of Court viz as per Bil allowed 18s 8d.

Thomas Selden appeales from this Judgment to the next Inferior Court of Common Pleas for this County and hath given Bond to 4£ with Hezekia Dickenson his surty, there to prosecute his appeale to efect:

[*The following September 26, 1693 entry in* Hamp. Rec. Ct. Pleas *8 records the hearing of Selden's appeal by the Inferior Court of Common Pleas for Hampshire.*]

Thomas Seldin of Hadley, formerly Constable of Hadley Plantiff; per contra Mr. Peter Goulding of Hadley Defendant, In an action of appeal from John Pynchon Esq. one of the Justices of this County In a Plea tried before him on the 25th of this Instant September, when said Goulding was Plantiff, and said Seldin was Defendant In a Plea of trespass upon the case for that said Seldin In September; last under colour of law, and countenance of authority by virtue of a Writt shewed, and called a Replevin, took out of said Gouldings Custody a certain swine taken dammage feisant, not regularly executing said Writt, and regardless of the commands, and directions of law; whereby; that is by Irregular taking away of said; and not acting according to law, The Plantiff said Goulding was damnified fourty shillings.

Thomas Selden Plantiff, and Mr. Peter Goulding Defendant, appeared In Court;

In the action of appeal depending between Thomas Selden of Hadley Plantiff, and Mr. Peter Goulding Defendant; It being committed to the Jury; They brought In their Verdict, that they find for the Plantiff the reversion of the former Judgement, and cost of Courts, as per bill on file allowed by Cort one pound fifteen shillings, and sixpence In money.

[*220] Dec. 9th 1693.   Mr. George Phillips against Jacob Adams.

Mr. George Philips (resident in Springfeild) Plantiff against Jacob Adams of Suffeild in action of Detinue for neglecting the payment of 27s. or thereabouts according to Summons, returned and read, and writ upon that Adams was warned on the .2d of December Instant.

The Defendant Jacob Adam .3. times called, appeared not. The Plantiff who appeared: declared that being to take a Journy to Long Island, he should leave the further prosecution to John Pynchon Junior as his attourny desiring him to take out a warrant of contempt directed to the Constable or other official to bring the contemner as wel to answer the said action as said Contempt and so Issued the present process til a new warrant.

Presently after, the Defendant Jacob Adams appeared when the Plantiff was present, and so the Case proceeded:

The evedences in the Case presented: It appeares that Ten shillings of it was Isack Cakebreads Rate, and by Isack Cakebread Paid into Jacob Adams by William Allyn who personelly came and declares it, said Adams not disowning it but acknowledging he had it: Six shillings was Samuell Cross his Rate, which Adams owns he had warrant to Levy as he had for others and as much as for any out Towneman, and that he Levyed it upon Cross his Land, but could not light of any man to Buy it: The eleven shillings of Adams his owne debt, He says it was comitted to Constable Mighil to Collect, and Constable John Mighil ordered him to pay it in to Goodman

Haiden of Windsor for Mr. Philips: which care is taken to have it done and If not it properly belongs to Constable Mighils Rate: So that it is at least to be suspended for the Present and not medling with that 11s Goodman Adams presented the Rate Isaac Cakebreads 10s and Cross 6s is down so that I find for the Plantiff (the .10s and 6d) Sixteene shillings and Costs of court as per Bil allowed .9s 11d.

March .1st 1693/94. William Symonds etc.

William Symonds of Enfeild appeared etc. Plantiff against Zachariah Booth of Enfeild defendant in a Plea of debt to the value of .36. or 40s or thereabouts as shalbe made appeare according to Summons returned by the Constable read, with this writ on it: This summons was served on Zacheriah Booth and he warned to attend the same this 22th of February 1693/94. By me Isack Morgan Constable of Enfeild.

The defendant Zachariah Booth .3. times called appeared not: The Plantiff who appeared after Long time of stay desyred (according to Law) a warrant of Contempt against the Defendant, which I Granted and to answer the Plantiff action to Morrow or on Saturday morning:

March .2d 1693/4. William Symonds against Zachariah Booth.

William Symonds Plantiff as also Zachariah Booth appeared (the Defendant not being wel: Issued the Contempt) The Plantiff producing the agreement betweene them about keeping the feild which is ownd to be 8 weeks within .2. days comes to 2.18s whereof is Paid 1£ 04s: so remains 1£ 14s as [*221] as per the Papers on File: I find for the Plantiff William Symonds one Pounds fourteene shillings in Indian Corne and Costs of Court as per Bil allowed 1£ 6s 2d.

April 23d 1694. Richard Waite against Josiah Dewey.

Richard Waite Plantiff against Josiah Dewey Junior of Westfeild in a Plea of Debt to the value of 14s money with damages according to Summons returned; both partys appearing: The evedences in the case being on File besides Richard Waite presenting his Booke of Josiah Dewey Debtor .20s silver for goeing downe to Saybrooke with a Raft of Bords: where there is Credit .6s so that remains .14s. To which Booke and account the said Waite made oath.

I find for the Plantiff 14s Money and Costs of Court 7s as per Bil allowed.

May .14th 1694. Joseph Wiliston against Thomas Taylor.

Joseph Williston Plantiff contra Thomas Taylor of Suffeild defendant in an action of Debt of .29s in corne due to the Plantiff by assignment from Benjamin Crane which was originally due to Josias Phelps of Windsor according to Atachment: As also in a Plea of debt of 12s remaining on a debt of Nathanel Phelps assigned to said Williston which was a greater sum for which Taylor Ingaged a Cart and wheeles and performed only the wheeles so that not making the Cart remains .12s: .29s the first action.

Thomas Taylor being .3. times caled, The Atachment was returned and Read: Returne being that it was served on a Red Cow of Thomas Taylors now in the hands of Nathanel Hermon of Suffeild, who owned that the Cow was Thomas Taylors: which the Sherrifs deputy Left under Nathanel Harmons care til the Tryal: returne also being that Summons in writing for said Taylors appearance now, was left at the House of Mistress Younglove which was the Last abiding place of said Taylor and notice given of what was Attached: I Proceded upon Joseph Willistons presenting his Booke to which he made oath to .29s remaining due to him in corne:

The other 12s his Testymonys not coming I adjourned it to to Morrow or next Thursday May 17th 1694 In case they come then.

I find for the Plantiff 29s in corne and Costs of Court viz 9s as per Bil allowed .4s 6d of it Joseph is to pay me and 2s to the execution, execution being accordingly Granted:

July .2d 1694.

John Sackcut of Westfeild Senior his Complaint against Benjamin Smith Junior on File with the Papers where (I waiving it what I might) see the Papers how far that I proceeded.

[*222] July .23. 1694.   Thomas Abbee against Elisha Kibbee.

Thomas Abbee of Enfeild Plantiff against Elisha Kibbee of Enfeild in a Plea of Debt (for Drink etc.) to the value of one Pounds nineteene shillings with damages etc: according to summons returned Both partys appearing The Pleas and Evedences in the Case were read which are on File: I find for the Plantiff Thomas Abbee: one Pounds Nineteene shillings (in pay the drink being reduced to pay) and Costs of Court as per Bil allowed .13s 6d.

Elisha Kibbee against Thomas Abbee.

Elisha Kibbee Plantiff against Thomas Abbee of Enfeild in a Plea of debt to the value of .40s or thereabouts as shall be made appeare Both partys appearing The Pleas and evedences in the case read, which are on File I find for the Plantiff Elisha Kibbee: .1£ 10s and Costs of Court: viz .9s as per Bil allowed: The defendant Abbee owning part of the acount to 30s though says overprised:

Aug. 6th 1694:

Elisha Kibbee Plantiff contra Isaac Morgan defendant in a Plea for unjust taking away Boards of his from the sawmil in Enfeild about one thousand Foote to forty shillings damages as shal appear according to Summons returned; Both partys appearing The Pleas and Evedences in the Case herd and read which are on File I find for the Plantiff .406. foote of Boards or Sixteene shillings in pay and Costs of Court as per Bil allowed viz: .16s 4d.

Isaac Morgan appeals from this Judgment to the Court of Pleas at Springfeild in September next and Samuell Terry of Enfeild with himself said Isaac Morgan Ingages in 40s as per Bond given to prosecute the appeale to efect.

[*The following September 25, 1694 entry in* Hamp. Rec. Ct. Pleas *23 records the hearing of Morgan's appeal by the Inferior Court of Common Pleas for Hampshire.*]

Isaac Morgan of Enfeild Appellant Vs. Elisha Kibbey of said Enfeild Appellee from the Judgment of John Pynchon Esq. on the 6th of August Last Upon a plea for the appellants Unjust Taking away about one thousand of Boards from the Sawmill In Enfeild to forty Shillings as per the Judgment aforesaid which was that the original Plantiff Should Recover against the Defendant 406 foot of Boards or 16 In Pay and Costs as per the original Process appears Both Parties now appearing and the Case after a full Hearing was Comitted to the Jury who Being Sworne to try the Same Returned there verdict that they find for the Appellant a Reversion of the former Judgment and Cost of Courts; The Court therefore Consider that the former Judgment be and hereby is Reversed, and that the appellant Shall Recover against the appellee Cost of Courts allowed at Two Pound Seven Shillings.

Sept. 11th 1694:

James Lawton of Suffeild, complaining to me of a kettle taken from him last Saterday and yesterday Having warrant, to the Constable to make Search for it: accordingly this day the Constable of Suffeild Having made search, Brought before me John Kent of Suffeild, who says That he tooke the kettle in way of distress by vertue of his office being Clerke of the Band at Suffeild, and for a Fine of six shillings which the Captain taxed upon said Lawton to pay for defects in Training and ordered him said Clerk of the Band to Levy: which Fine he several times demanded of said Lawton, and twice goeing to his House finding none at Home went away and a 3d time on Saterday last goeing againe to his House for it, and finding a kettle within Dores and none at Home: Tooke the kettle away and

presently afterwards went to the House againe and there met with
Lawtons wife whom I told of it that I had taken the Kettle in order
to the Fine and If her husband would goe to the Captain and pay the
fine or agree with him He should have his kettle againe: But Lawton
instead of coming to me, it seems went for a warrant, and brought
the Constable to my House to serch for a kettle that he said was
Stolen: I told him I had [*223] taken a kettle of Lawtons in way of
distress for his Fine by the Captains order, but knew of none stolen:
The Constable said to me I owning that I had the kettle of Lawtons:
I must goe along with him: and so brought me before you: and the
constable coming with him: says the same and That Kent owned, the
taking the kettle for the Fine or in order to obtaine the Fine and noe
otherwise:

James Lawton Insists upon it that the kettle was taken away un-
knowne to him; and his wife present with him, says shee did not
heare any thing of it: Though John Kent affirmes that he told her
that he tooke the Kettle for her husbands fine and If her husband
would but goe to the Captain and agree about it and sattisfie him He
would let him have the Kettle againe and give them in his fee and al
charges: and To the same Purpose the Testymonys on File speake etc.

Upon hearing the Case, I find the Kettle to be taken in way of distress according to Law: and Justifiable in John Kent the clerke.

But Inasmuch as after the Taking it the Drummer William
Pritchard hath given under his hand that he hath accepted of James
Lawton for the 6s Fine I order upon Lawtons Paying the Cost and
charges That John Kent shal restore the kettle to him againe:

The Charges and Constables attendance according to the Bil on
File being .6s.

Sept. 17. 1694.

James Mun Plaintiff against Joseph Ashly Defendant, for that
said Ashly Contrary to agreement (about Hay that said Mun was to
Mow in Ashlys meddow to Halves) Tooke away the best or the English Hay without deviding it, unjustly carrying away said Muns share
of English Hay to a delivery of said Hay which is Muns part, to the
value of 20s:

I apointed men to veiw and Judge the Hay what each party had
before I can give Judgment on the case viz. Jonathan Morgan and
Joseph Williston, who are to bring in to me which difference they
find in that share or part of the Hay which each of them had:

Joseph Ashly owning that he Mun Mowed the Meddow to Halves
and was to have halfe only that said Ashly was to have the first Load
yet that the devision was to be equal though he had the choise of the

1st Load. But Mun says he Joseph Ashly had al the English Hay: wherefore the difference is now to be Judged:

The men apointed to veiw and Judge the Hay or difference brought in their determination under their hands this 20th of Sept. 1694 which is on File: whereuppon: Joseph Ashley being present and James Mun also: Theire Pleas and argueing herd etc. I Find for the Plaintiff James Mun Five shillings in good English Hay or in good pay answerable: and Costs of Court as per Bil allowed viz .5s Money.

[*224] Sept. 24th 1694: Zachary Booth against Thomas Hayward.

Zachary Both of Enfeild Plantiff contra Thomas Hayward of Enfeild aforesaid Defendant in a Plea of unjust Impounding by said Hayward of a Mare and Colt and a .2. yeare old Colt of said Booth, (which said Booth hath Replevyed) to the value of forty shillings with due damages as shal be made appeare: according to summons returned and read.

The Plantiff .3. times called (and after that, Longe waiting) Hayward the defendant appearing and desyring his charges may be allowed. I Granted him accordingly as per his Bil of Costs viz Two shillings, on File with the summons etc:

The Plantiff presently after appeared before the defendant was gon, but the defendant having got his Cost Granted, would not stay but went away.

Afterward Both partys came, and agreed al past matters and I delivered up that which had reference to the Replevin, viz Booths Bond by Thomas Haywards Consent and ordering it, into Capt. Meachems hands.

Nov. 24th 1694.

John Buck the Indian examened, (whom upon the complaint of James Warrinar senior this day; That he had stolen his Horse and several other things from others was according to warrant persued after by Joseph Williston, James Mun and William Warrinar who overtooke him at Chikkuppy House and brought him back with several things) which are as followeth besides the Horse of James Warrinars a Saddle and Bridle of Joseph Willistons a Halter of James Muns .3. yards of [illegible] Homemade linnen of Mary Perrys a lace neck Handchercheife and a Muslene neckcloth of John Harris his a kettle of Mr. Pynchon besides several fowles about 10 etc a Loafe of Bread etc and other provissions etc the al which were delivered to the several owners.

As also Mr. John Pynchon Junior charges him with a Horse he stole from him.

Said Buck Examened saith That he tooke Goodman Warrinars Horse out of his yard last Night and Joseph Willistons Saddle and Bridle out of my Barne and having stored himselfe with provissions Intended to March off But being pursued came Back etc.

Question: Why did you come from New Yorke, where you were with a Master. Answer: I cannot tel why: what was your Masters Name: Answer: Thomas Milton: why did you leave him: I know not for I cannot fault him, But being come off: I tooke a Horse to goe further.

For his stealing and misdemeanors as abovesaid (tho none offered to prosecute him) and for that Hu en cry from Yorke was sent after him It now being Satturday Night, I Committed him to Prison til further order taken and delivered him to the sherifs Deputy to secure and put into the keepers hand according to Mittimus.

Joseph Williston undertooke to carry him to New Yorke to his Master To whom he was accordingly delivered:

[*225] Jan. 7th 1694/95.

Richard Waite Plantiff contra Timothy Moses Defendant both of Springfeild in a Plea of debt of five shillings in pay and .22d in Money due to said Waite with due damages according to Summons returned: Both partys appearing: the Pleas and evedences in the case heard and Read which are on File I find for the Plantiff five shillings in pay and Costs of Court:

Costs of Court as per Bil allowed is .6s 10d.

Timothy Moses appeales from this Judgment to the Court of Pleas at Northampton in March next: and Benjamin Sitton of Springfeild with Timothy Moses himselfe Ingages in 20s a peice as per Bond given to prosecute the said appeale to efect:

Afterward: January the .14. 1694 [1695]   Both partys came to me together and told me they had agreed: and desired to withdraw the appeale Praying me to deliver up the Bond for appeale: which Bond I accordingly delivered up and Timothy Moses Burnt it in Richard Waites presence and so Issued this matter.

Jan. 14th 1694 [1695].

Charls Ferrey Senior Plantiff Contra Samuell Bliss Senior both of Springfeild in a Plea of debt of about .24s for weaving   For that having reckned with each other about .2. Months since said Ferrey accounted only for the weaving of .2. peices when as he had woven .3. peices of cloth and forgot to account the middle peice: according to Summons returned. Both partys appearing the Pleas and evedences in the Case being herd and read, which are on File I find for the Plantiff in pay foure and Twenty shillings and Costs of Court.

They agreed to beare their owne time and Costs, except 4.8d allowed which Samuell Bliss Ingage to pay to John Pynchon.

Feb. 25th 1694/5.

Mistress Mary Parsons of Springfeild Widdow Plantiff against Timothy Moses Defendant in a Plea of debt to the value of 40s with damages according to Summons returned: that said Timothy Moses was warned:

The defendant Timothy Moses .3. times caled and not appearing.

Timothy Moses also Plantiff against Mistress Mary Parsons defendant in a Plea of debt to the value of 40s with damages according to Summons returned and served. The Plantiff Timothy Moses .3 times caled and not appearing: the defendant appearing and demanding charges or costs, and denying the oweing of any thing to Timothy Moses: I find for the Defendant .12d for attending.

Nov. 4th 1695.

Upon John Gun of Westfeild his Complaint of the Disorders of several young people at Westfeild in breaking downe Fences and laying open Inclosures and according to Summons served and Returned: appeared John Roote: Samuell Roote son of Thomas Rote, Samuell Roote son of widdow Roote, Eleazur Welles, Joseph Pixley.

Al being severally examind evaded the matter and put al upon profe: and so were dismissed excepting Joseph Pixley who was altogether Mute the Rest desyred to know their accusers and se the Proofe against them and all said things as very suspitious of their being gilty, only Samuel Roote son of widdow Roote expresly said he was wholy Ignorant and did noe damage to any Fence:

I Dismissed them al, only with a more severe check to Joseph Pixley for being wholy mute and rendering himselfe thereby the more suspitious:

[*226] Dec. 2d 1695.

George Granger of Suffeild Plantiff contra James King of Suffeild defendant in a Plea of Trespass and Battery for abusing him the said George Granger by Striking and wounding him on Thriesday, November 14. 1695 disenabling him for work to his damage at least 40s according to Summons which the Constable Served and returned. Both partys appearing according to Summons: The Pleas and evedences in the Case heard and read which are on File. I find for the Plantiff (who Pleads he hath lost a fortnights time and is stil disenabld and hath bene wounded the Care costing 10s so that I find 35s for the Plantiff Thirty five shillings in Corne pay [His Teame not being proved in al above 40s] [*Marginal notation.*] and Costs of Court money

viz the writ or Summons	2s	
Summons for .6. witnesses	1	.6s
Entry of the action	3	
Filing Papers	1	
for .6. witnesses coming up	12	
George Grangers time	2	
Coming up for the warrant		
Constable Serving it	2	
	22s	

He accepted of Kings paying him for it and so I meddle not with it.

Dec. 23.1695.

John Sackut of Springfeild Plantiff Contra Benjamin Smith of Westfeild, defendant in a Plea of

They appeared and agreed.

Dec. 30th. 1695.

James Petty of Springfeild Plantiff contra Edward Kibbee of Enfeild according to Attachment in a Plea of Detinue for with holding from said Petty a black steere of above a yeare old, to the vallue of 40s as shal appeare, with due Damages.

The Attachment returned and served on the said black steere and a mare of said Kibbees, as also that Summons was left at the House with Kibbees wife (he not being at Home).

The Plantiff appearing and also the Defendant, Both partys apearing The Pleas and Evedences in the Case being read which are on File I find for the Plantiff The steere in Controversy to be his in time demanding him and damages Sixe shillings with Costs of Court as per Bil allowed is Thirteene shillings eight pence.

Afterwards both Plantiff and Defendant came to me and made an agreement between themselves abating the charges and Issueing the matter as to Costs so that noe execution is to goe out Kibbee delivering the steere to Petty within .2. days.

Dec: 31.1695.

Fearenot King of Westfeild Plaintiff Contra Benjamin Smith of Westfeild weaver in a Plea of Detinue for that He said Benjamin Smith tooke away or detained certain yards of linnen Cloth from Fearenot King to his damage 40s with damage   Summons returned and both partys appearing the Pleas and evedences in the case being read which are on File: It appeares and is owned that Smith weaved the cloth and detained it only for his pay and that 4. or .5 days and that he did at last deliver it and that Fearenot King hath the Cloth: and yet Benjamin Smith is not paid   I find for the Defendant costs of Court. His attendanc 3. days 2s.

[*227] Feb. 14 1695/6.

Mr. James Mackman of Windsor making process against Josiah Marshfeild of Springfeild For 34s Money due to him from said Marshfeild By Bil: which Bil with Josiah Marshfeilds hand and seale to it attested per Josiah Willys and Samuell Beamon, being presented and payable the 20th Sept. 1694: Josiah Marshfeild owned and acknowledged or Confessed Judgment to prevent further procedure in Law By Costs: This done and acknowledged by Josiah Marshfeild Feb. 14th 1695/6 Before me

JOHN PYNCHON   Justice Peace.

So that upon non payment execution may goe out.

At same time a Bil of Like sum Payable to Mr Alexander Allyn of Windsor by said Josiah Marshfeild and witnessed as befor by the partys above named was also presented which Josiah Marshfeild owned and Confessed Judgment for 34s. Money due to Mr. Alexander Allyn   This acknowledgd by Josiah Marshfeild as also 6s more in Mony due to said Allyn upon Book in al 40s Mony he Confeses Judgment against himself etc. Feb. 14. 1695/6.

Before me   JOHN PYNCHON   Justice Peace.

Mr. Alexander Allin being at Springfeild February 1698/9 said they were like to agree with Josiah Marshfeild and this 24 February 1698/9 sent me a note subscribed Alexander Allin and Elizabeth Mackmen under both their hands that they had agreed with Marshfeild and both of them desired a vacant or voidness to be put upon the above.

Feb.24. 1695/6.

Thomas Abbee of Enfeild Plantiff contra William Randal of Enfeild defendant executor to Mr. Edward Whittington deceased in a Plea on account of Debt to the value of .21s 3d Due by Booke from said Mr. Edward Whittington whose Executor said Randal is and refuses or neglects to pay the same with al Due damages as shal be made appear: according to Summons returned: Both partys appearing accordingly: The Pleas and evedences in the Case heard and read which are on File: There appearing in Abbees Booke several particulars for October 1694 or in Anno 1694 amounting to the sum of 1. 1. 3.

And also in what William Randal presents viz a Paper for Schol-
ing wherein Thomas Abbee hath Ingaged .20s to Mr. Whittington
under his said Abbes hand for Keeping Schoole in the year 1694 viz
from the 19th of March 1693/4: which Randal owns that Mr. Whittington being taken of by the Towne with Space he wil abate 5s for
it and so brings it to 15s—o. 15. o.

The Remains to Thomas Abbee is .6s 3d.

So that I find for the Plaintiff .6 3d and Cost of Court.

Al things being frankly made appear If at al: I take Abbees demand and Randals account and grant and bring it to as above But
at last refered and adjourned the Court to Thirsday next at one of
the clock both partys having (as they say) further evedence.

Thirsday Feb. 27th 1695/6.

Plantiff and defendant appeared and their Pleas being heard and
what further they had to present, Read and Considered which are
on file I Find for the Plantiff Ten shillings eleven Pence and Costs
of Court as per Bil allowed—16s. 2d (Suspending the 10s 4d for
want of profe present of what is in the .2d. column of his acount) .

[*228] Feb. 27 1695/6.

Complaint being made against William Anthony for horible lying
If not adding cursing etc. I sent a warrant to apprehend him and
bring him before me to answer for the same.

And February 28. 1695/6.

William Anthony being apprehended and brought by the Constable and examined saith he remembers nothing about it and puts
al upon profe: which is evedenced by the Testymonys of Jehojahdah
Bartlet and Ephraim Bartlet which are on File whereuppon I sentence said William Anthony for his wittingly abusive reports (which
he is Common in) and so wilfully speaking falls by (Timothy Moses
being present and saying al is utterly false, and Anthony himselfe
granting it: and owning noe provocation)   That he the said William
Anthony shal Forthwith Pay a Fine of sixe shillings downe in Money
and pay the charges or else be whipt with Ten lashes by the constable
and If he doe not depart the Place within .2. days Then to be committed by the constable til he find surtys in five Pound Bond for his
good Behaviour.

   1s   the writ
   1s   to the Constable and
   1   for a man to watch over him.
   ——
   3s   [*Marginal notation.*]

Feb.27. 1695/6.

Mathew Noble of Westfeild Being Summoned to appeare this day to answer John Gun of Westfeild in a Plea of Trespass for Felling and Taking away Pine Trees of said Guns Ground Granted him by the Towne for turpentine to said Guns damage 40s.

John Gun absenting: The Defendant Mathew Noble demands his Costs and charges which by Reson of the constabls not returning the Summons: Three men (as on file) [which is on File viz Thomas Myryk, John Myryck, Adiya Dewey oaths (*Marginal notation.*)] made oath to the Constable Deputy John Sackcuts serving the summons: Read it and required Nobles appearing accordingly: Wheruppon I Grant the Defendant Mathew Noble his Costs viz 2s and a witness to himselfe that was summoned viz .2s Deacon Nathanel Dolbee appearing. For the plantiff to pay: unless he should make appeare that the defect is in the constable for not returning the summons and then said Noble is to pay it.

[*229] Dec: 1st 1696.

Mr. Nicholaus Aurault of Springfeild Plantiff against William Holmes Taylor (late Resident in Springfeild at the House of Hezekiah Dickenson) according to attachment (returned and served on a coate partly made) to the value of Three Pounds, for a debt due to said Nicholaus Aurault by Booke to the value of one Pound eleven shillings sixpence. William Holmes being Three times Caled. The Atachment was read which is on File and return being that it was served upon a certaine Broadcloth Cote of William Holmes (which cloth he had of Doctor Nicholaus Aurault) the coate in part made and one dozen and 8 Buttons, al apprised at .33s 8d and said Holmes Having notice of it according to Law by a Summons left at his place of aboad viz at the House of Hezekiah Dickenson in Springfeild where Holmes kept: said Summons being produced and sworne to: I proceded upon Doctor Auraults presenting his acount taken out of his booke produced; and sworne to the truth of it, and that it was a Just debt amounting to one Pound eleven shillings six pence, which account Compared with the Booke is on File: wherfore I Find accordingly for the Plantiff one Pound eleven shillings and Sixpence and Costs of Court as per Bil allowed, Seven shillings Sixpence.

JOHN PYNCHON

Execution Granted out the same day, and returned Dec .2d 1696: That he, Samuell Stebbin Constable of Springfeild had served it on a broad cloth cote and 20 Buttons Prised at .33s 8d and noe more delivered it accordingly to Nicholaus Ayrault and that noe more estate can be found nor the Body of said Holmes to sattisfie Costs.

Dec: 8th 1696.

Mr. Nicholas Ayrault of Springfeild Doctor, Plantiff against Thomas Roote of Northampton Senior according to attachment (returned by the Sheriff (that he had served it the .28th day of November 1696. upon a Cow in said Rootes yard which his wife said was his) to the value of (nere) Three Pounds and left Summons at the said Rootes house with his wife for his appearence accordingly this .8th of December at .9. of the Clock before noone, To answer Mr. Nicholas Ayrault of Springfeild in a Plea concerning Money long due to said Ayrault By Booke to the value of .29. or Thirty Shillings: etc. Thomas Roote being .3. times Caled The Attachment was read which is on File and said Rootes Having notice of it according to Law by Summons left with his wife as the Sherif his return attests: I proceeded upon Doctor Ayraults presenting his account taken out of his Booke said Booke being produced and Sworne to its being a true and Just debt amounting to the Sum of one Pound Nine shillings which account compared with the Booke is on File: wherefore I find accordingly for the Plaintiff one Pounds Nine shillings to be paid in Porke or otherwise to his Content and Costs of Court as per Bil allowed Eight shillings:

[*230] Jan. 28th 1696/7.

David Froe of Suffeild Plantiff contra James King of Suffeild Defendant (according to Summons returned served) in a Plea concerning 10s Money due to the Plantiff for Horse Hire to the value of Forty shillings damage as shalbe made appeare. The Plantiff appearing (The defendant James King .3. times Caled and not answering or appearing) upon the Plantiff urging to my proceeding: I Declared that James King the defendant had bene with me on the .26th day of this Instant January, and acknowledged a Judgment against himself, Confessing Ten shillings Money due from him to the Plantiff David Froe, which he said King said he would pay him: Therefore I said it would ease the charges in part, But giving in his Bil of Costs Just then James King the Plantiff [sic] came in and so I proceeded: The Defendant now in Court owning the oweing him Ten shillings money: which he paid downe to him in Court:

So there is only the Bil of Costs to be allowed, which being given in and is on File amounts to .9s 8d allowed as per Bil on File: and said King paid downe the Money viz the .9.8d costs to Froe.

April: 5: 1697.   10s Fine to the King:

William Peirce of Suffeild being brought before his Majesties Justices of the Peace Colonel John Pynchon, Esq. and John Holyoke and accused for that he did on the fourth day of this Instant April: Travel from Suffeild to Pequanicke (being the Lords Day) and there did enter the house of Nathanell Owen of said Pequanicke and did felloniously take away of said Owens goods viz porke Beife butter a bar of Lead and a pair of Ocurn Breetches also some powder, did Confess his theft and hath restored the said Goods to the owner: and said Owen not prosecuting said Peirce: yet It being needful to bear witness against such Crimes viz. such Robbery committed on the Lord day the said Justices do adjudg that said Peirce be whipt on the naked body with Eight stripes four as a punishment for his profaning the Sabbath day and four stripes for his said theft [*231] and that the Constable that brought him before the Justices do take said Peirce under his own custody to Suffeild, and so keep him til the said Punishment of Whiping be performed as aforesaid by said Constable also that said Peirce do pay al charges occasioned by the foresaid Crimes comitted by him: Saveing unless the said Peirce do pay as a Fine unto the said Constable viz Victory Sikes: fifteen shillings before he puts him said Peirce from his Custody, five shillings whereof he said Constable is to deliver to the Suffeild Town Treasurer for the use of their poor, and the other Ten shillings he is to deliver to said Justices.

Received the 10s of Victory Sikes the Constable April 10th. 1697. which Mr. Holyoke and I shared as part of our dues for the Sessions service.

April .12th 1697.

Luke Hitchcock of Springfeild Senior, Plantiff against John Trumbel of Suffeild Senior defendant (according to attachment returned served on a coverlid Rug, and warming Pan of said Trumbels) notice and warning thereof being left at said Trumbels House In a Plea concerning Twelve shillings Money due to the Plantiff Luke Hitchcock for .2. pair of shooes To the value of 24s damages as it shal appeare etc. The Plantiff appearing, The defendant John Trumbel .3. times Caled and not answering or appearing I adjourned to .2. aclock in the afternoone: when Victory Sikes in Trumbels behalfe appeared and tooke up the matter with Luke Hitchcok which Luke sent to me under his hand: and so Issued this case Victory Sikes paying 1s for the Atachment.

April 20th 1697.

Benjamin Dibble Summoned to appeare this day and Summons returned served and he warned on April 12th 1697. Said Dibbel not appearing to answer Samuel Howard (according as on File the summons appears:) I issued out a warrant of Contempt for taking his

Body and bringing him before me the 22th of this April at 10 of the clock as wel to answer Samuell Howards Plea as for this Contempt.

April.22. 1697.

Benjamin Dibble appearing (the Constable of Suffeild according to warrant of Contempt Bringing him and returning said warrant which is File), Says as to the matter of Contempt that he really mistooke the day Intended to come, and so the Constable says that when he tooke him he at first word said he was summoned for Thursday he tooke it not on Tuesday But Thirsday: and would have appeared This Thirsday wherefore as to the matter of Contempt I se cause to Pass it over: as to his answering Samuell Howard Plea he is ready and it proceeds as follows over the leafe.

[*232] April 22th 1697.

Samuell Howard of Hartford (appearing by his attourney Hezekiah Dickenson) Plantiff against Benjamin Dibbel of Suffeild Defendant: The Defendant desiring to agree which Hezekiah Dickenson accepted He withdrew his Plea: and Victory Sikes and Richard Austin giving Bil to pay Hezekiah Dickenson 25s Money by the 22 of July next who were secured By Benjamin Dibbel Mortgaging .1. acre of Land to said amount.

Henry Rogers of Springfeild making Complaint That certaine Baggs left in his custody by John Noble of Westfeild, and under his care were taken away by James Petty, Contrary to his the said Rogers his mind and in opposition to his said Rogers his son John who forbid James Petty his taking them away whereupon said Petty struck said son of Henry Rogers which also said Rogers Complaines of: upon which said Petty was Summoned to answer for his Misdemeanors This 20th of April 1697. as per Summons returnd and the Constable finding of the Baggs: which he was ordered upon finding them to deliver them to said Rogers and accordingly had done it: only That upon David Morgans Ingaging (because the Bags were ful and it would be Inconvenient to empty them in the open Boate) I permitted their going down with them on David Morgans Ingaging: That James Petty should appeare and answer al before me when Caled and appointed: which hath bene deferred til now this 10th of May 1697: [Henry Rogers coming to me May .8. 1697 That I would apoint a time which I did to be this 10 May 1697 the case being referred thereunto] [*Marginal notation.*] when They not having agreed matters, I proceed as followeth:

May .10th 1697.

David Morgan as Ingaging for James Petty appearing and James Petty also present and answering: Likewise Henry Rogers present as

Complainant against James Petty saith the Bags were disorderly taken away out of his Custody by James Petty and that James Petty struck his son John Rogers: etc. the summons returned which is on File.

The Bags were disorderly and violently taken away as per Testymonys on File, yet Inasmuch as it also appears that David Morgan had an allowance and hath Compounded with John Noble it abates the Injury so that I find or allow Henry Rogers his charges and Costs in this, and as to the other part of his Complaint against James Petty for striking his son which also is evidenced by the Testymonys of said John Rogers and John Miller which are on File I adjudge said James Petty To pay him said Rogers five shillings and also a Fine to the King of .3s 4d and Costs as per Bil alowed Henry Rogers 6s 8d.

3s 4d Fine to the King (not had) . [*Marginal notation.*]

[*233] May 11th 1697.

Mr. William Gibbons (late of Hartford now) of Boston Merchant, Plantiff contra Thomas Moorley of Westfeild according to attachment returned served on some land etc. To the value of .2£ 2s 6d for answering of a debt due on account as per Booke to the value of one Pound one shilling and 3d.

The Plantiff appearing, also the Defendant Thomas Moorely, who acknowledges a Judgment against himselfe Confessing one Pound one shillings and Three pence due from him to Mr. William Gibbons aforesaid, in eight bushels and halfe of Indian Corne at Hartford So there is only the Bil of Costs allowed which is the Atachment and Summons .2s. serving it .1s 4d and the acknowldges Judgment .1s which Mr Gibbons paid for him alis 4s 4d added and allowed.

JOHN PYNCHON

Memorandum Execution granted October 22. 1698 [*Marginal notation.*]

May 19th 1697. Thomas Mighil .6s. Fine: to the King.

Thomas Mighil of Suffeild being Summoned before me to answer his Breach of the Peace, in striking of Robert Old of Suffeild, beating and wounding him Sometime in February last which they have Compounded as to the Damage to Robert Old But it being a great Breach of the Peace: which said Thomas Mighil now appearing according to Summons and owning the Same Falling under it, Saying he was in a Pashon and thereby disordered so that he struck and wounded Robert Old which he is very sorry for as he says, and wil be more careful and orderly for time to come: acknowledging it, without putting any thing of it upon profe I se noe cause to Bind him over to the Sessions: only Fine him to the King Sixe shillings Money: and dismiss him he being Penitent and very Ingenious also Ingaging watchfulness and good cariage for future: But he is to pay the charges summons serving it and attendance al being about .4s.

July .1st 1697.

Thomas Huxley of Suffeild Plantiff against Edward Scot formerly of Suffeild now of New Haven: said Huxley declaring the defendant Edward Scot was absent I deferred Hearing the Case to the beginning of next weeke: If said Edward Scot might come by the .5th of July:

July .5th 1697.

Thomas Huxley of Suffeild (againe appearing as) Plantiff contra Edward Scot defendant according to attachment returned served, and prosecuting his Plea of Debt due by Booke to the value of Thirty nine shillings due to said Huxly: Edward Scot the defendant being .3. times Caled: The Atachment was read, and the return by the Constable of Suffeild being That it was served on the goods of Edward Scot viz Two chests and that within them and on an Iron Kettle and little wheele (now in the Constable of Suffeilds hands viz Quinton Stockwel Huxley declaring that he had Indeavored to send word of it and given notice to Edward Scot: I proceeded upon Thomas Huxly his presenting his account out of his Booke of accounts. To which said Thomas Huxly made oath that it was a True account and a true and Just debt ever since 1692 never having Received one Penny of it I find for the Plantiff Thomas Huxly .39s and Costs of Court as per Bil allowed .7s 6d.

Execution issued out same day for 2.6.6d and 2s the execution.

[*234] July .29th 1697.

Mr. Nathanel Bissal of Windsor Plantiff contra Benjamin Dibbel defendant, according to Summons returned served (which was read and is on File) in a Plea concerning dues to said Bissal by Booke to the Sum of one Pound Thirteene shillings .6d with due damages:

The Plantiff Nathanel Bissal appearing by his Attourney Hezekiah Dickenson.

The defendant Benjamin Dibbel .3. times caled not answering nor appearing upon the Plantiff urging because the Summons was duely served and so returned by the officer) That I would Issue out a warrant of Contempt (I could not deny it, But) deferred the same til another time If it be come for within a weeke or 10 days and so at present only tooke the account out of Bissals Booke which is on File Sworne unto per Bissal and to his Booke presented.

Oct. 28. 1697.

Michael Towsely of Suffeild Summoned to appeare before me this day to answer Benoni Banes of Suffeild his Plea about a mare valued at 39s Money Summons as also Atachment being returned served by the Constable of Suffeild under his hand: said Towsley not appearing being .3. times Caled: I Issued out a warrant of Contempt to the Constable of Suffeild for his Taking said Towslys Body and bringing him before me on the .8th of November ensueing at 10 of the clock in the Forenoone as wel to answer Benoni's Plea as for his said Towslys contempt in not appearing.

Memorandum: John Pynchon Register for Deeds etc. Sworne:

Mr. John Pynchon the .3d: Clerk of the Inferiour Court of Pleas in Hampshire Being allowed and appointed to be the Register of Deeds, Conveyances Morgages etc. within the same County: and ordered to take his oath before one or .2. of the Justices of said Court:

Dec. 28. 1697:

Said John Pynchon appearing Before Two of the Justices of said Court of Pleas viz Capt. Samuell Partrigg and Col. John Pynchon we administered the oath to him accordingly: wel truly and faithfully to Record and Register al Instruments proper to his office as Law Injoynes etc.

[*235A] Nov. 22th 1697.

Joseph Williston of Springfeild Plantiff contra John Kilum of Springfeild (according to Summons and Atachment returned served) in a Plea concerning the delivery of .2. yerling steeres Ingaged to be Joseph Willistons on the Middle of May 1697 In case Kilum did not pay .24s in Money or Tar at Money Price: The Plantiff appearing (the Defendant John Kilum .3. times caled not answering nor appearing) upon the Plantiff urging to proceed I find (the Plantiff producing the agreement which is on File) due said John Kilum: .24s to be paid the Plaintiff Joseph Williston in Money or Tar at Money price and in want thereof the .2. yerling steeres to be delivered to Joseph Wiliston within a weekes time in Case the Money 24s be not paid before that time and Costs of Court as per Bil allowed is Sixe shillings 6d.

They after agreed. [*Marginal notation.*]

March .21th 1697/8.

Hezekia Dickenson of Springfeild Plantiff contra Abraham Temple of Springfeild according to attachment and summons served and returned In a .3. fold Plea upon a Doble Writ the first writ conteining .2. actions.

.1st upon attachment to the value of fifty shillings To answer Hezekia Dickenson in a Plea concerning Dues to him for goods of John Nobles of Westfeild Delivered to Abraham Temple to the value of .24s as shal appeare etc: The Plantiff appearing and also the Defendant Abraham Temple appearing as also John Noble of Westfeild appearing and declaring that Hezekia Dickenson was his factor and Insisting upon the Debt due to him and He said Noble as also Hezekia Dickenson presenting their Booke of accounts wherein goods were delivered to Abraham Temple and part by Noble himselfe and part by Hezekia Dickenson and wife to the value of .23s 8d as in the Booke appeares, and sworne unto per Hezekia Dickenson and his wife who made oath that she delivered the 1st and last particular in the account and John Noble that he delivered the middle particular al amounting to 23s 8d. I find for the Plaintiff as due to John Noble one Pounds Three shillings and eight pence and Costs of Court as per Bil allowed 6s 6d. Abraham Temple appealed from said Judgment and gave Bond:

Temple ownes the .1st and last particular but evades the Middle particular because he says Dickenson delivered them not and so he would not Answer to him. [*Marginal notation.*]

[*The following September 6, 1698 entry in* Hamp. Rec. Ct. Pleas *63 records the hearing of Temple's appeal by the Inferior Court of Common Pleas for Hampshire.*]

Abraham Temple late of Springfeild Appellant Vs. John Noble Appellee From the Judgment Given against Him by John Pynchon Esq. on the 21st of March 1698. Upon an Action brought before the said Pynchon as per the original writt Dated March 7th 1698 etc appears on file.

Both Parties Now appeared And the Case after a full Hearing was Comitted to the Jury who Returned there Verdict that they find a Reversion of the Judgment and Cost of Courts Therefore it is Considered by the Court that the Said be and is Hereby Reversed and that the Said Temple Recover Costs against Said Noble Taxed at one pound Nineteen Shillings and four Pence.

2.ly For said Abraham Temple his Ingaging to cut Three load of wood and deliver to Hezekia Dickenson which said Temple neglects to performe: Temple owning the .3. load of wood and saying it is cut and ready in the wood: and that he gave Hezekiah Dickenson notice of it: I find the .3. load of wood to be delivered to Hezekia Dickenson by to Morrow night and Dickenson to receive it (the said loads) and Then Temple to be discharged: otherwise to make good .3 load of wood and Costs of Court.

[235B] 3dly Hezekia Dickenson Plantiff against Abraham Temple in a Plea of Defamation according to particular Summons Returned Served for his said Temple his Reproching said Dickenson by Saying writing or in a Libellous manner declaring or Publishing That Hezekia Dickenson was a Theife a lyar and whore Master as folks say, To his said Hezekiah Dickensons damage to the value of 40s as shal appeare.

I adjourne the Court to, to Morrow .12 o clock or halfe an houre after, when al partys are to appeare it being said (Barber who is an evedence is not wel) As also what concernes the King and are against his Laws according to particular Summons Then to be herd and Temple I accordingly warned ordered and Ingaged him then to appeare to answer to what shal then be objected against him on his Majesties behalfe.

March 22. 1697/8. Hezekia Dickenson Plantiff against Abraham Temple.

The Plantiff Hezekia Dickenson and the Defendant Abraham Temple appearing The Summons Read etc. The Pleas and evedences in the Case heard and read, which are on File: The defendant says to al, That he is charged with that which he is not guilty of: Yet I find to much Idle base and reprochful writing speeches and carriage by Abraham Temple in Publishing or spreading that which Tends to the defamation of the Plantiff But yet the damage to the Plantiff not being demonstrated what it is and supposing none beleeve any of the reports Concerning him. I therefore leave that matter at present, and Hezekia Dickenson to further process as he shal se cause, as also Temple to his owne way thereabo[ut] for the Future: Each of them now to beare their own charges in the action unless further process be [illegible].

And so Proceed to the other matter which Temple was [par]ticularly Summoned and ordered to answer unto (Namely for his offences or misdemeanors in the particulars aforementioned) that is To answer to the King for saying writing or in a libellous manner spreading or instigating Il reports to his disquieting the Peace of his Majesties subjects which al ought to maintaine.

Temple for Libelling and Criminous Reports Bound to the next Sessions.

Abraham Temple called and appearing I examined him Concerning his Making Publishing Divulging or spreading or promoting of Defamatory Libellous writing or speeches or his unlawful casting abroad Criminous reports: Read the Papers and demonstrations thereof (which are on File) Requiring him to make answer to what

Read and declared before him He said He is not Gilty of what he is charged with and Putting matters upon further profe, I told him John Barber would be an evedence but was not wel to come now, wherefore I ordered him to find Suretys for his good behaviour, and answering for al, and what further misdemeanors thereabouts should on his Majesties [*236A] Majesties behalfe be objected against him, at the next General Sessions of the Peace for this County of Hampshire whether al the Papers shal be Transmitted, and Barbers and other Testimony also: said Temple with Suretys Gave Bond accordingly, which is on File to be Transmitted to the next Sessions.

I likewise ordered Hezekia Dickenson to become Bound then to prosecute (said Temple) on his Majesties behalfe.

March .28. 1698. Present John Pynchon and John Holyoke Esquires .2. of his Majesties Justices of Peace.

Westwood Cooke of Hadly Having on March 10th 1697/8 made his Complaint to John Pynchon of Samuell Partrig of Hadly his Making or Publishing False reports tending to defamation of some persons; particularly That Samuell Partrig of Hadly should say That Westwood Cooke had given False evedence which was Sworne before Capt. Cooke in February last in the case about said Partrigs Servant Girl: etc. I (John Pynchon) Thereupon (at Westwood Cooks desire) sent my writ to the Sherif To Cause said Samuell Partrig Forthwith to appeare at my House in Springfeild or on the Munday following to answer to such matters of Misdemeanor as on his Majesties behalf shalbe objected against him: said writ Read etc.

March 28. 1698.

The Sherif Returns the writ and Says the providence of God hindered it at the Time and So sends him now to Springfeild.

Accordingly March .28. 1698. Samuel Partrig of Hadly appearing to answer to the writ as above which was read. Westwood Cooke also appearing they producing Papers in the Case and Testimonys which are on File.

Samuell Partrig saith That he was charged Falsly to have Struck the Girl and said he never struck her on the Head and that was False. this is that which he spake to that the evedence was false and doth not now owne, but denys that he struck the Girle as Westwood Cooke swears on the Head. However tho was but one evedence of it neither as he says:

Having Herd al that was alledged, read and considered al the Papers which are on file We Find very unmeete and Rash words in particular Samuell Partrig saying [*236B] of one of his Majesties Subjects that he had given a Testymony utterly false and noe truth in it as is testified against Samuell Partrig That he said it not only at that time but Somtime after the Hearing the Case before Capt. Cooke: which Reports tend to defame and abuse his Majesties people and occasion disturbance disquiet and unpeacableness contrary to his Majesties good Laws Wherefore we Fine him said Samuell Partrig to the King Ten Shillings and to beare and pay the charges of prosecuting against him: said Samuell Partrig upon Reading and declaring the Sentence above: Appeales from said Sentence unto the next Court of General Sessions of the Peace to be Held within said County and gave Bond according to Law.

14s. allowed as per Bil [*Marginal notation.*]

But afterward withdrew his appeale: standing to the (above) sentence: and so his Bond is void and al further prosecution ceases.

July .12th 1698.

Luke Hitchock of Springfeild Senior Cordwainer Plantiff against Joseph Wolcot late of Brookefeild Defendant according to attachment returned served (and Summons left at his said Woolcots Place of usual or last aboad there) on the 24th of June 1698, upon about .30. acres of Land of said Woolcots lying or being at the Place or Towne Caled Brookfeild when was present at the serving of it Benjamin Smith of Westfeild and John Gillet The summons left at Henry Gilberts Garrison for Giving Wolcot notice of it for his appearence accordingly this 12th day of July 1698 at .9. of the clock in the Forenoon:

Luke Hitchcock aforesaid appearing Atachment Read (which is on File) Joseph Woolcot .3. times caled and not answering or appearing waiting til .10. a clock, and past, I proceeded upon Luke Hitchcocks presenting his Booke of account wherein said Woolcot is Debtor .2. 8. 3. and hath Credit .1.10.1. To which account and Booke said Luke Hitchcock made oath which is on File so that I find accordingly for the Plantiff .18s and Costs of Court as per Bil allowed 12s 8d.

John Pynchon is .5s 8d. [*Marginal notation.*]

[*237] Aug. 12th 1698.

Joseph Williston of Springfeild Plantiff contra Mr. Pelatiah Glover of Springfeild defendant They withdrew and agreed:

Aug. 22th 1698. John Miller late Constable for not collecting the Towne Rates:

Presentment of the Selectmen Jonathan Burt and Ensign Joseph Stebbins, Samuel Bliss Senior, James Warriner.

Upon Complaint of the late Selectmen of Springfeild in the year

1697 and of the Towne Treasurer or Receiver for the Towne Rates in 1697 Ensign Joseph Stebbins:

That John Miller late Constable of Springfield in the yeare 1697 neglected and neglects to Collect the last yeares Towne Rates Committed to him for which Neglect according to Law he forfeits .20s per Month: said John Miller being convented before me and appearing: puts it upon profe of his neglect: whereupon The Selectmen present—Deacon Jonathan Burt etc. presented the Towne Booke or Selectmens booke of accounts wherein is writ Feb. .23d 1697/8 delivered to John Miller Constable to gather in the sum of .12£ 01s 10d it being unpaid part of the Rate for to pay the Schole Master and representative To which said Jonathan Burt, Samuel Bliss made oath this 22 August 1698 Before me John Pynchon also they affirm they gave out Warrants for collecting it   Hence it being evident That said John Miller late Constable hath neglected gathering in or clearing accounts of the Rates not only the first .3. months after his yeare expired, but hath neglected after that now more than .2. Months since and the law being Plaine that he is lyable to forfeite 20s per Month for every month afterward: His being very evidently lyable there I Doe find said John Miller Gilty of the breach of said Law or Forfeiture viz 20s per Month for .2. Months since sometime in June last, which is to say That John Miller is to pay in 40s accordingly: forthwith to the Selectmen or Towne Treasurer for the use of the Pore of the said Town of Springfeild and in case of said Miller's default or neglect of paying in said 40s it is to be Levyed by distress upon his goods and chattels.

John Miller appealed from said Sentence unto the next Sessions of the Peace to be held at Northampton and Gave Bond accordingly as is on File: [Se also over the leafe John Millers discharge (*Marginal notation.*)] Se over the leafe forward John Miller withdrawing his appeale.

Aug. 23. 1698.

John Ferry late constable of Springfeild in the yeare 1697 summoned together with the Selectmen appearing viz Decon Burt, Samuel Bliss, James Warriner, Towne Treasurer or Receiver Ensign Joseph Stebbins who complained against him that he said John Ferrey hath not collected or Issued his accounts of the last yeares Towne Rates Committed to him by said Selectmen and hath neglected it more than .2. Months besides the first .3. Months next after his year expired whereby he is by Required by Law to pay and forfeit 20s per Month for each Months neglect afterwards said Ferry appearing and answering saith That he denys it that he hath neglected: putting it to him whether he had Issued accounts about said Rates he said noe:

and said he doth not owne yet that he had a Rate either from the Treasurer or Receiver, or from the Selectmen and [*238] and they must make that appeare: upon which Deacon Burt said we affirm we delivered him the Rate and produced the Towne Booke etc. as in John Miller his answer on the former side wherin it was entered that they deliver him the Schole Masters Rate the 23 February 1697/8 with other accounts and Rates shewn then also as in Said Booke: and Decon Burt made oath both concerning the account in the Booke and to his or some of their delivering him the Rate that very day:

Sworn accordingly before JOHN PYNCHON

Joseph Stebbins further Testified that he saw the Rate several times in Constable John Ferrys hands with some of the Selectmens Names and hands to it, and that he said Ferry accounted with him said Stebbins concerning said sums therein and said Ferry gave him out of it (which I here show) several mens proportions and sums therein who were behind in it.

Sworne to before JOHN PYNCHON

The Select men Moreover say That they Gave the Constables John Miller and Joseph Ferry to each of them Two warrants one at the first when they gave them the Rates: with the Rates in February they gave them warrants John Miller His warrant He readyly tooke it But John Ferry would not take it so that we argued with him aboute neglecting Authority yet he would not take it from our hands, whereupon laying it on the Table he had it afterward as we can prove and he said himself afterward when we asked him to se it because we were Informed it was not sufficient and we would mend it and make it sufficient he then said If that be it you shant se it: nor would he let us have it. However we gave him another warrant which 2d warrant for the same Rates was dated and delivered March 3d 1697/98 as is in the Town Booke presented: which The said Lt. Hitchcock saw and Read per said Ferrys shewing it him (as also James Stevenson knows it) By al which it most evidently appeares (besides his taking in many Rates and crossing them) That said Joseph Ferry had the Rates and that he hath neglected to collect or Issue accounts about them for more than .2. Months since the beginning or end of June last, wherby he hath forfeited .40s per the Law and Doe accordingly Sentence him said Joseph Ferry .40s to be paid the Selectmen or Treasurer to the pore of the Towne of Springfeild and costs of Court.

Said John Ferry appeals from said Judgment to the Court of Sessions in Northampton next, and gave Bond accordingly which is on File.

With drawne and al fals.

[*239] John Miller came to me Aug. .29th 1698, and proposed That he might withdraw or let his appeale Fall, which is on the leafe back August 22. 1698: Inquiring whether it might not be: and he discharged of the Forfeiture which I sentenced him to pay to the Selectmen or Town Treasurer for the pore of the Town for not gathering in the Town Rates. I told him that the end of it that is of declaring that Forfeiture of 40s. was because of his neglect, and in Case he would Redeeme time and get in the Rates If he brought the Towne Treasurer or Receiver Ensign Joseph Stebbins to certifie that he had paid in the Rates or collected them to sattisfaction: I then thought that I might discharge him of the Forfeiture, and would because it was yet with me, So that the .40s declared forfeited Should be Nul and made void upon his withdrawing his appeale and performing the Collecting of said Rates committed to him and clearing his accounts about them with the Towne Treasurer or Receiver Ensign Joseph Stebbins: Upon my Receiving sattisfaction concerning it by Ensign Joseph Stebbins then his and his suretys Bond for prosecuting of his appeale at next Sessions should be delivered up: and the Selectmen Have notice of it That they might not appeare against him on the account at said Sessions:

Ensigne Stebbins came to me this .3d of Sept. 1698 and says That John Miller hath got in the Rates: speakes Pluraly saying They the Constables have got in the Rates that is have taken things and got security excepting of one or .2. of Suffeild or Enfeild which they wil also Looke after and get in, says That al wilbe discharged and fynished next Munday or very soone: and would not have matters proceed to the Sessions.

So I gave him up Millers Bond and have discharged him for appearance Says they have made distress upon al within their precincts and Miller told him he would apprize what distreined and make sale on Munday and pay the Rates delivering the over pluss to the owners.

John Ferrey also came to me this .3d Sept. 1698 (Ensign Joseph Stebbins present) and before Ensign Stebbins Ingaged to Issue al accounts about the Rates in Question and to pay in and Cleare al (of al persons within his precincts that is of the Towne) either on Munday or Tuesday or by this day Senight: to Issue al accounts and cleare al: upon which at his desire and his withdrawing his appeale: I doe dispence with his forfeiture and declare it Nul he performing as before Ingaged and doe deliver up his Bond to him: and set him at liberty from appearing at the Sessions.

He is to cleare al with the said Ensign Stebbins that are of the Towne and to doe his utmost to get in the due from al persons out of Towne and pay the same in to the Treasurer.

[*240] Feb. 8th 1698/9.

John Stedman of Wethersfeild appearing as attourney and in behalfe of Mr. Gershom Bulkley of Wethersfeild Phisitian: and presenting a Bil of 12s Mony due from Robert Old of Suffeild to said
Mr. Gershom Bulkley said Bil dated July .10th 1695 and payable the
last day of January ensueing witnessed per George Norton, Thomas
Treate. Robert Old of Suffeild appearing: and owning the Bil: Con-
fessess Judgment against himselfe for the Sum of .12s Money to Mr.
Gershom Bulkly (to be paid next May).

Feb. 14th 1698/9.

Alexander Allen of Windsor presenting a Bil of forty shillings
Money due to him from John Petty of Springfeild said Bil dated
14. Feb. 1695/6 payable the last day of April 1696 as witnessed per
James Mackman and Samuell Frost said John Petty appearing and
owning the Bil and his hand and seale thereunto: Confesses Judgment against Himselfe for said Sum of Forty shillings Money due to
the said Alexander Allin This done and acknowledged this 14th Feb.
1698/9:

Before me JOHN PYNCHON Justice Peace

With .12d more for the acknowledgement.

[*241] Feb. 20th 1698/9.

Major Jonathan Bul of Hartford Plantiff against Samuell Dewey
of Westfeild Defendant (according to Summons returned served) in
an action of Debt due by Bil to the value of thirty one Shillings. The
Plantiff appearing by his attourney Hezekia Dickenson Also the Defendant Samuell Dewey appeares and seing the Bil and acknowledging it, Confesses Judgment against himselfe for Thirty one shillings
due to Major Jonathan Bul of Hartford this 20th Feb. 1698/9.

attests JOHN PYNCHON

To be added

For taking the acknowledgement of Judgment	.1s od	
The writ	.1. o	4s which 4s
Serving it .1s and the Constable goeing 4 Mile More to serve it is 3 per mile	2. o	Samuell Dewey Paid to Dickenson Major Bulls at-tourney

March .6th 1698/9.

Major Jonathan Bul of Hartford Plantiff against Thomas Copley
of Suffeild (and his wife) as administrator to the estate of Samuell
Taylor of Suffeild deceased in an action of debt for moneys due to

said Bulle from Samuell Taylor deceased according to Summons returned served and for the Sum of .21s 5d. The Plantiff appearing by
his attourney Hezekia Dickenson Also the defendant Thomas Copley appearing: The Pleas and Evedences in the case herd and read
etc: The plantiff and defendant goeing together and discoursing:
The Plantiff Thomas Copley came and acknowledged the debt and
Confesses Judgment against himselfe on the account of Samuell Taylor for 21s 5d due to Jonathan Bul of Hartford: this 6th of March
1698/9.

attests John Pynchon.

To be paid by the last of June next in pay: he Ingages to pay it in
Bords as they goe for pay: also .5s charges Money viz .1s summons .1s
acknowledgment Judgment and .3s the Marshals serving it.

John Pynchon

Dickenson promised that If it were not ful 3s to the Marshal he
would allow it in abatement. [*Marginal notation.*]

March 15 1698/9.

Luke Hitchcock Senior of Springfeild Plantiff against Isaac Frost
of Springfeild husbandman according to Summons returned Served
in an action or Plea concerning Moneys due to said Hitchcock upon
Ballance of accounts about a Horse agreed: To the Sum of seventeen
shillings Money or there about according as shal appeare with damages Plantiff and defendant both appearing: The plantiff presenting
the Sale of the Horse and delivery of it to the defendant and that
payment towards it was to the sum of .5.13s as the plantiff ownes to
have Received: wanting 17s to make up the sum of sixe Pounds Ten
shillings the price of the Horse agreed: I find for the Plantiff Seventeene shillings money and Costs of Court as per Bil allowed Seven
shillings I say .7s.

[*242] July .31. 1699.

Joseph Williston of Springfeild Plantiff contra: Ephraim Bartlet
of said Springfeild (according to Summons returned served) in an
action or Plea of debt for seven days worke: etc The Plantiff .3. times
called and not appearing The defendant appearing after an houre
and more waiting, demanded his Costs: which I granted him according to Bil   .1s 10d ⎫
and Nonsute   1   0   ⎬ 2s 10d
                          ⎭
The constable present attested his serving it.

Aug. 12. 1699.

John Web of Springfeild Brought before me by the Marshal and
Sherifs Deputy: upon Samuell Cross of Windsor his having a writ
out against him for Stolen goods: which upon Serch a Gun barrel

being found in the Smiths shop at Westfeild Daniell Nash: who produced said small barrel of a Gun: and John Web being apprehended
and present, owned That he took the Gun from Samuell Cross his
house: and caryed the Barrel of it to Daniel Nashes (where he laid
it in the woods a Trees falling had broken the Stock and so he lost
the Lock there) which he said Web ownes he stole from Samuell
Cross in a Druken fit [illegible] nere .2. yeares since: not knowing
what he did then But now ownes it and is sorry for it etc. I fine him
for his said Misdemeanor Ten shillings, and to pay al charges in prosecution: and stand committed til the sentence be performed and
leave Samuell Cross to his Remydy in Law.

[*243] October .2d 1699.

Mr. William Gibbons sometime of Hartford now of Boston Merchant Plantiff Contra Abel Leanord of Springfeild Taylor in an action or Plea of debt Due to him said Gibbons To the Sum of Twenty
six shillings and .10d neglected to be paid to the damage of Forty
shillings Benjamin Leanord being .3. times Called and not appearing
Summons served returned and Read: the Sherrifs deputy present
who underwrit his Serving it and warning Leanord to appear attest-
ing the same also. After long waiting and .3. times called said Leanord not appearing. (His default I record: and the Plantiff producing
also his booke and making oath to it I find as per Coppy of the account from his Booke on File) .26s 10d [illegible] due to the Plantiff
and Costs of Court as per Bil allowed 14s al is .40s 10d.

[The above entry has been crossed out.]

This Sentence or Judgment I presently made void and Nul, be
for ever it was it was made known to said Benjamin Leanord in his
absence declaring to the Plantiff Mr. Gibbons that I revoke it the
same day and that because the Law is that If the defendant appeare
not upon Summons by a Justice a writ of Contempt is to goe out
and so left the plantiff to procede in that way: making Nul that above
this 2d Oct. 1699 as fully as If it had never been and so is noe Judgment at al being Imediately Recaled and not at al declared to the defendant. The next day they agreed and Issued all matters.

JOHN PYNCHON.

Oct .3d 1699:

Mr. William Gibbons sometime of Hartford now of Boston Merchant Plantiff:

[The remainder of the page is blank.]

[*244] Dec. 9th 1699.

Nathanel Treadway who was sent for by Summons on Dec. .1st
1699 To answer to some reflective speeches of his against Mr. Joseph

Hayward But then was not wel or able to come as the Constable then said. Now this .9th December said Treadway appearing Mr. Joseph Haward also present: Treadway desires God to forgive him al his sins and his uncle Mr. Joseph Hayward to forgive him for his speeches Concerning him reflecting on him, and acknowledges and says he had noe Cause to say anything of Mr. Hawards being Privy to his cloathes being gon (which were found in the house in which James Mirick Lived formerly by the Mil) Though How they Came there he says he knows not But doth noe way Impute it to Joseph Hayward: and is very sorry for what he said thereabouts and as now he cleares said Haward so If (or when ever caled to it He wil Publikely doe it also: and says what he said to Constable Tilly Mirick was partly from his said Miricks words to him and some mistaking of them, and desires forgiveness for al declaring That he never knew Mr. Hayward taxed or questioned about any such things as taking other mens things in any dishonest way acknowledging what he said looking that way to be very evill and intreates his uncle to forgive him and he wil be more watchful here after.

This Read to Nathanel Treadway he ownes and acknowledges before me.   JOHN PYNCHON
and so said Treadway was discharged at present.

His uncle Haward accepting his acknowledgement.

[*245] Hampshire July 12th 1700.

Joseph Cooley of Springfeild Husbandman Plantiff contra Edward Kibbey of Enfeild husbandman defendant (according to Summons returned Served) in an action or Plea of Trespass For That the said Edward Kibbee, hath Mowed or cutt downe his the said Cooleys grass on his Meddow at Fresh Water Brooke, and thereby defaced and hindred his the said Joseph Cooleys Improvement there to the damage of said Cooley forty shillings or as shal appeare with other due damages: Both partys appearing, Summons being Read and the defendant owning he was Summoned accordingly.

The Pleas heard and evedences in the Case produced by the said Plantiff read who Insists upon this That he had and came to the land or Meddow, which the defendant hath cut the Grass off: By and from his Father Benjamin Cooley deceased: his willing it to him This Meddow being that part which upon Devission of his Fathers Land, fel to him the Plantiff to be his share of what land his Father long Injoyed and Possessed for .30. or 40 years since to now From which time it hath ever bene in the Possession and Quiet Improvement of the said Benjamin Cooley and in his children since his the said Benjamin Cooleys death: And particularly this Meddow of about five

acres on Fresh Water Brook hath beene in his the said Joseph Cooleys Possession and Improvement always since the devission propor-
tioning or stateing each childs share or part in our Fathers Land
about or nere .13. yeares since So that the Land being his said Joseph
Cooleys and appearing by the Testimonys produced to which he refers to be in his said Coolys quiet and rightful Improvement and possession He is Trespassed upon by the defendant Edward Kibbee and
therefore sues and expects damages according to the Trespass appearing:

The defendant Replys he is noe Trespasser for that the Land
doth not appear to be Joseph Cooleys nor that he hath Legal right
to it To which I ansered we are not now to Judge Legal right to
Land but it appears that he said Cooly from his Father came to and
Injoyed this Land and hath ben in Posession of this without ejection
or any one Challenging and therefore it is necessary Kibbee plead
Title and wil prosecute at the Court of Pleas I find him the Plantiff
in Possession that the Trespass done him.

The defendant says only That He Judges The Plaintiff is not
seized in Law so as to have Trespass allowed though he declins
pleading title to the Land at present for That that He bring special
matter and partake against its being a Trespasse and so would waite
But [illegible] al that Defendant neglecting and refusing to become
Bound to prosecute Title at the [illegible] and the Law says in such
cases the Justice shal award Damages according to what shalbe made
out and costs. It appears and is owned by the defendant that he [il-
legible] the defendant hath cut about ½ an acre or nere one acre cut-
ing the grass thereon which hath been long in the plantiffs Improvement [illegible] about [illegible] and [illegible] I find for the Plantiff
Two shilings and costs of Court as per Bil allowed .15s 10d—3s 10d
of it is to my selfe.

The Defendant appeales from this Judgment and hath given
Bond to the [illegible] of foure Pounds to prosecute his appeale at
next Court of Pleas [illegible].

[*The following September 3, 1700 entry in* Hamp. Rec. Ct. Pleas
*98–99 records the hearing of Kibbee's appeal by the Inferior Court
of Common Pleas for Hampshire.*]

Edward Kibbee of Enfield In the County of Hampshire Husbandman
Appellant Vs. Joseph Cooley of Springfield Husbandman Appellee From
the Judgment of John Pynchon Esq. Justice of Peace upon In an action
or Plea of Trespass brought by the Appellee then Plaintiff against the
appellant Then Defendant (on the .12th July Last Past) For that the
Said Edward Kibbee Hath Mowed or Cut Down his the Said Cooleys

Grass in his meadow at Freshwater Brook etc Which said Judgment was Rendered the said Cooley Should Recover against said Kibbee Two Shillings and Costs Both Parties Now appeared; And The Appellant withdraws this action, It is by the Court therefore Considered the said Joseph Cooley Recover against the said Kibbee Two Shillings money Damage and Cost of Court Taxed at one pound one shillinge.

[*246] Hampshire July 29 1700.

Mr. Nathanel Bissel of Windsor husbandman Plantiff contra Andrew Miller of Enfeild Blacksmith defendant (acording to attachment returned) in an action or Plea of Trespase for unlawfully or unjustly taking away and withholding from him said Bissel his Plow Irons, to the damage of said Bissel .40s Money as shal appeare with other damages.

Having entered this upon the return of the Atachment to me expecting the appearance of the partys and waiting a while yet neither party appeared: so it drops and wholy Fals.

Aug. 9. 1700.

Eliakim Cooly of Springfeild husbandman Plantiff against Thomas and John Hale of Enfeild Husbandmen defendant in an action or Plea of Trespase (according to Summons returned served) For that the said Hale Mowed or Cut down said Eliakim Cooleys his Grass on his said Coolys Meddow at Fresh Water Brooke in Enfeild to the damage of said Cooly .20s or as shal appeare with other damages: Both partys appearing that is to say Plantiff and one of the defendants viz John Hale: (Thomas Hale being disabled as his Father who appeared gives account etc.) : The said defendant John Hale owning he was Summond and Thomas Hale Senior desyring he may answer for his sons both of them and particularly for Thomas absent: (Pleas herd and evedences in the Case Read which are on File) Having Herd this far, before further proceeding: the defendant John Hale and Thomas Hale also [illegible] by his attourney His Father Thomas Hale senior appearing for him not only Saying that Thomas Hale absent was his Son and under him but that he came for him and tooke the case as his owne his sons being under him and Imployed by him and desyred me to enter it and make a Record of it which accordingly I Doe that he for Thomas Hale the Father Joines Issue in the matter and Thereupon Pleads Title: and desires me to enter that which I here doe That he said Thomas Hale Senior as defendant joins Issue and doth demur and Justifie upon Plea of Title to the land whereby the matter of Fact by Law is taken pro Confesso: and the Partys Thomas Hale senior and John Hale, became Bound and enter in Recognizance with surety in the sum of Ten Pounds to persue his Plea and bring forward a Suite for Tryal of his Title to said land at Enfeild at the next Inferior Court of Comon Pleas to be holden for this County as per said Bond to Eliakim Cooly of 10s in case of not prosecuting.

So this case ended That I have only Hales Bond to present to the next Court of Pleas: giving back the Testimonys to Eliakim Coly as Hale had his also.

[*The following September 3, 1700 entry in* Hamp. Rec. Ct. Pleas *99–100 records the hearing of* Cooley v. Hale *by the Inferior Court of Common Pleas for Hampshire. Apparently the appeal taken from said court to the Superior Court of Judicature was not prosecuted.*]

In an action or Plea of Trespass brought before John Pynchon Esq. Justice of Peace on the 9th day of August Last Past by Eliakim Cooley of Springfield Husbandman then Plaintiff against Thomas Hale Junior and John Hale both of Enfield Husbandmen then Defendants for that the said Hales Mowed or Cut Down said Coolys [hay] on his Said Coolys meadow at Freshwater Brook in Enfielde to his Damage 20s as per the writ Dated the 1st day of said August. The Defendant Thomas Hale of said Enfielde Senior Father of said Thomas Hale Junior and John Hale appearing then before said Justice Desired He might be admitted Defendant In this Action by Reason that the said Thomas Hale Junior and John Hale were under him and Imployed by him etc who was accordingly, admitted Defendant then, by said Justice to Defend said Action, Who then Justified and Demurred upon Plea of Title to the said Land, Who became bound by way of Recognizance in the Sum of Ten pound to be well and truly Paid to the said Eliakim Cooley In Case he should fail of Prosecuting his said Plea and of bringing forward a Suit for the Tryall of his said Title to this Court, as per the Process of said Justice appears, Accordingly the said Thomas Hale Senior the Now Plaintiff appeared and brought forward his said Suit, and the said Eliakim Cooly the Now Defendant appeared appeared also. And the Case after a full Hearing of both parties was Committed to the Jury who Returned there verdict therein upon oath that they find for the Defendant four Shillings and Cost of Court.

It is Therefore Considered by the Court that the Defendant Eliakim Cooley Shall Recover against the Now plaintiff Thomas Hale Senior Four Shillings money Damage And Cost of Courts Taxed at one pound Fifteen Shillings and Nine Pence. The Plaintiff appeals.

Aug. 14th 1700:

Samuel Keepe of Springfield Husbandman Plantiff contra Edward Kibbee of Enfeild defendant according to Summons returned served (to which as entry of the action I refer) in a Plea of Trespass etc. as in the Summons. Both partys appearing: The Plantiff produces Testymony etc. But the defendant Edward Kibbee put a stop to further proceedings and so the Testymonys were Recalled. Justifying and demurring upon Plea of Title to the Meddow, which I here enter and make Record thereof accordingly: said Kibbee Ingaging to Bring forward his Plea at next Inferior Court of Pleas to be Holden at Springfeild in Hampshire.

And said Kibbee with Elisha Kibbee his Father Gave Bond or becomes Bound in the Sum of Ten Pounds to persue his Plea and bring forward his Suite accordingly at next Inferior Court as per said Bond on File and so the Case was dismist:

[*The following September 3, 1700 entry in* Hamp. Rec. Ct. Pleas *100–01 records the hearing of* Keep v. Kibbee *by the Inferior Court of Common Pleas for Hampshire. Apparently the appeal taken from said court to the Superior Court of Judicature was not prosecuted.*]

In an action or Plea of Trespass brought before John Pynchon Esq. one of his Majesties Justices of the peace for said County on the 14th Day of August Last Past by Samuel Keep of Springfield Husbandman then Plaintiff Vs. Edward Kibbee of Enfield Husbandman then Defendant for that the said Edward Kibbee hath Mowed or Cut Down about the Quantity of Two Load of said Samuel Keeps Grass on his said Keeps meadow on the North-Easterly branch of Freshwater Brook So Called within the Town or bounds of Enfield to his Damage Thirty five Shillings as per the writ is Set forth, the said Kibbee then Justified and Demurred upon Plea of Title to the said meadow and became bound before said Justice by way of Recognizance to the said Keep in the Sum of Ten pounds to be well and truly Paid to the said Keep In Case he the said Kibbee should fail of Pursuing his said Plea and of bringing forward a Suit for a Tryall of his said Title to this Court, accordingly the said Edward Kibbee (the Now Plaintiff) appeared In Court and brought forward his said Suit, And the said Samuel Keep the Now Plaintiff appeared also and the Case after a full hearing of both Parties was Comitted to the Jury who Returned there verdict therein upon Oath that they find for the Defendant Two Shillings Damage and Cost of Courts.

It is Therefore Considered by the Court that the Defendant Shall Recover against the said Edward Kibbee the Now plaintiff Two Shillings money Damage and Cost of Courts taxed at one pound Eight Shillings and Nine pence. The Now Defendant appeals.

[*247] Sept. 2d 1700.

Fearenot King of Westfield husbandman Plantiff contra John Sexton of Westfield (Son of James Sexton of Westfield) defendant in an action or Plea of defamation of him said Fearenot King in saying said King was a Theife and had Stolen a Trap from him said Sexton, which is to said Kings damage .20s (according to summons returned served) Both partys appearing Summons being Read Pleas herd and evedences in the Case produced by the Plantiff read (which are on File) I Find For the Plantiff Ten shillings and Costs of Court .11s 6d as per Bil allowed.

.11s 6d costs. [*Marginal notation.*]

The defendant John Sexton appeales from this Judgment his Father James Sexton also Joining Issue with him therein and hath given Bond according to law to the value of forty shillings to prosecute his appeale at next Inferior Court of Pleas at Northampton in December next.

[*The remainder of page is damaged.*]

Sept. 2d 1700.

John St[   ] William Gibbons formerl[   ] Lt. John Parson
    ] by Booke to the S[   ] summons returned [   ]s

Nov 11th 1700

    [   ]al Natha-[   ]al of West[   ] Westfield [   ]ner oft did [   ]ing to a feild Nathanel [   ] proprietors cral [   ]amage app[   ] other damages as shall an [   ]ned served: Both partys Son [   ]edences in the Case produced which are un[   ]nd for the defendant costs of Court

    [   ] Plantiff Contra Nathanel Bancroft of Westfield senior [   ] one him in his land at Westfeild in Posassick Lower field by said [   ]ing down his fence and or going through his Improved land on the 1st of this Instant N[   ]ing his said Land Common and open for Cattle going in To his damage Ten shillings: Both partys appearing, summons Read Pleas herd and evedences in the case produced and read, which are on File I find not the evedences to the Case and so Fynd for the Defendant Costs of Court .7s as per Bil allowed.

    [*248] Jan. 22th 1700/1.

Josiah Marshfeild came before me (John Pynchon) to acknowledge that he had sold strong Drink without lycense, which he desyred me to take notice of and enter it as Informing For the King against himselfe for breach of the Law, which he said was sometime since that he had formerly a Cask of Drink not now, (having not any or none to sell) He is convicted by his owne Confession.

[*The remainder of page is damaged.*]

He further Informes against Joseph Williston for Selling Strong Drink he or his wife or both contrary to Law which he likewise desyred me to Enter, and that he shal produce the time .2. or .3. Months

agoe and within [   ]e says he Informes for the King [   ] and
[   ].

This was before Doctor Read of Simsbury and a lad his uncles
Son whom Josiah Marshfeild brought along with him and in presence
of whom he spake it and declared it to me. [*Marginal notation.*]

[   ]called. and the above Infor[   ]iah Marshfeild present
[   ]trary to Law [   ] He said Williston [   ]hfeild to make
[   ] charged him with [   ]ared him [   ] Sessions [   ]bove)
Aug. .30th [1701].

The Sessi[   ]ld to make Joseph Willisto[   ]d him attendance
with [   ]o   When on the .2d of September 1701 [   ]ns out August .30 1701 [   ]ins should order and Injoyn him [   ] and this
busyness being now referred to the [   ] Sessions or There both
partys appeared with Marshfeild [   ]ere delt in, and Issued, both
as to Williston [   ] Sentence, where it is to be found [   ] said
Sessions.

I having writ out and laid before the said Sessions an attested copy
of my proceedings as above on the 22th of January 1700/1, and the
27th January 1700/1 as above.

[*The following September 2, 1701 entry in* Hamp. Rec. Ct. Pleas
*124 of a Court of General Sessions of the Peace held at Springfield
relates to the above information lodged by Josiah Marshfield against
Joseph Williston.*]

It appearing Upon Information and Confession of Joseph Wilistone
that he had Sold Strong Drink Contrary to Law ordered that he Pay a fine
of four pounds, Whereof forty shillings to Josiah Marshfield the Informer
and the other forty Shillings to the Use of Springfield School.

[*Pages 249 and 250 have been cut out.*]

[*251] Jan. 27 1700/1.

Josiah Marshfeild of Springfeild Brought before me, Being by
Joseph Williston accused of lying etc. in saying (as in the summons)
That he knew nothing of those goods of his taken in execution by or
for Mr. Porter, being hid or conveyed away and for saying at Night
the same day That he had told Col. Pynchon after they were found
that he would take them againe and said Pynchon did not Forbid
him taking them away and David Morgan lingred at the Colonels
house to give him opportunity That he might take them. Al which
being most false said Marshfield present, acknowledges his fault and
that he spake that which was most untrue about it and so prevented
the summoning the witness [Luke Hitchcock Senior, Daniel Morgan,
Theodore Mirick who because he owned it were not sent for] [*Mar-*

ginal notation.] owning what is Charged with in the Summons as above written and declared: His Submission and Sorrow for it saying that with Troble about the busyness He knew not wel, what he said and was a litle out in his head   I only fine him Ten shillings to the King and give him a Fortnights time to pay it.

Feb. 1. 1700/1 10s. fine abated and taken of.

Lt. Col. Partrig moveing in behalfe of Josiah Marshfeild that I would take of the Fine I did accordingly abate it wholy:
[*The remainder of the page is damaged.*]

Jan. 31. 1700/1.

Josiah Marshfield entring Complaint against Luke Hitchcock Senior and Joseph Williston of Springfield for that one or both of them in clandestine way tooke a Deed of Sale of Land by said Marshfeild to them, away out of Mr. Holyokes hand where it was left: from or without his said Marshfeilds delivery of the same or allowance they should have it, and before S[   ]ty given by them for certaine sums of money due or [   ] that Land said Deed of sale refers to: I thereupon [   ] said Hi[   ]cock and Willistons appearing before [   ] of Marshfeild: who appearing say [   ]ney and are ready to give Security [   ] the Deed was They said Mr. John [   ]th it to Record [   ] matter by giving Security for [   ] gave them time to draw aside for d[   ] matters betweene themselves or o[   ] wise to deliver [   ]eed into Mr. Holyoks hands where it was, and from whom it was taken sometime to Morrow and in meane time Forbide the Recorder from Recording it til agreement betwen al partys and matters Issued: al which I read to them and Read and declared it to and before the Register or Recorder and so dismissed al persons.

[*252] March .25. 1701.   Hampshire

Lt. Colonel Samuell Partrigg of Hatfield Esq. Plantiff contra Thomas Cooper late of Springfield husbandman Senior, according to Atachment which is on File returned served on the house lots That part that is orchards Reputed the Estate of said Thomas Cooper, and that a Summons on March 10th 1700/1. was put into and left in the house of said Thomas Cooper as his last place of aboad in Springfield on the west side of the great River at the Place called Agawam.

To answer said Lt. Col. Samuell Partrig in an action or Plea of Debt due by Booke to the Sum of one Pound Sixtene shilings .6d etc. The defendant Thomas Cooper .3. times called and not appearing The Plaintiff considering his remotness etc. was willing to stay and defer proceeding in the case to another time, and so I adjourned that to the .21th of May next at .8. of the clock in the Morning Supposing Thomas Cooper (having notice) wil agree and Issue with the Plaintiff at that time:

The Plantiffs Bil of Costs being on File til then:

Lt. Col Partrig of Hatfield etc. Plantiff contra Thomas Elgar of Suffield husbandman according to Summons returned Served, Both partys appearing Summons read, it being for Debt due by Booke to the Sum of .1£3s said Thomas Elgar confesses Judgment and acknowledges himselfe In debt to said Lt. Col. Partrigg the Sum of one Pound Three shillings in Current Pay and Bil of costs (on File) allowed is .5s al is .1.8.od.

Before me JOHN PYNCHON.

John Web (according to Summons read) Confesses Judgment against himselfe for 40s acknowledging himselfe indebted said Sum in Money to Lt. Col. Partrigg and Costs five shillings: al is .2£.5 .0.

Before me JCHN PYNCHON.

Michael Towsley of Suffield according to Summons Confesses Judgment against himselfe to Lt. Col. Samuell Partrig for .19s and Costs 9s al is one Pound Eight shillings:

Before JOHN PYNCHON.

[A portion of the page is damaged.]

April .7th 1701.

Andrew Miller of Enfield Blacksm[   ] Plantiff contra Nathanel Bissal of Windsor Defendant [   ] to Atachment returned served on the Body of said Bi[   ]e) To answer said Andrew Mil[   ] 40s Money due to him up [   ] Plow and Irons etc. Sold to said Bi[   ] which said Bissal neglects to pa[   ] appears (as per Atachment) Plantiff [   ] evedences in the Case being herd [   ] The Defendant ownes the Barg [   ] the Plaintiff ingaged 40s Money for it [   ]n he was to pay him in Money it remains that the Defendant [   ] payment and he read out of his Booke several, but the Plaintiff disownes many of the things and noe Coppey attested: and the plantiff says Bissal is in his debt and that he hath paid him al his booke account and presents an account out of his Booke of .1£ 18s 4d Bissal owes him, To answer Bissals account: and the 40s for the Plow remains.

Upon al the Pleas and hearring the which I find for the Plaintiff 40s Money Costs of Court as per Bil allowed .17s.

The Defendant appeales to the Inferior Court of Plees on the 3d Tuesday May next and hath given Bond 4£ for prosecuting at said cort to effect.

Ephraim Colton of Enfeild surety.

[*The following May 20, 1701 entry in* Hamp. Rec. Ct. Pleas *109 records the affirmance of Miller's judgment by the Inferior Court of Common Pleas for Hampshire.*]

Andrew Millar of Enfield Blacksmith Complainant Vs. Nathaniel Bissel of Windsor Shewing that on the 7th of April Last before John Pynchon Esq. he Recovered Judgment against said Bissel for 40s money and Cost from which Judgment the said Bissel appealed to this Court but not Prosecuting the Same the said Millars Prayed the said Judgment may be affirmed with Costs. It is by the Court therefore Considered that the said Millar Shall Recover against said Bissel the said Sum of Forty Shillings money Damage and Cost allowed at Forty Shillings and ten pence.

[*253] Sept. 1st 1701.

Mr. John Blackleach of Hartford [*illegible*] by his attourney John Stedman) Plantiff, contra John Noble of Westfeld defendant according to Summons returned Served in a Plea of debt due by Booke of one Pound Two shillings etc. The Plantiff apearing The defendant John Noble not appearing I adjourn the hearing of the case til to Morrow the Plantiff desiring it.

Sept. 2d [1701].

John Noble the defendant appearing: and the Plantiff viz John Stedman of Hartford as Mr. Blackleech attourny shewing his Power etc.) The Plantiff producing an account out of his Booke attested and sworne (which is on File) the defendant owning the debt (though he says he paid it yet giving no demonstration thereof I find for the Plantiff one Pound one shilling .10d $\frac{1}{2}$ in wheat and Pease: and Costs of Court as per Bil allowed eleven shillings which is on File.

October [1701].

Wiliston, about Josiah Marshfields selling Drink:

The both desiring it may be herd at the Sessions Marshfeild to become Bound in 5£ to appeare and answer it there: at Northampton on the first Tuesday of December next: And so I Transmit al the Papers thether and Dismissed them this .3d of November 1701 making noe further Record.

[*The following December 2, 1701 entry in* Hamp. Rec. Ct. Pleas *125 of a Court of General Sessions of the Peace held at Springfield records the hearing of Williston's complaint against Marshfield.*]

Joseph Wilistone Complainant Vs. Joseph Marshfield for Selling Strong Drink without Licence and Contrary to Law the said Marshfield appearing Pleaded not Guilty, and the Case after a full Hearing was Committed to the Jury who Returned there verdict therein on oath that the said Marshfield is Guilty, The Court therefore ordered Marshfield to Pay a fine of four pounds, forty Shillings Whereof to said Wilistone and forty shillings to the Use of the Grammar School in Springfield and Cost of Court Taxed at Nine Shillings.

October .31 1701. Mary Pengillys Fine .5s

Mary Penngilley wife of John Pengilley of Suffield according to writ to the Constable of Suffield being this day Brought before me John Pynchon and appearing accordingly.

Mrs. Younglove also (who was the complainant appearing by her Sons John: Samuell and James Younglove, Charge Mary Pengilly with saying that Mrs. Sarah Younglove came to Springfield to Sweare lyes and Publishing False reports, which Mary Pengilly Denys etc: yet according to the Testimonys which are on File I Proceed.

Mary Pengilly the wife of John Pengilly of Suffield being convicted (though somewhat Barely) of Publishing making uttering or spreading False reports tending to the defamation of particular persons, particularly of Mrs. Sarah Younglove thereby misleading or deceiving others contrary to his Majesties wholesome Laws of the Province: I Doe Fine, the said Mary Pengilley the sum of five shillings to be paid to his Majesty forthwith and upon Consideration of the circumstances of the case doe order each to beare their owne Charges in the Case.

Her hearing being extreme Bad and answering to questions mistaken in what she hath said, so that I Reckne the Fine with the most and therefore order noe costs.

The Testimonys Thomas Smith, John Younglove. Mary Pengillys fine 5s. [Marginal notations.]

Joseph Pomrey Ingages the Mony .5s shal be Paid and wil send it me presently:

[*254] Jan. 8th 1701/2.

Memorandum

Mrs. Mary Parsons widdow desyring to give oath to her Booke of accounts where were entred several things paid to her daughter Hannah now wife to Mr. Pelatiah Glover (as part of her Portion: The Booke being presented and the accounts read, and Considered and Mrs. Parsons cautioned and some amendments made: said widdow made oath to said Booke and accounts amounting to 81£ 06 .09 But upon Mr. Pelatiah Glover his Comming and objecting against one article of 20s for wintering cow and calves etc. shee yeilded to abate it wholy and give in that 20s and so brought the Sum in her

Booke paid to 80£ 6s 9d according as I have writ it in Mrs Parsons Booke and there under my hand attested it, as is to be seene, to which I refer, only enter it here as a Memento.

Jan. 9th 1701/02.

Mr Pelatiah Glover Complaining against Betty Negro for bad Language striking his son Pelatiah who came and was present Charging Betty that shee told him that his Grandmother had killed .2. persons over the River, and had killed Mrs. Pynchon and halfe killed the Collonel and that his Mother was half a witch To which Richard White and Tom Negro gave in evedence that shee so said on Munday Night the .5th of this Instant January, when then Betty owned it that shee had so said etc.

We Find her very Culpable and for her Base Toung and words as aforesaid (also striking said Pelatiah Glover Junior) we Sentence said Betty to be well whipped on the naked Body by the Constable with Ten Lashes wel laid on: which was performed accordingly by Constable Thomas Bliss: Jan.9. 1701/2

Present JOHN PYNCHON Justice Peace: Parson Justice Peace:

[*Pages 255 through 317 are blank or contain lists of marriages which have not been included.*]

[*318] The names of the Freemen in Springfeild this present .8th. of May 1663:

Captain John Pynchon: Leiutenant Elizur Holyoke: Ensigne Thomas Cooper: Joseph Parsons: Miles Morgan: William Branch: John Lamb: Reice Bedortha, John Dumbleton, Griffith Joanes, John Leonard, Jonathan Burt, John Lumbard, Thomas Bancroft; Mr. Pelatiah Glover, Deacon Samuell Chapin, William Warrinar, Thomas Stebbins, Benjamin Mun, Robert Ashley, Samuell Marshfeild, Nathaneel Ely, Benjamin Parsons, Laurence Bliss, Anthony Dorchester, Richard Sikes.

George Colton made free at the General Court May. 3d 1665.

Benjamin Cooly and Nathaneel Pritchard were then also admitted to freedome But being absent were referred to the County Court to be sworne who accordingly tooke their oathes at Springfeild Court, September .26. 1665.

Thomas Mirick admitted to freedome at the General Court in October 1665 and sworne at Springfeild Court, January 17th 1665 [1666] Per Adjournment.

Thomas Day: admitted to freedome, by the General Court in October 1668, and sworne March. 30th 1669 at Northampton Court.

John Keepe: admitted to freedome by the General Cort in May. 1669: and sworne 28th September 1669, at Springfeild Court.

John Barber: Charls Ferry: and John Riley admitted to freedome at the General Court in May 1671. and sworne September, 26. 1671 at Springfeild Court.

Joseph Crowfoote, admitted to freedome at the General Cort October 1672: and sworne at Springfeild Cort September 30 1673.

Mr. John Holyoke admitted to freedom at the General Court in May 1677 and sworne at Springfeild Court in September 1677.

Victory Sikes: Isack Cakebread and Luke Hitchcock admitted to freedome at General Court May 1678 were sworne at Springfeild Court September 1676.

James Warriner: and John Warner admitted to freedome October 1679: sworn at Northampton March .30. 1680.

Mr. Daniel Denton: Japhet Chapin and Samuell Ely admitted to fredome May 1680: sworn at Springfeild September 1680.

Joseph Stebbin: Ephraim Colton, Thomas Colton sworne September 27: 1681.

See .8. leaves further where is a list of Names of al the freemen, as they are this May 1691. [*Marginal notation.*]

[*319] March. 14th 1660/61.

At a meeting of the Freemen of this Towne of Sprigfeild for Nomination of Magistrates: choise of County Treasurer, etc.:

Captain Pynchon commissioner to carry the votes to the shire meeting [*Marginal notation.*]

The freemen according to Law proceeded to give in theire votes in distinct Papers; and choose and appointed Mr. John Pynchon to take their said votes, and to seale them up and carry them unto the shire meeting on the last .4th day of this Instant March: as Law injoynes:

Aprill .30th. 1661.

At a meeting of the Freemen of Springfeild Mr. Elizur Holyoke was Chosen to be theire Deputy for the Generall Court this yeare ensueing, unto whome they have Granted and Deputed full power to deale in all The affaires of this Common wealth wherein freemen have to doe According to Law:

Deputy: Mr. Holyoake:

At the same meeting the freemen gave in theire votes for Election of Magistrates to theire Deputy aforesaid to be by him sealed up and caryed to the Court of Elections according as Law provides:

John Hitchcock sworne to freedome at Springfeild Court September .25. 1683:

Samuell Ball sworne at Northampton Court September 1684.

Daniel Cooly and Increase Sikes Sworne at Springfeild Court September 1684.

See Further about .8. leaves where is a list of the Names of the Freemen in Springfeild according as they are this May 1691.

[*320] Springfeild: .March 13th. 1661/62.
According to Law the freemen of this Towne met togithir, and gave in theire Votes in distinct Papers, for Nomination of the .18. persons, out of whom the Magistrates are to be chosen, at the next Court of Election:
At which tyme also (according to law) they proceeded to choise of County Treasurer:
And appointed Mr. John Pynchon to take theire votes and seale them up, and carry them to the shire meeting on the last 4th day of this instant March as law injoynes:
Captain John Pynchon chosen Deputy:
At the meeting, the day above mentioned: The freemen (by Papers) choose Mr. John Pynchon to be theire Deputy (for the first Sessions of the Generall Court, the year ensueing viz) for the Court of Election unto whom they have granted and Deputed full Power to deale in all the affaires of this Common wealth wherein freemen may act by theire Deputy, according to Law:

April .24th 1662: The freemen met, and gave in theire votes for Asistants and to theire Deputy, who Received them into distinct Papers and sealed them up (according to Law) to Carry with him to the Court of Elections on the .7th of May Next:

[*321] Springfeild: March .10th 1662/63.
This Day the Freemen being called togither by the Constable to give in theire votes for Nomination of Assistants, And for choise of County Treasurer, They proceeded in the worke according to Law: And appointed Mr. Holyoke to carry theire votes sealed up to the shire Towne on the last .4th day of this Instant March:
They being Sealed up in the presence of the freemen and written on directed and attested by the Constable:

May 8th 1663.   Captain Pynchon chosen Deputy:

At a meeting of the Freemen of this Towne, They gave in theire votes by Papers for a Deputy for the Generall Court, and choss Captain John Pynchon to be theire Deputy for the next Court of Election unto whom they have given full Power to deale in all the affairs of this Common wealth wherein Freemen may act by theire Deputy according to Law:

At the same meeting: The freemen Gave in theire votes for election of Assistants and the General officers of the Countrey, Before the Constable and theire Deputy who Received them into distinct Papers and sealed them up to be Caryed to the Court of Election on the .27th day of this Instant May, according to Law:

[*Page 322 is blank.*]

[*323] August the 1st 1664.   Captain John Pynchon: Deputy.

According to a Warrant under the Secretaryes hand, the Constable assembled the freemen of this Town of Springfeild to choose a deputy for the Generall Corte to be held at Boston the .3d of this instant by Order of the Councill And Captain John Pynchon is Chosen Deputy for this Generall Corte aforementioned.

Mr. Elizur Holyoke Deputy

October .14th (1664) A warrant from the Secretary To the Constable to warne the Deputy of Springfeild to the General Court, to sit at Boston next Wednesday the .19th of this present October: occasioned the freemen to Assemble: who choose Mr. Holyoke theire Deputy for the Generall Court aforementioned:

[*324] Springfeild: March .13th 1664/65.

This Day the Freemen being called togithir by the Constable; to give in theire votes for Nomination of Assistants, and for choise of County Treasurer: They proceeded in the worke according to Law: And appointed Mr. Elizur Holyoke to carry theire votes sealed up to the shire meeting on the last .4th day of this Instant March: They being sealed up in the presence of the freemen Assembled: and Directed and Attested by the Constable:

Aprill 21st. 1665.   Captain Pynchon: Deputy who was taken of from that Service, by it etc.

At a meeting of the freemen of This Towne, they gave in theire votes by Papers for a Deputy for the Generall Court, and choose Captain Pynchon theire Deputy for the Court of Election on the .3d. of May next: for the first session thereoff unto whom they have Given full Power to deale in all the affaires of this Common wealth wherein Freemen may act by theire Deputy according to Law:

At the same meeting the Freemen gave in theire votes for election of Governour and Assistants, and the Generall officers of the Country, before the Constable and theire deputy, who Received them into distinct Papers and sealed them up to be caryed to the Court of Election of the .3d of May next according to Law:

The votes Received and sealed up, were the votes of .24. freemen:

[*325] July 26 1665.   Mr. Holyoke Deputy

The Constable Assembled the freemen by warrant from the Secretary to choose a Deputy for the Generall Court called the .1. of August 1665. And the freemen choose Mr. Elizur Holyoke to be theire Deputy for the General Court aforesaid.

Springfeild September .29th. 1665.   Deputy: Mr. Holyoke.

The Constable Having Assembled the Freemen to choose a Deputy for the next Generall Court The Freemen proceeded in the worke and choose Mr. Elizur Holyoke to that service For the Generall Court to be held at Boston on the .11th of October 1665.

Springfeild March .12th 1665/66.

This Day the freemen being called togithir by the Constable to give in theire votes for Nomination of Asistants and for choise of County Treasurer: They proceeded in the worke according to Law: And appointed Mr. Elizur Holyoke to carry theire votes sealed up to the Shire meeting on the last .4th day of this Instant March: The freemen also at the same tyme gave in votes for Associates for the County Corts and sent them By the same person to be opened at the shire meeting.

Aprill .20th 1666   Captain William Davis Deputy.

The freemen met togithir by warning from the Constable: and Proceeded to choise of a Deputy for the Court And Chose Captain William Davis of Boston Deputy (for Springfeild) for the Generall Court to Sit next May the first Sessions of it.

At the same Meeting the freemen gave in theire votes for election of the Generall officers of the Country before the Constable who Received them and sealed them up to be caryed to the Courts of Election next May the .23th 1666.

[*326] Springfeild March the .9th 1666/67.   Mr. Holyoke Commissioner to carry the votes to the shire meeting.

This day the freemen being Called togithir by the Constable according to Law, they accordingly assembled, and proceeded to give in theire votes for nomination of Magistrates Choise of Associates and County Treasurer: And choose and Appointed Mr Elizur Holyoke to carry theire votes sealed up to the shire meeting: on the last Wednesday of this Instant March according to Law:

May .1st: 1667.   Mr. Holyoke Deputy.

The freemen met togithir by warning from the Constable and proceeded to choise of a Deputy for the Generall Court.

And choose Mr. Elizur Holyoke for their Deputy for the next Generall Court to assemble at Boston on the .15th of May next, viz for the first Sessions thereoff: At the same meeting the freemen give in theire votes for Election of the Generall officers of the Country, before the Deputy who Received them and sealed them up in distinct Papers: to be by him caryed in to the Court of Election aforesaid.

[*327] Springfeild March the .11th 1667/68.   George Colton to carry the votes to the shire meting.

This Day the Freemen being Called togither by the Constable as Law directs they accordingly assembled and proceeded to give in theire votes for Nomination of Magistrates, choise of Associates and County Treasurer, And choose and appointed George Colton to carry their votes sealed up to the shire meeting on the last Wednesday of this Instant March according to Law:

Leiutenant Cooper, Deputy.

At the same meeting the freemen proceeded to choise of a Deputy for the Generall Court, and (by Papers according to Law) chose Leiutenant Thomas Cooper for theire Deputy for the next Generall Cort of Election viz the first sessions thereoff.

Aprill .22th 1668.

The Freemen met togithir by warning from the Constable, And gave in theire votes for Governour Asistants etc, to theire Deputy and Constable who Received them into distinct Papers and sealed them up (according to law) to carry with him to the Court of Elections at Boston on the .29th of this instant Aprill 1668.

March 12th 1668/69.   Samuell Marshfeild to carry the votes to the shire meeting.

This day the freemen being called togithir by the Constable as Law directs, they accordingly assembled: and proceeded to give in theire votes for Nomination of Magistrates, Choise of Associates; and County Treasurer, And chose and appointed Samuell Marshfeild to carry theire votes sealed up to the shire meeting on the last .4th. day of this Instant March according to Law.

George Colton Deputy.

At the same meeting the freemen proceeded to choise of a Deputy for the Generall Court and (by Papers according to law) chose

Quarter Master George Colton for theire Deputy for the first Sessions of the next Generall Court of Election:

October .4th 1669.

The Freemen Assembled (by warning from the Constable) and having Agreed to make choise of a Deputy for the Generall Court to sit now the next weeke: They proceeded to give in their votes, And (by Papers according to Law) Choose Quarter Master George Colton Deputy for the Generall Court which is to begin its sessions the .12th of this Instant October:

[*328] March .9th 1669/70. Mr. Holyoke to carry the votes to the Shire meeting:

This day the freemen being Called togithir by the constable (as Law directs) They proceeded to give in theire votes for Nomination of Magistrates choise of Associates and County Treasurer And chose and appointed Captain Holyoke to carry theire votes Sealed up to the shire meeting on the last Wednsday of this Instant March.

Samuell Marshfeild Deputy:

At the same Meeting the freemen proceeded to choise of a Deputy for the Court of Election And Choose Samuell Marshfeild theire Deputy for the next Generall Court of Election.

Captain Holyoke Deputy.

Samuell Marshfeild refusing the service of Deputy not being present at the choise and declaring his nonacceptance thereoff, To the Freemen, the 20th of Aprill 1670. At theire meeting by warning from the Constable, To give in votes for choise of Governour asistants etc.: The freemen were willing to proceed to a new choise, and for that end gave in Papers according to Law: and choose Captain Elizur Holyoke their Deputy for the next Court of Elections and for that Sessions of the Generall Court which is to begin on the .11th of May next: And at this Meeting gave in their votes to the Deputy and Constable (for election of Generall officers of the Country) who Received them into distinct Papers and sealed them up according to Law for the Deputy to carry with him to the Court in May next.

March .8th 1670/71. Mr. Holyoke to carry the votes to the shire meting

This Day the Freemen being Called togithir by the Constable (as Law directs) They proceeded to give in their votes for Nomination of Magistrates Choise of Associates for keeping the County Courts, and for choise of the County Treasurer according to Law: And Chose and appointed Captain Holyoke to carry their votes Sealed up to the shire meeting on the last Wednesday of this instant March.

Quarter Master Colton Deputy.

At the same Meeting the freemen proceeded to choise of a Deputy for the Court of Election: And choose Quarter Master George Colton their Deputy for the next Generall Court of Elections.

[*329] Aprill .19th 1671.

The Freemen met togithir by warning from the Constable and gave in their votes for Governour, Asistants etc, to their Deputy who Received them into distinct Papers according to Law to carry with him to the Court of Elections in May next:

At the same meeting the freemen agreed and by vote determined to have Two Deputys the next Generall Court, and so gave in their vote by Papers according to Law, and choose Captain William Davis of Boston for their Deputy: the other being George Colton: as aforesaid:

March .7th 1671/72.   Mr. Holyoke commissioner to carry the votes to the shire meeting.

This Day the Freemen being called togithir by the Constable (as law directs) They proceeded to give in their votes for Nomination of Magistrates, Choise of Associates for keeping the County Courts, and for choise of the County Treasurer according to Law: And choose and appointed Captain Holyoke to carry their votes sealed up to the shire meeting on the last Wednesday of this Instant March:

Captain William Davis Deputy.

At the same Meeting the freemen proceeded to choise of a Deputy for the Generall Court: And chose Captain William Davis of Boston their Deputy for next Court of Elections on the .15th of May next and so to stand their Deputy for the whole yeare ensueing:

[*330] Springfeild March .10th 1672/73.   Captain Holyoke Comissioner to carry the votes to the shire meeting.

This Day the Freemen being Called togithir by the Constable (as the Law directs) They proceeded to give in their votes for Nomination of Magistrates, Choise of Associates for keeping the County Courts, and for choise of the County Treasurer according to Law: And chose and appointed Captain Holyoke to carry their votes sealed up to the shire meeting on the last Wednesday of this Instant March.

Captain Holyoke Deputy:

At the same Meeting the Freemen proceeded to choise of a Deputy for the Generall Court for the yeare ensueing: and Chose Captain Elizur Holyoke for their Deputy:

March the .9th 1673/74

This day the Freemen being called togithir by the Constable (as the Law directs) They proceeded to give in their votes for Nomination of Magistrates, choice of Associates for the County Courts and County Treasurer according to Law: And Chose and appointed Mr. Pynchon to carry their votes (sealed up, which was done in presence of the freemen) unto their shire meeting which is on the last Wednesday of this Instant March.

Captain Holyoke Deputy:

At the same meeting the freemen proceeded to choise of a Deputy for the Generall Court, and chose Captain Elizur Holyoke for their Deputy for the next Court of Election:

March 10th 1674/75. Quarter Master Colton to carry the votes to the shire Meting.

This day the Freemen Met, being called togither by the Constable (as law directs) and gave in their votes for Nomination of Magistrates as also for Nomination of Associ[ates] for the County Courts and for choise of County Treasurer: And they chose and appointed Quarter Master George Colton, to carry their votes Sealed up to the shire Meeting on the last Wednesday of this Instant March:

Captain Holyoke: Deputy:

At the same Meeting the freemen proceeded to choise of a Deputy for the Generall Court and chose Captain Holyoke their Deputy for the next General Cort of Election that Sessions only:

March.8th 1675/76. Captain Davis Deputy.

This day the Freemen being called togithir by the Constable as the Law directs: They gave in their votes for Nomination of Magistrates and Associa[tes] and for choise of County Treasurer, And they chose and appointed Benjamin Parsons to carry their votes sealed up to their shire Meeting on the last Wednesday of this Mar[ch] Also the freemen by Papers chose Captain William Davis their Deputy for the Generall Court for the yeare ensueing.

Aprill 1676.

The freemen Meeting by warning from the Constable they gave in their votes for Governour Asistants etc.

[*331] Springfeild March .13th 1676/77.

This day the Freemen Met being called togither by the Constable as law directs; And gave in their votes for Nomination of Magistrates: and also of Associates for the County Court, and likewise for choise of County Treasurer: And they chose and appointed Samuell Marshfeild to carry their votes sealed up to their shire Meeting which is on the last Wednesday of this Instant March.

[*The next item has been crossed out.*]

Mr. Eliott Deputy.

At the same Meeting the freemen by Papers Chose Mr. Jacob Eliot of Boston (the Deacon of the .3d church) their Deputy for the first Sessions of the Generall Court in May next:

May .9th 1677.   George Colton Deputy.

The freemen met togithir by warning from the Constable and gave in their votes for a Deputy from among themselves (recalling the last vote for one in Boston) and made choise of Quarter Master George Colton for theire Deputy for the Court of Election next: At same tyme Gave in their votes for Governour Deputy Governour Asistants: etc.

March the .13th 1677/8.

The Freemen Met being called togither by the Constable as Law directs and Gave in their votes for Nomination of Magistrates, as also of Associats for the County Courts, and likewise for choise of County Treasurer: And Chose and apointed Samuell Marshfeild to carry the votes sealed up to the sheire Meeting on the last Wednesday of this Instant March according to Law And saw not cause to choose any Deputy for the Generall Court.

Aprill .24th 1678.

Being a Meeting of the Freemen by warning from the Constable They proceeded to give in their votes for choise of Governour Asistants etc. sealing them up in distinct Papers according to law, and so to be caryed to the next Court of Election to be on the 8th of May 1678:

October 16th 1678.

The freemen assembled by warning from the Constable by virtue of a speciall warrant for choise of a Deputy Governour etc. and sent their votes sealed to Boston to be opened 21st of October 1687. according to order of Generall Cort.

March 14, 1678/79.

The Freemen Met being called togither By the Constable as Law directs, and Gave in their votes for Nomination of Magistrates as also for Associates for the County Courts, and Likewise for choise of County Treasurer: And chose and appointed Jonathan Burt to carry the votes sealed up to the shire Meeting on the last Wednesday of this Instant March according to Law.

May 9th 1679.

The Freemen met by warning from the Constable and gave in their votes for Governour Asistants etc. sealing them up as Law directs to be caryed to the Court of Election, at Boston on the .28th of this Instant May:

[*332] Springfeild March .8. 1679/80. Mr. Samuell Marshfeild: Deputy.

This day the Freemen Met, being assembled by the Constable and Gave in their votes for Nomination of Associates: Choise of County Treasurer And chose Samuell Marshfeild to seale up the votes and carry them to the shire Meeting according to Law: Also at this Meeting they proceeded to Choise of a Deputy for the Generall Court: and made choise of Samuell Marshfeild for their Deputy for the next Court of Elections:

April 1680.

The freemen Met by warning from the Constable and Gave in their votes for choise of Governour Asistants etc: Sealing up all etc. according to Law:

December 24.th 1680. Mr. Joseph Pynchon chosen Deputy.

The Constable assembled the Freemen by warrant from the Secretary to choose a Deputy for the Generall Court which is called to Sit the .4th day of January next who Being Met together, made choise of Mr. Joseph Pynchon for their Deputy for the Generall Court aforesaid, and apointed Mr. John Holyoke to write to him to signifie the same to him:

April: 28 1681.

At a Meeting of the Freemen Mr. Joseph Pynchon was made choise off for the Deputy of this Towne for the General Court of Elections.

March .14: 1681/82.

This Day the freemen Met being assembled by the Constable according to law, and Gave in their votes for Nomination of Magistrates: as also for Nomination of Associates, choise of County Treasurer And ch[ose] and apointed Samuell Ely to carry the votes sealed up to the shire meeting they being sealed up in presen[ce] of the freemen according to law:

Mr. Joseph Pynchon Deputy.

Also At this Meeting the freemen proceeded to choise of a Deputy for the Generall Court, and made choise of Mr. Joseph Pynchon for their Deputy for the Generall Court of Elections.

March.13th 1682/3.   Samuell Ely: comissioner.

This day (as I was Informed I being at Boston) The freemen be-ing assembled by the Constable, Met and gave in their votes for Nomination of Magistrates as also for Nomination of Asociate choise of county Treasurer etc. and chose: Samuell Ely to carr[y] the votes to the shire Meeting on the last Wednesday of this Instant March.

Mr. Samuell Marshfeild Deputy.

At this meeting Samuell Marshfeild was chosen Deputy for the next Generall Court of Election in May next.

[*333] March 11th 1683/84.   Mr. Samuell Marshfeild Deputy.

This day the Freemen Met being assembled by the Constable ac-cording to law, and gave in their votes for Nomination of Magis-trates, as also for Nomination of Associates choise of County Treas-urer, And choose and apointed Samuell Marshfeild to carry the votes sealed up to the shire Meeting they being sealed up in presence of the freemen according to law. Also at this Meeting the freemen [pr]oceded to choise of a Deputy for the Generall Court, and [ma]de choise of Mr. Samuell Marshfeild for their Deputy [to] the Generall Court of Elections next ensueing:

May 13th 1691.

Mr. John Holyoke (at the meeting of the Freemen for giving in votes by Proxies for election) was Chosen Deputy for this Towne of Springfeild for the General Court of Elections next ensueing on the 20th of this Instant May, that is to say for the first Sessions of said General Court, and to act on their behalfe as their Deputy or Rep-resentative:

[*334] A list of the Names of all the Freemen in Springfeild as they are this 13th of May 1691.

Of the aunciant Freemen that are now remaining

Lieutenant Colonel John Pynchon, Mr. Pelatiah Glover, Mr. John Holyoke, George Colton, Thomas Mirick, Nathaniel Pritchard, Miles Morgan, Jonathan Burt Senior, Thomas Day Senior, Charls Ferry Senior, Luke Hitchcock, James Warrinar, John Warner (over the Great River), Japhet Chapin, Samuell Ely Senior, Joseph Steb-bins, Ephraim Colton, Captain Thomas Colton, Ensigne John Hitch-cock, Daniel Cooley, Increase Sikes: John Dumbleton (over the great River), Samuell Marshfeild, John Barber:

Admitted to the privileges of Freedom by the General Court Bos-ton December 19th 1690 and sworne at Springfeild Before John Pynchon: March .26.th 1691 and May .11.th and .13.th 1691 these persons following:

David Morgan, John Dorchester, James Dorchester, John Harmon, David Lumbard, Charls Ferry Junior, Isack Colton: Samuell Bliss Senior, Samuell Bliss .3d., Thomas Stebbins, Edward Stebbins, Benjamin Stebbins, Samuel Lamb, Daniel Lamb, Joseph Leanord, Benjamin Leanord, Edward Foster, Josiah Marshfeild, John Miller, Samuel Miller, Thomas Cooper.

Jonathan Ball, Joseph Bedortha, Samuell Bedortha, Joseph Ely: James ——, Thomas Day Junior, John Merick, Lieutenant Abel Wright, Eliakim Cooley, Joseph Cooley, Benjamin Cooley, Jonathan Morgan, Samuel Bliss Junior, Nathanell Bliss, John Colton, John Bliss Senior, Joseph Thomas, Nathanel Burt Senior, Jonathan Burt Junior, John Burt.

[*335] May 1692   Captain Belcher Mr. Holyoke our Deputys.

By vertue of a warrant from his excelency Sir William Phips the Governour of this Province to the Constable of Springfeild to Assemble the Inhabitants Freeholders to choose .2. persons to Represent them at the General Assembly apointed by his excelency to convene at Boston the .8th day of June 1692. The Freeholders etc. accordingly assembling together this —— and made choice of Mr. John Holyoke and Captain Andrew Belcher to represent them at the Generall Assembly on the 8th of this next June and to act therein, accordingly on their Behalfe:

May, 1693.

John Pynchon Esq. chosen the Representative for this Towne of Springfeild, who being taken of to the Council The Freeholders made a choise of Captain Benjamin Davis for their Representative:

1694
Nathanel Bliss chosen our Representative.

1695
Lieutenant Abel Wright chosen to Represent Springfeild.

1696
Mr. Luke Hitchcock chosen Representative.

Appendix

To the much Honored the County Corte of Middlesex

These may signify to this Honored Corte that Wee whose Names are Subscribed, being appointed by Order of Our much Honored the Generall Corte in May last past to heare and take examination of a great misdemeanor committed in NorthWottock at Northampton by Robert Bartlett against Sarah the wife of Christopher Smith both of the said town, and that if Wee should fynd the case only a misdemeanor and not Capitall, then to bynd over the said Bartlett, unto the County Corte of Middlesex, next ensueinge the date of the said Order, to answer for his fault: Wee have accordingly indeavored to attend the pleasure and said Order of our Honnored Corte and have examined the cause, and though the crime be of a grievous nature exceedingly to be lamented of all that heare it, yet we cannot judge the case Capitall; and therefore have bound over the said Bartlett to this Honored Corte to answer for his fault, and have sent the accusation and relation of the said Sarah Smith concerninge the said Crime, with the said confession of the said Bartlett therein:

The accusation relation of Sarah the wife of Christopher Smith of Nortwottuck at Northampton against Robert Bartlett of the same Town: wherein shee thus affirmeth that About the beginning of October 1655, I haveing occasion (my husband for some space being from [home] To goe into the Meddow to look after Two calves, because the wolves had done some hurt to some of our Neighboring Calves, it being the Lords day neere Sun-setting, I did accidentally meet with Robert Bartlett, whom I asked whether he saw any calves, he said he saw some, soe I went with him to see whether I had any there or noe, and they beinge none of my calves, he led me further thorow a swamp, and he goeinge before mee upon a suddayne he turned full butt upon mee and laid hold on mee, and grasped me in his Armes, soe that I was in a great fright, not knowinge what his aim and intent was: I was in an amazement to see such uncomely carriage by him, for that impudently and immodestly he kissed mee and after that he threw mee down and kissed mee, and lay uppon me with his mouth upon mine: on some part of my body he lay on how much I cannot tell, neyther can I tell whether he uncovered mee by taking up my coates, yea or noe, but he did shamefully handle my nakedness: I considering what his filthy unclean purpose was, by his shameful carriage towards mee, I was very earnest with him to lett mee goe he made mee some returne, but what he said I cannot tell: But after a little tyme he continuinge his opportunity to satisfy his filthy lust, and to defile me, I did then heare and remember what he said, persuinge mee earnestly to yeeld to his filthy abominable motion; I told him I would not, and then he said he would not doe it without my consent, but after this he did agayn desire to fulfill his filthy lust: but I refused earnestly intreating him to lett mee goe: and it pleased God to keep in mee a resolution not to yeeld: and he did at length lett mee goe: I beinge I beinge now in a strange place that he led mee into, where I never was before that I know of, and night being come on, I went after him homewards till I came neere home and knew where I was, but he did noe more offer ill to mee, only he told mee that he could have done it whether I would or noe, and further Shee Sayth not.

This is the true relation of Sarah Smith against Robert Bartlett beinge attested on oath the 26th of June 1656

Before us   JOHN PYNCHON
ELIZUR HOLYOKE

The Confession of Robert Bartlett Concerning the said Crime:
He saith he ownes the greatest part of this relation of Sarah Smith against him; but not all of it: He confesseth he laid hold on her through the violence of the tentation, and that he threw her down and kissed her and that he did handle her nakedness, but sayeth he did not lye on her but by her, only his arme was over her and it may be some part of his body, but never the weight of his body: and he saith that he did urge her twice or thrice to yeeld unto him, but that shee refused, and desired him to lett her goe, and at last he sayeth God smote him with a trembling that at last he lett her goe. This is the truth of Robert Bartletts Confession taken the 26th June 1656

Before us   JOHN PYNCHON
ELIZUR HOLYOKE

There was noe testimony on eyther side to testify anything concerninge this matter (The thinge being attempted about a mile from the Town) excepting something related by an Irish youth who could not be well understood besides what he said was contradictory to himself and he accorded not with the man and woman about the place where this wickedness was attempted, they agreeinge therein.

The premises Considered we bound out the said Bartlett to attend at the County Corte in Cambride to answer for his miscarriage ingaging 2 sufficient suretys for his personall appearance there which bond we have herewith Sent:

The aforesaid Christopher Smith being a poor man and something weak did not prosecute against this delinquent as he might yet he thinketh he may justly demand 10 damages at least against this Bartlett which wee leave to the judgment of this Honored Cort.

O that rivers of water might run down our eyes because men keep not Gods Law.

Much Honored we remayn

your most Humble Servants
JOHN PYNCHON
ELIZUR HOLYOKE

Springfeild
July the 8th 1656.

Index

Index

INDEX

100–101, 189, 315, 387; activities on Governor's Council, 52; justice of the peace, 52, 101–102, 113, 148, 166, 189–196, 375; commissioner, 63, 67, 93–99, 177, 227–228, 244; issuance of commission of oyer and terminer to, 85; associate of County Court, 101; judge of the Inferior Court of Common Pleas for Hampshire, 102, 353; binding over of offenders, 111, 112, 118–119, 127, 151–152; contempt of court cases, 120, 271; civil jurisdiction as magistrate, as member of the Council, and as justice of the peace, 159–160; significant role of, 197–200; empowered to give oaths to freemen, 215, 252; town treasurer, 220, 245; commissioners sworn in by, 253, 276, 277; improvement of House of Correction of Springfield, 257; receipt of military commissions from, 313–314; theft from, 341–342

Pynchon, Captain John v. Lockermans, Boltus Jacobus, 259–260

Pynchon, John v. Sackett, Widow as administratrix, 263

Pynchon, John v. Sackett and Blomefeild, 264

Pynchon, John, Jr., 4, 42n, 48n, 341–342; Boston business activities, 46; removal to Springfield, 59; inventory of law books, 157–158; attorney to take out warrant of contempt, 336

Pynchon, John, 3rd: clerk of Court of Oyer and Terminer, 85; sworn as Register of Deeds, Conveyance, Mortgages, etc., within the County of Hampshire, 353

Pynchon, Joseph, 39n, 46n; letters from his father, 48; death unmarried, 59; deputy to the General Court of Elections, 385

Pynchon Magistrate's Book. See Record.

Pynchon manuscript: acquisition, 3; contents, 3; authorship, 3; appearance, 3–4; modernization of text, rules for, 4; marriages, records of, 4–5. See also *Record*

Pynchon, Margaret, 29

Pynchon, Mary: marriage, 29, 60; death, 59, 62n

Pynchon Waste Book for Hampshire, 4n

Pynchon, William, 67, 224, 225; and *Record,* 3, 4; biographical sketch, 6–31; and Massachusetts Bay Company, 8–9; fur trade activities, 10–11, 14, 17–18; farming activities, 11; settlement at Agawam and on east bank, 12–13; com-

missioner for Connecticut River settlements, 13; alleged monopoly in corn, 14–15; and uniting of Connecticut plantations with Massachusetts Bay, 15, 16; government of Springfield, 17; judicial power in Springfield, 17; and Indian matters, 18; appointment and jurisdiction as magistrate, 19, 89–91, 159–160, 203; attitude toward political events of the 1640's, 19; letter to John Winthrop, 19–20; and witchcraft proceedings, 20–25; religious publications, 25, 28, 30; return to England, 28, 29; publication of second book, 28; death, 30; will, 30n; summary of work and accomplishments, 31; holding of courts by, 90, 109, 152–153, 163, 164, 177; General Court commission of 1641, to exercise judicial power, 91–92, 154, 174; General Court commission of 1643, judicial powers under, 92–93; punishment of sexual offenses, 104; defamation cases before, 117–118; familiarity with Fortescue, 157, 158; familiarity with Dalton, 157; authorized to make freemen in Springfield, 181; and witnesses, 182; significant role of, 197–200; and Samuell Terry, 226–227

Pynchon, William, record of accounts with early settlers and Indians carried forward from previous book around September, 1645 and to a new book around March, 1650, 17n

Pynchon, William v. Horton, Thomas, 204

Pynchon, William v. Merricke, Thomas, 204

Pynchon v. Collicott, 28n

Quabaug (later Brookfield), 18, 138; establishment, 34–35; abandonment threatened, 51; grant of lands to Indians, 61

Quakers: prosecution of, 74; banning of books and writings, 74n; law enforcement problem in western Massachusetts, 119; constable's power to apprehend without warrant, 131

Questions of fact or law, 179

Qui tam actions by informers, 129, 219, 374; matters covered, 137–138

Randal, William v. Peirce, John, 334
Randal, executor (Abbee v.), 345–346
Randall (Moore v.), 319–320
Randolph, Edward, 49–50
Rates. *See* Town rates

INDEX

Scire facias: proceeding against First Charter, 58; writ of, 185, 191–192

Scold: jurisdiction of offense of being, 70n; punishment of, 114, 150, 235–236

Scot, Ebenezar, 333–334

Scot, John v. Mirick, Thomas, 256–257

Scot, William, 331

Scot (Huxley v.), 352

Scott, Edward, oath of fidelity, 278

Scott (Scot), John, 257, 258, 269, 270, 309

Scott, John v. Miller, Obadiah, 248

Sealer of weights and measures, 229, 245, 261

Sear, John, 206

Search and seizure, search warrants, 142, 223

Searles, John, 172; juror, 204, 205; constable, 208

Searles, John, Jr., 212, 213

Searles, Widow, 172, 213

Second Charter of Massachusetts Bay colony: activities of John Pynchon, 53–59; judicial system under, 82–88; role of constable under, 131; tithingman, 136–137; necessity that *qui tam* actions be brought in court of record, 137; initial process in criminal matters, 143; commissions of the peace under, 144; right to jury trial, 145; standards of proof, 147; witnesses, 148–149; provision for appeal to Court of General Sessions of the Peace, 155; procedure in civil actions, 189–196

Security, posting for return of stolen goods, 150

Segar, Joseph, 308–309

Segregation of civil and criminal aspects of same case, 152

Selden (Seldon, Selding), Joseph, 116, 285–286; oath of fidelity, 278

Seldon (Seldin), Thomas, 335–336; constable of Hadley, 336

Seldon (Goulding v.), 169, 335–336

Selectmen of towns: judicial or quasi-judicial powers, 77–78; complaints or presentments by, 133

Selectmen of Springfield v. Sackett, John, 240

Self-incrimination, claim of privilege, 146

Selling or bartering guns, lead, or powder with Indians, 69, 122; jurisdiction over failure to pay fees for, 70n

Sentence, suspension of, 151

Sentencing, 149–153

Service: jurisdiction of assisting selectmen in putting orphans out to, 70n; putting

out to as punishment, 150. *See also* Putting out to service

Settlement by agreement, 328–329

Settlement of debt, 326–328

Settling and providing for poor persons, 70n

Sewall, Samuel, 48n, 49, 55n

Sewell, Besse, 23n

Sewell, Thomas, oath of fidelity, 217

Sewell (Parsons v.), 221

Sexton, George, 301; oath of fidelity, 269

Sexton (Dewey and Bancroft v.), 301

Sexton (King v.), 172, 318, 368–369

Sexton (Sackut v.), 291–292

Sheldon, Isaak, 120; freeman, 257

Sheriff, law-enforcement agency, 199

Shire meetings (Hampshire County), 34, 376–386

Sikes, Increase, freeman, 377, 386

Sikes (Sykes), Richard: selectman, 125; appraiser, 213, 220–221; juror, 214, 215, 222, 230, 246, 263; freeman, 215, 375; presenter, 228; informer, 228–229; sealer of weights and measures, 229; released from training, 255

Sikes, Victory, 349, 350; freeman, 376

Sikes, Victory v. King, James, 328–329

Sikes, Victory v. Taylor, Thomas, 291, 292

Sill, Captain, 41

Single magistrate: administration functions, 72–75; jurisdiction and appeal from, 72–75; power to marry, 73

Sitton, Benjamin, 342

Slander, action of, 170–172, 179, 180, 205, 207, 208, 238, 240, 244, 247, 250, 254, 259, 264, 304–308, 311–312, 317, 355–356, 368–369

Slander, as criminal offense, 116–118, 219–220, 236–237, 300, 356–357, 374, 375

Smith, Anne, 29, 29n, 30n, 36n

Smith, Benjamin, 357

Smith, Christopher, 389–390

Smith (Smyth), Henry, 25, 30n, 62, 67, 90n, 94, 96, 205, 212, 213, 220; Agawam, settlement, 9, 12; commissioner for Connecticut River settlements, 13; judicial authority, 22–23; return to England, 29, 30n; marriage of daughter Anne, 36n; commission as magistrate, 93; selectman, 125; juror, 204, 205, 206, 209, 211, 212, 215, 216, 221; fines for the poor paid to, 210; sealer of votes, 216; indentures to, 224, 225

Smith, John, 145n, 146n

Smith, Mary, 49

Smith, Mistress, 229–230

Smith, Phillip: freeman, 252; juror, 254